# Systems Programming

# Systems Programming

Editor:

Gerard Ian Prudhomme

ArclerPress

www.arclerpress.com

**Systems Programming**

*Editor: Gerard Ian Prudhomme*



**708 3rd Avenue, 6th Floor**
**New York**
**NY 10017**
**United States of America**
**www.arclerpress.com**

ISBN: 978-1-68094-454-9

Library of Congress Control Number: 2016951147



Arcler Press LLC publishes wide variety of books and eBooks. For more information about Arcler Press and its products, visit our website at www.arclerpress.com

# About the Editor

## Gerard Ian Prudhomme

Gerard I. Prudhomme has a graduate degree (M.S.) for Computer Science from University College London (UCL). He has also worked as a software programmer and tech writer for different Fortune 500 companies, and studied at UCL, Harvard, and Oxford.

# Contents

# List of Contributors

**Jianfang Cao**
Computer Science and Technology Department, Xinzhou Teachers University, Xinzhou, China,

**Hongyan Cui**
Computer Science and Technology Department, Xinzhou Teachers University, Xinzhou, China,

**Hao Shi**
College of Computer Science and Technology, Taiyuan University of Science and Technology, Taiyuan, China

**Lijuan Jiao**
Computer Science and Technology Department, Xinzhou Teachers University, Xinzhou, China,

**Radek Silhavy**
Faculty of Applied Informatics, Tomas Bata University in Zlin, Zlin, Czech Republic Nankai University, CHINA

**Petr Silhavy**
Faculty of Applied Informatics, Tomas Bata University in Zlin, Zlin, Czech Republic Nankai University, CHINA

**Zdenka Prokopova**
Faculty of Applied Informatics, Tomas Bata University in Zlin, Zlin, Czech Republic Nankai University, CHINA

**Yasar Abbas Ur Rehman**
NUSys Lab/ National University of Computer and Emerging Sciences (NUCES), Peshawar, KPK, Pakistan,
Department of Electrical Engineering/City University of Science and Information Technology, Peshawar,KPK, Pakistan

**Muhammad Tariq**
NUSys Lab/ National University of Computer and Emerging Sciences (NUCES), Peshawar, KPK, Pakistan,

**Omar Usman Khan**
NUSys Lab/ National University of Computer and Emerging Sciences (NUCES), Peshawar, KPK, Pakistan

**Quang Do**
Information Assurance Research Group, University of South Australia, Adelaide, Australia

**Ben Martini**
Information Assurance Research Group, University of South Australia, Adelaide, Australia

**Kim-Kwang Raymond Choo**
Information Assurance Research Group, University of South Australia, Adelaide, Australia

**Blazej Adamczyk**
Institute of Informatics, Silesian University of Technology, Gliwice, Poland.

**Andrzej Chydzinski**
Institute of Informatics, Silesian University of Technology, Gliwice, Poland.

**Shaofei Chen**
College of Mechatronics and Automation, National University of Defense Technology, China
School of Electronics and Computer Science, University of Southampton, UK

**Feng Wu**
School of Electronics and Computer Science, University of Southampton, UK

**Lincheng Shen**
College of Mechatronics and Automation, National University of Defense Technology, China

**Jing Chen**
College of Mechatronics and Automation, National University of Defense Technology, China

**Sarvapali Ramchurn**
School of Electronics and Computer Science, University of Southampton, UK

**Tianyang Dong**
School of Computer Science and Technology, Zhejiang University of Technology, Hangzhou, Zhejiang, China,
Key Laboratory of Visual Media Intelligent Processing Technology of Zhejiang Province, Hangzhou, Zhejiang, China

**Siyuan Liu**
School of Computer Science and Technology, Zhejiang University of Technology, Hangzhou, Zhejiang, China,
Key Laboratory of Visual Media Intelligent Processing Technology of Zhejiang Province, Hangzhou, Zhejiang, China

**Jiajia Xia**
School of Computer Science and Technology, Zhejiang University of Technology, Hangzhou, Zhejiang, China

**Jing Fan**
School of Computer Science and Technology, Zhejiang University of Technology, Hangzhou, Zhejiang, China,

**Ling Zhang**
Key Laboratory of Visual Media Intelligent Processing Technology of Zhejiang Province, Hangzhou, Zhejiang, China

**Mohsen Dorraki**
Department of Electrical Engineering, Amirkabir University of Technology, Tehran, Iran

**Gregory K. Cambrell**
Department of Electrical and Computer Systems Engineering, Faculty of Engineering, Monash University, Victoria, Australia

**Derek Abbott**
School of Electrical and Electronic Engineering, University of Adelaide, South Australia, Australia

**Lauro C. M. de Paula**
Institute of Informatics, Federal University of Goia´ s - UFG, Goia˜ nia, GO, Brazil,

**Anderson S. Soares**
Institute of Informatics, Federal University of Goia´ s - UFG, Goia˜ nia, GO, Brazil,

**Telma W. de Lima**
Institute of Informatics, Federal University of Goia´ s - UFG, Goia˜ nia, GO, Brazil,

**Alexandre C. B. Delbem**
Institute of Mathematical Sciences and Computing, University of Sa˜ o Paulo - USP, Sa˜ o Carlos, SP, Brazil,

**Clarimar J. Coelho**
Computer Science Department, Pontifical Catholic University of Goia´ s - PUC Goia´ s, Goia˜ nia, GO, Brazil,

**Arlindo R. G. Filho**
Department of System and Control, Technological Institute of Aeronautics - ITA, Sa˜ o Jose´ dos Campos, SP, Brazil

**Zoltan Gingl**
Department of Technical Informatics, University of Szeged, Szeged, Hungary

**Robert Mingesz**
Department of Technical Informatics, University of Szeged, Szeged, Hungary

**David Dı´az**
Dep. Lenguajes y Ciencias de la Computacio´n, Universidad de Ma´laga, Ma´laga, Spain,

**Francisco J. Esteban**
Servicio de Informa´tica, Universidad de Co´rdoba, Co´rdoba, Spain,

**Pilar Herna´ndez**
Instituto de Agricultura Sostenible (IAS-CSIC), Co´rdoba, Spain,

**Juan Antonio Caballero**
Dep. Estadı´stica, Universidad de Co´rdoba, Co´rdoba, Spain,

**Antonio Guevara**
Dep. Lenguajes y Ciencias de la Computacio´n, Universidad de Ma´laga, Ma´laga, Spain,

**Gabriel Dorado**
Dep. Bioquı´mica y Biologı´a Molecular, Universidad de Co´rdoba (Campus de Excelencia Internacional Agroalimentario), Co´rdoba, Spain

**Sergio Ga´lvez**
Dep. Lenguajes y Ciencias de la Computacio´n, Universidad de Ma´laga, Ma´laga, Spain,

**Adam Gudys**
Institute of Informatics, Faculty of Automatic Control, Electronics and Computer Science, Silesian University of Technology, Gliwice, Poland

**Sebastian Deorowicz**
Institute of Informatics, Faculty of Automatic Control, Electronics and Computer Science, Silesian University of Technology, Gliwice, Poland

**Rajesh Poddar**
Department of Organismic and Evolutionary Biology, Harvard University, Cambridge, Massachusetts, United States of America, Center for Brain Science, Harvard University, Cambridge, Massachusetts, United States of America

**Risa Kawai**
Department of Organismic and Evolutionary Biology, Harvard University, Cambridge, Massachusetts, United States of America, Center for Brain Science, Harvard University, Cambridge, Massachusetts, United States of America

**Bence P. Ölveczky**
Department of Organismic and Evolutionary Biology, Harvard University, Cambridge, Massachusetts, United States of America, Center for Brain Science, Harvard University, Cambridge, Massachusetts, United States of America

**Juan A. Añel**
Smith School of Enterprise and the Environment, University of Oxford, Oxford, United Kingdom,
EPhysLab, Facultade de Ciencias, Universidade de Vigo, Ourense, Spain,

**Douglas R. Allen**
Naval Research Laboratory, Washington, District of Columbia, United States of America,

**Guadalupe Sa´enz**
Smith School of Enterprise and the Environment, University of Oxford, Oxford, United Kingdom
Departamento de Fısica, Facultad de Ciencias, Universidad de Extremadura, Badajoz, Spain

**Luis Gimeno**
EPhysLab, Facultade de Ciencias, Universidade de Vigo, Ourense, Spain

**Laura de la Torre**
EPhysLab, Facultade de Ciencias, Universidade de Vigo, Ourense, Spain

**Ram Vinay Pandey**
Institut für Populationsgenetik, Vetmeduni Vienna, Vienna, Austria

**Christian Schlötterer**
Institut für Populationsgenetik, Vetmeduni Vienna, Vienna, Austria

**Wei-Jen Wang**
Department of Computer Science and Information Engineering, National Central University, Taoyuan, Taiwan,

**I-Fan Hsieh**
Graduate Institute of Biomedical Engineering, National Central University, Taoyuan, Taiwan

**Chun-Chuan Chen**
Graduate Institute of Biomedical Engineering, National Central University, Taoyuan, Taiwan

**Thomas W. Schubert**
Department of Psychology, University of Oslo, Oslo, Norway,
Centro de Investigac¸a˜o e Intervenc¸a˜o Social, Instituto Universita´rio de Lisboa (ISCTE-IUL), Lisboa, Portugal

**Carla Murteira**
Centro de Investigac¸a˜o e Intervenc¸a˜o Social, Instituto Universita´rio de Lisboa (ISCTE-IUL), Lisboa, Portugal

**Elizabeth C. Collins**
Centro de Investigac¸a˜o e Intervenc¸a˜o Social, Instituto Universita´rio de Lisboa (ISCTE-IUL), Lisboa, Portugal

**Diniz Lopes**
Centro de Investigac¸a˜o e Intervenc¸a˜o Social, Instituto Universita´rio de Lisboa (ISCTE-IUL), Lisboa, Portugal

**Carlos Contreras Bolton**
Departamento de Ingenierı´a Informa´tica, Universidad de Santiago de Chile, Santiago, Chile,

**Gustavo Gatica**
Escuela de Informa´tica, Universidad Andre´s Bello, Santiago, Chile

**Vı´ctor Parada**
Departamento de Ingenierı´a Informa´tica, Universidad de Santiago de Chile, Santiago, Chile,

**Xin Li**
Nankai-Baidu Joint Laboratory, College of Information Technical Science, Nankai University, Tianjin, China,

**Douglas S. Stones**
Clayton School of Information Technology, Monash University, Victoria, Australia
School of Mathematical Sciences, Monash University, Victoria, Australia

**Haidong Wang**
Nankai-Baidu Joint Laboratory, College of Information Technical Science, Nankai University, Tianjin, China,

**Hualiang Deng**
Nankai-Baidu Joint Laboratory, College of Information Technical Science, Nankai University, Tianjin, China,

**Xiaoguang Liu**
College of Software, Nankai University, Tianjin, China

**Gang Wang**
Nankai-Baidu Joint Laboratory, College of Information Technical Science, Nankai University, Tianjin, China,

**Olawale Titiloye**
School of Computing, Mathematics and Digital Technology, Manchester Metropolitan University, Manchester, United Kingdom

**Alan Crispin**
School of Computing, Mathematics and Digital Technology, Manchester Metropolitan University, Manchester, United Kingdom

**Guillermo Vega-Gorgojo**
Department of Informatics, University of Oslo, Oslo, Norway,

**Martin Giese**
Department of Informatics, University of Oslo, Oslo, Norway

**Simen Heggestøyl**
Department of Informatics, University of Oslo, Oslo, Norway

**Ahmet Soylu**
Faculty of Computer Science and Media Technology, Norwegian University of Science and Technology, Gjøvik, Norway

**Arild Waaler**
Department of Informatics, University of Oslo, Oslo, Norway

# Preface

Standard system programs consist of the OS, as well as firmware, compilers, interpreters, assemblers, loaders, schedulers, as well as linkers, in addition to the run-time libraries of the personal computer. Creating software programs that stretch or perhaps increase the operating of an operating system, akin to drivers, changes to an OS, or perhaps a completely new OS. Systems programming includes creating applications that enable the personal computer to interact with the computer programmer as well as the end user. Therefore, it enables the functioning of practical application software programs on the platform. Essentially, whatever is a member of the operating system, that is not a program, is systems programming.

Just how these kinds of programs work collectively, how they are invoked, just what restraints are available on the tools that a computer programmer makes use of, as well as just what APIs as well as utilities and so forth that are supplied for users: these are generally all of the areas of systems programming. It largely includes the administration of memory space; I/O procedures in the broadest meaning of the expression, i.e.: networks, documents having access to the machine, etc.; device control ( tasking , administration of processes, and so forth ). User<->system communication strategies as well as end user administration are also part of systems programming. Systems programming represents the design, and modelling, of the programs, and services, that can make up an OS. The improvement and control of methods which can be an integral part of an OS are part of systems programming as well. Systems programming requires a large amount of hardware knowledge relative to applications programming. Systems programming is designed to create software program which offers services to the personal computer's hardware. The first chapter peruses BP neural networks. Chapter 2 analyzes approximation techniques that can be employed to approximate the difficulty of computer software engineering ventures. Chapter 3 scrutinizes Wireless Multimedia Sensor Networks. Chapter 4 suggest an antagonistic strategy to assist forensic research of mobile handsets. Chapter 5 puts emphasis on the timer device features offered by 5 diverse VMMs. Chapter 6 evaluates a multi-agent patrolling situation. Chapter 7 peruses time-critical variable method for viewing naturally occurring scenarios. Chapter 8 probes a consistent transmission line of limited duration. Chapter 9 evaluates choice algorithms in multivariate calibration that may be enhanced utilizing Graphics Processing Units. Chapter 10 figures out the noise attributes required for unquestionable safety for a perfect Kirchhoff-Law-Johnson-Noise ( KLJN ) protected key supply method. Chapter 11 gives an outline of the MC64-ClustalWP2, a fresh rendering of the Clustal W algorithm. Chapter 12 analyzes a version of the MSAProbs algorithm for graphics processors. Chapter 13 views a completely computer-controlled common objective method for high-throughput coaching. Chapter 14 features a fresh algorithm to calculate equal latitude. Chapter 15 scrutinizes DistMap - an incorporated workflow to map scans in the dispersed Hadoop structure. Chapter 16 is designed to develop the efficiency of Dynamic Causal Modeling for Event Related Potentials ( DCM for ERP ) in MATLAB. Chapter 17 scrutinizes ScriptingRT, a fresh open source application to accumulate reaction latencies in on the web tests of simple human cognition. Chapter 18 deals with vertex coloring problems. Chapter 19 explains how to delivery a network motif identification software package. Chapter 20 analyzes a combinatorial optimization strategy motivated by quantum mechanics. Chapter 21 studies a handy application for researching semantic datasets prepared for conventional end users.

**Editor**
**Gerard Ian Prudhomme**
**Hawaii, US**

CHAPTER 1

# BIG DATA: A PARALLEL PARTICLE SWARM OPTIMIZATION-BACK-PROPAGATION NEURAL NETWORK ALGORITHM BASED ON MAPREDUCE

Jianfang Cao[1] , Hongyan Cui[1], Hao Shi[2] , Lijuan Jiao[1]

[1] Computer Science and Technology Department, Xinzhou Teachers University, Xinzhou, China,

[2] College of Computer Science and Technology, Taiyuan University of Science and Technology, Taiyuan, China

## ABSTRACT

**A back-propagation (BP) neural network can solve complicated random nonlinear mapping problems; therefore, it can be applied to a wide range of problems. However, as the sample size increases, the time required to train BP neural networks becomes lengthy. Moreover, the classification accuracy decreases as well. To improve the classification accuracy and runtime efficiency of the BP neural network algorithm, we proposed a parallel design and realization method for a particle swarm optimization (PSO)-optimized BP neural network based on MapReduce on the Hadoop platform using both the PSO algorithm and a parallel design. The PSO algorithm was used to optimize the BP neural network's initial weights and thresholds and improve the accuracy of the classification algorithm. The MapReduce parallel programming model was utilized to achieve parallel processing of the BP algorithm, thereby solving the problems of hardware and communication overhead when the BP neural network addresses big data. Datasets on 5 different scales were constructed using the scene image library from the SUN Database. The classification accuracy of the parallel PSO-BP neural network algorithm is approximately 92%, and the system efficiency is approximately 0.85, which presents obvious advantages when processing big data. The algorithm proposed in this study demonstrated both higher classification accuracy and improved time efficiency, which represents a significant improvement obtained from applying parallel processing to an intelligent algorithm on big data.**

## INTRODUCTION

A Back-Propagation (BP) neural network is a type of multi-layered feed-forward neural network that learns by constantly modifying both the connection weights between the neurons in each layer and the neuron thresholds to make the network output continuously approximate the desired output [1]. Because a BP neural network is robust and can realize any complex nonlinear mapping relation, this technique has been widely used in many fields [2]. In terms of speed prediction, to better utilize wind power, Guo et al. [3] constructed a hybrid wind speed prediction model using a BP neural network that eliminates seasonal effects from actual wind speed datasets using a seasonal exponential adjustment. They conducted a case study in Minqin County, Gansu Province that satisfactorily eliminated the seasonal effects from the prediction results. Xu

**Citation:** Cao J, Cui H, Shi H, Jiao L (2016) Big Data: A Parallel Particle Swarm Optimization-Back-Propagation Neural Network Algorithm Based on MapReduce. PLoS ONE 11(6): e0157551. doi:10.1371/journal.pone.0157551

et al. [4] applied a BP neural network to debris flow control engineering and proposed a method for predicting the average velocity of debris flow. In the medical field, Zhang et al. [5] used a BP neural network to construct an m-order nonlinear model to describe the complex relationships between surface electromyogram signals and the joint angles of a human leg. The model inputs were preprocessed sEMG time series, and the outputs were the hip, knee and ankle joint angles, with an average angle estimation root mean square error of less than 5° for spinal cord injury patients. Cheng et al. [6] proposed a new method based on a BP neural network to predict facial deformation following a complete denture prosthesis. By analyzing the relationship between one third of the facial area and the completed denture, this method accurately predicted deformation of the facial soft tissue. To solve cotton pest problems in agricultural fields, Zhang et al. [7] designed a cotton disease and pest damage identification method based on rough sets and a BP neural network that accurately identified 4 cotton diseases. In digital image processing, Pan et al. [8] used a BP neural network to conduct automatic recognition of woven fabric patterns by extracting fabric texture features with a black and white co-occurrence matrix. In other areas, Hu [9] proposed a type of intrusion detection algorithm that used a BP neural network to solve the relatively high false negative rate and high false alarm rate problems with traditional intrusion detection algorithms. Liu et al. [10] applied a BP neural network to establish a forecasting model for port throughput and achieved good results when forecasting the port throughput in 2011 and 2012. However, the BP neural network algorithm is based on the idea of an error gradient descent function; thus, it does not have global search capability. In addition, the connection weights between the layers and the neuron's thresholds, which can take on random values between 0 and 1 in the initial training stage, lead to slow convergence by the algorithm and do not necessarily lead to an optimal solution [11]. Later, researchers gradually introduced some metaheuristic optimization algorithms. Wang et al. [12–14] presented an improved firefly algorithm, a biogeography-based krill herd algorithm and a chaotic krill herd algorithm to solve complex optimization tasks. Chiroma H. et al. [15] discussed the applications of a bio-inspired flower pollination algorithm, which motivated other researchers in the bio-inspired algorithms research community to further improve the effectiveness of the flower pollination algorithm as well as to apply the algorithm in other fields to solve optimization problems in engineering and industry. Saadi et al. [16] proposed a new metaheuristic algorithm called Ringed Seal Search that found the optimal solution. This algorithm searched and selected the best lair by performing a random walk to find new lairs. In recent years, optimization algorithms have usually been used to optimize the weights of neural networks and solve practical problems in various fields. Nawi et al. [17] used the PSO algorithm to optimize the weights of recurrent neural networks and conduct data classification. Chiroma et al. [18] applied an artificial neural network optimized by the PSO algorithm to predict OPEC $CO_2$ emissions. Chiroma H. et al. [19, 20] predicted crude oil prices using a neural network optimized by a genetic algorithm. The optimization and application of the initial weights and thresholds of the BP neural network have also been studied intensively. The most widely used optimization algorithms are the genetic algorithm (GA) and the particle swarm optimization (PSO) algorithm. Ding et al. [21] combined a GA with BP neural networks to accelerate the training of the BP network—which to a certain extent overcomes the disadvantages of the BP becoming easily stuck in a local minimum—and performed an experimental analysis of the UCI dataset. Yu et al. [22] also used a genetic algorithm to optimize a BP neural network. They improved the additional momentum factor and self-adaptive learning rate and established a natural gas load forecasting model to make short-term forecasts of natural gas loads in Shanghai. Gao et al. [23] used the GA to optimize the initial weights and thresholds of a BP neural network and was able to predict housing prices in Guiyang City with improved accuracy. Wang et al. [24] applied a PSO-optimized BP neural network algorithm to estimate the cost of plastic injection molding parts, improving both the convergence rate of the algorithm and the cost estimation accuracy rate. Similar to [3], Ren et al. [25] also predicted wind speed; however, in contrast to [3], Ren et al. first used a PSO algorithm to optimize the initial thresholds and weights of the BP neural network and then established a forecasting model that obtains improved accuracy compared to [3]. In addition, various other algorithms have been combined with the BP neural network to improve its performance. To improve classification results, Jia et al. [26] proposed a type of PLS-HCA-BP algorithm that uses partial least squares (PLS) to reduce the feature dimensions of samples, which simplifies the network structure and improves the speed of convergence in hierarchical cluster analysis (HCA), therein obtaining favorable experimental results. Wang et al. [27] established a target threat estimation model using Glowworm Swarm Optimization and the BP neural network. The above-mentioned studies, combined with other algorithms, have optimized BP neural networks and improved their performance. Compared with standalone BP neural networks, such combinations have achieved good results. However, regardless of the optimization employed, BP neural networks always show good performance when the sample size is small; however, when the sample set size increases, the time efficiency of these algorithms sharply and intolerably declines.

With the arrival of the big data era, sample datasets are becoming increasingly large. A bottleneck problem is being faced in terms of hardware capabilities for the above-mentioned traditional serial algorithm form of the BP neural network. Moreover, the training time for the algorithm becomes very lengthy. As a result, the efficiency of the system decreases significantly. Scholars are beginning to study parallel designs for traditional algorithms. Feng et al. [28] achieved a parallel form of an algorithm for a BP neural network on the Sunway Blue Light Supercomputer based on MPI techniques and made predictions of traffic flow. Zheng et al. [29] designed a type of multi-BP neural network parallel integration model and performed multi-semantic image classifications, therein obtaining good experimental results under the MPI Cluster environment. Liu [30] conducted parallel processing of a large-scale matrix operation in the PVM parallel environment, effectively reducing the time required for matrix operations. Guo et al. [31] designed a parallel BP neural network based on a field programmable gate array (FPGA) to address big data. Wang et al. [32] implemented an efficient GPU to train large-scale recurrent neural networks and achieved a good experimental result. However, the parallel design (based on

MPI, PVM, FPGA and GPUs) requires a clear understanding of the computer hardware architecture by the developers, and the communication between nodes is time consuming. These factors make such systems difficult to build and apply [33].

The MapReduce framework is based on Hadoop and has become popular in recent years. MapReduce is a type of parallel computing model oriented toward distributed environments. This model provides developers with a complete programming interface, does not require them to understand the computer architecture, and has gradually become a research hotspot for current studies on parallel algorithm design [34]. Therefore, researchers have proposed some algorithms for processing big data. Kim et al. [35] used a MapReduce model to design a density-based clustering algorithm suitable for processing big data and achieved good experimental results. Attribute reduction is an important research question in rough set theory. When addressing big data, the traditional attribute reduction algorithms appear to be inadequate. Jin et al. [36] proposed a hierarchical attribute reduction algorithm that executed in parallel using MapReduce on both data and tasks, therein saving a great deal of time. Scardapane et al. [37] proposed a decentralized training algorithm for Echo State Networks in distributed big data applications. To fulfill the potential of artificial neural networks for big data applications, Liu et al. [38] used the MapReduce framework to implement parallelized neural networks and solve existing problems faced by traditional artificial neural networks. Simultaneously, the applications of big data have gradually increased in various fields, especially in the biomedical fields. Zou et al. [39] applied the MapReduce framework to bioinformatics and used it to conduct next-generation sequencing. Subsequently, Zou et al. [40] used the MapReduce model to solve bottleneck problems in massive multiple sequence alignments (MSAs) of homologous DNA and genome sequences. Shen et al. [41] proposed a quantitative quality control method for radiotherapy and chemotherapy based on an artificial neural network to process medical big data. Chung et al. [42] used a parallel deep neural network to train big data on Blue Gene. Elsebakhi et al. [43] adopted functional networks based on propensity scores and Newton-Raphson maximum-likelihood optimizations as a new large-scale machine learning classifier to improve the classification performance when faced with biomedical big data. In other areas, to address increasing traffic flow data efficiently, Cheng et al. [44] proposed a prediction method to process distributed traffic flow using a parallel programming model based on MapReduce. Gu et al. [45] designed a parallel computing platform to make instant messaging deliveries. Stateczny et al. [46] solved the reduction problems of hydrographic big data. These studies, using MapReduce parallel processing, all do a good job of improving the time efficiency of their respective systems. Applications based on MapReduce are gradually increasing. However, there are few studies concerning the PSO algorithm or that investigate MapReduce distributed parallel processing of BP neural networks and their application to the semantic classification of digital images.

To solve the above-mentioned problems, this study proposes a parallel PSO-BP neural network algorithm and applies it to the classification of scene images. The parallel processing mechanism of this algorithm is based on the MapReduce parallel programming model and uses the PSO algorithm to optimize the initial weights and thresholds of the BP neural network. Then, different multiple optimized parallel BP neural networks are used to train different sample sets, which not only ensures that the BP neural network can obtain the optimal solution but also accelerates the convergence rate. This approach effectively reduces the impact of sample diversity and complexity on the performance of the BP neural network and shortens the required training time.

## PSO-BP NEURAL NETWORK ALGORITHM

The PSO algorithm, when introduced into a BP neural network to optimize its initial weights and thresholds, is well suited for addressing some of the deficiencies caused by the randomness of the initial weights and thresholds of BP neural networks [24].

### PSO-optimized BP Neural Network Model

The basic idea behind using the PSO algorithm to optimize the BP neural network is to combine them, using the initial connection weights between BP neural network layers and the initial thresholds between neural nodes, to optimize the distribution, execute global searches within the solution space, and find the optimal initial weights and thresholds of the BP neural network at a rapid convergence rate. Subsequently, the initial weights and thresholds obtained by the BP neural network can be used for training and testing the sample set. Fig 1 shows a flowchart of this optimized model.

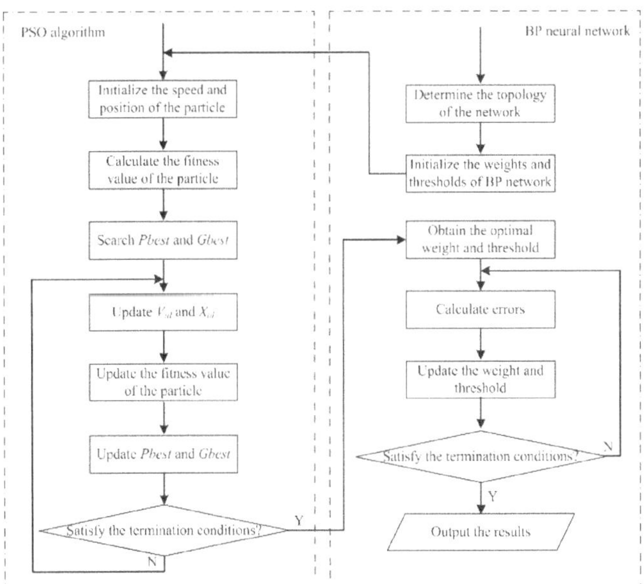


Figure 1. PSO-BP neural network algorithm model.

### Steps in the PSO-optimized BP neural network algorithm

The main steps of the algorithm are as follows:

Optimization phase of PSO algorithm:

- Initialize PSO parameters (population size, speed and position of particles and iterations).
- Determine the structure of the BP neural network and generate population particles. Particles: $X_i = (x_{i1}, x_{i2}, \ldots x_{iD})^T$, $i = 1,2,\ldots,n$

$$D = RD_1 + D_1D_2 + D_1 + D_2 \quad (1)$$

- where R, $D_1$ and $D_2$ represent the number of nodes in the input layer, hidden layer and output layer of the BP neural network, respectively.
- Design the fitness function. The BP neural network trains on the training samples in accordance with Particle $X_i$ in Eq (2) to set weights and thresholds until it generates the expected output $\bar{y}_i$ The fitness function of the individual, $X_i$, is defined as

$$fit_i = \sum_{j=1}^{M-1} (\bar{y}_j - y_j)^2 \ (i = 1, 2, \cdots, n) \quad (2)$$

- Calculate each particle's fitness value and evaluate Population *X*. Calculate the fitness value of each individual particle $X_i$.
- Update the individual's optimal fitness value *Pbest* and the particles' positions. For each particle $X_i$, if its current fitness value is smaller than its optimal fitness value*Pbest*, then use the current fitness value to update the optimal fitness value *Pbest* and the position of particle $X_i$.
- Update the population fitness value *Gbest*. For each particle $X_i$, if its fitness value is smaller than the optimal fitness value *Gbest* for the current population, then use the fitness value of the current particle to update the optimal fitness value *Gbest*.
- Iteratively update the speed and position of particles to generate new populations. According to Formulas (3) and (4), constantly update the speed and position of each particle $X_i$, as shown below:

$$V_{id}^{k+1} = \omega V_{id}^k + c_1 r_1 (P_{id}^k - X_{id}^k) + c_2 r_2 (P_{gd}^k - X_{id}^k) \ (d \in [1, D], i \in [1, n]) \quad (3)$$

$$X_{id}^{k+1} = X_{id}^k + V_{id}^{k+1} \ (d \in [1, D], i \in [1, n]) \quad (4)$$

- where  is the inertia weight; *k* is the number of iterations; $V_{id}$ is the speed of Particle$X_i$; $c_1$ and $c_2$ are acceleration factors, which are not smaller than zero; and $r_1$ and $r_2$ are arbitrary numbers between 0 and 1.
- Judge whether to halt the iteration based on whether the optimal initial weights and thresholds of the BP neural network have been generated. The overall fitness variance (Formula (5)) is used to judge whether the PSO algorithm converges. If the overall fitness variance of the particle population is smaller than the given threshold, then the algorithm has converged. The optimal solution is output as the initial weights and thresholds. Otherwise, the iterations continue.

$$\sigma^2 = -\sum_{i=1}^{n} (\frac{f_i - f_{avg}}{f})^2 \quad (5)$$

- where *n* is the number of particles in the current population, $f_i$ is the fitness value of particle $X_i$, and $f_{avg}$ is the average fitness of the current population particle.

The training phases of the BP neural network are as follows:

- Initialize the network. The network structure, expected output and learning rate are determined according to the sample characteristics. The PSO algorithm optimization is used to derive the optimal individual solution for the initial weight value and threshold of the network.
- Input the training sample and calculate the output of the network layers.
- Calculate the learning error of the network.
- Correct the connection weight values and thresholds of the layers.
- Judge whether the error satisfies the expectation requirements and whether the number of iterations has reached the set training limit. If either condition is met, then the training ends. Otherwise, the iterative learning process continues.

## PARALLEL IMPLEMENTATION OF THE PSO-BP NEURAL NETWORK ALGORITHM

The arrival of the big data era poses a challenge to traditional machine learning algorithms. In information technology, big data is a collection of datasets so large and complex that they become difficult to process using available database management tools or traditional data processing applications. Big data is usually composed of datasets with sizes beyond the ability of commonly used software tools, which are unable to capture, curate, manage, or process such data within a reasonable elapsed time [47]. The challenges include capture, curation, storage, search, sharing, analysis, and visualization. Therefore, both the time and space efficiency of traditional algorithms decrease dramatically when addressing big data.

Although the PSO-BP neural network algorithm improves the performance of the traditional BP neural network algorithm, as the data size increases, the BP neural network training time increases as well, eventually raising efficiency issues. The MapReduce parallel programming framework provides a type of distributed parallel calculation environment for big data processing. Faced with booming data growth in a big data environment, there is a need to improve the time efficiency and accuracy of BP neural networks. Therefore, this study's goals are to solve the low time efficiency problem and the poor data classification accuracy of traditional BP neural networks optimized by the PSO algorithm as proposed in [25]. To that end, this study conducts a parallel implementation of the PSO-BP neural network algorithm within the MapReduce framework.

### MapReduce Programming Model

MapReduce [47] is based on Hadoop, which is a type of distributed parallel programming model developed by Google Inc. for processing big data. MapReduce separates the calculation process for data into Map and Reduce stages, which correspond to the execution of a mapper() function and a reducer() function, respectively. The process requires data to be input in the form of key-value pairs (e.g., <key, value>, where the key can be regarded as the data serial number and the value can be regarded as the data value). In the Map stage, MapReduce segments data into Splits of identical sizes and processes each Split in the form of key value pairs *<k1, v1>* to create the formal input. It executes the mapper() function to generate intermediate results in the form of *<k2, v2>*, which are ranked according to the value of *k2*. The *v2* values whose *k2* values are the same are combined to form a new list *<k2, list(v2)>* and, finally, grouped according to the scope of *k2* to form Reduce tasks. In the Reduce stage, the outputs of the Map tasks are integrated and ranked, *<k2, list(v2)>* is taken as the input, and the reduce() function is executed to obtain the key value pair *<k3, v3>*, which is output to the Hadoop File System (HDFS). A flowchart of the MapReduce process is shown in Fig 2.

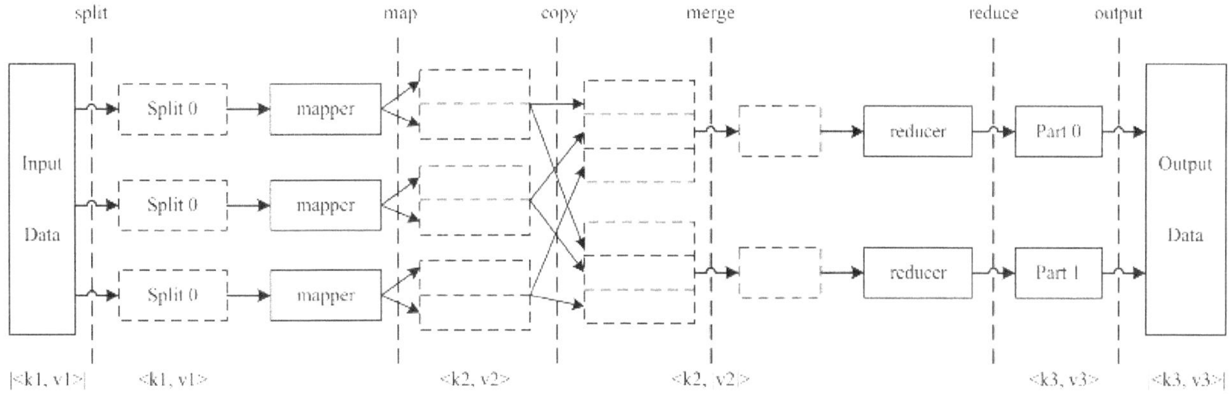


Figure 2. The MapReduce programming model process.

## Parallel design and realization of PSO algorithm

Design and realization of PSO-Map().

Due to the data input format utilized by the MapReduce programming model, this study first converts the data input by the PSO algorithm into the *<key, value>* format, where *key*represents the serial number of a particle and value represents the attribute of a particle. In the Map stage—particle initialization and fitness evaluation—the optimal particles for individual populations and other operations are calculated. The Map process for the PSO algorithm is designed as follows:

Input: particle id, particle attribute value

Output: key, optimal particle set

PSO-Map(particle id, particle attribute value)

{

For each particle, obtain its value;

fit-value = fit(value); //calculate the fitness value of the updated particle

//iteratively update the position and speed of particle

if (satisfy condition)

key = new-key(key);

output key, optimal particle set;

}

Design and realization of PSO-Reduce().

In the Reduce stage, the optimal particle sets generated by the Map tasks are received and integrated, and the position and speed of the optimal particle set are globally updated. If the termination condition is satisfied, the optimal particle of the whole population is output. The Reduce process for the PSO algorithm is designed as follows:

Input: key, optimal particle set

Output: key, optimal particles

PSO-Reduce(key, optimal particle set)

{

Obtain the fit-value of each optimal particle in the population;

//globally iteratively update population

if (the optimal solution of the problem is obtained|| and the maximum iteration times are reached)

output key, optimal particle;

}

When the parallel iterations of the PSO algorithm are complete, the optimal particles obtained are the initial weights and thresholds for the BP neural network.

## Parallel design and realization of the BP neural network

To overcome the shortcomings of the BP neural network, including hardware overhead and excessive training time, this study also conducts a parallel design for the BP neural network based on MapReduce, therein using Map and Reduce tasks to implement automatic parallel operations within the multi-layered BP neural network. This approach greatly reduces the training time and simultaneously improves the training precision. The model structure is shown in Fig 3.

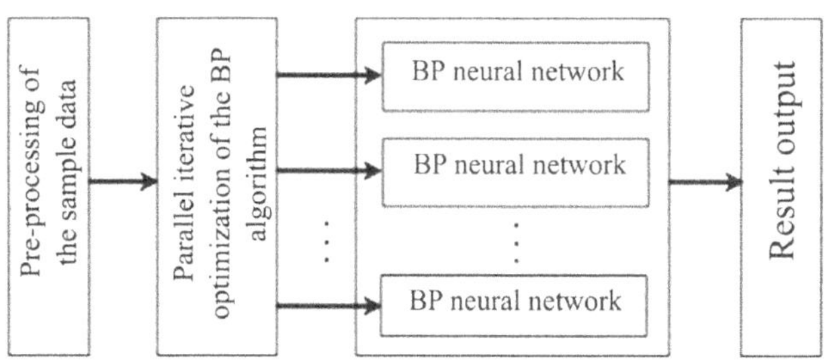


Figure 3. A parallel model of the BP neural network.

### *Design and realization of BP-Map().*

In the Map stage, based on the input, the Map tasks calculate the actual output of the network layer by layer. Then, the actual output and the expected output are compared to calculate the network learning error. Finally, based on the learning error, updated connection weight values in the network are calculated. The Map tasks for the BP neural network are designed as follows:

Input: sample id, sample feature value

Output: the corresponding weights $\omega$ of the sample and the amount $\Delta\omega$ by which the weights were updated

BP-Map(Sample id, sample feature value)

{

//For each sample,

calculate the output of network layers;

and calculate the learning error of the network;

For each connection weight $w$, calculate the updated amount $\Delta w$ for the weight;

Output($w$, $\Delta w$);

}

Design and realization of the BP-Combine() function.

In the MapReduce parallel programming model, the Combine() function can perform local processing of the intermediate result generated in the Map stage, thereby greatly reducing the communication overhead. As the size of the sample data that the BP neural network uses for training gradually increases, it becomes imperative to process the results generated by Map tasks using the Combine() function before using them as input in the Reduce tasks. In the parallel design process of the BP neural network, the Combine() function is designed as follows:

Input: key value pair <$w$, $\Delta w$>

Output: key value pair <$w$, $\Delta w$>

BP-Combine($w$, $\Delta w$)

{

Initial variable count = 0; //count the number of training samples

//resolve each training sample

and process the three-dimensional coordinate values of $\Delta w$;

count←count+1;

$w$←$w$;

Collect all the key value pairs whose $w$ values are the same, and conduct local reduction to derive $\Delta w$;

Output $w$←$w$;

}

## *Design and realization of BP-Reduce().*

In the Reduce stage, the output of the Combine() function is used as input. Next, the total number of samples whose weights are the same is calculated, and their weights are updated. The Reduce tasks for the BP neural network are designed as follows:

Input: the output of the Combine function: < ',Δ '>

Output: $< \omega', \sum_{i=1}^{n} \Delta\omega'/n >$

BP-Reduce ( ',Δ ')

{

Add the Δ ' of the samples whose ' s are the same to obtain $\sum_{i=1}^{n} \Delta\omega'$;

calculate the average amount with which to update every weight; and

output ', $\sum_{i=1}^{n} \Delta\omega'/n$ ;

}

Experiment and Results Analysis

To validate the performance of the parallel PSO-BP neural network algorithm proposed in this study, we tested it on a semantic classification task with a large number of scene images on the Hadoop platform.

## Experimental Environment and Data

The experimental environment was a Hadoop cluster composed of five computers in an intranet. One computer acted as the master node, and the other four computers acted as slave nodes. All the nodes were equipped with 4G dual-core processors, 1 TB hard disks, and the Ubuntu operating system. Configured as described, the system can obtain the desired results even when dealing with tens of thousands of images. As the size of the image database increases, additional processing power can be added by increasing the number of slave nodes in the Hadoop cluster [48].

The experimental data stemmed from the SUN Database image library (http://groups.csail.mit.edu/vision/SUN/), which consists of 131,067 images in 908 categories freely available to researchers. At present, the Sun database is available as a free big data image set. This study constructed 5 datasets (using a combination of random selection by a computer and artificial selection) and named them sequentially as "Data1" through "Data5." Data1 contained 300 scene images in 3 categories, Data2 contained 800 scene images in 5 categories, Data3 contained 2,000 scene images in 8 categories, Data4 contained 5,000 scene images in 12 categories, and Data5 contained 15,000 scene images in 15 categories. For processing convenience, we convert all experiment images into images of 300 pixels × 300 pixels, and the size of each image is approximately 265 KB. Thus, the size of the 15,000 images used in this paper is approximately 3.98 GB.

Because the color feature is the main characteristic reflecting the implied semantics of scene images [2], in the preprocessing stage for the sample data in this study, 60-dimensional color feature vectors were selected in the HSV color space in the OpenCV environment. In this paper, 60-dimensional color feature vectors are used as the input, and the image category is the output. Therefore, for the BP neural network, after the individual PSO was conducted, the number of input nodes $n_i$ was set to 60, and the number of output nodes was $n_o$ to 1. The number of hidden nodes $n_h$ was determined to be 8 through repeated experiments according toFormula (6). Then, the structure of an individual BP neural network was 60-8-1. Ten BP neural networks with the same structures and all optimized using the PSO algorithm were used in the study to perform parallel categorizations of the scene images.

$$n_h = \sqrt{n_i + n_o} + \alpha \quad \alpha \in [0, 1] \quad (6)$$

where is an arbitrary decimal value between 0 and 1.

## Experimental Results and Analysis

To validate the performance of the algorithm proposed in this study, we conducted experimental comparisons by evaluating aspects such as classification accuracy, speedup ratio, and efficiency.

***Classification Accuracy.***

Under different image scales, and using training samples to test sample ratios of 3:2, 2:1, 3:1 and 5:1, the traditional serial BP neural network algorithm, the PSO-BP neural network algorithm and the parallel PSO-BP neural network algorithm proposed in this study were compared in terms of their classification precision ratios and recall rates. The experimental results are shown in Table 1.

Table 1. Comparison of the classification performance of different algorithms under different data scales and data partition ratios.

| Dataset | Classification algorithm | Accuracy (%) | Data partition ratio | | | | Max | Min | Mean | Standard deviation |
|---|---|---|---|---|---|---|---|---|---|---|
| | | | 3:2 | 2:1 | 3:1 | 5:1 | | | | |
| Data1 | | | | | | | | | | |
| | BP | | | | | | | | | |
| | | Precision ratio | 84.5 | 87.6 | 90.4 | 92.6 | 92.6 | 84.5 | 88.8 | 3.04 |
| | | Recall rate | 89.6 | 92.2 | 94.7 | 95.1 | 95.1 | 89.6 | 92.9 | 2.21 |
| | PSO-BP | | | | | | | | | |
| | | Precision ratio | 91.9 | 93.4 | 95.1 | 96.3 | 96.3 | 91.9 | 94.2 | 1.67 |
| | | Recall rate | 93.8 | 95.4 | 97.0 | 98.5 | 98.5 | 93.8 | 96.2 | 1.76 |
| | Parallel PSO-BP | | | | | | | | | |
| | | Precision ratio | 95.2 | 95.9 | 96.6 | 97.1 | 97.1 | 95.2 | 96.2 | 0.72 |
| | | Recall rate | 97.2 | 98.0 | 98.7 | 99.3 | 99.3 | 97.2 | 98.3 | 0.78 |
| Data2 | | | | | | | | | | |
| | BP | | | | | | | | | |
| | | Precision ratio | 81.5 | 84.4 | 87.2 | 89.8 | 89.8 | 81.5 | 85.7 | 3.10 |
| | | Recall rate | 84.2 | 87.0 | 89.7 | 92.3 | 92.3 | 84.2 | 88.3 | 3.02 |
| | PSO-BP | | | | | | | | | |
| | | Precision ratio | 90.3 | 92.0 | 93.6 | 94.0 | 94.0 | 90.3 | 92.5 | 1.46 |
| | | Recall rate | 91.0 | 92.8 | 94.5 | 96.0 | 96.0 | 91.0 | 93.6 | 1.87 |
| | Parallel PSO-BP | | | | | | | | | |
| | | Precision ratio | 93.4 | 95.2 | 96.0 | 96.7 | 96.7 | 93.4 | 95.3 | 1.23 |
| | | Recall rate | 96.4 | 97.1 | 97.9 | 98.5 | 98.5 | 96.4 | 97.5 | 0.79 |
| Data3 | | | | | | | | | | |
| | BP | | | | | | | | | |
| | | Precision ratio | 76.2 | 79.3 | 82.3 | 85.2 | 85.2 | 76.2 | 80.8 | 3.35 |
| | | Recall rate | 78.7 | 82.0 | 84.9 | 87.9 | 87.9 | 78.7 | 83.4 | 3.41 |
| | PSO-BP | | | | | | | | | |
| | | Precision ratio | 84.1 | 86.4 | 88.6 | 90.3 | 90.3 | 84.1 | 87.3 | 2.32 |
| | | Recall rate | 86.3 | 88.5 | 90.7 | 92.6 | 92.6 | 86.3 | 89.5 | 2.36 |
| | Parallel PSO-BP | | | | | | | | | |
| | | Precision ratio | 92.2 | 93.3 | 94.3 | 95.2 | 95.2 | 92.2 | 93.8 | 1.12 |
| | | Recall rate | 94.1 | 95.3 | 96.3 | 97.1 | 97.1 | 94.1 | 95.7 | 1.12 |
| Data4 | | | | | | | | | | |
| | BP | | | | | | | | | |
| | | Precision ratio | 69.6 | 73.2 | 76.7 | 80.1 | 80.1 | 69.6 | 74.9 | 3.91 |
| | | Recall rate | 74.2 | 77.4 | 80.2 | 83.0 | 83.0 | 74.2 | 78.7 | 3.27 |
| | PSO-BP | | | | | | | | | |
| | | Precision ratio | 79.0 | 81.3 | 83.5 | 85.6 | 85.6 | 79.0 | 82.4 | 2.46 |
| | | Recall rate | 81.9 | 84.1 | 86.2 | 88.0 | 88.0 | 81.9 | 85.1 | 2.28 |
| | Parallel PSO-BP | | | | | | | | | |
| | | Precision ratio | 90.0 | 91.3 | 92.3 | 93.5 | 93.5 | 90.0 | 91.8 | 1.29 |
| | | Recall rate | 91.0 | 92.3 | 94.4 | 95.5 | 95.5 | 91.0 | 93.3 | 1.76 |
| Data5 | | | | | | | | | | |
| | BP | | | | | | | | | |
| | | Precision ratio | 59.5 | 63.9 | 68.1 | 72.2 | 72.2 | 59.5 | 65.9 | 4.73 |
| | | Recall rate | 62.0 | 66.8 | 71.1 | 75.4 | 75.4 | 62.0 | 68.8 | 4.98 |
| | PSO-BP | | | | | | | | | |
| | | Precision ratio | 68.9 | 72.3 | 75.5 | 78.4 | 78.4 | 68.9 | 73.8 | 3.55 |
| | | Recall rate | 70.2 | 74.5 | 77.4 | 80.1 | 80.1 | 70.2 | 75.6 | 3.67 |
| | Parallel PSO-BP | | | | | | | | | |
| | | Precision ratio | 88.0 | 89.4 | 90.5 | 91.8 | 91.8 | 88.0 | 89.9 | 1.40 |
| | | Recall rate | 90.1 | 91.3 | 92.5 | 93.8 | 93.8 | 90.1 | 91.9 | 1.38 |

doi:10.1371/journal.pone.0157551.t001

As shown in Table 1, under different data scales and data partition ratios, the classification effect of the algorithm proposed in this study is preferable to the algorithm of the traditional BP neural network and the PSO-BP neural network, showing that the accuracy improvement did not occur by chance. Furthermore, because the efficiency of the traditional BP and PSO-BP algorithms is dramatically reduced as the sample data size increases rapidly [44], the parallel PSO-BP algorithm exhibits the fewest sample fluctuations according to the statistical standard deviation results and achieves the best classification performance. In addition, as the data scale increases, although the classification accuracy rates of all algorithms decreased, the parallel PSO-BP neural network algorithm decreased only slightly, which indicates that the parallel programming model based on MapReduce achieves an excellent performance level, particularly with big data.

### *Speedup Ratio and Efficiency.*

For the parallel programming model based on MapReduce, two important indicators for measuring algorithmic performance are the speedup ratio and efficiency. The former refers to the ratio of the time required to run a task on a single calculating node to the time required to run that same task on multiple calculating nodes, while the latter refers to the ratio of the speedup to the number of calculating nodes [48]. Under ideal conditions, the speedup ratio increases linearly as the number of calculating nodes increases, and the efficiency remains constant at 1. However, because conditions can be affected by load balancing, communication overhead and other factors, the ratio does not increase linearly, and it is impossible for the efficiency to reach 1. Nevertheless, the study shows that when the efficiency reached 0.5, the system obtained very good performance [48]. Figs 4 and 5 present experimental comparisons of the speedup ratios and of the efficiencies of the algorithm proposed in this study, respectively, using datasets of different scales.

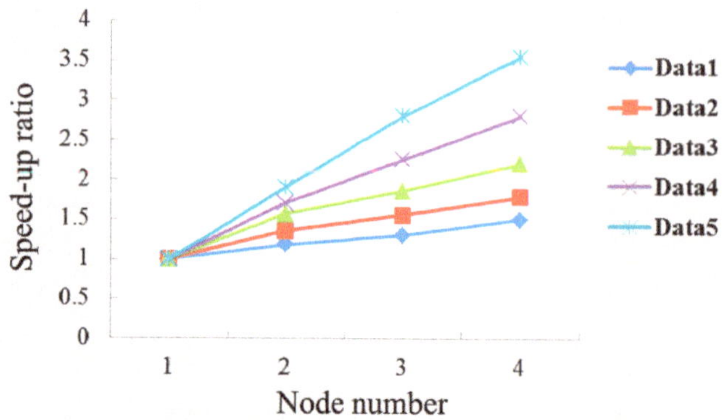


Figure 4. Comparison of speedup ratios with varying numbers of nodes.

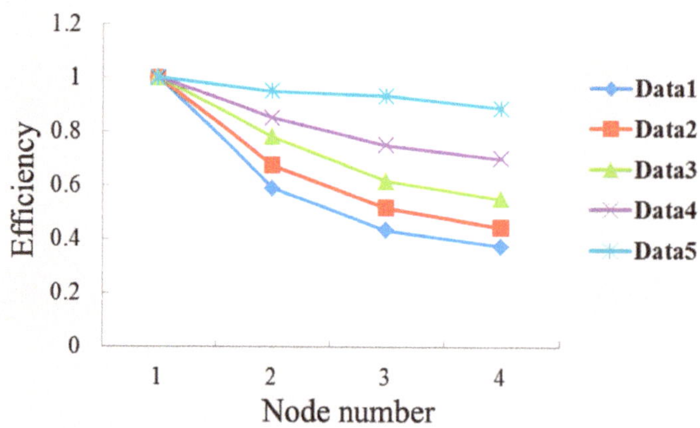


Figure 5. Comparison of system efficiency with varying numbers of nodes.

For the proposed algorithm in this paper, the training samples are assigned to a few processors from different slave nodes of the Hadoop cluster, and each processor trains the same BP neural network optimized by PSO and updates the network by counting all the training results. Consequently, on larger datasets, the algorithm's speedup ratio and efficiency performance are improved with increasing number of nodes [45].

In Fig 4, the speedup ratio follows an increasing trend as the number of calculating nodes increases, and increased data size results in an increased magnitude of the speedup ratio. For the same dataset, the processing speed of the system improves as the number of computing nodes increases. In other words, the system consumes less processing time; therefore, the speedup ratio follows an increasing trend. For the different datasets, the multi-computing nodes' performance increases with increasing amount of data [49]. Compared to a single-node computer, the processing speed is much higher. This result further indicates that larger datasets better demonstrate the performance of multiple calculating nodes.

Fig 5 validates the parallel system's efficiency. Its efficiency on smaller datasets is lower than its efficiency on larger datasets. As the number of calculating nodes increases, the system efficiency decreases more rapidly than when the dataset is smaller. As the size of the dataset gradually increases, the increase in calculating nodes results in a reduced system efficiency although with a smaller magnitude. The main reason for the reduction in system efficiency is that the increase in data size causes the system processing time to increase. In contrast, as the number of calculating nodes increases, the communication overhead between nodes also increases. However, the system efficiency is always greater than 0.5, which indicates that the algorithm has excellent parallel performance and expandability.

In addition, to validate the effectiveness of the proposed algorithm, this study performed image classification prediction on 10,000 randomly selected images from the SUN Database using the proposed algorithm and the algorithm presented in reference [25]. From an accuracy point of view, the average precision ratio and recall rate for the proposed algorithm reached 90.9% and 92.3%, respectively, when there were 4 slave nodes in the Hadoop cluster; however, when using the algorithm presented in [25], the average precision ratio and recall rate reached only 77.8% and 80.2%, respectively. Compared with the approach in [25], the average prediction precision ratio and recall rate based on our method increased by 13.1% and 12.1%, respectively. From the perspective of time overhead, the speedup ratio of the system reached 3.2 for the configuration of the Hadoop cluster in this paper. In other words, for the dataset including the randomly selected 10,000 images, the time cost of the proposed algorithm in [25] is 3.2 times that of our proposed algorithm. Moreover, the time efficiency of our approach has been greatly improved. These experimental results are presumably the result of the following. On the one hand, from a hardware perspective, this study adopted multiple computers to constitute a master-slave mode under a network environment and adopted a multiprocessor, parallel computing strategy to greatly increase the efficiency. On the other hand, from a software technology perspective, this paper uses not only the MapReduce parallel programming framework but also distributed data processing techniques. When the amount of processed data becomes very large, the running time of the traditional algorithm proposed in [25] would be excessive, and the classification accuracy would decrease sharply. These big data conditions reflect the superiority of the proposed algorithm in this paper even more clearly.

## CONCLUSIONS

Image classification is a complicated and time-consuming process. It requires more space and time to select, extract, and express features and to use the BP neural network to establish a classification model and classify images. In particular, when the image database size increases sharply, a single-machine environment cannot satisfy the time and space requirements of image classification. As an open-source and distributed computing platform, Hadoop has been widely used because it is convenient and cheap to create clusters and has a simple and easy-to-use computing model. The academic world and the industrial world are continuously studying how to adapt the traditional algorithms and applications developed under single-machine or mainframe environments to a Hadoop cluster environment.

This study conducted an in-depth exploration and analysis of the parallel design and implementation of a PSO-BP neural network algorithm. The study investigated the following three topics: optimizing the initial weights and thresholds for the BP neural network using the PSO algorithm, the PSO algorithm itself, and a parallel design and implementation of the BP neural network. The completed implementation was tested using image data from the SUN Database scene image library. The results verified the performance of the algorithm based on several aspects. The experimental results show that the algorithm proposed in this study achieves a good parallelization that can fully use distributed system resources and improve the algorithm's classification effectiveness. Furthermore, the distributed parallel system based on MapReduce greatly improved the performance compared with the serial version of the framework and fully demonstrates the powerful calculating capacity of parallel processing.

With the development of parallel technology, parallel computing plays an increasingly important role in addressing the complex problems involved in performing enormous amounts of calculations. The purpose of this study was to apply the MapReduce parallel programming framework to the BP neural network optimized by the PSO algorithm to improve the training speed of the BP neural network by creating a version of the algorithm that runs upon the parallel processing technology of Hadoop clusters. In the field of digital image analysis, using the powerful data processing ability of parallel computing to mine and analyze massive data is helpful for obtaining more accurate image information. This technique is important for image annotation, classification and retrieval and is of great significance in improving machine intelligence in understanding digital images.

As big data and cloud computing continue their rapid development, the processing and analysis of big data will remain a research hotspot for quite some time. The future goals of this study include (1) changing the number of nodes in the Hadoop distributed platform and adjusting related parameters to further improve the algorithm's efficiency; (2) improving the PSO algorithm to find the global optimal solution in a simpler and faster manner; and (3) optimizing the design of the Map and Reduce tasks for the algorithm to improve its classification accuracy.

## ACKNOWLEDGMENTS

This study was supported by the College Students' Innovative and Entrepreneurial Training Project in universities and colleges in Shanxi Province (2014383), the Natural Science Foundation of Shanxi Province (2013011017–2), the key discipline project of Xinzhou Teachers University (XK201308, XK201404), and the Youth Foundation Project of Xinzhou Teachers University (201209).

## AUTHOR CONTRIBUTIONS

Conceived and designed the experiments: JFC HYC. Performed the experiments: HS LJJ. Analyzed the data: HYC HS. Contributed reagents/materials/analysis tools: HS LJJ. Wrote the paper: JFC HYC HS LJJ.

## REFERENCES


1. Hu Y. The parallelism and application in data mining of BP algorithm. Chongqing: Chongqing University, 2003.
2. Cao JF, Chen LC. Fuzzy emotional semantic analysis and automated annotation of scene images. Computational Intelligence and Neuroscience. 2015;2015: 1–10. doi: 10.1155/2015/971039
3. Guo ZH, Wu J, Lu HY, Wang JZ. A case study on a hybrid wind speed forecasting method using BP neural network. Knowledge-based Systems. 2011;24(7): 1048–1056. doi: 10.1016/j.knosys.2011.04.019
4. Xu LM, Wang Q, Chen JP, Pan YZ. Forecast for average velocity of BP neural network. Journal of Jilin University (Earth Science Edition). 2013;43(1): 186–191.
5. Zhang F, Li PF, Hou ZG, Lu Z, Chen YX, Li QL, et al. sEMG-based continuous estimation of joint angles of human legs by using BP neural network. Neurocomputing. 2012;78(1): 139–148. doi: 10.1016/j.neucom.2011.05.033
6. Cheng C, Cheng XS, Dai N, Jiang XT, Sun YC, Li WW. Prediction of facial deformation after complete denture prosthesis using BP neural network. Computers in Biology and Medicine. 2015;66: 103–112. doi: 10.1016/j.compbiomed.2015.08.018. pmid:26386549
7. Zhang JH, Qi LJ, Ji RH, Wang H, Huang SK, Wang P. Cotton diseases identification based on rough sets and BP neural network. Transactions of the Chinese Society of Agricultural Engineering. 2012;28(7): 161–167.
8. Pan RR, Gao WD, Liu JH, Wang HB. Automatic recognition of woven fabric pattern based on image processing and BP neural network. Journal of the Textile Institute. 2011;102(1): 19–30. doi: 10.1080/00405000903430255
9. Hu MX. Intrusion detection algorithm based on BP neural network. Computer Engineering, 2012;38(6): 148–150.
10. Liu ML, Zhu MH. The port throughput forecast model based on the BP neural network. Journal of Systems Science. 2012;20(4): 88–91
11. Jing GL, Du WT, Guo YY. Studies on prediction of separation percent in electrodialysis process via BP neural networks and improved BP algorithms. Desalination. 2012;291: 78–93. doi: 10.1016/j.desal.2012.02.002
12. Wang GG, Guo L, Duan H, Wang H. A new improved firefly algorithm for global numerical optimization. Journal of Computational and Theoretical Nanoscience. 2014;11(2): 477–485. doi: 10.1166/jctn.2014.3383
13. Wang GG, Gandomi AH, Alavi AH. An effective krill herd algorithm with migration operator in biogeography-based optimization. Applied Mathematical Modelling. 2014;38(9): 2454–2462. doi: 10.1016/j.apm.2013.10.052
14. Wang GG, Guo L, Gandomi AH, Hao GS, Wang H. Chaotic krill herd algorithm. Information Sciences. 2014;274: 17–34. doi: 10.1016/j.ins.2014.02.123
15. Chiroma H, Shuib NLM, Muaz SA, Abubakar AI, Ila LB, Maitama JZ. A review of the applications of bio-inspired flower pollination algorithm. Procedia Computer Science. 2015;62: 435–441. doi: 10.1016/j.procs.2015.08.438
16. Saadi Y, Yanto IT, Herawan T, Balakrishnan V, Chiroma H, Risnumawan A. Ringed Seal Search for Global Optimization via a Sensitive Search Model. PLOS ONE. 2016;11(1): e0144371. doi: 10.1371/journal.pone.0144371. pmid:26790131
17. Nawi NM, Khan A, Rehman M, Chiroma H, Herawan T. Weight optimization in recurrent neural networks with hybrid metaheuristic Cuckoo search techniques for data classification. Mathematical Problems in Engineering. 2015;501: 868375. doi: 10.1155/2015/868375
18. Chiroma H, Abdul-Kareem S, Khan A, Nawi NM, Gital AYU, Shuib L, et al. Global warming: predicting OPEC carbon dioxide emissions from petroleum consumption using neural network and hybrid cuckoo search algorithm. PLOS ONE. 2015;10(8): e0136140. doi: 10.1371/journal.pone.0136140. pmid:26305483
19. Chiroma H, Gital AYU, Abubakar A, Usman MJ, Waziri U. Optimization of neural network through genetic algorithm searches for the prediction of international crude oil price based on energy products prices. In Proceedings of the 11th ACM Conference on Computing Frontiers (ACM). 2014.
20. Chiroma H, Abdulkareem S, Herawan T. Evolutionary Neural Network model for West Texas Intermediate crude oil price prediction. Applied Energy. 2015;142: 266–273. doi: 10.1016/j.apenergy.2014.12.045
21. Ding SF, Su CY, Yu JZ. An optimizing BP neural network algorithm based on genetic algorithm. Artificial Intelligence Review. 2011;36(2): 153–162. doi: 10.1007/s10462-011-9208-z
22. Yu F, Xu XZ. A short-term load forecasting model of natural gas based on optimized genetic algorithm and improved BP neural network. Applied Energy. 2014;134: 102–113. doi: 10.1016/j.apenergy.2014.07.104
23. Gao YM, Zhang RJ. Analysis of house price prediction based on genetic algorithm and BP neural network. Computer Engineering. 2014;40(4): 187–191.
24. Wang HS, Wang YN, Wang YC. Cost estimation of plastic injection molding parts through integration of PSO and BP neural network. Expert Systems with Applications. 2013;40(2): 418–428. doi: 10.1016/j.eswa.2012.01.166
25. Ren C, An N, Wang JZ, Li L, Hu B, Shang D. Optimal parameters selection for BP neural network based on particle swarm optimization: A case study of wind speed forecasting. Knowledge-based Systems. 2014;56: 226–239. doi: 10.1016/j.knosys.2013.11.015
26. Jia WK, Zhao DA, Shen T, Ding SF, Zhao YY, Hu CL. An optimized classification algorithm by BP neural network based on PLS and HCA. Applied Intelligence. 2015;43(1): 176–191. doi: 10.1007/s10489-
27. Wang GG, Guo LH, Duan H, Liu L, Wang HQ. Target threat assessment using glowworm swarm optimization and BP neural network. Journal of Jilin University (Engineering and Technology Edition). 2013;43(4): 1064–1069.
28. Feng JQ, Gu WD, Pan JS, Zhong HJ, Huo JD. Parallel

Implementation of BP Neural Network for Traffic Prediction on Sunway Blue Light Supercomputer. Applied Mechanics & Materials. 2014;614: 521–525. doi: 10.4028/www.scientific.net/amm.614.521

29. Zheng XW, Li YD, Ma MW. Parallelization Design of Image Semantic Classification Algorithm Under MPI Cluster Environment. Journal of Chinese Computer Systems. 2014;35(6): 1348–1352.

30. Liu J. Parallel computing based on the PVM. Journal of Guangdong University of Petrochemical Technology. 2012;12(4): 34–35.

31. Guo YH, Zhou DT, Qian XP, Zheng XQ. A Parallel BP Neural Network Based on the FPGA. Applied Mechanics & Materials. 2012;239–240: 1541–1545. doi: 10.4028/www.scientific.net/amm.239-240.1541

32. Wang Y, Li B, Luo R, Chen Y, Xu N, Yang H. Energy efficient neural networks for big data analytics. In the Proceedings of IEEE Conference on Design, Automation and Test in Europe Conference and Exhibition (DATE 2014), 1–2, 2014.

33. Roberge V, Tarbouchi M, Labonte G. Comparison of Parallel Genetic Algorithm and Particle Swarm Optimization for Real-Time UAV Path Planning. IEEE Transactions on Industrial Informatics. 2013;9(1): 132–141. doi: 10.1109/tii.2012.2198665

34. Mohamed H, Marchand-Maillet S. MRO-MPI: MapReduce overlapping using MPI and an optimized data exchange policy. Parallel Computing. 2013;39(12): 851–866. doi: 10.1016/j.parco.2013.08.010

35. Kim Y, Shim K, Kim MS, Lee JS. DBCURE-MR: An efficient density-based clustering algorithm for large data using MapReduce. Information Systems. 2014;42: 15–35. doi: 10.1016/j.is.2013.11.002

36. Jin Q, Lv P, Yue XD, Liu CH, Jing ZJ. Hierarchical attribute reduction algorithms for big data using MapReduce. Knowledge-based Systems. 2015;73: 18–31. doi: 10.1016/j.knosys.2014.09.001

37. Scardapane S, Wang D, Panella MA. A decentralized training algorithm for echo state networks in distributed big data applications. Neural Networks. 2015. doi: 10.1016/j.neunet.2015.07.006

38. Liu Y, Yang J, Huang Y, Xu L, Li S, Qi M. MapReduce Based Parallel Neural Networks in Enabling Large Scale Machine Learning. Computational Intelligence and Neuroscience. 2015; 501: 297672. doi: 10.1155/2015/297672

39. Zou Q, Li XB, Jiang WR, Lin ZY, Li GL, Chen K. Survey of mapreduce frame operation in bioinformatics. Briefings in Bioinformatics. 2014;15(4): 637–647. doi: 10.1093/bib/bbs088. pmid:23396756

40. Zou Q, Hu QH, Guo MZ, Wang GH. HAlign: Fast Multiple Similar DNA/RNA Sequence Alignment Based on the Centre Star Strategy. Bioinformatics. 2015;31(15): 2475–2481. doi: 10.1093/bioinformatics/btv177. pmid:25812743

41. Shen H, Meng JL, Yu LC, Fang XF, Chen TZ, Tan H, et al. A quantitative quality control method of big data in cancer patients using artificial neural network. In Proceedings of 2014 IEEE 3rd International Conference on Cloud Computing and Intelligence Systems (CCIS), 499–504, 2014.

42. Chung IH, Sainath TN, Ramabhadran B, Pichen M, Gunnels J, Austel V, et al. Parallel deep neural network training for big data on blue gene/Q. In Proceedings of 2014 International Conference for High Performance Computing, Networking, Storage and Analysis, IEEE Press, 745–753, 2014.

43. Elsebakhi E, Lee F, Schendel E, Haque A, Kathireason N, Pathare T, et al. Large-scale machine learning based on functional networks for biomedical big data with high performance computing platforms. Journal of Computational Science. 2015;11: 69–81. doi: 10.1016/j.jocs.2015.09.008

44. Chen C, Liu Z, Lin WH, Li S, Wang K. Distributed Modeling in a MapReduce Framework for Data-Driven Traffic Flow Forecasting. IEEE Transactions on Intelligent Transportation Systems. 2013;14(1): 22–33. doi: 10.1109/tits.2012.2205144

45. Gu R, Shen F, Huang Y. A parallel computing platform for training large scale neural networks. In Proceedings of 2013 IEEE International Conference on Big Data, 376–384, 2013.

46. Stateczny A, Wlodarczyk-Sielicka M. Self-organizing artificial neural networks into hydrographic big data reduction process. In Rough Sets and Intelligent Systems Paradigms, Springer International Publishing, 335–342, 2014.

47. Doulkeridis C, Norvag K. A survey of large-scale analytical query processing in MapReduce. VLDB Journal. 2014;23(3): 355–380. doi: 10.1007/s00778-013-0319-9

48. Zhu WS, Wang P. Large-scale image retrieval solution based on Hadoop cloud computing platform. Journal of Computer Applications. 2014;34(3): 695–699.

49. Yan J, Mu XX. Researching on Hadoop speedup performance model. Journal of Henan Normal University (NaturalScienceEdition). 2014; 42(2): 152–157.

CHAPTER 2

# ALGORITHMIC OPTIMISATION METHOD FOR IMPROVING USE CASE POINTS ESTIMATION

Radek Silhavy, Petr Silhavy, and Zdenka Prokopova

Faculty of Applied Informatics, Tomas Bata University in Zlin, Zlin, Czech Republic Nankai University, CHINA

## ABSTRACT

**This paper presents a new size estimation method that can be used to estimate size level for software engineering projects. The Algorithmic Optimisation Method is based on Use Case Points and on Multiple Least Square Regression. The method is derived into three phases. The first phase deals with calculation Use Case Points and correction coefficients values. Correction coefficients are obtained by using Multiple Least Square Regression. New project is estimated in the second and third phase. In the second phase Use Case Points parameters for new estimation are set up and in the third phase project estimation is performed. Final estimation is obtained by using newly developed estimation equation, which used two correction coefficients. The Algorithmic Optimisation Method performs approximately 43% better than the Use Case Points method, based on their magnitude of relative error score. All results were evaluated by standard approach: visual inspection, goodness of fit measure and statistical significance.**

## INTRODUCTION

Software development effort estimation plays an important role in the software engineering field. There are several approaches under investigation. The first is method-based Functional Points Analysis (FPA), which has an official technical standard [1] in ISO standardisation. This method depends on the ability and experiences of an analyst, who is responsible for evaluating parameters. The system is descripted as set of functions, but the analyst must understand the system in great detail. A tendency of personal influence on the estimation can be described in the case of each individual analysis. Functional analysis considers a system as a black box. It is not important to describe the platform, the development method or any hardware used. The results of the calculation estimate only the effort of each individual system function or ability. The personal opinion of the analyst, which influences the estimation, makes this method unsuitable for comparing productivity in system or software development. However, if the same analyst prepares the calculation, the quality of the original estimation can be measured. If the results of the analysis in each development phase are compared and the error curve is flat, then the estimation is calculated accurately. This method is based on interactions between computer systems.

FPA considers external inputs or outputs. The boundary is the border between two systems from the user perspective.

**Citation:** Silhavy R, Silhavy P, Prokopova Z (2015) Algorithmic Optimisation Method for Improving Use Case Points Estimation. PLoS ONE 10(11): e0141887. doi:10.1371/journal.pone.0141887

External inputs are processes that send data into the boundary. This input can be the control input or data input. The data may be used to maintain one or more internal logical files and can be either control information or business information. External outputs consider data from one or more internal logical files (ILFs) and external interface files. The input process does not update the ILFs, and the output side does not contain derived data.

An estimation technique for early stage estimation is called Use Case Points (UCP) method, which was developed by Gustav Karner [2]. His perspective addresses object-oriented design and is thus widely used. The method is based on use case models, which are commonly used as functional descriptions of proposed systems or software. A number of use case steps were initially involved in the estimation process. There have been several modifications of the original principles, such as use case size points [3], extended use case points [4], use case points modified [5], adapted use case points [6], and transaction or path analysis [7].

Karner's basic method is based on assigning weights to clustered actors and use cases. Karner's UCP method identifies three clusters–simple, average and complex. The sum of weighted actors creates a value called unadjusted actor weights (UAW), and in the same sense, the unadjusted use case weights (UUCW) value is calculated. Two coefficients, technical factors and environmental factors, are used to describe the project, related information and development team experience. Summing UAW and UUCW and then multiplying this value by the technical and environmental factor coefficients obtain the number of UCP. Finally, Karner [2] works with the productivity factor, i.e., the number of man-hours per point. This factor is one of the greatest issues with the methodology, as this final operation can change the estimate considerably.

Use case size points is investigated in [3]. The authors emphasise the internal structure of the use case scenario in their method. The primary actors take roles and classifications based on the adjustment factor. Fuzzy sets are used for the estimation.

Several authors have presented improvements to Karner's method based on identifying transactions instead of steps in use cases. In [7], the number of stimuli is equal to the number of transactions. A stimulus is an activity of an actor in a use case. The authors of [1] and [7] improve transactions by calculating paths. The final complexity of the transaction is based on the number of binary or multiple conditions used in the scenarios.

The second modification described here is prepared by Wang [4] and is called extended UCP. This approach employs fuzzy sets and a Bayesian belief network, which is used to set unadjusted UCP. The result of this approach is a probabilistic effort estimation model.

Diev [5] notes that if the actors and use cases are precisely defined, then unadjusted UCP can be multiplied by technical factors. Technical factors are used to establish a coefficient of base system complexity. According to [5], the effort of further activities must be added. These further activities are supportive tasks, such as configuration management or testing.

The next interpretation is called adapted UCP [6]. UCP are adapted to incremental development for large-scale projects. In the first increment, all actors are classified as average and all use cases as complex. The authors also propose the decomposition of use cases to smaller ones, which are classified into the typical three categories.

Use case-based methods of estimation have certain well-known issues [8]. Use cases are written in natural language, and there is no rigorous approach to allow for a comparison of the use case quality or fragmentation. Therefore, the number of steps may vary, which affects the estimation accuracy. In a single individual use case, there can be more than one scenario, which can influence the accuracy of the estimation. Thus, the use case model is critical for system functional or behavioural modelling, but for the purpose of estimation, use cases can be used only if the estimation approach can be adjusted or calibrated for individual work conditions and writing style. Here, we propose an algorithm of calibrating the model by setting the productivity factor according to historical data.

## METHODS

### UCP Method Description

In the UCP method [1, 2, 4, 9], actors and use cases are classified as simple, average or complex [2]. A simple actor typically represents an application programming interface (API) or, more generally, a non-physical system user. A system interconnected by network protocol is classified as average, and finally, physical users interacting with the system through a graphical user interface are complex actors. These factors are summarised in Table 1.

Table 1. Actor Classification and Actor Weighting Factor.

| Actor Classification (AC) | Weighting Factor (WFa) |
| --- | --- |
| Simple | 1 |
| Average | 2 |
| Complex | 3 |

doi:10.1371/journal.pone.0141887.t001

The total unadjusted actor weights (TUAW) are calculated according to the following formula:

$$TUAW = \sum AC \times WFa \quad (1)$$

Use cases are classified in a similar manner (see Table 2). The complexity of use cases is based on the number of steps, also called a transaction. However, a transaction typically refers to a path of activity, not a simple step in a structured scenario. Therefore, the term "step" is used here. The step counting process is not clear from the inline view. The original method counts steps in a primary scenario and in alternative scenarios. If the use case is extended (or included) by another use case, these steps are not counted: these use cases are counted as separate scenarios.

Table 2. Use Case Classification and Weighting Factor.

| Use Case Classification (UCC) | Number of Steps | Weighting Factor (WFb) |
|---|---|---|
| Simple | (0,4) | 5 |
| Average | <4,7> | 10 |
| Complex | (7, ∞) | 15 |

doi:10.1371/journal.pone.0141887.t002

The unadjusted use case weights (UUCW) are calculated according to the following formula:

$$UUCW = \sum UCC \times WFb \quad (2)$$

Technical factors (first correction value) are then applied to the unadjusted UCP (UUCP). The technical complexity is already known in the FPA method. The second correction value is based on environmental factors. This factor describes non-functional requirements. Table 3presents the technical factors, and Table 4 presents the environmental factors, as they are known in UCP.

Table 3. Technical Factors.

| Factor ID | Description | Weight (WFc) | Significance (Sla) |
|---|---|---|---|
| T1 | Distributed System | 2 | <0,5> |
| T2 | Response adjectives | 2 | <0,5> |
| T3 | End-User Efficiency | 1 | <0,5> |
| T4 | Complex Processing | 1 | <0,5> |
| T5 | Reusable Code | 1 | <0,5> |
| T6 | Easy to Install | 0.5 | <0,5> |
| T7 | Ease to Use | 0.5 | <0,5> |
| T8 | Portable | 2 | <0,5> |
| T9 | Easy to Change | 1 | <0,5> |
| T10 | Concurrent | 1 | <0,5> |
| T11 | Security Feature | 1 | <0,5> |
| T12 | Access for Third Parties | 1 | <0,5> |
| T13 | Special Training Required | 1 | <0,5> |

doi:10.1371/journal.pone.0141887.t003

Table 4. Environmental Factors.

| Factor ID | Description | Weight (WFd) | Significance (Slb) |
|---|---|---|---|
| E1 | Familiar with RUP | 1.5 | <0,5> |
| E2 | Application Experience | 0.5 | <0,5> |
| E3 | Object-oriented Experience | 1 | <0,5> |
| E4 | Lead Analyst Capability | 0.5 | <0,5> |
| E5 | Motivation | 1 | <0,5> |
| E6 | Stable Requirements | 2 | <0,5> |
| E7 | Part-Time Workers | -1 | <0,5> |
| E8 | Difficult Programming Language | 2 | <0,5> |

doi:10.1371/journal.pone.0141887.t004

Factors T1-T13 and E1-E8 have fixed weights. Moreover, for each factor, the significance can be set in the interval from 0 to 5, where 0 indicates no impact, 3 indicates an average impact, and 5 indicates a strong impact. The technical complexity factor (TCF), that is, the first correction coefficient, can be calculated according to the following formula [7]:

$$TCF = 0.6 + (0.01 \times \sum_{T13}^{T1} WFc \times SIa) \quad (3)$$

The second correction coefficient is called the environmental complexity factor (ECF). The formula for calculation is similar to the above:

$$ECF = 1.4 + (-0.03 \times \sum_{E8}^{E1} WFd \times SIb) \quad (4)$$

The final result of the estimation is called adjusted UCP (AUCP) and represents the project (system or software) size in points. The unadjusted value of points from actors and points from use cases are summarised, and then, the TCF and ECF are applied. The following formula is used [1, 2, 4, 9]:

$$UCP = (TUAW + UUCW) \times TCF \times ECF \quad (5)$$

The UCP value represents a system size, but a man-hour value is used to measure the work effort. Therefore, UCP is typically multiplied by 20 (according to [2]) or, more generally, by 15–30 man-hours per point. This value is a productivity factor of the development team.

Transactions in a use case scenario have been investigated as a method of tuning the traditional UCP concepts. Robiolo et al. and Ochodek et al. [7, 10] introduce transaction-based methods. According to [7], a transaction is a part of a use case scenario that represents a stimulus. As an example, a scenario can be reduced to a set of pairs. If transactions are used, then the UUCW is different from that in an example with steps. Each use case scenario typically has more steps than transactions.

## Algorithmic Optimisation Method Design

The proposed Algorithmic Optimisation Method (AOM) design is motivated by investigating the possibility of solving issues with the standard estimation process, which are described in the UCP method description section. Therefore, we have applied an optimisation method based on increasing the correction coefficients accuracy by multiple least squares regression [11].

Furthermore, we simplify the estimation process itself and make it less sensitive to personal ability and experiences. New approach indeed brings straightforward approach, which is based on historical data. This principal idea allows minimalizing an error as integral part of estimation process.

The AOM is based on a widely used version of the UCP method, which was previously described in the text.

AOM brings tree-phases design, as can be seen in Fig 1. The Preparation Phase (Phase I) is used for calculation of the $(a_1, a_2)$ correction coefficients. Least Squares Regression (LSR), or, more precisely, multiple linear regression is used for obtaining these coefficients $(a_1, a_2)$. Following formula is applying for calculation:

$$\begin{pmatrix} y_1 \\ \vdots \\ y_n \end{pmatrix} = \begin{pmatrix} x_{11} & x_{12} \\ \vdots & \vdots \\ x_{n1} & x_{n2} \end{pmatrix} \times \begin{pmatrix} a_1 \\ a_2 \end{pmatrix} \Rightarrow \begin{pmatrix} a_1 \\ a_2 \end{pmatrix} = (X^T \times X)^{-1} \times (X^T \times Y) \qquad (6)$$

Where $x_{i1}$ and $x_{i2}$, $i = 1 \ldots n$, are as follows:

$$x_{i1} = (TUAW_i \times TCF_i \times ECF_i) \qquad (7)$$

$$x_{i2} = (UUCW_i \times TCF_i \times ECF_i) \qquad (8)$$

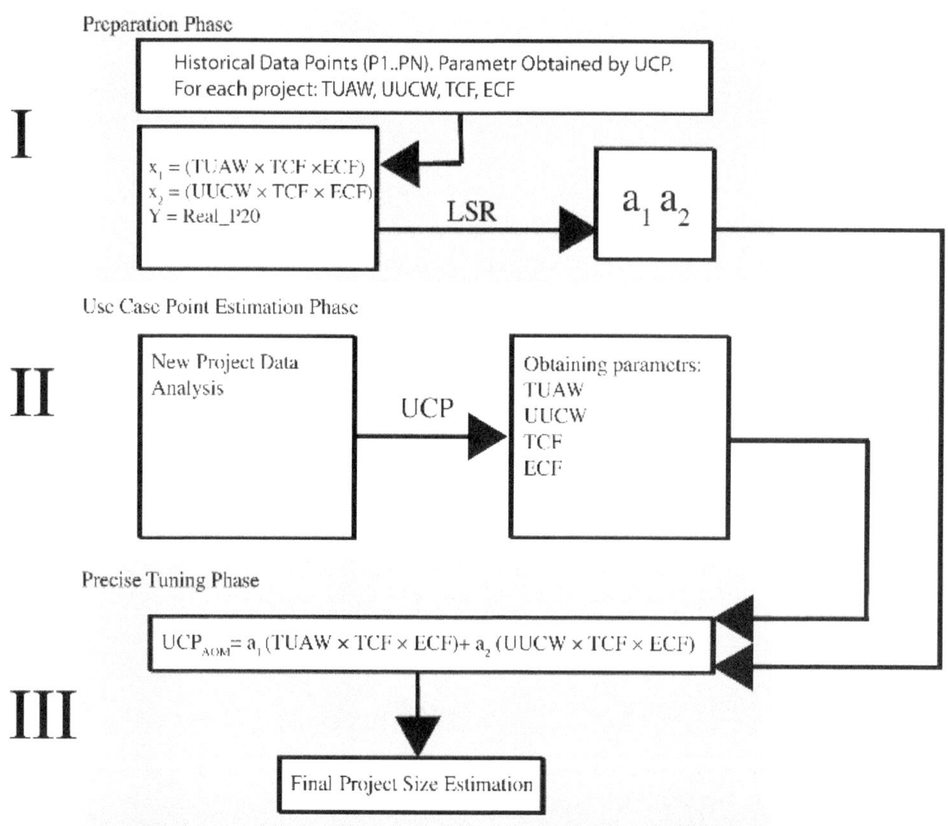


Figure 1. Algorithmic Optimisation Method Schema.

And $y_i$ represents real size (Real_P20 values), which is real size of software projects form historical dataset (see Table 5). Therefore values of $a_1$, $a_2$ can be different for each individual dataset or generally for each project pool and developers. The values $a_1$, $a_2$ are not generally valid and their numerical values cannot be applied to other dataset or project. This method can be used only, if the historical data points exist. It is inevitable for correction functioning of AOM to perform Preparation Phase again, when historical dataset expands. New data points can be added to historical dataset only, if there is new finished project and its real size is known.

Table 5. Raw Project Data [9, 12].

| Project No. | TUAW | UUCW | TCF | ECF | Est_P | Real_P20 |
|---|---|---|---|---|---|---|
| 1 | 12 | 375 | 0,92 | 0,78 | 277,7112 | 151,85 |
| 2 | 10 | 85 | 0,75 | 0,81 | 57,7125 | 95,85 |
| 3 | 6 | 115 | 0,9 | 1,05 | 114,345 | 58,65 |
| 4 | 9 | 205 | 0,85 | 0,89 | 161,891 | 37,1 |
| 5 | 12 | 160 | 0,82 | 0,79 | 111,4216 | 30,7 |
| 6 | 9 | 115 | 0,85 | 0,88 | 92,752 | 24,6 |
| 7 | 6 | 85 | 0,78 | 0,51 | 36,1998 | 13,85 |
| 8 | 14 | 515 | 0,94 | 1,02 | 507,2052 | 179,65 |
| 9 | 12 | 185 | 1,03 | 0,8 | 162,328 | 84,05 |
| 10 | 12 | 290 | 0,71 | 0,73 | 156,5266 | 67,2 |
| 11 | 9 | 150 | 1,05 | 0,95 | 158,6025 | 61 |
| 12 | 12 | 135 | 0,78 | 0,79 | 90,5814 | 36 |
| 13 | 4 | 60 | 0,96 | 0,96 | 58,9824 | 25,7 |
| 14 | 15 | 160 | 0,9 | 0,91 | 143,325 | 19,85 |
| 15 | 15 | 355 | 1,125 | 0,77 | 320,5125 | 184,2 |
| 16 | 18 | 145 | 1,08 | 0,77 | 135,5508 | 99 |
| 17 | 12 | 325 | 1,095 | 0,95 | 350,56425 | 197,5 |
| 18 | 6 | 90 | 1,02 | 1,085 | 106,2432 | 96,25 |
| 19 | 9 | 125 | 1,025 | 0,98 | 134,603 | 108,75 |
| 20 | 9 | 120 | 1,118 | 0,995 | 143,50089 | 111,3 |
| 21 | 12 | 200 | 1 | 0,92 | 195,04 | 132 |
| 22 | 9 | 175 | 0,95 | 0,92 | 160,816 | 128,4 |
| 23 | 12 | 245 | 0,89 | 1,19 | 272,1887 | 152,1 |
| 24 | 6 | 140 | 0,965 | 0,755 | 106,37195 | 84,8 |
| 25 | 7 | 180 | 0,81 | 0,84 | 127,2348 | 183,5 |
| 26 | 7 | 155 | 0,9 | 0,94 | 137,052 | 143 |
| 27 | 5 | 210 | 0,72 | 0,67 | 103,716 | 137 |
| 28 | 6 | 340 | 0,8 | 0,74 | 204,832 | 168 |

doi:10.1371/journal.pone.0141887.t005

Secondly the basic UCP parameters are calculated. Eqs (1–4) are used for obtaining of TUAW, UUCW, TCF and ECF parameters.

Adopting the part of UCP estimation methodology supports consistency early processes of estimation. These parameters can be obtained from various CASE tools.

Thirdly, Precise Tuning Phase is performing. $UCP_{AOM}$ value represents final estimated project size, which should be used for project planning and later on for effort estimation. $UCP_{AOM}$ is obtained according Eq (9).

$$UCP_{AOM} = a_1(TUAW \times TCF \times ECF) + a_2(UUCW \times TCF \times ECF) \quad (9)$$

## Experiment planning

The experiment in our study deals with evaluating AOM principles, which may significantly improve prediction model based on Use Case Points.

In order to validate effectiveness of AOM an empirical validation was conducted. The first model, which was evaluated, is a Use Case Points (UCP). UCP was used as simple base model for setting basic performance level.

The second model, which may be called, advanced is AOM. Finally, the accuracy of prediction of two presented models was compared.

Let assume, that the prediction error of AOM will be significantly lower, that error of UCP method and optimal values of correction coefficients $a_1$, $a_2$, will be set.

Our task is not to offer generally valid coefficients. This paper will demonstrate that AOM is applicable to several projects pool.

In order to decide whether the model is more capable for prediction, a statistical hypothesis was tested:

$H_0$: UCP = AOM, There is no difference in the capability of prediction between UCP and AOM models. No difference in estimation errors.

### Alternative hypothesis:

$H_1$: UCP ≠ AOM, there is difference in prediction capability between UCP and AOM models. There is a difference in estimation errors.

This paper compares the accuracy of the AOM model with that of the UCP model using t-test. The t-test is used as a test of the null hypothesis that the means of two normally distributed populations are equal. The t-test will be used for evaluation of MRE.

## Adopted Metrics for Performance Evaluation

Magnitude of Relative Error (MRE), Mean Magnitude of Relative Error (MMRE) and Percentage of Prediction (PRED(0.25)) is accepted as standard evaluation in size prediction and effort estimation techniques. In this paper are used this methods for purpose of future cross comparison to other approaches.

We also adopted Total Sum of Squares (TSS), which as metric for evaluation of the prediction models and median of errors. Following equations are used for obtaining this performance metrics:

$$\text{MRE} = \frac{|PredictedSize - Real\_P20|}{Real\_P20} \quad (10)$$

$$\text{MMRE} = \frac{\sum_i^N MRE}{N} \quad (11)$$

$$\text{PRED}(0.25) = \frac{A}{N} \quad (12)$$

$$\text{TSS} = \sum_{i=1}^{n} (Real\_P20 - PredictedSize)^2 \quad (13)$$

*PredictedSize* value stands for values of predicted project size. This value is a value of UCP or AOM. A "N" in Eqs (11) and (12) stands for number of observed projects. Next metric is a PRED(0.25). An "A" in Eq (12) stands for number of projects, which have MRE<0.25.

Goal for results is to keep MMRE and TSS minimalized and PRED(0.25) maximized. For purpose of our evaluation the most important criterion is minimal value of TSS, because it means that LSR algorithm achieved optimal performance.

## RESULTS AND DISCUSSION

In this paper the UCP method [2] and our proposed method, called the Algorithmic Optimisation Method (AOM) were compared.

Table 5 summarises the raw project data. The TUAW, UUCW, TCF and ECF are known from UCP. Est_P is an estimation (in points) according UCP method (see Eqs (1–5)) a Real_P20 is a value, which represents real project size, which were measured in points, when project were finished.

The results were evaluated against three datasets, which take role as simulated software project pools. Each testing dataset were constructed as random selection of 10 projects for Phase I (see Table 6) from raw project data (see Table 5). These datasets takes role as historical dataset. For the evaluation we have used rest of dataset. Our evaluation will at $\alpha = 0.05$ significance level.

Table 6. Preparation Phase Datasets Characteristics.

| Test Case | Historical Data Points | Real-P20 (Min) | Real-P20 (Max) | Mean | Standard Deviation |
|---|---|---|---|---|---|
| Test1 | P23,P6,P4,P26,P18,P3,P8,P16,P17,P2 | 24,6 | 197,5 | 108,37 | 55,76 |
| Test2 | P20,P1,P8,P2,P3,P24,P12,P9,P27,P18 | 36 | 179,65 | 103,54 | 40,9 |
| Test3 | P19,P1,P24,P27,P20,P22,P2,P11,P9,P5 | 30,7 | 151,85 | 99,37 | 34,48 |

doi:10.1371/journal.pone.0141887.t006

Results of evaluation are based on rest of the dataset. It means that for evaluation were used:

Test1: P1, P5, P7, P9, P10, P11, P12, P13, P14, P15, P19, P20, P21, P22, P24, P25, P27, P28

Test2: P4, P5, P6, P7, P10, P11, P13, P14, P15, P16, P17, P19, P21, P22, P23, P25, P26, P28

Test3: P3, P4, P6, P7, P8, P10, P12, P13, P14, P15, P16, P17, P18, P21, P23, P25, P26, P28

Projects, which were used during a Preparation Phase, were omitted. The obtained results are presented in Table 7. Real_P20 were obtained from Table 5 and estimated size was calculated according Eq (9) for AOM or according Eq (5) for UCP.

Table 7. Comparison of the Estimation Methods Performance.

| | Test1 | Test2 | Test3 |
|---|---|---|---|
| MMRE-UCP | 1,17 | 1,39 | 0,69 |
| MMRE-AOM | 0,69 | 0,83 | 0,69 |
| PRED(0.25)-UCP | 0,17 | 0,17 | 0,17 |
| PRED(0.25)-AOM | 0,39 | 0,34 | 0,34 |
| TSS-UCP | 97229,35 | 129109,46 | 224825,52 |
| TSS-AOM | 52041,24 | 51708,79 | 50679,76 |

doi:10.1371/journal.pone.0141887.t007

Fig 2 shows the Magnitude of Relative Error of the AOM for the Test1-3 datasets and compares them to UCP performance on same datasets. Table 7 and Fig 2 illustrate that AOM produces significantly better estimates than UCP. The mean MRE is 0.74 in the case of AOM, which is more than 43% better then result obtained UCP method. According to PRED(0.25) AOM is more then twice better.

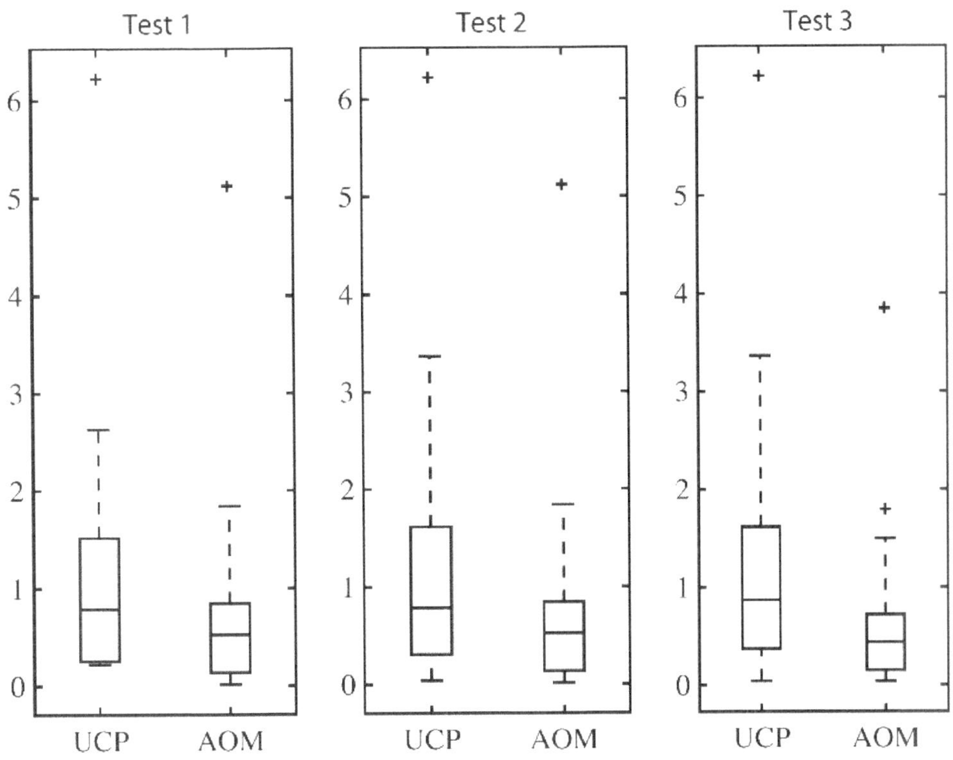


Figure 2. Box Plot on MRE Results obtained from testing datasets.

Fig 3 describes a low correlation between Error and AOM predicted Size. The AOM performs consistently better as can be seen from Fig 2 (MRE distribution) and from Fig 4, which shows a Total Sum of Squares.

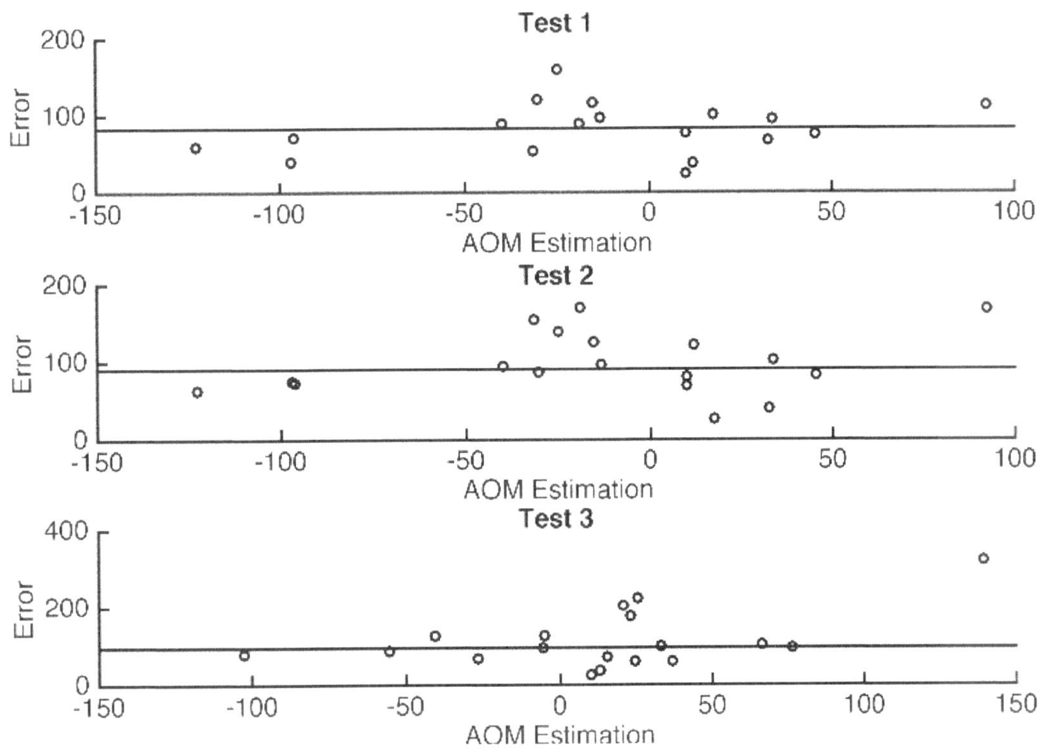


Fig 3. Error and AOM (PredictectSize) Correlation.

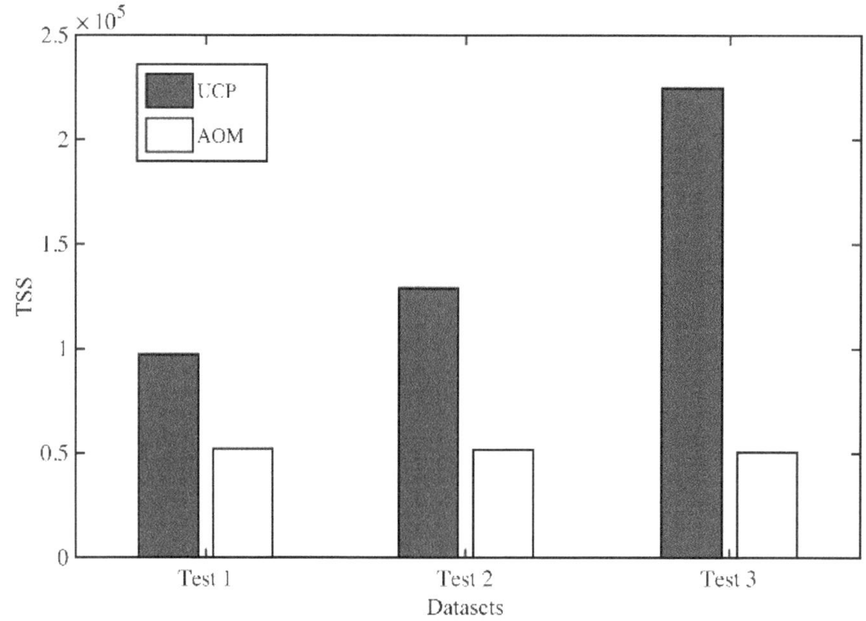


Figure 4. Total Sum of Squares.

## Results Interpretation

Results, which are presented, in previous section show, that AOM model can produce significantly better estimations. AOM produce more reliable and more consistent results. The result of the t-test for MRE is given in Table 8. All datasets (Test1, Test 2 and Test3) were tested independently.

Table 8. Results of t-test for MRE.

| | Test 1 | Test 2 | Test 3 |
|---|---|---|---|
| SD | 0.5992 | 0.6373 | 0.6685 |
| Degree of freedom | 17 | 17 | 17 |
| t value | -3.3393 | -3.7059 | -4.3011 |
| p value | 0.0039 | 0.0018 | 0,00048385 |
| h value | 1 | 1 | 1 |

doi:10.1371/journal.pone.0141887.t008

Results of t-test for MRE as a computational results (MRE, MMRE, PRED and TSS) show, that AOM performs significantly better. MRE was tested at significance level 0.05 and null hypothesis can be rejected. Performance of AOM and UCP is not equal.

## Validity Treats

There is an issue connecting with size of dataset. Use Case points dataset is not broadly available and therefore all studies are perform on relatively small datasets. We have used 28 data points, which were divided into two parts randomly. Three (Test 1, Test 2 and Test 3) dataset were created.

Our data points represent small and medium projects and for this should be a limitation. Therefore further investigation based on broad project pool and for bigger projects will be needed. Whereas it becomes apparent, that project size and project size variance is important parameter for model construction.

The main aim of this paper was to show that AOM approach could lead to more precise and consistent prediction than UCP. UCP is used as valuable initial estimation, from which some parameters are used for AOM estimation.

## Case Study

The following case study will illustrate real-life situation of using AOM. Case Study is descripted in phases according Fig 1.

### Preparation Phase.

Lets assume that there are 10 projects in historical dataset. Table 9 illustrates historical project data.

Table 9. Case Study Historical Data Points.

| | Test 1 | Test 2 | Test 3 |
|---|---|---|---|
| SD | 0.5992 | 0.6373 | 0.6685 |
| Degree of freedom | 17 | 17 | 17 |
| t value | -3.3393 | -3.7059 | -4.3011 |
| p value | 0.0039 | 0.0018 | 0,00048385 |
| h value | 1 | 1 | 1 |

doi:10.1371/journal.pone.0141887.t008

These data points are used for setting $x_1$ and $x_2$ as is declared in Eqs (7) and (8). Real_P20 represents know value of real project effort.

Next step is to obtain ($a_1$, $a_2$) values. These are calculated by using multiple linear regressions. Values are as follows: $a_1$ = 0.96737, $a_2$ = 0.64416.

Use Case Points Estimation Phase.

Values of TUAW, UUCW, TCF and ECF for the project, which is estimated, are obtained by UCP Eqs (1–4). Parameters values are: TUAW = 12, UUCW = 245, TCF = 0,89, ECF = 1,19.

Precise Tuning Phase.

Finally project size estimation can be obtained by using Eq (9). For our project Equation is$UCP_{AOM}$ = 0,96737 × (12 × 0,89 × 1,19) + 0.64416 × (245 × 0,89 × 1,19). Therefore, new project estimation is 179 use case points.

## CONCLUSIONS

In this article, we presented a new estimation approach based on a three-phase algorithm, called AOM. In the first phase, we applied a calculation based on UCP to obtain set of parameters (TUAW, UUCW, TCF, ECF) for each of historical project. Next we have obtain a correction values ($a_1$, $a_2$). These values were obtained via least squares regression. This approach employs historical project data to refine the estimation. By applying the least squares regression approach, the algorithm penalises errors in the estimation caused by human factors and company practice.

The AOM is significantly better than UCP estimation methods, with a mean MRE that is 43% better than that obtained with UCP.

Results of AOM are better and according Fig 4, results are significantly more consistent than those obtain by UCP.

The AOM represents an estimation workflow and describes approach how a size of software project could be estimated. AOM employs correction values ($a_1$, $a_2$), which are making a model less sensitive to introduction a personal errors.

As results clearly shows AOM produce consistent predictions. Ability of adaptation to individual project characteristics is improvement too.

A comparison drawn with regard to a number of descriptive characteristics has shown that datasets can influence the quality of the estimation. Therefore, in our future research, we will focus on dataset expansion and clustering projects into homogenised segments, which should improve the accuracy of the estimation.

## Author Contributions

Conceived and designed the experiments: RS PS ZP. Performed the experiments: RS PS ZP. Analyzed the data: RS. Contributed reagents/materials/analysis tools: RS PS ZP. Wrote the paper: RS.

## REFERENCES

1. Robiolo G, Orosco R. Employing use cases to early estimate effort with simpler metrics. Innovations in Systems and Software Engineering. 2008;4(1):31–43. doi: 10.1007/s11334-007-0043-y.
2. Karner G. Metrics for objectory', December 1993, Diploma, University of Linkoping, Sweden, No. LiTH-IDA-Ex-9344. 21.
3. Braz MR, Vergilio SR, editors. Software effort estimation based on use cases. Computer Software and Applications Conference, 2006 COMPSAC'06 30th Annual International; 2006: IEEE.
4. Wang F, Yang X, Zhu X, Chen L. Extended Use Case Points Method for Software Cost Estimation. 2009:1–5. doi: 10.1109/cise.2009.5364706.
5. Diev S. Use cases modeling and software estimation. ACM SIGSOFT Software Engineering Notes. 2006;31(6):1. doi: 10.1145/1218776.1218780.
6. Mohagheghi P, Anda B, Conradi R. Effort estimation of use cases for incremental large-scale software development. 2005:303–11. doi: 10.1109/icse.2005.1553573.
7. Robiolo G, Badano C, Orosco R. Transactions and paths: Two use case based metrics which improve the early effort estimation. 2009:422–5. doi: 10.1109/esem.2009.5316021.
8. Azevedo S, Machado RJ, Bragança A, Ribeiro H. On the refinement of use case models with variability support. Innovations in Systems and Software Engineering. 2011;8(1):51–64. doi: 10.1007/s11334-011-0177-9.
9. Ochodek M, Nawrocki J, Kwarciak K. Simplifying effort estimation based on Use Case Points. Information and Software Technology. 2011;53(3):200–13. doi: 10.1016/j.infsof.2010.10.005.
10. Ochodek M, Alchimowicz B, Jurkiewicz J, Nawrocki J. Improving the reliability of transaction identification in use cases. Information and Software Technology.

2011;53(8):885–97. doi: 10.1016/J.Infsof.2011.02.004 pmid:WOS:000292176300007.

11. Pindyck RS, Rubinfeld DL. Econometric models and economic forecasts: Irwin/McGraw-Hill Boston; 1998.

12. Subriadi A, Ningrum P. Critical review of the effort rate value in use case point method for estimating software development effort. Journal of Theroretical and Applied Information Technology. 2014;59(3):735–44.

CHAPTER 3

# IMPROVED OBJECT LOCALIZATION USING ACCURATE DISTANCE ESTIMATION IN WIRELESS MULTIMEDIA SENSOR NETWORKS

Yasar Abbas Ur Rehman[1,2], Muhammad Tariq[1], Omar Usman Khan[1]

[1] NUSys Lab/ National University of Computer and Emerging Sciences (NUCES), Peshawar, KPK, Pakistan,

[2] Department of Electrical Engineering/City University of Science and Information Technology, Peshawar,KPK, Pakistan

## ABSTRACT

**Object localization plays a key role in many popular applications of Wireless Multimedia Sensor Networks (WMSN) and as a result, it has acquired a significant status for the research community. A significant body of research performs this task without considering node orientation, object geometry and environmental variations. As a result, the localized object does not reflect the real world scenarios. In this paper, a novel object localization scheme for WMSN has been proposed that utilizes range free localization, computer vision, and principle component analysis based algorithms. The proposed approach provides the best possible approximation of distance between a wmsn sink and an object, and the orientation of the object using image based information. Simulation results report 99% efficiency and an error ratio of 0.01 (around 1 ft) when compared to other popular techniques.**

## INTRODUCTION

The accessibility of low cost and low complexity multimedia hardware like cameras and microphones has allowed for the transformation of existing Wireless Sensor Networks (WSN) to Wireless Multimedia Sensor Networks (WMSN). Although the variability in services provided by recent WMSN have surpassed traditional WSN, there are certain constraints which are imposed by the properties inherited from traditional WSN [1–3]. These constraints include limited processing capabilities, battery power, bandwidth, and on-board memory. Since, both WSN and WMSN involve battery powered devices, the need for energy conservation to prolong sensor lifetime is an important design parameter when modeling and designing protocols, algorithms and services for these networks. One important technique that is used in designing these services is the localization of individual sensor nodes or objects within the network [4]. Amongst the various node localization techniques, range free methods have gained wide-spread attention due to their ability to localize devices with an acceptible error tolerance without the need for any specialized hardware component [5, 6]. Object localization involves estimation of an object's position within a network as it traverses a path in-between individual WSN nodes [7].

A key problem in WMSN is the isolation of objects from image backgrounds [8]. Most approaches assume static

**Citation:** Ur Rehman YA, Tariq M, Khan OU (2015) Improved Object Localization Using Accurate Distance Estimation in Wireless Multimedia Sensor Networks. PLoS ONE 10(11): e0141558. doi:10.1371/journal.pone.0141558

nodes and thus rely on simple background subtraction based methods [9–12]. Another approach takes into account fusion of information from multiple WMSN nodes to compensate for localization error [13]. In real-time, however, the assumption of static nodes can lead to false results due to uncontrollable environmental variations. Another source for false detection can be attributed to lack of consideration to the geometry and orientation of an object. This false information is then eventually conveyed to sink nodes. The orientation of a node with respect to an object is mostly unpredictable and involves the fusion of disparate WMSN nodes [14].

The central theme of this paper is to effectively isolate and locate objects from images by fusing range free techniques with machine learning and computer vision algorithms. The objective would be to increase object localization accuracy in the real-world from images received at the sink node by utilizing coordinate information of sensor nodes using Principle Component Analysis (PCA) and computer vision algorithms. The energy consumption footprint of this method will also be minimized in order to prolong the WMSN lifetime. The proposed method will be analyzed and compared to other existing techniques.

The rest of this paper is organized as follows: The related work discusses the state of the art work done in range free localization techniques and object localization techniques. The methadology section defines the proposed methodology of object localization in a localized WMSN. The results are discussed and analyzed in simulation results section. The paper is then concluded with a direction to the future work.

## RELATED WORK

Since WMSN essentially involve WSN with multimedia equipped devices [15], it can therefore be assumed that they can inherit traditional range free based localization algorithms. This assumption inspires us to review some of related state of the art work in the area.

The basic aim of range free localization algorithms is to locate individual sensor nodes by utilizing existing resources without depending on additional hardware infrastructure [16]. This localization process is completed in three steps; determining the relative distances between individual nodes, approximating position of nodes by solving a set of linear equations simultaneously, and finally, refining the position by utilizing position information from neighboring nodes [17]. For efficiency, the localizing scheme must be robust and energy efficient in areas of low sensor density, or when obstacles are present between sensing nodes. Likewise, the scheme must also hold against un-determinant nodes [18–20]. However, since WSN deployments are usually random, therefore anisotropic patterns and holes can pose a challenge. For these deployment related constraints, detour path angular information (DPAI) based localization can be used [21].

For object localization, computer vision based algorithms are predominantly used for the purpose of detection, recognition, and tracking [22–25]. As can be anticipated, vision based algorithms in a distributed setup would not only involve processing overhead, but also constrain image transmission on limited bandwidths. As such, data compression would be natural [26]. The processing overhead would be associated with algorithmic complexity. For tracking based applications, continuous capture of a target would entail a significant energy footprint. Various solutions exist to minimize this footprint; ranging from rotational camera sensors [27] to time-stamped varying information capture using single static cameras [28]. Another approach to reduce transmission latency and conserve energy is the adoption of cluster based approach for communication with the aid of Kalman filters [29]. As such, each cluster will track objects using cooperative communication between cluster elements in order to aggregate data.

The real-world coordinates of objects can be estimated using image based coordinates using intrinsic and extrinsic properties of cameras [28]. However, numerous difficulties arise in this transformation process, for instance, the disturbance of camera positions due to strong winds, the presence of moving artefacts, or shadowing effects. It is, therefore, not sufficient to send image based information to sink node's but object meta-data from the image must also be conveyed [30]. To extract this information, a straight-forward approach based on frame differencing can be possible [9–12] assuming static nodes. However, in the scenarios just mentioned, this method will be less efficient. To cope with this problem, this paper proposes to localize objects in WMSN using image information received from different nodes at the sink node. The orientation of the object will then be carried out with respective to the sink. The proposed methodology utilizes a fusion of range free localization, PCA, and computer vision based algorithms to accurately localize a target object while respecting energy constraints of the WMSN nodes.

## METHODOLOGY

Consider a heterogeneous WMSN network with m multimedia and s sensor nodes deployed randomly in a field. To localize an object o traversing a path inbetween the nodes, it is important that the other WMSN nodes, including the sink node are also aware of their positions. The WMSN node positions are localized using the DPAI procedure [21] by obtaining location information of anchor nodes in the network. Once the nodes are localized, the sink node floods its unique identity to all nodes in the network. Upon receipt of an identity packet, WMSN multimedia nodes will start the object localization process. This process is illustrated in Algorithm 1.

**Algorithm 1**: In-Node Process

**Input**: $V = \{v_1 \ldots v_n\}$: Set of WMSN nodes with unknown location

$D_{xd,yd}$: Sink node location

$F_i$: Frame captured by $v_i$ node

**Output**: $V_{X,Y} = \{v_{1x,y}, v_{2x,y}, \ldots, v_{nx,y}\}$: Localized nodes with location information

$LL1_i$: Low-Low level 1 sub-band corresponding to frame i

**Node Localization** localize()

**for** i = 1 → n **do**

calculate(x, y) ∈ $v_i$; Using **DPAI** [21]

**Frame Capture & Transmit** captureTransmit()

captureF$_i$;
extract(LLI$_i$, Sub − Band);
packetize{LLI, $v_{1x,y}$};
transmit{LLI, $v_{1x,y}$};

An example scenario is depicted in Fig 1, where a multimedia node with location ($X_n$, $Y_n$) captures an image of the scene containing a target object. This image is then decomposed into four multi-resolution images using 2D Discrete Wavelet Transform (2D-DWT). Of these decomposed images, only the coarse level coefficient image, i.e., the Low-Low level 1 (LL1) sub-band is transmitted to the sink using a multi-hop route. The selection of the LL1 sub-band has multiple advantages as it entails minimum processing, storage, and transmission energy. The small size is thus ideal when considering the limited bandwidth properties of the WMSN. The sink-node, upon receipt of the LL1 sub-band image, performs post-processing using computer vision algorithms aided by PCA technique. This process extracts an object from the received image, and is shown in Algorithm 2.

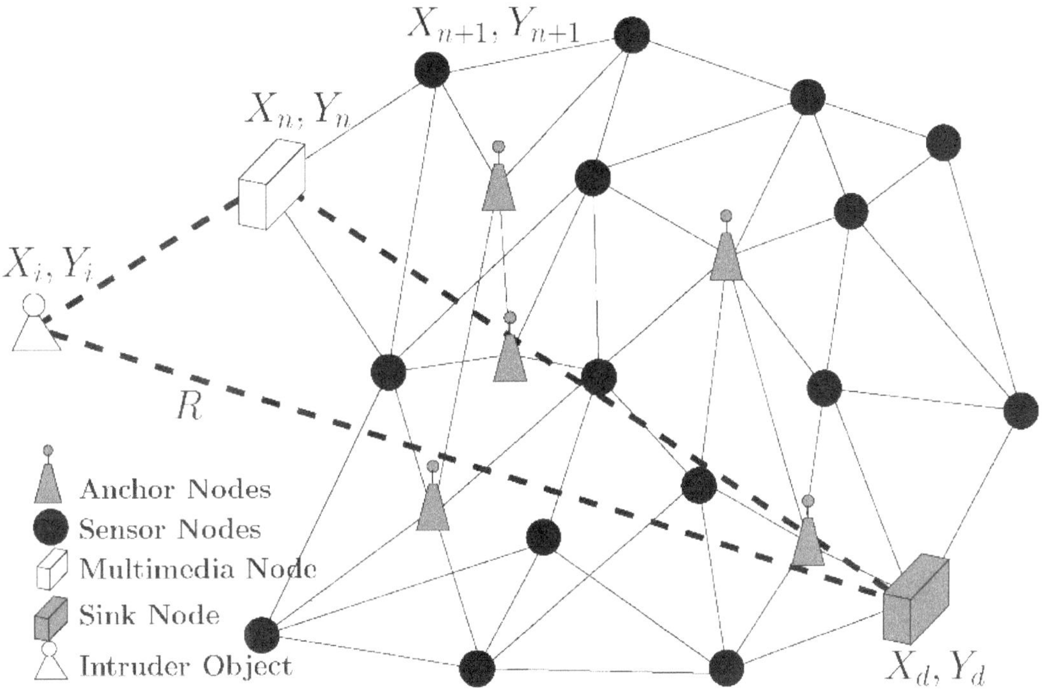


**Figure 1.** WMSN Network with m **multimedia nodes and** s **sensor nodes.**

**Algorithm 2**: Object Localization at Sink Node

**Input**: $V_{X,Y} = \{v_{1x,y} \ldots v_{nx,y}\}$: Localized nodes along with location information

LL1$_i$: Low-Low level 1 sub-band corresponding to node i

**Output**: $d_{min(i)}$: Minimum distance to object from $v_i$ node

$C_{D,O}$: Distance from $D_{Xd,Yd}$ to object $O_i$

$\beta^T$: Angle between object and sink node

**Select Object Close to Node** $v_i$ selectObject()

**for** i = 1 → n **do**

extract $O_i$(LL1$_i$);

**if** $O_i$ = = 1 **then**

$v_{i(x,y)} = v_{i(Xs,Ys)}$;

Calculate $B_{D,N}$;

Calculate $O_{max(i)}$;

**Compute** $D_{min}$ **from** $v_i$ **to** $O_i$ computeDMin()

Calculate $P = A - \mu$;

Calculate $U = P^T \cdot EGV_{1,\ldots,20}$;

Calculate $D_i = normF_i - U$;

Calculate $D_{mini} = \{D_i\}$;

$A_{O,N} = D_{mini}$;

## Compute Orientation & Distance from Object to Destination

DestinationOrientation()

Calculate $C_{D,O}\sqrt{A^2_{O,N} + B^2_{D,N}}$;

**if** $C_{D,O} > B_{D,N}$ **then**

$\beta^T = \tan^{-1}\frac{A_{O,N}}{B_{D,N}} + \tan^{-1}\frac{dp'}{db'}$;

**else**

**if** $C_{D,O} < B_{D,N}$ **then**

$$\beta^T = \tan^{-1}\frac{A_{O,N}}{C_{D,O}} + \tan^{-1}\frac{dp'}{db'};$$

**else**

**if** $C_{D,O} == B_{D,N}$ **then**

$$\beta^T = \tan^{-1}\frac{dp'}{db'};$$

To obtain location information of the object, it is necessary to estimate it's distance from the WMSN node. This distance is obtained by preparing the information set $\mathfrak{R}$ from the received image, given as:

$$\mathfrak{R} = \{(o_i, h_i) | i \in m\} \quad \textbf{(1)}$$

where, $o_i$ is the size of the i[th] object, and $h_i$ is its respective height from the baseline of the image, received from the i[th] WMSN node camera. Only one object per image will be considered. As such, the object closest to the WMSN node camera will be preferred. This object will either have maximum size or minimum height. An example is illustrated in Fig 2, where an image received from node i contains two objects $o_i$ and $o'_i$. After prioritizing the objects based on their size and height, $o_i$ is ultimately selected.

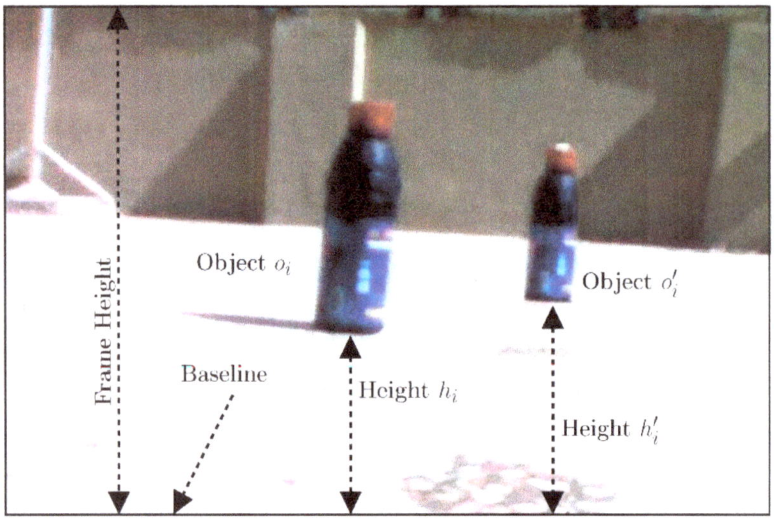


**Figure 2.** Object $o_i$ has maximum size and minimum height $h_i$ as compared to object$o'_i$ with height $h'_i$.

Before discussing various cases, it is important to describe the indexing process of the various parameters used for prioritizing the objects. The object sizes are arranged such that the object with smallest index i is the object having maximum area with respect to other objects in the same image. The object height index i′ are arranged such as the smallest index i′correspond to the minimum height of the object from the base line. In the present case the objects with minimum heights are given priority however, the addition of object size parameter reliably select the objects in case of multiple objects sharing same height and size parameters. The selection process is shown in Fig 3, where three possibilities can arise in the entire process.

- If the index i of a maximum object size and i′ of minimum object height are the same, then the object corresponding to index i is selected.
- If the index i of a maximum object size and i′ of minimum object height are not the same, then the object corresponding to index i′ is selected.
- If there are multiple objects with same maximum object size, or with same minimum object height, then priority is assigned to the object having the least index i amongst the participating indices.

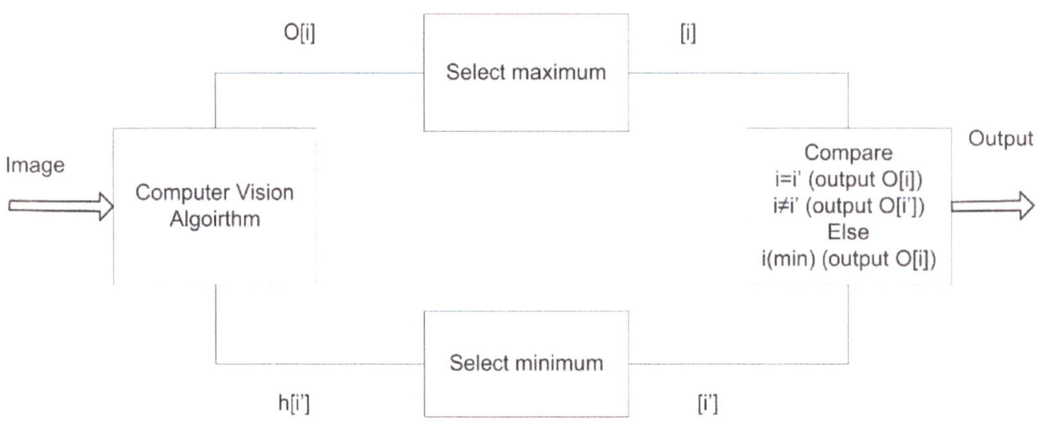


**Figure 3.** Selecting objects for initial distance estimation.

Upon selection of an appropriate object from a received image, the distance between the object and the WMSN node is then estimated. A referential frame is designed for this purpose, as shown in Fig 4(a). The sink at location $D(x_d, y_d)$ is treated as the origin point. The distance between the sink and the WMSN multimedia node would already have been estimated using the DPAI algorithm [21].

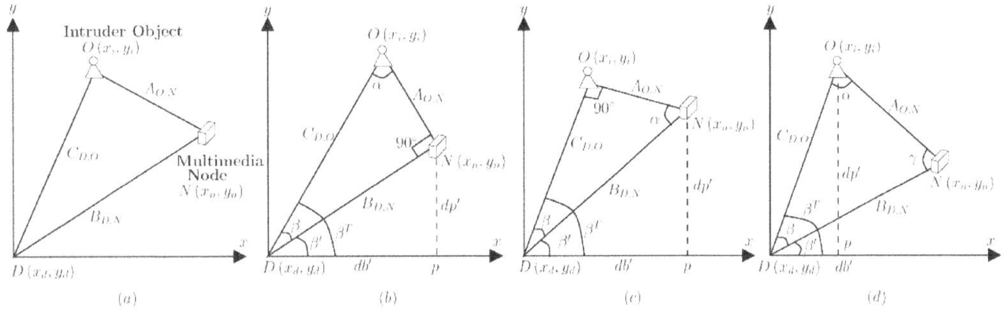


**Figure 4.** (a) Referential frame for estimating location of an object. (b) Case where object distance from the sink node is greater as compared to monitoring WMSN node $C_{D,O} > B_{D,N}$. (c) Case where object distance from the sink node is smaller as compared to monitoring WMSN node $C_{D,O} < B_{D,N}$. (d) Case where object distance from the sink node is equal to the monitoring WMSN node $C_{D,O} == B_{D,N}$.

The distance $A_{O,N}$ between the object $O(x_i, y_i)$ and the WMSN multimedia node $N(x_n, y_n)$ is estimated from the image received at the sink node using PCA. For this, a predefined matrix Mof n objects bearing size variations obtained at various distances between 1 upto 10 feet is defined:

$$M = \begin{bmatrix} S_{11} & \cdots & S_{1n} \\ \vdots & \ddots & \vdots \\ S_{n1} & \cdots & S_{nn} \end{bmatrix}, \qquad (2)$$

where, each element $S_{i,j}$ represents the size of the ith object at a distance of j ft. The mean $\mu$, variance var, and covariance cov of the vectorized form $S = [S_{11}, S_{12}, \ldots, S_{nn}]$ of matrix Mare given as:

$$\mu = \frac{1}{n^2}\sum_i^n\sum_j^n S_{i,j} \qquad (3)$$

$$var(S) = (S_i - \mu) \qquad (4)$$

$$cov(S) = \frac{1}{n}\sum_i^n (S_i - \mu)\cdot(S_i - \mu)^T \qquad (5)$$

Then, the eigen vectors for the covariance matrix are calculated and arranged in descending order as: $E = [E_{g1}, E_{g2}, \ldots, E_{gn}]$. Of these, the first twenty larges eigen vectors are selcted. A new feature set F is then obtained as:

$$F = var(S)^T \cdot E_{1\ldots20} \qquad (6)$$

For a given object size $o_i$ the variance P, feature vector U and distance $d_i$ can be given as:

$$P = o_i - \mu \qquad (7)$$

$$U = P^T \cdot E_{1\ldots20} \qquad (8)$$

$$d_i = \text{norm}F_i - U \qquad (9)$$

Finally, the minimum distance from the set $d_i$ is computed as:

$$d_{\min i} = \{d_i\} = A_{O,N} \qquad (10)$$

where, $d_{mini}$ corresponds to the closest match for U in $F_i$ in the given vectorized matrix S. Thus, $d_{mini} = A_{O,N}$ is taken as the distance between source WMSN multimedia node and the object. After computing $A_{O,N}$, the coordinates of object O can be obtained as:

$$(x_i, y_i) = (x_n, y_n) + A_{O,N} \qquad (11)$$

Finally, the distance $C_{D,O}$ between the sink node D and the object O can be computed using the distance formula:

$$C_{D,O} = \sqrt{(x_d - x_i)^2 + (y_d - y_i)^2} \qquad (12)$$

Once all the distances $B_{D,N}$, $A_{O,N}$ and $C_{D,O}$ are computed, the object orientation $\beta^T$ is then calculated. For this purpose, the edges of triangle formed by the coordinates of WMSN multimedia node N, object O, and sink node D are analyzed. For the case where distance $C_{D,O}$ is equal to $B_{D,N}$, triangle $\Delta DOP$ (See Fig 4d) can be used to compute the orientation $\beta^T$ as:

$$\beta^T = \begin{cases} \tan^{-1}\frac{dp'}{db'} & C_{D,O} == B_{D,N} \\ \beta + \beta' & otherwise \end{cases} \qquad (13)$$

For cases where the two distances are un-equal, orientation $\beta^T$ is computed as a sum of angles $\beta$ and $\beta'$ of two constituent triangles; $\Delta DNO$ and $\Delta DPN$ (See Fig 4b and 4c). These are given as:

$$\beta = \begin{cases} \tan^{-1}\frac{A_{O,N}}{B_{D,N}} & C_{D,O} > B_{D,N} \\ \tan^{-1}\frac{A_{O,N}}{C_{D,O}} & C_{D,O} < B_{D,N} \end{cases} \qquad (14)$$

$$\beta' = \begin{cases} \tan^{-1}\frac{dp'}{db'} & C_{D,O} > B_{D,N} \\ \tan^{-1}\frac{db'}{dp'} & C_{D,O} < B_{D,N} \end{cases} \qquad (15)$$

## SIMULATION RESULTS

To analyze the performance of the proposed method with, we randomly deployed 10 WMSN sensor nodes, including the destination node in a 100 × 100 meter field as shown in Fig 5. The radio range is set to 25 meters to increase probability of maximum number of neighbors for each node. The nodes are first localized using the DPAI method [21]. After localization, every sensor node transmits an LL1 sub-band image (acquired after a 2D-DWT) of the monitored scene to the sink node. The sink node then performs a computer vision algorithm to find and extract any objects of interest. If found, these are recorded in set $\mathfrak{R}$ along with their size and height from image baseline. For multiple objects in the same image, a priority selection process is performed to select only one candidate object. This information is then fed to the PCA algorithm, which, based upon its predefined database, provides a distance estimate for the given size.

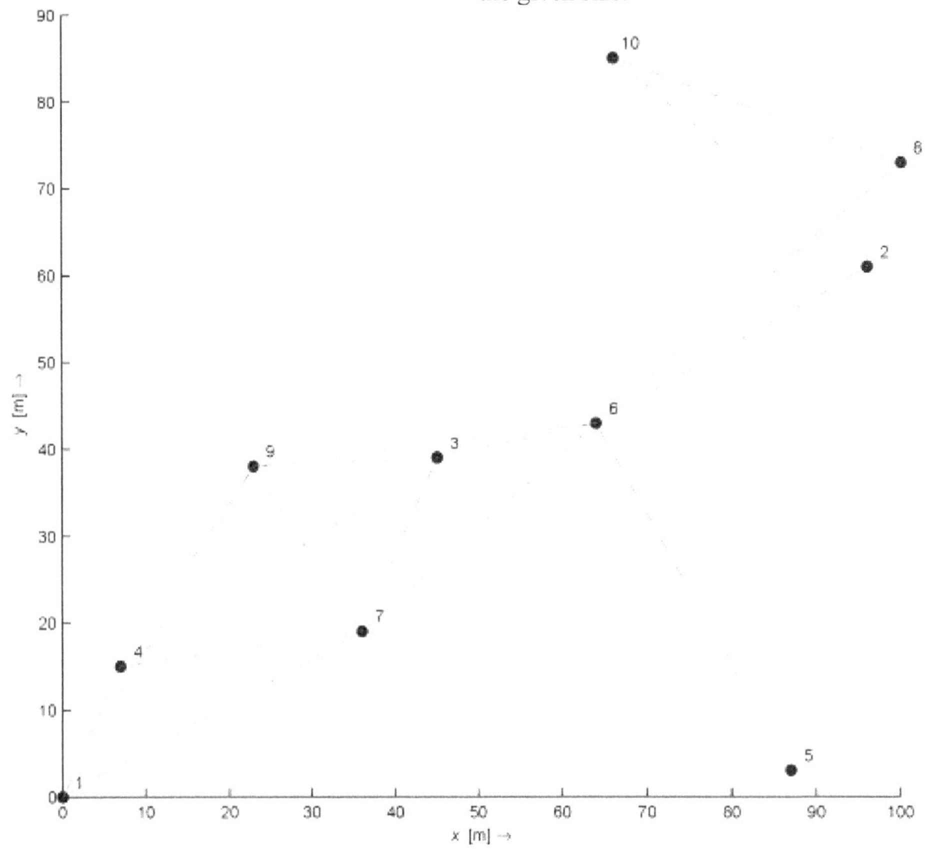


Figure 5. Network Map.

To further investigate the geometry of the object in the received frame, the variation in size of the isolated objects with respect to distance is studied. For a specific object, the object size varies exponentially with distance from the camera as shown in the Fig 6. For the farthest distances, the object size can be observed to be of almost 1 pixel.

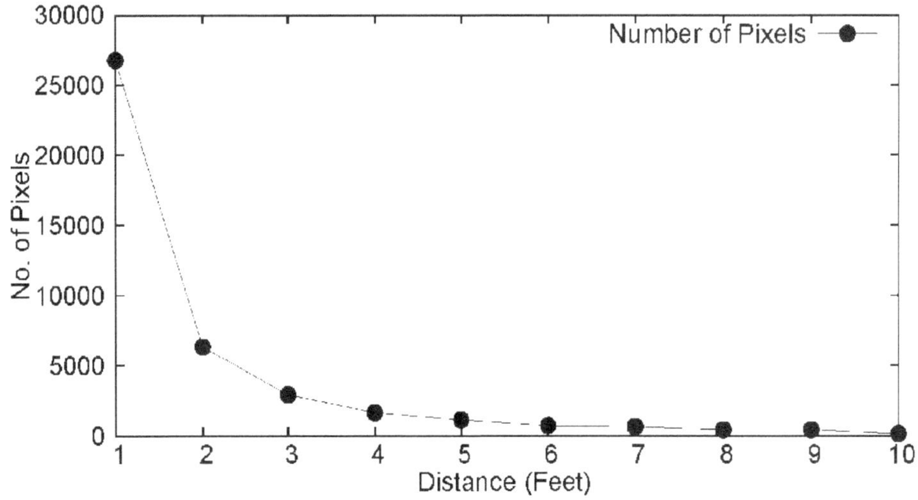


**Figure 6.** Variation of Object Size with Distance.

To calculate the distance between the object and the sink node, the PCA algorithm is trained initially with 10 different objects. During the training phase, each object image is taken at a distance of 1 to 10 feet from the camera. From these images, the respective object size is extracted. A marix M of the objects is then constructed Eq (2). For M, a feature set F and distance $d_1$ is then computed using Eqs (6)–(9). For an unknown object size, the minimum distance between the sink node and WMSN node is estimated using Eqs (11) and (12).

## Distance Estimation between WMSN node and Object

Tables 1 and 2 show the computed object distance and size using PCA. This is also compared to a regression based technique and Oztarak et al. [28]. For simplicity, variation of a single object's size with respect to a distance from 1, upto 10 feet is taken. As seen in Table 1, the frequency of error in the PCA based localization is reported as 1/10, compared to other localization techniques. This error is attributed towards uncertainty in the object's size at the farthest distance. Therefore, PCA technique computes the same distance at 9 and 10 feet.Table 2 shows object size calculation in term of pixels of the object given that the distance of the object is in ft. In this case, the error in PCA based technique is exactly 0 as compared to other.

**Table 1.** Distance estimation and associated error.

| Distance (feet) | Object Size | PCA | Regression | Oztarak et. al | Error (PCA) | Error Regression | Error Oztarak et. al. |
|---|---|---|---|---|---|---|---|
| 1 | 27328 | 1 | 1.06347 | 0.50065 | 0 | 0.06347 | 0.49935 |
| 2 | 6399 | 2 | 6.06899 | 0.97627 | 0 | 4.06899 | 1.02373 |
| 3 | 3114 | 3 | 6.85465 | 1.35593 | 0 | 3.85465 | 1.64407 |
| 4 | 1647 | 4 | 7.20551 | 1.87744 | 0 | 3.20551 | 2.12256 |
| 5 | 1189 | 5 | 7.31505 | 2.2704 | 0 | 2.31505 | 2.7296 |
| 6 | 746 | 6 | 7.421 | 2.87139 | 0 | 1.421 | 3.12861 |
| 7 | 574 | 7 | 7.46214 | 3.14926 | 0 | 0.46214 | 3.85074 |
| 8 | 465 | 8 | 7.48821 | 3.61582 | 0 | 0.51179 | 4.38418 |
| 9 | 364 | 9 | 7.51236 | 4.0678 | 0 | 1.48764 | 4.9322 |
| 10 | 288 | 10 | 7.53054 | 4.64891 | 1 | 2.46946 | 5.35109 |

doi:10.1371/journal.pone.0141558.t001

**Table 2.** Estimation of object size and its associated error.

| Distance (feet) | Object Size | PCA | Regression | Oztarak et. al | Error (PCA) | Error Regression | Error Oztarak et. al. |
|---|---|---|---|---|---|---|---|
| 1 | 27328 | 27328 | 83678 | 32235 | 0 | 56349.92238 | 4907.80618 |
| 2 | 6399 | 6399 | 27671 | 7999 | 0 | 21271.86142 | 1600.37498 |
| 3 | 3114 | 3114 | 28336 | 4017 | 0 | 31450.19953 | 903.83225 |
| 4 | 1647 | 1647 | 84343 | 2110 | 0 | 85990.26049 | 463.32888 |
| 5 | 1189 | 1189 | 140350 | 1482 | 0 | 141539.32145 | 293.72081 |
| 6 | 746 | 746 | 196357 | 928 | 0 | 197103.3824 | 182.64202 |
| 7 | 574 | 574 | 252364 | 742 | 0 | 252938.44336 | 168.70721 |
| 8 | 465 | 465 | 308372 | 582 | 0 | 308836.50431 | 117.22418 |
| 9 | 364 | 364 | 364379 | 457 | 0 | 364742.56527 | 68.38182 |
| 10 | 288 | 288 | 420386 | 356 | 0 | 420673.62622 | 68.38182 |

doi:10.1371/journal.pone.0141558.t002

Figs 7–9 show the distance between the WMSN node and the object using PCA, Regression and Oztarak et al. [28] based localization techniques. In Fig 7, the error between the actual distance and the distance estimated by PCA technique is almost zero. Fig 10 show the error in distance estimation between Regression, PCA and Oztarak et. al. [28] based localization technique. Again, it can be observed that the error in PCA based technique is almost zero.

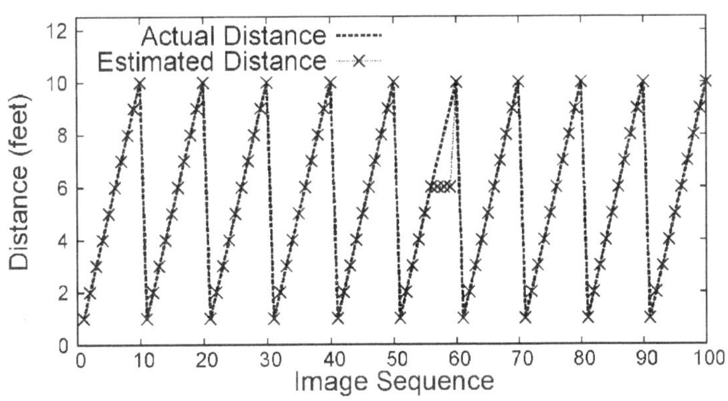


**Figure 7.** PCA based localization.

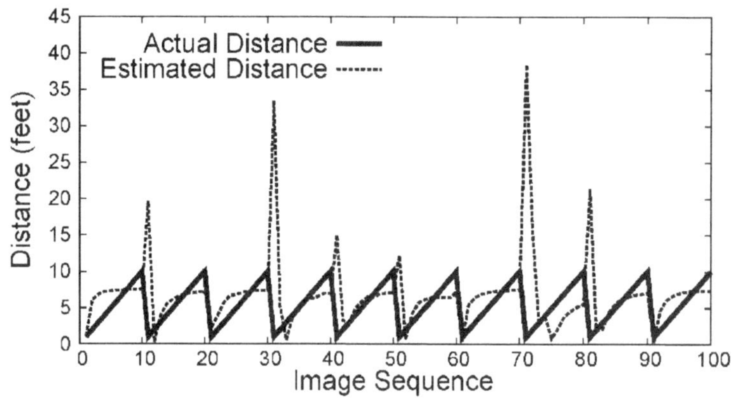


**Figure 8.** Regression based localization.

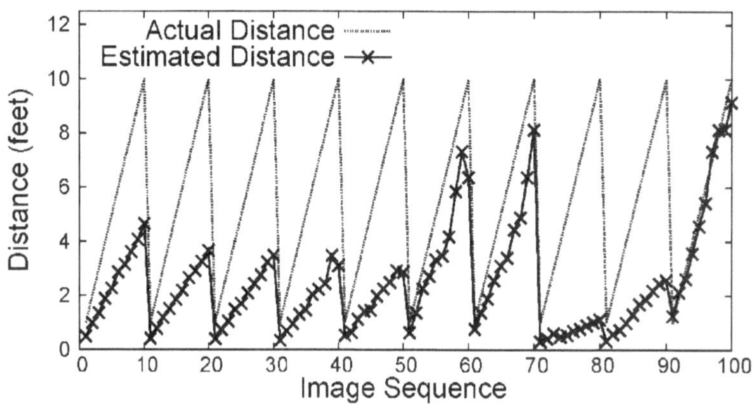


**Figure 9.** Localization results by Oztarak. et. al. [28].

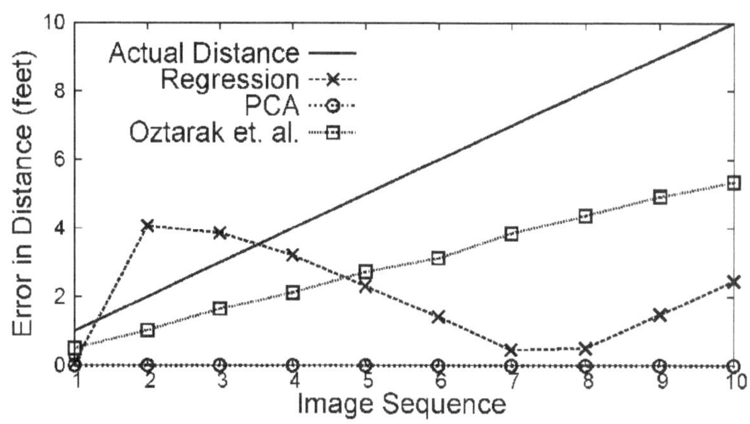


**Figure 10.** Error in distance estimation between regression, PCA, and Oztarak. et. al. based localization methods.

The efficiency η of the proposed method is calculated as:

$$\eta = \frac{T - T_{noError}}{T} \times 100, \quad (16)$$

where T represents the total observations, and $T_{noError}$ represents the number observations where an error was reported. With this, it can be observed that the percentage efficiency of calculating distance between the object and the source WMSN node is 40% using the method by Oztarak et al. [28], 59% using regression, and 99% using our PCA based approach. Fig 11shows the complete result of the normalized object size variation with distance.

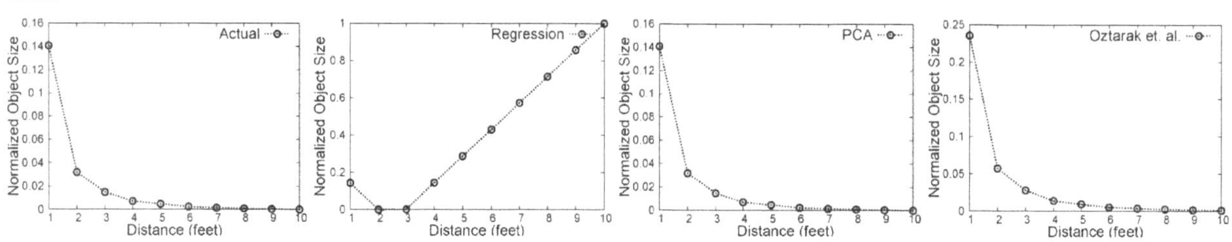


**Figure 11.** Normalized object sizes against distance (in feet).

Fig 12 shows the distance estimation under noisy measurements, where it can be observed that the distance estimated using PCA based technique provides a statisfactory result as compared to Regression and Oztarak et. al. [28] based techniques. Fig 13 shows the result of object orientation with respect to sink node. Here, it can be observed that the orientation using all three localization methods is close to the actual orientation.

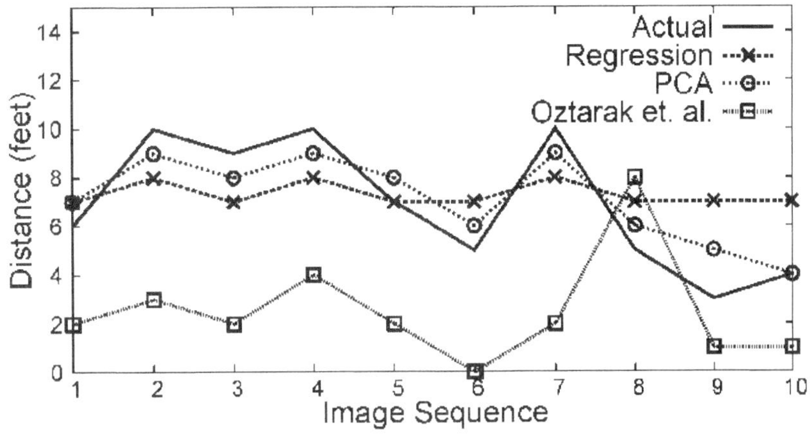


**Figure 12.** Distance estimation under received noisy measurement.

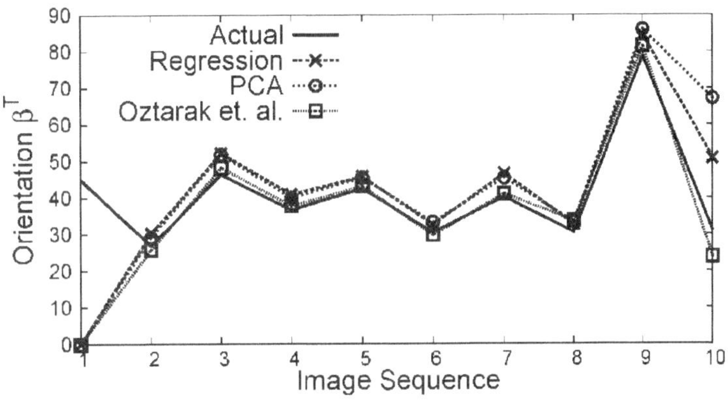


**Figure 13.** Object orientation $\beta^T$ **obtained at sink node from various image sources** i.

Table 3 reports the comparison of PCA, Regression and Oztarak et. al. [28] techniques in terms of various parameters such as size and camera orientation. To calculate the efficiency of these techniques, a tolerance of 2 feet for distance estimation and 200 pixels for size estimation has been considered. The ratio ρ is given as:

$$\rho = \frac{T_{error}}{T_{noError}} \quad (17)$$

**Table 3.** Comparison of various techniques.

| Technique | Object Actual Size | Camera Parameters | $\mu$ in calculating distance | Distance Error Ratio $\rho$ | $\mu$ in calculating size | Size Error Ratio $\rho$ |
|---|---|---|---|---|---|---|
| PCA | No | No | 99% | 0.01 | 100% | 0 |
| Regression | No | No | 59% | 0.69 | 2% | 49 |
| Oztarak et. al. | Yes | Yes | 40% | 1.5 | 61% | 0.64 |

doi:10.1371/journal.pone.0141558.t003

Table 4 shows the estimated object location by using PCA, Regression and Oztark et. al. [28] based technique. As can be depicted in Table 4 the error is reduced to 1 feet by using PCA based technique.Fig 14 shows the final result in the Network Map.

**Table 4.** Localization comparison of different schemes.

| | Actual | | PCA | | Regression | | Oztarak et. al | |
|---|---|---|---|---|---|---|---|---|
| Sensor # | X | Y | X | Y | X | Y | X | Y |
| 1 | 6 | 6 | 7 | 7 | 7 | 7 | 1 | 1 |
| 2 | 81 | 41 | 80 | 40 | 79 | 39 | 74 | 32 |
| 3 | 65 | 68 | 64 | 67 | 63 | 66 | 58 | 60 |
| 4 | 86 | 64 | 85 | 63 | 84 | 62 | 79 | 56 |
| 5 | 107 | 98 | 108 | 99 | 107 | 98 | 102 | 92 |
| 6 | 102 | 60 | 103 | 61 | 104 | 62 | 97 | 55 |
| 7 | 64 | 54 | 63 | 53 | 62 | 52 | 56 | 45 |
| 8 | 102 | 60 | 103 | 61 | 104 | 62 | 104 | 58 |
| 9 | 15 | 75 | 17 | 77 | 19 | 79 | 13 | 72 |
| 10 | 10 | 6 | 10 | 6 | 13 | 9 | 7 | 2 |

doi:10.1371/journal.pone.0141558.t004

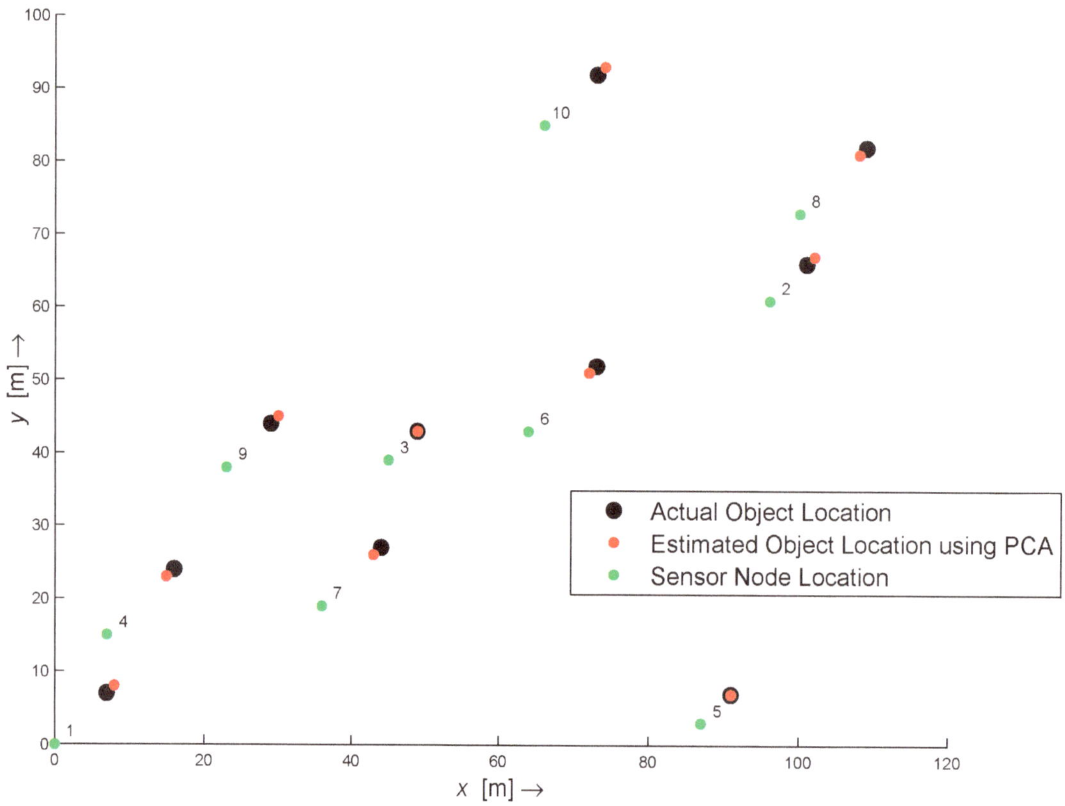


**Figure 14.** Final Result.

## CONCLUSION

This manuscript presents a method for object localization in wireless multimedia sensor networks that uses range free localization, machine learning, and computer vision based techniques. Object localization is an important component of many popular applications of WMSN. As such the first step is to localize the WMSN nodes. The image acquisition process then begins where all images are processed before being delivered to the sink node. The main objective of this processing is to reduce network bandwidth, and is performed by application of a 2D Discrete Wavelet Transform 2D Discrete Wavelet Transform composes the image into various sub-bands of varying sizes and quality. The sink employs a PCA based technique to localize the object. Node orientation and object geometry are taken into account in the entire process. Simulation results report 99% efficiency and an error ratio of 0.01 (around 1 ft) when compared to other popular techniques.

## REFERENCES


1. Akyildiz IF, Melodia T, Chowdhury KR. A Survey on Wireless Multimedia Sensor Networks. Comput Netw. 2007 Mar;51(4):921–960. Available from:http://dx.doi.org/10.1016/j.comnet.2006.10.002.
2. Costa DG, Silva I, Guedes LA, Vasques F, Portugal P. Availability Issues in Wireless Visual Sensor Networks. Sensors. 2014;14(2):2795–2821. Available from:http://www.mdpi.com/1424-8220/14/2/2795. doi: 10.3390/s140202795. pmid:24526301
3. Liu X. A Survey on Wireless Camera Sensor Networks. In: Li S, Jin Q, Jiang X, Park JJJH, editors. Frontier and Future Development of Information Technology

in Medicine and Education. vol. 269 of Lecture Notes in Electrical Engineering. Springer Netherlands; 2014. p. 1085–1094. Available from: http://dx.doi.org/10.1007/978-94-007-7618-0_106.

4. Tran DA, Nguyen T. Localization In Wireless Sensor Networks Based on Support Vector Machines. Parallel and Distributed Systems, IEEE Transactions on. 2008 July;19(7):981–994. doi: 10.1109/TPDS.2007.70800.

5. Chandrasekhar V, Seah WK, Choo YS, Ee HV. Localization in Underwater Sensor Networks: Survey and Challenges. In: Proceedings of the 1st ACM International Workshop on Underwater Networks. WUWNet'06. New York, NY, USA: ACM; 2006. p. 33–40. Available from: http://doi.acm.org/10.1145/1161039.1161047.

6. El Assaf A, Zaidi S, Affes S, Kandil N. Range-Free Localization Algorithm for Anisotropic Wireless Sensor Networks. In: Vehicular Technology Conference (VTC Fall), 2014 IEEE 80th; 2014. p. 1–5.

7. Gao D, Zhu W, Xu X, Chao HC. A hybrid localization and tracking system in camera sensor networks. International Journal of Communication Systems. 2014;27(4):606–622. Available from: http://dx.doi.org/10.1002/dac.2492.

8. Bouwmans T. Traditional and recent approaches in background modeling for foreground detection: An overview. Computer Science Review. 2014;11–12(0):31–66. Available from: http://www.sciencedirect.com/science/article/pii/S1574013714000033. doi: 10.1016/j.cosrev.2014.04.001.

9. Li W, Portilla J, Moreno F, Liang G, Riesgo T. Improving target localization accuracy of wireless visual sensor networks. In: IECON 2011 - 37th Annual Conference on IEEE Industrial Electronics Society; 2011. p. 3814–3819.

**10.** .Nguyen T, Jeong Y, Trinh D, Shin H. Location-aware visual radios. Wireless Communications, IEEE. 2014 August;21(4):28–36. doi: 10.1109/MWC.2014.6882293.

11. O'Rourke D, Moore D, Wark T. Demo abstract: Fusion of audio and image information for efficient object detection and capture. In: Information Processing in Sensor Networks, 2009. IPSN 2009. International Conference on; 2009. p. 401–402.

12. Alaei M, Barcelo-Ordinas JM. A hybrid cooperative design for energy-efficient surveillance in Wireless Multimedia Sensor Networks. In: European Wireless, 2012. EW. 18th European Wireless Conference; 2012. p. 1–7.

13. J R Martinez-de Dios AJG, Ollero A. Localization and Tracking Using Camera-Based Wireless Sensor Networks. In: Thomas C, editor. Sensor Fusion - Foundation and Applications. InTech; 2011.

14. Öztarak H, Akkaya K, Yazici A. Providing Automated Actions in Wireless Multimedia Sensor Networks via Active Rules. In: Gelenbe E, Lent R, Sakellari G, editors. Computer and Information Sciences II. Springer London; 2012. p. 185–190. Available from: http://dx.doi.org/10.1007/978-1-4471-2155-8_23.

15. Tavli B, Bicakci K, Zilan R, Barcelo-Ordinas J. A survey of visual sensor network platforms. Multimedia Tools and Applications. 2012;60(3):689–726. Available from:http://dx.doi.org/10.1007/s11042-011-0840-z.

16. Huang Q, Selvakennedy S. A Range-Free Localization Algorithm for Wireless Sensor Networks. In: Vehicular Technology Conference, 2006. VTC 2006-Spring. IEEE 63rd. vol. 1; 2006. p. 349–353.

17. Langendoen K, Reijers N. Distributed Localization in Wireless Sensor Networks: A Quantitative Comparison. Comput Netw. 2003 Nov;43(4):499–518. Available from:http://dx.doi.org/10.1016/S1389-1286(03)00356-6.

18. Paul AK, Sato T. Effective Data Gathering and Energy Efficient Communication Protocol in Wireless Sensor Network. In: Wireless Personal Multimedia Communications (WPMC), 2011 14th International Symposium on; 2011. p. 1–5.

19. Wang C, Xiao L. Locating Sensors in Concave Areas. In: INFOCOM 2006. 25th IEEE International Conference on Computer Communications. Proceedings; 2006. p. 1–12.

20. Liu C, Wu K. Performance evaluation of range-free localization methods for wireless sensor networks. In: Performance, Computing, and Communications Conference, 2005. IPCCC 2005. 24th IEEE International; 2005. p. 59–66.

21. Paul AK, Sato T. Detour Path Angular Information Based Range-Free Localization in Wireless Sensor Network. Journal of Sensor and Actuator Networks. 2013;2(1):25–45. Available from: http://www.mdpi.com/2224-2708/2/1/25. doi: 10.3390/jsan2010025.

22. Hu W, Tan T, Wang L, Maybank S. A survey on visual surveillance of object motion and behaviors. Systems, Man, and Cybernetics, Part C: Applications and Reviews, IEEE Transactions on. 2004 Aug;34(3):334–352. doi: 10.1109/TSMCC.2004.829274.

23. Wang L, Huang K, Huang Y, Tan T. Object detection and tracking for night surveillance based on salient contrast analysis. In: Image Processing (ICIP), 2009 16th IEEE International Conference on; 2009. p. 1113–1116.

24. Lee JK, Kim JJ, Jun MS. Design and Realization for Security System of Facility Management Based USN. In: Ubiquitous Computing and Multimedia Applications (UCMA), 2011 International Conference on; 2011. p. 30–34.

25. Vittal KP, Ajay Pai P, Ajay Shenoy B, Rao CHS. Computer Controlled Intrusion-Detector and Automatic Firing-Unit for Border Security. In: Computer and Network Technology (ICCNT), 2010 Second International Conference on; 2010. p. 289–293.

26. Kimura N, Latifi S. A survey on data compression in wireless sensor networks. In: Information Technology: Coding and Computing, 2005. ITCC 2005. International Conference on. vol. 2; 2005. p. 8–13 Vol. 2.

27. De D, Gupta MD, Sen A. Energy Efficient Target Tracking Mechanism using Rotational Camera Sensor in {WMSN}. Procedia Technology. 2012;6(0):674–681. 2nd International Conference on Communication, Computing & Security [ICCCS-2012]. Available from:http://www.sciencedirect.com/science/article/pii/S2212017312006263.

28. Oztarak H, Akkaya K, Yazici A. Lightweight Object Localization with a Single Camera in Wireless Multimedia Sensor Networks. In: Global Telecommunications Conference, 2009. GLOBECOM 2009. IEEE; 2009. p. 1–6.

29. Medeiros H, Park J, Kak AC. Distributed Object Tracking Using a Cluster-Based Kalman Filter in Wireless Camera Networks. Selected Topics in Signal Processing, IEEE Journal of. 2008 Aug;2(4):448–463. doi: 10.1109/JSTSP.2008.2001310.

30. Boulanouar I, Rachedi A, Lohier S, Roussel G. Energy-aware object tracking algorithm using heterogeneous wireless sensor networks. In: Wireless Days (WD), 2011 IFIP; 2011. p. 1–6.

CHAPTER 4

# A FORENSICALLY SOUND ADVERSARY MODEL FOR MOBILE DEVICES

Quang Do , Ben Martini , Kim-Kwang Raymond Choo

Information Assurance Research Group, University of South Australia, Adelaide, Australia

## ABSTRACT

**In this paper, we propose an adversary model to facilitate forensic investigations of mobile devices (e.g. Android, iOS and Windows smartphones) that can be readily adapted to the latest mobile device technologies. This is essential given the ongoing and rapidly changing nature of mobile device technologies. An integral principle and significant constraint upon forensic practitioners is that of forensic soundness. Our adversary model specifically considers and integrates the constraints of forensic soundness on the adversary, in our case, a forensic practitioner. One construction of the adversary model is an evidence collection and analysis methodology for Android devices. Using the methodology with six popular cloud apps, we were successful in extracting various information of forensic interest in both the external and internal storage of the mobile device.**

## INTRODUCTION

Human beings have become increasingly dependent on information and communication technologies (ICTs) not just for work and commercial functions, but also for many daily activities. The advent of Web 2.0, since around the mid-2000s, marked the introduction of pervasive interconnectivity, otherwise known as an 'always-on' lifestyle. This has made ICT (e.g. mobile devices and apps) paramount to everyday life, such that any significant technical glitch or outage in internet access or mobile transmission would lead to mass frustration, confusion, and even panic.

**Citation:** Do Q, Martini B, Choo K-KR (2015) A Forensically Sound Adversary Model for Mobile Devices. PLoS ONE 10(9): e0138449. doi:10.1371/journal.pone.0138449

Holt and Bossler [1] explained that "[a]s technology increasingly permeates all facets of modern life, there are substantive risks to the safety of digital information and computer networks". For example, the increasing popularity of mobile devices including smart phones (e.g. iOS and Android devices) constitutes an opportunity for cybercriminals.

Technological advances should not, however, be blamed for any increase in criminal exploitation of ICT. Cyber threats and windows of vulnerability evolve over time, partly in response to defensive actions or crime displacement. Therefore, we need to maintain persistent pressure on cybercriminals to safeguard the security and privacy of our data (e.g. stored on mobile devices) even though we may never be able to completely eradicate cybercrime.

To increase the risks of detection and successful prosecution due to the ability to collect evidence from mobile devices, it is important to stay ahead of the race between device (i.e. hardware) and software releases by providers, and software and hardware modifications made by end users to complicate or prevent the collection and analysis of digital evidence.

During investigations of crimes involving mobile devices, there is usually some accumulation or retention of data on the device that will need to be identified, preserved, analyzed and presented in a court of law—a process known as digital or mobile forensics (also known as cyber forensics) [2].

Potential evidential data that could be recovered from mobile devices includes login credentials for cloud storage and other online accounts, and metadata such as when and where a photo or video was taken (i.e. geolocation) using the mobile device or stored in the cloud.

Studies of digital forensic toolkits currently available to law enforcement agencies reveal significant challenges and complications in extracting evidence from newer devices, with attempts to extract information from various mobile devices using a range of mobile forensic tools producing differing results [3, 4].

There is little doubt that governments will continue to be under pressure to deliver more with less. This will apply to the provision of law enforcement services no less than other government services. Therefore, to keep pace with this growth and the changing face of criminal activity, particularly to ensure that evidential data can be forensically recovered from mobile devices, we propose a forensic adversary model for mobile device data collection and analysis. Forensic practitioners, like adversaries, are subject to certain constraints. In the case of a forensic practitioner, these constraints relate to "forensic soundness". These constraints help to ensure that evidence remains valid and suitable for presentation to a court of law and that it remains untainted. We integrate the constraints of forensic soundness into our adversary model, resulting in a forensically sound adversary model.

The remainder of the paper is organized as follows. The next section discusses related work. Section 3 outlines our research motivations. We then present our mobile forensic adversary model and a construction of this model, the Android evidence collection and analysis methodology (see also [5]), in Section 4. We discuss the utility of our construction in Section 5. The last section concludes this paper and outlines future work.

## RELATED WORK

### Adversary Models

Adversary models have long been an important part of designing and validating cryptographic and secure systems (e.g. used to prove or disprove the properties of a cryptographic protocol). An adversary generally has capabilities, such as the ability to listen to all messages transmitted by a target. One of the most recognized and utilized adversary models is, perhaps, the Dolev-Yao model [6]. An adversary in this particular model has capabilities that verge on omnipotence, including the ability to intercept messages from a target, modify these messages and even initiate a connection with the target. Similarly, Bellare and Rogaway's adversary model [7] provided the adversary with comparable capabilities. The adversary has the capacity to control all communications between the interacting parties. All messages produced by the parties are observable and modifiable by the adversary. The adversary is even capable of controlling the delays between messages, replaying messages, employing multiple sessions and corrupting an honest user in the system. Some may criticize that both adversary models are too strong, and hence, unrealistic.

Adversary models have also been used in network security to replicate and simulate attacks on communications protocols. Syverson, et al. [8] presented an adversary model for networks utilizing onion routing. The capabilities of this model include the ability to: observe (sniff) a connection, delay or corrupt a connection, initiate or destroy a connection and modify a connection's traffic at will. This model differs somewhat from those designed for cryptographic protocols. The adversary's main aim is to compromise connections between parties instead of manipulating the data of the actual traffic itself. Similarly to the cryptographic-based adversary models, this model is somewhat specific to the field of network security.

In the field of privacy preservation, adversary models have been used to model privacy invasions. Heiber and Marron [9] considered the privacy of users in context-aware systems and presented a framework for the modelling of privacy within these systems. In order to demonstrate their model, the authors utilized an adversary model capable of over-hearing all wireless transmissions in a network and also having full access to the context-aware system's location service. The specificity of this model makes it difficult to use outside of this research.

Within the field of Android security, a number of researchers have also utilized adversary models within their work. For example, both Wu, et al. [10] and Zhou, et al. [11] utilize adversary models that involve the adversary simulating a malicious third-party app installed on an Android device. The adversary model of Zhou, et al. [11] can only request non-sensitive permissions and the adversary model of is unable to request for any permissions. Such specific adversary models cannot be used to generalize or model other types of security attackers.

Other research that makes use of adversaries often informally defines an adversary or an adversary's capabilities, or refers to the adversary in passing. The use of loosely defined adversaries (e.g. a "strong adversary") and/or adversary capabilities means that the research lacks a concrete adversary which would be useful in other research environments. Bugiel, Heuser and Sadeghi [12] presented a security architecture for access control on Android devices. In doing so, the authors provided an adversary model that exhibited a "strong" adversary able to "access sensitive data" and "launch software attacks". Although their research does not focus on the adversary model, the formalization concerning the capabilities of their proposed adversary model is somewhat lacking.

As described above and shown in Table 1, there are many different use cases for adversary models (with varying levels of competence). These different use cases also prompt researchers to design their own adversary models that may be incompatible with other research both inside and outside of their field of study. For example, Syverson, et al. [8] focused on the security of onion routing networks which are designed to provide anonymity. Cryptographic protocols, on the other hand, are intended to provide secure communications between parties—the identity of each party would be known before communication had even commenced. Further differences arise when comparing a cryptographic or networking adversary to a smartphone adversary. Take, for example, a user with a smartphone which is connected to an onion routing network who wishes to perform a secure transaction with another party. A smartphone adversary typically wishes to obtain sensitive user data (e.g. contact phone numbers, location information and login details), message or call premium numbers or otherwise obtain some data of (monetary) value whilst the onion routing adversary seeks to determine the identity of the user. The cryptographic adversary would like to decrypt the secure communications between the smartphone and the other party. Table 1 demonstrates the differences in adversary models with regards to the ways they are defined, including their goals and assumptions (and the levels of detail provided).

**Table 1.** A comparison of adversary models.

| | Adversary Capabilities Fully Defined? | Adversary Goals | Adversary Assumptions | Adversary Model Limitations |
|---|---|---|---|---|
| Dolev and Yao [6] (Cryptographic protocols) | Yes | The adversary seeks to obtain the plaintext for encrypted messages on the network. | The adversary can read any message on the network, and can initiate a two-way connection with any other user. | Very powerful, making it difficult to model weaker adversaries. |
| Bellare and Rogaway [7] (Cryptographic protocols) | Yes | Similarly to the Dolev-Yao model, the adversary aims to obtain the long-term secret key and/or the ephemeral / session key. | The adversary has similar capabilities to the Dolev-Yao model, including the ability to delay or replay messages. | Very powerful, but also flexible due to the notion of "queries" (i.e. adversary capabilities). |
| Syverson, et al. [8] (Network security) | No | The aim of the adversary is to determine the identity of (i.e. de-anonymize) the traffic flowing through its compromised nodes. | The adversary is assumed to have control of one or more nodes (known as Core Onion Routers). | Adversary capabilities are not formally defined. Furthermore, this model is specific to onion routing (e.g. compromised nodes), and cannot be generalizable. |
| Heiber and Marron [9] (Network security) | Yes | The adversary's goal is to collect personal or private data (e.g. location information) from a network. | The adversary is designed such that it is only able to view data (i.e. it cannot modify it). | A weak adversary that is formally defined using inference rules. |
| Wu, et al. [10] (Android security) | No | The adversary aims to steal money from the user, gather sensitive information or destroy data on the device. | The adversary cannot initially request any "sensitive" permissions. | The adversary is defined very loosely. This means it cannot be used for formal proofs. |
| Zhou, et al. [11] (Android security) | No | The adversary aims to accurately determine the locations and behaviors of the user. | The adversary cannot request *any* permissions initially. | This adversary is also very loosely defined. |
| Bugiel, Heuser and Sadeghi [12] (Android security) | No | The adversary's goals are to obtain sensitive data and compromise apps on the device (both system and third-party) | The adversary is assumed to be "strong". | This adversary lacks meaningful detail. |

doi:10.1371/journal.pone.0138449.t001

## Android Data Collection

There have been a number of data collection methodologies designed specifically for Android devices. These are a combination of techniques (methods or approaches), often with an underlying process (model or framework) in order to bring them together.

Most notable of the current methodologies proposed is the general collection methodology for Android devices presented by Vidas, Zhang and Christin [13]. It comprises a process for obtaining data from an Android device that relies on a bootable image which is flashed onto the Android device. The images differ based on the phone model and are required to be flashed over the original recovery image on the Android device. This custom recovery mode is able to extract all data from the NAND and any attached SD cards of the device without requiring root access. One major problem with this approach is that newer phones (released after the publication of [13] in 2011) have locked bootloaders, generally requiring the device be wiped in order to unlock them (if indeed there are ways to unlock the bootloader at all).

Lessard and Kessler [14] presented a process for obtaining all the data from an Android NAND (Negated AND) flash. One technique proposed allowed for collecting a bit-for-bit copy of the NAND flash itself in order to perform data recovery on deleted items. Their process requires rooting the device in order to perform a "dd" image of the relevant partitions and storing these on an external SD card attached to the device, and then analyzing these dumps for potential evidence. One issue with this technique is that it requires rooting the device and the disadvantages to the forensic process that it brings in order to create these images and the technique also requires the device to have a microSD card slot. Many popular Android devices, such as the Nexus 5, Samsung Galaxy S6 and LG G2, do not have the ability to accept SD cards, rendering this process infeasible on these devices.

Chen, Yang and Liu [15] suggested that physical data acquisition on an Android device can be performed without modifying the Android device in almost any manner and presented a process to do so. The authors use the Android device's recovery mode in order to run their own "update.zip" (generally used by carriers and phone manufacturers to issue Android OS updates) package which is stored on an external SD card. As the "update.zip" package runs as a root process, it is able to perform a physical data acquisition of the Android device and dump it onto the SD card. Two major problems arise with this suggested method. Firstly and most importantly, this method relies on the Android device having already have flashed a third-party recovery mode on the recovery partition. This is unlikely to be the case as the user would have to unlock the bootloader of the device and flash this software manually. The reason a third-party recovery mode software is required is that first-party recovery modes generally have signature checking which is used to make sure the "update.zip" files were packaged by the appropriate authority (carriers or phone manufacturers). Such an "update.zip" package designed by the authors would refuse to run on first-party recovery modes. In addition to requiring a third-party recovery mode, this method also requires the device have an SD card slot.

A methodology for collecting data from Android devices was presented by Votipka, Vidas and Christin [16]. They suggested that a custom recovery image could be built which can be easily ported to many Android devices. This image contains forensic tools that can extract all the required data in a forensically sound manner from the Android device. In order to bypass a locked bootloader, the authors rely on the forensic practitioner having the ability to obtain the manufacturer key used to sign legitimate bootloader images. In most cases, device manufacturers are unlikely to be in the same jurisdiction as the forensic practitioner and may not be legally obligated to provide the key. This makes it highly infeasible that a forensic practitioner would be able to obtain the key. Furthermore, flashing this custom recovery image overwrites the original first-party recovery mode on the device, reducing the forensic soundness of this process.

Similarly, Son, et al. [17] proposed a data acquisition process for Android that relied on the use of a custom recovery mode image that was flashed onto the boot partition. Flashing the boot partition with a custom recovery mode image will render the device unable to boot into the original Android OS. The authors state that the boot image must be flashed with the original boot image of the device, which may be difficult (and not forensically sound depending on the source) to obtain. They also designed an application that extracts user data stored within the Android device via ADB after the custom recovery mode image was installed. Although their process should be capable of collecting most of the data from the Android device's NAND flash, the authors focus on obtaining user and app data.

Finally, a crucial stage that the majority of contemporary data collection methodologies currently lack is the analysis of the collected data. Without accurate analysis, the collected data cannot be utilized to its full extent. In addition, without an adequate analysis of the collected evidence, the forensic practitioner may omit critical evidential data.

## RESEARCH MOTIVATIONS

As discussed in the previous section, adversary models exist for a range of fields in the security and cryptography disciplines. However, adversary models have not yet been adopted in digital forensics. We hope to contribute to filling this gap in this paper as we believe that the role of the traditional security 'adversary' represented in existing models and a forensic practitioner conducting investigations have significant parallels.

Generally, adversary models are designed for use in a particular field, each of which has different specific requirements and capabilities. This holds true for digital forensic adversary models, where an overriding principle must be maintained, that is, the principle of ensuring that evidence sources remain unmodified wherever possible [2]. Where a change to an evidence source is required to collect evidence, these changes must be discrete (i.e. the practitioner must be able to report upon the exact actions they performed and the transient and persistent effect(s) this had on the device, preferably at the bit level for persistent changes) and kept to an absolute minimum [2]. This requirement significantly constrains the ability for forensic practitioners to utilize a range of invasive attack techniques (particularly attacks developed by unknown individuals, with only compiled code released) that would be available to traditional adversaries.

For example, when collecting evidence from secure devices, practitioners often need to bypass operating system (OS) or hardware security features (e.g. app / process sandboxing). In the case of smartphones, this is achieved via 'rooting' or 'jailbreaking' the device. These processes generally rely upon security flaws to escalate the privileges of the attack code, and in turn, the device's user. However, in most cases, the source code underlying the privilege escalation procedure is not released. This makes it particularly difficult for a forensic practitioner to report on the discrete operations that are being undertaken on the device. In practice, this could result in the destruction or modification of evidence on the device, either intentionally or inadvertently, by the privilege escalation procedure.

In contrast, while many adversary models constrain the adversary by requiring that attacks be executed remotely (e.g. via a network link), such restrictions do not apply to forensic practitioners. In most cases, forensic practitioners are able to 'seize' the physical device being analyzed and, as such, have access to capabilities that require physical access/control of the device. This is a reasonable and necessary ability for forensic practitioners in most cases, even in circumstances where the only apparently feasible option is remote collection of evidence [18]. This is apparent, for example, in the case of cloud computing evidential data, which is commonly stored on remote servers outside of the jurisdiction of the investigating law enforcement agency (LEA). However, despite the primary evidence source being remotely located, evidential data generally exists on the client devices (e.g. laptops, tablets and smartphones) that are used to connect to the remote cloud service. These client devices are generally located within the jurisdiction of the investigating LEA and within the possession or control of the individual being investigated (drawing a physical link between the electronic evidence and the suspect [19]).

The contribution of an adversary model in the field of digital forensics allows for a more formal approach to the development of forensic methodologies. The model can be used as a basis for ensuring that a practitioner can conduct an investigation using only the forensically sound capabilities available to them (e.g. mapping adversary capabilities in combination with an existing forensic model to develop a forensically sound methodology).

## MOBILE FORENSIC ADVERSARY MODEL

### The Proposed Model

As described in Section 3, one of the primary constraints on the forensic adversary is in ensuring that all actions on the evidence item are forensically sound. As such, it should be noted that all of the above capabilities are discrete (i.e. the practitioner is aware of the precise effect they will have on the device being analyzed) and documented as part of standard forensic reporting procedures. Based on the definitions of McKemmish [20] and Casey [21], we formalize the definition of forensic soundness in Definition 1.

**Definition 1** (Forensic Soundness) A process is forensically sound if it satisfies all of the following key criteria described by McKemmish [20] and Casey [21]:

- *Meaning*: Meaning refers to the fact that evidence that is collected as part of digital forensic investigations must retain its original meaning and interpretation. However, it should be noted that "[i]mposing a paradigm of "preserve everything but change nothing" is impractical and doing so can create undue doubt in the results of a digital evidence analysis, with questions that have no relation to the merits of the conclusions" [21].
- *Errors*: Errors refer to the need to identify the existence of errors, when they occur, and, explain and justify that their existence has not affected the core validity of the evidence. Hashes are a common method of detecting errors during forensic collection processes.
- *Transparency and Trustworthiness*: Transparency and trustworthiness highlight the need for independent oversight into the forensic processes used. For example, a court may wish to validate the integrity of the process.
- *Experience*: Experience refers to the need for individuals undertaking forensic investigations to have sufficient experience, such that their findings can be relied upon.

The forensic soundness criteria (Definition 1) are considered in the selection of available capabilities, outlined below, and specific constraints raised by these criteria are noted as part of our capability descriptions.

Following the approaches of Dolev and Yao [6] and Bellare and Rogaway [7], we introduce an adversary model for mobile forensic data collection and analysis. In this model, there exists an adversary with physical access to a mobile device and capabilities to exploit device security vulnerabilities. The adversary aims to obtain confidential data from a target device within the constraints of forensic soundness (Definition 1). These capabilities are described below:

- **Corrupt** (*Target device*) allows the adversary to take over the Target device. Such a capability, typically used to capture insider attacks in cryptographic protocols and network security, allows the adversary to learn the complete internal state of the device. Under a strict implementation of the forensic soundness criteria, this capability would be constrained to functions that do not introduce *errors* (e.g. modification of evidential data sources) or result in a loss of *transparency and trustworthiness* (e.g. the execution of unknown operation sequences on the Target device).
- **Delete** (*Target device*, *Target data*) enables the adversary to delete data (*Target data*) stored on the *Target device*. Under a strict implementation of the forensic soundness criteria, this capability would be significantly constrained to functions that do not result in the introduction of *errors* or a loss of *meaning* (e.g. deletion operations on evidential data sources).
- **Encrypt/Decrypt** (*Target device*, *Target data*, *Key*) allows the adversary to either encrypt or decrypt a message (*Target data*) from the *Target device* with the *Key*. For theDecrypt function, the decryption key is obtained using another capability (e.g.Forensic Examination). It may not necessarily be feasible to obtain the decryption key for all encrypted items (e.g. the keys may be stored remotely). A strict implementation of the forensic soundness criteria would not significantly affect this capability as it operates on data that has been collected (e.g. Forensic Copy), rather than evidence source data.
- **Exploit** (*Target device*, *Entry-point*) allows the adversary to exploit the *Target deviceusing* a known exploit. Under a strict implementation of the forensic soundness criteria, this capability would be constrained to functions that do not introduce *errors* or result in a loss of *transparency and trustworthiness*.
- **Forensic Copy** (*Target device*) allows the adversary to make a logical or physical forensic copy of the *Target device*. This capability intrinsically meets the criteria for forensic soundness. The capability would be designed to ensure that *errors* are avoided and identified where they are encountered as part of the copy procedure.
- **Forensic Examination** (*Target device*, *Target data*, *Method*) allows the adversary to undertake a forensic examination of *Target data* on the *Target device* using a specific*Method* (e.g. keyword searches). The operation of the capability would be subject to the forensic soundness criteria, particularly the *meaning* criteria, in ensuring that the true meaning of any data examined is maintained. This is fundamentally related to the*experience* of the forensic practitioner.
- **Inject** (*Target device*, *Entry-point*, *Message*) allows the adversary to inject or infiltrate a *Message* (i.e. binary data such as code) onto the *Target device* via an entry-point (e.g. infiltrated app). For example, an adversary could add code into the Keyboard app (*Entry-point*) on the *Target device* to facilitate other attacks (e.g. Transmit) [22]. Under a strict implementation of the forensic soundness criteria, this capability would be constrained to functions that do not introduce *errors* or result in a loss of *transparency and trustworthiness* or *meaning*.
- **Listen** (*Target device*) allows the adversary to passively monitor a communication channel on the *Target device*. This capability must be utilized with consideration for the requirement to obtain data with a known *meaning*, ensure that *errors* in collection are avoided and identified where unavoidable, and that the process for interception is subject to *transparent* review.
- **Modify** (*Target device*, *Target data*, *Message*) allows the adversary to modify an existing message (*Target data*) on a *Target device*, replacing it with a new message (*Message*). An example would be an adversary replacing configuration or modifying app execution on a device. Under a strict implementation of the forensic soundness criteria, this capability would be constrained to functions that do not introduce *errors* or result in a loss of *transparency and trustworthiness* or *meaning*.
- **Transmit** (*Target device*, *Message*) permits the adversary to transmit and/or exfiltrate a *Message* (i.e. binary data such as code and SMS) from the *Target device*. As with the**Listen** capability, this capability

must be utilized with consideration for the requirement to transmit data with a foreknown effect (i.e. *meaning*), ensure that *errors* in transmission are avoided and identified where unavoidable, and that the process for transmission is subject to *transparent* review.

Based on the definition of forensic soundness and the proposed adversary capabilities, we introduce two levels of forensic soundness: strict and standard. A forensic practitioner requiring a strict level of forensic soundness can only utilize constrained adversary capabilities (with the constraints outlined above). A strict adherence to forensic soundness should be the initial stage in any investigation in order to reduce modification of evidence sources. The less stringent standard level of forensic soundness could be utilized if a strict investigation does not provide sufficient evidence. It is at this level that forensic practitioners should use the capabilities to their full potential to obtain evidential data, while meeting the constraints of forensic soundness (Definition 1).

## A Construction

The following section provides a brief outline of our Android evidence collection and analysis methodology [5]–see Fig 1. The methodology is constructed using the mobile forensic adversary model (outlined in Section 4.1).

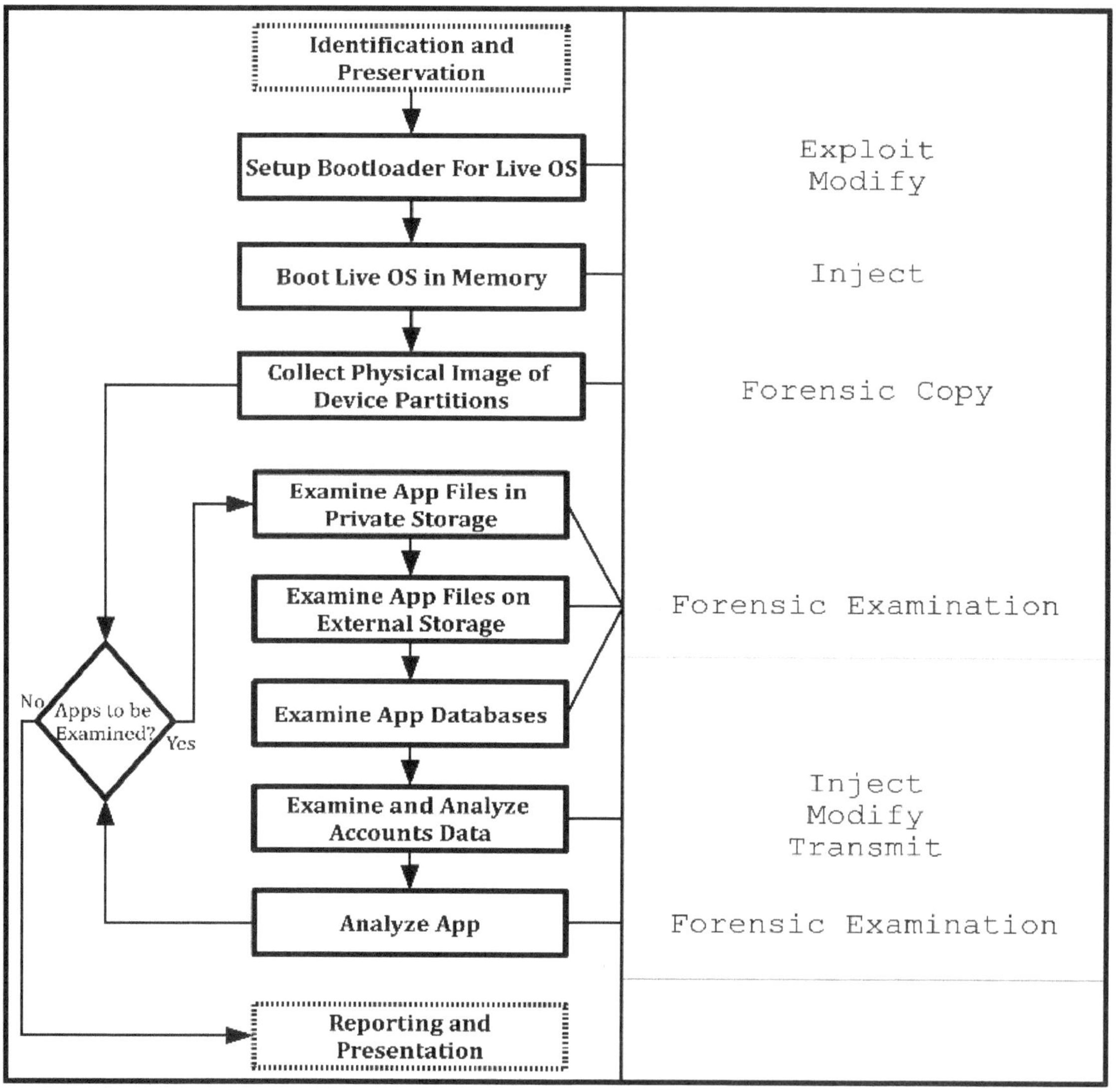


**Figure 1.** Android evidence collection and analysis methodology (adapted from [5]).

After identification and preservation of the mobile device has been completed, evidential data collection must be undertaken. Collection commences with the configuration of the bootloader, which must be setup to allow the booting of a live OS. This recovery image is booted and then used to collect the physical image(s) of the device partition(s).

Using the images obtained as part of the initial collection stages, we then undertake examination and analysis procedures of a forensic copy of the data stored on the device. Once a practitioner has determined the apps that they wish to investigate, they begin by examining the files stored by the app in its private storage, followed by any files stored in the device's external storage (e.g. SD card). During this examination, it is common to find databases which are examined as part of the next stage. Finally, if the app being examined has an online component (e.g. cloud sync), the account data stored on the device is examined and analyzed to obtain any relevant credentials. If the practitioner has any doubts as to the *meaning* of the data obtained during the examination, they will then undertake an analysis of the app which involves examining the app memory heap in a virtual environment and decompilation of the app code to gain an understanding of the code's operation. Once all relevant data has been obtained and its meaning and provenience (i.e. the source of the evidential data) is fully understood, the practitioner will report and present their findings. The practitioner may also appear as an expert witness in a court of law.

With regards to forensic soundness, the Android evidence collection and analysis methodology should meet the strict level of forensic soundness as defined in Section 4.1, dependent on the implementation used and the *experience* of the forensic practitioner. Even though this methodology requires modifications to be made to the evidence source, all modifications should be fully known by the practitioner and therefore follow the strict adversary capability constraints (see Table 2).

**Table 2.** A mapping of methodology stages to adversary capabilities, constraints and adherence to forensic soundness constraints.

| Methodology Stage [5] | Adversary Capabilities Utilized | Key Forensic Soundness Constraints | Adherence to Forensic Soundness Constraints |
|---|---|---|---|
| Setup Bootloader for Live OS | `Exploit` and `Modify` | *Errors, Transparency and Trustworthiness*, and *Meaning* | Implementation dependent for *Errors*, adheres for *Transparency and Trustworthiness*, and *Meaning* |
| Boot Live OS in Memory | `Inject` | *Errors, Transparency and Trustworthiness*, and *Meaning* | Adheres to all applicable forensic soundness constraints |
| Collect Physical Image of Device Partitions | `Forensic Copy` | N/A | N/A |
| Examine App Files in Private Storage | `Forensic Examination` | *Meaning* | *Experience* dependent |
| Examine App Files on External Storage | `Forensic Examination` | *Meaning* | *Experience* dependent |
| Examine App Databases | `Forensic Examination` | *Meaning* | *Experience* dependent |
| Examine and Analyze Accounts Data | `Inject`, `Modify` and `Transmit` | *Errors, Transparency and Trustworthiness*, and *Meaning* | Adheres to all applicable forensic soundness constraints |
| Analyze App | `Forensic Examination` | *Meaning* | *Experience* dependent |

doi:10.1371/journal.pone.0138449.t002

The third and fourth columns of this table are especially pertinent as they provide the specific forensic soundness constraints for a stage and whether the stage adheres to the constraints, respectively. For example, the modification and exploitation of the evidence source to allow the bootloader to accept the forensic practitioner's custom live OS has three constraints: the process must not introduce *errors*, it must be clear (i.e. *transparent and trustworthy*) what modifications are being made and it must not affect the *meaning* of the evidence. Depending on how the device is modified, *errors* may be introduced (e.g. by flashing boot partitions). Ideally, no *errors* should be introduced if the device has been successfully exploited.*Transparency and trustworthiness*, and *meaning* of the evidence are not affected by this stage. Further along the methodology are the three stages that relate to examining data on the evidence source's external and internal (private) storage. The *meaning* of the evidence obtained is directly linked to the forensic practitioner's *experience* in dealing with similar devices and knowledge of what constitutes evidential data.

## DISCUSSION

In order to verify the Mobile Forensic Adversary Model when applied to the Android evidence collection and analysis methodology [5], we analyzed a Google Nexus 4 mobile device (see sections 5.1–5.3) and six popular cloud apps, namely, Dropbox, Box, OneDrive, OneNote, Evernote and ownCloud [23] (see sections 5.4–5.8). The relationship between our findings and the adversary's capabilities and forensic soundness constraints is presented in the following subsections.

### Setup Bootloader for Live OS

After the identification and preservation stages have been completed, the first step is toExploit the security features in the device bootloader with a view to booting an alternative, forensically sound, operating system on the mobile device. This Exploit generally requires the modification (i.e. use of the Modify capability) of low level parameters within the device flash, which are configured by default to prevent the execution of unsigned operating systems. Constraints on the Modify and Exploit capabilities must be adhered to as part of this process, for example, ensuring that *errors* in the evidence source are not inadvertently introduced during the modification of the bootloader configuration parameters. The process used must be subject to *transparent and trustworthy* verification, which limits the capacity for forensic practitioners to utilize existing exploits where the detailed operation of the exploit is unknown.

### Boot Live OS in Memory

Once the bootloader has been appropriately configured, the Inject capability is used to execute the OS code for the forensically sound operating system in device memory. Similar forensic soundness constraints apply to this stage as those for setting up the bootloader. For example, the operating system used must be *transparently* verifiable, not introduce unavoidable *errors* and be designed by a practitioner with sufficient *experience*.

### Collect Physical Image of Device Partition

Using the operating system that has been injected into memory, we are now able to utilize ourForensic Copy capability to collect a physical image of the device's flash storage. Hashes (such as MD5 and SHA1) are utilized to verify the forensic soundness of the copy operation and to ensure that *errors* are not introduced in the transmission. Stages that utilize theForensic Examination capability will use the output of the Forensic Copy capability.

## Examine App Files in Private Storage

We utilized the Forensic Examination capability to examine the files stored within the apps' private directories. We were successful in locating a number of notable artefacts, including personally identifiable information (PII), authentication tokens, encryption keys and cached data. In terms of PII, we located usernames, email addresses and geolocation information, along with any PII stored in the files cached by the apps. Authentication tokens were a particularly interesting finding as, combined with the capabilities in the "Examine and Analyze Accounts Data" stage (see Section 5.7), the information can be used to collect data from remote sources. This, however, requires the use of the Transmit and Listencapabilities, to communicate with external systems, and the associated constraints on the operation of these capabilities apply. Combining the encryption keys that we located with app data collected from the external storage, we were able to use the Decrypt capability to access files which had been protected by apps, presumably to prevent external viewing. Finally cached data presented a particularly rich valuable source within the internal storage, in terms of potential evidence data.

## Examine App Files on External Storage

Again utilizing the Forensic Examination capability, we were able to locate files stored by the examined apps. The majority of these files were cached versions of files stored on the respective online services by the users and were stored unprotected. However, a subset of these files was stored using encryption, with the encryption key generally being stored within private storage.

## Examine App Databases

The Forensic Examination of app databases resulted in the location of numerous artefacts of PII and file related metadata. PII data included user identifiers such as usernames and email addresses, access times, and geolocation data. The majority of data stored by the apps related to the files accessed and cached by them. File metadata included typical entries such as filename, paths, access, modification, deletion, synchronization and creation timestamps, and file types. The databases also stored a range of more esoteric metadata such as sharing, ownership and permissions metadata, encryption metadata, file hashes, JSON encoded data and file URLs. Forensic practitioners can combine select data, such as file URLs, with the Listen and Transmit capabilities to access data stored on remote systems. This may include files stored by the user or public information stored by the service about the user (such as avatars). However, consideration must be given to the constraints on these capabilities. For example, the forensic soundness requirement to ensure that *meaning* is preserved may be difficult to maintain when the precise purpose of a URL, located within an app's database, is unknown.

## Examine and Analyze Accounts Data

Examination and analysis of accounts data utilizes a number of adversary capabilities, which if used without due consideration, may result in a breach of forensic soundness principles. For example, to extract accounts information, which is protected by Android's OS security, requires the use of the Inject capability. Inject is used, in concert with Modify, to add code to and modify the existing underlying OS frameworks, which ultimately results in the bypassing of security checking code (usually used to validate that the app which is requesting access to stored credentials is the same app that originally stored them). These functions would often need to be utilized on the evidence source device. This has the obvious consequence of potentially introducing *errors* and violating the associated forensic soundness requirements dealing with data modification. To avoid this circumstance, practitioners must ensure that the code being used is subject to *transparency and trustworthiness* constraints (i.e. having the code independently verified to ensure that it does not result in unknown modification to evidential data) and logging the operation of the code to ensure that the output is free of *errors*. *Experience* is another forensic soundness constraint that must be considered in the operation of these capabilities. A practitioner with *experience* in the development and operation of the Injected and Modified code is less likely to cause *errors* and ensure that*meaning* is maintained. After the data has been collected, the Transmit capability can be used to transfer the data from the mobile device to a forensic workstation for further examination and use.

While host-based intrusion detection systems (HIDS) [24] and other similar heuristic technologies are not yet prevalent on mobile devices, it is reasonable to assume that they may be introduced in the future as device performance improves [25]. With this in mind, the inclusion of a HIDS in a mobile device OS may increase the difficulty for a forensic practitioner when attempting modifications, such as this one, on the mobile device. This highlights the importance of live booting a forensic OS, which would bypass any HIDS implemented on the native OS. It should be possible to modify the OS frameworks on a forensic OS to allow for the extraction of credentials; however, this would significantly increase the level of per device customisation required for the forensic OS.

Examination of accounts data, in our case, returned a range of data including refresh tokens, access tokens, usernames, passwords, emails and timestamps. Refresh tokens are requested from the app servers using the users credentials and stored by apps to request updated access tokens which are, in turn, used to access protected resources (e.g. user files and records stored on remote systems).

## Analyze App

After all available evidential data has been extracted from private and external storage, databases and OS accounts storage, a forensic practitioner may choose to conduct further analysis on the apps themselves. This analysis may be necessary to meet the *meaning*forensic soundness requirement as, although data may have been extracted, its precise meaning is not necessarily known. For example, timestamps may be recorded for "access" to an app or file, however it may not always be clear how "access" is defined by the app developers.

Detailed analysis of the app would answer this question. This analysis was achieved in our case using both the decompilation of the app source code (static analysis) and analysis of the memory and operation of the app while it is running on a physical or emulated device (dynamic analysis). Using these techniques, we were able to locate various items of interest such as URLs for authentication, app secrets and protected information, which would otherwise be obfuscated during normal app operation.

## Comparative Summary

Table 3 presents a comparison of this Android evidence collection and analysis methodology with similar methodologies in the literature.

**Table 3.** A comparison of Android data collection methodologies.

| Requirements or Outcomes | Our Adversary Model Derived Methodology [5] (Fig 1) | Votipka, Vidas and Christin [16] | Vidas, Zhang and Christin [13] | Son, et al. [17] | Lessard and Kessler [14] | Chen, Yang and Liu [15] |
|---|---|---|---|---|---|---|
| Require device to be rooted? | **No** | No | No | No | Yes | No |
| Recovery/boot partition flashed | **No** | Yes, recovery partition | Yes, recovery partition | Yes, boot partition | No | Yes, recovery partition |
| Collects bit-for-bit physical copy? | **Yes** | Yes | Yes | No | No | No |
| Collects secure credential storage? | **Yes** | No | No | No | No | No |
| External SD Card required? | **No** | No | No | No | Yes | Yes |
| Analyzes collected data? | **Yes** | No | No | No | Yes | No |

doi:10.1371/journal.pone.0138449.t003

As the work by and Chen, Yang and Liu [15] require the Android device to have an external SD card slot, they are unable to perform bit-for-bit physical copies of devices that do not allow for external SD cards. Furthermore, there may already be data on the obtained device's SD card. Their work cannot be applied to devices that do not have an SD card slot. Our methodology is applicable to devices with and without SD card slots and is able to perform bit-for-bit copies of both kinds of devices.

## CONCLUSION

Mobile devices and apps are an increasingly ubiquitous tool used throughout the daily lives of people worldwide. However these devices and apps can present a genuine security and privacy threat to mobile device and app users, due to their capacity to access sensitive data and personally identifiable information. In addition, as the use of mobile devices and apps grows, so too does their use by criminals, particularly in areas of sophisticated and organized crime where ongoing secure communications is critical for the operation of a criminal syndicate.

In this paper, we proposed a forensic adversary model which, to the best of our knowledge, is the first adversary model to be used in a forensic context. By utilizing the McKemmish [20] model for forensic soundness as a base in terms of selecting capabilities, the adversary model formalizes the real world capabilities of a forensic practitioner in obtaining evidential data from mobile devices. A key difference between our forensic adversary model and the adversary model(s) used in security and cryptography research is the constraint of forensic soundness (see Table 3).

We demonstrated how this adversary model can be used to derive an Android evidence collection and analysis methodology. This methodology facilitates the presentation of valid evidence. Using the methodology, we analyzed a number of cloud-based apps for potential evidential data. We then summarized the relationship between our findings, including the key forensic artefacts that we were able to locate, and the adversary's capabilities and forensic soundness constraints. We also found that it was possible to obtain a significant amount of evidential data using our methodology whilst also maintaining the required level of forensic soundness (outlined in Definition 1).

Future work includes deploying the forensic adversary model in a range of forensic case studies and investigations.

## ACKNOWLEDGMENTS

The views and opinions expressed in this paper are those of the authors alone and not the organizations with whom the authors are or have been associated. The authors would also like to thank the anonymous reviewers for providing constructive and generous feedback. Despite their invaluable assistance, any errors remaining in this paper are solely attributed to the authors.

## AUTHOR CONTRIBUTIONS

Conceived and designed the experiments: QD BM KKRC. Performed the experiments: QD BM. Analyzed the data: QD BM. Contributed reagents/materials/analysis tools: QD BM KKRC. Wrote the paper: QD BM KKRC.

## REFERENCES

1. Holt TJ, Bossler AM. Examining the Relationship Between Routine Activities and Malware Infection Indicators. Journal of Contemporary Criminal Justice. 2013;29(4):420–36. doi: 10.1177/1043986213507401
2. McKemmish R. What is Forensic Computing? Trends & Issues in Crime and Criminal Justice. 1999;118:1–6.
3. Glisson WB, Storer T, Buchanan-Wollaston J. An empirical comparison of data recovered from mobile

forensic toolkits. Digital Investigation. 2013;10(1):44–55. doi: 10.1016/j.diin.2013.03.004

4. Tassone C, Martini B, Choo K-KR, Slay J. Mobile device forensics: A snapshot. Trends & Issues in Crime and Criminal Justice. 2013;460:1–7.

5. Martini B, Do Q, Choo K-KR. Conceptual Evidence Collection and Analysis Methodology for Android Devices. In: Ko R, Choo K-KR, editors. Cloud Security Ecosystem. Waltham, MA, USA: Syngress, an Imprint of Elsevier; 2015. p. 285–307.

6. Dolev D, Yao AC. On the Security of Public Key Protocols. IEEE Transactions on Information Theory. 1983;29(2):198–208. doi: 10.1109/tit.1983.1056650

7. Bellare M, Rogaway P. Entity Authentication and Key Distribution. In: Stinson DR, editor. Advances in Cryptology—CRYPTO' 93. Lecture Notes in Computer Science. 773: Springer Berlin Heidelberg; 1993. p. 232–49.

8. Syverson P, Tsudik G, Reed M, Landwehr C. Towards an Analysis of Onion Routing Security. In: Federrath H, editor. Designing Privacy Enhancing Technologies. Lecture Notes in Computer Science. 2009: Springer Berlin Heidelberg; 2001. p. 96–114.

9. Heiber T, Marron PJ. Exploring the relationship between context and privacy. Privacy, Security and Trust within the context of Pervasive Computing: Springer; 2005. p. 35–48.

10. Wu L, Grace M, Zhou Y, Wu C, Jiang X. The Impact of Vendor Customizations on Android Security. Proceedings of the 20th Conference on Computer and Communications Security: ACM; 2013. p. 623–34.

11. Zhou X, Demetriou S, He D, Naveed M, Pan X, Wang X, et al. Identity, Location, Disease and More: Inferring Your Secrets from Android Public Resources. Proceedings of the 20th Conference on Computer and Communications Security. 2516661: ACM; 2013. p. 1017–28.

12. Bugiel S, Heuser S, Sadeghi A-R. Flexible and Fine-grained Mandatory Access Control on Android for Diverse Security and Privacy Policies. Proceedings of the 22nd USENIX Security Symposium: USENIX; 2013. p. 131–46.

13. Vidas T, Zhang C, Christin N. Toward a general collection methodology for Android devices. Digital Investigation. 2011;8(Supplement):S14–S24. doi: 10.1016/j.diin.2011.05.003

14. Lessard J, Kessler G. Android Forensics: Simplifying Cell Phone Examinations. Digital Device Forensics Journal. 2010;4(1):1–12.

15. Chen S-W, Yang C-H, Liu C-T. Design and implementation of live SD acquisition tool in android smart phone. Proceedings of the 5th International Conference on Genetic and Evolutionary Computing: IEEE; 2011. p. 157–62.

16. Votipka D, Vidas T, Christin N. Passe-Partout: a General Collection Methodology for Android Devices. IEEE Transactions on Information Forensics and Security. 2013;8(12):1937–46. doi: 10.1109/tifs.2013.2285360

17. Son N, Lee Y, Kim D, James JI, Lee S, Lee K. A study of user data integrity during acquisition of Android devices. Digital Investigation. 2013;10(Supplement):S3–S11. doi: 10.1016/j.diin.2013.06.001

18. Martini B, Choo K-KR. Remote Programmatic vCloud Forensics. Proceedings of 13th IEEE International Conference on Trust, Security and Privacy in Computing and Communications: IEEE; 2014. p. 935–42.

19. Martini B, Choo K-KR. An integrated conceptual digital forensic framework for cloud computing. Digital Investigation. 2012;9(2):71–80. doi: 10.1016/j.diin.2012.07.001

20. McKemmish R. When is Digital Evidence Forensically Sound? In: Ray I, Shenoi S, editors. Advances in Digital Forensics IV. IFIP—The International Federation for Information Processing. 285: Springer US; 2008. p. 3–15.

21. Casey E. What does "forensically sound" really mean? Digital Investigation. 2007;4(2):49–50. doi: 10.1016/j.diin.2007.05.001

22. Do Q, Martini B, Choo K-KR. Exfiltrating Data from Android Devices. Computers & Security. 2015;48:74–91. doi: 10.1016/j.cose.2014.10.016

23. Martini B, Do Q, Choo K-KR. Mobile Cloud Forensics: An Analysis of Seven Popular Android Apps. In: Ko R, Choo K-KR, editors. Cloud Security Ecosystem. Waltham, MA, USA: Syngress, an Imprint of Elsevier; 2015. p. 309–45.

24. Creech G, Hu J. A Semantic Approach to Host-based Intrusion Detection Systems Using Contiguous and Discontiguous System Call Patterns. IEEE Transactions on Computers. 2014;63(4):807–19. doi: 10.1109/tc.2013.13

25. Miettinen M, Halonen P, Hatonen K. Host-Based Intrusion Detection for Advanced Mobile Devices. Proceedings of the 20th International Conference on Advanced Information Networking and Applications; 18–20 April 2006: IEEE; 2006. p. 72–6.

CHAPTER 5

# ACHIEVING HIGH RESOLUTION TIMER EVENTS IN VIRTUALIZED ENVIRONMENT

Blazej Adamczyk[1] and Andrzej Chydzinski[1]

[1]Institute of Informatics, Silesian University of Technology, Gliwice, Poland.

## ABSTRACT

**Virtual Machine Monitors (VMM) have become popular in different application areas. Some applications may require to generate the timer events with high resolution and precision. This however may be challenging due to the complexity of VMMs. In this paper we focus on the timer functionality provided by five different VMMs—Xen, KVM, Qemu, VirtualBox and VMWare. Firstly, we evaluate resolutions and precisions of their timer events. Apparently, provided resolutions and precisions are far too low for some applications (e.g. networking applications with the quality of service). Then, using Xen virtualization we demonstrate the improved timer design that greatly enhances both the resolution and precision of achieved timer events.**

## INTRODUCTION

Throughout the years time keeping techniques for common operating systems have evolved several times. Some changes were caused by the introduction of a new timer hardware into PC architecture. Processor and motherboard manufacturers have created several different devices to keep the track of time, in particular: the Programmable Interval Timer (*PIT*) [1], Real Time Clock (*RTC*) [2], Local Advanced Programmable Controller (*lapic*) [3], Advanced Configuration and Power Interface (*ACPI*) (also called *chipset timer*) [4], Time Stamp Counter (*TSC*) (see RDTSC instruction in [5]) and High Precision Event Timers (*HPET*) [6]. Each of the above was designed to serve a different purpose. Some provide advanced interrupt functionality while others are based on a simple counter register without any asynchronous notifications. Other changes in time handling techniques originated from architectural changes, like the introduction of Linux *Tickless* kernel mode. Previously, the kernel required a periodic timer interrupt to be delivered in order to work properly. The tickless mode allows the kernel to have longer inactivity periods and saves it from unnecessary interrupts and context switches while still maintaining good performance and time synchronization [7]. Another important modification to Linux timing functionality was the introduction of High Resolution Timers (*hrtimers*) [8]. This is a universal mechanism for scheduling timer events on currently available hardware thus allowing for a good resolution. It has become very popular and it is currently widely used among various kernel modules.

**Citation:** Adamczyk B, Chydzinski A (2015) Achieving High Resolution Timer Events in Virtualized Environment. PLoS ONE 10(7): e0130887.

Today's computer systems are often being virtualized to increase the hardware utilization and to decrease maintenance costs. Thus the programmers are faced with many new challenges related to the virtualization concept. Usually, in such environments one main operating system has a direct access to the hardware and is responsible for sharing it among other virtual machines. Naturally, this additional software layer influences the performance and may be crucial for the time-related functionality.

As for the related literature, the implementation of *hrtimers* in Linux operating system (without virtualization) is well described and discussed (e.g. in [8] or [9]). However, considering virtualized environments the emulation of timer hardware becomes a very important factor which influence is not well described. For instance, there is very little information available about the timer implementation in Kernel-based Virtual Machine (*KVM*). The authors of [10] while trying to achieve the virtualization with real-time processing explained and analyzed the timer mechanism but only briefly and with no measurements of the accuracy or precision. The VMWare VMM implementation of the timers is described in detail in [11]. Unfortunately, no measurements of the resolution or precision are presented either. In a VMWare virtual machine several different timer devices are being emulated. The emulation mechanism, time synchronization issues and the distribution of timer events among several virtual processors (VCPU) may have significant, as well as negative impact on the precision. Regarding Xen available literature is missing a detailed description of the Xen timer implementation. Moreover, we could not find any studies regarding Xen timer precision or accuracy. In [12] a detailed description of the Xen internals is presented, yet with only a brief explanation of the timer mechanism itself.

Depending on the application timer resolution and precision are not always considered as the most important. Several papers focus on decreasing timer resolution in virtualized environments in order to achieve other goals. In [13] for example the authors evaluate the influence of the timer events on the overall power consumption. In such a situation it is good to minimize the number of timer events and their processing complexity. Sometimes, the elimination of the fine grained timers in virtual environments can increase the security, as it was shown in [14]. In case of this study the situation is opposite—we are interested in high timer resolution and precision. As VMMs are general purpose systems, the potential applicability of precise timers is wide.

As it will be shown presented virtualization platforms provide timer events at a resolution of hundreds of microseconds. For some applications this resolution may be far too low. In networking, for instance, the transmission of a typical packet (1500 bytes) on a typical interface (1 Gb/s) takes only $12\mu s$ while the resolution of the timer events in the examined virtualization platforms may be a few orders of magnitude lower than that. Therefore, we cannot design applications with a high quality of service requirements, e.g. providing the total packet processing time below $20\mu s$.

We faced this problem while implementing a time-based network scheduler for the virtualized networking infrastructure described in [15]. However, there are many other applications where high resolution timers may be required, e.g. CPU scheduling [16], automotive platforms [17] and others.

The purpose of this paper is twofold. Firstly, we present the measurements of the resolution and precision of the timer events in some commonly used virtual machine monitors: VMWare [18], VirtualBox [19], Qemu [20], Xen [21], and KVM [22]. Secondly, we propose our own implementation of the virtual timer interrupts for Xen which provides far better resolution and precision comparing to the original measurements of all five platforms.

The detailed outline of the paper is as follows. In Section *Evaluated Virtualization Systems*, all five evaluated virtualization platforms are briefly described. Section *Experiments* presents the performed measurements of timer event resolution and precision for all mentioned VMMs. We also compare and discuss the results in this section. Beginning with Section *Xen VMM* we focus on Xen VMM by describing its architecture and the timer implementation. Then, in section *New High Resolution Timer*, we present how Xen sources can be modified to achieve much better resolution and precision by creating a separate timer mechanism. Naturally, measurements of the resolution and precision of the proposed implementation are also presented. Finally, the conclusion is presented in section *Conclusion*.

## Virtual Machine Monitors

Virtualization systems fall into two categories: full virtualization and paravirtualization. Before hardware virtualization support technologies (namely the Intel VT-x and AMD SVM, later called AMD-V), the x86 architecture was not easy to virtualize (the architecture did not meet the virtualization requirements stated by Popek and Goldberg in [23]), as some crucial CPU instructions could be executed from outside the privileged mode without causing a trap. To tackle this problem some virtualization engines (e.g. VMWare) use the so called "binary rewrite" method (see [12]) which results in significant performance penalty, due to all forbidden instructions have to be detected and rewritten at run-time. On the other hand, paravirtualization (e.g. Xen) approaches the problem differently by rewriting the problematic instructions at the design time—it means that the guest operating system has to be modified in advance to work properly. Xen was one of the first virtualization platforms that used the concept of paravirtualization.

Both approaches have their advantages and disadvantages. Full virtualization is much more portable and allows to virtualize any operating system, but at the expense of performance. Paravirtualization does not require the emulation of the hardware and allows many hardware-related operations to be performed more efficiently.

Nowadays, after the virtualization support technologies were introduced (thus eliminating the mentioned x86 virtualization problems) the distinction between full and paravirtualization has significantly blurred. For example, Xen utilizes Intel VT-x and AMD-V to support full virtualization. Kernel-based Virtual Machine (KVM), which was designed to implement strictly full virtualization, has started to use paravirtual drivers to achieve better IO operations performance.

Another factor which differentiates Virtual Machine Monitors is their architecture. Some VMMs (like Xen, VMWare vSphare Hypervisor—previously called VMWare ESXi, and Microsoft Hyper-V) use a dedicated small operating system called hypervisor that is responsible for the virtualization of the main resources, such as CPU and memory. Other VMMs (such as KVM, Qemu, VirtualBox, VMWare Workstation/Player or Microsoft Virtual PC) utilize an existing host operating system to perform this task.

Usually, in hypervisor-based virtualization the user interacts first with the virtual machine, not the hypervisor itself, as it does not provide any user interface. Such small purpose-built hypervisors allow for better implementation without any limits placed by an existing generally purposed operating system. On the other hand, all hardware related mechanisms need to be reimplemented which may cause problems with stability and efficiency. In contrast, the VMMs based on an existing operating system inherit the implementation and corrections from the operating system which is usually mature and well tested.

## EVALUATED VIRTUALIZATION SYSTEMS

For our experiments we chose five free virtualization platforms which represent mentioned groups: Xen—a hypervisor based paravirtualization, KVM—Linux kernel-based full virtualization with the use of the hardware virtualization technology, Qemu—Linux quick emulator with full software virtualization, VirtualBox—Open Source full virtualization software maintained by Oracle company, and VMWare Player—host operating system based full virtualization technology. The evaluated products are widely used around the world and certainly are among the most popular virtualization platforms. A short description of each will be presented in the following sections.

### VMWare Player

VMWare Player is a free version of the VMWare virtualization platform which is based on the same core functionality as VMWare Workstation. It is available for Windows and Linux based host operating systems. According to the End User License Agreement [24] it can be used for personal and non-commercial purposes, or for distribution or other use by written agreement. The first version of VMWare Player was released in June 2008. It was based on version 6 of VMWare Workstation. The roots of VMWare Workstation date back to 1999, when the initial version was released. The latest stable release of VMWare Player at the time of writing this article is version 7.1.0.

VMWare software can be run on an existing host operating system. It is possible to run VMWare virtual machines on Microsoft Windows, Linux and Mac OS X host operating systems. Because it performs a full virtualization, by means of emulation and binary rewriting, it is possible to run any x86 and x86–64/AMD64 compatible operating systems [25].

### VirtualBox

VirtualBox is an open source full virtualization platform. In terms of architecture and design it is very similar to VMWare products. The first version of VirtualBox was released by Innotek GmbH in 2007. Since the beginning an Open Source Edition of VirtualBox has been available with the GNU General Public License, version 2. The project was bought by Sun Microsystems in 2008 and later in 2010 with the acquisition of Sun by Oracle it was renamed to "Oracle VM VirtualBox".

VirtualBox supports the common host operating systems: Microsoft Windows, Mac OS X, Linux and Solaris. Similarly to VMWare, the full virtualization is achieved by binary rewriting ring 0 privileged instructions using the Code Scanning and Analysis Manager (CSAM) and the Patch Manager (PATM). The latest stable release of VirtualBox is 4.3.26.

### Qemu

The Quick Emulator called Qemu is an open source project which allows for emulation of different hardware platforms and run fully virtualized guest operating systems. It can emulate CPU of the following platforms: x86, MIPS, 32-bit ARMv7, ARMv8, PowerPC, SPARC, ETRAX CRIS and MicroBlaze. It can also emulate hardware devices to let for full support of common operating systems.

Qemu by itself can be used to run userspace programs compiled for different platforms or to fully emulate a computer system with all necessary hardware. Qemu is also employed in Xen and KVM in hardware (other than CPU) emulation tasks. The Qemu project was started by Fabrice Bellard in 2004, is available for free, and is mainly licensed under GNU General Public License. It can be compiled and run on most major host operating systems. Current stable version of Qemu is 2.2.0.

### KVM

KVM (Kernel-based Virtual Machine) is a virtualization platform based on the Linux kernel in the role of a hypervisor. KVM is an open source project established in 2006 by Qumranet, Inc. and currently maintained by the Open Virtualization Alliance. It is licensed with either GNU General Public License or GNU Lesser General Public License. It provides full virtualization capabilities but only for processors with hardware virtualization support (Intel VT-x or AMD-V). Although KVM provides only full virtualization of CPU and memory, it additionally allows the use of different kinds of IO device virtualization:

- Emulation—the devices are fully emulated which allows for great portability, but at the expense of the performance.
- Paravirtualization—the device drivers used in the virtual machine are aware of being virtualized and utilize the virtualization interface to perform IO operations much more effectively; this approach requires the use of special drivers for the guest operating system.
- Pass-through—the device is assigned to a certain virtual machine and is not intended to be shared.

KVM is a kernel module and is a part of Linux kernel sources since version 2.6.20. The module exposes the */dev/kvm* interface which can be used by user-space programs (e.g.*qemu-kvm*) to perform virtualization.

### Xen

The initial release of Xen hypervisor was created at Cambridge University in 2003. The product was initially supported by XenSource Inc. which in 2007 was acquired by Citrix Systems, a company that supports the development of a free version of Xen but additionally sells an enterprise edition to commercial clients. Currently, Xen open source software called Xen Project is maintained as a collaborative project by the Linux Foundation consortium.

Xen provides a hypervisor-based virtualization. Initially, it allowed for paravirtualization only but with the introduction of hardware virtualization extensions, Xen also allows full virtualization mode. The core of Xen software is the hypervisor. It is a purpose-built, small operating system that provides virtualization of CPU and memory and delegates control to the first, privileged virtual machine called *Domain0*. The user may run and manage all virtual machines from within*Domain0*. All IO devices are handled by privileged domains which use paravirtual drivers to share them with other virtual machines. Such architecture makes the system very stable, as the hypervisor does not handle device drivers or other functionalities which usually cause problems.

## EXPERIMENTS

To check the resolution and precision of the clock event devices we performed several tests. In all of them we used Linux Gentoo 3.17.8 as both host and virtual machine operating system. We performed the experiment on several hardware platforms but the results presented here are based on an Intel Xeon E5645 @ 2.4GHz, 24GB RAM with Supermicro X8DTN motherboard. The timer events were scheduled using *hrtimers* within a virtual machine. We have created a special Linux kernel module which was used to perform and gather the results of measurements.

In the experiments we installed version 6.0.0 of the VMWare Player, version 4.3.18 of the VirtualBox and version 2.1.2 of the Qemu, all installed from Linux Gentoo repository (we used the most recent stable versions of all three products available in the repository). For KVM, we used the version of KVM available with the host kernel version i.e. 3.17.8. Finally, to test Xen we used version 4.5.0 of Xen hypervisor. Additionally, we have also performed the experiment on a plain Linux Gentoo 3.17.8 without using virtualization.

Considering Xen, it is important to note that the default Xen implementation sets a slop variable (*timer_slop*) that allows merging of the timer events from certain time ranges into one interrupt. The default value of *timer_slop* is set to $50\mu s$, what is good for general purposes and unloads the processor from unnecessary interrupt handling and context switching. Moreover, the Xen sources of Gentoo kernel version 3.17.8 also use a similar slop constant (*TIMER_SLOP*) which is set to $100\mu s$. Both slop settings can be changed to obtain more fine-grained timer events with the cost of more interrupts and context switches. For the purpose of this experiment, we have changed the slop value to $1ns$ in the hypervisor and in the guest domain kernel sources. Without changing this value, the timer events in Xen virtual machines were merged and fired with the resolution of $100\mu s$.

The presented measurements consist of three parts which are supposed to show what is the timer resolution and precision under the different circumstances. In the first part, all virtualization platforms were tested in a scenario of an idle system—the system was not performing any intense IO or CPU operations. In the second test, the system was loaded with a set of CPU loads. Finally, the last part presents the influence of intense IO disk operations which were causing many additional interrupts to be handled by the processor at the same time.

The results show that heavy CPU load does not influence the precision of the timer events very much. This was to be expected as the timer events are handled as interrupts. Thus, the incoming interrupts result with CPU preemption no matter what is the actual load level of the CPU. The case is different when the system is loaded with other interrupts.

Historically Linux kernel was dividing the interrupt handling routines into 'slow' and 'fast' handlers. This allowed 'slow' interrupts to be preempted by 'fast' ones in order to improve the performance of time critical functions. Such distinction between the interrupts originated from not properly designed device drivers that were consuming too much CPU time inside the interrupt handlers. This was systematically fixed by removing the time consuming parts of the drivers into separate kernel tasklets running outside of the interrupt handlers. Finally, since version 2.6.35 the Linux kernel switched all interrupt handlers to be run as 'fast' (the*IRQF_DISABLED* flag was marked as deprecated) meaning that an interrupt cannot be preempted. In general this was a very good decision as it simplified the interrupt handling mechanisms and freed the kernel from handling nested interrupts. Considering high resolution timers however, this change could have a negative influence on timer precision. Obviously, even the fast interrupt handlers still consume some CPU time. Thus, some other interrupts occurring right before the timer event on the same CPU may introduce additional delays.

The third part of the experiments proves that other interrupts may have a strong impact on the timer precision. We chose to create IO interrupts by reading the disk, but the problem could have been demonstrated using other type of interrupts as well.

It is worth noting the following consequence of the fact that the timer performance depends on the interrupts: the number of virtual machines running on the hypervisor does not influence directly the timer resolution and accuracy. They are influenced only by the number of and types of interrupts generated by them.

## THE DETAILED RESULTS ARE PRESENTED IN THE FOLLOWING SECTIONS.

### Idle system

Firstly, in an idle system, 4500 timer events were scheduled every *d* microseconds. During our study we have performed many different experiments with different values of *d*. In this article we present only the border values of *d* which were hard to achieve by most of the tested platforms.

For every scheduled event the actual time interval was measured. Then the mean value, the sample uncorrected standard deviation, and the 99% confidence intervals were computed.

All results are gathered together in Table 1 on page 17. A detailed representation for VMWare Player for an interval duration of $50\mu s$ is additionally depicted in Fig 1. The graph for VMWare is similar for all measurements greater than $50\mu s$, with the measured time being usually delayed by around $80 \mu s$ from the expected value. Such results could be expected because the timer device is being emulated by VMWare software which causes the additional delay.

Table 1. Summary of all measured statistics for each timer version discussed.

| Experiment | Timer implementation | Mean measured time [μs] | Standard deviation [μs] | Confidence interval for the mean $\alpha$ = 99% |
|---|---|---|---|---|
| **timer setting = 150μs idle system** | VMWare | 228.999 | 7.987 | (228.764,229.234) |
| | VirtualBox | 218.370 | 71.147 | (216.268,220.473) |
| | Qemu | 190.415 | 4.492 | (190.282,190.548) |
| | KVM | 164.593 | 1.029 | (164.562,164.623) |
| | native Xen | 150.213 | 0.282 | (150.204,150.221) |
| | new timers | 150.151 | 0.175 | (150.146,150.156) |
| | Linux kernel | 150.025 | 0.073 | (150.023,150.027) |
| **timer setting = 100μs idle system** | VMWare | 175.908 | 9.867 | (175.617,176.198) |
| | VirtualBox | 159.232 | 9.252 | (158.959,159.506) |
| | Qemu | 140.259 | 3.832 | (140.145,140.372) |
| | KVM | 114.087 | 0.753 | (114.064,114.109) |
| | native Xen | 100.221 | 0.339 | (100.211,100.231) |
| | new timers | 100.074 | 0.118 | (100.071,100.078) |
| | Linux kernel | 100.103 | 0.070 | (100.101,100.105) |
| **timer setting = 50μs idle system** | VMWare | 123.951 | 7.110 | (123.742,124.161) |
| | VirtualBox | 97.749 | 7.633 | (97.524,97.975) |
| | Qemu | 82.768 | 9.912 | (82.475,83.061) |
| | KVM | 65.310 | 1.526 | (65.265,65.355) |
| | native Xen | 50.108 | 0.085 | (50.105,50.110) |
| | new timers | 50.071 | 0.094 | (50.068,50.073) |
| | Linux kernel | 50.056 | 0.083 | (50.053,50.058) |
| **timer setting = 10μs idle system** | VMWare | 24.497 | 4.269 | (24.371,24.622) |
| | VirtualBox | 54.370 | 46.192 | (53.005,55.735) |
| | Qemu | 66.450 | 11.418 | (66.113,66.788) |
| | KVM | 21.762 | 2.637 | (21.685,21.840) |
| | native Xen | 10.127 | 0.078 | (10.125,10.130) |
| | new timers | 10.060 | 0.062 | (10.058,10.062) |
| | Linux kernel | 10.076 | 0.175 | (10.070,10.081) |
| **timer setting = 150μs system with heavy IO** | VMWare | 669.971 | 10.026K | (374.986,964.957) |
| | VirtualBox | 214.700 | 63.933 | (212.811,216.589) |
| | Qemu | 232.981 | 84.149 | (230.494,235.467) |
| | KVM | 177.355 | 21.907 | (176.708,178.003) |
| | native Xen | 152.796 | 10.177 | (152.496,153.097) |
| | new timers | 150.172 | 0.182 | (150.167,150.178) |
| | Linux kernel | 152.091 | 7.513 | (151.869,152.313) |
| **timer setting = 100μs system with heavy IO** | VMWare | 485.224 | 4.266K | (359.720,610.727) |
| | VirtualBox | 156.717 | 13.720 | (156.311,157.122) |
| | Qemu | 177.905 | 80.585 | (175.524,180.287) |
| | KVM | 119.712 | 9.869 | (119.421,120.004) |
| | native Xen | 105.312 | 17.797 | (104.786,105.838) |
| | new timers | 100.151 | 0.168 | (100.146,100.156) |
| | Linux kernel | 101.454 | 6.340 | (101.267,101.641) |
| **timer setting = 50μs system with heavy IO** | VMWare | 427.037 | 3.558K | (322.353,531.722) |
| | VirtualBox | 99.504 | 14.097 | (99.088,99.921) |
| | Qemu | 116.652 | 67.896 | (114.646,118.659) |
| | KVM | 76.398 | 21.001 | (75.778,77.019) |
| | native Xen | 54.214 | 17.628 | (53.694,54.735) |
| | new timers | 50.054 | 0.156 | (50.049,50.058) |
| | Linux kernel | 51.767 | 8.180 | (51.525,52.009) |
| **timer setting = 10μs system with heavy IO** | VMWare | 491.723 | 3.960K | (375.207,608.239) |
| | VirtualBox | 58.146 | 45.545 | (56.800,59.492) |
| | Qemu | 71.087 | 32.459 | (70.128,72.046) |
| | KVM | 25.015 | 12.234 | (24.653,25.376) |
| | native Xen | 11.274 | 10.643 | (10.959,11.588) |
| | new timers | 10.053 | 0.096 | (10.050,10.056) |
| | Linux kernel | 10.568 | 5.071 | (10.418,10.718) |

doi:10.1371/journal.pone.0130887.t001

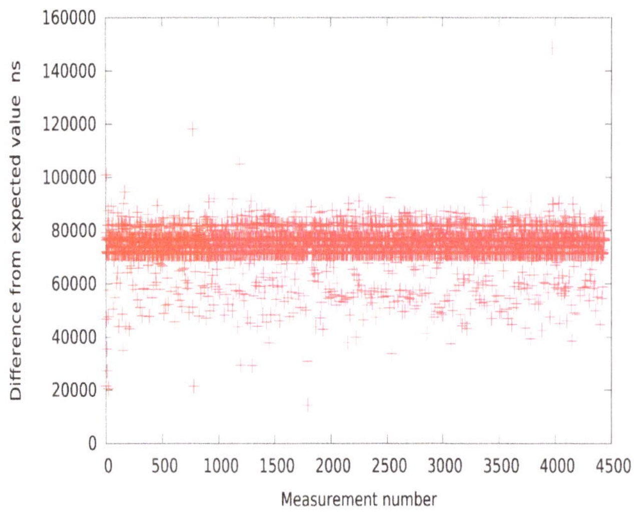


**Figure 1.** The difference between the measured timer interval and its expected value 50$\mu s$ **in VMWare (idle system).**

Analogically, the graph for VirtualBox is presented in Fig 2. As it can be observed by looking atTable 1, VirtualBox is usually (for all delays greater than 10$\mu s$) delayed by about 37 – 60$\mu s$from the expected value what is slightly better in terms of resolution than VMWare Player but still very inaccurate and imprecise.

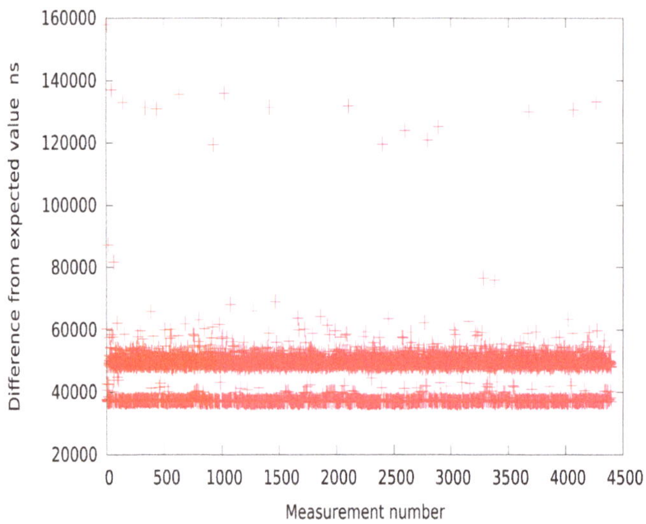


**Figure 2.** The difference between the measured timer interval and its expected value 50$\mu s$ **in** VirtualBox (idle system).

Further, the Qemu provides again a slightly better resolution. The results, presented in Fig 3, show that for the intervals greater than 50$\mu s$ the timer events are usually delayed by about 40$\mu s$. Thus, we may summarize that all emulated userspace full virtualization platforms (i.e. VMWare Player, VirtualBox and Qemu) provide similar timer resolution at the level of tens of microseconds within an idle system.

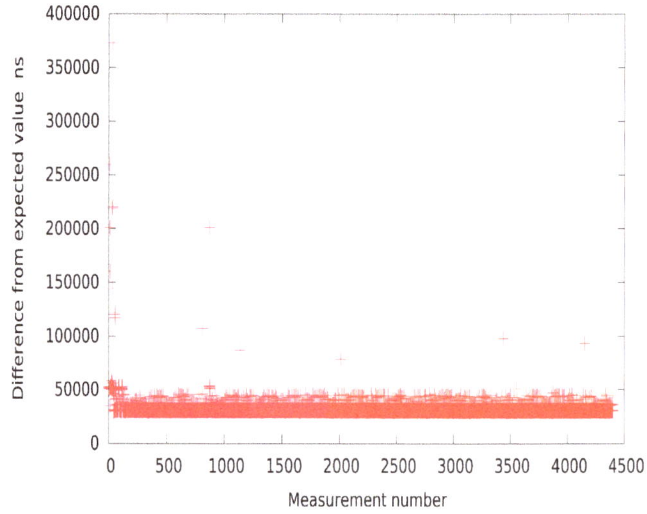


**Figure 3.** The difference between the measured timer interval and its expected value 50$\mu s$ **in** Qemu (idle system).

Continuing, the graph for KVM for an interval of 50$\mu s$ is shown in Fig 4. It can be easily observed that the resolution of the timer events in KVM is more fine-grained than in the case of VMWare Player, VirtualBox and Qemu. The difference between the expected and measured timer intervals is at the level of 12 – 16$\mu s$.

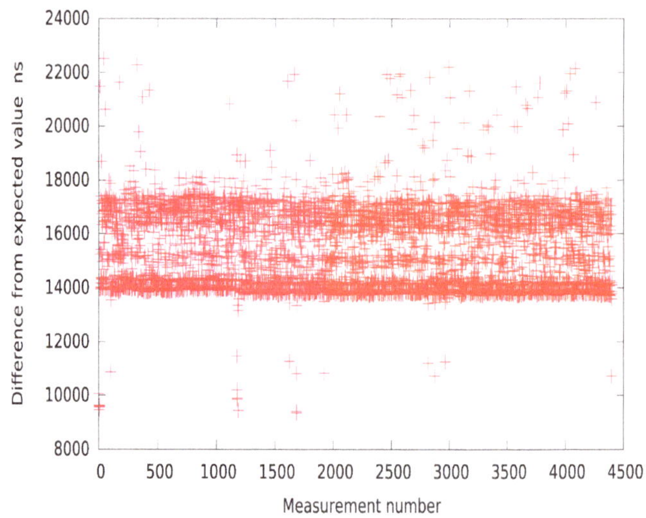


**Figure 4.** The difference between the measured timer interval and its expected value 50$\mu s$ **in KVM (idle system).**

Next we performed the same experiment in a Xen based virtual machine. Again the results are presented in Table 1 and for an interval duration of 50$\mu s$ additionally depicted in Fig 5. As one can observe, the resolution of Xen is much better when compared to KVM and all other tested virtualization platforms.

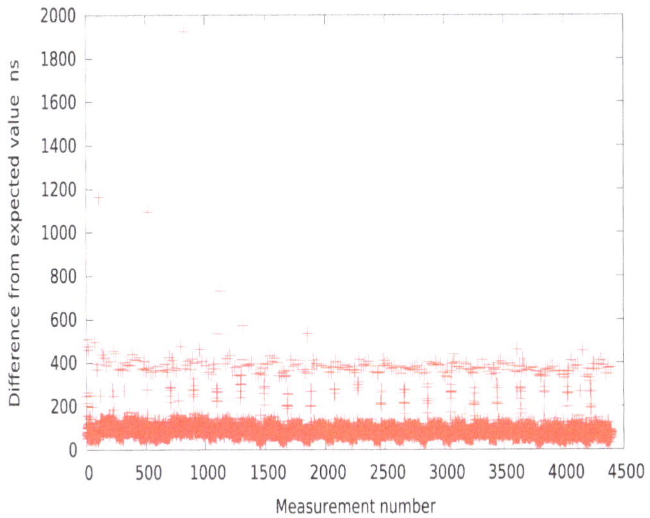


**Figure 5.** The difference between the measured timer interval and its expected value 50$\mu s$ **in** Xen (idle system).

Finally, the experiment was also repeated within bare Linux kernel without any virtualization. The results are depicted in Fig 6. As it was to be expected the resolution is at a similar level but the precision is even better than in case of Xen. The standard deviation for a bare Linux kernel is at the level of one-tenth of a microsecond.

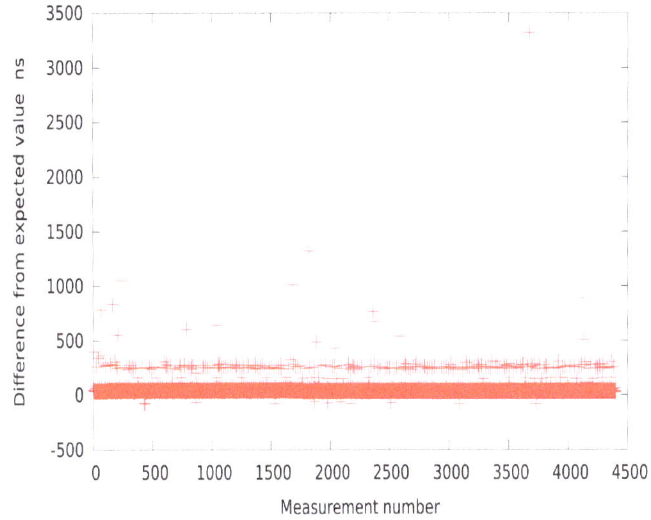


**Figure 6.** The difference between the measured timer interval and its expected value 50$\mu s$ **in Linux kernel without virtualization (idle system).**

## Influence of CPU load

Results presented in the previous section are valid for an idle system—i.e. a system without any substantial IO operations or CPU load. As it was already stated intense CPU load should not have a significant influence on the timer resolution because the timer events are being executed as interrupts and thus the CPU is preempted independently of the current CPU state. Nevertheless, we decided to perform an additional experiment to show that this is in fact the case.

The test for 10$\mu s$ similar to the one described in the previous section was repeated for Xen platform for 3 different values of CPU load. The CPU load was generated on all 24 cores of the machine with the use of Linux *stress-ng* tool [26]. The results are presented in Table 2.

**Table 2.** CPU load influence.

| CPU load | Timer implementation | Mean measured time [$\mu s$] | Standard deviation [$\mu s$] |
|---|---|---|---|
| 30% CPU load | native Xen | 10.217 | 0.375 |
| | new timers | 10.039 | 0.067 |
| 60% CPU load | native Xen | 10.188 | 0.398 |
| | new timers | 10.148 | 0.262 |
| 100% CPU load | native Xen | 10.151 | 0.313 |
| | new timers | 10.100 | 0.312 |

doi:10.1371/journal.pone.0130887.t002

As it can be observed the resolution is similar to the one obtained in an idle system and stays at the level of one microsecond. The additional load has some small influence on the precision of the timer events but the effect is marginal. It can be related with several aspects. Firstly, when a processor is under load the interrupt may occur more frequently under different CPU states: idle or running. In both cases the number of instructions to be executed before the actual timer handling routine may vary. Thus, the standard deviation is bigger and the timer duration is less precise. Secondly, additional variation may be introduced because of the power-saving functions, as well as temperature control logic.

## Influence of other interrupts

Similarly to the idle system test experiments with four values of *d* and 4500 timer events were repeated in a system with heavy IO usage. Namely, heavy disk operations within the virtual machine were triggered in attempt to induce a negative effect of the other IO interrupts on the timer accuracy and precision. This was achieved by clearing the disk caches and using the *dd*Linux utility to read data from disk. To make the difference more visible the disk driver interrupt was pinned to the same processor as the timer event device using the Linux *smp_affinity*interrupt mask. To present the impact of disk read operations on the number of interrupts of a single CPU, we gathered the interrupt statistics for both, the idle system and the system with heavy IO usage. Fig 7 presents the number of interrupts per second in both cases.

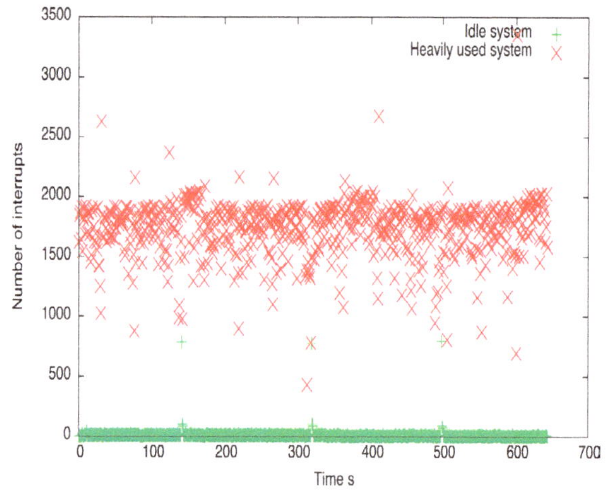


**Figure 7.** The number of interrupts per second in the idle system and in the system with heavy IO load.

The average number of the interrupts per second for an idle system is 11.52 and for the system with heavy IO load is 1733.35. As we can see, due to the disk read operations many additional disk interrupts are handled by the CPU. According to the arguments presented in Section *Experiments*, if these interrupts are executed on the same CPU just before the scheduled timer interrupt, then they cause the timer events to be delayed.

The results of the experiment for the system with heavy IO load are again presented in Table 1on page 17. As it can be observed the additional interrupts have significant impact on the resolution and precision of the timers in all virtualization platforms.

For VMWare, the influence of IO operations is very noticeable. First of all, the resolution seems to be out of the microsecond scale (it is around half of a millisecond). The precision is also very low. Detailed results presented in Fig 8 additionally show that there were few outlier events triggered after tens to hundreds of milliseconds, which may be unacceptable for some time depended applications.

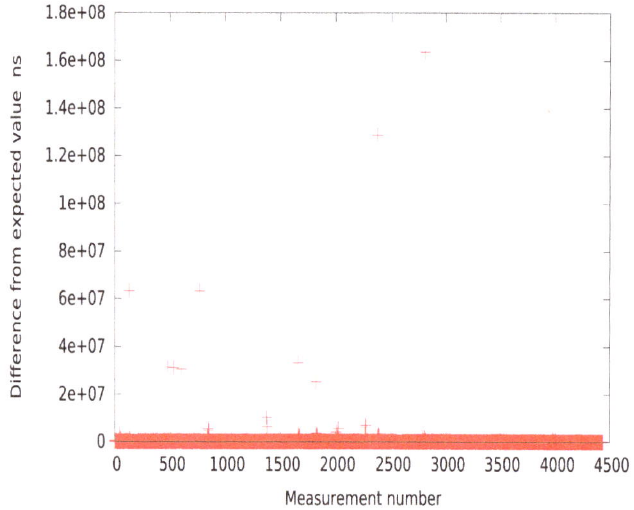


**Figure 8.** The difference between the measured interval and its expected value $50\mu s$in VMWare (system with heavy IO load).

As far as VirtualBox is concerned the influence of additional IO interrupts is also visible. Again, the detailed results for $50\mu s$ interval are presented in Fig 9. In contrast to VMWare there are no outliers above $200\mu s$. This makes the standard deviation much smaller. There are however more values between $60 - 200\mu s$ comparing to the idle system which are probably caused by the additional interrupts.

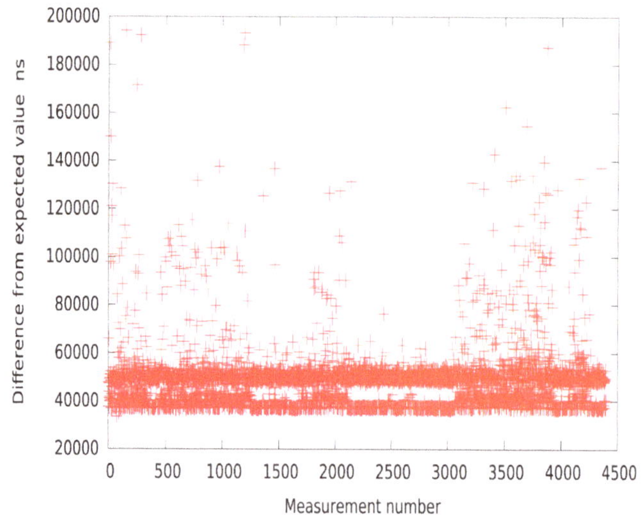


**Figure 9.** The difference between the measured interval and its expected value $50\mu s$in VirtualBox (system with heavy IO load).

Qemu results are presented in Fig 10 as well as in the Table 1. Here, similarly to VMWare the influence of IO interrupts is clearly visible. The impact is not as strong as in case of VMWare but much stronger than in VirtualBox. The standard deviation is from around 3 (in the best case) to around 21 (in the worst case) times greater comparing to the idle system.

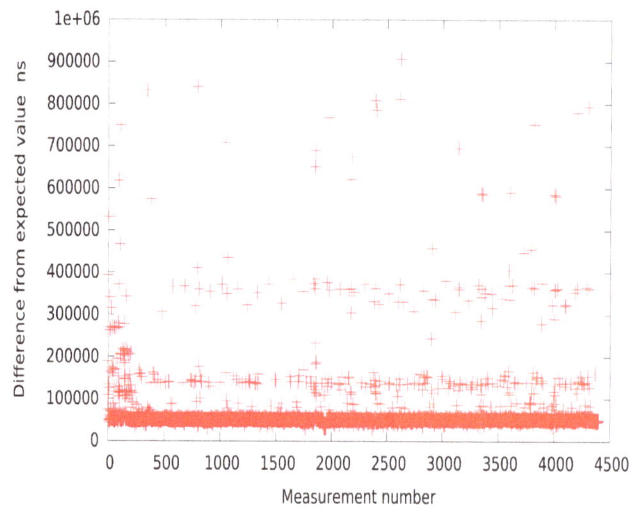


**Figure 10.** The difference between the measured interval and its expected value $50\mu s$in Qemu (system with heavy IO load).

In the case of KVM the results for a system with high IO load presented in Table 1 and in Fig 11 show that the majority of events occur at around $16\mu s$ (similarly to the idle system case) but there are also many values concentrated at the level of $55 - 70\mu s$ what is probably caused by the additional disk interrupts. To sum up, looking at the standard deviation we may conclude that the KVM timer events precision is from around 5 (in case of $10\mu s$ intervals) to around 21 (for $150\mu s$ intervals) times worse than in case of an idle system.

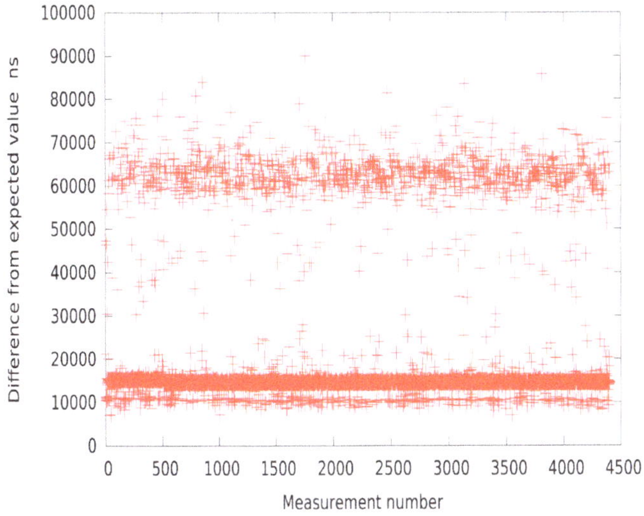


**Figure 11.** The difference between the measured interval and its expected value 50$\mu s$in KVM (system with heavy IO load).

The heavy IO operations also have an influence on the Xen timer events. As it is presented inTable 1 and Fig 12 the resolution is maintained but the precision is worse than in case of the idle system. There are multiple events over 50$\mu s$, which may be unacceptable for some applications. Nevertheless, Xen still proves to be better in resolution and precision when compared to all other virtualization platforms.

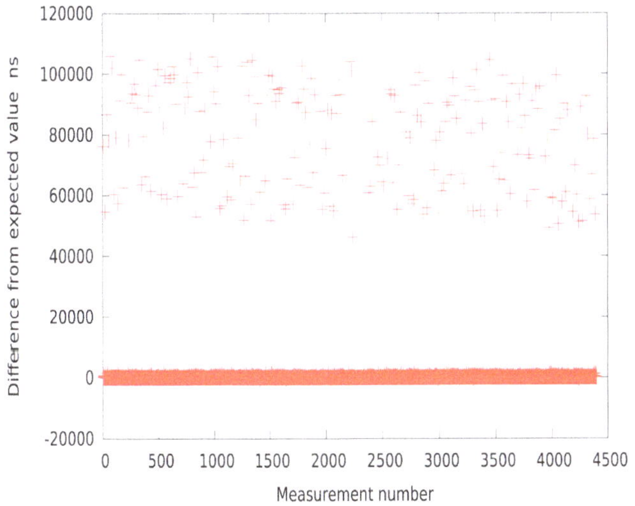


**Figure 12.** The difference between the measured interval and its expected value 50$\mu s$in Xen (system with heavy IO load).

Linux kernel without virtualization shows similar behavior to Xen. The results are also presented in Table 1 and Fig 13. Comparing to Xen the bare Linux kernel provides around 2 times better precision of the timer events in the case of a system with heavy IO load.

As we can see, heavy disk operations cause additional negative effects on the timer precision in all of the tested virtualization platforms. The effect is observed most significantly in VMWare and Qemu. The least affected were Linux kernel without virtualization and Xen.

Taking these results into consideration, we can say that among all the examined virtualization environments the most accurate timer events can be obtained by using Xen virtualization. However, modification of the *timer_slop* variables is required. Unfortunately, this change affects the number of delivered timer interrupts in all *hrtimer* usages inside all the virtual machines. Without this modification, Xen timer events have resolution of 100$\mu s$.

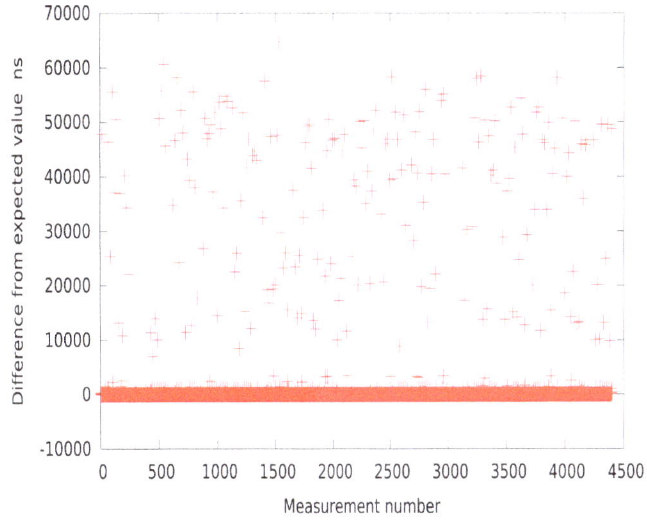


**Figure 13.** The difference between the measured interval and its expected value 50$\mu s$in Linux kernel without virtualization (system with heavy IO load).

Summarizing, we can state that achieving the timer events with resolution of a about ten microseconds with high precision in the heavy IO load is not possible in any of the examined virtualization platforms. Even without the virtualization, the Linux kernel does not provide good precision with high IO loads. To solve this problem we decided to create a separate timer implementation in Xen which would be used only for special purposes, providing better resolution and precision while not affecting the overall system performance, and other hrtimer events.

In the following sections, we will describe the general Xen architecture and the timer event device implementation. Further we will show how we have implemented our own timer event device and present an evaluation of this implementation similar to the experiments shown above.

## Xen VMM

Xen was created to virtualize x86 architecture with good performance thanks to paravirtualization. As it has been already stated, this approach has several advantages over full virtualization mode. First of all, there is no run-time binary rewriting. Additionally, as the guest operating system requires to be modified, the changes can also eliminate certain device emulation, improving the performance even further.

Additionally Xen was one of the first virtualization platforms with hypervisor-based architecture. Instead of running an existing operating system directly on the hardware (i.e. in *Ring0*), it uses a small *hypervisor*, see Fig 14. After start, the hypervisor runs the first virtual machine,*Domain0*, in a less privileged mode (depending on architecture this could be *Ring1* or *Ring3*). In fact, this is the first OS that the user has contact with, because the hypervisor does not contain any user interfaces. The *Domain0* is a privileged virtual machine (VM) which can control and manage the hypervisor, and has a permission to access the IO devices. As*Domain0* can run any of the supported operating systems, it can use the existing device drivers to access the real devices. Moreover, it is responsible for sharing them with other VMs. This is achieved by the *Backend/Frontend* drivers (see Fig 14). Such design provides good reliability and stability of the system. The hypervisor controls only the CPU and memory, while the device drivers (which are the cause of most kernel errors) are separated from the hypervisor. Therefore their errors do not influence other VMs stability. Xen can be configured also to provide device access to certain VMs called *Driver Domains*. In this way the administrator can separate even a single device driver, so that a fatal system error in one of the driver domains would not affect any other.

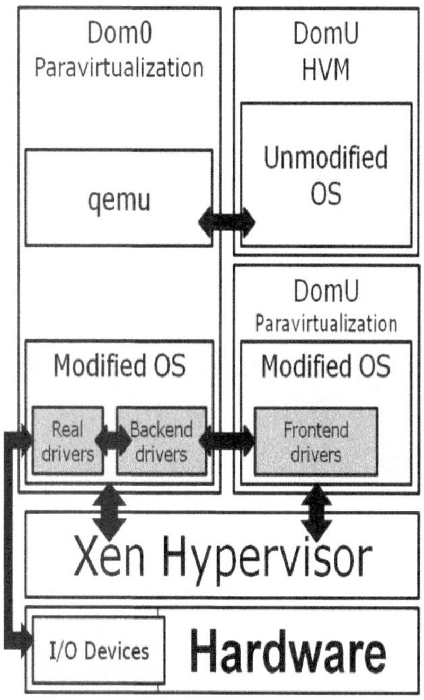


**Figure 14.** Xen VMM architecture.

## Xen timer implementation

In order to run a virtual machine, the VMM has to provide timer events to the guest operating systems. In contrast to other VMMs that achieve this through emulation of the existing timer devices, Xen again uses paravirtualization. The modified guest kernel contains a new *Clock Event Device* which schedules a timer interrupt in the hypervisor using *hypercalls* (see [12] or [27]). Further, the hypervisor sets local APIC timer accordingly. Of course, such an implementation requires not only a very fast delivery of the interrupt into the VM, but also some control mechanism for the scheduled events from all virtual machines.

### *Timers in the hypervisor.*

The Xen hypervisor uses local APIC for scheduling the timer events. The virtualized event device can work in two modes: *singleshot* and *periodic*. In order to schedule a new event, the VM has to call the *VCPUOP_set_singleshot_timer* or *VCPUOP_set_periodic_timer* hypercall accordingly. All scheduled timer events are stored in two data structures: (faster) heap and (slower) linked list. Each time the *lapic* interrupt occurs, the handler executes the expired timer events and, at the end, schedules next *lapic* interrupt looking for the earliest deadline timer. To improve the performance and lower the number of the timer interrupts, a *timer_slop* parameter is used. It denotes the amount of the time (in nanoseconds) that the timer can be late. All timers from such interval will be executed in a single *lapic* interrupt. The *timer_slop* is set by default to 50000*ns*.

### *Virtual timer interrupt.*

All interrupts in Xen are handled by the hypervisor. It then delivers them to guest OSs using so called *event channels* [12]. There are three types of the events: Physical IRQ, Virtual IRQ (VIRQ) and inter-domain events. Different hardware interrupts are delivered using Physical IRQs event channels. This is done to make the standard device drivers work correctly and map real IRQs inside the guest kernel. In the case of virtual devices, such as the aforementioned timer event device, the Virtual IRQs are used. There is a special virtual timer interrupt called *VIRQ_timer*.

A simplified process of handling hardware interrupt and delivering it to the VM using an event channel is presented in Fig 15.

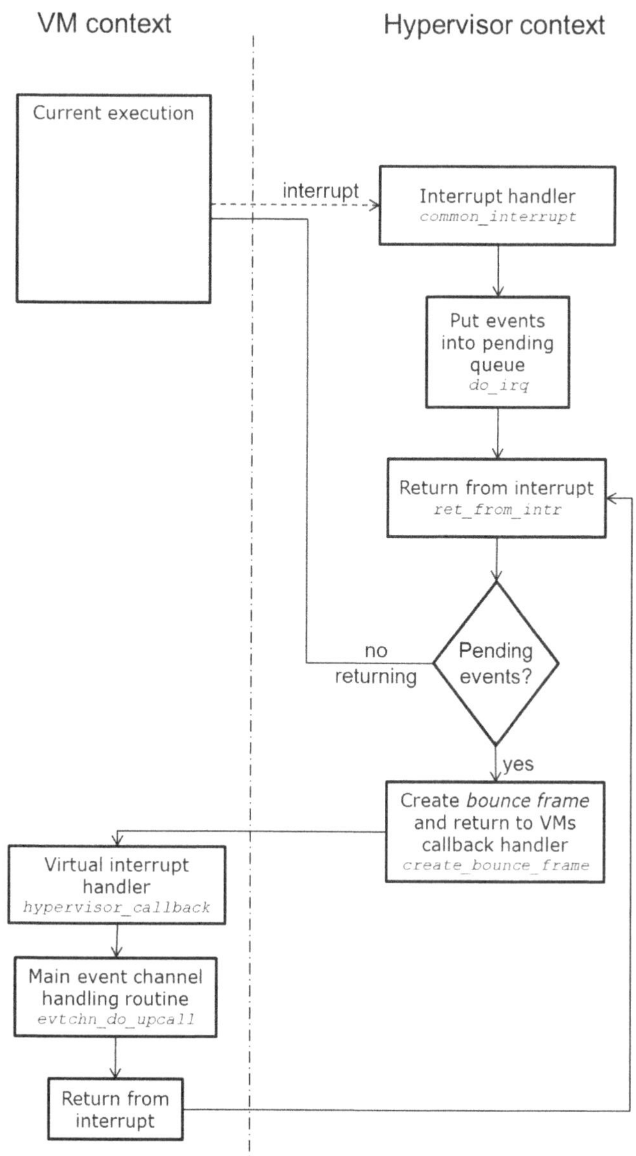


**Figure 15.** Simplified hardware interrupt handling process with propagation to VM using event channel.

Inside the hypervisor, all hardware interrupts are handled using the *common_interrupt* routine (defined in *xen/arch/x86/x86_64/entry.S* file). This macro is a wrapper for the real handler. It performs common interrupt tasks (like saving registers before executing the handler) but also returns to the VM context afterwards. The *ret_from_intr* assembly routine is used to execute the pending event channel requests and, at the end, return to the previously executed VCPU process. This is actually done every time the hypervisor returns to certain VCPU context, no matter what the cause of previous preemption was (it could be the mentioned hardware interrupt, but also Xen CPU scheduler preemption for different VCPU), to allow the VCPU receive the pending events as soon as possible. If an event is pending for the returning VCPU then the hypervisor has to return to the event handling routing in guest VM. This is done by creating a special *bounce frame* on the guest stack, so that the return will restore the instruction pointer to the event handling function (usually called *xen_hypervisor_callback*—the guest OS, while initiating has to register it using the *CALLBACKOP_register* operation of the*HYPERVISOR_callback_op* hypercall) with appropriate arguments. Further, the context switches to guest OS and executes the xen_hypervisor_callback routine which is a wrapper around the *xen_evtchn_do_upcall* function. The latter, using the arguments received in the bounce frame from the hypervisor, executes an appropriate handler for the given event channel.

As it was already stated, the timers in Xen are paravirtualized using a new clock event device (usually called *xen_clockevent* defined in *xen/time.c*). This virtual clock event device registers an event channel handler for the VIRQ_timer virtual interrupt. Further it becomes the default clock event device and thus it is used by all event related kernel mechanisms (one of them are*hrtimers*). Every time the timer event is scheduled the device sends the*VCPUOP_set_singleshot_timer* hypercall setting the next *VIRQ_timer* interrupt time.

Such a design has some drawbacks which may affect the timers resolution and precision. Firstly, all the scheduled timers are delivered using the same mechanism and the same virtual interrupt. In practice we need much less fine grained timers for some purposes than for the other, so using the same high resolution mechanism may result in decreased accuracy for the crucial applications. Additionally, other virtual interrupts may also delay the timer event (if they are fired just before *VIRQ_timer*). Secondly, the CPU scheduler may delay the virtual timer interrupt until the receiver VCPU will be scheduled again. Further, Xen creates a *virtual time*which is synchronized with the hypervisor real time on every VIRQ_timer interrupt. This normally does not introduce any shift. However, in some cases the absolute timer timeout may be calculated before the virtual time synchronization but scheduled after, so that would make the timer event shift. Finally, the clock event device is optimized (similarly as in the hypervisor) with the *TIMER_SLOP* constant. All timers falling in the range of a single*TIMER_SLOP* are handled by the same single interrupt. The constant is set to $100\mu s$ which is fine in many cases but in some applications may be too large. For example, we have implemented a network scheduler which required timer events with resolution of tens of microseconds. In this case proposed value would be $10\mu s$.

## NEW HIGH RESOLUTION TIMER

To overcome the precision problems we decided to create our own timer implementation, which might be used only in cases when it is really required. For example in applications highlighted in the introduction other system processes might still use standard timer implementation built in the virtualization platform.

The idea was to introduce a new virtual interrupt *VIRQ_custom_timer* which would be handled before any other interrupts. Moreover, the other interrupts, as well as VCPU rescheduling, should be avoided near the custom timer timeout, so that it would not be disturbed. To achieve this we created a separate event channel to allow any guest domain to bind and register the*VIRQ_custom_timer* handler. This was done by defining the new virtual interrupt and increasing the number of all VIRQs in the Xen hypervisor header file xen/include/public/xen.h.

The new virtual interrupt should be delivered to a single, predefined VCPU, rather than to any of them, so that the guest domain can expect the interrupt and avoid all other interrupts near the timer deadline only on this predefined VCPU. This is possible when the function*virq_is_global* returns 0 for the *VIRQ_CUSTOM_TIMER* parameter.

Such binding of the VIRQ to a single chosen virtual processor can also help to avoid the VCPU reschedules that can be achieved in two different ways depending on the application being run and the amount of available resources:

- By assigning a single physical processor to the single VCPU which is responsible for handling timer interrupts, thus disabling the VCPU scheduler completely on this virtual processor (the *vcpu-pin* command).
- By modifying the Xen CPU scheduler to ensure that the correct VCPU is scheduled near the timer deadline.

The first method requires much less modifications and does not depend on the CPU scheduler algorithm, therefore it can be recommended (especially for the multicore systems). This method was also used for the purpose of this study.

The final hypervisor modification is the actual timer scheduling and handling functionality. The guest operating systems are allowed to schedule the new timer events via the same *hypercall*(i.e. *VCPUOP_set_singleshot_timer*), as in the case of standard timers but with an additional flag *SS_CUSTOM_TIMER*.

The modified version of *VCPUOP_set_singleshot_timer* uses the existing Xen LAPIC timer functions defined in *xen/timer.h* to schedule timer events at the requested time. Finally, the hypervisor handler—*custom_timer_fn* sends the *VIRQ_CUSTOM_TIMER* interrupt to appropriate guest VCPU.

All above modifications to the hypervisor kernel allow the guest domain to bind and handle the new timer events. This code can be used in any kernel module and allows for scheduling and handling the new timer events.

As it was already stated, it is important to treat the *VIRQ_CUSTOM_TIMER* interrupt with highest priority, to achieve the best precision.

Finally the most important change is to avoid execution of other interrupts near the timer deadline.

Because this implementation will not be used as a general clock event device, all other timer requests will not use this functionality. This is a great advantage because the *timer_slop*variables can be left untouched and the system will not be flooded by different timer interrupts.

To verify our timer implementation and compare it with the native implementation tested previously we performed again the same set of experiments, using the new timer. The detailed results for all tested scenarios are shown in Table 1 (the "new timers" rows relate to the proposed timer implementation).

As we can note, the new timer has no problem to achieve resolutions up to $10\mu s$. What is more, a significant improvement in the precision (compared to the native Xen) is gained. Especially for the system with heavy IO load the precision may be improved in some cases by two orders of magnitude (e.g., for $50\mu s$ we have StdDev = $0.156\mu s$ versus $17.628\mu s$ in the native Xen). The results for the $10\mu s$ setting are depicted also in Figs 16 and 17. As we can see, for both idle system and system with heavy IO operations, the results look much better than for the native Xen implementation. All the events are gathered near the expected time and only a few measurements cross the $1\mu s$ delay.

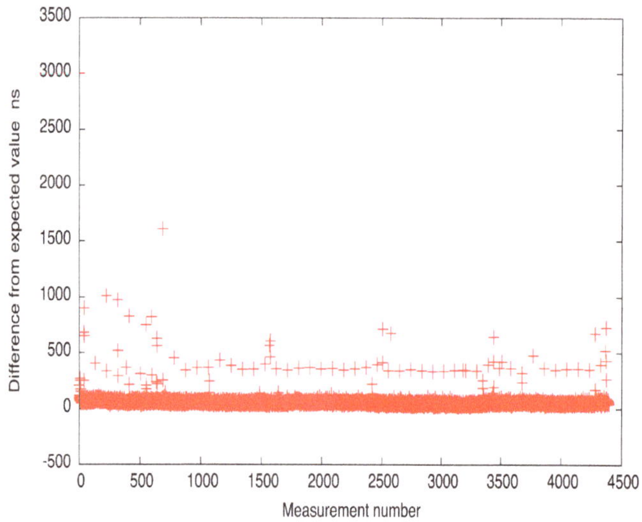


**Figure 16.** The difference between the measured timer interval and its expected value $10\mu s$ **for the new timer implementation (idle system).**

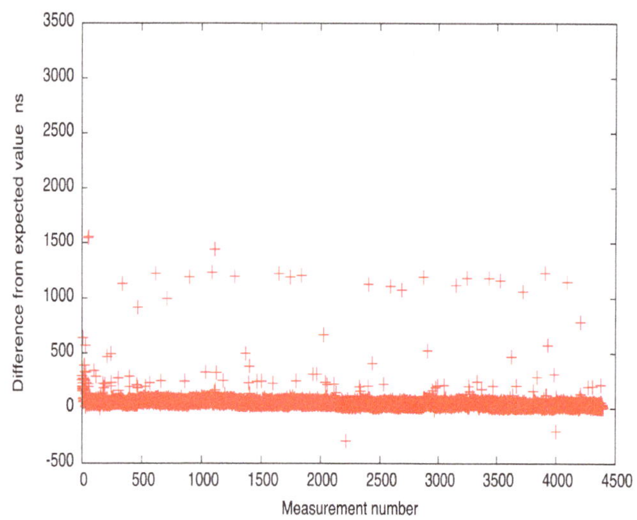


**Figure 17.** The difference between the measured timer interval and its expected value $10\mu s$ **for the new timer implementation (system with heavy IO load).**

Finally, Figs 18 and 19 present all the results for intervals of $50\mu s$ in the system with high IO load gathered on one graph to allow visual comparison between all considered virtualization systems. In particular, in Fig 18 the new timer implementation is compared with platforms of low resolution (Qemu, KVM, VMWare and VirtualBox), while in Fig 19 with platforms of higher resolution (Xen and Linux kernel).

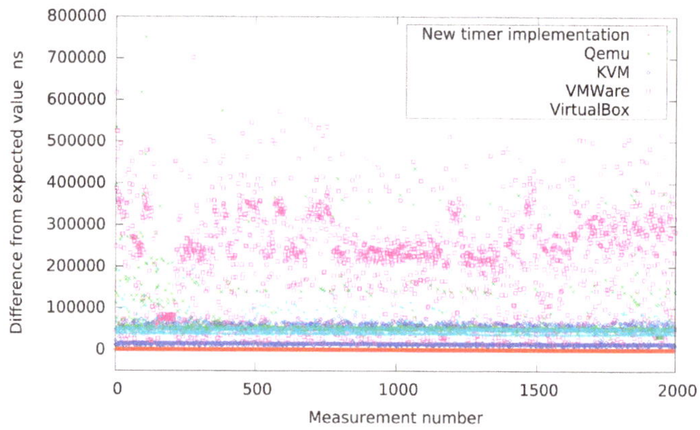


**Figure 18. The difference between the measured timer interval and its expected value $50\mu s$ for platforms with low resolution (systems with heavy IO load).**

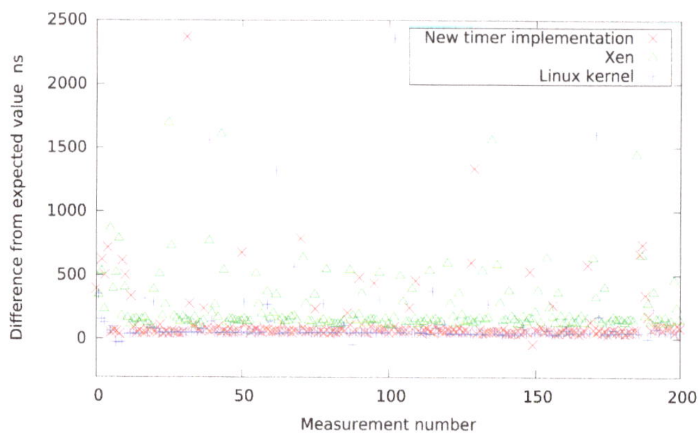


**Figure 19.** The difference between the measured timer interval and its expected value $50\mu s$ **for platforms with higher resolution (systems with heavy IO load).**

## CONCLUSION

We presented a study on high resolution timer events inside virtual machines using different virtualization platforms, i.e. Xen, KVM, Qemu, VirtualBox and VMWare. As shown in our experiments the timer resolution provided by those VMMs may not be sufficient for some purposes, especially under high interrupt load.

In particular, VMWare provided the worst resolution and precision of the timer events. KVM provided better resolution than VMWare, but still at the level of tens of microseconds. Resolution provided by Xen can be of ten microseconds but this requires changing the slop value to $1ns$ in the hypervisor and in the guest domain kernel sources. Without these changes the resolution is of a hundred microsecond. On the other hand, such changes may have a deep impact on the overall system behavior and performance.

In all studied platforms, the timer precision was strongly affected by other IO interrupts.

In order to enhance resolution and significantly reduce the impact of other IO interrupts on the precision we proposed a new timer implementation based on Xen VMM. We believe that modifications based on the same general idea can be applied analogically in the standalone Linux kernel, as well as in KVM.

Creating a separate purpose-built timer event device may prove to be the only solution for very demanding applications. In the case of open source platforms, this can be achieved by modifying the sources. However, in the case of closed solutions, such as VMWare it is not possible. As shown in the experiments, the new implementation in Xen provides a very good resolution and precision even in highly interrupted system.

## AUTHOR CONTRIBUTIONS

Conceived and designed the experiments: BA AC. Performed the experiments: BA AC. Analyzed the data: BA AC. Contributed reagents/materials/analysis tools: BA AC. Wrote the paper: BA AC.

## REFERENCES


1. Intel Corporation. 8254/82C54: Introduction to Programmable Interval Timer; 2004. Available from: http://www.intel.com/design/archives/periphrl/docs/7203.htm.
2. Maxim Integrated Products. Real-Time Clocks Product Guide; 2011. edition 2.
3. Intel Corporation. MultiProcessor Specification; 1997. version 1.4.
4. Hewlett-Packard Corporation, Intel Corporation, Microsoft Corporation, Phoenix Technologies Ltd, Toshiba Corporation. Advanced Configuration and Power Interface Specification; 2011. revision 5.0.
5. Intel Corporation. Intel 64 and IA-32 Architectures Software Developer's Manual: Instruction Set Reference; 2012. volume 2.
6. Intel Corporation. IA-PC HPET (High Precision Event Timers) Specification; 2004. revision 1.0a.
7. Siddha S, Pallipadi V, Van De Ven A. Getting maximum mileage out of tickless. In: Proceedings of the Linux Symposium, Ottawa, Ontario, Canada; 2007. p. 201–208.
8. Gleixner T, Niehaus D. Hrtimers and beyond: Transforming the linux time subsystems. In: Proceedings of the Ottawa Linux Symposium, Ottawa, Ontario, Canada. vol. 1; 2006. p. 333–346.
9. Oberle V, Walter U. Micro-second precision timer support for the Linux kernel. Relatório técnico, IBM Linux Challenge Winner of an IBM Linux Challenge Award. 2001;.
10. Kiszka J. Towards Linux as a Real-Time Hypervisor. In: Eleventh Real-Time Linux Workshop; 2009.
11. VMware, Inc. Timekeeping in VMWare Virtual Machines; 2008.
12. Chisnall D. The Definitive Guide to the Xen Hypervisor. Prentice Hall Press, Upper Saddle River; 2007.
13. Wei G, Liu J, Xu J, Lu G, Yu K, Tian K. The on-going evolutions of power management in Xen. Intel Corporation; 2009.
14. Vattikonda BC, Das S, Shacham H. Eliminating fine grained timers in Xen. In: Proceedings of the 3rd ACM Workshop on Cloud Computing Security Workshop; 2011. p. 41–46.
15. Burakowski W, Tarasiuk H, Beben A, Danilewicz G. Virtualized Network Infrastructure Supporting Co-existence of Parallel Internets. In: 2012 13th ACIS International Conference on Software Engineering, Artificial Intelligence, Networking and Parallel Distributed Computing (SNPD); 2012. p. 679–684.
16. Davis RI. A review of fixed priority and EDF scheduling for hard real-time uniprocessor systems. ACM SIGBED Review. 2014;11(1):8–19. Available from:http://dl.acm.org/citation.cfm?id = 2597458. doi: 10.1145/2597457.2597458.
17. Hamayun MM, Spyridakis A, Raho DS. Towards Hard Real-Time Control and Infotainment Applications in Automotive Platforms. OSPERT 2014. 2014;p. 39. Available from: https://mpi-sws.org/~bbb/proceedings/ospert14-proceedings.pdf#page=39.
18. VMware, Inc. VMWare Player;. Available from:http://www.vmware.com/pl/products/player.
19. Oracle Corporation. Oracle VM VirtualBox;. Available from: https://www.virtualbox.org/.
20. QEMU team. QEMU;. Available from: http://wiki.qemu.org/Main_Page.
21. Xen Project. Xen Hypervisor;. Available from: http://www.xenproject.org/.
22. Open Virtualization Alliance. Kernel-based Virtual Machine;. Available from:http://www.linux-kvm.org/.
23. Popek GJ, Goldberg RP. Formal requirements for virtualizable third generation architectures. Communications of the ACM. 1974;17(7):412–421. Available from:http://dl.acm.org/citation.cfm?id = 361073. doi: 10.1145/361011.361073.
24. VMware, Inc. VMware End User License Agreement;. Available from:https://www.vmware.com/pl/download/eula/universal_eula.html.
25. VMware, Inc. Understanding Full Virtualization, Paravirtualization, and Hardware Assist; 2007.
26. King C. Stress-ng;. Available from: http://kernel.ubuntu.com/~cking/stress-ng/.
27. Barham P, Dragovic B, Fraser K, Hand S, Harris T, Ho A, et al. Xen and the art of virtualization. ACM SIGOPS Operating Systems Review. 2003;37(5):164–177. Available from: http://dl.acm.org/citation.cfm?id = 945462. doi: 10.1145/1165389.945462.

CHAPTER 6

# MULTI-AGENT PATROLLING UNDER UNCERTAINTY AND THREATS

Shaofei Chen[1,2] , Feng Wu[2] , Lincheng Shen[1] , Jing Chen[1] , and Sarvapali Ramchurn[2]

[1] College of Mechatronics and Automation, National University of Defense Technology, China

[2] School of Electronics and Computer Science, University of Southampton, UK

## ABSTRACT

**We investigate a multi-agent patrolling problem where information is distributed alongside threats in environments with uncertainties. Specifically, the information and threat at each location are independently modelled as multi-state Markov chains, whose states are not observed until the location is visited by an agent. While agents will obtain information at a location, they may also suffer damage from the threat at that location. Therefore, the goal of the agents is to gather as much information as possible while mitigating the damage incurred. To address this challenge, we formulate the single-agent patrolling problem as a Partially Observable Markov Decision Process (POMDP) and propose a computationally efficient algorithm to solve this model. Building upon this, to compute patrols for multiple agents, the single-agent algorithm is extended for each agent with the aim of maximising its marginal contribution to the team. We empirically evaluate our algorithm on problems of multi-agent patrolling and show that it outperforms a baseline algorithm up to 44% for 10 agents and by 21% for 15 agents in large domains.**

## INTRODUCTION

Unmanned Aerial Vehicles (UAVs) are increasingly becoming essential tools to carry out situational awareness tasks in a number of real-world applications ranging from disaster response [1–3] and security surveillance [3–5]. In these scenarios, multiple UAVs may be deployed to gather information at specific locations as quickly as possible in order to support an ongoing operation. However, such problems are often liable to a high degree of dynamism (e.g., fires may spread, wind direction may change) and uncertainty (e.g., it may not be possible to completely observe the causes of fires or the location of casualties may not be exactly known), and may also contain a number of hazards or threats for the UAVs (e.g., UAVs may fly close to buildings on fire or debris may fall on the UAVs).

In this paper, we consider the scenario where a set of UAVs aim to patrol the area to gather as much information as possible while minimising the negative impact of threats. Crucially, they aim to do so within an environment that is partially observable (i.e., the features of the locations are only fully observable where the UAV is located and partially observable at other locations). Hence, when planning the sequence of locations to visit, UAVs have the difficult task

**Citation:** Chen S, Wu F, Shen L, Chen J, Ramchurn SD (2015) Multi-Agent Patrolling under Uncertainty and Threats. PLoS ONE 10(6): e0130154. doi:10.1371/journal.pone.0130154

of estimating the information to be gained and threats to be encountered at these locations. This problem is compounded by the fact that the dynamism inherent to the environment may cause the information and threats at each location to change over time (i.e., the environment is stochastic). For example, when UAVs visit a building in a disaster area, the building states (intact, about to collapse, collapsing, or collapsed) may correspond to threat states (levels) for UAVs, and the threat at each location may be changing stochastically, such that it switches between "about to collapse" to "collapsed" due to an aftershock [6]. The information in the environment may also change dynamically (e.g., a victim may get out of danger or the fire may get close to a victim).

To date, a number of approaches to information gathering with teams of UAVs have been proposed. However, most of the work [3, 7, 8] focus on developing algorithms for UAVs gathering information in dynamic environments where the model of the features of the environment is fully observable and stationary (see Related Work section for more details). Furthermore, none of these approaches have considered how threats may affect the information gathering process while the environment is partially observable and non-stationary. Unless such issues are tackled, we believe it is unlikely that large UAV deployments in real major disaster will be feasible.

In recent years, agent-based modelling has been effectively used to formulate and solve the problems of planning in environments characterized by uncertainties [9]. In agent-based models, an agent is an encapsulated computer system that is situated in some environment and that is capable of flexible, autonomous action in that environment in order to meet its design objectives [10]. Such agents are either software or hardware (e.g., robots or unmanned autonomous systems (UAS)). In particular, operating in uncertain environments, autonomous agents have to deal with executing actions that may not have the intended results, with environments that change while the agent is operating, and with making observations that might not be completely accurate.

Against this background, we propose a agent-based model for patrolling under uncertainty and threats and go on to develop a novel algorithm to solve the planning problem that it poses. In more detail, we first model the information and threats on a graph representing the environment, where the information and threat at each location are independently modelled asmulti-state Markov chains (which captures the non-stationary feature), whose states are not observed until the location is visited by an agent (which captures the partially observable feature). Then, we cast the single-agent patrolling problem as a Partially Observable Markov Decision Process (POMDP), which provides a rich model for planning and acting in partially observable stochastic domains [11]. Unfortunately, existing POMDP solvers are very inefficient to solve our POMDP formulation due to the exponential growth of the number of possible paths of agents in the size of the graph and the number of the possible observations along each possible path (see Related Work section for more detail). Hence, we propose an online algorithm to solve the patrolling problem for one agent at a time. (In computer science, an online algorithm is one that can process its input piece-by-piece in a serial fashion, i.e., in the order that the input is fed to the algorithm, without having the entire input available from the start. In contrast, an offline algorithm is given the whole problem data from the beginning and is required to output an answer which solves the problem at hand.) In particular, the algorithm utilises a predictive heuristic that only refers to the possible paths (looking ahead several steps) from the current position of the agent. Building upon this, to compute patrolling policies for multiple agents, the single-agent algorithm is extended for each agent with the aim of maximising its marginal contribution to the team. In summary, this paper advances the state of the art in the following ways:

We propose the first algorithm for multi-agent patrolling under uncertainty and threats. Our formulation does not only capture the partially observable and non-stationary features of the dynamic environment, but also accounts for the health status of the patrolling agents.

- We design a predictive heuristic to estimate the value of each possible path from current position of the agent and provide an online algorithm to solve the patrolling problem for one agent at a time. Moreover, we propose a multi-agent algorithm that sequentially computes policies for individual agents. In particular, we also show that our multi-agent algorithm scale to larger environments (i.e., more than 10 agents) than existing solutions.
- We evaluate our algorithms in simulations and show that our algorithm outperforms a baseline algorithm up to 44% for 10 agents and by 21% for 15 agents.

The remainder of this paper is structured as follows. First, we review the literature on patrolling problems. We then present our model for the problem of multi-agent patrolling under uncertainty and threats. Given this, we formulate the single-agent patrolling problem as a POMDP and provide an algorithm that computes policies for individual agents. Finally, we propose our multi-agent algorithm and evaluate it in the simulations of multi-agent patrolling in a large environment.

## RELATED WORK

In this section, we review related work on agent based model and approaches for multi-agent patrolling problems.

In general, methods to gather situational awareness without considering threats are typically categorised as a class of information gathering problem[3], in which agents aim to continuously collect and provide up-to-date situational awareness. For these dynamic environments, previous work [3, 7, 8] consider fully observable (agents can directly observe the underlying state of the environment) stationary models (joint probability distribution of its states do not change when shifted in time). A partially observable model has been proposed in [12], where an agent can only perceive the exact state at its current position. Game-theoretic approaches [13–18] have focused on patrolling to guard important targets in the presence of strategic evaders or intruders; a problem that is characterised by (possibly multiple) attackers attempting to avoid capture or breach a perimeter. The agents' main challenge in such cases is to detect and capture these attackers in an effort to minimise loss. However, these approaches do not consider the health status of the agents and the damage that agents can suffer while patrolling.

Stationary models of the information/threats are considered in previous work. The work on information gathering in dynamic environments [8] have focused on specific environmental phenomena (e.g., monitoring algal bloom growth in lakes and salt concentration in rivers) rather than stochastic events as in our scenarios. Markov models are widely used to model non-stationary stochastic states in the world, such as the specific ground targets for aircraft [12,19, 20] and sensors [21], physical activities in wireless network [22], and channel memory in communication systems [23, 24]. However, a number of strict assumptions are made in these works in terms of the Markov models used. For example, each target at each period can be in one of only two states [12, 23] and the matrix of the Markov models must satisfy some special formations [24].

Among these works, a Markov Decision Process (MDP) based algorithm that computes policies for individual agents has been proposed in [3] to solve continuous information gathering in fully observable environments. Our formulation in this paper mainly extends [3] to patrolling under threats in partially observable and on-stationary environments and cast the single-agent patrolling problem as a POMDP. However, solving this formulation using current POMDP solvers [25] for all but the smallest instances is impossible due to the exponential growth in the number of possible paths of agents that can be traced in the environment and the number of the possible observations along each path. The POMCP algorithm has been proposed in [26] and has been shown to generate good solution quality and scale to large POMDPs. However, to the best of our knowledge, developing scalable approaches that extend POMCP to solve multi-agent POMDPs is still a open problem. As these possible benchmarks are unable to scale to multi-agent instances of our formulation, we design a baseline algorithm that greedily select the policy for one time step as a benchmark.

## METHODS

In this section, we present the model for the problem of multi-agent patrolling under uncertainty and threats. Specifically, we first model the physical environment in which the agents operate and then go on to describe the decision problem faced by the agents.

## The Patrolling Problem

We formulate the patrolling problem by defining the physical environment and patrolling agents. In particular, we present the Markov models of information and threat at in the environment to capture the non-stationary feature.

### The physical environment.

The physical environment is defined by its spatial, temporal and dynamic properties. In particular, in the aftermath of a disaster, a number of specific sites might need urgent attention and access to these sites may be limited to certain areas (e.g., due to trees, debris, or natural obstacles). Hence, we can capture such features in terms of paths along which agents can travel from one disaster site to another. Specifically, the spatial property of the environment is encoded by a graph, which specifies how and where agents can move.

**Definition 1 (Graph)** We model an area of the environment as an undirected graph G = (V,E), where each vertex V representing spatial coordinates are embedded in Euclidean space and edges E encode the movements that are possible between them. Here, we denote N = |V|.

In disaster response, each disaster site is a vertex in the graph, and a traversable area between a pair of sites is an edge of the graph.

**Definition 2 (Time)** Time is modelled by a set of time steps {1,2,…,T} and at each time step t ∈ {1,2,…,T} the agents visit some sites in the environment.

To capture the dynamic attributes of the environment, we assume that each vertex holds two states: one for information and one for threats.

**Definition 3 (Information State Variable)** An information state variable indicates different levels of the information at a given vertex.

For example, how many people need help and what is the status of a bridge are information state variables in disaster response scenario.

**Definition 4 (Threat State Variable)** A threat state variable reflects the level of damage an agent suffers when visiting a given vertex.

For example, the level of fire and the degree of smog are typical threat state variables in disaster response.

**Definition 5 (Markov Model of Information and Threat)** The two state variables at each vertex change over time according to discrete-time multi-state Markov chains.

To capture the transitions of the state variables, we employ a Markov chain model. Specifically, for a Markov chain with K states $S = (S_1, S_2, \ldots, S_K)$, the matrix of transition probabilities for pairs of states is defined as:

$$P = \begin{bmatrix} p_{11} & \cdots & p_{1K} \\ p_{21} & \cdots & p_{2K} \\ \vdots & \ddots & \vdots \\ p_{K1} & \cdots & p_{KK} \end{bmatrix} = \begin{bmatrix} P_1 \\ P_2 \\ \vdots \\ P_K \end{bmatrix}$$

where $p_{ij}$ is the probability that threat state $S_i$ transitions to $S_j$ in one time step and $S_i, S_j \in S$. An example of information and threat models at a vertex is shown in Fig 1. Thus, Fig 1(a)shows a threat model with 2 states (i.e., $R_1$ and $R_2$) and Fig 1(b) shows an information model with 3 states (i.e., $I_1$, $I_2$ and $I_3$), where the probabilities of each information/threat state changes over a time step are given (e.g., the probability of $R_1$ changes to $R_2$ is 0.1).

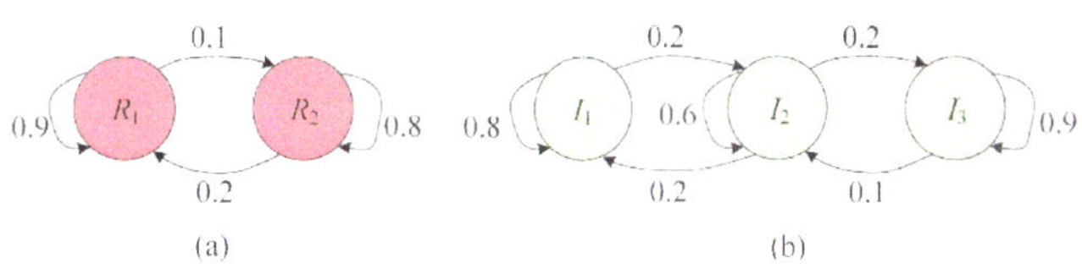


**Figure 1.** Example of information and threat models at a vertex.

(a) A threat model with 2 states (i.e., $R_1$ and $R_2$) and (b) an information model with 3 states (i.e., $I_1$, $I_2$ and $I_3$), where the probabilities of each information/threat state changes to another over a time step are given (e.g., the probability of $R_1$ changes to $R_2$ is 0.1).

The set of information states $I^n = \{I_1^n, I_2^n, \ldots, I_{K_I^n}^n\}$ for location $v_n$ correspond to an amount $K_I^n$ of information which agents obtain when visiting $v_n$. The value of information is determined by the function $f^n:I^n \rightarrow \mathbb{R}^+$, and $f(I_k^n)$ increases monotonically with $k \in \{1, \ldots, K_I^n\}$, which indicates that the states of information are ordered in terms of their value. The information state at a given vertex independently evolves as a $K_I^n$-state Markov chain model with a matrix of transition probabilities $P_I^n$.

Similarly, the set of threat states $R^n = \{R_1^n, R_2^n, \ldots, R_{K_R^n}^n\}$ indicate the $K_R^n$ threat levels of vertex $v_n \in V$. The "damage" that an agent suffers when visiting vertex $v_n$ is captured by the function $c^n:R^n \rightarrow \mathbb{R}^+$, and $c(R_k^n)$ increases monotonically with $k \in \{1, \ldots, K_R^n\}$. The threat state at a given vertex independently evolves over time as a $K_R^n$-state Markov chain and the matrix of transition probabilities is $P_R^n$.

Having modelled the environment in which the agents operate, we next elaborate on the agents' goals.

## PATROLLING AGENTS.

We define a patrolling agent (agent for short) as a physical mobile entity situated in the environment defined above, capable of gathering information, and maybe damaged by the threat when visiting a vertex. The set of all agents is denoted as A = {1,...,|A|}. Then, the movement and visit capabilities of agents are formulated as follows. When patrolling in a graphG, each agent is positioned at a given vertex in G at each time step t. The movement of each agent is atomic, i.e., takes place within the interval between two subsequent time steps, and is constrained by G, i.e., agent m positioned at a vertex $v_i \in V$ can only move to a vertex $v_i' \in adj_G(v_i)$ that is adjacent to $v_i$ in G. We assume that $\forall v_i \in V$, $v_i \in adj_G(v_i)$, i.e., an agent can also stay at the same vertex. The speed of the agents is sufficient to reach an adjacent vertex within a single time step. Time can be discretised according to the speed of the UAVs. Thus if the UAVs can travel between sites in a five minutes, then a time step may be set at 5 minutes in the model.

Given this, an agent visits a vertex $v_n$ when it is positioned at that vertex. On the one hand, a visit results in the agent being aware of the current information and threat state at $v_n$, such as $I_i^n$ and $R_j^n$ respectively. On the other hand, this agent obtains a reward $f^n(I_i^n)$ and suffers a loss $c^n(R_j^n)$ for a visit. The time it takes to visit a vertex is assumed to be negligible. We let $F^n = [f^n(I_1^n), \ldots, f^n(I_{K_I^n}^n)]$ denote the information value vector, where $f^n(I_k)$ is the information value that an agent could get if the information state is $I_k^n$ (e.g., information at a vertex has 3 states and corresponds to 3 information values [0, 2, 5]). Similarly, we let $C^n = [c^n(R_1^n), \ldots, c^n(R_{K_R^n}^n)]$ denote as the damage value vector at vertex $v_n$, where $c^n(R_k^n)$ is the damage value that an agent will lose if the threat state is $R_k^n$ (e.g., fire level at a position has 4 states which corresponds to 4 levels of damage [0, 4, 6, 10], and smog degree at a position has 3 states which corresponds to 4 levels of damage [0, 2, 5]). For each visit, the information at that vertex is obtained by the agent and we regard that the information state at a given vertex $v_n$ will reset to $I_1^n$ when an agent visits this vertex ($I_1^n$ is the information state which means no new information was generated at $v_n$ after last visit). As the states at each vertex change over time and agents can only access the exact states at the vertices that they visit, the patrolling environment can be considered non-stationary (i.e., joint probability distribution of its states may change when shifted in time) and partially observable.

Furthermore, in this paper, we make two assumptions about the communication and cooperation among agents as follows.

**Assumption 1** All the agents can share their collected observations with each other via communication. Such peer to peer communication is free of noise, costs, and delays.

Consider a centralised station is organized to coordinate a team of UAVs for monitoring the continuously changing state of a disaster area, where each UAV can full communication with this station and Assumption 1 is satisfied in these domains. However, in some real scenarios, UAVs can only coordinate with each other using limited communication and decentralised approaches may be more appropriate (but this is beyond the scope of this paper and will be considered in future work).

**Assumption 2** When more than one agent is visiting a vertex, only one information value is obtained for the team but each agent suffers the same damage that may be generated at that vertex.

This assumption is satisfied in the scenarios where the information gathering capability of one agent at a vertex is equal to that provided by multiple agents with the same sensors, and agents independently suffer the damage caused by threats. In future work, a model of information fusion for multiple (heterogeneous) agents will be considered. Thus, the team of agents need to coordinate with each other based on their observations while patrolling. Specifically, the goal of the agents is to gather as much information as possible while minimise the damage incurred.

We now provide a simple example to explain how the agents would operate in this scenario. Consider an agent that enters into a building on fire. In our setting, this is equivalent to the agent visiting a node in the graph. The fire level (threat state variable) and valuable information about victims and assets (information variable) changes over time. While exploring the building, the agent may acquire some information and suffer some damage due to the fire. At each time step, an agent selects one adjacent building to visit based on the estimated information value and the prior observation of threat states at each location. It then obtains a reward based on the value of the information, and suffers a loss which is associated with the threat state. Then, the information state at the visited vertex is immediately reset.

Having defined the patrolling problem, we now need to plan the sequential patrolling actions for agents based on the history of actions and observations, and the model of the environment. Hence, in what follows, we first propose a POMDP formulation for single-agent patrolling within a graph and design an algorithm to solve it. Building upon this, we propose a scalable multi-agent patrolling algorithm.

## Single-Agent Patrolling

In this section, we first formulate the POMDP based framework for single-agent patrolling problem. POMDPs imply that the agent does not know the exact state it is in, and the agent requires to keep track of each observation received, in order to maintain a probability distribution, known as the belief state, over the possible states [11]. Thus, we analysis that a standard representation of belief state makes the POMDP computational intractable and then present a compact representation of belief state for our POMDP formulation. Given this, we propose a predictive heuristic and an online single-agent algorithm.

## The POMDP Framework.

We now set up the single-agent patrolling problem as a POMDP $\langle \mathcal{S},,, T, \Omega, r \rangle$ as follows:

- $\mathcal{S}$ is the set of states. A state is defined as a tuple $s = [v, (s_R^1, \ldots, s_R^N), (s_I^1, \ldots, s_I^N)] \in \mathcal{S}$, where v is the current position of the agent, $s_R^N \in R^n$ and $s_I^N \in I^n$ are the threat and information states at vertex $v_n \in V$. We denote $s_e = [(s_R^1, \ldots, s_R^N), (s_I^1, \ldots, s_I^N)] \in \mathcal{S}_e$, as the state that captures the information and threat states at all of the positions. Given this, the number of the states in $\mathcal{S}$ increases exponentially with the number the vertices.
- $\mathcal{A}$ is the set of all actions. The agent select an adjacent vertex to visit as an action.
- $\mathcal{O}$ is the set of observations. We define an observation $o = (v_i, s_I^i, s_R^i) \in \mathcal{O}$ as the current position $v_i$ and the information and threat state at this position.
- $\mathcal{T}$ is the set of conditional transition probabilities. We assume that v is deterministic and only determined by the destination of movement of the agent. Based on the Markov models defined in the patrolling problem, $s_e$ follows a discrete-time Markov process with $\prod_{n=1}^{N} K_R^n K_I^n$ states.
- $\Omega$ is the set of observation probabilities. As an observation o is directly a part of some states, the observation probability $\Omega(o|s', a) = 1$ if o is consistent with the corresponding part of s' and $\Omega(o|s', a) = 0$ otherwise.
- $r: \mathcal{A} \times \mathcal{O} \rightarrow \mathbb{R}$ is a reward function. r(a, o) is the sum of the rewards obtained by the agent which associates to the action a and observation o:

$$r(a, o) = \alpha f^i(s_I^i) - (1 - \alpha) c^i(s_R^i) \quad (1)$$

where α is a weight parameter of the two objectives.

The objective of the agent is then to choose the movement actions sequentially to maximize the total expected reward accumulated over Tsteps.

In this model, the states are not directly observable. Hence, a standard belief vector $B(t) = [b_1(t), \ldots, b_M(t)]$ is defined as the posterior probability distribution over the possible states S, where $b_m(t)$ is the conditional probability that the environment state is at the mth state at the current time step t. For any t, it has been shown in [27] that this belief vector is a sufficient statistic for the design of the optimal action for each time step. A policy π specifies the action that will be executed in any given belief state and the optimal policy π* is a policy by which the agent gets the maximum total expected reward accumulated over T steps. However, as each environment state is an joint state of the information and threat states at all of the vertices, the number of possible states S that defined in our POMDP is $\prod_{n=1}^{N} K_R^n K_I^n$, which increases exponentially with the number the vertices. Moreover, as the belief vector is defined as the posterior probability distribution over these possible states, the dimension of this belief vector also increases exponentially with the number the vertices.

To address this, we propose an online method by introducing a belief vector of reduced dimension and develop a predictive heuristic to reduce the search space and still produce high quality solutions (as we show later).

## COMPACT BELIEF REPRESENTATION.

As the threat state and information state variables at each vertex evolve independently and vis deterministic, we can find a sufficient statistic for the optimal policy whose dimension linearly grows with N, similar to [23, 24]. We introduce a compact representation of belief state and its transition function in this section.

We define a sufficient statistic belief vector of the environment states at time t as the vector of the conditional probabilities (conditioned on the observation and decision history) $\Psi(t) = [\Psi_R(t), \Psi_I(t)]$, where $\Psi_R(t)$ is defined as:

$$\begin{cases} \Psi_R(t) &= (w_R^1(t), \ldots, w_R^N(t)) \\ w_R^n(t) &= (w_{R1}^n(t), \ldots, w_{RK_R^n}^n(t)) \end{cases} \quad (2)$$

where $w_{Rk_1}^n(t)$ is the probability that the threat state at vertex $v_n$ is $R_{k_1}^n$, $k_1 = 1, \ldots, K_R^n$ and $\Psi_I(t)$ is defined as:

$$\begin{cases} \Psi_I(t) &= (w_I^1(t), \ldots, w_I^N(t)) \\ w_I^n(t) &= (w_{I1}^n(t), \ldots, w_{IK_I^n}^n(t)) \end{cases} \quad (3)$$

where $w_{Ik_2}^n(t)$ is the probability that the information state at vertex $v_n$ is $I_{k_2}^n$ and $k_2 = 1, \ldots, K_I^n$. Then Ψ(t) is a sufficient statistic of optimal decision making [23, 24]. By exploiting the statistical independence among vertices, we reduce the dimension of the sufficient statistic from $\prod_{n=1}^{N} K_R^n K_I^n$ to $\sum_{n=1}^{N} (K_R^n + K_I^n)$, which grows with N linearly. This allows us to reduce the computational and storage complexity of the optimal patrolling policy from exponential to linear.

**Theorem 1** For any time t, Ψ(t) is a sufficient statistic for the design of optimal policy for our POMDP formulation.

**Proof** We show that when the information and threat at the N vertices evolve independently, each element $b_m(t)$ in the standard belief vector B(t) can be obtained from Ψ(t), where $b_m(t)$ is the conditional probability that the environment state is at the ith state. Without loss of generality, we consider N = 2. Let $\mathcal{I}(t)$ denote the history up to the beginning of slot t. Let $\tau_n$ denote the most recent time instant when vertex $v_n$ is visited. We can thus write an entry of $b_m(t)$ as in Eq (4). Quantities in Eq (4) are entries of Ψ(t). Hence, Ψ(t) is a sufficient statistics.

$$\begin{aligned} &\Pr\left[s_R^1(t)=i', s_R^1(t)=i'', s_I^1(t)=j', s_I^2(t)=j'' \mid \mathcal{I}(t)\right] \\ =\; &\Pr\left[s_R^1(t)=i', s_R^2(t)=i'', s_I^1(t)=j', s_I^2(t)=j'' \mid s_R^1(\tau_1)=o_R', s_R^2(\tau_2)=o_R'', \tau_1, \tau_2\right] \\ =\; &\Pr\left[s_R^1(t)=i' \mid s_R^1(\tau_1)=o_R'\right]\Pr\left[s_R^2(t)=i'' \mid s_R^2(\tau_2)=o_R''\right] \\ &\Pr\left[s_I^1(t)=j' \mid \tau_1\right]\Pr\left[s_I^2(t)=j'' \mid \tau_2\right] \end{aligned} \tag{4}$$

Initially, we assume that we have probabilistic information about the state of each of the Nvertices $\Psi(0) = [\Psi_R(0),\Psi_I(0)]$. Then, the elements of belief vector Ψ(t) are updated to Ψ(t+1) upon action a = $v_i$ and observation $o = (v_i, s_I^i, s_R^i)$ as:

$$w_R^n(t+1) = \begin{cases} \tilde{I}_k & \text{if } v_n = v_i, s_R^i(t) = R_k \\ w_R^n(t)P_R^n & \text{if } v_n \neq v_i \end{cases}$$
$$w_I^n(t+1) = \begin{cases} \tilde{I}_1 & \text{if } v_n = v_i \\ w_I^n(t)P_I^n & \text{if } v_n \neq v_i \end{cases} \tag{5}$$

where $\forall v_n \in V$, $R_k^n \in R^n$, $I_k^n \in I^n$, and $\tilde{I}_k$ is a unit vector with the k[th] item is 1, $P_R^n$ and $P_I^n$ are respectively the matrices of transition probabilities of threat and information at position $v_n$. As shown in Eq (5), the threat belief vector $w_R^n(t+1)$ at one vertex $v_n$ that some agent is visiting is updated to $\tilde{I}_k$ based on the observation $R_k^n(h)$ at this vertex, while $\mathbf{w}_R^n(t+1)$ at some other vertex that no agent is visiting is updated by the current threat belief vectors $\mathbf{w}_R^n(t)$ and threat Markov model $P_R^n$ at this vertex. A similar explanation holds for the update to the information belief $w_I^n(t+1)$, as for $v_n \in V$.

Based on the transition function above, a policy π specifies a sequence of actions π = [π(1),π(2),…], where π(t) is the position selected to visit at time t. Given this, the optimal policy can be computed as:

$$\pi^* = \arg\max_{\pi} \mathbb{E}^{\pi}\left[\sum_{t=1}^{\infty} \gamma^t \mathcal{R}^{\pi(t)}(\Psi(t)|\Psi(0))\right] \tag{6}$$

where $\mathcal{R}^{\pi(t)}(\Psi(t))$ is the reward obtained when the belief state is Ψ(t) and γ ∈ [0, 1] is the discount factor.

Although the dimensionality of the belief state is reduced, the problem is still a POMDP and finding the optimal solution is intractable. Based on this reduced belief vector, we next develop a predictive heuristic and present the online single-agent algorithm that implements this heuristic.

## THE PREDICTIVE HEURISTIC

In order to develop a predictive heuristic for online policy selection, we first introduce the assumption that the Markov state transition matrices are monotone matrices, which means that the higher the information/damage value of the vertex's current state the higher is the likelihood that the next state of this vertex will be of high information/damage value. Then, we show how to define the predictive heuristic as the predictive expected future reward based on the monotonicity of the transition matrices.

Stochastic dominance is a central theme in a wide variety of applications in economics, finance and statistics [28]. Similar assumption has been made to model the states of the channels in communication systems [23, 24] and the states at targets for UAVs monitoring [12]. Stochastic dominance ≻ between two Z dimension probability vector x, y is defined as x≻ y, if:

$$\sum_{j=i}^{Z} x(j) \geq \sum_{j=i}^{Z} y(j), \quad \text{for } i = 2, 3, \ldots, Z \tag{7}$$

We assume that the Markov information model and Markov threat model are monotonic matrices, i.e., the matrix of transition probabilities $P_R^n$ and $P_I^n$ satisfies:

$$P_{RK_1}^n \succ P_{RK_1-1}^n \succ \ldots \succ P_{R_1}^n$$
$$P_{IK_2}^n \succ P_{IK_2-1}^n \succ \ldots \succ P_{I_1}^n \tag{8}$$

If the matrix of transition probabilities $P_R^n$ and $P_I^n$ satisfy the assumption above, then $P_R^n$ and $P_I^n$ aremonotone matrices[29]. Under this assumption, the higher the information value of the state of the current vertex the higher is the likelihood that the next state of this vertex will be of high information value, i.e., if $w_I^n(t) \succ w_I^{n'}(t)$, then $w_I^n(t)P_I^n \succ w_I^{n'}(t)P_I^{n'}$. From (5), we know that probability vectors for information states of two vertices keep the relationship of stochastic dominance when no agent visits any of them. Obviously, if $w_I^n(t) \succ w_I^{n'}(t)$, then $w_I^n(t)F^n \geq w_I^{n'}(t)F^{n'}$, which means that a stochastically dominant information belief vector is likely to have a higher information value. The same is true that a stochastically dominant threat belief vector is likely to have a higher damage value. In particular, as the information state at a given vertex will reset to $I_1$ when there is an agent visiting this vertex, the belief vector of information states (1,0,…,0) is stochastically dominated by the belief vector of any vertex which is not being visited, so the more recently visited vertex always has a lower expected information value.

To note, our monotonicity assumption is not a constraint that makes the information value (or the damage of the threat) increasing with time, but a model that the probability vector of the information (or threat) transition matrices satisfy the feature of stochastic dominance. We now provide a example of a 4-state Markov threat model at a vertex as follows:

$$P_R = \begin{bmatrix} 0.8 & 0.1 & 0.1 & 0 \\ 0.4 & 0.5 & 0.0 & 0.1 \\ 0.2 & 0.1 & 0.6 & 0.1 \\ 0 & 0.0 & 0.4 & 0.6 \end{bmatrix}$$

It can be seen that the Vectors of $P_R$ satisfy the condition of Eq (8), i.e., $P_{R4} > P_{R3} > P_{R2} > P_{R1}$, where for $P_{R3} > P_{R2}$ as an example, the elements of $P_{R2}$ and $P_{R3}$ match the condition for stochastic dominance of Eq (7) as:

$$0.1 + 0.6 + 0.1 \geqq 0.5 + 0.0 + 0.1$$

$$0.6 + 0.1 \geqq 0.0 + 0.1$$

$$0.1 \geqq 0.1$$

For example, if the threat states at vertices $v_1$ and $v_2$ are respectively $w_R^1 = [0.1, 0.2, 0.5, 0.2]$ and $w_R^2 = [0.2, 0.4, 0.3, 0.1]$, i.e., $w_R^1 \succ w_R^2$. Then, $v_1$ is likely to have a higher next threat state than $v_2$. However, after a time step, it is possible that any threat state may switch to not only a higher state, but also a lower state.

Then given the monotonicity assumption, we can use the relationship between the belief states at different vertices in order to "predict" the belief state at an unvisited node. Hence, we can estimate the expected reward agents may get from one vertex of the graph when visiting it at a near future step. We denote a feasible policy of length D at time t as $\pi_D(t) = (\pi_{t+1}, \ldots, \pi_{t+D})$, which consists of D consecutive deterministic vertices/actions.

Here, we define the predictive heuristic as the predictive expected future reward $\mathbb{E}[\hat{\mathcal{R}}(\pi_D(t))]$ for policy $\pi_D(t)$, which is the aggregate of the expected reward of each step in $\pi_D(t)$ as:

$$\mathbb{E}[\hat{\mathcal{R}}(\pi_D(t))] = \sum_{i=1}^{D} \gamma^i (\alpha w_I^{\pi_{t+i}}(t+i) F^{\pi_{t+i}} - (1-\alpha) w_R^{\pi_{t+i}}(t+i) L^{\pi_{t+i}}) \quad (9)$$

where, $[\hat{w}_I^{\pi_{t+i}}(t+i), \hat{w}_R^{\pi_{t+i}}(t+i)]$ is the predictive belief vector at the vertex $\pi_{t+i}$ and time t+i. For the step t+1, we can get the predictive belief vector $[\hat{w}_I^{\pi_{t+1}}(t+1), \hat{w}_R^{\pi_{t+1}}(t+1)]$ by the current belief vector $\Psi(t)$, current action a(t) and observations $\theta(t)$, i.e. $\Psi(t+1) = \delta(\Psi(t) \mid a_t^*, \theta(t))$, which is the belief vector at t+1 and obtained from Eq (5). For {t+2,..., t+D}, we get the predicted belief vector based on a transition which omits observations in Eq (5) as follows:

$$\hat{w}_R^n(\tau+1) = \hat{w}_R^n(\tau) P_R^n$$

$$\hat{w}_I^n(\tau+1) = \begin{cases} P_{I1}^n & \text{if } v_n = \pi_\tau \\ \hat{w}_I^n(\tau) P_I^n & \text{if } v_n \neq \pi_\tau \end{cases} \quad (10)$$

where $\tau = \{t+1, \ldots, t+D-1\}$.

Given the predictive heuristic and policies that looks ahead D time periods, the agent compares all feasible paths of length D and chooses the next location to visit according to the path that gives the highest predictive expected reward gained over that path. The details of how to use the heuristic in our online single-agent algorithm is presented in the next section.

## The Online Algorithm.

Based on the predictive heuristic, we propose an online algorithm for single-agent patrolling problem (Algorithm 1) in this section.

**Algorithm 1** Single-Agent Patrolling

**Require:** $\{P_R^n\}$: the Markov threat models

**Require:** $\{P_I^n\}$: the Markov information models

**Require:** $\Psi(t)$: the belief state of current time step

**Require:** o(t): the observation at the current position

**Require:** v(t): current position.

**Ensure:** $a^*(t+1)$: next action of the agent

▷ Step 0: get all feasible policies $\Pi_D(t)$;

▷ Step 1: computing best policy:

1: **for** $\pi_D(t) \in \Pi_D(t)$ **do**

▷ Step 1.1: Get predictive belief state for next D steps:

2: $\Psi(t+1) \leftarrow \delta(\Psi(t) \mid v_t, \theta(t))$

3: **for** $\tau \in \{t+1, \ldots, t+D-1\}$ **do**

4: **for** $v_n \in V$ **do**

5: $\hat{w}^n(\tau+1) \leftarrow \hat{\delta}(\hat{w}^n(\tau) \mid \pi_\tau(\tau))$

6: **end for**

7: **end for**

▷ Step 1.2: Compute the predictive reward for $\pi_D(t)$:

8: $\mathbb{E}[\hat{\mathcal{R}}(\pi_D(t))] = \alpha w_I^{\pi_{t+i}}(t+i) F^{\pi_{t+i}} + \beta w_R^{\pi_{t+i}}(t+i) L^{\pi_{t+i}}$

▷ Step 1.3: Compare $\pi_D(t)$ with the stored best policy:

9: **if** $\mathbb{E}[\hat{\mathcal{R}}(\pi_D(t))] > \mathbb{E}[\hat{\mathcal{R}}(\pi_D^*(t))]$ **then**

10: $\pi_D^*(t) \leftarrow \pi_D(t)$

11: **end if**

12: **end for**

▷ Step 2:return the next action from the best policy $\pi_i^*$

13: **return** $a^*(t+1) \leftarrow \pi_{t+1}^*$

First, we compute $\Pi_D(t)$, which is the set of all the feasible policies that start from current position v(t) (step 0), where we name the parameter D as the maximum horizon, i.e. the number of horizons we look ahead in the POMDP. Then, we compute the predictive expected reward for all the policies. For each policy, the belief state at t+1 is updated by the belief state, position and observations at t by Eq (5) (line 2) and the predictive belief state at {t+2,..., t+D} is computed by Eq (10) (line 3–7). Given this, we compute the predictive reward for the policy (line 8). Thus, the best policy is:

$$\pi_D^*(t) = \arg\max_{\pi_D(t)} \mathbb{E}[\hat{\mathcal{R}}(\pi_D(t))] \quad (11)$$

The best next action here is computed as $a^*(t+1) = \pi^*_{t+1}$, which is the first action of best policy (line 13).

Having defined the online single-agent algorithm for our formulation of patrolling under uncertainty and threats, we extend it to compute policies for multi-agent problems next.

## Multi-Agent Patrolling

For multi-agent patrolling, we assume all the agents can share their collected observations with each other with full communication. Thus, team of agents may not only obtain more information about the environment, but each agent may also make decisions given observations are shared by other agents. Given this, we formulate the multi-agent patrolling problem as a Multi-agent POMDP (MPOMDP) and design an scalable online multi-agent algorithm to coordinate the actions of agents in their patrolling tasks.

A MPOMDP with complete communication can be reduced to a POMDP with a single centralised controller that takes joint actions and receives joint observations [30]. We now set up our problem of multi-agent patrolling in a graph as a POMDP ⟨$\mathcal{M}$,,,, T,Ω, r⟩ as follows.

- $\mathcal{M}$ is the set of the agents.
- $\mathcal{S}$ is the set of states. A state is defined as a tuple $\vec{s} = [\vec{v}, (s_R^1, \ldots, s_R^N), (s_I^1, \ldots, s_I^N)] \in \mathcal{S}$, where $\vec{v}$ is the current positions of agents, $s_R^N \in R^n$ and $s_I^N \in I^n$ are the threat and information states at vertex v ∈ V. We denote $\vec{s_e} = [(s_R^1, \ldots, s_R^N), (s_I^1, \ldots, s_I^N)] \in \mathcal{S}_e$, as the state that captures the information and threat states at each position.
- $\mathcal{A}$ is the set of all joint actions. The agents select adjacent vertices to visit as an joint action.
- $\mathcal{O}$ is the set of joint observations. For current positions of the agents and the information and threat states of their current positions, we define a joint observation $o = \{\vec{v}, \{o^i | \forall v_i \in \vec{v}\}\} \in \mathcal{O}$, where $o^i = (s_R^i, s_I^i)$ is the observation of agent i.
- $\mathcal{T}$ is the set of conditional transition probabilities. We assume that $\vec{v}$ is deterministic and only determined by the destinations of the joint movement of agents. $\vec{s_e}$ follows a discrete-time Markov process with $\prod_{n=1}^{N} K_R^n K_I^n$ states.
- Ω is the set of observation probabilities. As an observation $\vec{o}$ is directly a part of some states, the observation probability $\Omega(\vec{o}|\vec{s}\,', \vec{a}) = 1$ if $\vec{o}$ is consistent with the corresponding part of $\vec{s}\,'$ and $\Omega(\vec{o}|\vec{s}\,', \vec{a}) = 0$ otherwise.
- r:$\mathcal{A} \times \mathcal{O} \rightarrow \mathbb{R}$ is a reward function. $r(\vec{a}, \vec{o})$ is the sum of the reward obtained by the agents which associates to the joint action $\vec{a}$ and observation $\vec{o}$ : $r(\vec{a}, \vec{o}) = \sum_{v_i \in \vec{v}} \left( \alpha \frac{1}{n_{v_i}} f^i(s_I^i) - (1-\alpha) c^i(s_R^i) \right)$ where $n_{vi}$ is the number of agents who are visiting $v_i$.

The objective of the agents is then to choose the movement actions sequentially to maximize the total expected reward accumulated over Tsteps.

Then, we note that, while the state variable described in Eqs (2) and (3) can be used to express the belief vector of the environment states for a multi-agent POMDP, the joint action space of the POMDP is the Cartesian product of the action and observation spaces of the individual agents. However, in so doing, the size of the joint action space and joint observation space grows exponentially with the number of agents $|\mathcal{M}|$, allowing only the smallest of problem instances to be solved. Instead, sequentially computing policies for individual agents as in our multi-agent algorithm avoids this problem of computing a joint policy for the team at the expense of solution quality. However, a bounded optimal of this multi-agent algorithm is guaranteed (we analyse this later).

Similar methods have been successfully used to solve multi-agent problems [3, 8]. As these formulations are different from our partially observable scenarios, a straightforward application of their methods is not possible. Hence, we consider how to sequentially compute policies for individual agents in partially observable problem using our online single-agent algorithm.

When sequentially computing policies for individual agents using our predictive heuristic, there implicitly exists an order in which the agents make actions; agent 1 completes D step actions of its best policy, agent 2 second, etc.. The expected future reward of a policy $\pi_D^i(t)$ of agent i is conditioned on position $v_i(t)$, belief vector Ψ(t) and the best policies of the previously computed policies of agents $\mathcal{M}_{-i}$ = {1,..., i−1}.

The best online patrolling policy for agent i in a multi-agent setting is recursively defined as:

$$\hat{\pi}_1^* = \arg\max_{\hat{\pi}_1} \mathcal{R}'(v_1(t), \Psi(t))$$

$$\hat{\pi}_2^* = \arg\max_{\hat{\pi}_2} \mathcal{R}'(v_2(t), \Psi(t), \hat{\pi}_1^*)$$

$$\vdots$$

$$\hat{\pi}_i^* = \arg\max_{\hat{\pi}_i} \mathcal{R}'(v_i(t), \Psi(t), \hat{\pi}_1^*, \ldots, \hat{\pi}_{i-1}^*) \quad \textbf{(12)}$$

where we use $\hat{\pi}_i^*$ denotes the best policy of agent i.

To ensure the reward function only takes into account the marginal reward value, we need to exclude double counting. There are two types of double counting. First, synchronous doublecounting, which occurs when two agents patrol the same cluster within the same time step. In this case the reward for patrolling the vertex is received twice. Second, asynchronous double counting, which occurs when agent i decides to visit vertex $v_n$ at $t_1$, and there was an action of visiting $v_n$ by agent j (j < i) at $t_2$ ($t_1 < t_2$) during the D horizon i.e., the agent j will visit vertex $v_n$ after agent i. For the situation where agent j visits vertex $v_n$ before agent i (i.e. $t_1 \geq t_2$), it has been accounted when calculating $\mathbb{E}[\hat{\mathcal{R}}(\pi_D(t))]$ in Eq (9).

Here, we show how to deal with the asynchronous double counting, i.e., agent i decides to visit vertex $v_n$ at $t_1$ and there was an action of visiting $v_n$ by agent j (j < i) at $t_2$ ($t_1 < t_2$) during the Dhorizon. Without loss of generality, we consider the situation that only $v_n$ in $\pi_D^i(t)$ of agent i has been visited by agent j. If more than one agent of $\mathcal{M}_{-i}$ = {1,..., i−1} has an action to visit $v_n$, we assume the time $t_2$ is nearest to $t_1$ (only the nearest one needs to be taken into account and this can be deduced from the transition Eq (10)). Based on this assumption, we can see that the expected information reward of agent j for visiting vertex $v_n$ is overestimated, as it is unaware that the i will reset the information at the time $t_1$. Thus, we introduce a penalty $\hat{p} \in \mathbb{R}^+$ for agent i that compensates for the reduction of reward of agent j, as follows:

$$\mathcal{R}_i'(v_i(t), \Psi(t), \hat{\pi}_1^*, \ldots, \hat{\pi}_{i-1}^*) = \mathbb{E}[\hat{\mathcal{R}}(\pi_D(t))] - \hat{p} \quad \textbf{(13)}$$

where $\mathbb{E}[\hat{\mathcal{R}}(\pi_D(t))]$ is the expected reward function defined in Eq (9), and $\hat{p}$ is the loss incurred by agent jthat will visit the vertex $v_n$ after i, which is defined as follows:

$$\hat{p} = \hat{r}_{\text{expected}} - \hat{r}_{\text{revised}} \quad \textbf{(14)}$$

where the $\hat{r}_{\text{expected}} \in \mathbb{R}^+$ is the expected reward that agent j computes for visiting vertex $v_n$ and the $\hat{r}_{\text{revised}}$ is the revised expected reward of agent j visiting vertex $v_n$ as computed by agent i considering only its action. We define the revised expected belief states at vertex $v_n$ and between time $[t_1+1,\ldots, t_2]$ are $\{\tilde{w}'^n(t_1+1), \ldots, \tilde{w}'^n(t_2)\}$, which are obtained by the transition Eq (10) based on the predictive belief state $\tilde{w}'^n(t_1)$ and action $a(t_1) = v_n$. Then the revised expected reward is as follows:

$$\hat{r}_{\text{revised}} = \gamma^{t_2}(\alpha \tilde{w}'^n_I(t_2)F^n - (1-\alpha)\tilde{w}'^n_R(t_2)L^n) \quad \textbf{(15)}$$

Now, using the algorithm to compute the policy of length D as before, we obtain an action for each individual agent. A team action is formed by combining these individual actions. This team action is not optimal, as the policy of agent i is computed greedily with respect to the policies of agents $\mathcal{M}_{-i}$. However, we can still bound the the performance guarantees compared with the policy obtained by searching the joint action space.

We use the theorem from [31] to obtain a bound on the value of the greedily selected policies:

**Theorem 2** Let $g:2^E \rightarrow \mathbb{R}$ be a non-decreasing sub-modular set function. The greedy algorithm that iteratively selects the element $e \in E$ that has the highest incremental value with respect to the previously chosen elements $I \in E$:

$$e = \arg\max_{e \in E \setminus I} g(e \cup I) - g(I) \quad \textbf{(16)}$$

until the resulting set I has the desired cardinality k, has an approximation bound $\frac{g(I_G)}{g(I^*)}$ at least $1-\left(\frac{k-1}{k}\right)^k$,where $I^* \in E$ is the optimal subset of cardinality k that maximises f.

For the number of agents $|\mathcal{M}|$ in our formulation, the approximation bound of the greedy algorithm is $1-\left(\frac{|\mathcal{M}|-1}{|\mathcal{M}|}\right)^{|\mathcal{M}|}$. It has been shown in [3] that this approximation bound is monotonically decreasing with $|\mathcal{M}|$, and thus as, for $|\mathcal{M}| \rightarrow \infty$, the multi-agent policy yields at least ≈ 63% of the reward obtained using the best policy that searches the joint policy space for $|\mathcal{M}|$ agents.

Having formulated the problem and designed both single-agent and multi-agent algorithms, we will evaluate our methods in the next section.

## Empirical Evaluation

To empirically evaluate our approach, we applied it to 10 and 15 agents continuously patrolling in a large graph, which contains 350 vertices and 529 edges. The online computing time limit is 0.5s because agents must decide which locations to visit at each time step within that time limit. As the single-agent algorithm in the paper can be seen as a special case of the multi-agent algorithm, we just present the results of the multi-agent algorithm here. In the aforementioned graph, we simulated two scenarios:

- **Scenario A:** we use the same Markov information and threat models for every vertex in the graph;
- **Scenario B:** we apply 3 different information and threat models to different vertices in the graph.

Notice that for Scenario A the information and threat models at different locations are homogeneous. However, as these information and/or threat are non-stationary, the information/or threat state are various among these locations. We use Scenario A aiming to capture the situation where the locations in the environment hold same types of information and threat. For Scenario B, the information and threat models at different locations are heterogeneous, i.e., different locations in the environment may hold various types of information and threat.

We set the parameters in reward function (i.e., Eq 1) and value function (i.e., Eq 6) as: the weight parameter $\alpha = 0.33$ and the discount factor $\gamma = 0.9$. More specifically, in Scenario A, we define the two Markov chains as follow:

$$P_R = \begin{bmatrix} 0.9 & 0.1 & 0 \\ 0.4 & 0.4 & 0.2 \\ 0.0 & 0.2 & 0.8 \end{bmatrix}$$

$$P_I = \begin{bmatrix} 0.8 & 0.1 & 0.1 & 0 & 0 \\ 0.2 & 0.7 & 0.0 & 0.1 & 0 \\ 0.1 & 0.1 & 0.7 & 0.1 & 0 \\ 0 & 0.0 & 0.1 & 0.8 & 0.1 \\ 0 & 0 & 0.0 & 0.1 & 0.9 \end{bmatrix}$$

Here, the transition function $P_R$ and $P_I$ satisfies monotonic assumption of Eq (7). For example, the first two rows in $P_R$ satisfy the constraints in Eq (8) that $0.9 \geq 0.4$, $0.9+0.1 \geq 0.4+0.4$ and $0.9+0.1+0.0 \geq 0.4+0.4+0.2$. The information and threat value vectors are respectively set as F= [0 1 2 3 4] and L = [0 1 2]. In Scenario B, we attribute several different Markov models to different vertices. A problem of 15 agents patrolling is shown in Fig 2, where the size of the circle of each location denotes the absolute value of instance reward of each vertex, the colour denotes its sign (black is positive and red is negative), the green circles are agents' current locations and "R" and "r" in lower right of each vertex denotes the threat state of this vertex is "2" and "1" respectively.

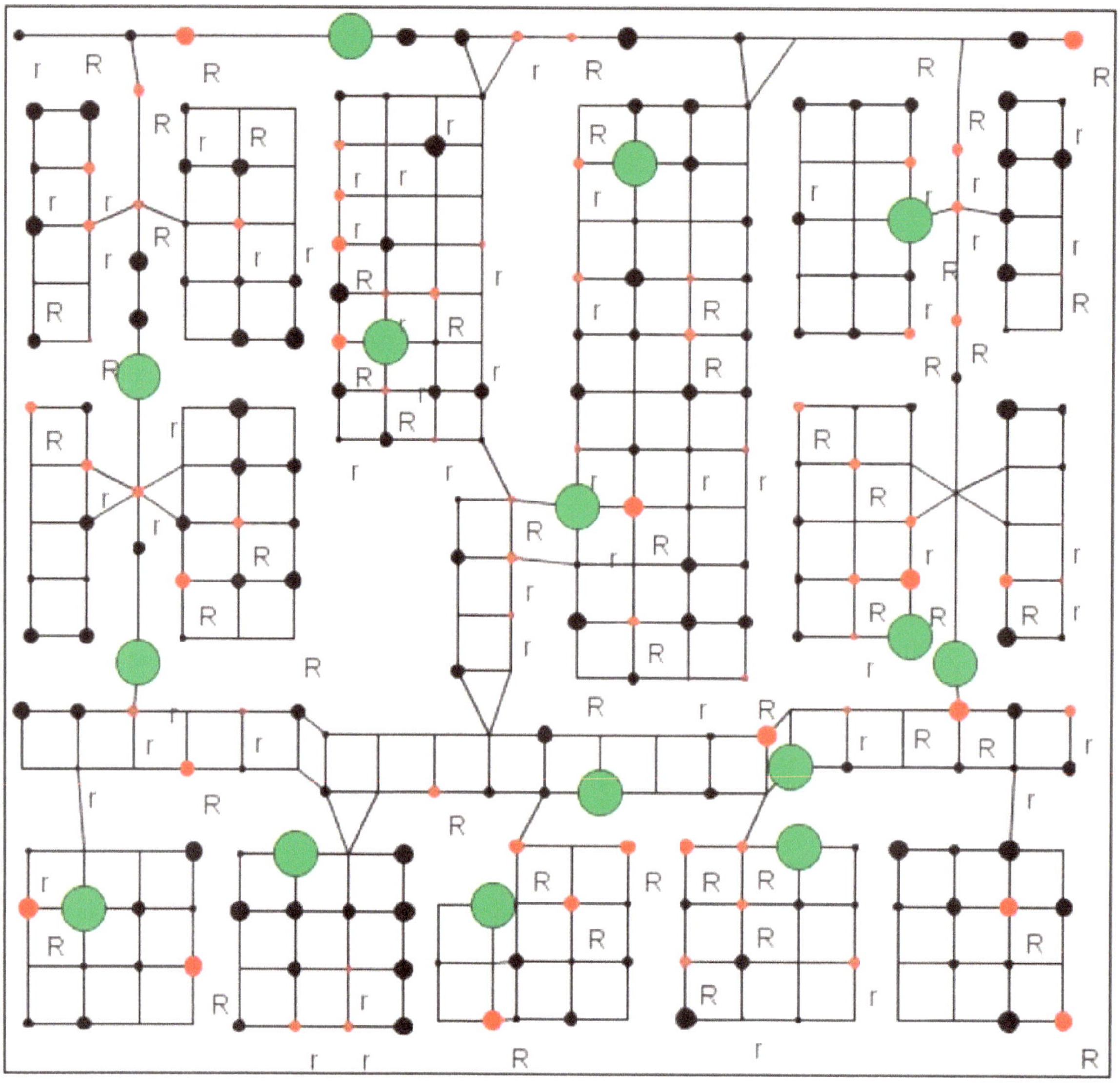

**Figure 2.** Scenario of 15 agents patrolling.

For standard POMDP solvers such as POMCP, the size of the joint action space and joint observation space grow exponentially with the number of agents, which makes them are intractable for our multi-agent patrolling problem with large number of actions and observations. Hence, we benchmark against a random algorithm (Random) and a baseline algorithm (Baseline), and measure the total reward of the information value and the damage suffered of agents using them. Specifically,

- **Random** moves the agents to a random location adjacent to the agents' current position.
- **Baseline** moves the agents to the adjacent location with the highest value in the next step. We assume the baseline algorithm sequentially computes policies for individual agents to avoid different agents selecting the same vertex, which is similar to PH-1.
- **PH-D** is our multi-agent patrolling algorithm, where D is the maximum horizon, i.e. the number of horizons we look ahead. We adjust maximum horizon D from the set {2,4,8} to investigate the extra computation involved for higher values of maximum horizon. We illustrated the results of our algorithms of different maximum horizon.

The initial locations of the agents are randomly distributed in the graph. Agents patrol continuously for 3000 time steps in the stochastically changing graph. For each scenario and each algorithm we ran 1000 rounds and plotted the results in Figs 3 and 4 where the error bars depict the 95% confidence intervals around the means. Non-overlapping error bars invalidate the null hypothesis with $\alpha = 0.05$. In both scenarios, Random performs poorly and its total reward never reaches more than 30% of the reward obtained by the other two algorithms. In Scenario A, both PH-8 and Baseline perform well, and PH-8 outperforms than baseline algorithm by at least 5%. However, for the graph with different Markov models in Scenario B, our algorithm is significantly better than all the other algorithms, and PH-8 outperforms the baseline algorithm by more than 44% for 10 agents and by 21% for 15 agents. In addition, with different maximum horizon D from {2,4,8}, the reward obtained by PH-D increases with D as well as its computation time increases with D exponentially. For $D > 8$, the computing time for each step is out of our time limit for online decision making. Thus, we can conclude that the use of our predictive heuristic in Ph-D has a significant impact on performance and that D can be adjusted to trade-off between quality and computation time while still outperforming baseline algorithms.

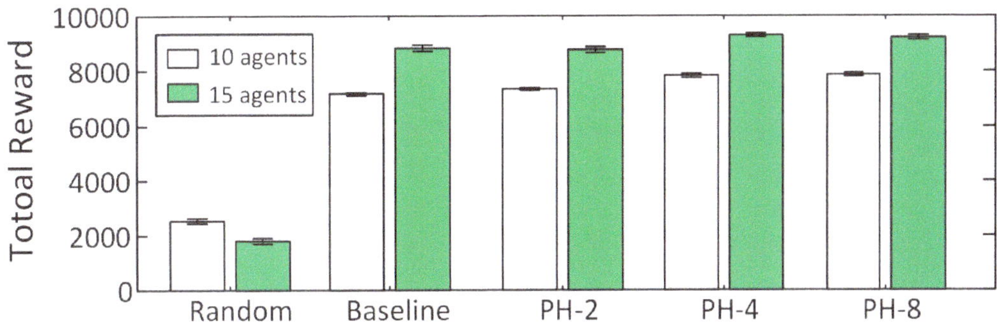


Figure 3. Rewards in Scenario A.

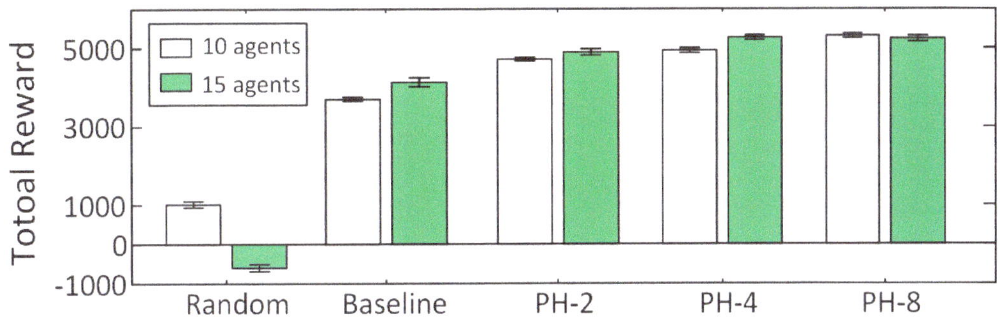


**Figure 4.** Rewards in Scenario B.

## CONCLUSION

In this paper, we developed an online multi-agent patrolling algorithm for large partial observable and stochastic environment where the information are distributed with threats. Specifically, a predictive heuristic is defined to evaluate the policies of looking ahead several steps. For the multi-agent algorithm, we extended the sequential policy computation method for individual agents to deal with partially observable problems. We empirically showed that for 10 agents in a large graph, our algorithm outperforms the baseline algorithm by more than 44%. In our future work, on the one hand, as this is the first algorithm for patrolling with uncertainty and threats, we plan to devise a better heuristic and algorithms that provide theoretical performance guarantees in our future work. One the other hand, as our formulation is a basic model of UAVs patrolling under uncertainty and threats, we will consider that the communication system of the agents may locally break down by suffering from harms or some agents may get destroyed due to cumulated harms.

## REFERENCES

1. Maza I, Caballero F, Capitán J, Martínez-de Dios J, Ollero A (2011) Experimental results in multi-uav coordination for disaster management and civil security applications. Journal of intelligent & robotic systems 61: 563–585. doi: 10.1007/s10846-010-9497-5.
2. Delle Fave FM, Rogers A, Xu Z, Sukkarieh S, Jennings NR (2012) Deploying the max-sum algorithm for decentralised coordination and task allocation of unmanned aerial vehicles for live aerial imagery collection. In: 2012 IEEE International Conference on Robotics and Automation. pp. 469–476.
3. Stranders R, de Cote EM, Rogers A, Jennings NR (2013) Near-optimal continuous patrolling with teams of mobile information gathering agents. Artif Intell 195: 63–105. doi: 10.1016/j.artint.2012.10.006.
4. Pöllänen R, Toivonen H, Peräjärvi K, Karhunen T, Ilander T, et al. (2009) Radiation surveillance using an unmanned aerial vehicle. Applied radiation and isotopes 67: 340–344. doi: 10.1016/j.apradiso.2008.10.008. pmid:19046635
5. Watts AC, Ambrosia VG, Hinkley EA (2012) Unmanned aircraft systems in remote sensing and scientific research: Classification and considerations of use. Remote Sensing 4: 1671–1692. doi: 10.3390/rs4061671.
6. Balakirsky S, Carpin S, Kleiner A, Lewis M, Visser A, Wang J, et al. (2007) Towards heterogeneous robot teams for disaster mitigation: Results and performance metrics from robocup rescue. Journal of Field Robotics 24: 943–967. doi: 10.1002/rob.20212.
7. Farinelli A, Rogers A, Petcu A, Jennings NR (2008) Decentralised coordination of low-power embedded devices using the max-sum algorithm. In: AAMAS. pp. 639–646.
8. Singh A, Krause A, Guestrin C, Kaiser WJ (2009) Efficient informative sensing using multiple robots. Journal of Artificial Intelligence Research 34: 707.
9. Schut M, Wooldridge M, Parsons S (2002) On partially observable mdps and bdi models. In: Foundations and Applications of Multi-Agent Systems, Springer. pp. 243–259.

10. Jennings NR (2000) On agent-based software engineering. Artificial intelligence 117: 277–296. doi: 10.1016/S0004-3702(99)00107-1.
11. Kaelbling LP, Littman ML, Cassandra AR (1998) Planning and acting in partially observable stochastic domains. Artificial intelligence 101: 99–134. doi: 10.1016/S0004-3702(98)00023-X.
12. Ny JL, Dahleh M, Feron E (2008) Multi-uav dynamic routing with partial observations using restless bandit allocation indices. In: American Control Conference, 2008. IEEE, pp. 4220–4225.
13. Agmon N, Kraus S, Kaminka GA, Sadov V (2009) Adversarial uncertainty in multi-robot patrol. In: IJCAI. pp. 1811–1817.
14. Basilico N, Gatti N (2011) Automated abstractions for patrolling security games. In: AAAI.
15. An B, Kempe D, Kiekintveld C, Shieh E, Singh SP, Tambe M, et al. (2012) Security games with limited surveillance. In: AAAI.
16. An B, Brown M, Vorobeychik Y, Tambe M (2013) Security games with surveillance cost and optimal timing of attack execution. In: AAMAS. pp. 223–230.
17. Vorobeychik Y, An B, Tambe M, Singh SP (2014) Computing solutions in infinite-horizon discounted adversarial patrolling games. In: ICAPS.
18. Qian Y, Haskell WB, Jiang AX, Tambe M (2014) Online planning for optimal protector strategies in resource conservation games. In: AAMAS. pp. 733–740.
19. Yost KA, Washburn AR (2000) The lp/pomdp marriage: Optimization with imperfect information. Technical report, DTIC Document.
20. Whittle P (1988) Restless bandits: Activity allocation in a changing world. Journal of Applied Probability 25: 287–298. doi: 10.2307/3214163.
21. Castanón DA (2005) Stochastic control bounds on sensor network performance. In: IEEE Conference on Decision and Control. IEEE, pp. 4939–4944.
22. Zois DS, Levorato M, Mitra U (2013) Energy-efficient, heterogeneous sensor selection for physical activity detection in wireless body area networks. IEEE Transactions on Signal Processing 61: 1581–1594. doi: 10.1109/TSP.2012.2236320.
23. Zhao Q, Tong L, Swami A, Chen Y (2007) Decentralized cognitive mac for opportunistic spectrum access in ad hoc networks: A pomdp framework. IEEE Journal on Selected Areas in Communications 25: 589–600. doi: 10.1109/JSAC.2007.070409.
24. Ouyang Y, Teneketzis D (2014) On the optimality of myopic sensing in multi-state channels. IEEE Transactions on Information Theory 60: 681–696. doi: 10.1109/TIT.2013.2288636.
25. Kurniawati H, Hsu D, Lee WS (2008) Sarsop: Efficient point-based pomdp planning by approximating optimally reachable belief spaces. In: Robotics: Science and Systems. volume 2008.
26. Silver D, Veness J (2010) Monte-carlo planning in large pomdps. In: NIPS. pp. 2164–2172.
27. Smallwood RD, Sondik EJ (1973) The optimal control of partially observable markov processes over a finite horizon. Operations Research 21: 1071–1088. doi: 10.1287/opre.21.5.1071.
28. Sandholm WH (2010) Orders of limits for stationary distributions, stochastic dominance, and stochastic stability. Theoretical Economics 5: 1–26. doi: 10.3982/TE554.
29. Keilson J, Kester A (1977) Monotone matrices and monotone markov processes. Stochastic Processes and their Applications 5: 231–241. doi: 10.1016/0304-4149(77)90033-3.
30. Pynadath DV, Tambe M (2002) The communicative multiagent team decision problem: Analyzing teamwork theories and models. Journal of Artificial Intelligence Research 16: 2002. doi: 10.1145/544862.544946
31. Nemhauser GL, Wolsey LA, Fisher ML (1978) An analysis of approximations for maximizing submodular set functions—i. Mathematical Programming 14: 265–294. doi: 10.1007/BF01588971.

CHAPTER 7

# A TIME-CRITICAL ADAPTIVE APPROACH FOR VISUALIZING NATURAL SCENES ON DIFFERENT DEVICES

Tianyang Dong[1,2], Siyuan Liu[1,2], Jiajia Xia[1], Jing Fan[1], Ling Zhang[2]

[1]School of Computer Science and Technology, Zhejiang University of Technology, Hangzhou, Zhejiang, China,

[2]Key Laboratory of Visual Media Intelligent Processing Technology of Zhejiang Province, Hangzhou, Zhejiang, China

## ABSTRACT

**To automatically adapt to various hardware and software environments on different devices, this paper presents a time-critical adaptive approach for visualizing natural scenes. In this method, a simplified expression of a tree model is used for different devices. The best rendering scheme is intelligently selected to generate a particular scene by estimating the rendering time of trees based on their visual importance. Therefore, this approach can ensure the reality of natural scenes while maintaining a constant frame rate for their interactive display. To verify its effectiveness and flexibility, this method is applied in different devices, such as a desktop computer, laptop, iPad and smart phone. Applications show that the method proposed in this paper can not only adapt to devices with different computing abilities and system resources very well but can also achieve rather good visual realism and a constant frame rate for natural scenes.**

## INTRODUCTION

With the development of the means to acquire plant data from natural scenes, such as with the use of photogrammetry and laser scanning, the accuracy of acquiring data and the speed of modeling natural scenes have improved rapidly, resulting in improvements in the details of natural scenes and increases in the complexity and data volume of scenes. However, the hardware for 3D display has not yet satisfied the increasing demand for large amounts of scene data. Even top-of-the-line hardware cannot display all scene data in real time. A variety of devices have appeared continuously due to the development of hardware; even devices of the same type have different system performances.

The tree is a typical and common plant in natural scenes. When modeling large-scale natural scenes, tree models with abundant details of geometric information are very large and also difficult to render rapidly [1]. The realistic rendering of trees uses large amounts of system resources and rendering time. Currently, 3D graphics acceleration technology has rapidly developed, but it can hardly meet the requirements of rendering complex natural scenes. In the real-time visualization of natural scenes, the challenge of automatically adapting to different requirements and software-hardware environments for generating satisfactory natural scenes has already become a hot topic for 3D interactive games, digital city and virtual forest simulation.

**Citation:** Dong T, Liu S, Xia J, Fan J, Zhang L. A Time-Critical Adaptive Approach for Visualizing Natural Scenes on Different Devices. Ji R, ed. PLoS ONE. 2015;10(2):e0117586. doi:10.1371/journal.pone.0117586.

An adaptive visualization system automatically adopts the appropriate condition to present the best visual effect based on its resources, equipment, and scene data. Most adaptive rendering acceleration methods mainly speed up the frame rate while they maintain the quality of images [2]. However, visual effect and rendering speed is a pair of interactional factors. The better the visual effect is, the lower the rendering speed is. On the contrary, if we reduce the rendering time, the visual effect will decrease accordingly. The adaptive visualization of interactive natural scenes should synthetically consider the computing power of the device, rendering time of the scene and the visual effect. The visual effect is properly reduced to ensure that the rendering of natural scenes can be completed within a limited time.

Because of the high complexity and large spatial spans of dynamic natural scenes, it takes a long time to render each frame of a natural scene. This delay leads to the visualization of natural scenes obviously lagging behind the movement of a user's point of view. The delay in visualization will lead to poor human visual perception of the natural scene. In addition, heterogeneity usually exists in the distribution of trees in a dynamic natural scene. The trees in some places may grow very densely, while the trees in other places may grow relatively sparsely. When the eye moves between the area of dense trees and that of sparse trees, there will be a sudden slowing down or a sudden speed up because of the unbalanced rendering time of the scene. The question of how to automatically adapt to the changes of the complex scenes within a specified time and dynamically adjust simulation information to generate the best natural scene is very important in the visualization of interactive natural scenes.

To automatically adapt to all types of devices that have different software and hardware configurations, this paper proposes a device-independent and time-critical adaptive visualization method for natural scenes. In this method, the best rendering strategy is selected by estimating the rendering time of trees based on their visual importance. To demonstrate the effectiveness of this method, it is applied on different devices, such as a desktop computer, laptop, Pad, and smart phone. Applications show that the method can adapt to devices of different computing powers and system resources, preserve the reality of natural scenes, achieve better visual realism and realize the persistent frame rate when roaming natural scenes.

## RELATED WORK

### Adaptive visualization

The mechanism of time-critical computing is that the computing process should be completed before the deadline. The system makes a comprehensive consideration of the resources and computing power currently available, as well as the time and quality requirements of computing. A simple calculation method and reduction of visual quality are adopted when it is necessary to ensure that the computing be completed in a specified time period [3].

To adaptively adjust to image quality while maintaining a stable and constant frame rate, Funkhouser proposed an adaptive algorithm for interactive frame rates in rendering complex virtual scenes through the management of discrete level of details (LODs) [4]. The algorithm performs a constrained optimization to choose a level of detail and rendering algorithm for each potentially visible object to generate the best possible image within the target frame time. Martin described the design and development of an adaptive environment for rendering of 3D models over networks [5]. This environment monitors the distribution of the available resources and selects the appropriate transmission and representation modalities to match these resources. Later Li et al. proposed a time-controlling algorithm for large-scale terrain rendering [6]; it guarantees that each frame is rendered at a preset time and is independent of the terrain or the viewpoint. XF Cao presented a generic solution for remote adaptive streaming and rendering of large terrain [7] that avoids loading irrelevant or redundant data and requests the most important data first. Park et al. proposed an adaptive rendering engine that renders high spatial resolution satellite images for streaming services on the web and manages large-scale satellite image data in current system resources [8]. Bao et al. proposed a framework for rendering large-scale forest scenes realistically and quickly that can automatically extract the level of detail (LOD) tree models [9]. To progressively render virtual scenes from a blurred state to a clear state, sequences of LOD models are transferred from coarse to fine. Reference [10] proposed a novel kd-tree based on a parallel adaptive rendering approach. A two-level framework for adaptive sampling in parallel is introduced to reduce the computation time and to lower the memory usage. In the field of digital city, Zhang applied an adaptive visualization method to the digital city models that can adapt to the changes of virtual scenes in the intended time and achieve good visual effect [11]. Shen et al. proposed an adaptive partitioning of image façade that used a series of horizontal or vertical planes to divide the input point cloud data and automatically extract high-level structure [12]. Scherzer D, et al. introduced the notion and main concepts of TC and described a general approach of image-space reprojection, which facilitates the reuse of shading information by the adjacent frames [13].

Most of the existing adaptive visualization methods are aimed at the stage where data are transmitted from the client's memory to the display terminal. Usually, the computing power is not the same in different clients; a large amount of data needs to be computed and time needs to be budgeted. The key technologies to address these issues are a gradual rendering mechanism, the compression and management of 3D models, the time-critical rendering algorithm and rendering efficiency optimization strategy.

### Simplified representation for 3D tree models

Irrespective of the type of device that is used, to achieve the reality of scene visualization in real-time, it is necessary to simplify 3D tree models and to reduce the complexity of scenes. Therefore, some researchers have put forward a series of simplification methods for 3D tree models. The basic idea is to gradually reduce the number of meshes and to preserve the appearance of tree models from the original fine tree models. The existing simplification methods of 3D tree models include geometry-based static simplification and view-dependent progressive representation.

The methods of geometry-based static simplification usually adopt pre-generated different LOD models to represent the same object. Compared with the original model, each model retains a certain level of detail. This method selects different resolution models to render in real time based on the viewpoint, stadia and the area size of models in a virtual scene. To simplify the geometric models with a large number of discrete leaves, a foliage simplification algorithm (FSA) was proposed by Remolar [14]. This algorithm iteratively selects two similar leaves to merge into one leaf for the sake of foliage simplification. Xiaopeng Zhang proposed a method for hierarchical union of organs, introducing the botanical knowledge about leaf phyllotaxy and flower anthotaxy (HUO) [15]. Then, Qingqiong et al. adopted a hybrid polygon model to represent leaves according to the morphological characteristics of leaves (broad leaf or conifer). The hybrid polygon/line model can achieve a higher level of geometric compression and can reduce the amount of meshes [16]. Guanbo Bao et al. proposed a new leaf modeling method that uses textures to simplify triangular meshes of leaves [17] so that the visual effect and model complexity can be balanced well; it can render a large scale forest containing thousands of trees in real time. The method of geometry-based static simplification is a good way to reduce the complexity of tree models. However, the simplified model still contains many meshes, and takes a long time to calculate illumination and real-time shadow, which still will be a heavy burden in the rendering process of large scale forest scenes. In a virtual ramble, the different resolution models in a continuously changing scene often occur as hopping. Hopping will affect the human vision perception of natural scenes [18].

The method of view-dependent progressive representation takes the locations between trees and viewpoints in virtual scenes into account and simplifies tree models in real time according to the dynamic viewpoint of a virtual scene. Cook et al. proposed a stochastic simplification of aggregate detail [19]. By using this method, scenes are rendered by randomly selecting a subset of the geometric elements and by altering those elements statistically to preserve the overall appearance of a virtual scene. The amount of simplification depends on a number of factors, including screen size, motion blur, and depth of field. Gumbau presented a view-dependent multi-resolution model for the foliage of the trees [20]. This method interactively reduces the amount of geometric patches that represents the foliage by using a view-dependent multi-resolution scheme. These existing methods of view-dependent progressive representation can solve the hopping problem, but they cannot reflect human vision perception of tree models that can embody topological semantics in a dynamic simulation.

## METHODS

### Simplified Representation of Tree Models for Different Devices

The geometric representation and simplification technology based on LOD can effectively reduce the surface details of models and generate multi-resolution LOD models. However, the simplified model still contains many meshes, and it needs a long time to calculate illumination and real-time shadow. That delay is a heavy burden on the rendering process of a natural scene. However, the image-based rendering method can be used to solve this problem. It renders natural scenes under any viewpoint through the blending of multiple images [21]. It has a great simplification degree because the complexity of models is only related to the number of sampling images, and it has nothing to do with the complexity of original models [22]. However, due to the limitations of image resolution, the models will be fuzzy when observed from a close distance. It is difficult to cope with dynamic changes in light conditions, and the method cannot generate the dynamic effects of natural scenes [23]. Therefore, this paper combines the visual perception features of tree models and adopts a hybrid representation method of geometry and image for different devices to achieve the balance between model simplification and visual quality.

Based on the different performances of all types of devices, this paper uses a hybrid representation method of geometry and image to construct a tree model. This method can achieve the rapid simplification of tree models and effectively compress the data of models, thus reducing the complexity of a natural scene. Because of different organizational structure, texture color and material properties between the trunk and the crown of tree models, trees can be separated into two different parts: the trunk and branch and the leaf. The hybrid representation method of geometry and image for 3D tree models is shown in Fig. 1.

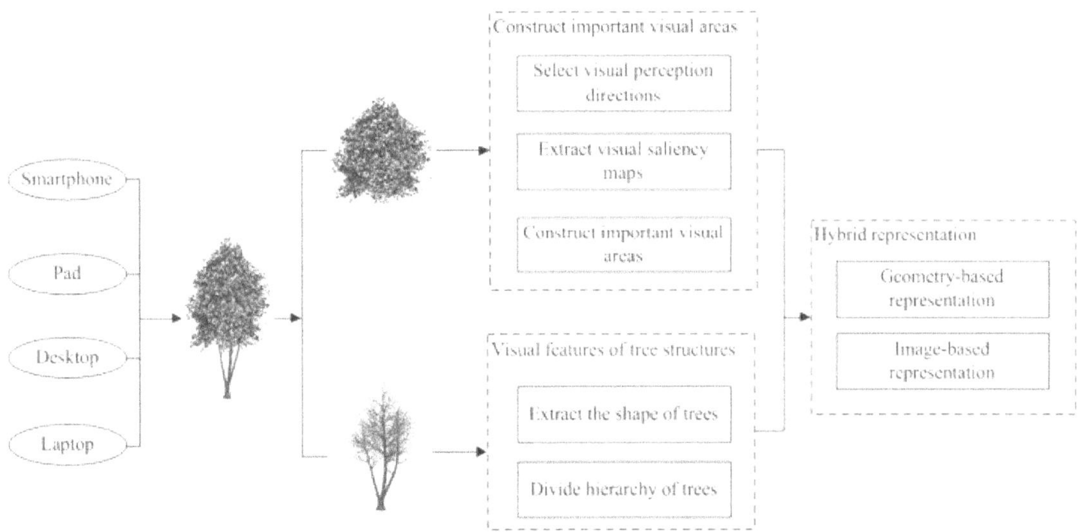


**Figure 1:** Hybrid representation of a tree model.

Tree models are represented using two different parts: topological structure and crown. Only the trunks and main branches of the trees are retained to maintain topological structure, while the branches, twigs and other levels of detail are pruned. As for the simplification of the crown, the saliency map is extracted from the original image for every visual perception direction in turn, and the crown is divided into several important visual areas and unimportant visual areas based on the visual attention model. Furthermore, two different approaches are adopted to represent tree models: geometric representation and image-based representation.

As for the trunk and branches, we divide different hierarchies of tree models based on its unique topological semantics, including trunk, main branches, branches, twigs and so on. To simplify the tree models, we only retain the trunks and main branches of trees, while the branches, twigs and other levels of detail are pruned. As for the crown, based on the visual attention model [24], we select several typical visual perception directions according to the space structure of tree models that form the sequence of the original images used in visual perception. We extract the saliency map from the original image for every visual perception direction in turn and divide the crown into important visual areas and unimportant visual areas.

Finally, based on the partition of the important visual areas for the crown, this paper adopts a heterogeneous simplification method to achieve the geometric simplification of the crown. To preserve the visual perception of tree models and to maintain the important visual leaves with high visual attention, this paper uses the geometric culling method. Textures are used to represent the unimportant visual leaves, greatly reducing the amount of geometric data of unimportant visual leaves and decreasing the complexity of the crown.

However, considering the difference in computing power and system resources between different devices, we adjust the percentage of geometry representation and image representation for the tree models adaptively, according to the graphics hardware performance.

Fig. 2 displays ten Platanus orientalis models with different levels of detail. The geometric patch numbers of the Platanus orientalis models in Fig. 2a are 6563, 4250, 2137, 925 and 312. However, we use more images to represent the Platanus orientalis models in Fig. 2b, and their geometric patch numbers greatly decrease. The number of geometric patches for Platanus orientalis models in Fig. 2b is 356, 178, 96, 58 and 9. As for the equipment with better graphics hardware configurations, such as desktop computers, we use more meshes to represent tree models, such as the Platanus orientalis models shown in Fig. 2a. As for mobile devices, the proportion of image representation for tree models is higher, and we will adopt the Platanus orientalis models (S1 Dataset) as shown in Fig. 2b.

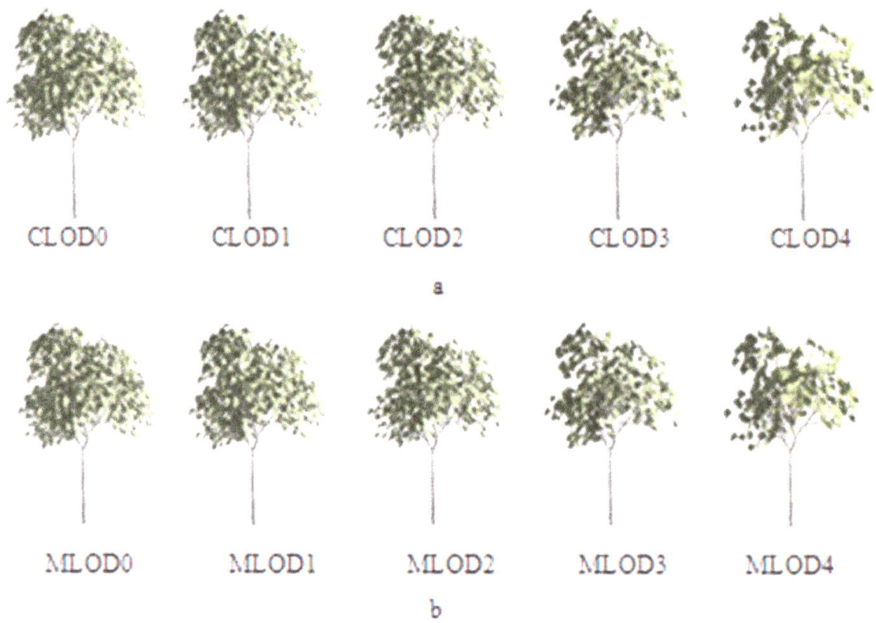


**Figure 2:** LOD models of Platanus orientalis.

a. LOD models for a computer. These models with fine details may consume more rendering time and resources, but they can describe more details of trees. They can be used on computers. b. LOD models for mobile devices. These models are simplified by using LOD technology because mobile devices usually have worse performance than computers.

## Dynamic Culling Based On Visual Importance of Leaves

The existing tree models usually contain a large amount of geometric detail to represent their elaborate shapes and complex structure. Currently, many 3D graphics acceleration technologies have been proposed, but they cannot render complex virtual scenes in real time. Therefore, irrespective of the device used to visualize natural scenes, we must dynamically cull tree models to further improve the rendering efficiency and real-time roaming speed.

This paper uses a geometry culling method for the simplification of important visual leaves to reduce the number of meshes of the crown. For preserving the visual perception of pruned leaves, we adopt a culling equation, as shown in Formula (1), to dynamically prune the leaves [25].

$$\varepsilon(l) = k1*dis(l,c) + k2*\cos(l,cam) + k3*area(l)$$

**(1)**

where $l$ is a leaf of tree model, c is the geometric center point of crown, and cam is the visual perception direction. *dis(l, c)*, *cos(l, cam)*, *area(l)* are the culling factors, where dis *(l, c)*represents the distance between the geometric center of leaf and crown, *cos(l, cam)*represents the orientation angle between the normal vector of leaf and the visual perception direction, *area(l)* represents the geometric area of leaves. The value of each factor is between 0 and 1, and $k_{1+k2+k3} = 1$. In this paper, the weight values of $k_{1,k2,k3}$ are 0.3, 0.4 and 0.3, respectively.

In the dynamic culling of leaves based on visual importance, the method first calculates culling factors for each leaf and obtains the value of *(l)* according to Formula (1). Then, it sorts the important visual leaves in descending order according to the value of *(l)* and stores the information of sorted leaves into a queue. Finally, based on the distance *d* between the viewpoint and tree models, the rendering rate λ of the important visual leaves is calculated, as shown in Formula (2).

$$\lambda = \frac{1}{Ln(d)}$$

**(2)**

where *Ln(d)* is the natural logarithm,*d* is the distance between the viewpoint and the geometric center of tree model. If the number of important visual leaves is *N*, it will dynamically render the first *N* leaves in the sorted queue. Thus, it can decrease the geometric data of tree models and improve rendering speed [25].

Some leaves are pruned after the above operation, which makes the crown appear sparse and decreases the density of leaves. To preserve the density of leaves and the area similarity of the crown, it is necessary to enlarge the areas of other remaining leaves and to maintain the crown areas. If the number of important visual leaves is *N*, the average area of leaves is *a*, and the sum of area is *S* = *Na* For maintaining the crown areas, if the average area of leaves after pruning is *a*', the equation *Na* = *Na*' is established. Then, the area of leaves after pruning is $a' = \frac{1}{\lambda}a$. According to the comparison of the experimental results [25], if the area of leaves after pruning is $a' = \frac{1}{\sqrt{\lambda}}a$, it will be better than the former. So, the area s' of all leaves after pruning will enlarge to $\frac{1}{\sqrt{\lambda}}$, as shown in Formula (3).

$$s' = \frac{1}{\sqrt{\lambda}}s$$

**(3)**

where  is the rendering rate, *s*' is the area of all leaves after pruning, and *s* is the area of all leaves before pruning.

The geometry culling method of leaves in this paper calculates the culling factors of important visual leaves and sorts them according to the value of visual perception importance. Then, it dynamically prunes the leaves according to the distance between the viewpoint and the tree models. With the viewpoint observing the trees from near-field to far-field, the number of leaves will decrease, and the area of leaves will gradually enlarge, and vice versa.

## Adaptive Visualization of Natural Scenes

This section mainly discusses how to automatically adapt and generate a satisfactory natural scene on different devices. There are some key technologies, such as model selection, the estimation of rendering time, and the evaluation of object importance.

### Selection of Tree Models

When rendering the same data on different devices, there will be a difference in rendering speed because of the differences in system performance (such as graphic card, memory, CPU, and operating system). Therefore, the original configuration parameters will no longer be applicable, and they should be reconfigured.

The traditional method of model selection chooses the appropriate models for trees according to the distance to a viewpoint [17]. When the distance to a viewpoint is near, the refined 3D models are used to render. Because of the limit of the visual field, there are not too many trees that are rendered at the same time. Usually, there will be about two or three refined 3D tree models. When the distance to a viewpoint is far away, the simplified geometric LOD models are used. And the farther the tree is to the viewpoint, the rougher the LOD model is. When the distance to a viewpoint is much farther, the visual perception of individual trees is not so obvious, and textures are adopted to represent trees, generally using billboard technology. If there are n + 1 different resolutions of LOD models for each tree, from the highest resolution to the lowest, each model is named as *CLOD0, CLOD1...CLODn.* The models used on mobile devices are named as *MLOD0, MLOD1...MLODn*. Which model is selected depends on the distance to a viewpoint in a virtual scene, as shown in Formula (4).

$$M = \begin{cases} CLOD_0 \, or MLOD_0, 0 \le d \le d_1 \\ CLOD_1 \, or MLOD_1, d_1 \le d \le d_2 \\ \vdots \\ CLOD_n \, or MLOD_n, d_n \le d \end{cases}$$

**(4)**

Where $0 \le d_{1 \le d2 \le \ldots \le dn}$ and $d_i$ ($i$ = 1, 2, ..., $n$) represents the threshold of model selection, and *d* represents the distance from the tree to the viewpoint.

### Estimation of Rendering Time

To reduce the instability of the rendering time of natural scenes and to make the rendering time to be in a reasonable range of user-specified time, it must estimate the rendering time of a virtual scene.

At present, most of the researches on rendering time estimations of geometric objects are free of textures. Funkhouser [4] presented a linear expression for rendering time of a geometric object that contains a vertex number, polygon number and pixel number. Wimmer and Schmalstieg [26] noted that the expression proposed by Funkhouser only gives the lower limit of the rendering time and that the actual rendering time is related to vertex transformation and rasterization. Therefore, the time estimation function is a linear expression of the polygon vertex number and the pixel number.

With the increase of natural scene complexity, an increasing proportion of texture is used in the visual model of a natural scene. If the resolution of tree texture is much higher, the conversion time and scheduling time in a graphics card will not be ignored. To obtain a more accurate estimation time, the rendering time of a 3D model is expressed as [27]:

$$T = c_1 \times v\_num + c_2 \times t\_size \tag{5}$$

where *v_num* is the polygons of tree model, *t_size* is the amount of textures needed to be rendered, $c_1$ and $c_2$ depend on the hardware and software environment of a device and are adaptively adjusted according to the device.

In the process of estimating the rendering time for a natural scene, it first selects n trees of the same level. Then, it computes the amount of polygons, textures and rendering time of the selected n trees. The information of tree *i* is ($T_{i,\ v\_num_i}$, $t\_size_i$). For tree *i*, it can get the rendering time $T_i$ by using the amount of polygons ($v\_num_i$), and the amount of textures ($t\_size_i$), as shown in Formula (6).

$$\begin{cases} T_1 = c_1 \times v\_num_1 + c_2 \times t\_size_1 \\ T_2 = c_1 \times v\_num_2 + c_2 \times t\_size_2 \\ \vdots \\ T_{n-1} = c_1 \times v\_num_{n-1} + c_2 \times t\_size_{n-1} \\ T_n = c_1 \times v\_num_n + c_2 \times t\_size_n \end{cases} \tag{6}$$

Therefore, *n* trees will obtain n equations, and any two equations can obtain a set of $c_1$ and $c_2$. Take $T_i$ and $T_j$ as an example, we can get $c_1 = (T_i \times t_size_{j}_T_j \times t_size_j)/(t_size_{j \times v_numi - t_size \times v_numj})$and. $c_2 = (T_i \times v\_num_{j - Tj \times v\_numi})/(t\_size_{i \times v\_numi - t\_sizej \times v\_numi})$

For the applicability of this evaluation method, this paper computes any two equations, and calculates the average values of $c_1$ and $c_2$. The average values of $c_1$ and $c_2$ can be represented as Formula (7) and Formula (8) respectively.

$$c_1 = \frac{\sum_{i=1}^{n-1}\sum_{j=i+1}^{n} \frac{(T_i \times t\_size_j - T_j \times t\_size_i)}{(t\_size_j \times v\_num_i - t\_size_i \times v\_num_j)}}{C_n^2} \tag{7}$$

$$c_2 = \frac{\sum_{i=1}^{n-1}\sum_{j=i+1}^{n} \frac{(T_i \times v\_num_j - T_j \times v\_num_i)}{(t\_size_i \times v\_num_j - t\_size_j \times v\_num_i)}}{C_n^2} \tag{8}$$

where $C_n^2$ means the combination of selecting two trees from n trees. When rendering a natural scene, it collects the monitoring data of rendering time. The time estimation function is dynamically adjusted according to the collected monitoring data, and making the time estimation more accurate. The amended *ci* (*i* = 1, 2) is defined in Formula (9).

$$c_i' = (1 + \beta \times \frac{t_{act} - t_{est}}{t_{est}}) \times c_i \tag{9}$$

where $t_{est}$ is the estimated time of all trees in view frustum, $t_{act}$ is the actual rendering time needed, and  is a value between 0 and 1, which reduces the volatility of this feedback algorithm [27].

To evaluate the error between estimated time and actual time [27], suppose the estimated time is *t_est* and the actual time is *t_act*, then the error between them is defined in Formula (10).

$$error = \frac{|t\_act - t\_est|}{t\_act} \tag{10}$$

Table 1 presents the comparison between the estimated time and the actual time when there are 30 trees in view frustum. The testing is conducted on a desktop computer with the following configuration: Intel(R) Core(TM) i3 CPU 550@3.20GHz, 512M graphic card memory, 2G memory. In Table 1, the first column is the five moments sampled when roaming in a natural scene, ET is the estimation time, AT is the actual time, and error is the error between them. The value of error is controlled in a reasonable range, demonstrating that the method of estimating rendering time proposed in this paper is feasible. Table 2 and Table 3 are the comparison of the iPhone and iPad.

**Table 1:** Comparison between estimated time and actual time on computers (unit: s)

| Time | ET*(s)* | AT*(s)* | error |
|---|---|---|---|
| t1 | 0.0695 | 0.0769 | 9.6% |
| t2 | 0.0657 | 0.0603 | 8.9% |
| t3 | 0.0616 | 0.0679 | 9.3% |
| t4 | 0.0687 | 0.0729 | 5.7% |
| t5 | 0.0636 | 0.0696 | 8.6% |

Table 2: Comparison between estimated time and actual time on the iPhone (unit: s)

| Time | ET*(s)* | AT*(s)* | error |
|---|---|---|---|
| t1 | 0.0598 | 0.059 | 1.4% |
| t2 | 0.0599 | 0.066 | 9.2% |
| t3 | 0.0599 | 0.062 | 3.4% |
| t4 | 0.0600 | 0.066 | 9.1% |
| t5 | 0.0601 | 0.065 | 7.5% |

**Table 3:** Comparison between estimated time and actual time on the iPad (unit: s)

| Time | ET(s) | AT(s) | error |
|---|---|---|---|
| t1 | 0.0626 | 0.070 | 10.5% |
| t2 | 0.0684 | 0.075 | 8.8% |
| t3 | 0.0674 | 0.071 | 5.1% |
| t4 | 0.0660 | 0.072 | 8.3% |
| t5 | 0.0695 | 0.075 | 7.3% |

## Evaluation of Tree Importance

The evaluation of tree importance is a crucial aspect to realize adaptive visualization. When the estimated rendering time exceeds the specified time, it can reduce the LOD levels for relatively unimportant trees to shorten rendering time. When the estimated rendering time is less than the specified time, it can improve the LOD levels for important trees to increase rendering time, thus making the rendering time stable.

The tree importance calculation based on the distance is simple and efficient. Trees near the viewpoint have a higher importance, while those far from the viewpoint have a lower importance. However, in actual visual effects, the detail degree of a tree is not only related to its viewpoint location but also related to visual angle. The area in the direct sight is distinct, and the area observed out of the direct sight is relatively vague. As shown in Fig. 3a, there are two trees, P1 and P2, and they have the same distance to the viewpoint. The blue dotted line represents the distance between the tree and the viewpoint, and the sight direction is along VP1. Obviously, the level of detail for tree P1 should be higher than that of tree P2. That is, with the same distance to the viewpoint, the bigger the visual angle is, the less detail it has. Trees near the sight direction have sensitive visual effects and more details.

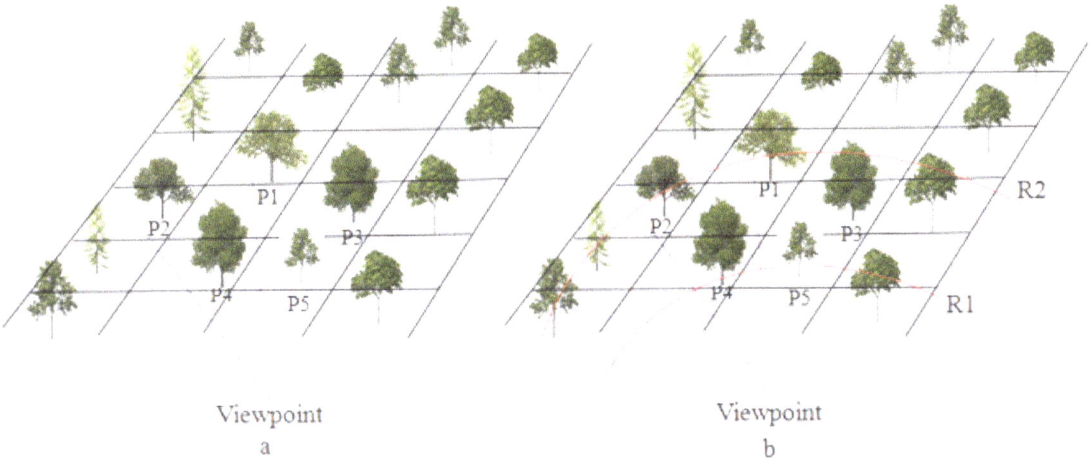


**Figure 3:** Evaluation of tree importance.

a. Our method to evaluate tree importance. The level of detail for a tree is related to viewpoint, tree position, visual angle and tree size. P4 has a higher level of LOD than P3 because P3 has a longer distance to viewpoint. P1 has the same distance to viewpoint as P2, but P1 has a higher level of LOD because it has a smaller visual angle. Although P4 and P5 have the same distance to viewpoint and the same visual angle, P4 has a higher level of LOD than P5 because P4 has a larger crown. b. Comparison with traditional LOD. Using traditional LOD method, P1 and P3 between range R1 and R2 have lower LOD level than P5, which is different from the result of our method.

Compared with traditional LOD, the method proposed in this paper to evaluate the importance of tree can achieve better visual effects. For the traditional LOD, trees in the range of R1 usually have more details than those trees between the range R1 and R2, as shown in Fig. 3b. However, P1 and P3 between range R1 and R2 can be seen more easily than P5 in the range of R1. Therefore, to take the visual angle and size of a tree into consideration is necessary.

This paper uses the projection area of tree crown to measure the size of a tree. As shown inFig. 3a, there are two trees, P4 and P5, which are assumed to have the same distance to the viewpoint and the same visual angle. Because the tree crown of P4 is larger than that of P5, the visual effect of P4 is obviously better than P5. Therefore, this paper synthetically considers the influences of distance, visual angle and the size of tree crown to express visual effect [27]. A determiner factor related to visual angle is introduced, that is, *factor* = tan . The formula for the improved measurement of tree importance is as follows:

$$I = \frac{B}{\alpha_1(1+\tan\theta) \times d + \alpha_2 \times \frac{100}{s}} \quad (11)$$

where $_1$ and $_2$ are weight coefficients, *B* is the benchmark value of importance, *d* represents the actual distance of a tree from the viewpoint and *s* represents the projection area of tree crown. The value of *B* is calculated from a tree (called a benchmark tree) in the importance-critical area, as shown in Formula (12).

$$B = \alpha_1(1 + \tan\theta_0) \times d_0 + \alpha_2 \times \frac{100}{s_0} \quad \textbf{(12)}$$

where $_0$ is the visual angle of the benchmark tree, $d_0$ is its distance to the viewpoint, and $s_0$is the crown size of the benchmark tree. The larger the value of $I$ is, the greater the visual importance is. When the value of $I$ is more than 1, it means that the visual effect of this tree is more important, and it is not allowed to reduce its LOD level.

Take tree P1 as the benchmark tree and its importance value as 1; for the marked five trees inFig. 3a, their importance values are shown in Table 4, where $d$ is the distance to viewpoint, is visual angle, $s$ is the projection area of the tree crown, and $I$ is the visual importance value.

**Table 4:** Importance information (α1 = 0.6, α2 = 0.4)

| Tree position | d | θ | S | I |
|---|---|---|---|---|
| P1 | 15 | 0 | 6 | 1 |
| P2 | 15 | 30 | 6 | 0.75 |
| P3 | 15 | 45 | 9 | 0.69 |
| P4 | 9 | 25 | 11 | 1.35 |
| P5 | 9 | 25 | 5 | 0.98 |

To verify this evaluation method of tree importance have better visual effects, this paper provides a comparison about the temporal coherence with traditional LOD method. Fig. 4ashows the scene rendered by using traditional LOD method at viewpoint p1, and Fig. 4b shows the same scene after walking forward at viewpoint p2 (S2 Dataset). The scene rendered by using the method proposed in this paper is shown in Fig. 5. Fig. 5a shows the scene at viewpoint p1, and Fig. 5b shows the same scene as Fig. 4b at viewpoint p2. According to these scenes, the LOD level of Tree 1 and Tree2 in Fig. 4a is LOD2, while the LOD level of Tree 1 and Tree2 in Fig. 4b is LOD1. However, the LOD level of Tree 1 and Tree2 is LOD1, no matter in Fig. 5a and Fig. 5b. That means our method can keep better temporal coherence than traditional LOD method, especially for the important objects.

**Figure 4:** Natural scene of traditional LOD.

a. Scene at viewpoint p1 with traditional LOD. With traditional LOD method, at viewpoint p1, the LOD level of Tree 1 and Tree2 is LOD2. b. Scene at viewpoint p2 with traditional LOD. At viewpoint p2, the LOD level of Tree 1 and Tree 2 is LOD1.

**Figure 5:** Natural scene of our LOD method.

a. Scene at viewpoint p1 with our method. With our method, the LOD level of Tree 1 and Tree 2 is LOD1. b. Scene at viewpoint p2 with our method. At viewpoint p2, the LOD level of Tree 1 and Tree 2 is LOD1.

## Time-Critical Adaptive Visualization

Because of the specified time, not all tree models will be rendered using the most elaborate LOD model in a natural scene. The proper LOD model is selected for each tree by using the device-independent and time-critical adaptive visualization algorithm. To render natural scenes within a limited time, the model decreases the LOD level of some tree models to reduce rendering time. Certainly we will not decrease the LOD of the trees that have important visual effect [27]. The workflow of the device-independent and time-critical adaptive visualization approach is shown in Fig. 6.

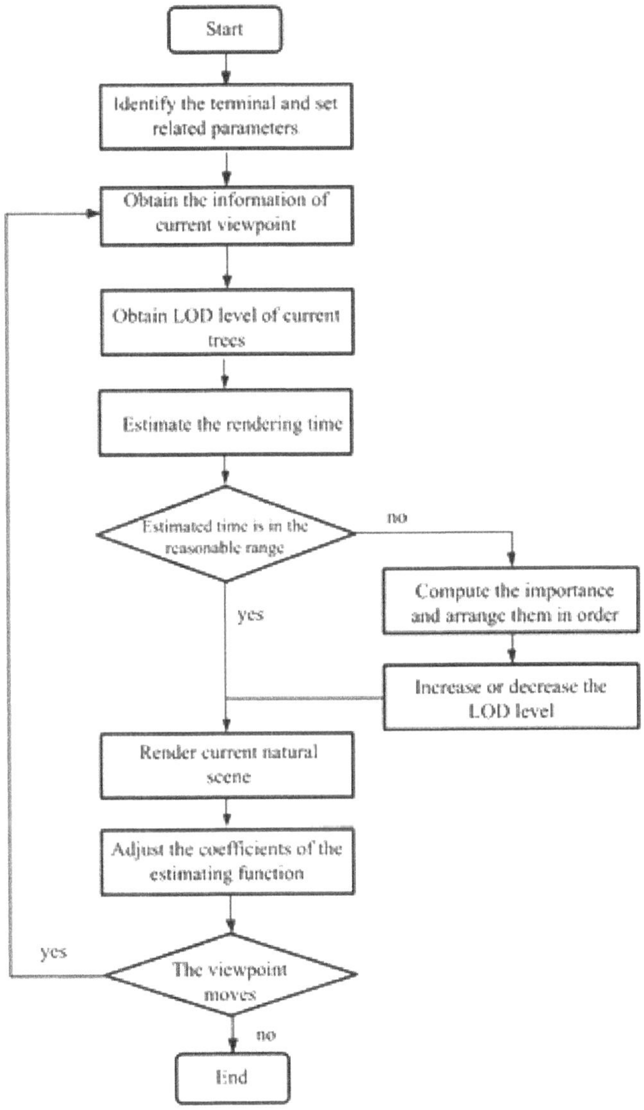


**Figure 6:** Workflow of time-critical adaptive visualization

This adaptive visualization approach chooses an initial set of tree models with different LODs according to the device type and then estimates the rendering time of the trees in view frustum under the current level of detail. If the estimated rendering time is not in the reasonable range of a specified time, it will adjust the level of LOD for tree models and render natural scenes using the appropriate level of detail.

The steps of the adaptive visualization approach are as follows:

1. Step1: Identify the types of device and set the corresponding parameters for the device.
2. Step2: Obtain the viewpoint information when the roaming begins, and the LOD level of the trees is obtained by the distance to the viewpoint.
3. Step3: Estimate the rendering time of the trees in view frustum under the current LOD level.
4. Step4: Adjust the models of trees. If the estimated rendering time is in the reasonable range of a specified time, the scene is rendered directly. If the estimated time is less than the reasonable range of a specified time, it arranges the trees in the order of importance value from large to small, and increases the LOD level of trees in turns, until all trees are rendered or until all trees reach the highest LOD level. If the estimation time is more than the reasonable range of a specified time, it arranges the trees in the order of importance value from small to large and decreases the LOD level of trees in turns, until the estimated rendering time approximates the specified time.
5. Step5: Render the natural scene using the appropriate LOD level described in Step 4 and collect the monitoring data of the actual rendering time. The coefficients of the time estimation function are adjusted according to the monitoring data, thus improving the accuracy of the time estimation algorithm.
6. Step6: Judge whether the viewpoint moves. If the viewpoint moves, then jump to Step 1 and obtain the information of the current viewpoint. If the viewpoint does not move, then the roaming is finished.

# RESULTS AND DISCUSSION

## Rendering Framework of Interactive Natural Scenes

The interactive natural scene simulation system in this paper realizes the adaptive rendering on different devices. This system automatically adapts to different user requirements and device configurations to generate satisfied visual results. The system framework is shown in Fig. 7 and is divided into three levels: user interaction layer, system core layer, and data layer. The application of hierarchical structure can make the system logic level more clear. Different modules interact with each other by transmitting data and messages; this interaction will reduce dependences and coupling relationships.

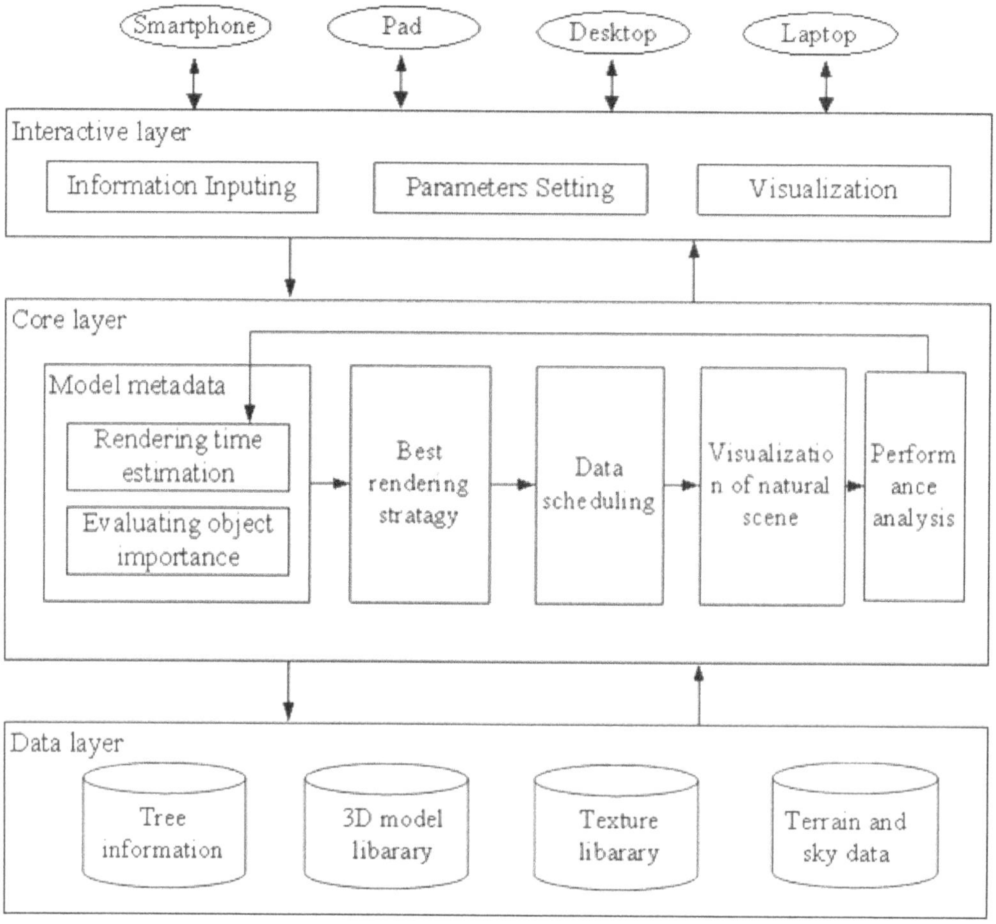


**Figure 7:** Rendering framework of natural scene.

The framework includes three layers: interactive layer, core layer and data layer. In the interactive layer, users set initial data based on their requirements and roam virtual scenes. In the core layer, the system adjusts the rendering strategy according to the data set in the interactive layer and then renders natural scenes. The tree models, textures and other data used in the core layer are all stored in the data layer.

Interactive layer: this layer provides the interactive functions between the system and the users, including data initialization, display of natural scenes and virtual roaming. Users initialize the parameters for complex natural scenes through this layer, including the number of trees in the scene, planting mode, expected frame rate, etc. After the initialization, it renders the initial natural scene according to these parameters, and users can roam in the natural scene.

Core layer: this layer mainly includes a rendering time estimation module, object importance evaluation module, best rendering strategy module, data scheduling module, visualization module and performance analysis module. The rendering time estimation module is used to estimate the rendering time and to provide the time information to the rendering strategy module. The object importance evaluation module computes the importance of each object for choosing the appropriate level of models. According to the estimated rendering time of each tree model and the results of the object importance evaluation, the best rendering strategy module selects an appropriate model level for each object in the case of total rendering time within the limited time and provides the best visual effect possible. The data scheduling module uses viewpoint parameters to retrieve model data within the current sight ranges from multi-scale databases in real time. The visualization module renders the trees on a 3D terrain based on their settled location after the calculation and realizes the visualization of complex natural scenes in the computer. The performance analysis module collects the monitoring data of every frame and provides an analysis data set for the time evaluation module, subsequently transmitting the analysis results to the rendering time evaluation module.

Data layer: this layer mainly focuses on data access logic (data definition, updating, management, and maintenance, etc). It is used to separate data access and data source and mainly includes the tree information, terrain data, 3D tree model library, texture library, etc. The tree information includes the position, species, heights, ages, biomass and diameter at breast height, etc. A 3D model library stores all tree models with different levels of detail. The texture library includes all types of textures, including that of the sky, landscape and trees.

## Simulation Experiment and Discussion

The tree models for applications on different devices are shown in Fig. 8 and Fig. 9; they are Lycium barbarum and Quercus pyrenaica, respectively. The models in Fig. 8a and Fig. 9a are used on computers, and those in Fig. 8b and Fig. 9b are used on mobile devices, such as the iPhone and the iPad. Each tree has 8 different LODs ordered by the resolution from high to low. The subtitle is the level of LOD and the number of polygons for the models.

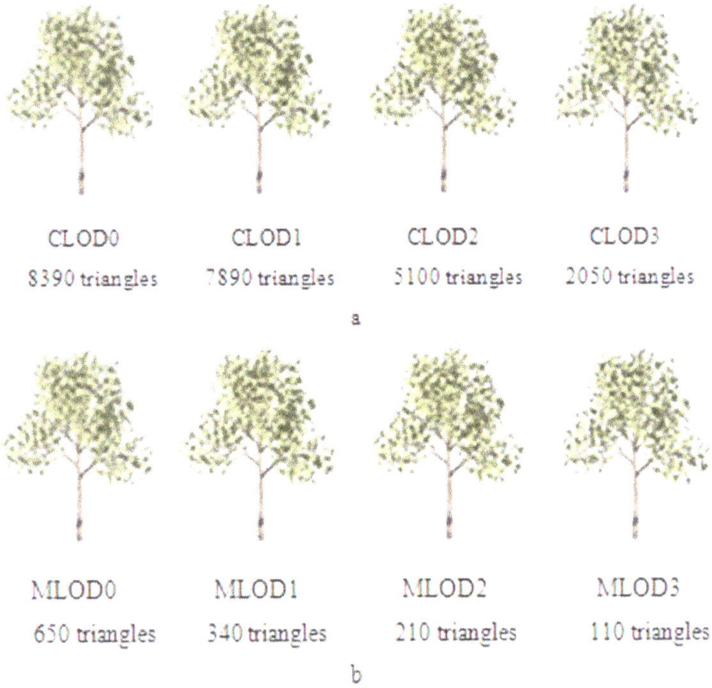


**Figure 8:** LOD models of Lycium barbarum.

a. Tree models with different LODs on a computer. Tree models are represented by triangles, and the number of triangles for each model is shown. The tree model with more details has larger amount of triangles, but it costs more time to render. b. Tree models on mobile device. These models have lower levels of detail than those models used on a computer because mobile devices usually have worse computing power and less system resources.

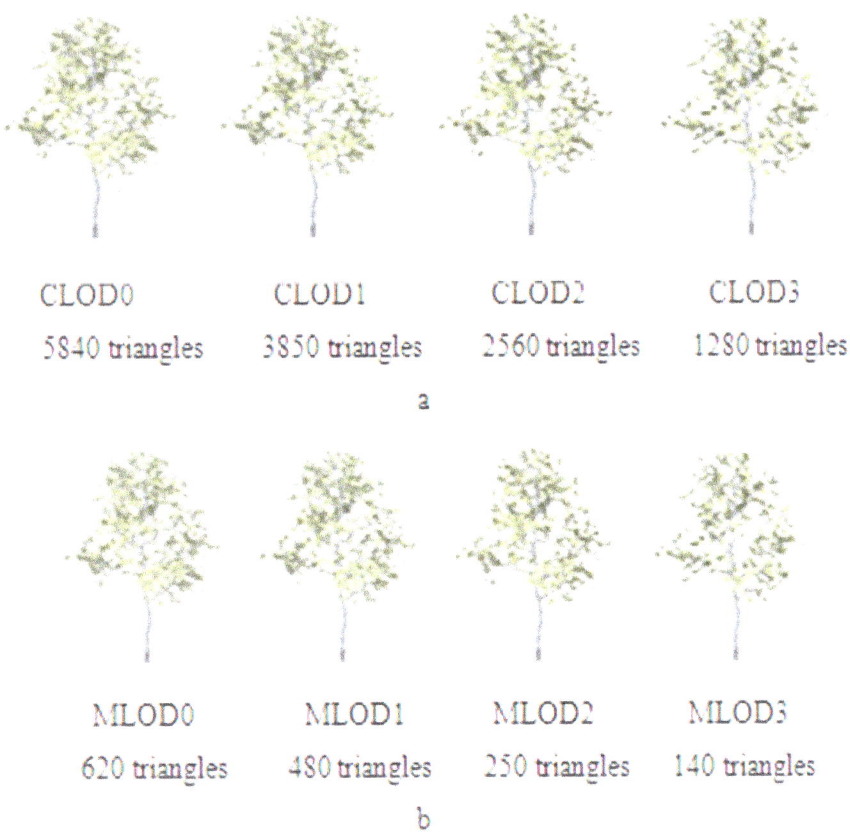


**Figure 9:** LOD models of Quercus pyrenaic.

a. Tree models with different LODs on a computer. b. Tree models on mobile device. This figure shows another type of tree, and the models applied on mobile devices also have a lower level of detail than those models used on a computer.

We have tested this method on different devices, including computers, the iPhone, and the iPad. To reach a satisfactory roaming rate of 15 fps, that is 0.067 s of the specified time, we compared the rendering time of using or not using the time-critical adaptive visualization approach. The natural scene is planted with Lycium barbarum and Quercus pyrenaic, which are distributed randomly. There are approximately 30~100 trees in the view frustum, and the natural scenes are rendered using these two approaches. The walkthrough of the natural scene is in the same path. The walkthrough distance consists of 500 frames, with every 5 frames as a sample.

Table 5 is the average frame rate before and after using the adaptive visualization approach on different devices. The average frame rate keeps at approximately 15 fps on the devices with different configurations (the configurations are shown in Table 6, Table 7, Table 8 and Table 9). This result demonstrates that the adaptive visualization approach proposed in this paper can dynamically display good visual effects depending on the system resources, the amount of data and so on.

**Table 5:** Average frame rate on different devices.

| Device | Before (fps) | After (fps) |
|---|---|---|
| Computer 1 | 10.06 | 14.93 |
| Computer 2 | 10.32 | 14.89 |
| iPhone | 11.23 | 15.38 |
| iPad | 9.01 | 13.89 |

**Table 6:** Configuration of computer 1

| Device Name | Configuration |
|---|---|
| Graphic card | ATI Radeon HD 4550, 512M |
| Memory | 2G (DDR2 SDRAM) |
| CPU | Intel(R) Core(TM) i3 CPU 550@3.20GHz |
| Operating system | Windows XP 32bit |

**Table 7:** Configuration of computer 2

| Device Name | Configuration |
|---|---|
| Graphic card | Nviidia Quadro 600, 1G |
| Memory | 4G (DDR3) |
| CPU | Intel(R) Xeon(R) CPU E5506 @2.13GHz quad-core |
| Operating system | Win 7 32bit |

**Table 8:** Configuration of iPhone4s

| Device Name | Configuration |
|---|---|
| Graphic card | Imagination PowerVR SGX543 |
| Memory | 512M(RAM) 16G(ROM) |
| CPU | Apple A5 1GHz |
| Operating system | iOS 5.0 |

**Table 9:** Configuration of iPad4

| Device Name | Configuration |
|---|---|
| Graphic card | Imagination PowerVR SGX543MP4 |
| Memory | 1G(DDR3) 32G(ROM) |
| CPU | Apple A6X 1.4GHz |
| Operating system | iOS 6.0 |

Fig. 10 is the rendering time before and after using the time-critical adaptive visualization approach on computer 1. There are 30~100 trees in the view frustum. The blue curve represents the rendering time of the natural scene before using the adaptive visualization approach, while the red curve represents the rendering time after using the approach. It can be observed from Fig. 10 that after using the adaptive visualization approach, the rendering time of the natural scene is reduced, and it approximates the specified time. Fig. 11, Fig. 12 andFig. 13 show the rendering time before and after using the time-critical adaptive visualization approach on computer 2, the iPhone and the iPad, respectively.

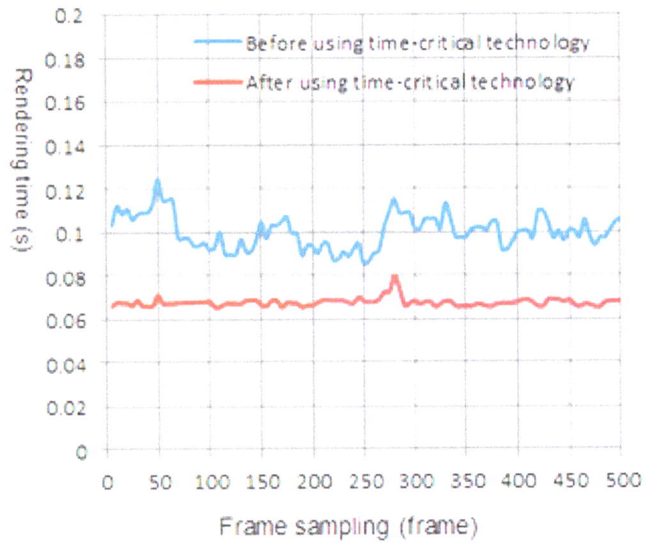


**Figure 10:** Comparison of rendering time on computer 1.

The blue line represents the rendering time before using time-critical technology on computer 1, while the red line represents the rendering time after using time-critical technology. The red line is much smoother, and it takes less time to render natural scenes than the blue line, indicating that time-critical technology is effective and reasonable.

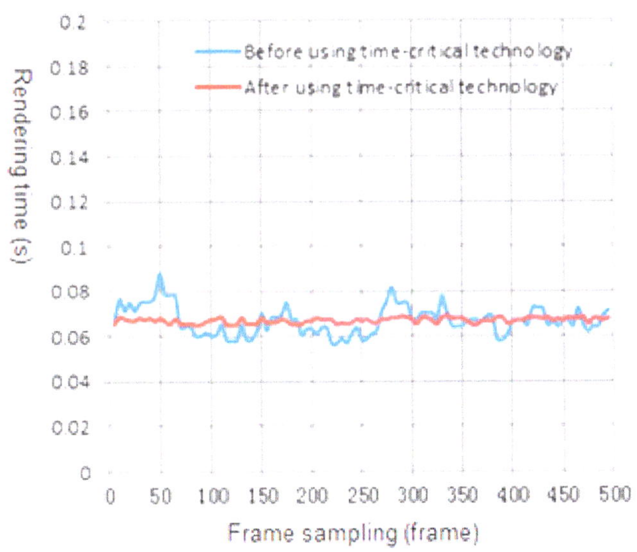


Figure 11: Comparison of rendering time on computer 2.

The blue line represents the rendering time before using time-critical technology on computer 2, while the red line represents the rendering time after using time-critical technology. Even if their rendering time is similar, the red line is smoother; indicating that time-critical technology can provide a more stable frame rate.

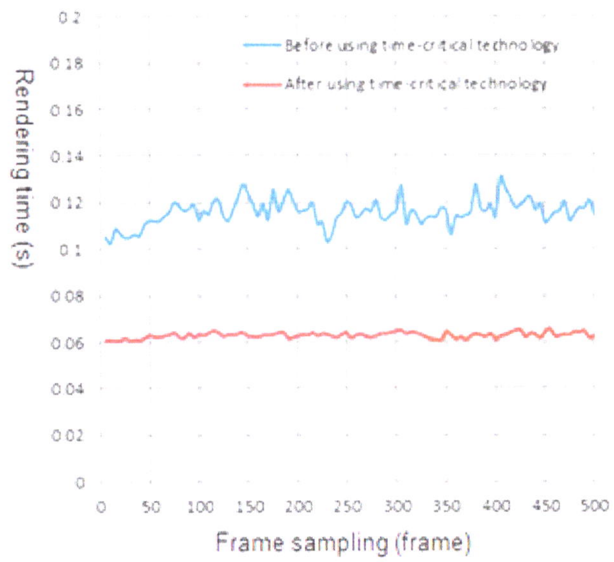


**Figure 12:** Comparison of rendering time on iPhone.

The blue line represents the rendering time before using time-critical technology on iPhone, and it always takes more rendering time than the red line. Furthermore, the red line is also smoother than the blue line; indicating that time-critical technology is effective and reasonable.

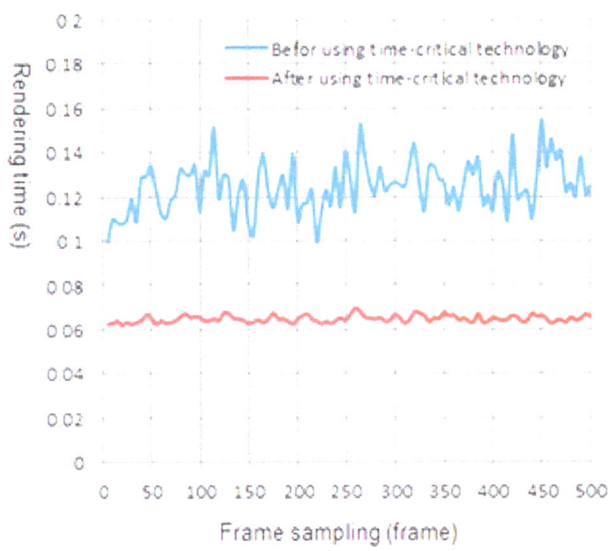


**Figure 13:** Comparison of rendering time on iPad.

The red line representing the rendering time after using time-critical technology is much smoother than the blue line, while it also costs much less rendering time than the blue line.

Table 10 presents the LOD distribution of trees before and after using this adaptive visualization approach on computer 1. T1~T5 are five different moments, and there are approximately 30 trees in view frustum. Before using the adaptive visualization approach, there are too many LODs of fine details, making the rendering time much longer. After using the adaptive visualization approach, the LODs of fine detail decreased, and the LODs of less detail but with more textures increased. Therefore, the rendering rate of natural scenes is improved by decreasing the LOD level of trees with less visual importance. Table 11, Table 12 and Table 13 present the LOD distribution of trees before and after using this adaptive visualization approach on computer 2, the iPhone and the iPad.

Table 10: LOD distributions on computer 1

| | Before | | | | After | | | |
|---|---|---|---|---|---|---|---|---|
| Time | clod0 | clod1 | clod2 | clod3 | clod0 | clod1 | clod2 | clod3 |
| *T1* | 2 | 3 | 9 | 17 | 1 | 2 | 5 | 23 |
| *T2* | 1 | 2 | 11 | 16 | 1 | 2 | 5 | 23 |
| *T3* | 1 | 4 | 10 | 16 | 0 | 2 | 6 | 24 |
| *T4* | 2 | 4 | 9 | 15 | 1 | 3 | 4 | 23 |
| *T5* | 2 | 3 | 10 | 18 | 1 | 3 | 2 | 24 |

**Table 11:** LOD distributions on computer 2

| | Before | | | | After | | | |
|---|---|---|---|---|---|---|---|---|
| Time | clod0 | clod1 | clod2 | clod3 | clod0 | clod1 | clod2 | clod3 |
| *T1* | 1 | 3 | 11 | 17 | 1 | 3 | 10 | 16 |
| *T2* | 2 | 4 | 9 | 15 | 2 | 5 | 9 | 17 |
| *T3* | 2 | 3 | 12 | 14 | 1 | 4 | 11 | 15 |
| *T4* | 1 | 2 | 12 | 15 | 2 | 2 | 13 | 13 |
| *T5* | 2 | 4 | 8 | 16 | 1 | 5 | 9 | 17 |

**Table 12:** LOD distributions on the iPhone

| | Before | | | | After | | | |
|---|---|---|---|---|---|---|---|---|
| Time | clod0 | clod1 | clod2 | clod3 | clod0 | clod1 | clod2 | clod3 |
| *T1* | 0 | 10 | 12 | 8 | 1 | 8 | 0 | 21 |
| *T2* | 2 | 8 | 16 | 4 | 2 | 6 | 1 | 21 |
| *T3* | 2 | 10 | 14 | 4 | 2 | 6 | 1 | 21 |
| *T4* | 2 | 10 | 16 | 2 | 2 | 4 | 4 | 20 |
| *T5* | 4 | 8 | 18 | 0 | 4 | 2 | 3 | 21 |

**Table 13:** LOD distributions on the iPad

| | Before | | | | After | | | |
|---|---|---|---|---|---|---|---|---|
| Time | clod0 | clod1 | clod2 | clod3 | clod0 | clod1 | clod2 | clod3 |
| *T1* | 0 | 10 | 14 | 6 | 0 | 3 | 1 | 26 |
| *T2* | 2 | 8 | 14 | 16 | 2 | 0 | 1 | 27 |
| *T3* | 2 | 10 | 14 | 4 | 2 | 0 | 1 | 21 |
| *T4* | 4 | 8 | 14 | 4 | 2 | 0 | 1 | 27 |
| *T5* | 2 | 8 | 8 | 12 | 2 | 1 | 0 | 15 |

Because of the better performance of computer 2 compared with computer 1, computer 2 reaches the average frame rate 16.14 fps before using the adaptive visualization approach. As shown in Fig. 11, the application in computer 2 has unstable fluctuations before using the adaptive visualization approach. After using the time-critical adaptive visualization approach, the frame rate is much more stable. Comparing Table 10 with Table 11, the number of high level LODs on computer 2 is greater than on computer 1. This result is because the computing power of computer2 is better than that of computer 1. Computer 2 decreases the rendering rate by increasing the number of more elaborate models, which keeps the frame rate at the specified value.

Table 14 is the frame rate of the adaptive visualization approach for different tree numbers (30, 50, and 80) tested on computer 1. When there are 30 trees in view frustum, the average frame rate is approximately 15 fps. When there are 50 or 80 trees in view frustum, the average frame rates are correspondingly improved, but they cannot reach 15 fps. There are two important factors that affect the frame rate. One factor is the importance threshold, which may not permit decreasing the LOD level of the trees for the essential visual effect; the other factor is the rendering time of tree models with the least detail. The rendering time of natural scenes must be equal to or greater than the value of the tree number multiplied by the rendering time of the least detailed model. Table 15, Table 16 and Table 17 display the frame rates of adaptive visualization, which is tested on computer 2, the iPhone and the iPad.

**Table 14:** Frame rates for different tree numbers on computer 1

| Number of trees | Before (fps) | After (fps) | Improvement |
|---|---|---|---|
| 30 | 10.06 | 14.93 | 48.4% |
| 50 | 6.70 | 11.22 | 67.5% |
| 80 | 4.55 | 7.90 | 73.6% |

**Table 15:** Frame rates for different tree numbers on computer 2.

| Number of trees | Before (fps) | After (fps) | Improvement |
|---|---|---|---|
| 30 | 10.32 | 14.89 | 44.3% |
| 50 | 6.85 | 11.37 | 66% |
| 80 | 4.63 | 7.94 | 71.5% |

**Table 16:** Frame rates for different tree numbers on the iPhone

| Number of trees | Before (fps) | After (fps) | Improvement |
|---|---|---|---|
| 30 | 11.23 | 15.38 | 37.0% |
| 50 | 8.33 | 10.87 | 30.5% |
| 80 | 5.0 | 7.14 | 42.8% |

**Table 17:** Frame rates for different tree numbers on the iPad

| Number of trees | Before (fps) | After (fps) | Improvement |
|---|---|---|---|
| 30 | 9.01 | 13.89 | 54.1% |
| 50 | 6.14 | 9.8 | 59.6% |
| 80 | 4.55 | 7.04 | 54.7% |

Fig. 14 (S3 Dataset) displays the natural scenes at the moment T1 of Table 10 and Table 11.Fig. 14a is the nature scene using the adaptive visualization approach on computer 1. There are 30 trees in view frustum. Fig. 14b is the nature scene using the adaptive visualization approach on computer 2.

a

b

**Figure 14:** Natural scenes on computers.

a. Adaptive visualization approach on computer 1. b. Adaptive visualization approach on computer 2. These two nature scenes are rendered using the adaptive visualization approach presented in this paper. The applications show that the adaptive visualization approach can improve the quality and speed of rendering effectively.

http://dx.doi.org/10.1371/journal.pone.0117586.g014

Additionally, this time-critical adaptive approach for visualizing natural scenes is applied on both iPhone and iPad, as shown in Fig. 15 (S1 Dataset and S3 Dataset). The natural scenes can also be rendered at a constant frame rate.

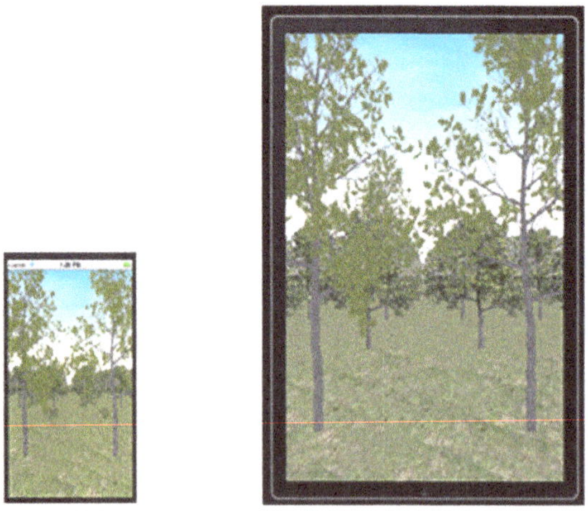


**Figure 15:** Natural scenes on mobile devices.

a. Natural scenes on the iPhone. b. Natural scenes on the iPad. These two nature scenes on mobile devices are also rendered using the adaptive visualization approach presented in this paper. The applications show that the adaptive visualization approach is suitable for mobile devices, and it can improve the quality and speed of rendering effectively.

## CONCLUSION

This paper describes a hybrid representation method of 3D tree models that are suitable for different devices. The geometry-based and image-based rendering method is used to simplify a 3D tree model to reach a balance between model simplification and visual quality. Then, an approach based on the device-independent and time-critical adaptive generation of interactive natural scenes is proposed. By estimating rendering time and computing tree importance, the appropriate LOD tree models are selected to render in natural scenes. The rendering time is controlled in a reasonable range of a specified time. Moreover, the speed of eye movements is an essential factor influencing object importance in a natural scene. The fast moving trees in natural scenes can only be observed in a short time, leading to the vague visual effects. The speed of eye moving should be taken into account in future research because it is closely related to visual importance.

In addition to the application in natural scene rendering, the time-critical adaptive approach proposed in this paper can be applied in some related fields, such as augmented reality and mobile visual search. Many augmented reality systems are designed with vision-based wide-area registration algorithm, and dynamically enhance the real scenes with objects data stored on devices [28–31]. Taking an augmented city guide or navigational tool as an example, people use location-based service on mobile devices to enhance their experience. The augmented reality system should fully consider the features of mobile devices, including limited computing abilities, battery capacity, and user's response time. Therefore, the time-critical adaptive approach can be extended to render the augmented reality scenes and make GPS positioning; thus the augmented reality system can provide better user experience.

Mobile visual search or mobile visual location recognition [31] is a kind of location-based service, which can be applied in many fields of our lives, such as hygiene, outdoor object search, entertainment, etc. By using the mobile visual location recognition applications, the users can get more information about the objects with its image of the landmark. And the system can do the recognition operations just using the query image of landmark. The existing mobile location recognition applications commonly use the image retrieval method to do the location recognition operations. For example, mobile landmark search [32–35] extracts compressed visual descriptors on mobile devices, which only consider the visual and location information. At the same time, these mobile retrieval methods [32–33] usually use image retrieval and compressed descriptors to identify the location. The compressed descriptors [36–38], such as tags, image of landmark, are also based on visual and local feature information. These applications can adopt an extended time-critical adaptive approach to get better user experience, such as taking the viewpoint, distance or size into consideration. What's more, these applications applied on different devices also can consider the different capabilities of mobile devices, which are taken into account in this paper. For example, compression ratio of image can be decided by the devices. The devices with better computing abilities can have a relatively low compression ratio. Therefore, a suitable mobile visual search strategy can be adopted for different devices.

## REFERENCES

1. Liu XQ, Cao WQ, Zhan L (2010) The modeling and animation of complex 3D forestry scenarios. Image & Graphics 15(1): 136–141.
2. Zach C, Mantler S, Karner K (2002) Time-critical rendering of discrete and continuous levels of detail. Proceedings of the ACM Symposium on Virtual Reality Software and Technology 2002, Shatin, NT, Hong Kong 1–8.
3. Wloka M (1993) Dissertation proposal: time-critical graphics. Providence, USA: Brown University.
4. Funkhouser TA (1993) Adaptive display algorithm for interactive frame rates during visualization of complex virtual environments. Proceedings of the 20th Annual Conference on Computer Graphics and Interactive Techniques, Anaheim, CA, USA: 247–254.
5. Martin IM (2002) Hybrid transcoding for adaptive transmission of 3d content. Proceedings of IEEE International Conference on Multimedia and Expo, Lausanne, Switzerland: 373–376.
6. Li LJ, Li FX, Huang TY (2006) A time-controlling terrain

rendering algorithm. 12th International Conference on Interactive Technologies and Sociotechnical Systems, Xi'an, China: 328–337.

7. Cao XF, Wan G (2010) Adaptive transmitting and rendering methods for large terrain. Proceedings of Second International Conference on Computer Modeling and Simulation, Washington, DC, USA: 327–330.
8. Park T, Shin J, Lee S, Nah Y (2013) Adaptive rendering system for large scale 3d-terrain data for streaming services. Information-an international Interdisciplinary Journal 16(1A): 393–405.
9. Bao GB, Li HJ, Zhang XP, Dong WM (2012) Large-scale forest rendering: real-time, realistic, and progressive. Computers & Graphics 36(3): 140–151.
10. Liu XD, Wu JZ, Zheng CW (2012) KD-tree based parallel adaptive rendering. The Visual Computer28(6–8): 613–623.
11. Zhang YT (2008) Time-critical adaptive visualization method of 3d city models. Wuhan, China: Wuhan University.
12. Shen HC, Huang SS, Hu SM (2011) Adaptive partitioning of urban facades. Computer-Aided Design & Computer Graphics 30(6): 149–151.
13. Scherzer D, Yang L, Mattausch O (2012) Temproal coherence methods in real-time rendering. Computer Graphics Forum 31(8): 2378–2408.
14. Remolar I, Chover M, Belmonte O, Ribelles J, Rebollo C (2002) Geometric simplification of foliage. Eurographics 2(1): 397–404.
15. Zhang X, Blaise F, Jaeger M (2006) Multiresolution plant models with complex organs. Proceedings of the 2006 ACM international conference on Virtual reality continuum and its applications, Shatin, Hong Kong 331–334.
16. DengQ,ZhangX,YangG,JaegerM(2010)Multiresolution foliage for forest rendering. Computer Animation and Virtual Worlds 21(1): 1–23.
17. Bao G, Li H, Zhang X, Che W, Jaeger M (2011) Realistic real-time rendering for large-scale forest scenes. 2011 IEEE International Symposium on VR Innovation (ISVRI), SUNTEC Convention Center, Singapore 217–223.
18. Zhu XY, Yang ZY (2013) Multi-scale spatial concatenations of local features in natural scenes and scene classification. PLOS ONE 8(9):e76393 doi: 10.1371/journal.pone.0076393
19. Cook RL, Halstead J, Planck M, Ryu D (2007) Stochastic simplification of aggregate detail. ACM Transactions on Graphics (TOG) 26(3): 791–798.
20. Gumbau J, Chover M, Remolar I, Rebollo C (2011) View-dependent pruning for real-time rendering of trees. Computers & Graphics 35(2): 364–374.
21. Tu C (2011) Real-time rendering of realistic trees in virtual reality systems. Computer Technology and Development 19(6): 206–209.
22. Liu F (2011) Real-time rendering and dynamic simulation of large-scale forest scenes. PhD. Thesis, China: Zhejiang University.
23. Zhang L (2008) Real-time simulation of swaying trees in large-scale forest scenes. PhD. Thesis, China: Zhejiang University.
24. Wang Y (2012) Research and application of visual attention model. M.Sc. Thesis, China: Shanghai Jiao Tong University.
25. Fan J, Fan YY, Dong TY (2013) Real-time information recombination of complex 3d tree model based on visual perception. Science China information Sciences 56(9): 1–14. doi: 10.1007/s11427-013-4521-1
26. Wimmer M, Schmalstieg D (1998) Load balancing for smooth LODs. Vienna State, Austria: Vienna University of Technology.
27. Dong TY, Xia JJ, Fan J (2013) Adaptive visualization of multi-style composition for complex forest scene. Journal of image and graphics 18(11): 1486–1496.
28. Guan T, Duan LY, Yu JQ, Chen YJ, Zhang X (2011) Real time camera pose estimation for wide area augmented reality applications. IEEE Computer Graphics and Applications 31(3): 56–68. doi:10.1109/MCG.2010.23
29. Guan T, He Y, Gao J, Yang J, Yu J (2013) On-device mobile visual location recognition by integrating vision and inertial sensors. IEEE Transactions on Multimedia 15(7): 1688–1699.
30. Guan T, He YF, Duan LY, Yu JQ (2014) Efficient BOF generation and compression for on-device mobile visual location recognition. IEEE Multimedia 21(2): 32–41.
31. Guan T, Fan Y, Duan LY (2014) On-device mobile visual location recognition by using panoramic images and compressed sensing based visual descriptors. PLOS ONE 9(6): e98806 doi:10.1371/journal.pone.0098806
32. Gao Y, Wang M, Ji RR, Wu XD, Dai QH (2014) 3D object retrieval with hausdorff distance learning.IEEE Transactions on Industrial Electronics 61(4): 2088–2098.
33. Gao Y, Wang M, Tao DC, Ji RR, Dai QH (2012) 3D object retrieval and recognition with hypergraph analysis. IEEE Transactions on Image Processing 21(9): 4290–4303. doi: 10.1109/TIP.2012.2199502
34. Ji R, Duan LY, Chen J, Yao H, Yuan J, Rui Y, Gao W (2012) Location discriminative vocabulary coding for mobile landmark search. International Journal of Computer Vision 96 (3): 290–314.
35. Wei BC, Guan T, Yu JQ (2014) Projected residual vector quantization for ANN search. IEEE Multimedia 21(3): 41–51.
36. Ji RR, Duan LY, Yao HX, Xie LX (2012) Learning to distribute vocabulary indexing for scalable visual search. IEEE Transactions on Multimedia 15(1): 153–166.
37. Ji R, Gao Y, Zhong B, Yao H, Tian Q (2011) Mining flickr landmarks by modeling reconstruction sparsity. ACM Transactions on Multimedia Computing, Communications, and Applications 7(1): Article 31, 1–22.
38. Ji R, Yao H, Liu W, Sun X, Tian Q (2012) Task-dependent visual-codebook compression. IEEE Transactions on Image Processing 21(4): 2282–2293. doi: 10.1109/TIP.2011.2176950

CHAPTER 8

# ANALYSIS OF THE TRANSIENT RESPONSE OF A DUAL-FED RC TRANSMISSION LINE

Mohsen Dorraki[1], Gregory K. Cambrell[2], Derek Abbott[3]

[1]Department of Electrical Engineering, Amirkabir University of Technology, Tehran, Iran,

[2]Department of Electrical and Computer Systems Engineering, Faculty of Engineering, Monash University, Victoria, Australia,

[3]School of Electrical and Electronic Engineering, University of Adelaide, South Australia, Australia

## ABSTRACT

**The transient analysis of a uniform transmission line of finite length is considered in this paper. For the first time this paper provides an analytical expression for the time-domain response of an RC transmission line, which is stimulated by a step function that is fed into both ends of the transmission line. In particular, we find an analytical expression for the step response at the center of the transmission line, in order to determine the worst-case rise time. This is of interest, for example, in large charge-coupled device (CCD) arrays, where long polysilicon lines are dual-fed in order to mitigate degradation in rise time. The analytical expressions for the RC transmission line are supported by computer-simulated lumped RC models.**

## INTRODUCTION

Integrated circuits have seen significant progress—from the early developments that contained only a few transistors to modern microprocessors that can contain billions of elements. This development has been made possible by the downscaling of circuit dimensions, which results in increased speed and reduced costs.

The disadvantage of this development is that the resistance of the wires between transistors increases disproportionately when their cross-sectional dimensions are reduced. Consequently, when they are scaled down, signal propagation speed becomes reduced.

Estimating interconnection delay is an important issue for present circuits. Many authors have modeled the wires inside integrated circuits as distributed RC lines. The analysis of finite RC interconnections under a step input is widely discussed in the literature, e.g. [1, 2]. The usual method is to calculate the transfer function, then the time-domain response is extracted for an RC transmission line with a step input. Many authors have adopted different approaches to obtain a time-domain response using the Laplace transform technique [3]. Kahng and Muddu presented the time-domain response for an RC transmission line with source and load impedances [3]. Moreover, they analyzed a finite transmission line for a ramp input [4], using a method based on solving the diffusion equation and applying the method of images [3]. Rao reviewed the step response of

**Citation:** Dorraki M, Cambrell GK, Abbott D. Analysis of the Transient Response of a Dual-Fed RC Transmission Line. Coles JA, ed. PLoS ONE. 2015;10(2):e0116993. doi:10.1371/journal.pone.0116993.

the semi-infinite distributed RC line and focused mainly on the step response of a finite-length RC line with a capacitive load termination, which is the most common model for a wire within present-day integrated CMOS chips [5]. Additionally, Gupta and Patnaik presented an exact analysis of the output response of a distributed RC interconnect under input signals that are polynomial in time [6].

None of these previous studies used the same step input fed simultaneously into both ends of the transmission line, while considering the behavior at the center of the line. This scheme is of interest for long interconnects on chips and also for long electrodes on charged-coupled devices (CCDs). For example, in order to mitigate a slow rise time, a circular clock bus can be fed from both ends, and it becomes of interest to have an analytical expression for the transient response at the center of the bus. Similarly, in order to reduce RC degradation of clock signals along long CCD electrodes, it is possible to feed the clock to both ends of the electrodes [7]. An analytical expression that predicts the worst-case rise time at the center of the electrode is therefore a useful design equation. Another example, where such an analytical expression is potentially useful, is in the design of A and J gates for future silicon quantum computers [8].

The rest of this paper is organized as follows. After reviewing the transient response of a semi-infinite RC transmission line and an RC line of finite length with open-circuit termination, we will derive the transient response of an RC line of finite length that is fed at both ends with the same step function. In particular, we will determine the improvement of the 63% rise time thereby achieved at the center of the line. The analytical expressions will be presented in two forms: a convergent series of trigonometric and exponential functions, and a convergent series of complementary error functions. Furthermore, it will be evident that the same expressions arise by applying the method of superposition. As a final confirmation of the derived analytical expressions, the distributed RC line of finite length is modeled by several lumped RC sections, and the step response at the center of the model is computed and compared with the analytical expressions.

## TRANSIENT RESPONSE OF RC TRANSMISSION LINES

### Semi-Infinite RC Transmission Line

An RC transmission line is shown in Fig. 1. This may, for example, be the model of a CCD electrode. Ignoring any propagation time due to inductance, the voltage across the line v(x, t) at position x along the line and at time t satisfies the well-known diffusion equation

$$\frac{\partial^2 v}{\partial x^2} = rc\,\frac{\partial v}{\partial t} \tag{1}$$

together with appropriate boundary conditions and initial condition. Here r and c are the uniform resistance and capacitance per unit length. It is a linear partial differential equation (PDE). The corresponding current in the line i(x, t) satisfies the same PDE and is related to the voltagev(x, t) by

$$i = -\frac{1}{r}\frac{\partial v}{\partial x}. \tag{2}$$

A particular integral for the diffusion equation is

$$v(x,t) = a\ \mathrm{erfc}\left((b \pm \frac{x}{L})/\sqrt{\frac{4t}{rcL^2}}\right) + cx + d \tag{3}$$

where a, b, c and d are constants and erfc(·) is the complementary error function defined by

$$\mathrm{erfc}(z) = 1 - \frac{2}{\sqrt{\pi}}\int_0^z e^{-y^2}\,dy. \tag{4}$$

A characteristic length L has been introduced so that the dimensionless (normalized) variables

$$\chi = \frac{x}{L} \tag{5}$$

And

$$\tau = \frac{t}{rcL^2} \tag{6}$$

can be used throughout the analysis. The corresponding dimensionless diffusion equation is

$$\frac{\partial^2 v}{\partial \chi^2} = \frac{\partial v}{\partial \tau}. \tag{7}$$

The unit step response of a semi-infinite line extending from x = 0 to infinity is found by imposing the boundary conditions

$$\mathrm{BC1}: v(0,t) = v_{\mathrm{in}}(t) = u(t) \quad \text{for all} \quad t \geqslant 0 \tag{8}$$

$$\mathrm{BC2}: i(\infty,t) = 0 \ \text{ or } \ \frac{\partial v}{\partial x}(\infty,t) = 0 \quad \text{for all} \quad t \geqslant 0 \tag{9}$$

where u(t) is the unit step function, and the initial condition

$$\mathrm{IC}: v(x,0) = 0 \quad \text{for all} \quad 0 < x < \infty. \tag{10}$$

Therefore a = 1, and b, c and d must be zero, and so the unit step response of the semi-infinite line is

$$v(x,t) = \mathrm{erfc}\left(\left(\frac{x}{L}\right)/\sqrt{\frac{4t}{rcL^2}}\right) \tag{11}$$

Or

$$v(\chi,\tau) = \mathrm{erfc}(\chi/\sqrt{4\tau}). \tag{12}$$

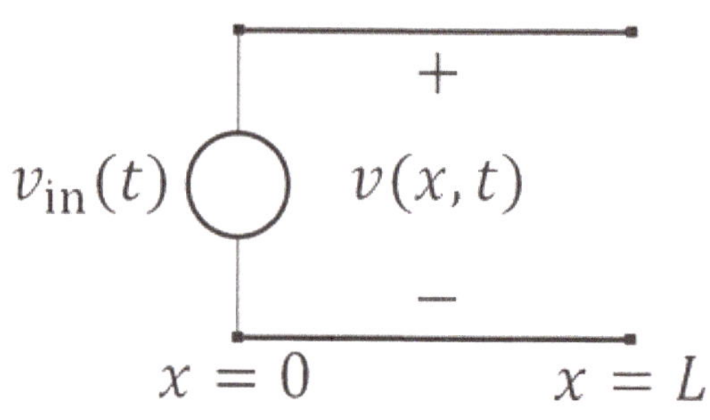


**Figure 1:** An RC transmission line.

## Finite RC Transmission Line with Open-Circuit Termination

Consider an RC transmission line of finite length L with open-circuit termination, as shown inFig. 1, fed with a unit step function of voltage. Rao has solved this case by using the Laplace transform technique [5]. For the Laplace transform of the voltage step response v(x, t) he obtains

$$\mathcal{L}\{v(x,t)\}_s^t = \int_0^\infty v(x,t)e^{-st}\,dt = V(x,s) = \frac{1}{s}\frac{\cosh\left(\left(1-\frac{x}{L}\right)\sqrt{rcL^2s}\right)}{\cosh(\sqrt{rcL^2s})} \tag{13}$$

for $0 \le x \le L$. By directly inverting this Laplace transform Rao obtains the following infinite series for the unit step response:

$$v(x,t) = 1 - \frac{2}{\pi}\sum_{n=1}^{\infty}\frac{1}{\left(n-\frac{1}{2}\right)}\left[\sin\left(\left(n-\frac{1}{2}\right)\pi\left(\frac{x}{L}\right)\right)\right]e^{-\left(\left(n-\frac{1}{2}\right)\pi\right)^2 t/(rcL^2)}. \tag{14}$$

Then, by using the expansion

$$\frac{1}{\cosh(y)} = \frac{2e^{-y}}{1+e^{-2y}} = 2\sum_{n=0}^{\infty}(-1)^n e^{-(2n+1)y} \tag{15}$$

so that

$$V(x,s) = \frac{1}{s}\sum_{n=0}^{\infty}(-1)^n\left\{e^{-\left(2n+\frac{x}{L}\right)\sqrt{rcL^2s}} +, e^{-\left(2n+2-\frac{x}{L}\right)\sqrt{rcL^2s}}\right\} \tag{16}$$

he performs an alternative inversion of the Laplace transform (13) and obtains another, but equivalent, infinite series for the unit step response:

$$v(x,t) = \sum_{n=0}^{\infty}(-1)^n\left\{\operatorname{erfc}\left(\left(2n+\frac{x}{L}\right)/\sqrt{\frac{4t}{rcL^2}}\right) + \operatorname{erfc}\left(\left(2n+2-\frac{x}{L}\right)/\sqrt{\frac{4t}{rcL^2}}\right)\right\}. \tag{17}$$

For the purpose of comparison, the following practical example will be considered here and later in the paper. Let $r = 1\ \Omega/m$, $c = 1\times10^{-6}$ F/m and $L = 1\times10^{-3}$ m. The unit step response at the center of this line will be of particular interest. Here, $x = 0.5\times10^{-3}$ m and $\chi = x/L = 0.5$. When evaluated at this position, the unit step response reaches (1–1/e) or 0.63212 of its final value of 1.0 in the time $t = 0.36283\times10^{-12}$ s, that is, when $\tau = t/(rcL^2) - 0.36283$. This is called the 63% rise time.

For interest, if this practical line were extended to infinity (becoming a semi-infinite line), the 63% rise time at the same position would increase to time $t = 0.54538\times10^{-12}$ s, that is, to $\tau = t/(rcL^2) = 0.54538$. The increased rise time is due to the need to charge the extra capacitance beyond x = L.

On the other hand, if this practical line is fed with the same step function of voltage into both ends of the line, charging of the capacitance within the finite line is potentially faster than when leaving the far end open.

## Analysis of Dual-Fed RC Transmission Line

Consider an RC transmission line of finite length L fed with the same step function of voltage at both ends, as shown in Fig. 2. The boundary and initial conditions now become

$$\text{BC1}: \ v(0,t) = u_1 \cdot u(t) \quad \text{for all} \quad t \ge 0. \tag{18}$$

$$\text{BC2}: \ v(L,t) = u_2 \cdot u(t) \quad \text{for all} \quad t \ge 0. \tag{19}$$

$$\text{IC}: \ v(x,0) = 0 \quad \text{for all} \quad 0 < x < L. \tag{20}$$

For generality, individual step amplitudes $u_1$ and $u_2$ have been introduced at each end of the RC line. They can both be set to unity at the end of the analysis.

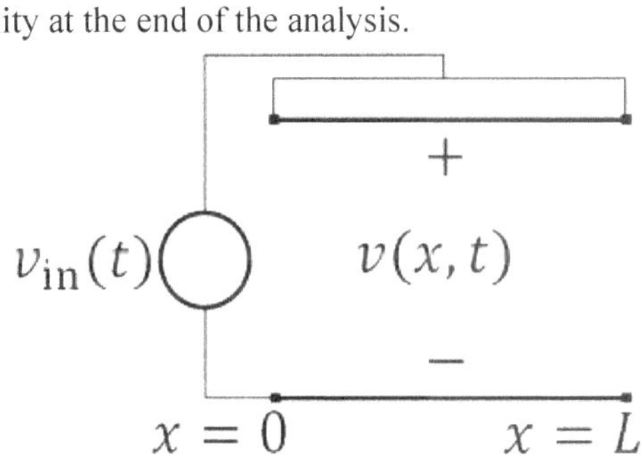


**Figure 2:** The RC transmission line is identical to that in Fig. 1, except that both ends are fed with the same step function $v_{in}(t)$.

The response of interest, v(x; t), is the voltage at the center of the line. The voltage at that position will possess the worst-case rise time.

Taking the Laplace transform of the diffusion Equation (1) and applying the initial condition (20) gives the wave equation

$$\frac{\partial^2}{\partial x^2}V(x,s) = rc\left[v(x,t)e^{-st}\right]_{t=0}^{t=\infty} + rcs\int_0^\infty v(x,t)e^{-st}dt = rcsV(x,s). \tag{21}$$

Its general solution in the Laplace transform domain is

$$V(x,s) = A(s)\ e^{x\sqrt{rcs}} + B(s)\ e^{-x\sqrt{rcs}} \tag{22}$$

where A(s) and B(s) do not depend on x and must be determined from the boundary conditions (18) and (19). Since the Laplace transform of the unit step function is 1/s, BC1 and BC2 become

$$V(0,s) = A(s) + B(s) = \frac{u_1}{s}, \tag{23}$$

$$V(L,s) = A(s)\, e^{L\sqrt{rcs}} + B(s)\, e^{-L\sqrt{rcs}} = \frac{u_2}{s}. \tag{24}$$

Thus

$$A(s) = \frac{-u_1 e^{-L\sqrt{rcs}} + u_2}{2s \sinh(L\sqrt{rcs})}. \tag{25}$$

$$B(s) = \frac{u_1 e^{L\sqrt{rcs}} - u_2}{2s \sinh(L\sqrt{rcs})} \tag{26}$$

so that

$$V(x,s) = \frac{1}{s}\cdot\frac{u_1 \sinh\left(\left(1-\frac{x}{L}\right)\sqrt{rcL^2 s}\right) + u_2 \sinh\left(\left(\frac{x}{L}\right)\sqrt{rcL^2 s}\right)}{\sinh\left(\sqrt{rcL^2 s}\right)} = u_1 F(L-x,s) + u_2 F(x,s) \tag{27}$$

Where

$$F(x,s) = \frac{1}{s}\cdot\frac{\sinh\left(\left(\frac{x}{L}\right)\sqrt{rcL^2 s}\right)}{\sinh\left(\sqrt{rcL^2 s}\right)}. \tag{28}$$

The inverse Laplace transform of F(x, s) is

$$f(x,t) = \mathcal{L}^{-1}\{F(x,s)\}_t^s = \frac{1}{2\pi j}\int_{\alpha-j\infty}^{\alpha+j\infty} F(x,s)e^{ts}ds = \frac{1}{2\pi j}\int_{\alpha-j\infty}^{\alpha+j\infty} \frac{1}{s}\cdot\frac{\sinh\left(\left(\frac{x}{L}\right)\sqrt{rcL^2 s}\right)}{\sinh\left(\sqrt{rcL^2 s}\right)} e^{ts}ds. \tag{29}$$

Though sinhz—√z is not analytic, the ratio of two such functions is lacking any double-valuedness and so there is no need for a cut along the negative-real axis. Note that this ratio has a line of first-order poles along this axis. For t < 0, the contour of the integration may be closed to the right, the integral at infinity goes to zero, and the value of the contour integral is zero. For t > 0, this is not permissible, the integral becoming exponentially large due to the $e^{ts}$factor. However, the contour may be closed to the left, thus enclosing the line of poles. The value of the new integral at infinity is still zero, and the contour integral that we are interested in takes on the value of the sum of the residues. The simple poles are located at

$$s_n = -\frac{(n\pi)^2}{rcL^2} \tag{30}$$

for each integer n ≥ 1. Therefore,

$$f(x,t) = \frac{x}{L} + \sum_{n=1}^{\infty} \frac{2}{jn\pi}\,\frac{\sinh(jn\pi x/L)e^{-(n\pi)^2 t/(rcL^2)}}{\cosh(jn\pi)} \tag{31}$$

so that

$$f(x,t) = \frac{x}{L} + \frac{2}{\pi}\sum_{n=1}^{\infty}\frac{(-1)^n}{n}\sin(n\pi x/L)e^{-(n\pi)^2 t/(rcL^2)}. \tag{32}$$

Hence the general step response is

$$v(x,t) = u_1\left(1-\frac{x}{L}\right) + u_2\left(\frac{x}{L}\right) + \frac{2}{\pi}\sum_{n=1}^{\infty}\frac{(-1)^n}{n}\left[u_1 \sin\left(n\pi\left(1-\frac{x}{L}\right)\right) + u_2 \sin\left(n\pi\left(\frac{x}{L}\right)\right)\right]e^{-(n\pi)^2 t/(rcL^2)}. \tag{33}$$

Finally, by setting $u_1$ = 1 and $u_2$ = 1, the unit step response of the dual-fed RC line is

$$v(x,t) = 1 + \frac{2}{\pi}\sum_{n=1}^{\infty}\frac{(-1)^n}{n}\left[\sin\left(n\pi\left(1-\frac{x}{L}\right)\right) + \sin\left(n\pi\left(\frac{x}{L}\right)\right)\right]e^{-(n\pi)^2 t/(rcL^2)}. \tag{34}$$

At the cnter of the line where $\chi$ = x/L = 0.5, the unit step response of the dual fed RC line is

$$v\left(\frac{L}{2}, t\right) = 1 - \frac{4}{\pi}\sum_{n=0}^{\infty}\frac{(-1)^n}{(2n+1)}e^{-((2n+1)\pi)^2 t/(rcL^2)} \quad (35)$$

Or

$$v(0.5, \tau) = 1 - \frac{4}{\pi}\sum_{n=0}^{\infty}\frac{(-1)^n}{(2n+1)}e^{-((2n+1)\pi)^2 \tau}. \quad (36)$$

Again let r = 1 Ω/m, c = $1\times10^{-6}$ F/m and L = $1\times10^{-3}$ m. The unit step response at the center of this dual-fed RC line reaches (1–1/e) or 0.63212 of its final value of 1.0 in the time t = $0.125795\times10^{-12}$ s, that is, when $\tau = t/(rcL^2) = 0.125795$.

Compared to the case when this line is left open at the far end, the 63% rise time at the center has been reduced by a factor of 2.8843, which is a significant improvement.

## Alternative Analysis of Dual-Fed RC Transmission Line

Following a method similar to that presented by Rao in [5], and using the expansion

$$\frac{1}{\sinh(y)} = \frac{2e^{-y}}{1-e^{-2y}} = 2\sum_{n=0}^{\infty}e^{-(2n+1)y} \quad (37)$$

the Laplace transform (28) can be expanded as

$$F(x, s) = \frac{1}{s}\sum_{n=0}^{\infty}\left\{e^{-(2n+1-\frac{x}{L})\sqrt{rcL^2 s}} - e^{-(2n-1+\frac{x}{L})\sqrt{rcL^2 s}}\right\}. \quad (38)$$

Then another, but equivalent, infinite series for the general step response of the dual-fed RC line is

$$v(x, t) = \sum_{n=0}^{\infty}\left\{u_1\left[\operatorname{erfc}\left((2n+\frac{x}{L})/\sqrt{\frac{4t}{rcL^2}}\right) - \operatorname{erfc}\left((2n+2-\frac{x}{L})/\sqrt{\frac{4t}{rcL^2}}\right)\right] + u_2\left[\operatorname{erfc}\left((2n+1-\frac{x}{L})/\sqrt{\frac{4t}{rcL^2}}\right) - \operatorname{erfc}\left((2n+1+\frac{x}{L})/\sqrt{\frac{4t}{rcL^2}}\right)\right]\right\}. \quad (39)$$

The unit step response is obtained by setting $u_1$ = 1 and $u_2$ = 1. At the center of the line where$\chi$ = x/L = 0.5, the unit step response of the dual-fed RC line is

$$v\left(\frac{L}{2}, t\right) = 2\sum_{n=0}^{\infty}\left\{\operatorname{erfc}\left(\left(2n+\frac{1}{2}\right)/\sqrt{\frac{4t}{rcL^2}}\right) - \operatorname{erfc}\left(\left(2n+\frac{3}{2}\right)/\sqrt{\frac{4t}{rcL^2}}\right)\right\} \quad (40)$$

Or

$$v(0.5, \tau) = 2\sum_{n=0}^{\infty}\left\{\operatorname{erfc}\left(\left(2n+\frac{1}{2}\right)/\sqrt{4\tau}\right) - \operatorname{erfc}\left(\left(2n+\frac{3}{2}\right)/\sqrt{4\tau}\right)\right\}. \quad (41)$$

This series has been found to converge faster than the series in Equation (36) for small values of $\tau$ but otherwise gives identical numerical values.

Some analytical results are shown in Table 1.

**Table 1:** Analytical results for the unit step response at the center of a dual-fed RC line

| $\tau$ | 0.01 | 0.02 | 0.03 | 0.05 | 0.07 | 0.10 | 0.12 | 0.13 | 0.15 | 0.20 | 0.50 |
|---|---|---|---|---|---|---|---|---|---|---|---|
| $v(0.5, \tau)$ (volt) | 0.001 | 0.025 | 0.082 | 0.228 | 0.363 | 0.526 | 0.610 | 0.647 | 0.710 | 0.823 | 0.991 |

## Analysis of Dual-Fed RC Transmission Line using Superposition

For any bilateral linear electrical network, lumped or distributed, the method of superposition is valid. In particular, the voltage at any point in an RC transmission line that is fed by two independent sources is the algebraic sum of the voltages caused by each independent source acting alone, where the other source is reduced to zero and replaced by its internal impedance. Thus, an ideal voltage source becomes a short-circuit when reduced to zero.

The problem of the dual-fed RC transmission line can now be solved by first finding the step response within the line when it is fed by a unit step voltage source at one end having terminated the other end of the line with a short-circuit. Because of the symmetry of the uniform RC transmission line, the step response when the unit step voltage source and the short-circuit load are swapped can be found by simply changing the position variable x to L—x, where L is the length of the line. By applying superposition, the step response of the dual-fed line is the algebraic sum of the step responses of the line when fed from just one end and terminated at the other end with a short-circuit.

Because of the symmetry of the uniform line the step response at the center will be the same whether it is fed from the left end and short-circuited at the right end or fed from the right end and short-circuited at the left end. Hence, the step response at the center of a dual-fed line is the same as that from a singly-fed line, terminated in a short-circuit, but fed with double the amplitude.

The step response of a forward-fed finite RC transmission line with short-circuit termination atx = L can obtained by setting $u_2$ = 0 in either Equation (33) or Equation (39). Similarly the step response of a backward-fed finite RC transmission line with short-circuit termination at x = 0 can obtained by setting $u_1$ = 0 in either Equation (33) or Equation (39). By superposition, the general step response of a dual-fed RC line is the algebraic sum of these two individual step responses. But that is exactly what appears in both Equations (33) and (39).

Furthermore, it is easily shown that the step response at the center of a dual-fed RC line is simply halved in amplitude when the source at either end is reduced to zero and replaced by a short-circuit. By linearity, that halved-response can be restored by doubling the amplitude of the remaining source. Shorting the far end of an RC line maximizes the current through the bulk of the transmission line, but at the same time causes the greatest voltage drop towards the far end. It follows that terminating the far end of the line with any finite value of resistance will improve the rise time within the RC line compared to when that far end is left open. The source amplitude can be increased to compensate for the extra voltage drop towards the far end.

## TRANSIENT RESPONSE OF LUMPED RC MODELS

A lumped approximation is used to model the distributed RC line as lumped resistors and lumped capacitors, as shown in Fig. 3. As the transmission line is uniform, the lumped model consists of several identical π sections in cascade.

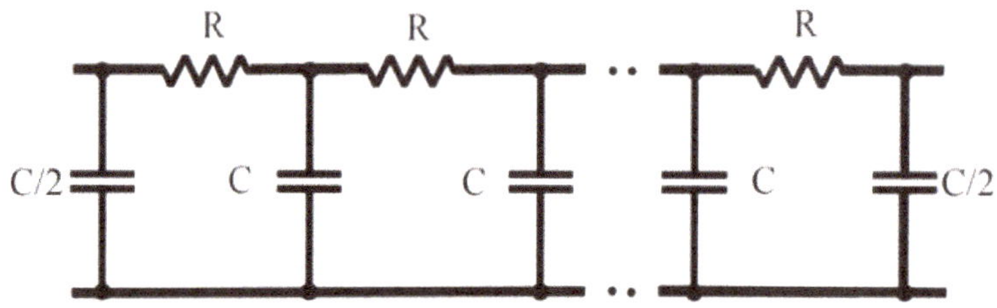


**Figure 3:** The lumped RC model.

A model with two π sections in cascade is the simplest approximation to the transmission line. A better approximation has four sections, wherein the transmission line is split into two halves, and each half is approximated by two π sections in cascade. The approximation continues to improve as the line is broken into smaller lengths, each piece being represented by a π section. Table 2 lists the computed results for the unit step response at the center of the dual-fed lumped model with N sections where N = 2,4,10 and 20. The example values of r = 1 Ω/m,c = $1\times10^{-6}$ F/m and L = $1\times10^{-3}$ m were used in the computations, but the results are shown for selected values of dimensionless (normalized) time $\tau = t/(rcL^2)$. The results for N = 2,4 and 20 are plotted in Fig. 4.

**Table 2:** Analytical and lumped model results for the unit step response at the center of a dual-fed RC line.

| τ | analytical | N = 2 | N = 4 | N = 10 | N = 20 |
|---|---|---|---|---|---|
| 0.01 | 0.001 | 0.077 | 0.021 | 0.004 | 0.002 |
| 0.02 | 0.025 | 0.148 | 0.069 | 0.034 | 0.027 |
| 0.03 | 0.082 | 0.213 | 0.129 | 0.091 | 0.085 |
| 0.05 | 0.228 | 0.330 | 0.258 | 0.232 | 0.229 |
| 0.07 | 0.363 | 0.429 | 0.378 | 0.365 | 0.363 |
| 0.10 | 0.526 | 0.551 | 0.528 | 0.526 | 0.526 |
| 0.12 | 0.610 | 0.617 | 0.608 | 0.610 | 0.610 |
| 0.13 | 0.647 | 0.647 | 0.643 | 0.646 | 0.647 |
| 0.15 | 0.710 | 0.699 | 0.704 | 0.709 | 0.710 |
| 0.20 | 0.823 | 0.798 | 0.815 | 0.822 | 0.823 |
| 0.50 | 0.991 | 0.982 | 0.989 | 0.991 | 0.991 |

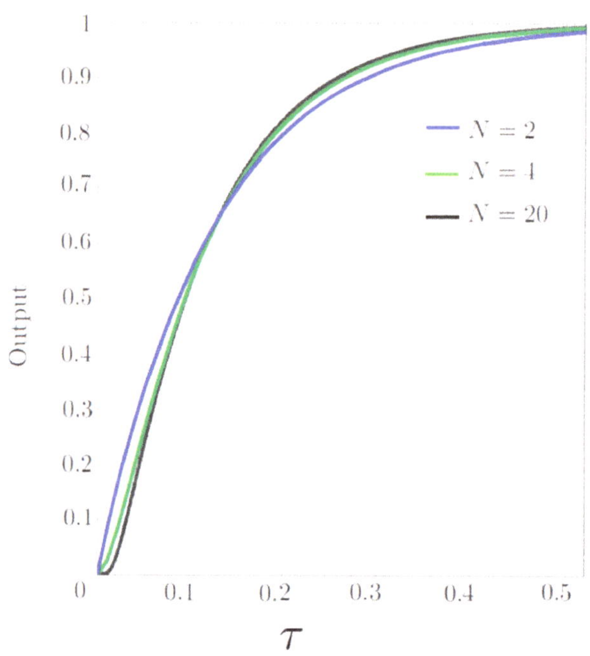


**Figure 4:** The voltage at the center of the dual-fed line, simulated with N = 2, 4 and 20 sections.

It is clear from these plots that the lumped approximation improves as the number of sections increases. In practice, for N = 20, the step response closely follows the analytical result.

For reference, the step responses of the first two models, N = 2 and N = 4, have explicit expressions:

$$v_2(0.5,\tau) = 1 - e^{-8\tau} \quad \textbf{(42)}$$

And

$$v_4(0.5,\tau) = 1 - \frac{\sqrt{2}+1}{2}e^{-(32-16\sqrt{2})\tau} + \frac{\sqrt{2}-1}{2}e^{-(32+16\sqrt{2})\tau} \quad \textbf{(43)}$$

The latter is the step response of an over damped second-order circuit with a natural frequency of $16\sqrt{2}/(rcL^2)$ rad/s and a Q-factor of $1/(2\sqrt{2}) = 0.354$.

## CONCLUSION

This paper derives analytical expressions for the transient time response of an RC transmission line under a step excitation fed into both ends of the line. Of particular interest is the response at the center of the line, where the rise time is the longest. Two forms of the analytical expressions are obtained by inverting the Laplace transform in two ways. Both forms are infinite series but one of them converges faster for small values of time. Furthermore, the expressions were presented in a form consistent with the method of superposition.

It is found that the 63% rise time at the center is reduced by a factor of 2.8843 when the RC line is dual-fed compared to the case when it is left open at the far end.

While closed-form analytical expressions now exist for the step response at the center of a dual-fed distributed RC line, lumped models with different numbers of sections were used to approximate the line. We demonstrated that the response errors from the lumped approximations reduce significantly as the number of sections in the $\pi$ model is increased, 20 sections being enough in practice to closely predict the step response of the distributed line.

## REFERENCES


1. Peirson RC, Bertnolli EC (1969) Time-domain analysis and measurement techniques for distributed RC structures. Impulse measurement techniques, J. App. Physics, 40:118–122.
2. Sakurai T (1983) Approximation of wiring delay in MOSFET LSI impulse measurement techniques. IEEE Journal of Solid-State Circuits, 18:418–426. doi: 10.1109/JSSC.1983.1051966
3. Kahng AB, Muddu S (1994) Delay analysis of VLSI interconnections using the diffusion equation model. Proc. ACM/IEEE Design Automation Conf., 2:563–569.
4. Kahng AB, Muddu S (1997) Analysis of RC interconnections under ramp input. ACM Transactions on Design Automation of Electronic Systems, 2:168–192. doi: 10.1145/253052.253137
5. Rao VB (1995) Delay analysis of the distributed RC line. Proc. ACM/IEEE Design Automation Conf., 370–375.
6. Gupta S, Patnaik LM (1999) Exact output response computation of RC interconnects under polynomial input waveforms. Twelfth International Conference on VLSI Design, 160–163.
7. Kamasz SR, Washkurak WD, Weale GP, Ma F, Smith CR et al. (1993) Design and electro-optical characterization of a 1024 × 1024 imager. Proc. SPIE Charge-Coupled Devices and Solid State Optical Sensors III, 1900:147–156. doi: 10.1117/12.148593
8. Ng J, Abbott D (2002) Introduction to solid state quantum computation for engineers. Microelectronics Journal, 33:171–177. doi: 10.1016/S0026-2692(01)00116-1

CHAPTER 9

# A GPU-BASED IMPLEMENTATION OF THE FIREFLY ALGORITHM FOR VARIABLE SELECTION IN MULTIVARIATE CALIBRATION PROBLEMS

Lauro C. M. de Paula[1], Anderson S. Soares[1], Telma W. de Lima[1], Alexandre C. B. Delbem[2] , Clarimar J. Coelho[3], Arlindo R. G. Filho[4]

[1]Institute of Informatics, Federal University of Goia´ s - UFG, Goia^ nia, GO, Brazil,

[2]Institute of Mathematical Sciences and Computing, University of Sa˜ o Paulo - USP, Sa˜ o Carlos, SP, Brazil,

[3]Computer Science Department, Pontifical Catholic University of Goia´ s - PUC Goia´ s, Goia^ nia, GO, Brazil,

[4]Department of System and Control, Technological Institute of Aeronautics - ITA, Sa˜ o Jose´ dos Campos, SP, Brazil

## ABSTRACT

**Several variable selection algorithms in multivariate calibration can be accelerated using Graphics Processing Units (GPU). Among these algorithms, the Firefly Algorithm (FA) is a recent proposed metaheuristic that may be used for variable selection. This paper presents a GPU-based FA (FA-MLR) with multiobjective formulation for variable selection in multivariate calibration problems and compares it with some traditional sequential algorithms in the literature. The advantage of the proposed implementation is demonstrated in an example involving a relatively large number of variables. The results showed that the FA-MLR, in comparison with the traditional algorithms is a more suitable choice and a relevant contribution for the variable selection problem. Additionally, the results also demonstrated that the FA-MLR performed in a GPU can be five times faster than its sequential implementation.**

## INTRODUCTION

Multivariate calibration refers to construction procedure of a mathematical model that establishes the relationship between the properties measured by an instrument and the concentration of a sample to be determined [1]. The building of a model from a subset of explanatory variables usually involves two conflicting objectives:

- Extracting as much information from a measured data with many possible independent variables;
- Decreasing the cost of obtaining data by using the smallest set of independent variables those results in a model with high accuracy and low variance.

The balance between these two commitments is achieve using variable selection techniques. The application of multivariate calibration had a breakthrough and nowadays are very popular[2]. One of the most interesting features of modern instrumental methods is the number of variables that can be measured in a single sample. Recently, devices as spectrophotometers have generated large amount of data with thousands of variables. As a consequence, the development of efficient algorithms for variable selection is important in order to deal with data even larger [3]–[5]. Furthermore, a high-performance computing framework can significantly contribute to efficiently construct an accurate model [6]. In this context, this paper presents an implementation of a modified Firefly Algorithm (FA) for variable selection in multivariate

**Citation:** de Paula LCM, Soares AS, de Lima TW, Delbem ACB, Coelho CJ, Filho ARG (2014) A GPU-Based Implementation of the Firefly Algorithm for Variable Selection in Multivariate Calibration Problems. PLoS ONE 9(12): e114145. doi:10.1371/journal.pone.0114145

calibration problems [4], [7], [8]. The FA is a metaheuristic inspired by the flashing behaviour of fireflies [9].

Several works have used FA to solve many types of problems. For instance, Yang [10] provided a detailed description of a new FA for multimodal optimization applications. Lukazik and Zak [11] provided an implementation of the FA for constrained continuous optimization. Yang [12] showed the use of the FA for nonlinear design problems. Senthilnath *et al.* [13] used the FA for clustering on benchmark problems and compared its performance with other nature-inspired techniques. Gandomi *et al.* [14] used the FA for mixed-continuous and discrete-structural optimization problems. Jati *et al.* [15] applied the FA for travelling salesman problem. Banati and Monika [16] proposed a new feature selection approach that combines the Rough Set Theory with the nature-inspired FA to reduce the dimensionality of data containing large number of features. Horng [17] proposed a new method based on the FA to construct the codebook of vector quantization for image compression. Finally, Abdullah *et al.* [18] introduced a new hybrid optimization method incorporating the FA and the evolutionary operation of the differential evolution method. In all these works, the experimental results showed that the FA scores over other algorithms in terms of computing time and optimality.

This paper also uses a Graphics Processing Unit (GPU) to parallelize the computation of the vector of regression coefficients in the problem of Multiple Linear Regression (MLR). GPUs can be employed to improve performance of computing applications usually handled by a Central Processing Unit (CPU) [5]. Husselman and Hawick [19], [20] are the only works we have found so far that present a GPU-based implementation of a FA. Moreover, estimates from the proposed FA (FA-MLR) are compared with predictions from the following traditional algorithms: Successive Projections Algorithm for MLR (SPA-MLR) [7], Genetic Algorithm for MLR (GA-MLR) [21], [22], Partial Least Squares (PLS) [23] and Bayesian Variable Selection (BVS) [24]. In addition, it is used three others criterions to determine the predictive ability of MLR models. The generalization ability of the models is also evaluated by adding artificial measurement noise to the independent variables.

The remaining of the paper is organized as follows. Section "Background" describes the multivariate calibration problem, the multicollinearity and variable selection problems, and the original FA. The FA-MLR and the processing on a GPU are presented in Section "The FA for Variable Selection". Section "Materials and Methods" describes the material and methods used in the experiments. Results are discussed in Section "Results and Discussion". Finally, Section "Conclusion" shows the conclusions of the paper.

## BACKGROUND

### Multivariate Calibration

The multivariate calibration model provides the value of a quantity $y$ based on values measured from a set of explanatory variables $\{x_1, x_2, \ldots, x_k\}^T$ [25], [26]. The model can be defined as:

$$y = \beta_0 + \beta_1 x_1 + \ldots + \beta_k x_k + \varepsilon, \quad (1)$$

where $\beta_0, \beta_1, \ldots, \beta_k$, $i=1, 2, \ldots, k$, are the coefficients to be determined, and $\varepsilon$ is a portion of random error.

A simple model to obtain the coefficients in Equation (1) based on calculation of partial least squares is known as MLR, which is a statistical technique used to build models describing reasonably relationships between several explanatory variables of a given process [27], [28]. This technique requires the number of observations greater than the number of variables. Nevertheless, the opposite may occur for some applications (more variables than samples) [8]. For instance, in problems involving spectrometric determination of a physical or chemical quantity the explanatory variables correspond to measurements taken at various wavelengths[29].

Equation (2) shows how the regression coefficients may be calculated using the Moore-Penrose pseudoinverse [30]:

$$\beta = (\mathbf{X}^T\mathbf{X})^{-1}\mathbf{X}^T\mathbf{y}, \quad (2)$$

where $\mathbf{X}$ is the matrix of samples and independent variables (collected by instruments used for construction of multivariate calibration models), $\mathbf{y}$ is the vector of dependent variables (or property of interest obtained in laboratory, which serves as a parameter for model calibration), and $\beta$ is the vector of regression coefficients.

As shown in Equation (3), predictive ability of MLR models comparing predictions with reference values for a test set from the squared deviations is calculated by Root Mean Squared Error of Prediction (RMSEP):

$$\text{RMSEP} = \sqrt{\frac{\sum_{i=1}^{N} (\mathbf{y}_i - \hat{\mathbf{y}}_i)^2}{N}}. \quad (3)$$

where $\mathbf{y}$ is the reference value of the property of interest, $N$ is the number of observations, and $\hat{\mathbf{y}} = \{\hat{y}_1, \hat{y}_2, \ldots, \hat{y}_k\}^T$ is the estimated value calculated as:

$$\hat{\mathbf{y}} = \mathbf{X}\beta. \quad \mathbf{(4)}$$

Another criteria to determine the predictive ability of MLR models that has been used is the Mean Absolute Percentage Error (MAPE) [31]. MAPE is a relative measure which express errors as a percentage of the actual data and is defined as:

$$MAPE = \frac{\sum \left|\frac{Y_i - \hat{Y}_i}{Y_i}\right|}{N}(100) = \frac{\sum \left|\frac{e_i}{Y_i}\right|}{N}(100). \quad (5)$$

where $Y_i$ is the actual data at variable $i$, $\hat{Y}_i$ is the forecast (using some model/method) at variable $i$, $e_i$ is the forecast error at variable $i$, and $N$ is the number of observations (or samples) used in computing the MAPE.

The biggest advantage of MAPE is that it provides an easy and intuitive way of judging the extent (or the importance) of errors. Furthermore, percentage errors are part of the every day language making them easily and intuitively interpretable [31]. This measure is widely used in forecasting as a basis of comparison. It can be used to measure how high or low are the differences between the predictions and actual data in regression models in a similar way to forecasting problems.

In statistics, there is also a technique called Predicted Residual Sums of Squares (PRESS) proposed by Allen [32]. PRESS is a useful statistic for comparing different models and is based on the leave-one-out technique [33]. It is also known as a form of cross-validation used in regression analysis to provide a summary measure of the fit of a model to a sample of observations that were not themselves used to estimate the model [32]. The PRESS also may be used as a measure of predictivity to compare and select the best model. However, one of the main problems of cross-validation techniques is their computational cost, which may become extremely higher and unviable [34]. Equation (6) shows how the PRESS is calculated:

$$PRESS = \sum_{i=1}^{N} (y_i - \hat{y}_i)^2. \quad (6)$$

where $y$ is a real value of concentration obtained by laboratorial methods, $\hat{y}$ is the result ofEquation (4) applied to measures of new observations (**X** measures), and $N$ is the number of observations.

## Multicollinearity Problem and Variable Selection

In prediction problems with regression model having many variables, most of them may not contribute to improve prediction precision. The selection of a reduced set with variables that positively influence in the regression model is important in order to improve the efficiency of algorithms for construction MLR models. Moreover, the identification of a small set of variables that are explanatory is usually desired in regression problems [3]. The problem of determining an appropriate equation associated to a subset of independent variables depends on the criteria used to: *i*) analyze the variables, *ii*) select the subset and *iii*) estimate the coefficients in Equation (2).

There are some model (or variable) selection criterias in the literature [35]. An approach is the use of information criteria such as Akaike Information Criteria (AIC) proposed by Akayke [36]or the Bayesian Information Criteria (BIC) proposed by Schwarz [37]. Equation (7) and (8) show how AIC and BIC may be calculated, respectively:

$$AIC = \ln(\hat{\sigma}_a^2) + r\frac{2}{N} + 1. \quad (7)$$

$$BIC = \ln(\hat{\sigma}_a^2) + r\frac{\ln(N)}{N}. \quad (8)$$

where $\ln(\hat{\sigma}_a^2)$ denotes the maximum likelihood estimate of $\hat{\sigma}_a^2$, $r$ denotes the number of parameters estimated in the model, including a constant term, and $N$ is the number of samples [35].

In the information criteria approach, models that yield a minimum value for the criterion are to be preferred. Generally, the AIC and BIC values are compared among various models as the basis for selection of the model. However, a disadvantage of this approach is that several models may have to be estimated by maximum likelihood, which is expensive and may require a huge computational effort [35].

In this context, a Firefly Algorithm is used in this paper to solve the problem of variable selection for the multivariate calibration problems, as described in Section "The Proposed FA for Variable Selection".

## Firefly Algorithm

Nature-inspired metaheuristics have shown to be powerful in solving various types of problems. The FA is a recently developed optimization algorithm proposed by Yang [9], [10]. This algorithm is based on the idealized behaviour of the flashing characteristics of fireflies. The FA simulates the attraction system of real fireflies. They produce luminescent flashes as a signal system to communicate with other fireflies, especially to prey attraction [16]. Algorithm 1 (Table 1) shows a pseudocode for the original FA.

**Table 1.** Algorithm 1. Original Firefly Algorithm

```
Initialize a population of fireflies x_i, i=1, 2,..., n
Calculate objective function f(x_i) for each firefly
Define light absorption coefficient γ
while t < MaxGeneration
   for i=1: n
     for j=1: n
       Light intensity I_i at x_i is determined from f(x_i)
       if (I_j > I_i)
       Calculate the attractiveness between i and j which varies with distance r via exp[−γr]
       Move firefly i towards j in all d dimensions according to the attractiveness between i and j
       end if
       Evaluate the new fireflies and update light intensities
     end for j
   end for i
   Rank the fireflies and find the current best
end while
Postprocess results
```

In the Algorithm 1 (Table 1), there are two important issues: the variation of light intensity and the attractiveness formulation. For simplicity, one can assume that the attractiveness of a firefly is determined by its brightness or light intensity which is associated with the encoded objective function [10]. The brightness $I$ of a firefly at a particular location $\mathbf{x}$ can be chosen as $I(\mathbf{x}) \Rightarrow f(\mathbf{x})$. However, the attractiveness $\omega$ is relative, which should be seen in the eyes of the beholder or judged by the other fireflies. Then, it should vary with the distance $r_{ij}$ between firefly $i$ and firefly $j$. As light intensity decreases with the distance from its source, and light is also absorbed in the media, so the attractiveness should vary with the degree of absorption[12]. In the simplest form, the light intensity $I(r)$ varies with the distance $r$ monotonically and exponentially as shown by Equation (9):

$$I = I_o e^{-\gamma r}, \tag{9}$$

where $I_o$ is the original light intensity and $\gamma$ is the light absorption coefficient.

As a firefly›s attractiveness is proportional to the light intensity seen by adjacent fireflies, one can define the attractiveness $\omega$ of a firefly by:

$$\omega = \omega_o e^{-\gamma r^2}, \tag{10}$$

where $\omega_o$ is the attractiveness at $r$=0.

It is worth pointing out that the exponent $\gamma r^2$ can be replaced by other functions such as $\gamma r^m$ when $m > 0$ [12].

The distance between any two fireflies is calculated using Cartesian distance in Equation 11.

$$r_{i,j} = \sqrt{(x_i - x_j)^2 + (y_i - y_j)^2}. \tag{11}$$

The firefly $i$ is attracted to brighter firefly $j$ and its movement is determined by

$$x_i = x_j + \omega_0 e^{-\gamma r_{i,j}^2}(x_j - x_i) + \alpha(\text{rand} - \frac{1}{2}). \tag{12}$$

In Equation (12), $x_i$ is the current position or solution of a firefly and the $\omega_0 e^{-\gamma r_{i,j}^2}(x_j - x_i)$ is attractiveness of a firefly to seen by adjacent fireflies. The $\alpha(\text{rand} - \frac{1}{2})$ is a firefly›s random movement. The coefficient $\alpha$ is a randomisation parameter determined by the problem of interest with $\alpha \in [0,1]$, while rand function is a random number obtained from the uniform distribution. Without the random movement, the reies would possibly be attracted to a rey that is not necessarily the brightest. The solution would be restricted to a local minima, directly toward the best solution in the local search space. Using the randomization term, the search over small deviations makes it possible to escape from local minima, having a higher chance of nding the global minimum of the function.

For most cases related in others works, they take $\omega_0 = 1$, $\alpha \in [0,1]$ and $\gamma = 1$. The parameter $\gamma$ characterizes the variation of attractiveness, and its value is crucially important in determining the speed of the convergence and how the FA algorithm behaves. In most applications, it typically varies from 0.01 to 100.

According with Yang [38], the algorithm is swarm-intelligence-based, so it has the similar advantages that other swarm-intelligence-based algorithms have. In fact, a simple analysis of parameters suggest that some particle swarm optimization (PSO) variants such as Accelerated PSO are a special case of firefly algorithm when $\gamma = 0$. However, according with Yang [38], firefly has two major advantages over other algorithms: automatical subdivision and the ability of dealing with multimodality. First, FA is based on attraction and atractiveness decrease with distance. This leads to the fact that the whole population can automatically subdivide into subgroups, and each group can swarm around each mode or local optimum. Second, this subdivision allows the fireflies to be able to find all optima simultaneously if the population size is sufficiently higher than the number of modes.

## The Proposed Multiobjective FA for Variable Selection

Based on the success of the works cited in "Introdution", one found out that FA can be used for selection of variables to solve multivariate calibration problems. Thus, this paper presents a FA for variable selection using MLR (FA-MLR). Algorithm 2 (Table 2) shows a pseudocode for the FA-MLR.

**Table 2.** Algorithm 2. Proposed FA-MLR

1. **Parameters**: $\mathbf{X}_{n \times m}$, $\mathbf{y}_{n \times 1}$, where $\mathbf{X}_{n \times m}$ is a matrix of samples by their corresponding variable values, $n$ is the number of rows, $m$ is the number of columns and $\mathbf{y}_{n \times 1}$ is a vector of dependent variables
2. $s \leftarrow$ the number of fireflies, determined by experimental analysis.
3. **for** $i = 1$: *MaxGeneration*
4. Generate randomly a population of $s$ fireflies, where each firefly is a set of $d$ indices for $d$ columns of $\mathbf{X}_{n \times m}$, $d \leq m$
5. Compute Equation (2) for each firefly (when using Algorithm 3 it is performed on the GPU)
6. Compute the number of variables used in the model
7. Calculate Equation (3) determining the light intensities of each firefly
8. If $i$-th firefly dominates $j$-th firefly
9. Move firefly $j$ towards $i$ using Equation (12)
10. Rank the fireflies and find the current best
11. **end for** $i$
12. Postprocess results, that is, calculate the prediction error for the best firefly and visualize the selected variables indicated by it.

The original formulation of FA uses the evaluation of a single objective. However, previous works [8], [39], [40] in multivariate calibration showed that while monoobjective formulation use a bigger number of variables, multiobjective algorithms use fewer variables with the less prediction error. Thus, in this work, we proposed a multiobjective optimization implementation. One classical way is to combine all objectives into a single objective so that algorithms for single objective optimization. Another way is to extend the firefly algorithm to produce Pareto optimal front directly. By extending the basic formulation of FA, we developed the following multiobjective firefly algorithm, based on [41], summarized in Algorithm 2 (Table 2).

In the multiobjective formulation of FA, the choice of current best is done in two steps. First, only the non-dominated solutions are selected. In mathematical terms, a feasible solution $x^1 \in X$ is said dominate another solution $x^2 \in X$ if:

- $f_i(x^1) \leq f_i(x^2)$ for all indices $i \in \{1,2,...,k\}$ and
- $f_j(x^1) \leq f_j(x^2)$ for at least one index $j \in \{1,2,...,k\}$

A solution $x^1 \in X$ is called Pareto optimal, if there does not exist another solution that dominates it. Among non-dominates solutions, we applied the multiobjective decision maker method described in [8] to choice the current best (step 10).

## Numerical Example

For illustration, let's consider a short variable selection problem with just five variables available and just three fireflies. Will be used, the first five variables available and the first three samples from matrix $\mathbf{X}$ and the first three samples from vector $y$ described in Materials and Methods Section, using $\alpha = 0.2$, $\gamma = 1$ and $\omega_0 = 0.97$. First, the fireflies are uniformly distributed random numbers in the range 0 to 1.

Firefly 1 = 0.95 0.48 0.45 0.44 0.92,

Firefly 2 = 0.23 0.89 0.01 0.61 0.73,

Firefly 3 = 0.60 0.76 0.82 0.79 0.17.

The variable selection is a binary problem, so each firefly must be encoded. Each variable information major than 0.5 is encoded to 1 (variable will be used in the regression model) and less or equal 0.5 is encoded 0 (variable will not be used in the regression model).

Encoded Firefly 1 = 1 0 0 0 1,

Encoded Firefly 2 = 0 1 0 1 1,

Encoded Firefly 3 = 1 1 1 1 0.

Now, each firefly will be evaluated using the Equation 2. This equation indicates the error of prediction. In Equation 2, just the columns of $\mathbf{X}$ indicated by firefly will be used in the regression. In our example the brightness is 6.82 10.97 9.22 for each firefly. Now, we compared all firefly each other, for example, the firefly 2 has major light intensity than firefly 1, so we must move firefly 1 toward firefly 2. For this proposes, first we must calculate the distance between the fireflies using Equation 11.

$r_{1,2}$ = 0.71 0.40 0.43 0.17 0.18

Using the distance between the fireflies, we can calculate the attractiveness using Equation 10. As a result, we updated firefly 1 and the encoded firefly 1. Worth noting that, the updated firefly 1 excluded the first variable used in the original solution and now use the second and fourth variables available after 'to walk' toward firefly 2.

Updated Firefly 1 = 0.44 0.75 0.02 0.53 0.67→

Updated Encoded Firefly 1 = 0 1 0 1 1

The iteration is repeated until all solutions have been updated. The updates allow the solutions to move towards to the current optimal solution. The solution that produces the best fitness (in this case the minor RMSEP value) is selected as the global best solution.

## Using a GPU with the CUDA-MATLAB integration for the FA-MLR

GPUs are microprocessors developed with a flow-oriented technology, optimized for calculations of data-intensive, where many identical operations can be performed in parallel on different data [42]. Graphics devices currently available represent a high performance computer hardware, flexible by enabling the execution of non-graphical applications [5]. While the current multicore architectures have two, four or eight cores, GPUs have hundreds or even thousands of processing cores [5]. GPUs can implement many parallel algorithms directly using graphics hardware and the current trend is to include in each new generation a significant number of additional cores [43].

Correspondingly the evolution of hardware, new programming models have been developed. Among them stand out Compute Unified Device Architecture (CUDA) [42] and Open Computing Language (OpenCL) [44]. In both, due to the availability of Application Programming Interface (API) to the programmer the implementation of efficient parallel applications is facilitated [5]. CUDA was the first architecture and programming interface, created by → in 2006 to allow GPUs could be used for a wide variety of applications [42].

Recently, using MATLAB for GPU computing can accelerate the applications more easily than by using the CUDA-C programming language [45]. This is possible because of the existence of MATLAB plug-in for CUDA (Parallel Computing Toolbox - PCT). Thus, with the familiar MATLAB language one can take advantage of the CUDA GPU computing technology [46].

Developments for GPUs using the PCT is in general easier and faster than using CUDA-C language, since several aspects of parallelization design are performed by the PCT [47], [48]. Furthermore, it is important to note that the PCT requires an *NVIDIA* graphics card.

Step 5 (that calculates the regression coefficients) in Algorithm 2 (Table 2) can be executed on a GPU. The parallel execution can be accomplished through MATLAB built-in functions. Algorithm 3 (Table 3) shows the pseudocode for Step 5 using a *NVIDIA* GPU.

**Table 3.** Algorithm 3. Step 5 of the FA-MLR

1. **Parameters**: $\mathbf{X}_{n\times m}$, $\mathbf{y}_{n\times 1}$ and fireflies $\mathbf{x}_1,\ldots,\mathbf{x}_s$
2. **for** $i=1:s$
3. Obtain submatrix $\mathbf{X}_{n\times d}$ that contains only $d$ columns of $\mathbf{X}_{n\times m}$ indexed by $\mathbf{x}_i$
4. Allocate matrices $\mathbf{X}_{n\times d}$ and $\mathbf{X}^T_{n\times d}$ and vector $\mathbf{y}_{n\times 1}$ on the GPU memory
5. Calculate Equation (2) on the GPU
6. **end for** $i$

## MATERIALS AND METHODS

The Firefly algorithm was implemented using $i$, $\alpha=0.2$ and $\gamma=1$. We have used for RMSEP, MAPE, PRESS, AIC and BIC comparison the Successive Projections Algorithm for MLR (SPA-MLR) [7], the standard Genetic Algorithm for MLR (GA-MLR) [21], the Partial Least Squares (PLS) [23] and the Bayesian Variable Selection (BVS). The BVS code was obtained at the following URL: https://github.com/pcarbo/varbvs [24].

Proposed by Araújo *et al.* [49], the goal of SPA-MLR is to select a subset of variables with low collinearity that allow the construction of a MLR model with a capacity of adequate prediction. SPA-MLR comprises three main phases. Phase 1 consists of projection operations carried out on the matrix of instrumental responses ($\omega_0 = 0.97$). These projections are used to generate chains of variables with successively more elements. Each element in a chain is selected in order to display the least collinearity with the previous ones. In Phase 2, candidate subsets of variables are extracted from the chains and evaluated according to the predictive performance (RMSEP) of the resulting MLR model. Such a performance can be assessed by using cross-validation or a separate validation set. Finally, Phase 3 consists of a variable elimination procedure aimed at improving the parsimony of the model.

In GA-MLR, the RMSEP guide the evaluation of a subset of variables used in the calibration model and allows us to choose models more suitable to prediction [21]. Genetic algorithms (GA) are a global search heuristic inspired on the natural evolution of species and in the natural biological process. Basically, a GA creates a population of possible solutions to the problem being solved and then submit these solutions to the evolution process. Genetic operators are applied to transform the population in every generation, in order to created better individuals. The main operators responsible for the population diversification well known in the literature are crossover (or recombination) and mutation.

Partial Least Squares (PLS) is a technique that generalizes and combines features from principal component analysis and MLR [30]. It is a statistical method that bears some relation to principal components regression. Instead of finding hyperplanes of minimum variance between the response and independent variables, it finds a linear regression model by projecting the predicted variables and the observable variables to a new space. Because both the $\mathbf{X}$ and $\mathbf{X}$ data are projected to new spaces, the PLS family of methods are known as bilinear factor models.

Bayesian Variable Selection (BVS) is a tool to variable selection in MLR used for tackling many scientific problems [24]. In the BVS, the model selection problem is transformed to the form of parameter estimation: rather than searching for the single optimal model, a Bayesian will attempt to estimate the posterior probability of all models within the considered class of models. A probability distribution is first assigned to the dependent variable through the specification of a family of prior distributions for the unknown parameters in the regression model. For each regression coefficient subject to deletion from the model, the prior distribution is a mixture of a point mass at 0 and diffuse uniform distribution elsewhere.

The Kennard and Stone [50] algorithm was applied to the resulting spectra to divide the samples into calibration, validation and prediction sets with 389, 193 and 193 samples, respectively. The validation set was employed to guide the selection of variables in SPA-MLR and GA-MLR. The prediction set was only employed in the final performance assessment of the resulting MLR models. In the PLS study, the calibration and validation sets were joined into a single modeling set, which was used in the leave-one-out cross-validation procedure. The number of latent variables was selected on the basis of the cross-validation error by using the F-test criterion of Haaland and Thomas [23]. The prediction set was only employed in the final evaluation of the PLS model.

All calculations were carried out by using a desktop computer with an Intel Core i7 2600 (3.40 GHz), 8 GB of RAM memory and a $\mathbf{Y}$ GeForce GTX 550Ti graphics card with 192 CUDA cores and 2 GB of memory config. The Matlab 8.1.0.604 (R2013a) software platform was employed throughout.

We present two studies, one simulated and a real problem, to present the proposed algorithm. The details of the data sets are presented below.

### Simulated Data Set

The simulated data set used in this work was generated using the matlab code showed. The algorithm uses a random numbers generation for building the matrix *NVIDIA* (independents variables). The seed of the random generator was setted with value 0 (zero), thus, the experiment can be reproduced in any computer. To generate the matrix responses $\mathbf{X}$, we choose a number of variables from $\mathbf{Y}$ to be correlated with $\mathbf{X}$ (dependents variables). The values of $\mathbf{Y}$ are generated using random weights applied over the variables chosen. We create two scenarios: the first five variables are randomly chosen to be correlated with $\mathbf{Y}$ and in the second, ten variables are used. The challenge of variable selection algorithm is to find the variables used to generate $\mathbf{Y}$. These variables explain the

**Y** variability and the best result can be obtained selecting only these variables.

## Real Data Set

The real dataset employed in this work consists of whole grain wheat samples, obtained from vegetal material from occidental Canadian producers. The standard data were determined at the Grain Research Laboratory as in work of [7], [5] and [51]. The data set for the multivariate calibration study consists of 1090 Near-Infrared (NIR) spectra of whole-kernel wheat samples, which were used as shoot-out data in the 2008 International Diffuse Reflectance Conference (http://www.idrc-chambersburg.org/shootout.html).

Protein content was chosen as the property of interest (matrix **Y**). The spectra were acquired in the range 400–2500 nm with a resolution of 2 nm (matrix **Y**). In this work the NIR region in the range 1100–2500 nm was employed. In order to remove undesirable baseline features, first derivative spectra were calculated by using a Savitzky-Golay filter with an **X** order polynomial and an 11-points window [52].

The reference values of protein concentration in samples of wheat were determined in the laboratory by the Kjeldahl method [53]. This method uses the destruction of organic matter with concentrated sulfuric acid in the presence of a catalyst and by the action of heat, with subsequent distillation and titration of nitrogen from the sample. The use of indirect instrumental methods such as NIR spectroscopy and mathematical models such as MLR allow the protein to be determined without destruction of the sample.

# RESULTS AND DISCUSSION

## Simulated Study

In the simulated study, the challenge of the variable selection algorithms is to find the variables in $2^{nd}$ that explain the **X** variance. We did two studies, one with five variables generating **Y**, and other with ten variables generating **Y**.

Table 4 presents the results of all algorithms in the simulated data. As can be seen, the FA-MLR has the minor value of RMSEP, MAPE and PRESS, in both studies, using five and ten variables generating **Y**. This measures indicates better prediction ability using the variables selected by FA. FA-MLR use less variables than SPA-MLR and BVS. According with AIC and BIC measure, FA-MLR has better parsimony between predictive capacity and number of variables in the model. In some applications the predictive ability is critical, in others the number of variables used or even the parsimony between both.

**Table 4.** Results of the FA-MLR, SPA-MLR, GA-MLR, PLS and BVS, in simulated data

| | Number of Variables | RMSEP | MAPE | AIC | BIC | PRESS |
|---|---|---|---|---|---|---|
| Five variables generating Y | | | | | | |
| PLS | 4 | 1.11 | 3.7% | 1279 | 1330 | 29.29 |
| SPA-MLR | 2 | 1.05 | 3.53% | 1005 | 1020 | 26.82 |
| GA-MLR | 26 | 1.85 | 4.0% | 1981 | 2013 | 45.42 |
| BVS | 4 | 0.98 | 3.4% | 1201 | 1301 | 21.02 |
| FA-MLR | 3 | 0.97 | 3.3% | 956 | 972 | 19.98 |
| Ten variables generating Y | | | | | | |
| PLS | 4 | 1.91 | 3.5% | 1054 | 1093 | 69.05 |
| SPA-MLR | 4 | 1.75 | 3.2% | 1004 | 1021 | 61.26 |
| GA-MLR | 35 | 2.01 | 4.80% | 1791 | 1807 | 74.36 |
| BVS | 7 | 1.95 | 3.3% | 1149 | 1201 | 70.95 |
| FA-MLR | 3 | 1.67 | 3.1% | 901 | 933 | 57.5 |

Table 5 shows the variable selected by each one of the algorithms. For the first case, the variables used to generating **Y** is 22, 32, 34, 40 and 99. For the second case, the variables used were 4, 11, 39, 46, 48, 66, 67, 69, 85 and 189. According with results, for the two cases SPA-MLR and FA-MLR are the more conservative algorithm. SPA-MLR selected just two variables (32 and 99) for the first case, but did not select the other three variables correlated with the response matrix **Y**. FA-MLR selected three variables (22, 32 and 40), all correlated whit the response matrix **Y**, generating a prediction error lower than SPA-MLR. In the second case, SPA-MLR selected three variables (11, 39 and 85) correlated with the response and one wrong variable. FA-MLR selected three variables (4, 46 and 189) all of them related with the response variable. Although the SPA-MLR algorithm use a elimination procedure, described in[54], the multiobjective formulation of FA-MLR was able to balance between prediction error and number of variables. The results of AIC and BIC show that FA-MLR algorithm has better parsimony of MLR models than models builded by SPA-MLR.

**Table 5.** Variable Selected by the Algorithms

| Algorithm | Variables Found |
|---|---|
| **Five variables generating Y** | |
| PLS | - |
| SPA-MLR | **32**, **99** |
| GA-MLR | **22**, 23, 29, 35, 38, 39, 46, 47, 55, 66, 69, 71, 78, 84, 90, 111, 127, 129, 136, 140, 158, 167, 174, 176, 188, 193 |
| BVS | **22**, 31, **99**, 144 |
| FA-MLR | **22**, **32**, **40** |
| **Ten variables generating Y** | |
| PLS | - |
| SPA-MLR | **11**, **39**, **85**, 99 |
| GA-MLR | 2, 7, 17, 17, 23, 26, 29, 32, 35, 38, **39**, 40, 42, **46**, 47, 52, 58, 66, 69, 71, 78, 84, **99**, 111, 127, 129, 136, 140, 158, 167, 174, 176, 181, 188, 193 |
| BVS | **4**, **11**, 31, 99, 158, 167, **189** |
| FA-MLR | **4**, **46**, **189** |

The best result of RMPSEP, MAPE and PRESS were obtained by FA-MLR in both cases. The algorithm selected more variables correlated with the response matrix (3 in both cases) reducing the prediction error. FA-MLR works individually each firefly and finds a better position for itself in consideration with its current position as well as the position of other fireflies. Thus, it escapes from the local optima and finds a global optimum is less number of iterations. However, the algorithm requires a correct adjustment of the parameters, while SPA-MLR, PLS and BVS not.

The worst result was obtained by GA-MLR algorithm. It selected much wrong variables and few variables correlated with the response matrix. The model produce by this algorithm is large and with low prediction ability. PLS uses linear transformation of original variables to build new latent variables. In this process is not possible separate the original variables used, thus, we do not have the results of which original variables used to build the regression model.

## Real Problem

Fig. 1 shows that the FA-MLR is able to perform the reduction of the RMSEP as the iterations are performed. The curve in the graph refers to the average error of all the fireflies.

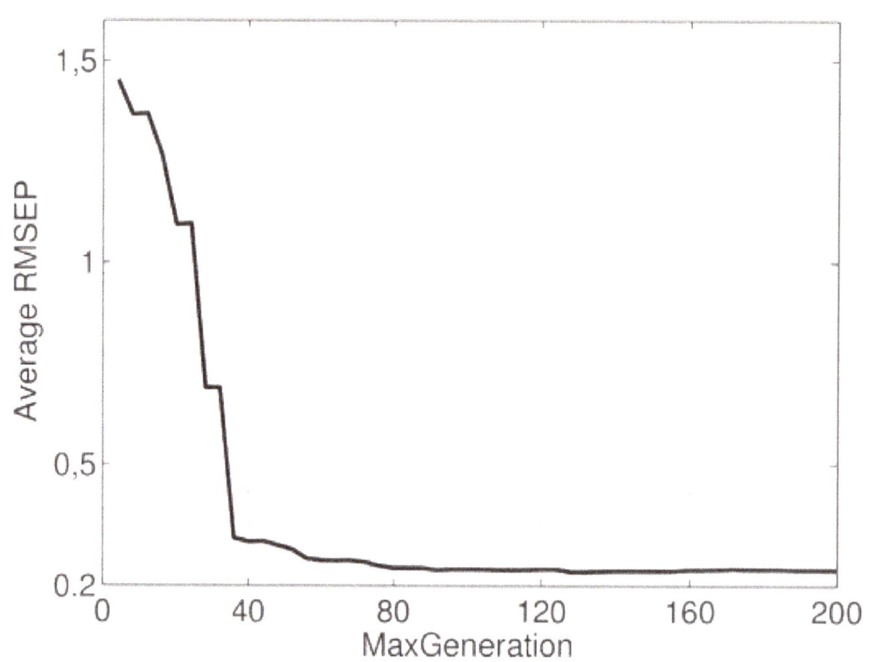


**Figure 1.** Behavior of average RMSEP versus **Y**.

Fig. 2 presents how the number of fireflies affects the RMSEP. It is possible to note that we need a number between 400 and 500 fireflies to achieve the best results.

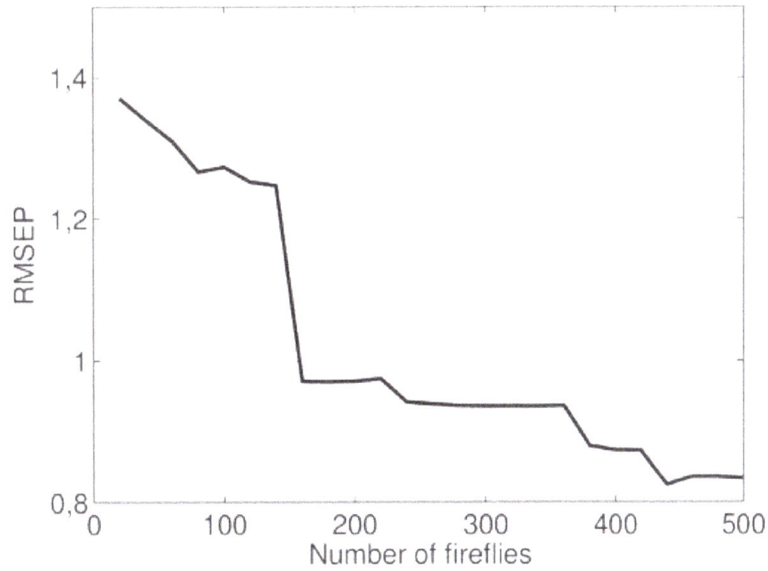


**Figure 2.** Behavior of RMSEP versus number of fireflies.

The selected variables in the best firefly obtained can be visualized in Fig. 3. This result indicates that these regions are the most promising to use in the spectrophotometer. In practice, this result implies a smaller number of wavelengths measures in spectrophotometer for quantify the protein concentration property in real samples.

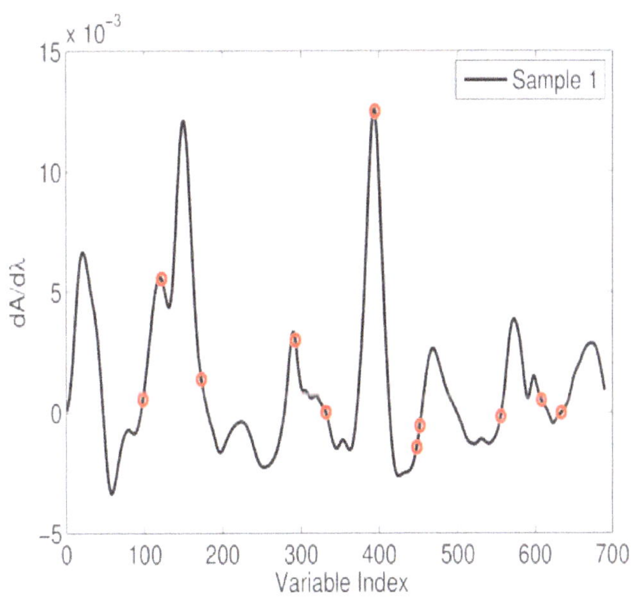


**Figure 3.** Visualization of selected variables.

## Comparison with Traditional Algorithms

The comparison among the FA-MLR and traditional algorithms (SPA-MLR, GA-MLR, PLS and BVS) are presented in Table 6. As can be seen, the results of SPA-MLR, GA-MLR and PLS are relatively similar in terms of RMSEP, MAPE and PRESS. The results of BVS in terms of RMSEP and MAPE were relatively smaller in comparison to the results of SPA-MLR, GA-MLR and PLS. However, the FA-MLR has the lower RMSEP (0.09), MAPE (0.8%) and PRESS (4.08) using just 11 variables while BVS has 0.15, 1.07% and 6.96, of RMSEP, MAPE and PRESS, respectively, using 29 variables. The FA-MLR presents the lower AIC and BIC values, that is, the best parsimony. Indeed some scientists may prefer a smaller number of variables. In this case, the FA-MLR or PLS would be a more viable choice. However, despite to select a relatively small number of variables PLS uses all the original variables to build the new latent variables [55].

**Table 6.** Results of the FA-MLR, SPA-MLR, GA-MLR, PLS and BVS

| | Number of Variables | RMSEP | MAPE | AIC | BIC | PRESS |
|---|---|---|---|---|---|---|
| PLS | 15 | 0.21 | 1.50% | 1379 | 3630 | 10.09 |
| SPA-MLR | 13 | 0.20 | 1.43% | 45.54 | 120.58 | 9.95 |
| GA-MLR | 146 | 0.21 | 1.50% | 291.58 | 767.93 | 10.86 |
| BVS | 29 | 0.15 | 1.07% | 49.70 | 131.26 | 6.96 |
| FA-MLR | 11 | 0.09 | 0.8% | 31.45 | 96.34 | 4.08 |

Fig. 4 plots the real values in the compound versus predictions using the SPA-MLR (red plus) and FA-MLR (blue balls), that produced the best performance among the rival-tested algorithms. Zero differences between predictions and actual concentrations result in points over the straight line of the plot. The predicted concentrations are near the real concentrations for both methods. Nevertheless, the model using the variables selected by FA-MLR are in general closer to the straight line than SPA-MLR predictions. This result also indicates that the MLR model obtained using the variables selected by FA-MLR can produce less RMSEP and MAPE in average.

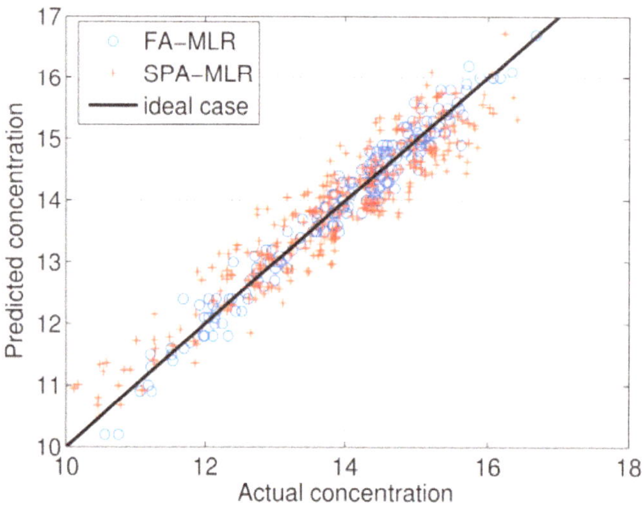


**Figure 4.** Comparison between actual and predicted concentration using the FA-MLR and the SPA-MLR.

Fig. 5 shows the PRESS values for all algorithms. To calculate the PRESS we used only the difference between the real ($y$) and predicted ($\hat{y}$) values of the property of interest. Using only the difference between $\hat{y}$ and $y$ one can obtain a more exact residual value. It is possible to note that the PRESS values of the FA-MLR are more together and nearby from zero. This indicates that, in fact, the proposed FA-MLR is more robust to outliers observations and can provide a model with a better predictive ability.

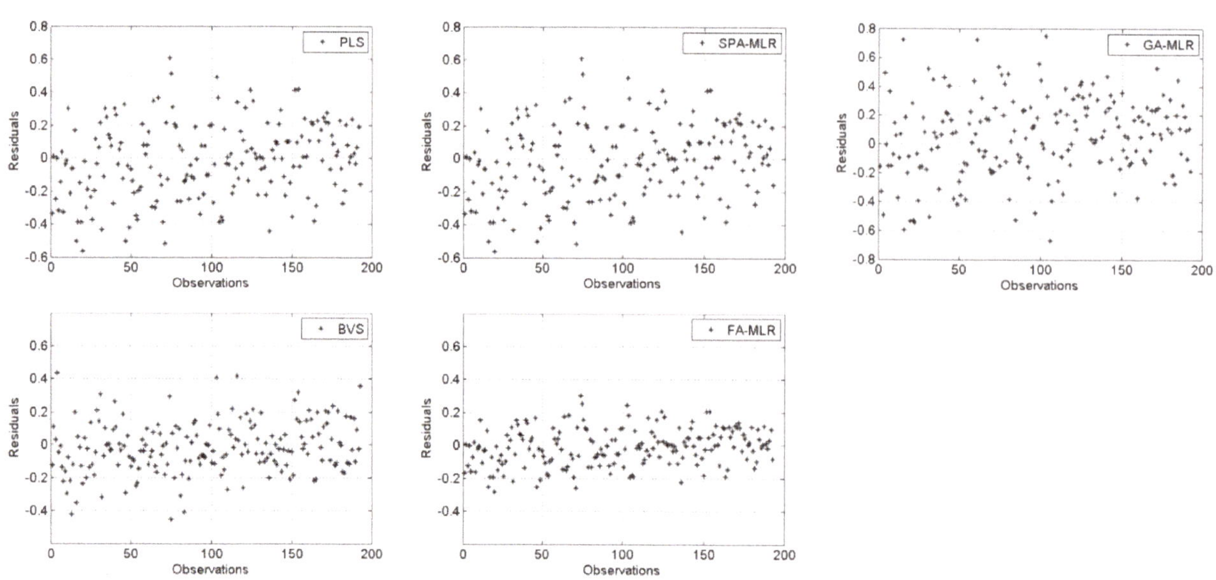


**Figure 5.** PRESS values for all algorithms: (a) PLS; (b) SPA-MLR; (c) GA-MLR; (d) BVS; and (e) FA-MLR.

In order to assess the sensitivity of the regression models to measurement noise, the matrix x in the prediction set was contaminated with artificial zero-mean white gaussian noise. In each column, the standard deviation of the additional noise was set to 0.1 times the standard deviation of the actual value. As can be seen in Table 7, the results of FA-MLR and SPA-MLR remained largely unaltered after introduction of the artificial noise. On the other hand, the performance of GA-MLR, PLS and BVS was noticeably degraded, as compared to Table 6. Such a result can be ascribed to the fact that FA-MLR and SPA-MLR is aimed at minimizing multi-collinearity problems, which are known to increase the propagation of noise.

**Table 7.** Accuracy of regression models with artificial noise addition

| | RMSEP | MAPE |
|---|---|---|
| PLS | 0.29 | 2.08% |
| SPA-MLR | 0.23 | 1.64% |
| GA-MLR | 0.35 | 2.51% |
| BVS | 0.21 | 1.50% |
| FA-MLR | 0.11 | 0.74% |

## Speedup for FA-MLR using GPU

Fig. 6 shows the computational performance of the FA-MLR execution using CPU and also GPU. Table 8 presents the comparison of computational time for FA-MLR according to the number of fireflies. The results showed that the FA-MLR using GPU is around five times faster than the FA-MLR using CPU.

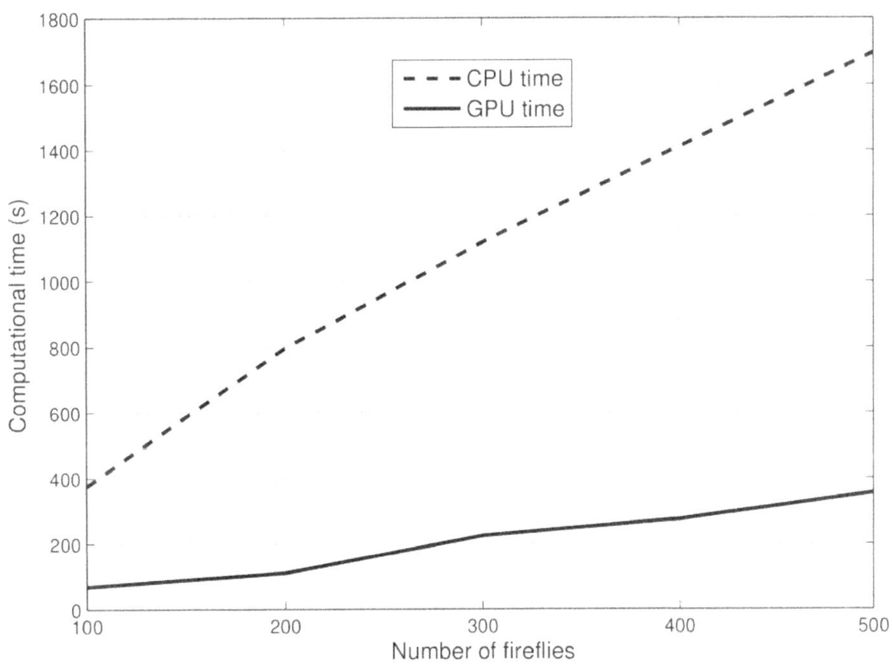


**Figure 6.** Comparison of computational performance between the FA-MLR using CPU and GPU.

**Table 8.** Computational time (seconds) for each implementation of the FA-MLR

| | Number of Fireflies | | |
|---|---|---|---|
| | 100 | 300 | 500 |
| FA-MLR using GPU | 69.34 | 223.56 | 355.34 |
| FA-MLR using CPU | 374.51 | 1119.63 | 1697.78 |

Table 9 presents a comparison of computational time between SPA-MLR, GA-MLR, PLS, BVS and FA-MLR according to the number of selected variables. It is possible to note that FA-MLR using GPU provides the lowest time.

**Table 9.** Computational time (seconds) for SPA-MLR, GA-MLR, PLS, BVS and FA-MLR

| | Time |
|---|---|
| PLS | 2834.15 |
| SPA-MLR | 533.66 |
| GA-MLR | 372.22 |
| BVS | 315.68 |
| FA-MLR using GPU | 185.34 |
| FA-MLR using CPU | 931.45 |

The computational times in Table 9 represent the spent time for selecting up to 150 variables for SPA-MLR, GA-MLR, PLS and BVS, and using 250 fireflies for the FA-MLR. For PLS we have used the cross-validation technique to determine the number of latent variables, which explains the higher computational cost. Moreover, as can be seen the time spent for the proposed FA-MLR using GPU is the lowest in comparison with the others.

## CONCLUSIONS

Several studies have used the Firefly Algorithm (FA) to solve various types of problems. Based on the success of such works, one found out that using a modified FA is also possible to select variables in multivariate calibration problems. Thus, this paper presented a GPU-based FA (FA-MLR) for selection of variables in protein determination problem in whole grain wheat samples. In addition a variable selection problem in simulated study was presented.

Using a multiobjective formulation of FA, our implementation was able to perform the reduction of all measures in all tests. In terms of RMSEP, PRESS, AIC and BIC the FA-MLR showed the lower values while compared with SPA-MLR, GA-MLR, PLS and BVS. Furthermore, the FA-MLR using GPU showed a significant speedup in relation to its CPU implementation. The speedup gain was 5.25x. Therefore, the FA-MLR would be a more suitable implementation for the problem of variable selection in multivariate calibration problems.

In future works, larger multivariate calibration problems may be solved. In addition, alternatives to CUDA-MATLAB integration such as OpenCL could be investigated for comparative studies.

## REFERENCES


1. Brown SD, Blank TB, Sum ST, Weyer LG (1994) Chemometrics. Analytical chemistry 66:315–359. doi: 10. 1021/ac00084a014
2. Ferreira MMC, Antunes AM, Melgo MS, Volpe PLO (1999) Quimiometria I: calibracao multivariada, um tutorial. Quimica Nova 22:724–731. doi: 10. 1590/ s0100-40421999000500016
3. George EI (2000) The variable selection problem. Journal of the American Statistical Association 95:1304–1308. doi: 10. 1080/01621459. 2000. 10474336
4. Coifman RR, Wickerhauser MV (1992) Entropy-based algorithms for best basis selection. Information Theory, IEEE Transactions on 38:713–718. doi: 10. 1109/18. 119732
5. Paula LCM, Soares AS, Lima TW, Martins WS, Filho ARG, et al. . (2013) Partial parallelization of the successive projections algorithm using compute unified device architecture. In: Internation Conference on Parallel and Distributed Processing Techniques and Applications. pp. 737–741.
6. Chau FT, Liang YZ, Gao J, Shao XG (2004) Chemometrics: from basics to wavelet transform, volume 234. Wiley. com.
7. Galvão Filho AR, Galvão RK, Araújo MCU (2011) Effect of the subsampling ratio in the application of subagging for multivariate calibration with the successive projections algorithm. Journal of the Brazilian Chemical Society 22:2225–2233. doi: 10. 1590/s0103-50532011001100029
8. Lucena DV, Lima TW, Soares AS, Delbem ACB, Galvao AR, et al. . (2013) Multi-objective evolutionary algorithm for variable selection in calibration problems: A case study for protein concentration prediction. In: Proceedings of 2013 IEEE Congress on Evolutionary Computation. pp. 1053–1059.
9. Yang XS (2008) Nature-inspired metaheuristic algorithms. Luniver Press.
10. Yang XS (2009) Firefly algorithms for multimodal optimization. In: Stochastic algorithms: foundations and applications, Springer. pp. 169–178.
11. Lukasik S, Zak S (2009) Firefly algorithm for continuous constrained optimization tasks. In: Computational Collective Intelligence. Semantic Web, Social Networks and Multiagent Systems, Springer. pp. 97–106.
12. Yang XS (2010) Firefly algorithm, stochastic test functions and design optimisation. International Journal of Bio-Inspired Computation 2:78–84. doi: 10. 1504/ ijbic. 2010. 032124
13. Senthilnath J, Omkar S, Mani V (2011) Clustering using firefly algorithm: Performance study. Swarm and Evolutionary Computation 1:164–171. doi: 10. 1016/j. swevo. 2011. 06. 003
14. Gandomi AH, Yang XS, Alavi AH (2011) Mixed variable structural optimization using firefly algorithm. Computers & Structures 89:2325–2336. doi: 10. 1016/j. compstruc. 2011. 08. 002
15. Jati GK, Suyanto (2011) Evolutionary discrete firefly algorithm for travelling salesman problem. In: Adaptive

and Intelligent Systems, Springer. pp. 393–403.

16. Banati H, Bajaj M (2011) Fire fly based feature selection approach. International Journal of Computer Science Issues 8:473–480.
17. Horng MH (2012) Vector quantization using the firefly algorithm for image compression. Expert Systems with Applications 39:1078–1091. doi: 10. 1016/j. eswa. 2011. 07. 108
18. Abdullah A, Deris S, Anwar S, Arjunan SN (2013) An evolutionary firefly algorithm for the estimation of nonlinear biological model parameters. PloS one 8:e56310. doi: 10. 1371/journal. pone. 0056310
19. Husselmann AV, Hawick K (2012) Parallel parametric optimisation with firefly algorithms on graphical processing units. In: Proc. Int. Conf. on Genetic and Evolutionary Methods (GEM12). Number CSTN-141, Las Vegas, USA, CSREA (16–19 July 2012). pp. 77–83.
20. Husselmann A, Hawick K (2014) Geometric firefly algorithms on graphical processing units. In: Cuckoo Search and Firefly Algorithm, volume 516 . pp. 245–269.
21. Soares AS, Delbem ACB, Lima TW, Coelho CJ, Soares FAAMN (2013) Mutation-based compact genetic algorithm for spectroscopy variable selection in the determination of protein in wheat grain samples. Eletronic Letters 49:80–92. doi: 10. 1049/el. 2013. 3284
22. Soares AS, de Lima TW, Soares FAAMN, Coelho CJ, Federson FM, et al. (2014) Mutation-based compact genetic algorithm for spectroscopy variable selection in determining protein concentration in wheat grain. Electronics Letters 50:932–934 (2). . doi: 10. 1049/el. 2013. 3284
23. Haaland DM, Thomas EV (1988) Partial least-squares methods for spectral analyses. 1. relation to other quantitative calibration methods and the extraction of qualitative information. Analytical Chemistry 60:1193–1202. doi: 10. 1021/ac00162a020
24. Carbonetto P, Stephens M (2012) Scalable variational inference for bayesian variable selection in regression, and its accuracy in genetic association studies. Bayesian Analysis 7:73–108. doi: 10. 1214/12-ba703
25. Martens H (1991) Multivariate calibration. John Wiley & Sons.
26. Westad F, Martens H (2000) Variable selection in near infrared spectroscopy based on significance testing in partial least squares regression. Journal of Near Infrared Spectrosc 8:117–124. doi: 10. 1255/jnirs. 271
27. Naes T, Mevik BH (2001) Understanding the collinearity problem in regression and discriminant analysis. Journal of Chemometrics 15:413–426. doi: 10. 1002/cem. 676
28. Cortina JM (1994) Interaction, nonlinearity, and multicollinearity: Implications for multiple regression. Journal of Management 19:915–922. doi: 10. 1177/014920639301900411
29. Beebe KR, Pell RJ, Seasholtz MB (1998) Chemometrics: a practical guide. Wiley-Interscience Series on Laboratory Automation, 341 pp.
30. Lawson CL, Hanson RJ (1974) Solving least squares problems, volume 161. SIAM doi: 10. 1137/1018100
31. Hibon M, Makridakis S (1995) Evaluating accuracy (or error) measures. INSEAD
32. Allen DM (1974) The relationship between variable selection and data agumentation and a method for prediction. Technometrics 16:125–127. doi: 10. 1080/00401706. 1974. 10489157
33. Tarpey T (2000) A note on the prediction sum of squares statistic for restricted least squares. The American Statistician 54:116–118. doi: 10. 1080/00031305. 2000. 10474522
34. Bartoli A (2009) On computing the prediction sum of squares statistic in linear least squares problems with multiple parameter or measurement sets. International journal of computer vision 85:133–142. doi: 10. 1007/s11263-009-0253-x
35. Box GEP, Jenkins GM, Reinsel GC (2013) Time series analysis: forecasting and control. Wiley. com.
36. Akaike H (1974) A new look at the statistical model identification. Automatic Control, IEEE Transactions on 19:716–723. doi: 10. 1109/tac. 1974. 1100705
37. Schwarz G (1978) Estimating the dimension of a model. The annals of statistics 6:461–464. doi: 10. 1214/aos/1176344136
38. Yang XS, He X (2013) Firefly algorithm: recent advances and applications. International Journal of Swarm Intelligence 1:36–50. doi: 10. 1504/ijsi. 2013. 055801
39. de Lucena DV, de Lima TW, da Silva Soares A, Coelho CJ (2012) Multi-objective evolutionary algorithm nsga-ii for variables selection in multivariate calibration problems. International Journal of Natural Computing Research 3:43–58. doi: 10. 4018/jncr. 2012100103
40. Anderson da Silva Soares AdS, de Lima TW, LuPcena DVd, Salvini RL, Laureano GT, et al. (2013) Spectroscopic multicomponent analysis using multiobjective optimization for variable selection. Computer Technology and Application 4:465–474.
41. Yang XS (2013) Multiobjective firefly algorithm for continuous optimization. Engineering with Computers 29:175–184. doi: 10. 1007/s00366-012-0254-1
42. CUDA N (2011) NVIDIA CUDA C Programming Guide. 2701 San Tomas Expressway Santa Clara, CA 95050: NVIDIA Corporation, 4. 0 edition.
43. Luebke D, Humphreys G (2007) How gpus work. Computer 40:96–100. doi: 10. 1109/mc. 2007. 59
44. Tsuchiyama R, Nakamura T, Iizuka T, Asahara A, Son J, et al. . (2010) The OpenCL Programming Book. Fixstars.
45. Little J, Moler C. Matlab gpu computing support for nvidia cuda-enabled gpus. Available: http://www. mathworks. com/discovery/matlab-gpu. html. Accessed 2013 Nov 3.
46. *MathWorks*. Matlab gpu computing support for nvidia cuda-enabled gpus. Available:http://www. mathworks. com/discovery/matlab-gpu. html. Accessed 2013 Nov 3.
47. Reese J, Zaranek S. Gpu programming in matlab. Available:http://www. mathworks. com/company/newsletters/articles/. Accessed 2013 Nov 3.

48. Liu X, Cheng L, Zhou Q (2013) Research and comparison of cuda gpu programming in matlab and mathematica. In: Proceedings of 2013 Chinese Intelligent Automation Conference. Springer, pp. 251–257.

49. Araújo MCU, Saldanha TCB, Galvão RKH, Yoneyama T, Chame HC, et al. (2001) The successive projections algorithm for variable selection in spectroscopic multicomponent analysis. Chemometrics and Intelligent Laboratory Systems 57:65–73. doi: 10. 1016/s0169-7439(01)00119-8

50. Kennard RW, Stone LA (1969) Computer aided design of experiments. Technometrics 11:137–148. doi: 10. 1080/00401706. 1969. 10490666

51. Soares AS, Galvao RKH, Araujo MCU, Soares SFC, Pinto LA (2010) Multi-core computation in chemometrics: case studies of voltammetric and nir spectrometric analyses. Journal of the Brazilian Chemical Society 21:1626–1634. doi: 10. 1590/s0103-50532010000900005

52. Savitzky A, Golay MJ (1964) Smoothing and differentiation of data by simplified least squares procedures. Analytical chemistry 36:1627–1639. doi: 10. 1021/ac60214a047

53. Bradstreet RB (1965) The Kjeldahl method for organic nitrogen.

54. Galvao RKH, Araujo MCU, Fragoso WD, Silva EC, Jose GE, et al. (2008) A variable elimination method to improve the parsimony of {MLR} models using the successive projections algorithm. Chemometrics and Intelligent Laboratory Systems 92:83–91. doi: 10. 1016/j. chemolab. 2007. 12. 004

55. Tobias RD (1995) An introduction to partial least squares regression. In: Proceedings of Ann. SAS Users Group Int. Conf. , 20th, Orlando, FL. pp. 2–5.

CHAPTER 10

# NOISE PROPERTIES IN THE IDEAL KIRCHHOFF-LAW-JOHNSON-NOISE SECURE COMMUNICATION SYSTEM

Zoltan Gingl , Robert Mingesz

Department of Technical Informatics, University of Szeged, Szeged, Hungary

## ABSTRACT

**In this paper we determine the noise properties needed for unconditional security for the ideal Kirchhoff-Law-Johnson-Noise (KLJN) secure key distribution system using simple statistical analysis. It has already been shown using physical laws that resistors and Johnson-like noise sources provide unconditional security. However real implementations use artificial noise generators, therefore it is a question if other kind of noise sources and resistor values could be used as well. We answer this question and in the same time we provide a theoretical basis to analyze real systems as well.**

## INTRODUCTION

Communication security is getting more and more important in many different applications including electronic banking, protecting personal data, securing intellectual property of companies, transmission of medical data and many more. The Kirchhoff-Law-Johnson-Noise (KLJN) protocol was introduced as a low cost unconditionally secure key exchange protocol using only passive components: four resistors, two switches and interconnecting wires [1]. The protocol is based only on the laws of classical physics and has been introduced as an inexpensive alternative to quantum communicators. The first real implementation has been shown a few years after its discovery [2], [3] and it has inspired the development of another secret key exchanged method [4]. There are many potential applications including securing computers, algorithms and hardware (memories, processors, keyboards, mass storage media)[5], key distribution over the Smart Grid [6], ethernet cables [7], uncloneable hardware keys[8]. Several attack methods has been discussed [9]–[14], however the ideal KLJN system is found to be secure. Debates are still going on [15], [16] and recent papers discuss practical considerations for the applications [17], [18].

The KLJN key exchange protocol is rather simple. During the communication a secret key is generated and shared between the two communicating parties, Alice and Bob. The system consists of two communicators and a transmission wire, see Fig. 1. Each communicator includes two resistors $R_L$ and $R_H$ and two series voltage noise sources $V_{LA}(t)$, $V_{HA}(t)$ and$V_{LB}(t)$, $V_{HB}(t)$ representing the thermal noise of the resistors at Alice and Bob, respectively:

**Citation:** Gingl Z, Mingesz R (2014) Noise Properties in the Ideal Kirchhoff-Law-Johnson-Noise Secure Communication System. PLoS ONE 9(4): e96109. doi:10. 1371/journal.pone.0096109

$$S_L(f) = 4kTR_L \qquad (1)$$

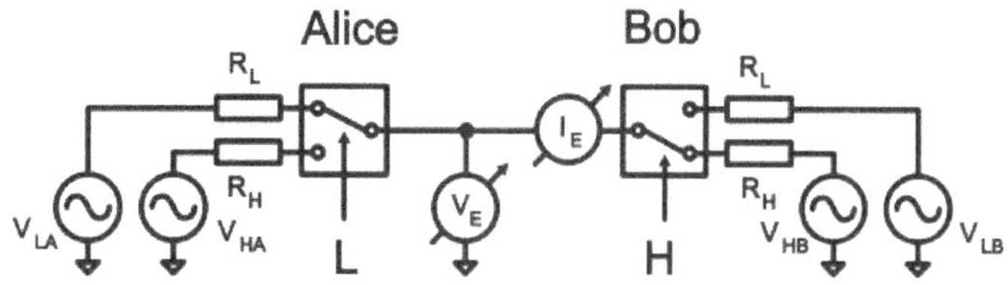


**Figure 1.** The KLJN secure communication system.

$$S_H(f) = 4kTR_H \qquad (2)$$

where $S_L(f)$ is the power spectral density of the voltage noise sources $V_{LA}(t)$, $V_{LB}(t)$ and $S_H(f)$ is the power spectral density of the voltage noise sources $V_{HA}(t)$, $V_{HB}(t)$; k is the Boltzmann constant and T is the temperature.

A switch is used to select one of the resistors to be connected to the wire connecting the two communicators, see Fig. 1. At the beginning of each bit exchange, both Alice and Bob connect a resistor ($R_H$ or $R_L$) to the wire. If both, Alice and Bob connect the higher value resistor, the voltage noise level will be high in the wire. If they both connect the low value resistor, the voltage noise will be low. If they connect different value resistors, the noise level will be intermediate and this is invariant if the resistors are swapped. [1], [13]. This level can also be identified by the eavesdropper, Eve, however she cannot determine who has chosen the low value resistor. For this reason, this is the secure state that can be used for key exchange.

Note that in real applications the noise would be too small, therefore artificial noise generators are used to provide large enough signals in a given frequency band. In this case, the noise equivalent temperature is above $10^9$ K [1]. On the other hand generators can enhance the security and offer new schemes with higher practical security in the non-ideal situations [17].

## RESULTS

According to the papers about the KLJN communication method the artificial noise generators are only used to emulate high temperatures, so they must generate Johnson-like noise. Therefore the security proof based on physical laws remains valid [1]. Our approach is in some sense opposite to the previous ones, when security has been proven for the given noise properties. Here we determine what the requirements of noise properties for unconditional security are. On the other hand, our analysis is based on statistical methods instead of physical laws of thermodynamics, therefore it can be more easily understandable for computer engineers and software engineers.

Let us assume that the system is operated in the LH situation, when Alice has switched on the lower value resistor and noise, while Bob uses the higher value resistor and noise as shown inFig. 1.

In this case Eve measures the following voltage $V_E(t)$ and current $I_E(t)$ (flowing from Bob's side towards Alice) in the wire:

$$V_E(t) = \frac{V_{LA}(t) \cdot R_H + V_{HB}(t) \cdot R_L}{R_L + R_H} \qquad (3)$$

and

$$I_E(t) = \frac{V_{HB}(t) - V_{LA}(t)}{R_L + R_H} \qquad (4)$$

where $V_{LA}(t)$ and $V_{HB}(t)$ are the voltage noise signals at Alice and Bob, respectively. She can have two hypotheses: the correct one and the opposite. She can calculate the statistics of Alice's voltage noise for both cases. Since she knows the resistor values and the used voltage noise statistics, it is clear, that she will know that her assumption is wrong, if she gets invalid values during her calculations. For the correct assumption she must get correct results of course. Let us see what happens in the case of the wrong hypothesis. In this case Eve assumes that the high value resistor has been chosen by Alice. Therefore she calculates Alice's noise voltage $V_A(t)$ as:

$$V_A(t) = V_E(t) - I_E(t) \cdot R_H = \frac{V_{LA}(t) \cdot R_H + V_{HB}(t) \cdot R_L}{R_L + R_H} + \frac{V_{HB}(t) - V_{LA}(t)}{R_L + R_H} R_H \qquad (5)$$

$$V_A(t) = \frac{V_{LA}(t) \cdot 2 \cdot R_H + V_{HB}(t) \cdot (R_H - R_L)}{R_L + R_H} \qquad (6)$$

$$V_A(t) = V_{LA}(t) \cdot \frac{2 \cdot R_H}{R_L + R_H} + V_{HB}(t) \cdot \frac{R_H - R_L}{R_L + R_H} \qquad (7)$$

The variance is given by the sum of variances:

$$\sigma_A^2 = \sigma_L^2 \cdot \left( \frac{2 \cdot R_H}{R_L + R_H} \right)^2 + \sigma_H^2 \cdot \left( \frac{R_H - R_L}{R_L + R_H} \right)^2 \qquad (8)$$

where $\sigma_A^2$ is the variance of $V_A(t)$ and $\sigma_L^2$ and $\sigma_H^2$ are the variances of the voltage noise$V_{LA}(t)$ and $V_{HB}(t)$, respectively.

The communication can only be secure if $\sigma_A = \sigma_H$, otherwise Eve will know that Alice connected the low value resistor and voltage generator to the wire. Substituting this into Eq. (8) yields:

$$\frac{\sigma_H^2}{\sigma_L^2} \left( 1 - \left( \frac{R_H - R_L}{R_L + R_H} \right)^2 \right) = \left( \frac{2 \cdot R_H}{R_L + R_H} \right)^2 \qquad (9)$$

$$\frac{\sigma_H^2}{\sigma_L^2} = \frac{(2 \cdot R_H)^2}{(R_L + R_H)^2 - (R_H - R_L)^2} = \frac{4 \cdot R_H^2}{R_L^2 + 2 \cdot R_L \cdot R_H + R_H^2 - (R_H^2 - 2 \cdot R_L \cdot R_H + R_L^2)} \qquad (10)$$

$$\frac{\sigma_H^2}{\sigma_L^2} = \frac{R_H}{R_L} \qquad (11)$$

or in other form

$$\frac{\sigma_H}{\sigma_L} = \sqrt{\frac{R_H}{R_L}} \qquad (12)$$

Therefore the noise amplitude must depend on the resistance as in the case of thermal noise; it must be proportional to the square root of the resistance. Otherwise the communication is certainly unsecure.

In the following we check how the security depends on the probability distribution of the noise. When the eavesdropper makes the correct assumption, she can calculate the noise signal that Alice is using exactly; therefore she gets the correct probability distribution of course. When she makes the wrong assumption then she obtains:

$$V_A(t) = V_L(t) \cdot \frac{2 \cdot R_H}{R_L + R_H} + V_H(t) \cdot \frac{R_H - R_L}{R_L + R_H} \qquad (13)$$

The probability density $p_A(x)$ of $V_A(t)$ is given by the convolution of the probability densities of the two independent terms in Eq. (13). If p(x) is the probability density function with unity variance,

$$\alpha = \sigma_L \cdot \frac{2 \cdot R_H}{R_L + R_H} \tag{14}$$

and

$$\beta = \sigma_H \cdot \frac{R_H - R_L}{R_L + R_H} \tag{15}$$

then

$$\sigma_A^2 = \alpha^2 + \beta^2 \tag{16}$$

where σA² is the variance of $V_A(t)$, and

$$p_A(x) = \int_{-\infty}^{\infty} \frac{1}{\alpha} p\left(\frac{x'}{\alpha}\right) \cdot \frac{1}{\beta} p\left(\frac{x - x'}{\beta}\right) dx' \tag{17}$$

If Eq. (12) is satisfied, then $\sigma_A = \sigma_H$, that is needed for secure communication. Furthermore$p_A(x)$ measured by Eve must also be identical to the probability density function $p_H(x)$ of the noise voltages $V_{HA}(t)$ and $V_{HB}(t)$, otherwise Eve can detect that her assumption is wrong. Therefore using Eqs. (16) and (17) $p_A(x)$ can be expressed

$$p_A(x) = p_H(x) = \frac{1}{\sigma_H} p\left(\frac{x}{\sigma_H}\right) = \frac{1}{\sqrt{\alpha^2 + \beta^2}} p\left(\frac{x}{\sqrt{\alpha^2 + \beta^2}}\right) \tag{18}$$

as.

and finally we get

$$\frac{1}{\sqrt{\alpha^2 + \beta^2}} p\left(\frac{x}{\sqrt{\alpha^2 + \beta^2}}\right) = \int_{-\infty}^{\infty} \frac{1}{\alpha} p\left(\frac{x'}{\alpha}\right) \cdot \frac{1}{\beta} p\left(\frac{x - x'}{\beta}\right) dx' \quad . \tag{19}$$

## DISCUSSION

Eq. (19) is valid for normal distribution only [19], therefore we can conclude that the noise sources $V_{LA}(t)$, $V_{LB}(t)$ and $V_{HA}(t)$, $V_{HB}(t)$ must have normal distribution and the ratio of their amplitude must be equal to the square root of the ratio of the corresponding resistor values. In other words, Johnson-like noise must be used for the secure key exchange in the KLJN system. Note that although several other distributions – for example Cauchy-distribution – satisfy the condition that the convolution in Eq. (19) does not change the type of distribution, however the finite variance required by energetic considerations is only provided by normal distribution.

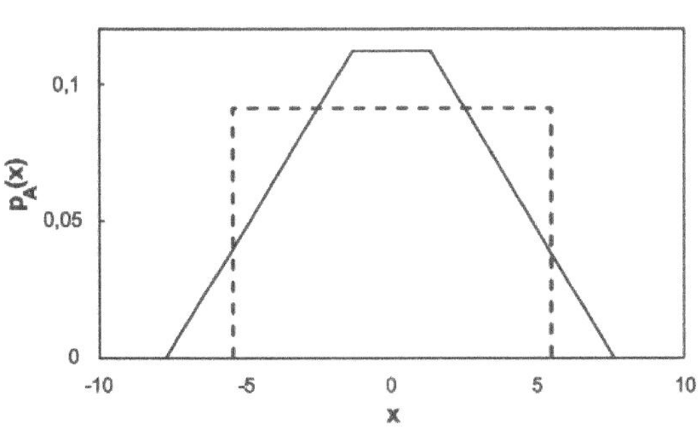


**Figure 2.** The probability density function $p_A(x)$ in the case of uniform distribution (solid line) strongly differs from $p_H(x)$ (dashed line).

It is easy to see that for example random numbers with uniform distribution can't be used for secure communication. In this case Eq. (17) gives a trapezoidal probability density function for$p_A(x)$ as shown on Fig. 2, therefore its deviation from $p_H(x)$ can be very easily detected. We have developed a simple software application written in LabVIEW that can be used to simulate the KLJN protocol [20]. Normal or uniform distribution can be selected and the values of $R_L$,$R_H$, amplitude of $V_{LA}(t)$, $V_{LB}(t)$ and $V_{HA}(t)$, $V_{HB}(t)$ can be arbitrarily chosen. The application performs Eve's calculation of $V_A(t)$ for both hypotheses, and plots the corresponding measured amplitudes and probability densities.

## LIMITATIONS AND OPEN QUESTIONS

We have presented a mathematical statistical approach to determine the noise properties and resistor values required for secure communication and the results are in agreement with the original physical approach [1]. On the other hand our work does not address the question of complete security.

Considerable additional work could be carried out to investigate several attack types with similar approach. For example, in practical applications the effect of resistor inaccuracies, wire resistances can also be analyzed using our method; Eq. (8) can be applied to find the difference between the observed and expected variances, $\sigma_A^2$ and $\sigma_H^2$, respectively. This means that the information leak due to these inaccuracies can be estimated. On the other hand, if the desired security level is given, the required resistor values and accuracy of the components can be obtained.

Furthermore one can consider correlation properties, bandwidth of the noise sources that is important in practical applications and discussed in several publications.

## CONCLUSIONS

In this paper we have shown a mathematical statistical approach to find out what kind of noise sources are required for secure communications in the Kirchhoff-Loop-Johnson-Noise unconditionally secure key exchange system. In agreement with the results can be found in the literature we found that the noise amplitude must scale with the square root of the corresponding resistor value and Gaussian noise sources must be used.

Note that our approach can serve as a starting point to quantitatively analyze several attack types in practical applications.

## ACKNOWLEDGMENTS

Zoltan Gingl thanks Béla Szentpáli for drawing his attention to the problem. Discussions with Gyula Pap about probability distributions are greatly appreciated.

## REFERENCES

1. Kish LB (2006) Totally secure classical communication utilizing Johnson(-like) noise and Kirchhoff's law. Phys. Lett. A 352: 178–182 doi: 10.1016/j.physleta.2005.11.062.
2. Mingesz R, Gingl Z, Kish LB (2008) Johnson(-like)-noise-Kirchhoff-loop based secure classical communicator characteristics, for ranges of two to two thousand kilometers, via model-line, Phys Lett A. 372: 978–984 doi: 10.1016/j.physleta.2007.07.086.
3. Mingesz R, Kish LB, Gingl Z, Granqvist CG, Wen H, et al. (2013) Unconditional security by the laws of classical physics. Metrology & Measurement Systems XX: 3–16 DOI:10.2478/mms-2013-0001 Available:http://www.

degruyter.com/view/j/mms.2013.20.issue-1/mms-2013-0001/mms-2013-0001.xml.

4. Liu PL (2009) A key agreement protocol using band-limited random signals and feedback. IEEE J Lightwave Technol 27: 5230–5234 doi: 10.1109/jlt.2009.2031421.
5. Kish LB, Saidi O (2008) Unconditionally secure computers, algorithms and hardware. Fluct Noise Lett 8: L95–L98 doi: 10.1142/s0219477508004362.
6. Gonzalez E, Kish LB, Balog RS, Enjeti P (2013) Information theoretically secure, enhanced Johnson noise based key distribution over the smart grid with switched filters. PLOS ONE 8(7): e70206 doi: 10.1371/journal.pone.0070206.
7. Lin PK, Ivanov A, Johnson B, Khatri SP (2011) "A novel cryptographic key exchange scheme using resistors." In Computer Design (ICCD), 2011 IEEE 29th International Conference on, 451–452. IEEE, doi: 10.1109/ICCD.2011.6081445.
8. Kish LB, Kwan C (2013) Physical uncloneable function hardware keys utilizing Kirchhoff-Law-Johnson-Noise secure key exchange and noise-based logic, Fluctuation and Noise Letters, 12, 1350018 http://dx.doi.org/10.1142/S0219477513500181, Available: http://vixra.org/abs/1305.0068.
9. Hao F (2006) Kish's key exchange scheme is insecure. IEE Proc. Inform. Soc. 153: 141–142 doi: 10.1049/ip-ifs:20060068.
10. Kish LB (2006) Response to Feng Hao's paper "Kish's key exchange scheme is insecure". Fluct. Noise Lett. 6: C37–C41 doi: 10.1142/s021947750600363x.
11. Scheuer J, Yariv A (2006) A classical key-distribution system based on Johnson (like) noise – How secure? Phys. Lett. A 359: 737–740 doi: 10.1016/j.physleta.2006.07.013.
12. Kish LB (2006) Response to Scheuer-Yariv: "A classical key-distribution system based on Johnson (like) noise – How secure?". Phys. Lett. A 359: 741–744 doi: 10.1016/j.physleta.2006.07.037.
13. Kish LB, Horvath T (2009) Notes on recent approaches concerning the Kirchhoff-law-Johnson-noise-based secure key exchange. Phys. Lett. A 373: 901–904 doi: 10.1016/j.physleta.2009.05.077.
14. Kish LB, Scheuer J (2010) Noise in the wire: The real impact of wire resistance for the Johnson(-like) noise based secure communicator. Phys. Lett. A 374: 2140–2142 doi: 10.1016/j.physleta.2010.03.021.
15. Bennett CH, Riedel CJ (2013) On the security of key distribution based on Johnson-Nyquist noise. Available: http://arxiv.org/abs/1303.7435.
16. Kish LB, Abbott D, Granqvist CG (2013) Critical analysis of the Bennett–Riedel attack on secure cryptographic key distributions via the Kirchhoff-Law–Johnson-Noise scheme. PLOS ONE 8(12): e81810 doi:10.1371/journal.pone.0081810.
17. Kish LB (2013) Enhanced secure key exchange systems based on the Johnson-noise scheme. Metrology & Measurement Systems XX: 191–204 Available:http://www.degruyter.com/view/j/mms.2013.20.issue-2/mms-2013-0017/mms-2013-0017.xml?format=INT.
18. Saez Y, Kish LB (2013) Errors and their mitigation at the Kirchhoff-Law-Johnson-Noise secure key exchange. PLOS ONE 8(11): e81103 doi:10.1371/journal.pone.0081103.
19. Feller W (1968, 1971), An introduction to probability theory and its applications, Vol. 1 and Vol. 2, John Wiley & Sons, ISBN 0 471 25708-7 and 0 471 25709-5.
20. Kirchhoff's-Law-Johnson-Noise secure key distribution simulation software.

CHAPTER 11

# MC64-CLUSTALWP2: A HIGHLY-PARALLEL HYBRID STRATEGY TO ALIGN MULTIPLE SEQUENCES IN MANY-CORE ARCHITECTURES

David Dı´az[1], Francisco J. Esteban[2], Pilar Herna´ndez[3], Juan Antonio Caballero[4], Antonio Guevara[1], Gabriel Dorado[5], Sergio Ga´lvez[1].

[1]Dep. Lenguajes y Ciencias de la Computacio´n, Universidad de Ma´laga, Ma´laga, Spain,

[2]Servicio de Informa´tica, Universidad de Co´rdoba, Co´rdoba, Spain,

[3]Instituto de Agricultura Sostenible (IAS-CSIC), Co´rdoba, Spain,

[4]Dep. Estadı´stica, Universidad de Co´rdoba, Co´rdoba, Spain,

[5]Dep. Bioquı´mica y Biologı´a Molecular, Universidad de Co´rdoba (Campus de Excelencia Internacional Agroalimentario), Co´rdoba, Spain

## ABSTRACT

**We have developed the MC64-ClustalWP2 as a new implementation of the Clustal W algorithm, integrating a novel parallelization strategy and significantly increasing the performance when aligning long sequences in architectures with many cores. It must be stressed that in such a process, the detailed analysis of both the software and hardware features and peculiarities is of paramount importance to reveal key points to exploit and optimize the full potential of parallelism in many-core CPU systems. The new parallelization approach has focused into the most time-consuming stages of this algorithm. In particular, the so-called progressive alignment has drastically improved the performance, due to a fine-grained approach where the forward and backward loops were unrolled and parallelized. Another key approach has been the implementation of the new algorithm in a hybrid-computing system, integrating both an Intel Xeon multi-core CPU and a Tilera Tile64 many-core card. A comparison with other Clustal W implementations reveals the high-performance of the new algorithm and strategy in many-core CPU architectures, in a scenario where the sequences to align are relatively long (more than 10 kb) and, hence, a many-core GPU hardware cannot be used. Thus, the MC64-ClustalWP2 runs multiple alignments more than 18x than the original Clustal W algorithm, and more than 7x than the best x86 parallel implementation to date, being publicly available through a web service. Besides, these developments have been deployed in cost-effective personal computers and should be useful for life-science researchers, including the identification of identities and differences for mutation/polymorphism analyses, biodiversity and evolutionary studies and for the development of molecular markers for paternity testing, germplasm management and protection, to assist breeding, illegal traffic control, fraud prevention and for the protection of the intellectual property (identification/traceability), including the protected designation of origin, among other applications.**

## INTRODUCTION

The amount of genomic data is growing exponentially, due to the advances in technology and the evolution in the so-called "Next-Generation" Sequencing (NGS), including the latest second- and third-generation equipment. Thus, the former bioinformatics tools from the genic era are evolving

**Citation:** Díaz D, Esteban FJ, Hernández P, Caballero JA, Guevara A, Dorado G, et al. (2014) MC64-ClustalWP2: A Highly-Parallel Hybrid Strategy to Align Multiple Sequences in Many-Core Architectures. PLoS ONE 9(4): e94044. doi:10.1371/journal.pone.0094044

to handle the current genomic data. These include alignment algorithms for sequence comparison like the Needleman-Wunsch [1] pairwise global-alignment algorithm, which has evolved both from a biological point of view, as the Smith-Waterman local aligners[2] or Gotoh affine gaps [3], and also from a computational point of view, as the Hirschberg linear space approach [4] or Driga FastLSA [5].

Yet, these computational improvements in pairwise-alignment algorithms cannot properly handle long or very long sequences, like some partial or complete chromosomes and genomes. Thus, some heuristic strategies have been developed to overcome the large amount of memory and execution time required to align such sequences. The Fast Alignment Sequence Tools (FAST)-All (FASTA) [6] and Basic Local Alignment Search Tool (BLAST) [7]are examples of this trend. The heuristics are able to obtain approximate alignments with acceptable accurate results in much less time, so they can be useful to compare long sequences. Nonetheless, the quality of the alignment may be compromised in some instances[8], and therefore non-heuristic aligners may be needed to guarantee the optimal alignment from a computational point of view.

Additionally, the "optimal" pairwise aligners can be ported to new computing architectures to overcome the previous limitations. Though an alternative to speedup algorithms is to use supercomputers, grid computing and clustering using several nodes [9], more affordable options are available nowadays. That is the case of the multi-core architectures, where several threads or processes run independent code in parallel, albeit requiring the programmers to develop new approaches when porting, adapting and optimizing the existing alignment algorithms to the new parallel architectures. In fact, the number of cores is increasing exponentially, giving birth to the concept of "many-core" architectures, where tens, thousands and even millions of them are available.

At this point it is important to distinguish between multi-core and many-core microprocessors. Thus, in many-core architectures, the execution cores are small Central Processing Units (CPU) with fewer resources than a standard multi-core CPU; so in order to extract the full potential of the former, specific parallelism strategies for them should be developed. Besides, the many-core microprocessors can be classified into two different groups: many-core Graphical Processing Units (GPU), and many-core CPU. The former ones have thousands of Stream Processors Units (SPU), sometimes named cores, distributed in a hierarchical way: a GPU has several Thread Processing Clusters (TPC), where each one consists of an array of Stream Multiprocessor Units (SMU), having each one eight SPU. The resources are shared between the SMU in these models. On the contrary, the many-core CPU microprocessors have a matrix of uniform CPU with their own resources, usually interconnected via a high-throughput network. A graphical comparison of both architectures can be seen in Figure 1. Unfortunately, such architectural differences require also different programming methodologies, being the Compute-Unified Device Architecture (CUDA) a specific model to exploit the parallelism in General-Purpose GPU (GPGPU) [10] and the standard C being usually deployed in many-core CPU architectures. In the field of cluster computing, the C language is sometimes complemented by some kind of standard or proprietary Application Program Interface (API), to extend some parallelism abilities like message passing, shared memory or abstract channel communications.

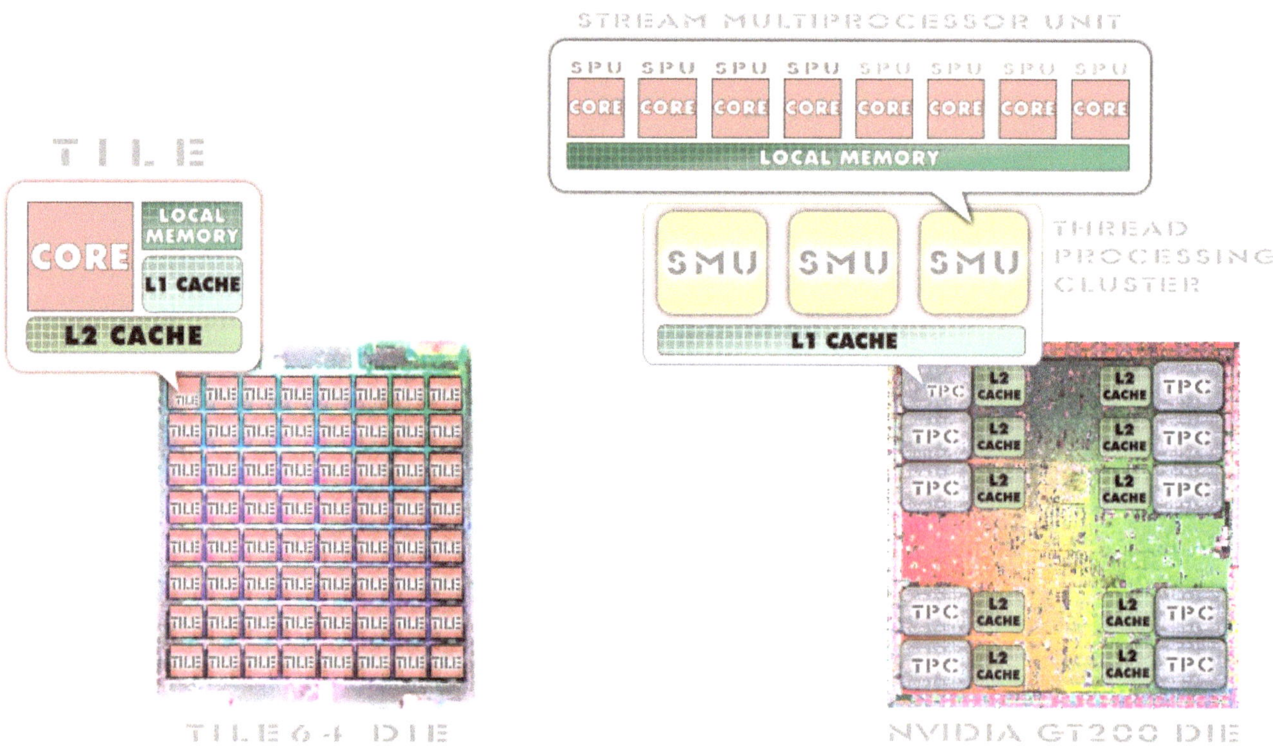


**Figure 1.** Block diagram of many-core CPU and GPU architectures.

The shown dies are boarded on nVidia GT 200 GPU series and Tilera Tile64 Peripheral Component Interconnect express (PCIe) cards. The cores in the many-core CPU architectures are interconnected through a high-bandwidth mesh, whereas the ones in the many-core GPU are isolated.

There are experimental and commercial many-core CPU models. They include the Adapteva Epiphany IV with 64 cores [11], the Sun Microsystems UltraSPARC T2 Pro with eight cores and eight threads per core [12], and the models from Intel, the leader company in this research field with the Many-Integrated Cores (MIC) architecture. At first, they created the Intel Terascale microprocessor with 80 cores [13], and then experimental models like the Single-chip Cloud Computing (SCC) [14] with 48 cores and the Knights Ferry [15] with 32 cores. From the experience obtained from this models and the Larrabee hybrid CPU-GPU project, a new model codenamed Knights Corner and eventually named Xeon Phi was developed with 61 cores and 22 nm 3-D tri-gate process fabrication process. The second generation of Xeon Phi products (Knights Landing) is expected in the near future as a coprocessor or a host processor (CPU), manufactured with 14 nm node technology and second-generation 3-D tri-gate transistors.

Following this trend, Tilera has developed a many-core CPU architecture known as the Tile64 microprocessor, being a 90 nm Reduced Instruction Set Computing (RISC) System-on-Chip (SoC) microprocessor with 64 general-purpose CPU called tiles, each one being able of running an independent operative system (Linux). Each core runs at 500–866 MHz and can reach a global 0.166 Tera-Instructions Per Second (TIPS). The tiles are interconnected through a high-throughput network called intelligent Mesh (iMesh) with 31 Terabits per second (Tbps) bandwidth. As seen in Figure 1, each tile contains its own Level 1 (8 KB for data and 8 KB for instructions) and Level 2 (64 KB) caches. Furthermore, all the Level 2 caches become a larger Level 3 common cache [16]. Lately, Tilera has announced a future branch of microprocessors called Tile-Gx [17] with 16 to 100 cores using a 40 nm fabrication process.

Thus, thanks to the emerging many-core technologies, new approaches are available to address the increasing demand of computational power. This allows to tackle the bioinformatics analyses required for the exponentially increasing data generated by the new sequencing methodologies. That is the case of the previously mentioned Needleman-Wunsch (NW) [1] and Smith-Waterman (SW) [2] pairwise aligners, where GPU parallel approaches have been presented by Manavski [18] and Liu [19]. However, most of these implementations are designed to align a single query sequence against a huge number of small sequences like those from peptides (eg., proteins), yet cannot align sequences longer than 59,000 residues. This is due to the intrinsic "Single Instruction, Multiple Data" (SIMD) characteristics of the GPGPU, where pipelining allows a great speedup factor, yet intense memory usage may lead to bottlenecks.

Indeed, although some many-core CPU microprocessors with tens of cores have recently arisen, there are only a few bioinformatics developments deployed in such architectures, as the ones that we have previously published for the Tile64 microprocessor [20]–[22]. Such developments were carried out with TILExpress-20G cards including the Tile64 microprocessor and 8 GB of RAM, for which we have empirically demonstrated some limits: 7.8 GB for Solid State Disk (SSD), 2.8 GB for local memory and 1.9 GB for shared memory. Such cards have high-bandwidth communication ports and a very good performance per watt [20]. Among others, we have developed a parallel version of the NW/SW algorithm, named Multicore64-NeedlemanWunsch/SmithWaterman (MC64-NW/SW), using a FastLSA strategy [5], which we have thoroughly optimized taking into account the hardware and algorithm features and peculiarities. This implementation achieved a gain of ~1,000% against the same algorithm on a x86 multi-core architecture, allowing to align sequences of one Megabase (Mb) length in 23 minutes approximately [20], [22].

In this report, we have extended our work to the popular Multiple-Sequence Alignment (MSA) algorithm known as Clustal W. The new parallel version of Clustal W exploits the high-throughput parallelism in many-core CPU architectures, optimizing the most time-consuming stage of the original algorithm. This has been accomplished taking into account both the existing parallel versions of the Clustal W for multi-core and many-core GPGPU architectures, as well as our previous experience when developing the parallel MC64-NW/SW [20]. Thus, the new algorithm, called MC64-ClustalWP2 for Many-Core64-Clustal W Phase 2 (of parallelization), was implemented for the Tilera Tile64 microprocessor, as described below.

Different benchmarks were run to test the new algorithm against the previous developments and to quantify its performance. Since the MC64-ClustalWP2 algorithm was developed to align relatively large sequences, for instance, from 10 kilobases (kb) to 300 kb, it was tested with a family of organisms whose genome lengths fall into such a range. It should be noted that this approach would require an excessive execution time in a multi-core system or would not even be allowed in a GPGPU architecture, due to the length of the sequences. The MC64-ClustalWP2 source code is available under the General Public License (GPL) license at the <http://galactus.uma.es/manycore> web site [23], where the algorithm can be also remotely invoked through web services.

## Multiple-Sequence Alignments

The multiple-sequence alignments allows the comparison of two or more sequences, in contrast to the pairwise aligners like Smith-Waterman, which are limited to just a couple of them. Therefore, the former are particularly useful to identify identities (similarities) and divergences (differences) between many sources, allowing to build evolutionary phylogenetic trees (dendrograms). Thus, the identification of small and large variations, mutations or polymorphisms like base changes and insertions/deletions (indels), duplications or amplifications, recombinations and rearrangements like translocations can be exploited to develop molecular markers for identification, including germplasm management and protection, paternity testing, marker-assisted selection and breeding, illegal traffic control, fraud prevention and traceability. This can be applied to the Protected Designation of Origin (PDO), which is a label of food products from some geographical areas, showing particular organoleptic or otherwise desirable characteristics, conferring them a higher quality than similar products from other sites.

However, generating a Dynamic-Program Matrix (DPM) in the sense of "optimal" pairwise aligners, but for more than two sequences, means a Nondeterministic Polynomial (NP) complete complexity problem in computation, and therefore no fast solution to it is known by definition. For this reason, several heuristic strategies were developed to simulate the behavior of the n-dimensional matrix, using a batch of pairwise alignments and simpler DPM. That is the case of MULTAN [24], being a Waterman [25] or Clustal [26] method. The latter has become very popular, due to its original performance and further developments and improvements. The Clustal algorithm is based on a progressive-alignment strategy of all the sequences, aligned by the order determined by a previously-calculated phylogenetic tree, generated from the similarities and differences among the sequences in an all-vs-all comparison matrix.

The first version of MULTAN was programmed in the FORTRAN language, but later on it was re-programmed in the C language, and a few new functionalities were added, like the generation of a dendrogram in the final stage [27]. More notable changes were introduced in the new Clustal W [28], which received the "W" for "weighting", since in this version the sequences were weighted in order to increase the sensibility of the algorithm. Later on, the version 2 was ported into C++, including two new minor-relevant features [29]. Besides the Clustal, there are other multiple-sequence alignment algorithms, like the T-Coffee [30] and MUSCLE [31], which may obtain accurate-enough results for large sequences using heuristics, modifying the progressive alignment method and adding new refinements.

Furthermore, as with pairwise aligners, quicker MSA heuristic methods which do not rely on a DPM have been also developed, as the Multi-LAGAN general anchoring-based method [32]. In addition, new multiple-sequence alignment approaches have been published, including the so-called genome MSA methods, capable of dealing with very long similar sequences, like MGA[33] or MAVID [34]. These methods are very fast, but they are usually not accurate when the aligned sequences have highly polymorphic regions (e.g., with high mutation-rates). Therefore, they can be useful to align restricted or local similar regions, but not to globally align any set of sequences [35]. More recent methods like the progressive Mauve [36] are able to deal with some sequence variations (like rearrangements), but not with all of them, as is the case for duplications [37]. A further review of the most important MSA algorithms can be found at [38].

On the other hand, the Clustal W design is divided into three main stages: the distance matrix generation, the guide tree generation and the progressive alignment. It can be easily determined that the most time-consuming stages are the first and the last ones [39]. Indeed, they require most of the computation time as the number of sequences or their length increase. Therefore, their optimization represents the first theoretical choice to improve the algorithm performance. Thus, the Clustal W has been parallelized for SGI computers [40], multi-core platforms using threads [41], the hybrid multi-core Cell chip [42] and scalable clusters using the Message Passing Interface (MPI) [43]. However, none of them has really exploited the parallelism in the third stage, as it is pointed out in the next section.

## Clustal W Behavior Analyses

In order to properly optimize the Clustal W parallelization, each stage of the algorithm should be carefully analyzed. Traditionally, the Clustal W has been used to align short sequences of nucleic acids (DNA or RNA) and peptides, with high-performance implementations of Clustal W exploiting parallelism to obtain the best results for larger number of such sequences. However, as the MC64-ClustalWP2 focuses on longer DNA sequences (for instance, from 10 kb to 300 Mb), the parallelization and optimization strategies should be different.

As previously noted, the Clustal W is divided into three main stages, shown at the top ofFigure 2. The first stage fulfills the cells of a distance matrix with a score that represents the distance between every pair of sequences. Each score is calculated running a pairwise-alignment operation. The second stage generates a guide tree using a clustering method, like the Neighbor-Joining (NJ) [44] and, finally, the third stage progressively generates the multiple alignment, following the topology of the guide tree.

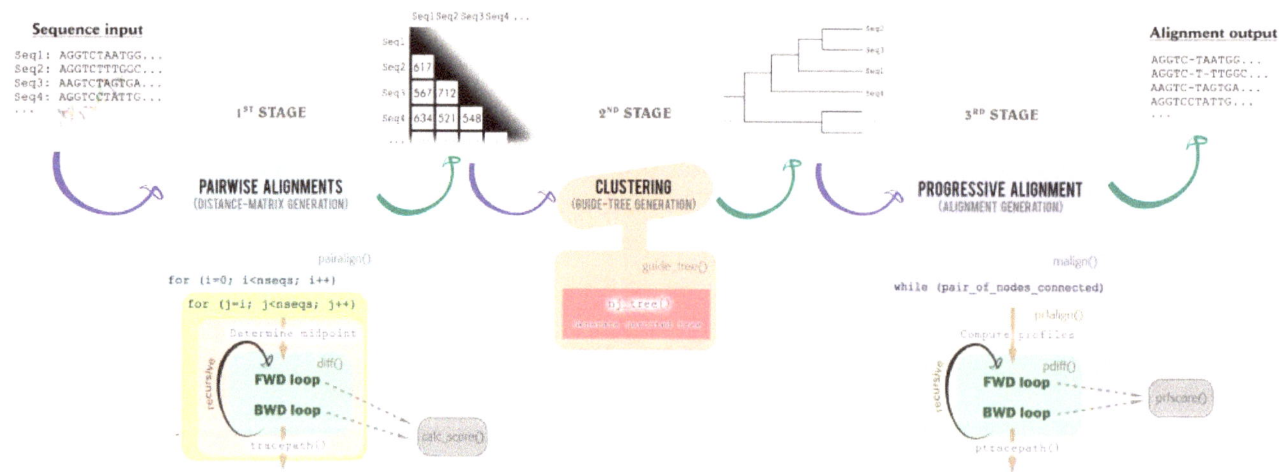


Figure 2. Global behavior of the Clustal W algorithm and its three main stages.

The top part shows the three main stages of the Clustal W showing both the data used and generated in each one. In the bottom part, the functions and high-level pseudo-code reveal the similarities between the most time-consuming and representative parts of the algorithm.

The pairwise alignments of the first main stage are calculated using the local Myers-Miller algorithm [45], a Smith-Waterman pairwise aligner that implements affine-gap penalties [3]. Its space complexity is linear, at the expense of doubling the execution time when compared to other standard pairwise aligners. The multiple alignment of n sequences requires to complete the distance matrix, performing n/2*(n−1) alignment operations between each pair of sequences. There are no dependencies between them, so they can be executed in parallel. The MPI-alike implementations for Personal Computer (PC) clusters usually assume this coarse-grained approach [46]. A more fine-grained approach is used by the MSA-CUDA [47], as each pairwise alignment is partially distributed among several executing threads, thus obtaining two levels of parallelism. Each alignment returns a score value, which is then stored into the corresponding cell of the distance matrix. In addition, the actual pairwise alignments are also required by Clustal W to fine-tune the distance matrix values.

The clustering stage builds a phylogenetic tree from the previously calculated distance matrix, returning an unrooted tree with the evolutionary distances between branches. This is the less time-consuming stage [39] and, when working with only a few sequences (n<100), it can be considered negligible, as its complexity only relies on the number of sequences to align. In any case, the algorithm used for this node-clustering phase is the Neighbor-Joining (NJ) method[44], which has been previously parallelized for GPU many-core systems [48]. Other methods like the Unweighted Pair Group Method with Arithmetic Mean (UPGMA) [49] can also be used.

Finally, the progressive-alignment stage globally aligns sequences in an iterative way, following the path described by the unrooted-guide-tree topology. This stage starts aligning the closest pairs of leaf sequences. Then, the resulting pairwise alignments must be aligned again, following the closest path given by the guide tree. This high-level alignment strategy is called profile-profile alignment, where a profile is obtained from a previous intermediate of the multiple alignment, following a path from the leaves to the top of the tree. Thus, a profile alignment presents a more advanced scoring system and is more computationally expensive than a common-pairwise alignment. Furthermore, dependencies in the tree do not allow parallelizing all alignments, as occurs in the first stage. Therefore, only independent parallel-branches of the tree can be simultaneously executed, and thus may be restricted by the tree shape. This low-parallelization factor is determined by the log *n* in a well-balanced tree of *n* nodes for the best-case scenario. In a deeper level, the core of the aligner can be divided as well into two independent loops to be run separately, corresponding to the forward and backward loops [50]. Some implementations take advantage of this fact to run both loops in parallel, as the ClustalW-MPI [43]. The result produced by this stage is the full alignment.

## A New Strategy to Parallelize Clustal W: MC64-ClustalWP2

In order to exploit the parallelism in the many-core architectures, the tasks to be executed must be spread among all the available cores, which should communicate between themselves at a high speed. Thus, the first step carried out in this work was considering Clustal as three main tasks to be independently parallelized. In addition, as we focus on aligning a few long sequences, the second stage can be ignored, because its execution time can be considered negligible. An exhaustive analysis of the Clustal W allowed us to identify the progressive alignment source-code that should be rewritten, in order to have a structure very close to that of the pairwise-alignments stage. A bird's eye Clustal W structure of such approach is shown at the bottom of Figure 2.

This chart reveals the inherent similarity between the first and the last stage, where the alignment of a pair of sequences is replaced by the alignment of a pair of profiles. These profile alignments make use of a more-advanced scoring system, and they are far-more computational expensive. In particular, the score calculus function, prfscore(), the hot spot of the aligner, is a time-consuming vector multiplication (whereas in the first stage, the corresponding operation is a straightforward access to an array cell).

## A new Parallel Approach of the Pairwise-Alignments Stage

In order to parallelize the first ClustalW stage in a previous work, we replaced it with an iterative call to the MC64-NW/SW pairwise aligner [21], obtaining more than a 60% performance speedup against the ClustalW-MPI executed in a quad-core Xeon system [43]. The resulting algorithm, named MC64-ClustalW, was a coarse-grained strategy, as only individual alignments were parallelized. Besides, a considerable percentage of the tiles were idle at the beginning and at the end of each alignment, due to the wave-front growth behavior of the algorithm. Furthermore, only a tile was used in the backward stage of a pairwise alignment, being therefore a waste of resources.

Following the Tile64 terminology, a geometry is a set of adjacent cores that forms a rectangular shape, behaving as an independent subset of the Tile64 chip from a functional point of view. The Tile64 can be partitioned into several geometries, but any tile can only belong to a particular geometry at a given time. In the present work, we propose a much more advanced and fine-grained approach, being a new phase in our efforts to improve the performance of Clustal W, in which the parallelism is exploited at two levels: i) several alignments are calculated simultaneously in different geometries of cores; and ii) inside each of them, the alignment is computed in parallel by all the cores contained in it.

To achieve this new run-distribution requires a higher-level controller to schedule alignments among all groups of geometries. This new design unrolls the two main loops in the pairalign() function, and replaces the original linear-space approach with a call to the MC64-NW/SW which, in turn, uses an advanced FastLSA strategy. With this unrolling method, each pairwise alignment is assigned to an available geometry, in the same way as our previous MC64-NW/SW works [20]. Therefore, the number of pairwise alignments that can be simultaneously calculated corresponds to the number of geometries into which the Tile64 core-array is divided. Nonetheless, forward and backward stages of the pairwise alignment are separated: geometries of *n* workers calculate the full DPM for the forward stage (*F-xx geometries* from this point on), but geometries of only one worker perform the backtracking and alignment generation (*B-xx geometries* from this point on). Thus, several working geometries of these two classes collaborate to calculate all the alignments, taking the most out of every available tile. Meanwhile, the high-level controller schedules and manages all the pending jobs. Furthermore, the temporary grid-cache data must be shared between their geometries, in order to communicate a forward stage job with its backward stage counterpart.

## A new Parallel Approach of the Progressive-Alignment Stage

With MC64-ClustalWP2 we propose as well a new parallelization strategy for the progressive-alignment stage. As stated above, Figure 2 shows that the progressive alignment is actually a Myers-Miller-like alignment algorithm, whose two main loops can be unrolled in a similar way as the pairwise alignment was done. Therefore, we propose to transform the linear-space recursive Myers-Miller into a quadratic-space sequential Needleman-Wunsch. In both cases, the corresponding progressive affine-gap algorithm must be applied. In a similar way as with the first stage, this sequential dynamic-programming strategy has been parallelized using the FastLSA approach, in order to reduce the constant multiplicative factor.

However, two levels of parallelism cannot be achieved in this progressive-alignment stage, because each alignment profile depends on the previous ones; these dependencies are given by the guide tree. Our parallel approach transforms the prfalign() function into a new parallel program, using the same FastLSA strategy to distribute a single alignment to all the available tiles in the many-core system. Thus, applying the wave-front parallel strategy and selecting an optimal *k value*, the speedup will depend on the number of available processing resources, as long as the scalability factor is very close to that of our previous MC64-NW/SW [20].

In this design, a controller tile is in charge of the management of the grid cache and the distribution of jobs among the rest of available worker tiles. The profiles of the original Clustal W are still used, so the profile initialization is performed by the controller tile, whereas the workers call the original prfscore() calculus-function profile. The new implementations of both the pairwise and progressive aligners, as well as their relative speedups, are discussed in the next sections.

## Deployment of the MC64-ClustalWP2 on the Tile64 Many-Core Microprocessor

The main asset of the many-core CPU Tile64 System-on-Chip is the execution of parallel programs, due to its 64 cores/tiles running at 866 MHz in a TILExpress-20G card. The drawback is that inherently sequential code is poorly performed by a single tile. Considering that the Clustal W contains purely sequential blocks of code, yet being potentially parallelizable, we have based our implementation on a heterogeneous programming model. In such an approach, the code is commonly executed in the host CPU, using many-core GPU cards as code accelerators, effectively exploiting the best complementary potential of each kind of microprocessor. Different standards and programming methodologies have been proposed to unify and schedule the tasks in these systems, like the OpenCL [51]. Albeit, no one supports the Tile64 architecture yet, due to the novelty of the many-core CPU technologies.

The Clustal W 1.83 source code, written in the C programming language, has been carefully adapted to support the heterogeneous programming approach, generating a x86-Tile64 implementation of the MC64-ClustalWP2 parallel algorithm. Thus, the MC64-ClustalWP2 is composed by three executables: one runs in the host and two run in the Tile64. The main one is executed in the host; it processes the input parameters, sets the internal variables and orchestrates the three stages of the algorithm, eventually producing the multiple alignment. The three stages of the Clustal W are scheduled between the host CPU and the many-core CPU, as follows:

- The pairwise alignments are launched in the Tile64 environment, following the schema previously described. The pairwise-alignments overseer is the previously named “high-level controller”, a Perl script launched in the host to supervise the work distribution among the geometries.
- Once every pairwise alignment and its score are obtained, the host performs the clustering algorithm, whose execution time is negligible compared to the other stages, since the number of sequences is reduced. Therefore, the parallelization is not worth the effort in this stage. The result is the phylogenetic tree.
- Again, each profile alignment of the progressive-alignment stage is executed in the Tile64 microprocessor, following the job distribution previously stated. Every intermediary result is processed by the host, in order to calculate the next one, until the final multiple alignment is obtained.

Therefore, this hybrid work distribution exploits both architecture strengths, thus running the sequential code in the PC host and the parallel code in the Tile64 microprocessor. The complete workflow can be seen in the Figure 3. Following this approach, the implementation requires communicating both platforms for pairwise and progressive alignments.

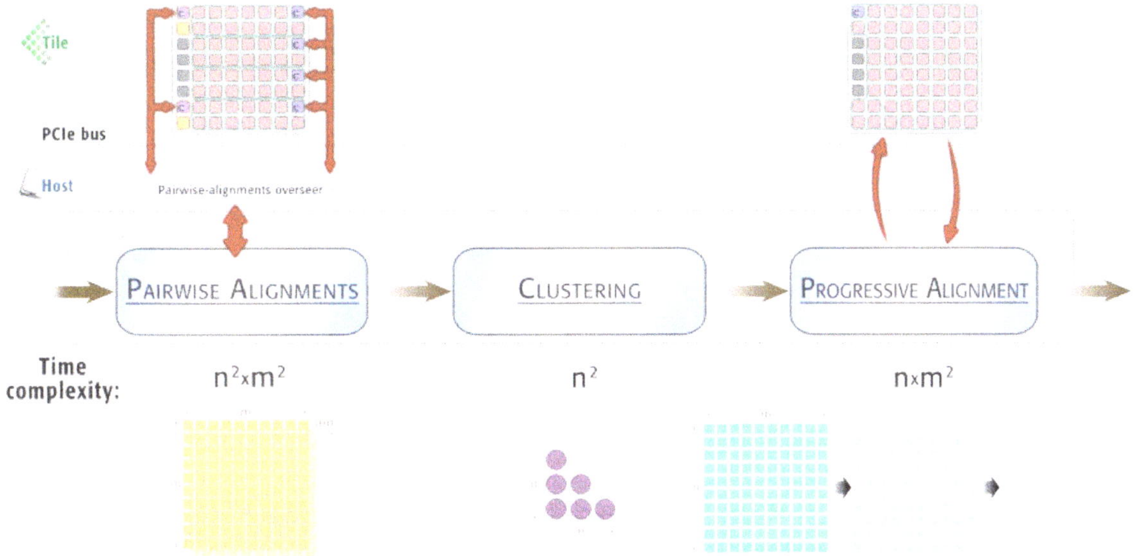


**Figure 3.** Heterogeneous programming model of the MC64-ClustalWP2 and each stage complexity.

The executable algorithm is run in the host machine: the pairwise-alignments stage communicates with an external host program, which schedules the alignments among tiles. The clustering stage is executed in the host, and the progressive-alignment stage is controlled by the host, by calculating each profile alignment in the Tile64 microprocessor. The time complexity of each stage is shown in the lower part.

## Implementation of the new Pairwise-Alignments Stage

The MC64-ClustalWP2 pairwise aligner design requires two different job classes to be run in the many-core platform; they deal with the forward and backward stages, respectively. In order to balance the developing effort versus the performance gain, the starting point was our local MC64-NW/SW pairwise aligner [20], where the necessary modifications were carried out to adapt it to the new requirements.

Both stages were decoupled, but keeping the same controller-worker strategy. So, in order to run any job, at least two tiles are needed in each stage: one acting as the stage controller and the other executing the code of the worker stage. With this approach, the same executable runs a forward or a backward stage, depending on a flag parameter: the forward stage is launched on a *F-xx geometry*, whereas the backward stage is launched on a *B-xx* one. This requires to share data between the two controllers of the same alignment (now decoupled), by temporarily storing the grid cache and the internal variables in the TILExpress-20G card 8 GB SSD file system. On the other hand, the original MC64-NW/SW used 6 bytes per cell, since gap penalties are never greater than 128 [5]. However, the pairwise alignment in Clustal W uses bigger values, so the grid-cache cell structure was modified as well to support it. Now, 12 bytes are used and the absolute values are stored instead of the relative differences in the case of the two auxiliary matrices. This is translated into more memory/file-system usage and less performance, due to the Tile64 instruction characteristics. As a collateral effect, the optimal *k values* calculated in the MC64-NW/SW parallelization are invalid and must be recalculated.

Taking into consideration that four cores are reserved for the internal management of the chip and communications with the host, the 60 remaining available cores are distributed into a number of static geometries. Different empirical tests have demonstrated that the optimal geometries to use are four forward stage geometries of 7×2 tiles and two backward stage geometries of 2×1 tiles. The rationale of such result is that the forward stage is far more computationally expensive than the backward one. Nonetheless, when the number of pairwise alignments is between five and eight, it is better to use eight 7×1 F-xx geometries, because this optimizes the workload by avoiding a second batch of alignments with idle geometries.

To achieve two levels of parallelism, a "high-level" controller is needed to manage several alignments simultaneously; this controller appears in Figure 3 with the name Pairwise-alignments overseer. This controller runs in the host because it must communicate with the tile-monitor command-line tool which Tilera provides in its Multicore Development Environment (MDE), in order to manage the tile geometries. To take apart this functionality from the Clustal W source code, this task is carried out by a Perl script, which is called from the host main executable with the proper parameters: sequences to align, scoring matrix, etc.

Although other kinds of communications would be possible, like a telnet access, a client-server approach using the available Ethernet ports or a serial console, the communication between the Perl script and the Tile64 is performed via the more straightforward tile-monitor command line tool: when the Perl script starts a new tile-monitor session, it takes input/output communication channels through which the commands and results are sent. The Perl script manages pending jobs and available geometries, in order to schedule workload. Finally, when every pairwise alignment has been calculated, the MC64-ClustalWP2 pairalign() function gets all of them from the Perl script. Starting from them, the scoring matrix is computed as the original Clustal W does.

## Implementation of the new Progressive-Alignment Stage

The implementation of the progressive aligner requires as well communicating the MC64-ClustalWP2 program, run in the host, with the parallel code executed in the Tile64. However, an intermediate script is not needed this time, as long as the algorithm has only one level of parallelism (every tile works for the same profile alignment and, thus, no fine-grained tile-monitor control is required).

This stage is controlled by the host main executable, which launches each profile alignment on the Tile64 environment. To do this, many internal variables must be shared between these both hardware environments. In total, 37 different variables and structures are needed, in order to rebuild the profiles and run the algorithm in the Tile64; other five are updated and returned to the host. To perform these communications and, at the same time, to avoid spreading dependencies throughout the code, we have built an intermediate layer library, called MC64-NWProfile_ParameterManagement, that encapsulates data structures and communication functions. This layer carries out communications using properly-formatted plain-text files. This facilitates uploading the required data into the Tile64, as well as download from it when required. In addition, the MC64_ParameterManagement provides the implementation of the profile-alignment algorithm, which is executed in the Tile64 microprocessor, as seen in Figure 3. Thus, the Clustal W malign() remains nearly the same, but the prfalign() function has been replaced by the needed calls to the parameter management library functions, which wait for the Tile64 program to finish before continuing.

The profile alignment algorithm for the Tile64 microprocessor has been developed starting from the MC64-NW/SW code, and applying several major changes to align profiles instead of sequences. For internal purposes, we have called MC64-NWProfile this new sub-algorithm, due to its global behavior. Each profile is a bi-dimensional structure of 35×m, where the height (35) is determined by all the possible residues plus gaps, whereas the width (m) is determined by the profile length; i.e., the length of the globally aligned sequences in the block. The progressive alignment is based on the alignment of these structures, with the prfscore() function determining the score for position i,j of the DPM from the vector multiplication of the profile1[i] row and the profile2[j] row.

Firstly, the MC64-NWProfile computes the profiles using the internal variables passed to it. Once calculated, the algorithm follows the same controller-workers approach than the MC64-NW/SW, using a similar wave-front parallelism. However, the prfscore() is now a vector-multiplication operation instead of an indirect-access operation. Additionally, the cells are 12 bytes instead of 6 bytes, so the job-partition optimal *k values* for each pair of profiles are completely different from those calculated in the pairwise-alignments stage. Thus, new optimal*k values* for significant profiles lengths must be pre-calculated, and, when a pair of profiles is to be aligned, the actual *k value* is interpolated from these ones.

To calculate a cell›s content in this parallel approach, each worker requires accessing to the profile structures to compute the scores and alignment. However, for relatively long sequences, each profile can take several megabytes (for example, to align 200 kb sequences, each profile requires 24 MB), so a new problem arises: the location of these two profiles in memory. A direct approach to overcome such limitation is to store a single copy of the profiles in the shared memory, being accessible by both the controller and every worker. Yet, unfortunately, the shared memory access is very slow (can consume tens of CPU cycles) in comparison to the local memory access. Therefore, a better approach is to copy the profiles into the local memory of each tile. This simple modification represents an 8x speedup in execution time, though it requires much more memory (following the 200 kb example, 24 MB×2×59 workers =2.8 GB), and thus restricts the range of valid *k values*. Indeed, both the grid cache and the profile copies coexist in the available 8 GB (used as SSD shared and local memory). As a consequence, the available memory to store the grid cache decreases using this approach, and then, a low *k value* may produce a memory overflow.

In contrast, the MC64-NWProfile obtains a better performance with lower *k values*. Therefore, an intermediate approach is to only copy the necessary fragments for the current job to the worker local memory. Hence, when a worker receives a new job, it brings these fragments of the profiles to the local memory and when finished, it frees the memory. This approach opens the door to use small *k value* sizes, though the handicap is that the same fragments are eventually copied in the same worker several times for each alignment. In spite of this, using low *k values* instead of bigger ones, allows obtaining an additional 1.5x overall speedup, as it has been empirically demonstrated (data not shown). Finally, when the alignment is obtained, the local Clustal W variables are modified and returned to the host, which generates the intermediary multiple alignment and continues the process, following the guide-tree topology to progressively generate the next alignments.

## RESULTS AND DISCUSSION

Once the algorithm was developed and implemented using the approach stated above, the MC64-ClustalWP2 was tested to benchmark its performance against the original algorithm and other parallel implementations, using different architectures and approaches. At first, we launched stress tests with ten sequences of different sizes and measured the speedup of the MC64-ClustalWP2 against other Clustal W implementations. A further test was carried out to analyze families of long sequences, which are aligned in much less time than with other general global MSA strategies, as discussed below.

### Heterogeneous Tile64/PC MC64-ClustalWP2 speedup tests

In order to test the relative performance of the new MC64-ClustalWP2 parallel strategy implementation with the many-core Tile64 microprocessor, the original Clustal W algorithm and other parallel implementations were compared using a set of sequences with different sizes. In particular, the tested algorithms were the Clustal W 1.83 (originally written in C language) [28]and two parallel implementations: the ClustalW-MTV (the latest version of MT-ClustalW for multi-threaded systems) [41] and the ClustalW-MPI (focused on multi-core systems and PC clusters using the MPI library) [43]. The Clustal W many-core GPU implementations, as the MSA-CUDA [47], were excluded from this test, since they are unable to align such large sequences. The dataset used for the experiment is composed of 10 sets of artificial sequences whose lengths range between 25 and 300 kb. The alignment of hundreds or thousands of sequences with lower lengths is not the focus of our parallel approach (and neither its strength), so it is not worthy to carry out any test on such sets of sequences. In these cases, the scientist may choose from a different set of tools specifically developed for the purpose, including the above-mentioned GPU implementations and programs like MAFFT (the PartTree algorithm [52]) and Clustal-Omega [53].

All of the algorithms tested were run in the same environment (Intel Xeon Quad Core 2.0 GHz PC with 8 GB of quad-channel DDR2 memory), providing the same results but with rather different execution times. The MC64-ClustalWP2 used the Tile64 microprocessor on-boarded in a TilExpress-20G card with 8 GB RAM. The execution time and minimum-gain ratio of the MC64-ClustalWP2 algorithm against the other ones is shown for each set of sequences inFigure 4.

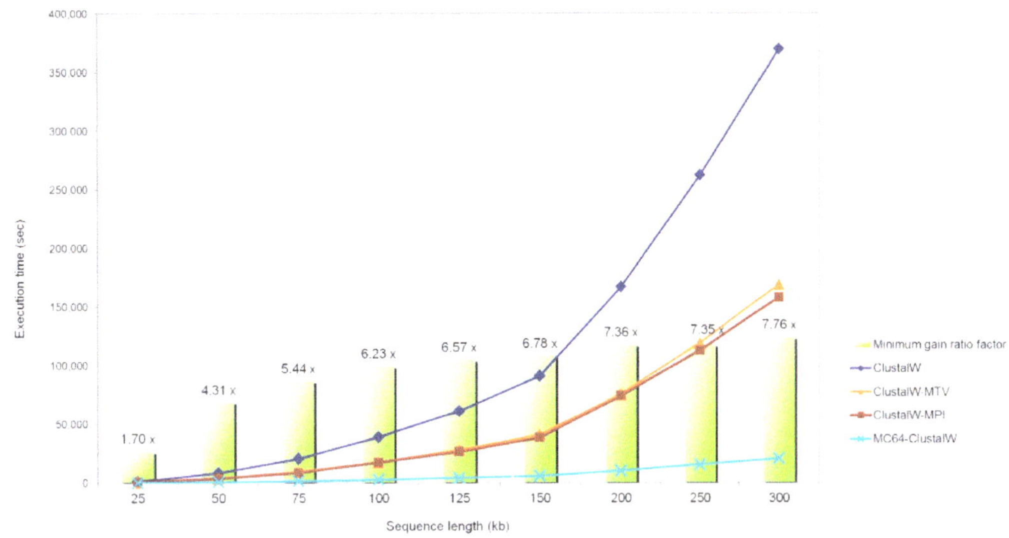


**Figure 4.** Execution time of the alignment of sets of ten randomly-generated sequences of different sizes, using Clustal W implementations.

The tested algorithms are the original Clustal W 1.83, the MC64-ClustalWP2 for Tile64 and PC, and two parallel implementations for x86 systems (MT-ClustalW and ClustalW-MPI). In addition, the minimum gain ratio of the MC64-ClustalWP2 against all the other implementations is exposed for each set of sequences.

The results reveal the best performance of the MC64-ClustalWP2 against every other implementation. This tendency increases with the length of the sequences, because a higher parallelization factor is obtained. Thus, the MC64-ClustalWP2 reaches a speedup of more than 7x when compared to the best multi-core implementation (ClustalW-MPI). In particular, both multi-core approaches present very similar behaviors with differences only appreciable when aligning 300 kb length sequences. On the other hand, the MC64-ClustalWP2 obtains a speedup factor of more than 18x when compared to the original algorithm. The Figures 5 and 6show the relative acceleration factor in both the first and third stages against ClustalW and ClustalW-MPI, which reveals that our work-distribution strategy for the third stage yields much more parallelism than other methods.

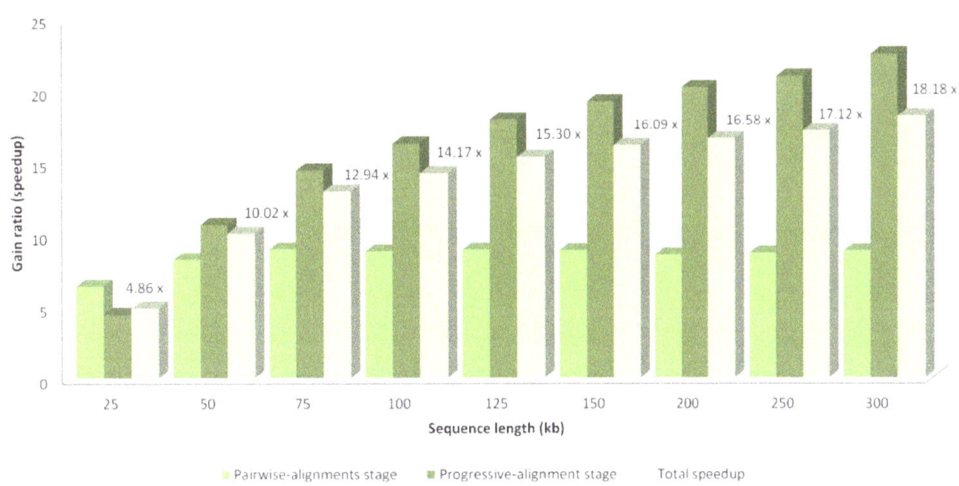


**Figure 5.** Speedup of the MC64-ClustalWP2 against Clustal W 1.83.

The speedup is shown both for each relevant stage and for the full execution when aligning sets of ten randomly-generated sequences of different sizes.

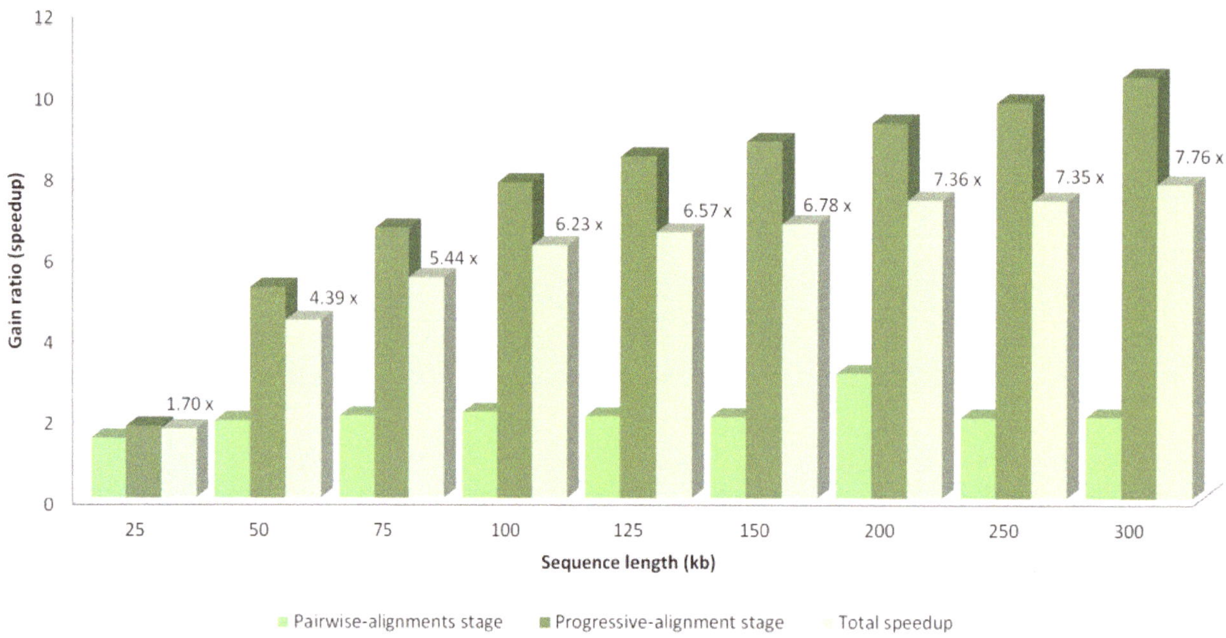


**Figure 6.** Speedup of the MC64-ClustalWP2 against ClustalW-MPI.

The speedup is shown both for each relevant stage and for the full execution when aligning sets of ten randomly-generated sequences of different sizes.

## Variation Analyses of the Human Herpesvirus 1 Genomes

As a final test, the MC64-ClustalWP2 was used to run an experiment whose execution time is near prohibitive when non-parallel or less-efficient parallel MSA methods are applied. In this stress test, 37 different human herpesvirus 1 (*Herpes simplex* virus type 1; HHV-1) genomes, publicly available at GenBank <http://www.ncbi.nlm.nih.gov/genbank>, were selected to be aligned. The complete genome of the HHV-1 is about 152 kilobase pairs (kbp), and the different strains should *a priori* present several mutation areas, due to the high mutation-rates of this kind of DNA viruses. Therefore, such alignments can be carried out with dynamic-programming algorithms like Clustal W.

The MC64-ClustalWP2 aligned the 37 sequence genomes in 36,103 seconds (10.03 h; 21,742 seconds for the first stage, nearly zero for the second one and 14,360 seconds for the third stage). The final phylogenetic tree is shown in Figure 7. The upper part of the dendrogram includes the reference genome, which appears twice in the database (GenBank accession numbers NC_001806.1 and X14112.1) and was modeled from the strain 17 sequencing (GenBank accession number JN555585.1).

To calculate the multiple alignment of the genomes in this tree, MC64-ClustalWP2 run 7.59 times faster than its closest competitor (ClustalW-MPI).

The quality of the alignments provided by any MSA algorithm, including Clustal W, depends on many factors, being an issue open for discussion [38], [54]. As expected in this case, the resulting alignment highlighted the polymorphisms between the virus strains. The most divergent strain was the TFT401 ocular one (GenBank accession number JN420337.1), also showing a low sequencing-coverage [55]. The alignment hereby presented confirms the previously reported sequencing results. As an example, a review of these genomes in relation to their glycoproteins coding genes has been published elsewhere [56].

**Figure 7.** Phylogenetic tree of 37 different genomes of HHV-1.

This alignment was also performed with other global MSA algorithms, and even with other Clustal W implementations (which provides exactly the same alignment), but the quickest among them (ClustalW-MPI) required 274,149 seconds (3.17 days) to complete the alignment, being 7.59 times slower than our approach which, hence, becomes the only one capable to deal with this type of alignments in a reasonable time. On the other hand, some of the MSA algorithms do not generate an evolutionary tree of the genomic sequences, as they are oriented to find only the similar regions. Besides, they lack accuracy when the aligned sequences have highly polymorphic regions (e.g., with high mutation-rates), which is typical for most viruses [35].

## Conclusions and Future Work

We have developed a new parallel strategy for Clustal W, which is one of the most relevant algorithms in bioinformatics for multiple-sequence alignments and dendrogram generation. This algorithm uses the pairwise-alignment operation as its core. Our work has focused on large sequences, a field where the resources of a GPGPU architecture have proven insufficient but, in contrast, our previous developments in many-core technologies for bioinformatics, like the MC64-NW/SW, have shown a high performance [20], [22]. In this scenario, we have separately redesigned and parallelized the two most time-consuming stages of Clustal W, using a new approach that exploits parallelism in systems with many cores. This new model, named MC64-ClustalWP2, allows aligning large sequences in a relatively short period of time on a personal computer, obtaining a global speedup of more than 18x against the original Clustal W, and more than 7x against the best x86 parallel implementation to date. This allows aligning more and larger sequences and, thus, enhances the range of problems that can be addressed in an affordable time.

The MC64-ClustalWP2 has been implemented for the heterogeneous standalone system x86-Tile64, using the Tile64 many-core microprocessor. Thus, within a single computer, the MC64-ClustalWP2 offers an impressive performance, being scalable to larger many-core systems using the same parallel strategy. This represents also a proof of concept that new parallel strategies can be exploited to harness the new developments in the many-core microprocessors to analyze the increasing amount of data generated by the second- and third-generation sequencing platforms. Thus, the Clustal W dynamic-programming approach that we have developed (MC64-ClustalWP2) can align genomes with highly polymorphic regions [35], which cannot be accomplished by the MSA heuristic aligners of genomes.

These developments allow to identify identities and differences to generate dendrograms for biodiversity and evolutionary studies, and to develop molecular markers like the ones based, for instance, on Single Nucleotide Polymorphisms (SNP), as well as on microsatellites, also known as Short Tandem Repeats (STR) in animals and as Simple Sequence Repeats (SSR) in plants, for germplasm management, breeding, identification and protection of the intellectual property, PDO, illegal traffic control and fraud prevention, as we have described for the olive oil[57].

Additionally, the MC64-ClustalWP2 strategy can be deployed for any many-core system with very little effort, like the current and future Intel Xeon Phi and the Tilera microprocessors. In particular, we have already developed a threaded version of MC64-NW/SW for the Intel i7 processor, and we are planning to use it as starting point to take full advantage of every Intel Xeon Phi core, where several threads must be executed to achieve an instruction-per-cycle performance. Furthermore, the approach can be escalated, both in processor and in memory resources, interconnecting several TilExpress-20G cards through their 10GBase-CX4 connectors to build a powerful cluster of Tile64 microprocessors, with thousands of cores, increasing both the number and the length of the sequences to align. We have already designed such a cluster, which is currently being evaluated [58].

On the other hand, a possible optimization in order to improve even further the parallelism of the first stage is to get rid of the intermediate Perl script and to transfer its high-level controller functionalities to a core of the many-core system. This allows using a single geometry where each worker is independent (i.e., may indistinctively work for any alignment), receiving in each case the data from the input sequences to be aligned. This new approach would maximize the core usage in the first stage, but would require more data transfers and memory resources in the overall system, which is strongly limited to 8 GB of RAM in the case of the Tile64 hardware. As an additional optimization for the alignment of thousands of sequences, the clustering stage could be parallelized as stated in [59]. However, we are not dealing with such an scenario now, since the MC64-ClustalWP2 is oriented to align long sequences.

On the other hand, the MC64-ClustalWP2 should be considered as a complementary tool to heuristic algorithms like the MGA [33] for the alignment of large sequences with highly polymorphic regions. In this regard, a more complex and "intelligent" alignment system could be built in a heterogeneous environment, in order to distribute and optimize the alignment tasks and stages, attending to the sequence characteristics. These developments should enhance the current tools in the bioinformatics arsenal.

Lastly, the MC64-ClustalWP2 algorithm is freely accessible to the scientific community and can be remotely executed on our server (a system that integrates the TilExpress-20G card) by means of a web service at <http://galactus.uma.es/manycore>. In the same way, the MC64-ClustalWP2 project is available under the GNU General Public License (GPL), and its source code can be downloaded from the same website.

## ACKNOWLEDGMENTS

We are grateful to Tilera for providing hardware and software tools <http://www.tilera.com>.

## AUTHOR CONTRIBUTIONS

Conceived and designed the experiments: DD FJE PH GD SG. Performed the experiments: DD FJE. Analyzed the data: DD FJE PH JC AG GD SG. Contributed reagents/materials/analysis tools: JC AG GD. Wrote the paper: DD FJE PH JC AG GD SG. Software design: DD FJE SG. Web deployment: DD AG SG.

## REFERENCES

1. Needleman SB, Wunsch CD (1970) A general method applicable to the search for similarities in the amino acid sequence of two proteins. Journal of Molecular Biology 48: 443–453. doi: 10. 1016/0022-2836(70)90057-4
2. Smith TF, Waterman MS (1981) Identification of common molecular subsequences. J Mol Biol 147: 195–197. doi: 10. 1016/0022-2836(81)90087-5
3. Gotoh O (1982) An improved algorithm for matching biological sequences. Journal of Molecular Biology 162: 705–708. doi: 10. 1016/0022-2836(82)90398-9
4. Hirschberg DS (1975) A linear space algorithm for computing maximal common subsequences. Commun ACM 18: 341–343. doi: 10. 1145/360825. 360861
5. Driga A, Lu P, Schaeffer J, Szafron D, Charter K, et al. (2006) FastLSA: A Fast, Linear-Space, Parallel and Sequential Algorithm for Sequence Alignment. Algorithmica 45: 337–375. doi: 10. 1007/s00453-006-1217-y
6. Pearson WR, Lipman DJ (1988) Improved tools for biological sequence comparison. Proceedings of the National Academy of Sciences of the United States of America 85: 2444–2448. doi: 10. 1073/pnas. 85. 8. 2444
7. Altschul S, Gish W, Miller W, Myers E-M, Lipman D (1990) Basic local alignment search tool. J Mol Biol 215: 403–410. doi: 10. 1016/s0022-2836(05)80360-2
8. Pearson WR (1991) Searching protein sequence libraries: comparison of the sensitivity and selectivity of the Smith-Waterman and FASTA algorithms. Genomics 11: 635–650. doi: 10. 1016/0888-7543(91)90071-l
9. Mirto M, Fiore S, Epicoco I, Cafaro M, Mocavero S, et al. (2008) A Bioinformatics Grid Alignment Toolkit. Future Generation Computer Systems 24: 752–762. doi: 10. 1016/j. future. 2008. 02. 001
10. Goetzmann JF (2007) Massively Parallel Contact Simulation on Graphics Hardware using NVIDIA CUDA [Bacherlor's Thesis]. Institute for Computer Science, Universität Mainz.
11. Adapteva (2011) Epiphany Multicore IP. Available:http://www. adapteva. com/index. php?option=com_content&view=article&id=72&Itemid=79. Accessed 2013 Jul 16.
12. Shah M, Barreh J, Brooks J, Golla R, Grohoski G, et al. (2007) UltraSPARC T2: A highly-treaded, power-efficient, SPARC SOC Asian Solid-State Circuits Conference. (ASSCC07): 22–25. doi: 10. 1109/asscc. 2007. 4425786
13. Mattson TG, Wijngaart RVD, Frumkin M (2008) Programming the Intel 80-core network-on-a-chip Terascale processor. Proceedings of the 2008 ACM/IEEE conference on Supercomputing. Austin, Texas: IEEE Press. pp. 1–11.
14. Intel (2010) The SCC Platform Overview. Available:http://techresearch. intel. com/spaw2/uploads/files/SCC-Overview. pdf. Accessed 2013 Jul 16.
15. Intel (2010) Intel's Teraflops Research Chip. Available:http://download. intel. com/pressroom/kits/Teraflops/Teraflops_Research_Chip_Overview. pdf. Accessed 2013 Jul 16.
16. Wentzlaff D, Griffin P, Hoffmann H, Bao L, Edwards B, et al. (2007) On-Chip Interconnection Architecture of the Tile Processor. IEEE Micro 27: 15–31. doi: 10. 1109/mm. 2007. 4378780
17. Tilera (2011) Product Brief: TILE-Gx 8000 Series.

Available:http://www. tilera. com/sites/default/files/productbriefs/TILE-Gx8000Series Brief_0. pdf. Accessed 2013 Jul 16.

18. Manavski SA, Valle G (2008) CUDA compatible GPU cards as efficient hardware accelerators for Smith-Waterman sequence alignment. BMC Bioinformatics 9 Suppl 2: S10. doi: 10. 1186/1471-2105-9-s2-s10
19. Liu Y, Schmidt B, Maskell DL (2010) CUDASW++2. 0: enhanced Smith-Waterman protein database search on CUDA-enabled GPUs based on SIMT and virtualized SIMD abstractions. BMC Research Notes 3: 93. doi: 10. 1186/1756-0500-3-93
20. Díaz D, Esteban FJ, Hernández P, Caballero JA, Dorado G, et al. (2011) Parallelizing and optimizing a bioinformatics pairwise sequence alignment algorithm for many-core architecture. Parallel Computing 37: 244–259. doi: 10. 1016/j. parco. 2011. 03. 003
21. Esteban FJ, Díaz D, Hernández P, Caballero JA, Dorado G, et al. (2013) Direct approaches to exploit many-core architecture in bioinformatics. Future Generation Computer Systems 29: 15–26. doi: 10. 1016/j. future. 2012. 03. 018
22. Gálvez S, Díaz D, Hernández P, Esteban FJ, Caballero JA, et al. (2010) Next-Generation Bioinformatics: Using Many-Core Processor Architecture to Develop a Web Service for Sequence Alignment. Bioinformatics 26: 683–686. doi: 10. 1093/bioinformatics/btq017
23. Agrifood Biotechnology ("Biotecnología Agroalimentaria") Research Group (2009) Many-core bioinformatics algorithms development. Available:http://galactus. uma. es/manycore/. Accessed 2013 Sep 11.
24. Bains W (1986) MULTAN: a program to align multiple DNA sequences. Nucleic Acids Research 14: 159–177. doi: 10. 1093/nar/14. 1. 159
25. Waterman MS (1986) Multiple sequence alignment by consensus. Nucleic Acids Research 14: 9095–9102. doi: 10. 1093/nar/14. 22. 9095
26. Higgins DG, Sharp PM (1988) CLUSTAL: a package for performing multiple sequence alignment on a microcomputer. Gene 73: 237–244. doi: 10. 1016/0378-1119(88)90330-7
27. Higgins DG, Bleasby AJ, Fuchs R (1992) CLUSTAL V: improved software for multiple sequence alignment. Computer applications in the biosciences: CABIOS 8: 189–191. doi: 10. 1093/bioinformatics/8. 2. 189
28. Thompson JD, Higgins DG, Gibson TJ (1994) CLUSTAL W: improving the sensitivity of progressive multiple sequence alignment through sequence weighting, position-specific gap penalties and weight matrix choice. Nucleic Acids Res 22: 4673–4680. doi: 10. 1093/nar/22. 22. 4673
29. Larkin MA, Blackshields G, Brown NP, Chenna R, McGettigan PA, et al. (2007) Clustal W and Clustal X version 2. 0. Bioinformatics 23: 2947–2948. doi: 10. 1093/bioinformatics/btm404
30. Notredame C, Higgins DG, Heringa J (2000) T-coffee: a novel method for fast and accurate multiple sequence alignment. Journal of Molecular Biology 302: 205–217. doi: 10. 1006/jmbi. 2000. 4042
31. Edgar RC (2004) MUSCLE: multiple sequence alignment with high accuracy and high throughput. Nucleic Acids Research 32: 1792–1797. doi: 10. 1093/nar/gkh340
32. Brudno M, Do CB, Cooper GM, Kim MF, Davydov E, et al. (2003) LAGAN and Multi-LAGAN: efficient tools for large-scale multiple alignment of genomic DNA. Genome Res 13: 721–731. doi: 10. 1101/gr. 926603
33. Hohl M, Kurtz S, Ohlebusch E (2002) Efficient multiple genome alignment. Bioinformatics 18: S312–320. doi: 10. 1093/bioinformatics/18. suppl_1. s312
34. Dewey CN (2007) Aligning multiple whole genomes with Mercator and MAVID. Methods Mol Biol 395: 221–236. doi: 10. 1385/1-59745-514-8:221
35. Chain P, Kurtz S, Ohlebusch E, Slezak T (2003) An applications-focused review of comparative genomics tools: Capabilities, limitations and future challenges. Briefings in Bioinformatics 4: 105–123. doi: 10. 1093/bib/4. 2. 105
36. Darling AE, Mau B, Perna NT (2010) progressiveMauve: Multiple Genome Alignment with Gene Gain, Loss and Rearrangement. PLoS ONE 5: e11147. doi: 10. 1371/journal. pone. 0011147
37. Paten B, Earl D, Nguyen N, Diekhans M, Zerbino D, et al. (2011) Cactus: Algorithms for genome multiple sequence alignment. Genome Res 21: 1512–1528. doi: 10. 1101/gr. 123356. 111
38. Notredame C (2007) Recent Evolutions of Multiple Sequence Alignment Algorithms. PLoS Comput Biol 3: e123. doi: 10. 1371/journal. pcbi. 0030123
39. Vandierendonck H, Rul S, Questier M, De Bosschere K (2008) Experiences with Parallelizing a Bio-informatics Program on the Cell BE High Performance Embedded Architectures and Compilers. In:Stenström P, Dubois M, Katevenis M, Gupta R, Ungerer T, editors: Springer Berlin/Heidelberg. pp. 161–175.
40. Mikhailov D, Cofer H, Gomperts R (2001) Performance optimization of Clustal W: parallel Clustal W, HT Clustal, and MULTICLUSTAL. Silicon Graphics, Inc.
41. Chaichoompu K, Kittitornkun S, Tongsima S (2006) MT-ClustalW: multithreading multiple sequence alignment. Proceedings of the 20th Parallel and Distributed Processing Symposium (IPDPS 2006). pp. 8.
42. Vandierendonck H, Rul S, De Bosschere K (2010) Accelerating Multiple Sequence Alignment with the Cell BE Processor. The Computer Journal 53: 814–826. doi: 10. 1093/comjnl/bxp086
43. Li K-B (2003) ClustalW-MPI: ClustalW analysis using distributed and parallel computing. Bioinformatics 19: 1585–1586. doi: 10. 1093/bioinformatics/btg192
44. Saitou N, Nei M (1987) The neighbor-joining method: a new method for reconstructing phylogenetic trees. Molecular Biology and Evolution 4: 406–425.
45. Myers EW, Miller W (1988) Optimal alignments in linear space. Comput Appl Biosci 4: 11–17. doi: 10. 1093/bioinformatics/4. 1. 11
46. Cheetham J, Dehne F, Pitre S, Rau-Chaplin A, Taillon

PJ (2003) Parallel CLUSTAL W for PC clusters. Proceedings of the 2003 international conference on Computational science and its applications: Part II. Montreal, Canada: Springer-Verlag. pp. 300–309.

47. Yongchao L, Schmidt B, Maskell DL (2009) MSA-CUDA: Multiple Sequence Alignment on Graphics Processing Units with CUDA. Proceedings of the 20th IEEE International Conference on Application-specific Systems, Architectures and Processors (ASAP 2009). pp. 121–128.
48. Yongchao L, Schmidt B, Maskell DL (2009) Parallel reconstruction of neighbor-joining trees for large multiple sequence alignments using CUDA. Proceedings of the IEEE International Symposium on Parallel and Distributed Processing (IPDPS 2009). pp. 1–8.
49. Michener CD, Sokal RR (1957) A quantitative approach to a problem of classification. Evolution 11. doi: 10. 2307/2406046
50. Isaza S, Sanchez F, Gaydadjiev G, Ramirez A, Valero M (2010) Scalability Analysis of Progressive Alignment on a Multicore. Proceedings of the International Conference on Complex, Intelligent and Software Intensive Systems (CISIS 2010). pp. 889–894.
51. Stone JE, Gohara D, Shi G (2010) OpenCL: A Parallel Programming Standard for Heterogeneous Computing Systems. Computing in Science and Engineering. pp. 66–73.
52. Katoh K, Toh H (2007) PartTree: an algorithm to build an approximate tree from a large number of unaligned sequences. Bioinformatics 23: 372–374. doi: 10. 1093/ bioinformatics/btl592
53. Sievers F, Wilm A, Dineen D, Gibson TJ, Karplus K, et al. (2011) Fast, scalable generation of high-quality protein multiple sequence alignments using Clustal Omega. Mol Syst Biol 7: 539. doi: 10. 1038/msb. 2011. 75
54. Higgins DG, Blackshields G, Wallace IM (2005) Mind the gaps: progress in progressive alignment. Proc Natl Acad Sci U S A 102: 10411–10412. doi: 10. 1073/pnas. 0504801102
55. Kolb AW, Adams M, Cabot EL, Craven M, Brandt CR (2011) Multiplex sequencing of seven ocular herpes simplex virus type-1 genomes: phylogeny, sequence variability, and SNP distribution. Invest Ophthalmol Vis Sci 52: 9061–9073. doi: 10. 1167/iovs. 11-7812
56. Norberg P, Bergstrom T, Rekabdar E, Lindh M, Liljeqvist JA (2004) Phylogenetic analysis of clinical herpes simplex virus type 1 isolates identified three genetic groups and recombinant viruses. J Virol 78: 10755–10764. doi: 10. 1128/jvi. 78. 19. 10755-10764. 2004
57. Perez-Jimenez M, Besnard G, Dorado G, Hernandez P (2013) Varietal tracing of virgin olive oils based on plastid DNA variation profiling. PLoS One 8: e70507. doi: 10. 1371/journal. pone. 0070507
58. Esteban F, Díaz D, Hernández P, Caballero J, Dorado G, et al. (2013) MC64-Cluster: A Many-Core CPU Cluster for Bioinformatics Applications. In: Rocha Á, Correia AM, Wilson T, Stroetmann KA, editors. Advances in Information Systems and Technologies: Springer Berlin Heidelberg. pp. 819–825.
59. Du Z, Lin F (2006) pNJTree: A parallel program for reconstruction of neighbor-joining tree and its application in ClustalW. Parallel Computing 32: 441–446. doi: 10.1016/j.parco.2006.05.001

CHAPTER 12

# QUICKPROBS—A FAST MULTIPLE SEQUENCE ALIGNMENT ALGORITHM DESIGNED FOR GRAPHICS PROCESSORS

Adam Gudyś, Sebastian Deorowicz

Institute of Informatics, Faculty of Automatic Control, Electronics and Computer Science, Silesian University of Technology, Gliwice, Poland

## ABSTRACT

**Multiple sequence alignment is a crucial task in a number of biological analyses like secondary structure prediction, domain searching, phylogeny, etc. MSAProbs is currently the most accurate alignment algorithm, but its effectiveness is obtained at the expense of computational time. In the paper we present QuickProbs, the variant of MSAProbs customised for graphics processors. We selected the two most time consuming stages of MSAProbs to be redesigned for GPU execution: the posterior matrices calculation and the consistency transformation. Experiments on three popular benchmarks (BAliBASE, PREFAB, OXBench-X) on quad-core PC equipped with high-end graphics card show QuickProbs to be 5.7 to 9.7 times faster than original CPU-parallel MSAProbs. Additional tests performed on several protein families from Pfam database give overall speed-up of 6.7. Compared to other algorithms like MAFFT, MUSCLE, or ClustalW, QuickProbs proved to be much more accurate at similar speed. Additionally we introduce a tuned variant of QuickProbs which is significantly more accurate on sets of distantly related sequences than MSAProbs without exceeding its computation time. The GPU part of QuickProbs was implemented in OpenCL, thus the package is suitable for graphics processors produced by all major vendors.**

## INTRODUCTION

Multiple sequence alignment (MSA) is an essential task in molecular biology. It is performed for both, nucleotide and protein sequences. Its field of applications covers phylogenetic analyses, gene finding, identification of functional domains, prediction of secondary structures, and many others. Rapidly increasing size of sequence databases allowed by the development of high throughput sequencing technologies provides biologists with the opportunity to analyse in silico enormous sets of data. Hence, the constant pressure for developing more accurate and faster MSA algorithms. As multiple sequence alignment problem is NP-hard [1], [2], exact methods are infeasible for practical applications due to excessive computation time. Therefore, many heuristics have been developed including progressive [3], iterative [4], or hidden Markov model-based [5] strategies. One of the most popular multiple sequence alignment software is ClustalW [6].

**Citation:** Gudyś A, Deorowicz S. QuickProbs—A Fast Multiple Sequence Alignment Algorithm Designed for Graphics Processors. Guo J-T, ed. PLoS ONE. 2014;9(2):e88901. doi:10.1371/journal.pone.0088901.

It is a classic representative of progressive algorithms, and works according to the scheme:

- Estimate evolutionary distances between all pairs of sequences.
- Build a guide tree on the basis of the distances.
- Align sequences in the order described by the tree.

Calculation of an evolutionary distance is done either by performing pairwise sequence alignment between sequences (default mode) or by employing $k$-tuple matching (fast mode).

Many researches aimed at refining ClustalW accuracy by extending the idea of progressive alignment. An important breakthrough was the introduction of T-Coffee algorithm [7] which incorporated a consistency-based objective function. The principle was employing knowledge of some symbols being aligned from all pairwise alignments and was confirmed to improve significantly quality of a final result. Other techniques acquired by MSA algorithms include identification of homologous regions using fast Fourier transform (MAFFT [8]) or iterative refinement of a final alignment (MUSCLE [9]). There is a group of methods that improved calculation of a pairwise alignment by using suboptimal alignments. These are Probcons [10]and Probalign [11] which compute posterior probability matrices for all pairs of sequences using pair hidden Markov models (pair-HMMs) and partition functions, respectively. Both of them are also equipped in a consistency scheme which makes them very accurate. Recently published MSAProbs algorithm combines pair-HMM and posterior function approaches with a consistency transformation and an iterative refinement leading to the highest quality amongst all presented packages [12]. However, experiments show that even most accurate methods fail to find a proper alignment when analysed sequences are distantly related, particularly in so called 'twilight zone', when sequence similarity drops below 30%. Some algorithms addressed this issue by introducing to the alignment procedure additional knowledge. E.g., 3D-Coffee extends T-Coffee by using mixture of pairwise sequence and structure alignments [13]. MSACompro introduces to MSAProbs pipeline secondary structures, residue-residue contact maps, and solvent accessibility which elevates accuracy [14].

Our research, however, focuses on methods exploiting only sequences themselves. An important issue related to accurate MSA algorithms like T-Coffee, ProbCons, or MSAProbs is that superior results are produced at the cost of significant increase in complexity: all the above-mentioned methods are inferior to ClustalW in fast mode in terms of time and memory requirements. This is a serious disadvantage when processing large sequence sets, which is often the case, as it has been proven that introducing homologous sequences to MSA improves quality of a final result [15]. Moreover, there are applications which require huge number of multiple alignments to be computed. E.g., PhylomeDB database [16] gathers currently almost 1.9 million of MSAs. As alignment times varied from several seconds to several minutes, computation of all alignments required tens of months of CPU time [17]. Taking into account increasing availability of genomic and proteomic data, this number is expected to grow dramatically in close future. Hence, it is desirable to have algorithms able to align large sequence sets or perform large number of alignments in a reasonable time.

For aforementioned reason, some algorithms aimed at improving alignment quality without sacrificing time and memory efficiency of ClustalW. These are for example Kalign [8] and Kalign2 [19] which instead of $k$-tuple matches employ respectively, Wu-Manber [20] and Muth-Manber [21] approximate string matching algorithms. Kalign2 turns out to be faster and more memory efficient than ClustalW in fast mode and also significantly more accurate (not as accurate as consistency-based methods, though). Kalign-LCS [22] further improved alignment accuracy and execution time by exploiting a bit-parallel longest common subsequence measure for distance calculation. The new version of MAFFT introduces PartTree algorithm[23] which allows a guide tree to be constructed without calculating all pairwise distances. A similar strategy was acquired by the recently published algorithm Clustal$\Omega$ [24] that joins HMMs with mBed [25], a method of dimensionality reduction called sequence embedding. As a result, the number of pairwise alignments in both these packages is decreased from $\Theta(k^2)$ to $\Theta(k \log k)$ with respect to the number of sequences $k$. This makes MAFFT and Clustal$\Omega$ the only methods which are able to align tens of thousands of sequences in a reasonable time.

Nevertheless, experiments clearly show that if alignment quality is of paramount importance, consistency-based methods are out of competition. In order to overcome their greatest disadvantage, i.e., large execution times, many algorithms utilise multi-core architecture of modern CPUs. One of the best examples is MSAProbs which assessed on quad-core CPU turned out to be faster than its less accurate serial competitors like ProbCons or Probalign. Yet, parallelisation on central processors has its limitations. Nowadays, a typical desktop PC is equipped with four- or six-core CPU and to further decrease execution times, expensive multi-processor architectures have to be used. One of the ways of addressing this issue is using a potential of graphics processors in general purpose computing. Since computational power of current GPUs is more than order of magnitude greater than power of central processors, developing GPU-suited versions of algorithms has become popular in many computational demanding tasks also in bioinformatics. One must keep in mind, that differences in architectures of graphics processors and CPUs are fundamental. GPUs have thousands of cores, several types of memory and utilise massively parallel execution model. This makes designing algorithms customised for GPUs a challenging task that cannot be accomplished by adapting serial or parallel methods destined for CPU execution.

Heretofore, GPU customisation of multiple sequence alignment algorithms concerned mainly ClustalW [26], [27] and different variants of MSA problem like constrained MSA investigated by authors of this paper [28] or regular expression MSA [29]. The only attempt to parallelise on graphics processor an accurate, consistency-based multiple sequence alignment method was G-MSA [30], a variant of T-Coffee algorithm. The authors, however, focused on decreasing execution times and introduced some modifications that lowered quality of an output alignment. As a result, G-MSA turned out to be very fast (even 193 times faster than its predecessor), but inferior in terms of accuracy not only to original T-Coffee, but also to some non-consistency algorithms like MUSCLE. The aim of our research is different. We selected MSAProbs, the most accurate from existing MSA methods as our starting point and developed QuickProbs. It is a variant of MSAProbs algorithm suited for graphics processors preserving outstanding accuracy of its predecessor.

The algorithm executes on GPU the most time consuming parts of MSAProbs pipeline, i.e., the posterior probability matrices calculation and the consistency transformation. These stages are parallelised in MSAProbs on CPU with a use of OpenMP [31]. The parallelisation is, however, based on inter-task execution model which is unsuitable for graphics processors because of their massively parallel architecture. Therefore, GPU-specific algorithms for these stages had to be designed.

The posterior calculation stage executes dynamic programming methods like *forward-backward*algorithm for pair-HMMs or partition function calculation. The dynamic programming (DP) was a subject of GPU customisation multiple times, also in bioinformatics. It concerned pairwise sequence alignment [32]–[37], short read alignment [38], RNA folding [39], phylogeny [40], etc. Each application has some specific features that require suited algorithms, though. In MSAProbs these features include presence of several dependant DP layers, different storage patterns for different layers, a complex form of recursive expression making GPU code register-bound.

The consistency transformation stage incorporates a set of sparse matrix multiplications. There are algorithms and libraries for this task [41]–[43]. The multiplication procedure exploited by MSAProbs has however some specific features. Firstly, many multiplications of small matrices is performed, while previously published solutions are optimised for large matrices. Secondly, the consistency transformation does not allow new elements to be introduced to output matrices. Due to these reasons existing methods cannot be used directly for our aims.

QuickProbs uses new, graphics processor specific, intra-task parallel algorithms for both, posterior matrix calculation and consistency transformation. Additionally, we parallelised on CPU the alignment construction and refinement stage, which in MSAProbs is performed serially. As a result, our package is several times faster than MSAProbs. This allows user to process larger datasets in a reasonable time without sacrificing alignment quality. Additionally we present a tuned variant of method called QuickProbs-acc. It significantly outperforms MSAProbs in terms of accuracy on sets of distantly related sequences without exceeding its running times.

# MATERIALS AND METHODS

## Problem Formulation

Let $U=\{u^1,u^2,\dots,u^k\}$ be the set of input sequences. Multiple sequence alignment problem consists in arranging sequences from $U$ by putting gaps between symbols in the way that homologous residues are aligned together in columns. Homologous residues are those which share three dimensional structural position and diverge from common ancestral residue[44]. The problem of MSA is that for majority of cases it is impossible to identify a single correct alignment. This is because both structures and sequences evolve and some residues cannot be superposed in any way. This must be taken into account when assessing multiple sequence alignment algorithms. Therefore, a subset of key residues and core structural blocks that can be unambiguously aligned is identified and used for evaluation. The most commonly used assessment measures calculated on these regions are sum-of-pairs (SP) and total-column (TC) scores [45]. They denote percentage of properly aligned residue pairs and columns, respectively, and a reference alignment is required to compute them. In the case of real sequences it is usually constructed manually. If testing sets are generated synthetically with a use of evolution modelling software like ROSE [46], the reference alignment is built during artificial evolutionary process by the software itself.

## General Purpose Computing on GPU

Computational power of current graphics processors is several times greater than power of CPUs. Rapid development of programming interfaces like CUDA [47] or OpenCL [48] allows this power to be employed in general purpose computing. Due to this fact, designing algorithms customised for graphics processors has recently become an important method of speeding up analyses of large datasets as an alternative to using expensive multi-processor architectures based on CPUs. In QuickProbs, GPU computing is performed with a use of OpenCL library since, unlike CUDA, it is suitable for graphics processors produced by both major vendors, NVidia and AMD. Hence, in the following description we hold to the OpenCL nomenclature providing CUDA terms in parentheses.

The reason why designing algorithms suited for GPU execution is a challenging task is a great difference between architectures of central and graphics processors. Unlike CPUs that contain few cores, modern GPUs are composed of thousands of *processing elements* (*cores*) gathered in several *compute units* (*multiprocessors*). Processing elements within compute units operate according to a single instruction-multiple data or single program-multiple data paradigm. From logical point of view a GPU program (known as a *kernel* in both OpenCL and CUDA) consists of many *work-items* (*threads*) gathered in *workgroups* (*blocks*). An important fact is that synchronisation between work-items can be done only within a workgroup. Thus, matching the number and the size of workgroups for a particular task is a crucial issue when developing GPU-suited algorithms. After execution of a kernel, a hardware *scheduler* maps work-items in the way that a workgroup is executed on a single compute unit, while one unit can handle multiple workgroups. OpenCL does not specify how workgroups are run by hardware but in order to efficiently utilise computational power of GPU, knowledge of workgroup execution at the device level is necessary. The smallest amount of work that is physically performed on AMD GPUs consists of 64 work-items and is called a *wavefront*; on NVidia devices it has 32 items and is known as a *warp*. Therefore, it is important to make the group size multiplicity of these portions. There is no guarantee in which order wavefronts (warps) are executed—this is decided by the scheduler dynamically. An important consideration is that all work-items within that portion must share exactly the same execution path. A divergence in a wavefront (warp) caused, e.g., by the presence of conditional statements is realised by executing instructions from all paths with some work-items being masked when necessary. Hence, data dependant branching inside wavefronts (warps) increases kernel execution time and should be avoided. Another important issue when developing algorithms on GPU is providing sufficient *occupancy*of a device. In order to hide delays of arithmetic instructions and, most importantly, memory accesses it is recommended to invoke a few times more work-items than the number of processing elements. On modern devices this results in as much as $10^4$ work-items per kernel.

An important difference between CPU and GPU concerns memory architecture. GPU is equipped with few gigabytes of *global memory* which is an equivalent of main memory at CPU. Maximal throughput of global memory is several times greater than main memory bandwidth. However, it can be achieved only in the case of coalesced accesses when consecutive work-items utilise data from contiguous 128-byte area. In such situation whole portion of data can be read in one transaction. Since latency of global memory is large, non-coalesced accesses often result in lower bandwidth than at CPU. This issue has been partially solved in recent graphics processors by caching. Nevertheless, compared to CPUs which have several megabytes of cache per core, amount of cache on GPU is much smaller—hundreds of bytes per processing element. Another limitation concerning global addressing space is lack of virtual memory on GPU: programmer is responsible for fitting all necessary data in a limited storage area. Each compute unit contains additional amount (tens of kilobytes) of fast, directly addressable *local memory* (*shared memory*) which can be used for buffering frequently accessed data. Graphics processors contain much more registers than CPUs (tens of thousands per compute unit). The size of local memory and the number of registers allocated by work-items are important for execution time as they affect the maximum size of workgroup as well as GPU occupancy.

Concluding, graphics processor execution model differs significantly from CPU. Presence of thousands of cores at GPU device requires fine-grained algorithm parallelisation. Programmer needs to take care of coalesced accesses to global memory to maximise throughput. Careful use of local memory and registers is necessary to keep GPU occupancy at desired level. Finally, calculations should be organised in the way, that eliminates branching within the same wavefront (warp). As a result, algorithms destined for graphics processors often use different data structures and computation schemes than methods suited for central processors, even those exploiting multi-core architectures. Due to this fact algorithms for GPUs must be designed and implemented from the scratch rather than be adopted from CPU.

## MSAProbs Algorithm Principals

MSAProbs is currently the most accurate multiple sequence alignment software. It is a progressive strategy based on the following stages:

- Calculation of posterior probability matrices and distances for all pairs of sequences.
- Construction of a guide tree upon distances and calculation of sequence weights.
- Performing weighted consistency transformation on all posterior matrices.
- Building final alignment using the guide tree and posterior matrices followed by the iterative refinement.

The algorithm scheme can be found on Figure 1. Stages I and IV were divided in the diagram into two sub-stages in order to present data dependencies. At the beginning, the algorithm computes posterior probability matrices (stage I.a) which contain detailed information of residue alignments for all sequence pairs and are used for distances calculation (stage I.b). Many progressive algorithms estimate distance between two sequences on the basis of a maximum probability alignment computed with Viterbi algorithm [49]. The main disadvantage of this approach is that it takes into account only one possible alignment of the sequences, thus it is error-prone. In contrast, MSAProbs computes for each pair of sequences a posterior probability matrix which is further used for calculation of a maximum expected accuracy alignment [44]. As it takes advantage of suboptimal alignments, it improves quality of results. As in all progressive methods, distances are required for guide tree construction (stage II). This is done with a variant of UPGMA algorithm [50]. Before MSAProbs constructs a final alignment it performs so called consistency transformation (stage III). Single posterior matrix computed in stage I contains information only from pairwise alignments of two sequences, which may cause errors in the result if some residues are aligned improperly. The consistency transformation relaxes posterior matrices over other sequences. Thanks to this, matrices contain information of residue alignment from pairwise alignments of all sequences. This reduces the probability of misaligning some symbols during construction of the final result. Number of consistency iterations is one of the algorithm parameters. Afterwards, sequences are aligned greedily in the order described by the tree (stage IV.a). At each tree node, a profile-profile alignment is performed with a use of relaxed posterior matrices calculated previously. When the alignment is constructed, the refinement stage begins (stage IV.b). It randomly splits the alignment horizontally and realigns resulting profiles. Thanks to this, the algorithm is able to remove some errors introduced in previous stages. The number of refinement iterations is also a parameter. Summing up, MSAProbs has three features crucial for its accuracy:

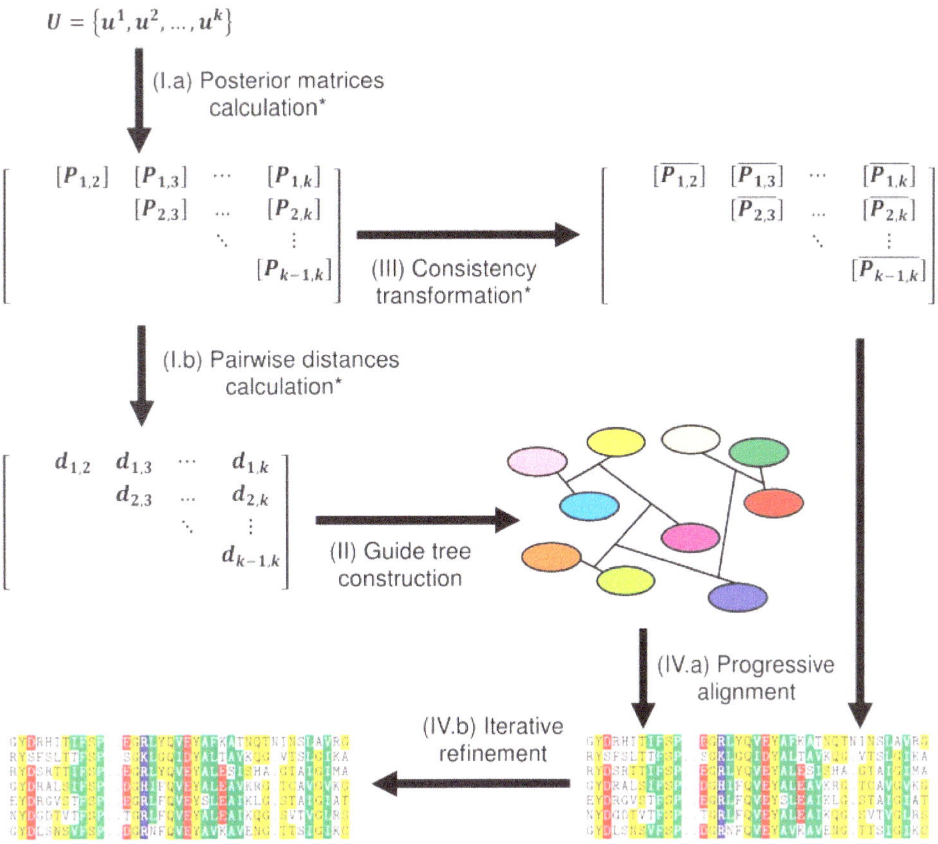


**Figure 1:** MSAProbs algorithm computation scheme.

Stages denoted with (*) are run in parallel with a use of OpenMP.

- exploiting maximum accuracy criterion during pairwise alignments,
- relaxing posterior matrices over other sequences,
- performing the iterative refinement.

First two methods decrease probability of misaligning given pair of residues by utilising information from suboptimal pairwise alignments and alignments of other sequences. If misalignment occurs, third feature gives the opportunity to correct it.

Predominance of MSAProbs over previously published methods is obtained at the cost of computation time. The most time consuming stages are those performed for all pairs of sequences, that is the posterior matrix calculation (I) and the consistency transformation (III). The worst-case time complexities of these stages are $\Theta(k^2n^2)$ and $\Theta(k^3n^3)$, respectively, for sequences of length $\Theta(n)$. In order to decrease computation time, those operations were chosen in MSAProbs to be parallelised using OpenMP. Following subsections describe all MSAProbs stages with a special stress put on stages I, III, and IV which were redesigned in QuickProbs.

**Posterior matrix calculation.** This stage of MSAProbs consists of calculating set of posterior probability matrices for all pairs of sequences $x, y \in U, x < y$, where '<' indicates an ordering relation of sequences within $U$. Let $x_i$ and $y_j$ denote $i$'th and $j$'th symbols of $X$ and $Y$sequences, respectively. Elements of posterior probability matrix $P_{xy}$ express $x_i \sim y_j$, that is a probability of symbols $x_i$ and $y_j$ being aligned in the true alignment of $X$ and $Y$. In MSAProbs, $P_{xy}$ elements are root mean squares (RMS) of posterior probabilities calculated using pair hidden Markov models ($P^a_{xy}$) and partition function ($P^b_{xy}$):

$$P_{xy}(x_i \sim y_j) = \sqrt{\frac{P^a_{xy}(x_i \sim y_j)^2 + P^b_{xy}(x_i \sim y_j)^2}{2}}. \quad (1)$$

After posterior matrix computation, the Needleman-Wunsch algorithm [51] with no gap penalties is applied on $P_{xy}$ in order to determine distance $d_{xy}$ between sequences. As majority of $P_{xy}$ elements are close to 0, in order to save space and accelerate the consistency transformation, posterior matrices are translated to a sparse form by filtering out all elements less than $cutoff = 0.01$. For convenience, sparse representation of $P_{xy}$ matrix will be referred to as $S_{xy}$. Let us denote the calculation of particular $P_{xy}$ and $S_{xy}$ as a posterior task, resulting in $k(k-1)/2$ tasks to be processed. Parallelism of posterior stage in MSAProbs is provided by distributing tasks among several OpenMP threads. As each thread calculates one or more tasks, this parallelisation model can be referred to as *inter-task*.

***Tree Construction and Sequence Weighting*:** The guide tree construction in MSAProbs is performed with a use of UPGMA algorithm. After that sequences are weighted in the order described by the tree using ClustalW weighting scheme. The weight of sequence $x \in U$ will be denoted as $w_x$.

**Consistency transformation.** The consistency transformation stage in MSAProbs relies in relaxing all posterior matrices calculated in stage I over sequences from $U$. The transformation is repeated $C$ times (2 by default).

The procedure of updating $S_{xy}$ matrix will be referred to as a relaxation task and requires a set of $k-2$ sparse-sparse matrix multiplications. It is done according to the formula:

$$S'_{xy} = \frac{(w_x + w_y) S_{xy} + \sum_{z \in U, z \neq x,y} w_z S_{xz} S_{zy}}{\sum_{z \in U} w_z}. \quad (2)$$

An important note is that MSAProbs does not allow any new elements to be introduced to $S'_{xy}$ matrix. More precisely, it may happen, that in a row of $S'_{xy}$ an element appears such that there is no element with the same column number in a corresponding row of $S_{xy}$. Such elements are filtered out from $S'_{xy}$ after multiplication. Moreover, the elements with values below *cutoff* are dropped. As a result $S'_{xy}$ always has less or equal number of elements than $S_{xy}$. MSAProbs performs consistency for $S_{xy}$ matrices such that $x<y$, i.e., the input and output of the relaxation procedure is only an upper triangle of a matrix table. As a consequence, the algorithm chooses one of the three versions of multiplication procedure depending on the ordering of $X$, $Y$, and $Z$ sequences, i.e., $x<z<y$, $z<x<y$, and $x<y<z$. Matrices that are being relaxed are temporarily stored in the dense form $P'_{xy}$ and translated back to the sparse representation $S'_{xy}$ at the end of the task. After all of the tasks finish, $S_{xy}$ matrices are replaced by $S'_{xy}$. Parallelism in the consistency transformation is provided, similarly to stage I, by inter-task execution: an OpenMP thread is responsible for relaxation of one or more $S_{xy}$ matrices. The posterior matrices after performing $c$ consistency transformations will be referred to as $\overline{S_{xy}}$ (on Figure 1 we neglect the fact that matrices are stored in the sparse form, thus $P_{xy}$ symbol is used).

***Final alignment construction and refinement***: The last stage of all progressive methods is the computation of final alignment according to the guide tree constructed during stage II. At each tree node a weighted profile-profile alignment (referred to as a progressive step) is performed. When aligning two profiles $X$ and $Y$ posterior probability matrix $P_{XY}$ is calculated using $\overline{S_{xy}}$ matrices for all pairs of sequences $(x,y)$ such that $x \in X$ and $y \in Y$. Then, the profile-profile alignment is constructed with a use of posterior probabilities $P_{XY}(x_i \sim y_j)$ of aligning $X_i$ and $Y_j$ profile residues. This is done according to the following dynamic programming recursion:

$$D(i,j) = \max \begin{cases} D(i-1,j-1) + P_{XY}(x_i \sim y_j), \\ D(i-1,j), \\ D(i,j-1). \end{cases} \quad (3)$$

Calculation of the final alignment is followed by the refinement, one of the classic techniques of progressive methods. In MSAProbs it is called a post-processing stage. It was designed as a solution for one of the greatest problems of progressive strategies—wrong choice of sequences or profiles to be aligned in early steps of the final result construction. Such misalignments cannot be corrected in the following progressive steps and affect overall accuracy of the method. The refinement tries to solve this problem by splitting final alignment horizontally into two random profiles. Then, the columns containing only gaps are removed and the profiles are realigned in the same way as in the final alignment stage. The aforementioned procedure is repeated $r$ times (10 by default). The more refinement iterations, the greatest the chance of removing errors introduced during progressive construction.

In MSAProbs the final alignment and refinement procedures are executed serially.

## QuickProbs Algorithm

The main goal of our study was to speed up the most time-consuming stages of MSAProbs (posterior matrices calculation and consistency transformation) by redesigning them for GPU execution using OpenCL. Additionally, we decided to parallelise on CPU the last stage of MSAProbs algorithm which previously was implemented in a serial manner. This is because the construction and refinement of final alignment, if executed serially, would be the most time consuming part of QuickProbs. In the following subsections we present how stages I, III, and IV were modified in QuickProbs. The separate subsection is devoted to QuickProbs-acc, a specialised variant of our package which aims at improving MSAProbs quality.

***Posterior matrix calculation***: The posterior matrix calculation in QuickProbs is, similarly to MSAProbs, based on tasks. However, massively parallel architecture of graphics processors requires smaller portions of work to be done by a work-item. Therefore, it was assumed that each task is processed by a single workgroup. That computation scheme can be denoted as*intra-task* parallelisation (one task—many work-items). As work-items within workgroup can synchronise and exchange data through local memory, they are able to properly handle data dependencies present in a task. Another important difference is that modifications made in QuickProbs algorithm at the consistency stage result in the necessity of calculating $S_{xy}$ for all $x \neq y$, not only $x<y$. As $P_{xy} = P^T_{yx}$, it is sufficient to calculate in the dense form only one of these two matrices (either $P_{xy}$ or $P_{yx}$) and then transform it to both $S_{xy}$ and $S_{yx}$. Therefore, QuickProbs posterior task takes as an input two sequences $x,y \in U$ and consists of three steps:

- calculate dense posterior matrix $P_{xy}$ (or $P_{yx}$, depending on sequence lengths) and pairwise distance $d_{xy}$,
- build sparse matrix $S_{xy}$ on the basis of $P_{xy}$ ($P_{yx}$),
- build sparse transposed matrix $S_{yx}$ on the basis of $P_{xy}$ ( $P_{yx}$).

Let $|u|$ indicate the length of sequence $u$ increased by 1. Size of $P_{xy}$ posterior matrix is $|x| \times |y|$ (sequences $X$ and $Y$ correspond to vertical and horizontal dimensions, respectively). QuickProbs parallelisation scheme assumes that each work-item in a workgroup calculates a single column of posterior matrix. Thus, the width $|y|$ of $P_{xy}$ matrix that can be processed on GPU is limited by the maximum number of work-items in a workgroup $I_{max}$ for a particular device. In current graphics processors like Radeon 7970 or GeForce 680 this limit is 1024 which is sufficient for majority of multiple sequence alignment problems. If $|y| > I_{max}$ and $|x| \leq I_{max}$, the algorithm calculates $P_{yx}$ matrix instead of $P_{xy}$. However, if $|x| > I_{max}$ and $|y| > I_{max}$, the task cannot be calculated at GPU and is scheduled for CPU execution.

At the beginning of posterior calculation stage, descriptions of all posterior tasks are prepared. As each task consists in computing two sparse matrices $S_{xy}$ and $S_{yx}$, there are $k(k-1)/2$ tasks in total. The orientation of a dense posterior matrix to be calculated by a task depends on lengths of sequences.

Namely, the shorter sequence corresponds to the horizontal dimension (task width) and the longer to the vertical dimension (task height). Tasks of width exceeding $l_{max}$ are scheduled for CPU execution. The rest is processed at GPU in batches. An important feature is that workgroups from different batches are scheduled independently. Therefore, workgroup resources, i.e., the number of work-items and the amount of local memory to be reserved are determined by the task with the largest horizontal dimension. Thus, the smaller divergence of task widths in a batch, the less GPU resources are wasted. Generally, the number of tasks in a batch is limited by the size of global memory available for a particular device $G_{max}$ (detailed description of task memory requirements is given later). Nevertheless, in order to produce smaller and less divergent batches, we lowered global memory limit to $G_{max}/4$ which produced best results in our preliminary experiments. Tasks are sorted in a descending order according to the width. Then, consecutive tasks are added to the current batch as long as its global memory requirement does not exceed $G_{max}/4$. If that happens, a new batch is created and procedure repeats until no task remains. Finally, to reduce width divergence in batches and improve GPU utilisation, QuickProbs transposes all tasks in a batch with heights smaller than the number of work-items in the workgroup (it does not affect required number of work-items but decreases columns length).

Step (1) of the posterior task consists in computation of matrix $P_{xy}$ as a root mean square of $P^a_{xy}$ and $P^b_{xy}$ matrices. Pair-HMM calculates posterior probability matrix $P^a_{xy}$ using *forward-backward* algorithm [44]. The procedure consists of two dynamic programming passes. They calculate matrices of forward and backward probabilities which are afterwards combined to form $P^a_{xy}$. $P^b_{xy}$ is calculated using values of partition functions of forward and reverse $X$ and $Y$alignments as in [11]. The procedure, analogously to pair-HMM, requires two dynamic programming passes. At the end of step (1) $P^a_{xy}$ and $P^b_{xy}$ are joined to form $P_{xy}$ and an additional DP pass calculates pairwise distance $d_{xy}$ from $P_{xy}$. In general, dependencies in the DP matrices in the above-mentioned procedures are

$$D(i,j) = \chi(D(i-1,j), D(i,j-1), D(i-1,j-1)) \quad (4)$$

And

$$D(i,j) = \chi(D(i+1,j), D(i,j+1), D(i+1,j+1)) \quad (5)$$

for forward and reverse passes, respectively, with different $\chi$ functions. The more detailed information about forms of a dynamic programming recursions used in $P_{xy}$ and $d_{xy}$ calculations is presented in Table 1. According to QuickProbs parallelisation scheme, each work-item within a workgroup calculates a single column of posterior matrix. Therefore, dynamic programming procedure must be executed according to an anti-diagonal pattern as presented in Figure 2. The whole matrix is processed in $|x|+|y|-1$ iterations in the way that $j$ 'th thread idles for $j$ and $|x|-1-j$ first iterations in forward and reverse passes, respectively. The idea of the dynamic programming computation scheme exploited by QuickProbs is presented in Table 2.

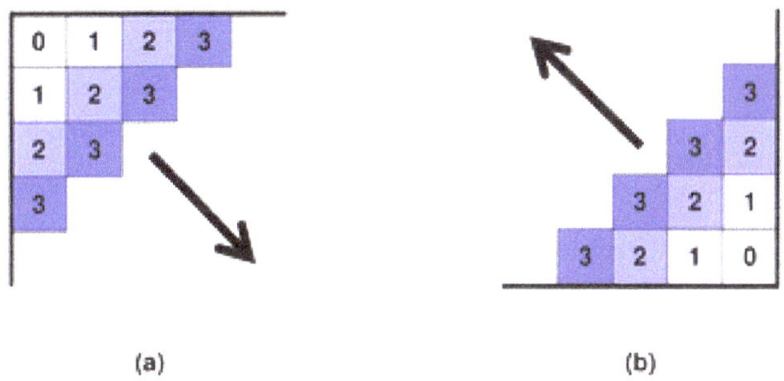


**Figure 2:** Scheme of traversing dynamic programming matrices in forward (a) and reverse (b) passes.

Cells contain numbers of iterations in which they are processed.

**Table 1:** Algorithm 1

**Input:** $x$, $y$—sequences for which posterior matrix is to be calculated, $j$—work-item identifier (column number).

**Output:** $d_{xy}$—distance between $x$ and $y$ sequences, $P_{xy}$—output posterior matrix in the dense form.

1: Initialise auxiliary matrices $F$ and $B$ of size $|x| \times |y|$.

2: Posterior function forward pass: $F(i,j) \leftarrow \chi_1(F(i-1,j), F(i,j-1), F(i-1,j-1))$

3: Posterior function reverse pass: $B(i,j) \leftarrow \chi_2(B(i+1,j), B(i,j+1), B(i+1,j+1))$

4: Combine forward and reverse matrices: $P^b_{xy}(i,j) \leftarrow \chi_3(F(i,j), B(i,j))$

5: Pair-HMM forward pass: $F(i,j) \leftarrow \chi_4(F(i-1,j), F(i,j-1), F(i-1,j-1))$

6: Pair-HMM backward pass: $B(i,j) \leftarrow \chi_5(B(i+1,j), B(i,j+1), B(i+1,j+1))$

7: Combine forward and backward matrices: $P^a_{xy}(i,j) \leftarrow \chi_6(F(i,j), B(i,j))$

8: Calculate final posterior matrix: $P_{xy}(i,j) \leftarrow \text{ROOT-MEAN-SQUARE}(P^a_{xy}(i,j), P^b_{xy}(i,j))$

9: Calculate final distance : $d_{xy}(i,j) \leftarrow \max(d_{xy}(i-1,j), d_{xy}(i,j-1), d_{xy}(i-1,j-1) + P_{xy}(i,j))$

10: $d_{xy} \leftarrow d_{xy}(|x|,|y|)$

Pseudo-code of the posterior matrix calculation procedure. Statements show only general form of data dependencies. Procedure requires execution of 6 anti-diagonal passes (lines 2, 3+4, 5, 6, 7, and 8+9). $P^b_{xy}$ is computed first due to greater memory requirements.

**Table 2**: Algorithm 2

```
Input: x, y—input sequences, j—work-item identifier (column number).
Output: D—matrix to be calculated.
function FORWARD
    Initialise D(0,□) and D(□,0)
    for iteration←0 to|x|+|y|−1 do
        i←iteration−j
        if i>0 and i<|x| and j<|y| then
            D(i,j)←α(D(i−1,j),D(i,j−1),D(i−1,j−1))
        end if
        SYNCHRONISE
    end for
    return D
end function

function REVERSE
    Initialise D(|x|−1,□) and D(□,|y|−1)
    for iteration←1to|x|+|y|−1 do
        i←|x|+|y|−j−iteration
        if i>0 and i<|x| and j<|y| then
            D(i,j)←α(D(i+1,j),D(i,j+1),D(i+1,j+1))
        end if
        SYNCHRONISE
    end for
    return D
end function
```

Pseudo-code of the generalised dynamic programming forward and reversed passes. $D(i,\square)$ and $D(\square,j)$ indicate $i$'th row and $j$'th column of $D$ matrix.

Note, that all intermediate matrices needed for $P_{xy}$ calculation must be stored in device global memory. Due to fact that dynamic programming requires accessing whole matrices with very limited data reuse, it will not take advantage of caching. Therefore, providing best possible global memory access pattern is a key issue for algorithm execution time. Taking into account anti-diagonal calculation scheme, simple row-major matrix representation results in a non-coalesced access which drastically decreases algorithm performance (each matrix cell is accessed in a separate transaction). Hence, a jagged memory layout of matrices elements was proposed (see Figure 3) in which consecutive work-items access consecutive memory cells resulting in perfect coalescing. Let $J$ indicate the size of the jag. The number of elements necessary for storing matrix for sequences $x$ and $y$ in the jagged form is

$$\delta(x,y)=(|x|+J-1)J\left\lceil\frac{|y|}{J}\right\rceil. \qquad (6)$$

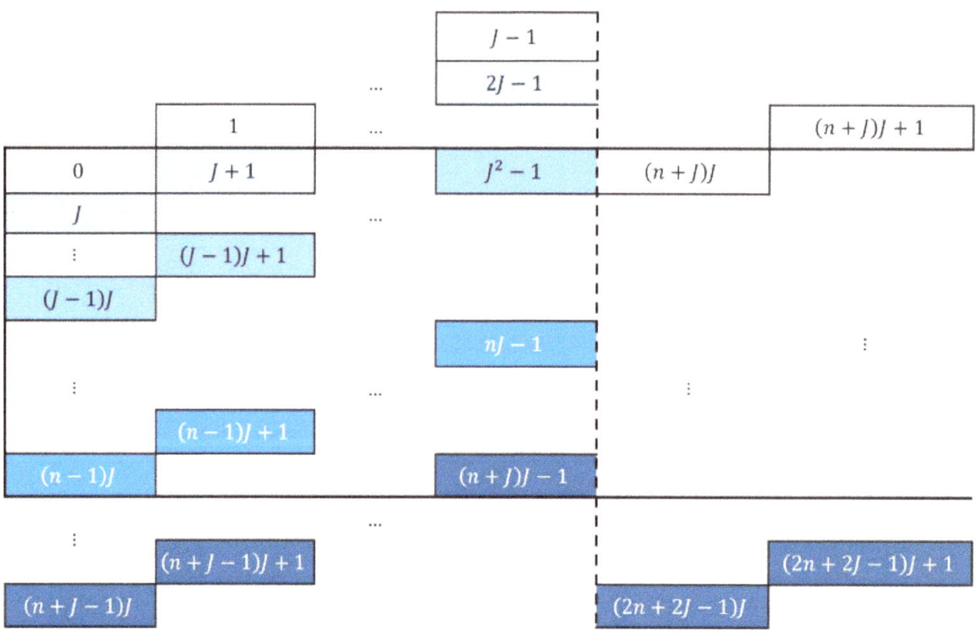


**Figure 3:** Jagged pattern of storing dense matrices in graphics device global memory. The size of jag is denoted as $J$.

For convenience an *element* is used as a basic memory unit in the paper. Sometimes it is referred to as a *dense element* to distinguish it from *sparse elements* defined later. Pair-HMM used in MSAProbs contains 5 states. MSAProbs stores whole DP matrices for all states resulting in $5|x||y|$ elements for both, forward and backward procedures. However, as we are only interested in full matrix at 0'th state, it is sufficient to store only two consecutive rows of layers 1–4 (they are required for the dynamic programming recursion). This reduces memory requirements for $P^{a}_{xy}$ calculation to $2\delta(x,y)+8|y|$, which is an important improvement, as it allows rows from layers 1–4 to be stored in fast local memory. Combination of forward and backward matrices can be done in place. The similar situation occurs in the case of partition function calculation. The difference here is that intermediate results are stored in a double floating-point precision. Therefore, in order to save space, reverse and combination passes are merged. The total memory footprint of calculating $P^{h}_{xy}$ is $3\delta(x,y)+8|y|$ elements. The calculation of a root mean square of $P^{a}_{xy}$ and $P^{h}_{xy}$ is done in place so it introduces no additional memory overhead. Eventually, the computation of $P_{xy}$ requires $3\delta(x,y)+8|y|$ elements in total. Note that $P^{h}_{xy}$ has to be computed first and stored so $P^{a}_{xy}$ can be calculated in the remaining space.

Steps (2) and (3) of the posterior task transform dense $P_{xy}$ matrix to sparse representations $S_{xy}$ and $S_{yx}$, respectively. The main component of $S_{xy}$ is an array of so-called *sparse elements* denoted as $data[S_{xy}]$. Each sparse element is a pair containing a column number and a floating-point value of posterior probability, referred to as *column* and *value*, respectively. Additionally, there are two vectors storing sizes of rows and starting indices of rows in the sparse elements array. They are denoted as  and $indices[S_{xy}]$. The $j$'th sparse element in $i$'th row of $S_{xy}$ matrix is denoted as $S_{xy}(i,j)$ and can be accessed by using the formula $data[S_{xy}](indices[S_{xy}](i)+j)$. Such representation has its impact on a sparse generation procedure. Namely, in order to store $P_{xy}(i,j)$ element in array $data[S_{xy}]$ the number of non-zeros are in all previous rows and part of $i$'th row before $j$'th element have to be known. The similar situation is during $S_{yx}$ generation but instead of rows we are interested in $P_{xy}$ columns. Therefore, the transformation to the sparse form is done in two passes. In the first pass the number of non-zero elements in $P_{xy}$ rows (or columns) is determined and stored in $sizes[S_{xy}]$ (or $sizes[S_{yx}]$). In the second pass $P_{xy}$ rows (columns) are transformed to the sparse form concurrently producing final $data[S_{xy}]$ (or $data[S_{yx}]$) arrays. As $P_{xy}$ matrix is stored in the jagged form, $P_{xy}$ is traversed anti-diagonally during both passes of $S_{xy}$ (or $S_{yx}$) generation. The procedure of transforming $P_{xy}$ dense matrix to sparse $S_{xy}$ form is presented in Table 3.

**Table 3:** Algorithm 3

**Input:** $P_{xy}$—dense matrix to be translated to sparse form, $j$—work-item identifier (column number)

**Output:** $S_{xy}$—output sparse matrix described by $data[S_{xy}]$, $sizes[S_{xy}]$ and $indices[S_{xy}]$ arrays.

```
Initialise in parallel sizes[S_xy] vector with 0.
SYNCHRONISE
for iteration ← 0 to |x| + |y| − 1 do                          ▷ First pass: fill sizes vector.
    i ← iteration − j
    if i ≥ 0 and i < |x| and j < |y| then
        if P_xy(i,j) ≥ cutoff then
            sizes[S_xy](i) ← sizes[S_xy](i) + 1
        end if
    end if
    SYNCHRONISE
end for

if j = 0 then
    indices[S_xy](0) ← 0
    for i ← 1|x| do
        indices[S_xy](i) ← indices[S_xy](i − 1) + sizes[S_xy](i − 1)
    end for
end if
SYNCHRONISE
Copy in parallel indices[S_xy] to auxiliary vector offsets.
SYNCHRONISE

for iteration ← 1 to |x| + |y| − 1 do                          ▷ Second pass: fill sparse elements array.
    i ← iteration − j
    if i > 0 and i < |x| and j < |y| then
        if P_xy(i,j) ≥ cutoff then
            data[S_xy](offsets(i)).column ← j
            data[S_xy](offsets(i)).value ← P_xy(i,j)
            offsets(i) ← offsets(i) + 1
        end if
    end if
    SYNCHRONISE
end for
```

Pseudo-code of the sparse matrix generation procedure.

If column numbers and indices are of the same size as matrix elements, storing $S_{xy}$ requires at most $2|x||y|$ elements for $data[S_{xy}]$ (if none of $P_{xy}$ elements is below $cutoff$) and $2|x|$ elements for $sizes[S_{xy}]$ and $indices[S_{xy}]$. Calculations of $S_{xy}$ and $S_{yx}$ matrices are serialised, i.e., the algorithm executes step (2), reads the resulting sparse matrix from device memory, executes step (3), and reads the result once again. Therefore, the same memory space can be reused for both $S_{xy}$ and $S_{yx}$ matrices. Taking into account space needed for storing the input dense matrix, total memory requirements for executing steps (2) and (3) is $\delta(x,y)+2|x||y|+2\max(|x|,|y|)$.

Assuming that $|x||y|+\max(|x|,|y|)<\delta(x,y)$, execution of a single task requires in total

$$3\delta(x,y)+8|x| \tag{7}$$

elements in device memory. The space for storing posterior layers and output sparse matrices, i.e., $3\delta(x,y)$ elements, is allocated in device global memory. Auxiliary rows consisting of $8|x|$elements are placed in local memory to reduce transfer overheads. Let $|x|=1024$ which is the maximum size of a workgroup that can be processed by modern GPUs. For such tasks the local memory requirement is 8,192 elements which equals 32 KB assuming 32-bit floating-point values. The last few generations of graphics processors are equipped in such amount of local memory. Thus storing auxiliary rows in local memory does not limit the size of datasets that can be processed by QuickProbs.

***Consistency transformation***: QuickProbs version of consistency transformation differs from its predecessor. First of all, as GPU computations are strongly memory limited, QuickProbs operates directly on sparse representations. As a result, the elements of $S'_{xy}$ that do not appear in $S_{xy}$ are discarded during multiplication procedure, not after, as in MSAProbs. Secondly, in order to eliminate divergence in kernel executions only one version of the sparse matrix multiplication procedure is implemented. This, however, requires all $S_{xy}, x\neq y$ matrices at the input of the consistency transformation. These are provided by the modified stage I of QuickProbs. Additionally, as the output of $i$'th consistency iteration is also the input to $(i+1)$'th, all $S'_{xy}, x\neq y$ must be computed in the consistency stage. Since computational effort of matrix transposition is irrelevant with respect to the relaxation, QuickProbs calculates on GPU $S'_{xy}$ matrices only for $x<y$ and then transposes them in parallel on CPU with a use of OpenMP generating $S'_{yx}$. The last difference concerns parallelisation scheme, which was changed to intra-task, i.e., each task is analysed by entire workgroup. As previously, after each transformation $S_{xy}$ matrices are replaced by $S'_{xy}$. Posterior matrices after performing all $c$ consistency transformations will be referred to as $\overline{S_{xy}}$.

At the beginning of the consistency transformation QuickProbs generates descriptions of all $k(k-1)/2$ relaxation tasks. In order to reduce GPU global memory requirements the relaxation is performed in batches, similarly to the posterior matrices calculation. Namely, set of sequences $U$ is divided in equally-sized subsets $V_i$. As a result, table of $S_{xy}$ matrices can be divided in square sectors denoted as $W_{ij}$. Afterwards, the execution of two nested loops begins. The outer loop iterates over sectors $W_{ij}$ to be computed. As QuickProbs calculates on GPU $S'_{xy}$ matrices only for $x<y$ sequences, the outer loop concerns sectors for which $i\leq j$. The inner loop iterates over all sequence subsets $V_k$ and performs on GPU relaxations of all matrices from $W_{ij}$ over all sequences from $V_k$. In order to perform the relaxation of particular $W_{ij}$ sector over $V_k$, $W_{ik}$ and $W_{kj}$ sectors are also required. As a result, for each calculated sector, a buffer for three sectors must be allocated at GPU. Sector sizes are adjusted in the way that buffer size does not exceed size of global memory $G_{max}$.

The relaxation procedure performed at GPU starts from weighting input matrix by $w_x+w_y$(sequence weights are computed during construction of the guide tree) and storing in $S'_{xy}$. After that $S'_{xy}$ is relaxed over all sequences $z\neq x,y$. The relaxation over single sequence consists in performing a sparse-sparse matrix multiplication and adding the result to $S'_{xy}$. Let $z$ be the sequence over which $S'_{xy}$ is relaxed. For simplicity let $S'_{xy}=C$, $S_{xz}=A$, and $S_{zy}=B$. The update is performed as follows: $C\leftarrow C+w_zAB$. The multiplication is done by traversing all elements of $A$, loading corresponding fragments of $B$ for each $a\in A$, making computations and adding result to $C$. Processing of $A$ matrix is performed in horizontal blocks called *stripes*. There are $s_{count}$ stripes executed concurrently, each having $s_{length}$ sparse elements. Let *subgroup* indicate a set of work-items which processes a stripe. As single sparse element is analysed by a single work-item, there are $s_{length}$ work-items in a subgroup and work-items in a workgroup. An important note is that consecutive subgroups are assigned to consecutive rows of $A$ matrix, thus at any given moment only one stripe in a row is being processed. The scheme of traversing $A$ matrix is presented in Figure 4.

$A$ There are $s_{count}$ subgroups, each assigned to a single row of $A$ matrix. Each row is divided into stripes having $s_{length}$ sparse elements. Subgroups process consecutive stripes of their rows. Stripes are represented by rectangles with corresponding subgroup identifier (upper left number) and their own identifier (bottom right number). Colours indicate stripes being calculated concurrently by a workgroup.

A detailed description of actions performed by a single subgroup is presented below. For convenience, let us introduce an additional notion: $A(i,\square)$—$i$'th row of $A$, $A(i,j)$—$j$'th element of $i$'th row of $A$, $A_{stripe}$—some stripe of $A$, $A_{stripe}(j)$—$j$'th element of $A_{stripe}$. At the beginning, each work-item computes an identifier of its subgroup $s_{id}$ and an offset within it $s_{offset}$. Then the subgroup sets itself on $i=s_{id}$ row and copies the first stripe $A_{stripe}$ of $A(i,\square)$ to local memory (each sparse element is copied by a single work-item). After that it iterates over sparse elements $a\in A_{stripe}$. Note, that for each element $a$ there is a corresponding row $B(j,\square)$ in $B$ such that $j=a.column$. In the following steps, the subgroup processes consecutive stripes of these rows. Each work-item reads its sparse element $b=B_{stripe}(s_{offset})$ of the current stripe, calculates $w_z\times a.value\times b.value$ and adds it to the proper element of $C$. In MSAProbs $C$ was temporarily stored in the dense form, therefore the algorithm updated directly $C(i,b.column)$.

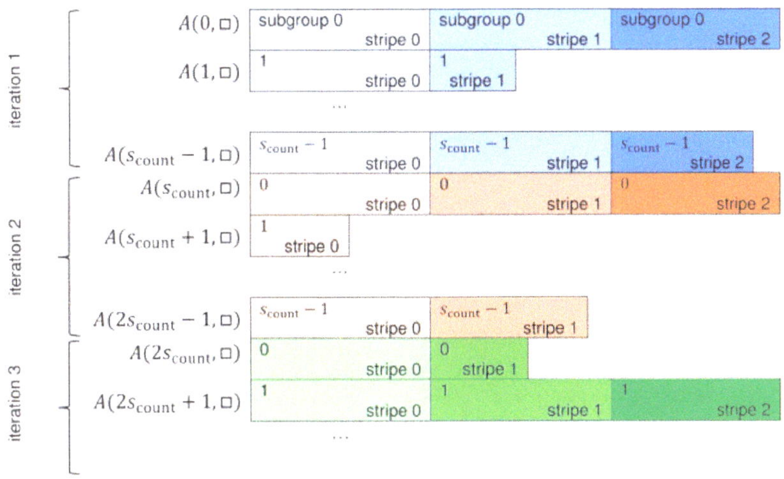


**Figure 4**: Scheme of traversing sparse matrix in multiplication procedure.

This approach is not used in QuickProbs as it renders inferior results. This is mainly because of increase in global memory requirements for a task which limits the size of a dataset that can be processed on a graphics processor. Moreover, as input matrices are sparse, accesses to $C$ are non-coalesced which decreases performance. An alternative solution is to use local memory for buffering in the dense form only $C(i,\square)$ row. Nevertheless, as tests show, this variant is also inappropriate for graphics processor execution. Since maximum length of a dense row is 1024 and a single element is a 32-bit floating-point value, 8 dense rows are sufficient to fill whole 32 KB GPU local memory limiting GPU occupancy.

After considering all these factors, we decided to store $C$ rows in local memory directly in the sparse form. The problem that emerges here concerns finding an element to be updated $C(i,\gamma)$, where $\gamma$ is index of a sparse element with column number equal to $b.column$. We examined two methods of overcoming this issue—hashing $C(i,\square)$ values according to column indices and performing binary search. As the latter turned out to be more efficient, it is employed in QuickProbs. If there is no index $\gamma$ such that $C(i,\gamma).column = b.column$, no update is performed (no new sparse elements can be introduced to $C$). After subgroup finishes processing $B$ rows for all elements $a \in A_{\text{stripe}}$, it reads another stripe of $A(i,\square)$. When processing of $A(i,\square)$ ends, $i$ is incremented by $s_{\text{count}}$ and the aforementioned scheme is repeated. After relaxing $S_{xy}$ matrix over all sequences $z \in U, z \neq x, y$, sparse elements smaller than $cutoff$ are filtered out. The pseudo-code of a single relaxation is presented in Table 4.

Table 4: Algorithm 4

```
Input:  U = {u^1, u^2, ..., u^k}—set of sequences, S_xy—sparse matrix to be relaxed, I_id—work-item identifier, s_count—number of stripes processed concurrently, s_length—stripe length.
Output: Matrix S'_xy after relaxation
s_id ← I_id / s_count
s_offset ← I_id mod s_count
Σ_w ← w_x w_y (w_x + w_y)
S'_xy ← S_xy × Σ_w
for all z ∈ U, z ≠ x, y do
    Σ_w ← Σ_w + w_z
    RELAX (S'_xy, S_xz, S_zy, w_z)
end for
S'_xy ← S'_xy / Σ_w

funtion RELAX(C, A, B, w)                                   ▷Function modifies C matrix
    for i = s_id height(C) do
        for all C_stripe ⊂ C(i,□) do
            Copy C_stripe(s_offset) to local memory
        end for
        SYNCHRONISE

        for all A_stripe ⊂ A(i,□) do
            Copy A_stripe(s_offset) to local memory.
            SYNCHRONISE
            for all a ∈ A_stripe do
                j ← a.column
                for all B_stripe ⊂ B(j,□) do
                    b ← B_stripe(s_offset)
                    γ ← BIANRY − SEARCH(C(i,□), b.column)
                    if γ ≥ 0 then
                        C(i,γ).value ← C(i,γ).value + w × a.value × b.value
                    end if
                end for
            end for
            SYNCHRONISE
        end for
        i ← i + s_count
    end for
end function
```

The relaxation of $S_{xy}$ requires $s_{count} \times \max(sizes[S_{xy}])$ sparse elements for buffering $S_{xy}$ rows and $s_{count} \times s_{length}$ sparse elements for $S_{xz}$ stripes. Additionally $|X|$ dense elements are needed for storing new sizes of $S_{xy}$ rows. Taking into account that a sparse element takes twice as much memory as a dense one, total local memory requirement for relaxation task equals

$$2s_{count}(\max(sizes[S_{xy}]) + s_{length}) + |X| \quad \textbf{(8)}$$

elements. In our preliminary experiments performed on both NVidia and AMD GPUs the best results were obtained for $s_{count} = 8$ and $s_{length} = 8$. As we observed, for default value of $cutoff = 0.01$, transforming matrix to sparse representation $S_{xy}$ retains on average 5–10% of $P_{xy}$ elements. Assuming that sequences are shorter than 1,000, which is often the case, $\max(sizes[S_{xy}])$ usually does not exceed 100. Local memory requirements are less than 12 KB/task assuming 32-bit elements. This results in better occupancy than in variant storing dense rows locally.

The most important disadvantage of the described method is its sensitivity for divergence of sparse matrices widths. This effect is especially visible for large datasets and is caused by multiplication algorithm containing several data-dependant nested loops. Branch divergence within a wavefront (warp) in outer-loop caused by different lengths of rows is very expensive, as alternative execution paths are time consuming. This effect is partially reduced by using stripes, but not entirely removed. To avoid waste of computational power, the diversity of sparse row lengths have to be minimised. The simplest way of obtaining it is gathering in sectors $W_{ij}$ matrices of similar size. We plan to implement this feature in the next release of QuickProbs.

Final alignment construction and refinement. In MSAProbs the last stage of the algorithm is executed serially, which is appropriate for small datasets when profiles contain few sequences. When the number of sequences is larger, the computation time of stage IV becomes comparable to the execution times of stages I and III. Since QuickProbs uses significantly faster algorithms for stages I and III, the last stage, if performed serially, would be the most time consuming part of the entire algorithm. Thus, we decided to parallelise this stage for multi-core central processors. There are two main parallelisation approaches possible.

The first one follows inter-task concurrency scheme utilised by original MSAProbs for stages I and III. The Eqn. (3) is computed for all pairs of sequences $(x, y)$ such that $x \in X, y \in Y$. Processing of each pair can be treated as an independent task. In the assumed parallelisation model each thread executes one or several tasks. Second parallelisation scheme can be referred to as intra-task and consists in parallel computation of Eqn. (3). In theory it would be profitable even for small datasets. However, such computation model requires tens or hundreds times more threads than inter-task. Central processors, unlike GPUs, are not massively parallel devices, hence the costs of invocation and synchronisation of threads could be higher than the gains from parallel processing. This is why QuickProbs utilises inter-task parallelisation based on OpenMP as more appropriate for architecture of multi-core CPUs. In the future release we plan to customise stage IV for graphics processor execution. In this case, intra-task parallelisation will be the choice.

Beside parallelisation, QuickProbs introduces a simple optimisation to the final alignment calculation. When MSAProbs computes Eqn. (3), the processing is row-wise or column-wise, depending on the indexes of sequences $X$ and $Y$, i.e., whether $S_{xy}$ or $S_{yx}$ matrix is available. Since in stage III of QuickProbs both of these matrices are computed, the recurrence is always solved in a row-wise manner, which uses cache memory more effectively.

In QuickProbs the refinement stage is also done in parallel with the use of the profile alignment inter-task algorithm described above.

***Accurate mode***: QuickProbs, similarly to MSAProbs, has two parameters influencing quality of a final alignment, the number of consistency transformations $c$ and the number of refinement iterations $r$. By default they equal 2 and 10, respectively. As QuickProbs in default settings turned out to be faster than its predecessor, we investigated whether it is possible to increase QuickProbs accuracy by tuning its parameters without exceeding MSAProbs computation times. At first we independently altered the number of refinement iterations to 20, 35, 50, 100, 150, 200 and the number of consistency transformations to 3, 4, 5. We established that increasing $r$ over default value 10 does not influence alignment accuracy, while increasing $c$ reduces results quality. This is because information loss caused by removing posterior elements below $cutoff = 0.01$ at the end of each transformation exceeds gains from the consistency. This was confirmed by the experiment in which $cutoff$ was set to $0.001$ resulting in much less posterior elements being discarded and elevated accuracy. Increasing in this scenario number of consistency transformations to $c = 3$ worsened accuracy. Even though, decrease is smaller than for $cutoff = 0.01$, it is still noticeable suggesting that default $c$ value produces best results.

The main disadvantage of approach based on global $cutoff$ value is that fraction of elements removed from posterior matrices differs across sequence pairs. Thus, information loss for distant sequences (those having small $S_{xy}$ values) is much higher than for closely related sequences. Therefore, we decided to test an alternative variant in which $cutoff$ value is computed independently for each posterior matrix in order to retain assumed fraction $\beta$ of elements. Such variant turned out to be a better compromise between computation time and result quality than static $cutoff$. Thus, in the accurate mode of QuickProbs algorithm (referred to as QuickProbs-acc) we decided to use the adaptive filtering with $\beta = 0.3$ as it gave the best results in our experiments.

## RESULTS

### Experimental Setting

Experiments were performed on several hardware configurations built upon three CPUs (Intel Xeon W3550, Intel Xeon E5-2630, and AMD Phenom II X6 1090) and four graphics cards (NVidia GeForce GTX 480, 560, 680, and AMD Radeon HD 7970). All computers used for the tests were controlled by Windows operating system. Detailed parameters of hardware used in the experiments can be found in Table 5. As majority of modern computers are equipped with quad-core processors, the basic experimental platform contained Xeon W3550 CPU which was coupled with GeForce 480, 680, and

Radeon 7970 GPUs. Another testing PC represented class of high-end desktop computers and consisted of Xeon E5-2630 hexa-core CPU and GeForce 680 which is one of the fastest single-chip graphic cards on the market. The experiments on quad-core PC reported Radeon 7970 to be faster than GeForce 680. However, AMD GPU was not supported properly by our hexa-core platform preventing us from testing it with Xeon E5-2630. Additional experiments were carried out on a mid-range hexa-core Phenom II X6 platform with GeForce 560. All examined processors are equipped with a dynamic overclocking feature which increases clocking frequency when CPU is not exceeding its thermal design power (this is usually the case when some cores are not loaded). Additionally, Intel processors utilise hyper-threading technology which improves task parallelism on a single core by duplicating some CPU logic. Operating system reports these processors to have twice as many cores as they physically posses.

**Table 5:** Characteristics of hardware used in the experiments

| Hardware | Frequency [GHz] | Cores | Cache L1 [KB] | Cache L2 [KB] | Cache L3 [MB] | Memory [GB] | Bandwidth [GB/s] | Local memory [KB] | GFLOPS |
|---|---|---|---|---|---|---|---|---|---|
| Xeon W3550 | 3.0–3.3 | 4[1] | 4×32 | 4×256 | 8 | 24.0 | 26 | — | 50 |
| Xeon E5-2630 | 2.3–2.8 | 6[1] | 6×32 | 6×256 | 15 | 32.0 | 43 | — | 110 |
| Phenom II X6 | 3.2–3.6 | 6 | 6×64 | 6×512 | 6 | 16.0 | 21 | — | 47 |
| GeForce 480 | 1.4 | 15×32 | 15×16[2] | 768 | — | 1.5 | 177 | 15×48[2] | 1345 |
| GeForce 560 | 1.8 | 8×48 | 8×16[2] | 512 | — | 1.0 | 128 | 8×48[2] | 1263 |
| GeForce 680 | 1.0 | 8×192 | 8×16[2] | 768 | — | 4.0 | 192 | 8×48[2] | 3090 |
| Radeon 7970 | 0.9 | 32×64 | 32×16 | 768 | — | 3.0 | 264 | 32×32 | 3789 |

Top three rows describe the CPUs. The bottom four rows describe the GPUs.
[1]CPUs are equipped with HT technology. Table gives the number of physical cores.
[2]On GeForce GPUs each compute unit posses 64 KB memory shared by L1 cache and local memory configured by default in ratio 16/48.

The main tests were performed on three popular benchmarks containing amino acid sequences, i.e., BAliBASE 3 [52], PREFAB 4 [9], and extended variant of OXBench [54]. All datasets were downloaded from Robert Edgar Web page in a standardised FASTA format [54]. All benchmarks are constituted of hundreds of sequence sets (see Table 6 for more details). As many algorithms were tuned on BAliBASE, sequence sets from this benchmark were shuffled randomly in order to remove potential bias. Additional experiments were carried out on real protein families downloaded from Pfam database [55]. The detailed characteristics of these datasets are presented in Table 7.

**Table 6:** Characteristics of amino-acid benchmarks used in experiments

| Dataset | | Sequence statistics $E(k)$ | $\sigma(k)$ | $E(\bar{n})$ | $\sigma(\bar{n})$ | No. sets |
|---|---|---|---|---|---|---|
| BAliBASE | RV11 | 6.9 | 3.1 | 294 | 143 | 38 |
| | RV12 | 9.0 | 5.8 | 389 | 256 | 44 |
| | RV20 | 45.6 | 20.0 | 391 | 204 | 41 |
| | RV30 | 63.2 | 34.1 | 359 | 155 | 30 |
| | RV40 | 27.1 | 14.9 | 479 | 255 | 49 |
| | RV50 | 27.9 | 13.8 | 488 | 138 | 16 |
| BAliBASE all | | 28.5 | 26.2 | 396 | 219 | 218 |
| PREFAB | | 45.2 | 10.8 | 289 | 126 | 1692 |
| OXBench-X | | 122.5 | 100.7 | 147 | 82 | 395 |

A single set of sequences is described by the number of sequences $k$ and the average sequence length $\bar{n}$.
Table presents means and standard deviations of these parameters for BAliBASE 3.0, PREFAB 4.0, and OXBench-X.

**Table 7:** Detailed characteristics of the protein families taken from Pfam database

| Dataset | $k$ | $\bar{n}$ | Description |
|---|---|---|---|
| PF02324 | 260 | 706 | glycoside hydrolase |
| PF04762 | 404 | 667 | IKI3 family |
| PF05110 | 483 | 611 | AF4/FMR2-related protein |
| PF07095 | 600 | 642 | growth attenuator protein |
| PF07520 | 283 | 878 | virulence factor SrfB |
| PF08689 | 144 | 741 | mediator complex subunit Med5 |
| PF10136 | 317 | 626 | site-specific recombinase |
| PF11573 | 204 | 794 | mediator complex subunit 23 |

Each set is described by the number of sequences $k$ and the average sequence length $\bar{n}$.

For each dataset we calculated sum-of-pairs (SP) and column-scores (TC) measures with a use of Qscore software [56]. Note that PREFAB benchmark is constructed in the way that SP and TC are equal. All experiments were divided into two phases. First one consisted in comparing execution times of MSAProbs and QuickProbs stages across different hardware platforms. The results are presented in Tables 8, 9, 10, and 11. We report times for stage I (posterior matrix calculation), III (consistency transformation), IV (construction and refinement of final alignment). Stage II (building a guide tree) is omitted on purpose—its execution times are irrelevant with respect to the other stages and do not differ across hardware platforms. The overall times of algorithm execution are also given. Note, that for benchmark datasets tables present sum of processing times of all sequence sets within benchmarks. SP and TC scores were only used for checking the correctness of QuickProbs and are not reported. In Tables 8,9, and 10 CPU results represent execution times of MSAProbs, while CPU+GPU configurations correspond to QuickProbs.

**Table 8:** Execution times for BAliBASE 3 benchmark reported in $minutes : seconds$ **format**

| Hardware | Stage I | | Stage III | | Stage IV | | Total(I-IV) | |
|---|---|---|---|---|---|---|---|---|
| | time | speed-up | time | speed-up | time | speed-up | time | speed-up |
| Xeon W3550 | 39:33 | | 5:08 | | 9:13 | | 53:54 | |
| Xeon W3550 + GeForce 480 | 10:28 | (×3.8) | 2:43 | (×2.2) | 4:28 | (×2.1) | 17:21 | (×3.1) |
| Xeon W3550 + GeForce 680 | 4:01 | (×9.9) | 2:12 | (×2.3) | 4:28 | (×2.1) | 10:42 | (×5.0) |
| Xeon W3550 + Radeon 7970 | 2:58 | (×13.3) | 1:06 | (×4.7) | 4:27 | (×2.1) | 8:33 | (×6.3) |
| Xeon E5-2630 | 30:35 | | 2:45 | | 10:05 | | 43:31 | |
| Xeon E5-2630 + GeForce 680 | 3:43 | (×8.2) | 2:10 | (×1.3) | 2:56 | (×3.4) | 8:51 | (×4.9) |
| Phenom II X6 | 51:38 | | 5:35 | | 11:27 | | 68:41 | |
| Phenom II X6 + GeForce 560 | 12:21 | (×2.9) | 3:26 | (×1.6) | 3:24 | (×3.3) | 19:13 | (×3.1) |

Speed-ups of QuickProbs (CPU+GPU) over MSAProbs (CPU) across different hardware configurations are also shown.

**Table 9:** Execution times for PREFAB 4 benchmark reported in *minutes* : *seconds* **format.**

| Hardware | Stage I | | Stage III | | Stage IV | | Total(I-IV) | |
|---|---|---|---|---|---|---|---|---|
| | time | speed-up | time | speed-up | time | speed-up | time | speed-up |
| Xeon W3550 | 169:19 | | 16:11 | | 23:15 | | 208:50 | |
| Xeon W3550 + GeForce 480 | 30:23 | (×5.6) | 9:15 | (×1.8) | 7:55 | (×2.9) | 47:40 | (×4.4) |
| Xeon W3550 + GeForce 680 | 13:41 | (×12.4) | 8:46 | (×1.8) | 8:00 | (×2.9) | 30:34 | (×6.8) |
| Xeon W3550 + Radeon 7970 | 8:47 | (×19.2) | 4:47 | (×3.4) | 7:55 | (×2.9) | 21:35 | (×9.7) |
| Xeon E5-2630 | 130:50 | | 9:39 | | 23:59 | | 164:36 | |
| Xeon E5-2630 + GeForce 680 | 13:31 | (×9.7) | 8:42 | (×1.1) | 5:21 | (×4.4) | 27:42 | (×5.9) |
| Phenom | 231:41 | | 18:34 | | 31:53 | | 282:16 | |
| Phenom + GeForce 560 | 40:01 | (×5.8) | 13:47 | (×1.4) | 7:36 | (×4.2) | 61:29 | (×4.6) |

Speed-ups of QuickProbs (CPU+GPU) over MSAProbs (CPU) across different hardware configurations are also shown.

**Table 10:** Execution times for OXBench-X benchmark reported in *minutes* : *seconds* **format.**

| Hardware | Stage I | | Stage III | | Stage IV | | Total(I-IV) | |
|---|---|---|---|---|---|---|---|---|
| | time | speed-up | time | speed-up | time | speed-up | time | speed-up |
| Xeon W3550 | 133:49 | | 89:12 | | 17:36 | | 240:58 | |
| Xeon W3550 + GeForce 480 | 12:42 | (×10.6) | 77:59 | (×1.1) | 6:41 | (×2.7) | 98:02 | (×2.5) |
| Xeon W3550 + GeForce 680 | 10:36 | (×12.7) | 71:28 | (×1.2) | 6:44 | (×2.6) | 89:26 | (×2.7) |
| Xeon W3550 + Radeon 7970 | 7:19 | (×18.3) | 27:29 | (×3.2) | 6:36 | (×2.7) | 42:03 | (×5.7) |
| Xeon E5-2630 | 101:03 | | 62:55 | | 18:09 | | 182:41 | |
| Xeon E5-2630 + GeForce 680 | 10:27 | (×9.7) | 70:57 | (×0.9) | 3:20 | (×5.4) | 85:28 | (×2.1) |
| Phenom | 184:03 | | 123:25 | | 24:35 | | 332:23 | |
| Phenom + GeForce 560 | 19:19 | (×9.5) | 110:50 | (×1.1) | 5:46 | (×4.3) | 136:04 | (×2.4) |

**Table 11:** Detailed results for the real-life datasets from Pfam database

| Dataset | MSAProbs | | | | QuickProbs | | | |
|---|---|---|---|---|---|---|---|---|
| | I | III | IV | Total | I | III | IV | Total |
| PF02324 | 21:30 | 2:39 | 7:08 | 31:17 | 0:59(×22.0) | 0:25(×6.3) | 1:10(×6.1) | 2:34(×12.2) |
| PF04762 | 46:54 | 13:37 | 16:45 | 77:18 | 1:54(× 24.7) | 3:30(×3.9) | 4:47(×3.5) | 10:42(×7.2) |
| PF05110 | 55:36 | 23:13 | 18:34 | 97:27 | 12:22(×4.5) | 6:27(×3.6) | 5:20(×3.5) | 25:32(×3.8) |
| PF07095 | 91:17 | 16:03 | 19:58 | 126:22 | 3:57(×23.0) | 3:46(×4.3) | 4:26(×4.3) | 12:11(×10.3) |
| PF07520 | 39:40 | 5:01 | 14:07 | 58:52 | 1:42(×23.3) | 0:39(×7.7) | 2:29(×5.7) | 4:53(×12.1) |
| PF08689 | 7:16 | 1:20 | 2:33 | 1:09 | 0:23(×18.7) | 0:13(×6.3) | 0:35(×4.4) | 1:12(×9.3) |
| PF10136 | 25:19 | 4:24 | 4:42 | 34:26 | 1:10(×21.6) | 1:05(×4.1) | 1:14(×3.8) | 3:37(×9.5) |
| PF11573 | 16:50 | 2:33 | 6:02 | 5:25 | 6:53(×2.4) | 0:19(×8.0) | 1:07(×5.4) | 8:20(×3.0) |
| All | 304:22 | 68:54 | 88:49 | 462:16 | 29:20(×10.4) | 16:24(×4.2) | 21:08(×4.2) | 69:01(×6.7) |

Times are given in *minutes* : *seconds* format.

The aim of the second experimental step was to compare base QuickProbs version and its accurate variant QuickProbs-acc with competing algorithms. SP and TC were used as quality measures and are reported together with total execution times in Table 12. Experiments were carried out on a machine equipped with Xeon W3550 and Radeon 7970. Packages that were chosen for experiments are MSAProbs 0.9.7, ClustalW v2.1, Clustal$\Omega$v1.2.0, Kalign2 v2.04, Kalign-LCS v1.0, MAFFT v7.053b, and MUSCLE v3.8.31. ClustalW was executed in the default and fast mode (distances calculated using full pairwise alignments and 2-tuple matches, respectively). MAFFT was run in the default mode without consistency and auto mode which selectively turns consistency on. MSAProbs algorithm in both experimental parts was compiled with a use of MinGW compiler due to support of long double floating-point precision which is used in the implementation. Additionally, we examined MSA-CUDA, a ClustalW variant suited for graphics processors. As CUDA is not supported by AMD GPUs, MSA-CUDA was run on a platform with Xeon W3550 and GeForce 680.

**Table 12:** Qualitative results for BAliBASE, PREFAB, and OXBench-X run on Xeon W3550 + Radeon 7970 (GeForce 680 was used for MSA-CUDA)

| Algorithm | BAliBASE | | | PREFAB | | OXBench-X | | |
|---|---|---|---|---|---|---|---|---|
| | time | SP | TC | time | SP/TC | time | SP | TC |
| QuickProbs-acc | 28:19 | 87.9 | 60.8 | 64:48 | 74.0 | 255:36 | 89.3 | 80.2 |
| MSAProbs | 53:54 | 87.8 | 60.8 | 208:50 | 73.7 | 240:58 | 89.1 | 80.0 |
| QuickProbs | 8:33 | 87.8 | 60.7 | 21:35 | 73.6 | 42:03 | 89.1 | 80.0 |
| MAFFT-auto | 21:49 | 86.7 | 58.3 | 77:49 | 72.3 | 22:01 | 87.7 | 78.4 |
| ClustalΩ | 7:33 | 83.6 | 54.8 | 23:07 | 70.0 | — | — | — |
| MUSCLE | 15:17 | 81.7 | 46.8 | 40:38 | 67.7 | 30:36 | 87.5 | 77.6 |
| Kalign-LCS | 0:27 | 82.9 | 50.4 | 1:47 | 65.9 | 0:36 | 86.8 | 76.4 |
| MAFTT-default | 3:47 | 81.3 | 46.2 | 24:54 | 67.7 | 6:02 | 86.1 | 75.6 |
| Kalign2 | 0:39 | 81.4 | 47.5 | 1:58 | 64.9 | 0:56 | 85.7 | 75.1 |
| ClustalW | 27:22 | 75.8 | 38.3 | 124:30 | 61.9 | 89:36 | 85.3 | 74.2 |
| ClustalW-quicktree | 6:25 | 73.7 | 37.1 | 22:19 | 61.9 | 8:04 | 84.9 | 73.8 |
| MSA-CUDA | — | — | — | 27:01 | 61.7 | 9:07 | 85.3 | 74.1 |
| MSA-CUDA-quicktree | 3:20 | 72.9 | 36.9 | 13:31 | 61.6 | 7:03 | 85.0 | 74.0 |

Aligners are sorted according to the average quality rank. Times are given in *minutes : seconds* format.

## Benchmark Datasets: Central Processor Running Times

The first observation when analysing results for benchmark datasets from Tables 8, 9, and 10is that relative execution times of original MSAProbs agree with relative theoretical computational power of CPUs used in the experiments. Xeon E5-2630 is the fastest central processor and it outperforms Xeon W3550 and Phenom II X6, respectively second and third CPU in the comparison. Nevertheless, when analysing results of stage IV of MSAProbs which is implemented in serial manner, it is apparent that quad-core Xeon performs better than its hexa-core counterpart. This can be explained by the fact, that single core of Xeon W3550 has a higher clock rate and is faster than E5-2630 even though the latter represents a newer CPU generation. When stage IV is parallelised with a use of OpenMP, as it is done in QuickProbs, E5-2630 takes the first place. An interesting observation is, that Phenom performs in this situation better than Xeon W3550. We believe, this may be caused by the memory access pattern in this part of the algorithm that prefers AMD CPU cache architecture over competitor. Another important conclusion is that parallel variant of stage IV does not scale perfectly with the number of cores—speed-ups with respect to the serial version are always lower. This is probably because some parts of stage IV were not subject to an OpenMP parallelisation and run for the same time independently of the number of cores.

## Benchmark Datasets: Graphics Processor Running Times

The shortest absolute execution times of analyses as well as highest speed-ups with respect to the original MSAProbs were obtained by Xeon W3550 + Radeon 7970 platform (see Tables 8, 9, 10). This coincides with a fact that Radeon has the greatest computational power from the examined GPUs. Since computations executed at graphic processor dominate in terms of execution time over CPU-parallel steps, this configuration is superior to the machine with faster CPU and slower GPU (E5-2630 + GeForce 680).

When detailed results for particular stages are analysed, the highest speed-ups are obtained for stage I. For Xeon W3550 + Radeon 7970 they vary from 13.3 (BAliBASE) to 19.2 (PREFAB). GeForce 680 turned out to be slower with speed-ups varying from 9.9 to 12.7. On hexa-core Xeon machine speed-ups are lower, but execution times are still superior to the original MSAProbs. Interesting observation comes from analysis of times obtained by GeForce 480 and 560, which are noticeably smaller than is suggested by the difference in computational power. After deeper investigation it became clear that the problem is caused by a number of registers in these GPUs which limits maximum size of a workgroup $l_{max}$ from 1024 to 576. Task can be processed at graphics processor if shorter of its sequence does not exceed $l_{max} - 1$. Therefore, smaller workgroups reduce performance as many tasks have to be calculated at CPU instead of GPU. Additionally, they limit occupancy for tasks executed at graphics processor preventing GPU computational power from full utilisation. In the case of stage III speed-ups of QuickProbs algorithm with respect to MSAProbs are lower than in stage I. For BAliBASE, PREFAB, and OXBench-X benchmarks run on quad-core CPU and Radeon 7970 they equal 4.7, 3.4, and 3.2, respectively. Significantly worse results were observed for GeForce 680 which indicates that parallelisation scheme of stage III prefers architecture of AMD GPUs. Another interesting observation is that differences between GeForce 480 cards and GeForce 680 are smaller than in the case of stage I. The explanation is that relaxation procedure is not limited by the register count. The worst speed-ups were reported for OXBench-X that contains large sets having hundreds of sequences. The consistency stage executed at GPU is vulnerable for divergence in width of sparse rows of input matrices. For large sets, the divergence is significant, thus lots of computational power is wasted resulting in lower speed-ups.

## Pfam Datasets Running Times

Experiments on real protein families were performed on our fastest testing platform equipped with Xeon W3550 CPU and Radeon 7970 GPU. Results are presented in Table 11. As in benchmark datasets, the best speed-ups are observed for stage I—in the majority of cases they exceed 20 with a maximum value of 24.7. The only exceptions are PF05110 and PF11573 with speed-ups equal to 4.5 and 2.4, respectively. This is caused by the presence of long sequences ($n > l_{max}$) that are processed on the CPU and dominate whole posterior calculation stage. Speed-ups for stage III are smaller which also coincides with the benchmark results. They vary from 3.6 to 8.0. In the case of stage IV which was parallelised for multi-core CPUs, execution times are 3.5 to 6.1 times shorter than in MSAProbs. An interesting fact is that for the majority of datasets speed-ups exceed 4, the number of physical cores in our testing platform. This differs from benchmark results where speed-ups were always lower than number of cores. There are many reasons for this. Firstly, families from Pfam are much larger than benchmark sequence sets, thus proportions between parallel and serial operations are better. Thanks to this, the modification that improved cache utilisation is also more beneficial. Finally, Xeon W3550 CPU is equipped with a hyper-threading technology which increases task parallelism of a single core. The overall QuickProbs speed-up on all families equals 6.7. One must keep in mind, that this result is strongly skewed by PF05110 and PF11573 sets for which performance is limited by the presence of long sequences (stage I is the most time consuming part of the algorithm). If we exclude them from the comparison, the speed-up increases to 9.7.

## Comparison with other Methods

Aligners from Table 12 were ranked on all datasets according to the result quality (SP and TC can be used interchangeably for this purpose as they generate identical ranks), and ordered by the average rank. The first group of algorithms gathers most accurate, consistency-based methods: QuickProbs in base and accurate variant, MSAProbs, and MAFFT-auto. The best aligner in terms of result quality is QuickProbs-acc which is superior to MSAProbs, the most accurate method so far. In order to statistically analyse observed differences in SP and TC, we performed Wilcoxon signed-rank tests [57] at the significance level $\alpha = 0.05$. If one considers entire benchmarks, the significance was reported for PREFAB only ($P$-value=0.000491). However, we suspected that adaptive filtering of sparse matrices used by QuickProbs-acc would be beneficial mainly for distantly related sequences, where static $cutoff$ may result in the information loss. Therefore, we clustered sets in benchmarks according to the average sequence identity and analysed differences on groups. In the case of OXBench-X it turned out that for 94 sets from twilight zone (average identity below 30%), the predominance of QuickProbs-acc with respect to MSAProbs was statistically significant ($P$-values equalled to 0.002074 and 0.024536 for SP and TC, respectively). Same analysis performed for PREFAB also revealed strong evidence that QuickProbs-acc is particularly suited for distantly related sequences: $P$-value for 535 twilight sets was two orders of magnitude lower than in the case of whole benchmark and equalled 0.000004. In the case of BAliBASE dataset, we compared different RV groups but no significant differences were discovered. An important observation is that all these results were obtained without exceeding MSAProbs execution times (in the case of BAliBASE and PREFAB QuickProbs-acc was much faster, for OXBench-X it was only 6% slower). This is important, since MSAProbs is the most time consuming from all tested algorithms.

In cases where MSAProbs accuracy is sufficient, default mode of QuickProbs should be used as it produces almost identical results as MSAProbs, at a fraction of the time. Small discrepancy in accuracies is caused by using double floating-point precision in partition function calculation at GPU instead of long double. This was confirmed by the fact, that MSAProbs compiled without long double support gives exactly the same results as QuickProbs. Fourth aligner in terms of quality rank was MAFFT in automatic mode. Additionally, it turned out to be slower than QuickProbs on BAliBASE and PREFAB benchmarks.

Second group of packages consists of algorithms without consistency: Clustal $\Omega$, Kalign-LCS, MUSCLE, MAFTT-default, Kalign2, and ClustalW. The first from aforementioned methods, Clustal $\Omega$ produces the best results on BAliBASE and PREFAB datasets, however, it failed to run properly on OXBench-X. The best algorithm which executed successfully on all datasets is MUSCLE. Its execution times may be an issue in some applications, though. Kalign-LCS, the modification of Kalign2, is inferior to MUSCLE only by a small margin. Moreover, it is the fastest method in the comparison outperforming also CUDA-based algorithms, which makes it the best choice when one is interested in aligning large sets of sequences. An interesting observation is that ClustalW performs significantly worse than other aligners in comparison. Taking into account relatively long execution times, it is clear that ClustalW, still the most popular MSA software, should be replaced in biological analyses by other packages. The ClustalW variant suited for GPU processing (MSA-CUDA) is characterised by much shorter execution times. Nevertheless, it is still inferior to fast and more accurate CPU aligners like Kalign-LCS. Additionally, its default variant failed to execute properly on BAliBASE benchmark.

## DISCUSSION

In the paper we present QuickProbs, a variant of MSAProbs algorithm suited for graphics processors. We designed and implemented GPU versions of two most time consuming stages of the strategy, which originally were customised for multi-core architecture with the use of OpenMP. These are the calculation of posterior probability matrices and the consistency transformation. Posterior matrices are calculated on the basis of pair hidden Markov models and partition functions. From algorithmic point of view the stage performs several dynamic programming passes. Customising computation scheme to massively parallel GPU architecture, optimising global memory accesses by using jagged pattern and exploiting advanced method of work balancing resulted in significant speed-ups at this stage. On the main testing platform equipped with a quad-core Xeon W3550 and Radeon 7970, QuickProbs calculated posterior matrices as much as 24.7 times faster than original CPU-parallel method. The consistency transformation stage relies on performing set of small sparse matrix multiplications. We designed an algorithm for this purpose customised for graphics processors. As experiments on the basic testing platform show, it outperforms its MSAProbs equivalent with speed-ups reaching 8.0. In order to further improve execution times, we additionally suited the last stage of QuickProbs for multi-core CPU architectures with a use of OpenMP. Thanks to this, the construction and refinement of final alignment is done even 6.1 times faster than previously.

Assessed on BAliBASE, PREFAB, and OXBench-X benchmarks, QuickProbs turned out to be respectively, 6.3, 9.7, and 5.7 times faster than MSAProbs. In the experiments on protein families from Pfam database, the overall speed-up was 6.7. This makes QuickProbs competitive to faster aligners like MAFFT, Clustal $\Omega$, or MUSCLE. In the research we additionally introduced QuickProbs-acc, a tuned version of QuickProbs which is significantly more accurate than MSAProbs on sequence sets from twilight zone (identity $<30\%$) without exceeding its running time. Unlike previously published GPU-suited multiple sequence alignment methods, computations in QuickProbs algorithm are performed in OpenCL making it suitable for graphics processors produced by both main vendors, NVidia and AMD.

Our future plans focuses three main tasks: (1) removing limitation of sequence lengths that can be processed at GPU at posterior stage, (2) redesigning consistency transformation to make it less vulnerable for divergence in sparse rows lengths, (3) customising final alignment construction and refinement procedures for graphics processors.

## REFERENCES


1. Wang L, Jiang T (1994) On the complexity of multiple sequence alignment. Journal of Computational Biology 1: 337–348
2. Just W (1999) Computational complexity of multiple sequence alignment with SP-Score. Journal of Computational Biology 8: 615–623
3. Feng DF, Doolittle RF (1987) Progressive sequence alignment as a prerequisite to correct phylogenetic trees. Journal of Molecular Evolution 25: 351–360
4. Barton GJ, Sternberg MJ (1987) A strategy for the rapid multiple alignment of protein sequences. Confidence levels from tertiary structure comparisons. Journal of Molecular Biology 198: 327–337
5. Krogh A, Brown M, Mian IS, Sjölander K, Haussler D (1994) Hidden Markov models in computational biology: applications to protein modeling. Journal of Molecular Biology 235: 1501–1531
6. Thompson JD, Higgins DG, Gibson TJ (1994) CLUSTAL W: improving the sensitivity of progressive multiple sequence alignment through sequence weighting, position-specific gap penalties and weight matrix choice. Nucleic Acids Research 22: 4673–4680
7. Notredame C, Higgins D, Heringa J (2000) T-Coffee: A novel method for fast and accurate multiple sequence alignment. Journal of Molecular Biology 302: 205–217
8. Katoh K, Misawa K, Kuma K, Miyata T (2002) MAFFT: a novel method for rapid multiple sequence alignment based on fast Fourier transform. Nucleic Acids Research 30: 3059–3066
9. Edgar RC (2004) MUSCLE: multiple sequence alignment with high accuracy and high throughput. Nucleic Acids Research 32: 1792–1797
10. Do C, Mahabhashyam M, Brudno M, Batzoglou S (2005) ProbCons: Probabilistic consistencybased multiple sequence alignment. Genome Research 15: 330–340
11. Roshan U, Livesay DR (2006) Probalign: multiple sequence alignment using partition function posterior probabilities. Bioinformatics 22: 2715–2721
12. Liu Y, Schmidt B, Maskell D (2010) MSAProbs: multiple sequence alignment based on pair hidden Markov models and partition function posterior probabilities. Bioinformatics 26: 1958–1964
13. O'Sullivan O, Suhre K, Abergel C, Higgins D, Notredame C (2004) 3DCoffee: Combining protein sequences and structures within multiple sequence alignments. Journal of Molecular Biology 340: 385–395
14. Deng X, Cheng J (2011) MSACompro: protein multiple sequence alignment using predicted secondary structure, solvent accessibility, and residue-residue contacts. BMC Bioinformatics 12: 472.
15. Katoh K, Kuma Ki, Toh H, Miyata T (2005) MAFFT version 5: improvement in accuracy of multiple sequence alignment. Nucleic Acids Research 33: 511–518
16. Huerta-Cepas J, Capella-Gutierrez S, Pryszcz LP, Denisov I, Kormes D, et al. (2011) PhylomeDB v3.0: an expanding repository of genome-wide collections of trees, alignments and phylogeny-based orthology and paralogy predictions. Nucleic Acids Research 39: 556–560
17. Capella-Gutierrez S (2012) Analysis of multiple protein sequence alignments and phylogenetic trees in the context of phylogenomics studies. Pompeu Fabra UniversityPh.D. thesis
18. Lassmann T, Sonnhammer E (2005) Kalign|an accurate and fast multiple sequence alignment algorithm.BMC Bioinformatics 6: 298
19. Lassmann T, Frings O, Sonnhammer E (2009) Kalign2: high-performance multiple alignment of protein and nucleotide sequences allowing external features. Nucleic Acids Research 37: 858–865
20. Wu S, Manber U (1992) Fast text searching: allowing errors. Communications of the ACM 35: 83–91
21. Muth R, Manber U (1996) Approximate multiple string search. In: Proceedings of the 7th Annual Symposium on Combinatorial Pattern Matching. pp. 75-86.
22. Deorowicz S, Debudaj-Grabysz A, Gudyś A (2014)

Kalign-LCS|more accurate and faster variant of Kalign2 algorithm for the multiple sequence alignment problem. In: Man-Machine Interactions 3, Springer Cham Heidelberg New York Dordrecht London. pp. 495-502.

23. Katoh K, Toh H (2007) Parttree: an algorithm to build an approximate tree from a large number of unaligned sequences. Bioinformatics 23: 372–374
24. Sievers F, Wilm A, Dineen D, Gibson T, Karplus K, et al. (2011) Fast, scalable generation of highquality protein multiple sequence alignments using Clustal Omega. Molecular Systems Biology 7: 539
25. Blackshields G, Sievers F, Shi W, Wilm A, Higgins D (2010) Sequence embedding for fast construction of guide trees for multiple sequence alignment. Algorithms for Molecular Biology 5: 21
26. Liu W, Schmidt B, Voss G, Muller-Wittig W (2006) GPU-ClustalW: Using graphics hardware to accelerate multiple sequence alignment. Lecture Notes in Computer Science 4297: 363–374
27. Liu Y, Schmidt B, Maskell D (2009) MSA-CUDA: Multiple sequence alignment on graphics processing units with CUDA. In: Proceedings of the 20th IEEE International Conference on Applicationspecific Systems, Architectures and Processors. pp. 121-128.
28. Gudyś A, Deorowicz S (2012) A parallel algorithm for the constrained multiple sequence alignment problem designed for GPUs. International Journal of Foundations of Computer Science 23: 877–901
29. Lin YS, Lin CY, Li ST, Lee JY, Tang CY (2010) GPU-REMuSiC: the implementation of constrain multiple sequence alignment on graphics processing units. In: Proceedings of the 2010 GPU Technology Conference. NVidia.
30. Blazewicz J, Frohmberg W, Kierzynka M, Wojciechowski P (2013) G-MSA|A GPU-based, fast and accurate algorithm for multiple sequence alignment. Journal of Parallel and Distributed Computing 73: 32–41
31. OpenMP ARB (2013) OpenMP Application Program Interface version 4.0. Available:http://www.openmp.org/mp-documents/OpenMP4.0.0.pdf
32. Manavski S, Valle G (2008) CUDA compatible GPU cards as efficient hardware accelerators for Smith-Waterman sequence alignment. BMC Bioinformatics 9: S10
33. Ligowski L, Rudnicki W (2009) An efficient implementation of Smith Waterman algorithm on GPU using CUDA, for massively parallel scanning of sequence databases. In: Proceedings of the 2009 IEEE International Symposium on Parallel&Distributed Processing. Washington,USA: IEEE Computer Society, pp. 1-8.
34. Liu Y, Schmidt B, Maskell D (2010) CUDASW++2.0: enhanced Smith-Waterman protein database search on CUDA-enabled GPUs based on SIMT and virtualized SIMD abstractions. BMC Research Notes3: 93
35. Khajeh-Saeed A, Poole S, Perot J (2010) Acceleration of the Smith-Waterman algorithm using single and multiple graphics processors. Journal of Computational Physics 229: 4247–4258
36. Blazewicz J, Frohmberg W, Kierzynka M, Pesch E, Wojciechowski P (2011) Protein alignment algorithms with an efficient backtracking routine on multiple GPUs. BMC Bioinformatics 12: 181
37. Liu Y, Wirawan A, Schmidt B (2013) CUDASW++ 3.0: accelerating Smith-Waterman protein database search by coupling CPU and GPU SIMD instructions. BMC Bioinformatics 14: 117
38. Liu CM, Wong T, Wu E, Luo R, Yiu SM, et al. (2012) SOAP3: ultra-fast GPU-based parallel alignment tool for short reads. Bioinformatics 28: 878–879
39. Chang DJ, Kimmer C, Ouyang M (2010) Accelerating the Nussinov RNA folding algorithm with CUDA/GPU. In: Proceedings of the 10th IEEE International Symposium on Signal Processing and Information. IEEE Computer Society, pp. 120-125: 20
40. Suchard MA, Rambaut A (2009) Many-core algorithms for statistical phylogenetics. Bioinformatics 25: 1370–1376
41. Demouth J (2012) Sparse Matrix-Matrix Multiplication on the GPU. In: Proceedings of the GPU Technology Conference 2012. NVidia.
42. NVidia (2013) CUSP library version 0.4.0. Available: https://developer.nvidia.com/cusp
43. NVidia (2013) cuSPARSE library version 5.5. Available: https://developer.nvidia.com/cusparse
44. Durbin R, Eddy SR, Krogh A, Mitchison G (1998) Biological Sequence Analysis: Probabilistic Models of Proteins and Nucleic Acids. Cambridge University Press.
45. Thompson JD, Plewniak F, Poch O (1999) A comprehensive comparison of multiple sequence alignment programs. Nucleic Acids Research 27: 2682–2690
46. Stoye J, Evers D, Meyer F (1998) Rose: generating sequence families. Bioinformatics 14: 157 163
47. NVidia (2013) CUDA Parallel Computing Platform version 5.5. Available:http://docs.nvidia.com/cuda/pdf/CUDA_C_Programming_Guide.pdf
48. Khronos Group (2013) The OpenCL Specification version 2.0. Available:http://www.khronos.org/registry/cl/specs/opencl-2.0.pdf
49. Viterbi A (1967) Error bounds for convolutional codes and an asymptotically optimum decoding algorithm. IEEE Transactions on Information Theory 13: 260–269
50. Sneath P, Sokal R (1973) Numerical Taxonomy. The Principles and Practice of Numerical Classification. San Francisco, USA: W.H. Freeman Limited.
51. Needleman S, Wunsch C (1970) A general method applicable to the search for similarities in the amino acid sequence of two proteins. Journal of Molecular Biology 48: 443 - 453.
52. Thompson J, Koehl P, Ripp R, Poch O (2005) BAliBASE 3.0: latest developments of the multiple sequence alignment benchmark. Proteins 61: 127–136
53. Raghava GPS, Searle S, Audley P, Barber J, Barton G (2003) OXBench: A benchmark for evaluation of

protein multiple sequence alignment accuracy. BMC Bioinformatics 4: 47.

54. Edgar RC (2009) Benchmark collection. Available: http://www.drive5.com/bench

55. Finn RD, Tate J, Mistry J, Coggill PC, Sammut SJ, et al. (2008) The Pfam protein families database.Nucleic Acids Research 36: D281–D288

56. Edgar RC (2009) QSCORE multiple alignment scoring software. Available:http://www.drive5.com/qscore

57. Wilcoxon F (1945) Individual Comparisons by Ranking Methods. Biometrics Bulletin 1: 80–83

# CHAPTER 13 A FULLY AUTOMATED HIGH-THROUGHPUT TRAINING SYSTEM FOR RODENTS

Rajesh Poddar[1,2], Risa Kawai[1,2], Bence P. Ölveczky[1,2]

[1]Department of Organismic and Evolutionary Biology, Harvard University, Cambridge, Massachusetts, United States of America,

[2]Center for Brain Science, Harvard University, Cambridge, Massachusetts, United States of America

## ABSTRACT

**Addressing the neural mechanisms underlying complex learned behaviors requires training animals in well-controlled tasks, an often time-consuming and labor-intensive process that can severely limit the feasibility of such studies. To overcome this constraint, we developed a fully computer-controlled general purpose system for high-throughput training of rodents. By standardizing and automating the implementation of predefined training protocols within the animal's home-cage our system dramatically reduces the efforts involved in animal training while also removing human errors and biases from the process. We deployed this system to train rats in a variety of sensorimotor tasks, achieving learning rates comparable to existing, but more laborious, methods. By incrementally and systematically increasing the difficulty of the task over weeks of training, rats were able to master motor tasks that, in complexity and structure, resemble ones used in primate studies of motor sequence learning. By enabling fully automated training of rodents in a home-cage setting this low-cost and modular system increases the utility of rodents for studying the neural underpinnings of a variety of complex behaviors.**

## INTRODUCTION

Studies exploring the neural mechanisms underlying higher-order cognitive and learning phenomena, including decision making[1], motor skill execution[2], and perceptual discrimination[3,4], have traditionally been done in non-human primates. Costs and regulations, however, make high-throughput experiments on monkeys difficult to justify[5]. Rodents, with their increasingly well-understood cognitive and learning capabilities, have emerged as an alternative model system for studying a variety of complex behaviors[6–15]. Rats and mice share the basic mammalian brain architecture with primates, and though cortical specializations may differ[16–18], recent studies suggest that many of the well-characterized cortical functions in primates have equivalents in rodents[7,9,12,13,15,19]. Sophisticated tools for measuring and manipulating brain activity[20–23] together with the many transgenic lines and disease models available in rodents further incentivize their use in mechanistic studies. Yet one of the main barriers for research on complex behaviors, both

**Citation:** Poddar R, Kawai R, Ölveczky BP. A Fully Automated High-Throughput Training System for Rodents. Schaefer A, ed. PLoS ONE. 2013;8(12):e83171. doi:10.1371/journal.pone.0083171.

in rodents and primates, lies in training animals - a process typically done under close supervision of researchers who frequently modify protocols and procedures on an animal-by-animal basis to improve learning rates and performance. This approach is labor-intensive and time-consuming, and makes the interaction between animal and researcher an integral part of the training process, possibly confounding comparisons of experimental outcomes across animals and labs[24].

Here we describe a method and experimental infrastructure that fundamentally transforms this traditionally arduous process, making it effortless, rigorous and amenable to high-throughput approaches. Our solution combines two main ingredients.

- *Automation of the training process*. Automation allows implementation of rigorously defined training protocols on a large scale without the vagaries and efforts associated with human-assisted training[25]. Such improvements in the quality and quantity of behavioral data enables powerful research approaches for addressing complex and slow-to-learn behaviors [19].
- *Training within the animal's home-cage*. Implementing automated training within the animal's home-cage eliminates the need for day-to-day handling of trained animals, making long training processes fully automated and largely effortless. Live-in home-cage training also enables long-term tethering of animals, making long-term uninterrupted neural recordings feasible.

While certain aspects of animal training have been automated, either through the use of custom-developed software or commercially available systems[19,26–30], most solutions lack the flexibility required to tackle broader sets of questions or behaviors. Existing solutions do not accommodate either complete automation of multi-stage training processes involving large numbers of animals or long-term neural recordings in the context of training. Thus the significant human involvement currently required for experiments on complex behaviors still represents a considerable impediment to large-scale rodent studies.

To further improve the efficiency of the training process, we developed a fully Automated Rodent Training System (ARTS) for reward-based learning (Figure 1). Our low-cost system is flexible, extensible, remotely administrable, and allows for simultaneous training of large cohorts of animals. ARTS is designed for deployment in animal facilities found in biomedical research centers, and requires no more human supervision than standard animal care. Training occurs in custom-designed home-cages that can be outfitted with a variety of sensors, manipulanda, water ports, and effectors (e.g. sensory stimulation devices), customized to the nature of the behavioral task (Figure 1A).

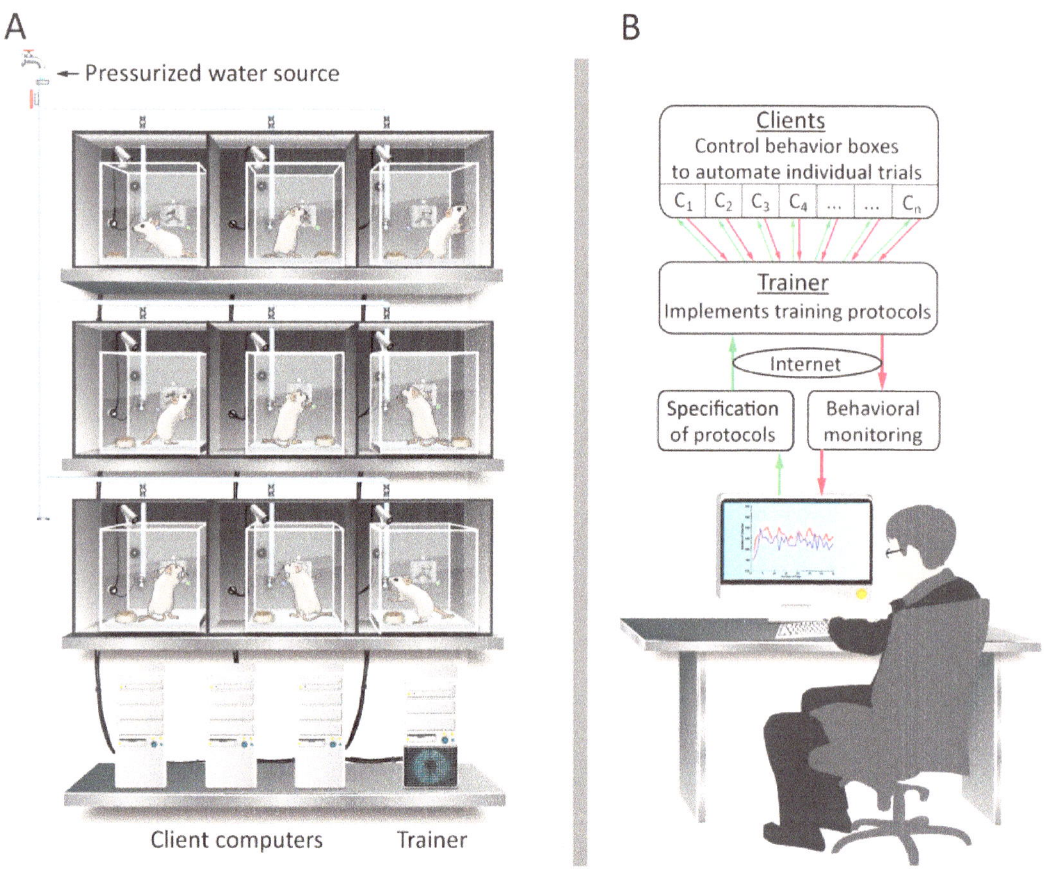


**Figure 1**: **A fully automated high-throughput training system for rodents.**

Below, we outline the general architecture and logic of ARTS and its current implementation and describe, validate, and benchmark its use for motor learning in rats.

## SYSTEM ARCHITECTURE

### Flexible and Modular Software Architecture for Control of High-Throughput Animal Training

The heart of our automated rodent training system is the software platform that interacts with individual home-cages and executes pre-specified training protocols. To allow for maximum flexibility and generality, the software suite is modular and hierarchical, with two different components controlling distinct aspects of the training process (Figure 1B). At the top of the hierarchy is the *Trainer*, which monitors overall performance and implements user-defined training protocols for individual behavioral boxes A 'protocol' is defined as a set of training stages and performance criteria for automatically transitioning between them. Each training stage is specified in the form of a finite state machine (FSM), a widely employed and intuitive abstraction for specifying behavioral tasks that consists of states linked by transitions[31]. Behavioral or environmental events, such as lever presses, nose pokes, or elapsed time, can trigger transitions between states, each of which can be associated with a set of actions (e.g. reward being dispensed, LEDs turning on/off).

The *Trainer* executes training protocols by supplying FSMs specifying reward contingencies and trial structure to lower level *Clients*, each of which controls a behavioral box. With this flexible and general program structure, automating a training protocol in ARTS reduces to having the *Trainer* supply the *Client*with the right FSMs at the right times.

Data acquired by the *Client* during the execution of an FSM, including high-resolution timing data and video, is stored in a central database. This allows multiple users to concurrently and efficiently read and write data to and from the database using SQL - an intuitive database language supported by all major programming languages. Centralized data storage also allows for easy backup, aggregation, analysis, and distribution of large amounts of behavioral data. A software package for ARTS complete with a user's manual can be downloaded from our server.

### Software Implementation

The entire software suite for ARTS is written in C#.Net, a simple, general-purpose, object-oriented programming language. The software (both source code and pre-compiled binaries) along with detailed step-by-step instructions on setting up the system can be downloaded fromhttp://olveczkylab.fas.harvard.edu/ARTS (the system is co-branded OpCon in the website and internally). Both the *Client* and *Trainer* can easily be extended to accommodate virtually any behavioral task or training protocol by simply writing add-on custom-scripts in any .NET compatible language, including C#, F#, J#, VB, and C++. Writing or using these plugins does not require a detailed understanding of the underlying software (the plugins and scripts included in the source code can serve as a starting point). Importantly, the software supports numerous extensions to basic FSMs, like custom plugins and concurrent execution of multiple FSMs[31], which enables specification of behavioral paradigms with probabilistic cues and complex reward contingencies.

In addition to the core components of ARTS (*Client*, *Trainer*, and the database), a suite of supporting software adds further functionality, making it a complete end-to-end high-throughput automated training system. A graphical user interface allows for easy and intuitive specification of training protocols. Behavioral monitoring, including querying the timing, duration, and saved video of each behavioral 'event' is made possible by an interactive data visualization tool. Furthermore, a suite of network services & scripts enables remote control and monitoring (including live streaming video onto the internet) of the system.

### A Cost-Effective Hardware Solution

The hardware requirements of ARTS are modest, making it cost-effective and easy to build and deploy (Figure 1). Our current system contains 48 behavior boxes controlled by 24 *Client*computers and two servers, all of which are housed in a temperature and humidity controlled animal facility. The reward port providing water reinforcement in each behavior box is connected to the animal facility's pressurized water system through solenoid valves, allowing us to dispense specific volumes of water by controlling the duration of valve openings through the *Client*. Aquarium pumps (Jehmco LPH 60) are used to ventilate behavior boxes at a ratio of one pump for every six boxes. To ensure acoustic and visual separation each box is placed in an enclosure, which is placed on the shelves of a standard wire racks.

Behavior boxes were custom designed using acrylic and aluminum extrusions. The boxes have a removable front panel holding all experimental equipment (sensors, indicators, manipulanda, water dispensing valves etc). The front panel is the only part of the system that needs to be customized for a given experimental paradigm. To ensure compatibility with invasive experiments (chronic electrophysiology etc.), the normal lid of the box can be exchanged with a custom lid having the experiment-specific equipment (e.g. commutator etc.). The hardware cost for building the boxes is ~$500/box.

Each low-cost *Client* computer runs Windows 7 and contains an Intel quad-core processor (Core i5-750 - 2.66GHz/core), 4GB of DDR3 SDRAM, and a 1.5TB 5900 RPM hard disk and controls and communicates with the behavior boxes at the ratio of two boxes per computer. Behavioral data (e.g. from manipulanda, lick sensors, and cameras) and signals for controlling peripherals such as speakers and LEDs are transferred between the box and the Client computer via a National Instruments data acquisition system (NI PCIe 6323 - DAQ card, 2 x RC68-68 – Ribbon Cable & 2 x CB-68LP – Connector Block). The *Client* computers, in turn, communicate with a central server, which runs the *Trainer* and hosts the database (Figure 1). Server computers (*Trainer*) contain a higher-end Intel quad-core processor (Core i7-950 – 3.06GHz/core), 12GB of DDR3 SDRAM, 3 1TB 7200 RPM hard disks. The servers run Windows Server 2008 R2 and host a SQL Server 2008 R2 database.

The total cost of our current ARTS set-up (48 boxes), including all hardware, computers, and electronics, is around $67K, i.e. $1400/box.

## Scalability and Safety

The number of behavior boxes per *Client* computer is primarily limited by the number of video cameras attached to each box since acquisition/processing of video data is fairly CPU intensive. ARTS supports multiple data acquisition cards per *Client* computer allowing a large number of behavior boxes to be controlled via a single computer if the *Client* does not need to process video data. Likewise the network bandwidth is dominated by uncompressed video data (17MBps per 30fps 640x480 webcam). The server can be scaled to support a larger number of clients by increasing the amount of available memory since this is the bottleneck for database performance.

In addition to free water at the end of every night (see section *Schedules and mode of reinforcement*) multiple layers of security checks are built into the system to prevent animals from dehydrating. Water is only dispensed upon licking the reward spout ensuring that the dispensed water is consumed. The behavior monitoring GUI prominently displays water consumption. A watchdog program continually monitors the*Client*, *Trainer* and database to detect any failures and displays this information in the monitoring GUI. Finally animals are periodically examined and weighed by the animal care staff to ensure they are adequately hydrated.

## Behavioral Training Methods

We have used *ARTS* to train more than 150 rats in a variety of behaviors including pressing a lever in precise temporal sequences, pressing a set of levers in spatiotemporal sequences on cue, and moving a joystick in various directions on cue. In this report we focused on a subset of 67 female Long Evans rats aged ~10-12 weeks at the start of the experiment, 30 of which were trained to perform a simplified version of the center-out task (Figures 2,3) 39 on a precise lever pressing task (Figure 4). Animals were kept on a daily 12h light cycle.

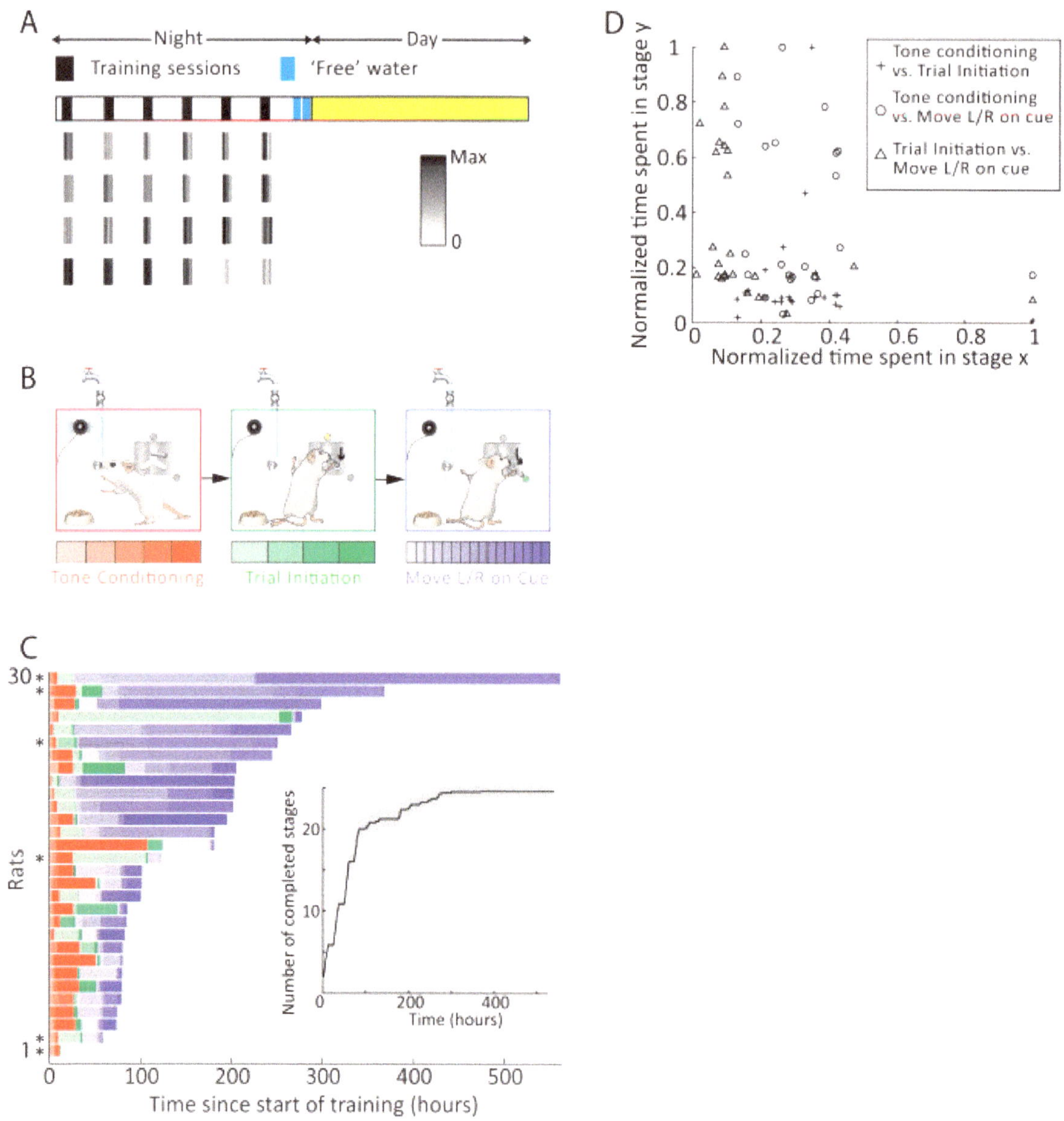


**Figure 2**: **Complete automation of a complex multi-step training protocol for a version of the center-out movement task (see Methods).**

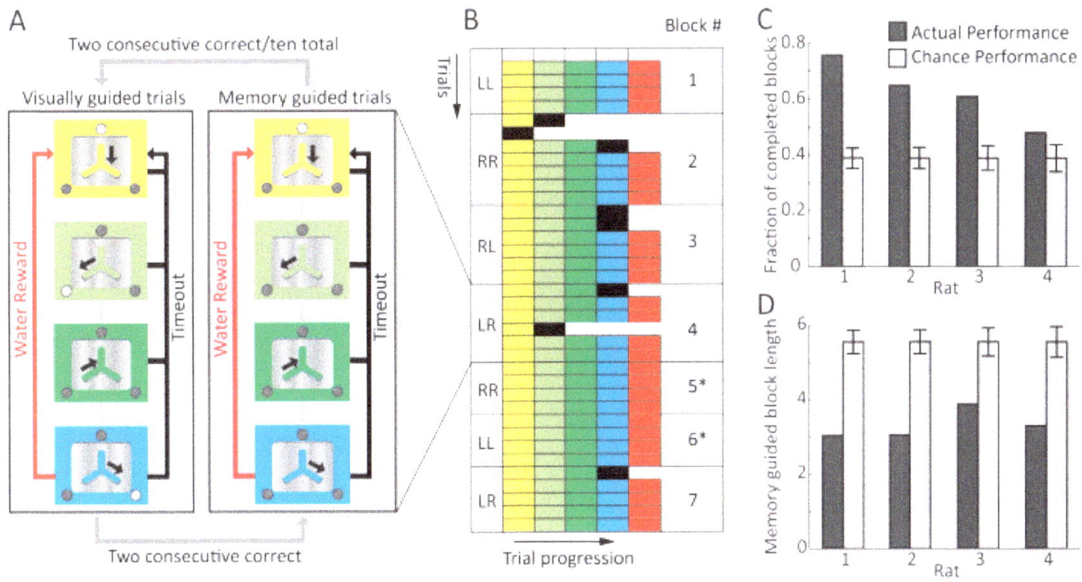


**Figure 3**: **Automated training of memory guided action sequences.**

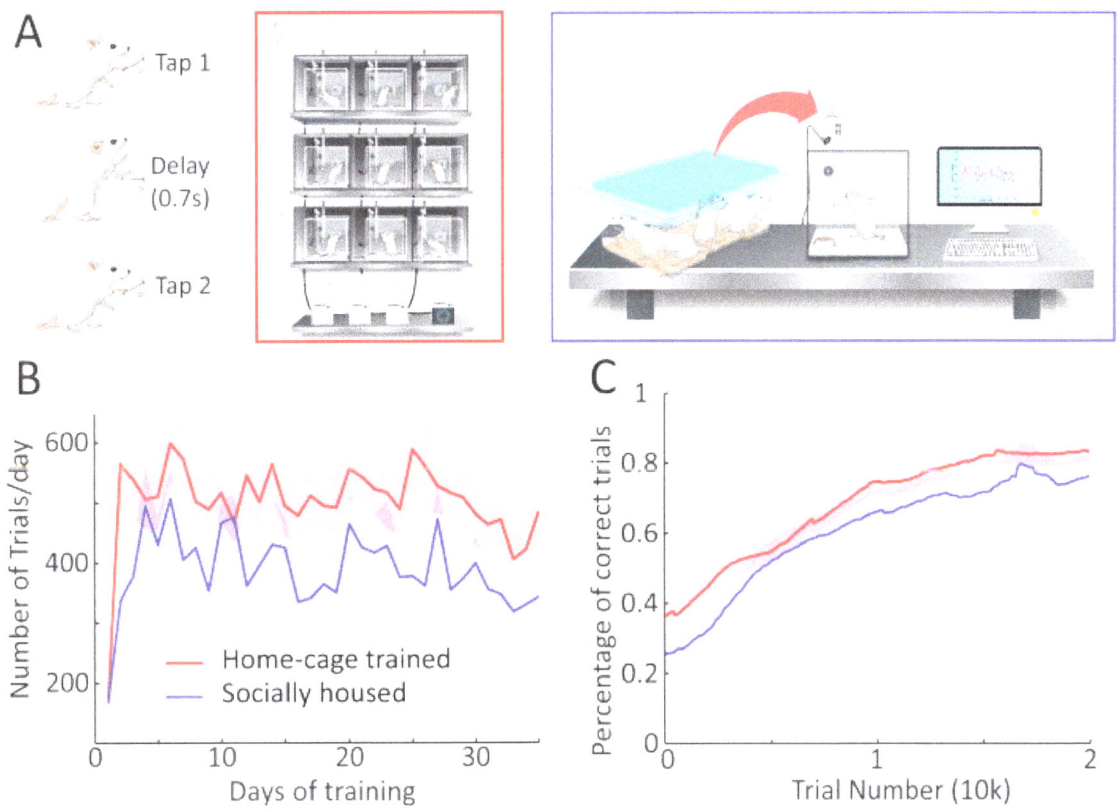


**Figure 4**: Fully automated live-in home-cage training is comparable to existing methods in terms of learning and performance.

## Ethics Statement

All experimental procedures were approved by the Harvard University Institutional Animal Care and Use Committee (protocol number: 29-15).

## *Schedules and mode of reinforcement*

Naïve rats were water-deprived for 8-10 hours before being transferred to their behavior boxes. After this, rats were trained for the next several weeks automatically by *ARTS* with no human involvement in the day-to-day training process. For the tasks in Figures 2 and 3, rats had 30-minute training sessions during their subjective night every 2 hours for a total of six training sessions. For the task in Figure 4, rats had 2 60-minute sessions per night. At the end of the night, ARTS automatically dispensed free water up to their daily minimum (5ml per 100g body weight). Rats also had a rest day every week during which water was dispensed *ad libitum*. Blinking house lights, a continuous 10s 1kHz pure tone and a few drops of water marked the beginning of each training and free water session.

### *Center-Out Task*

Rats were trained to move a 2D joystick left/right along two arms of an inverted-Y shaped slit (Figure 2). The equilibrium position of the joystick is at the top of the inverted-Y. Trial availability was indicated by the center LED; a rat could commence a trial by moving the joystick down by ~2 cm to the point where the two arms of the inverted-Y meet. Then, the left(right) LED turned on, and if the rat guided the joystick >5 cm along the left(right) arm of the slit, the trial was considered successful and a reward tone (1000Hz for 100ms) presented. The rat could then lick the reward spout to collect water and commence the next trial. If the rat moved in the wrong direction, a 7 second timeout was instituted before the next trial could be initiated.

### *Precise Lever Pressing Task*

Rats were trained to press a lever twice with a 700 ms delay between the presses. Animals could self-initiate the trial by pressing the lever. After learning to associate lever pressing with water, rats were rewarded for increasingly precise approximations to the target sequence, i.e. 2 lever presses separated by 700 ms. The reward contingencies were automatically updated based on performance to ensure that, on average, ~30-40% of the trials were rewarded. If the trial was successful, a reward tone was played and water reward dispensed upon licking of the reward spout. Animals had to wait 1.2s before initiating the next trial if the inter-press interval fell outside the rewarded range.

## SYSTEM VALIDATION

ARTS is designed for fully automated training of complex behaviors in a home cage environment and thus represents a significant departure from current practice. The day-to-day interaction of the researcher with experimental animals and training apparatus is eliminated as is the need for transferring animals back-and-forth between procedural chambers and holding rooms. Whether completely replacing the researcher with contextual cues can successfully get animals to learn complex tasks has not been evaluated. To ensure the feasibility of our approach as a general purpose solution for large-scale rodent training, we have done extensive testing and characterization of the system, including training more than hundred and fifty animals in a variety of sensorimotor tasks, a subset of which we report on below.

### Structure of Fully Automated Training

A major challenge presented by home-cage training is motivating animals to perform the behavioral task. In traditional reward-based training paradigms[10,15,27], the experimenter places a water- or food-deprived animal in the behavioral apparatus and rewards correct behaviors with liquids or foods. As hunger or thirst is satisfied, the researcher removes the animal and commences deprivation anew. We automate this process within the animal's home-cage by dispensing water as reward only during training sessions, the start and end of which are indicated to the animal by a set of salient sensory cues (e.g. flashing house lights). Time between sessions serves to deprive the animal of water and thus build up motivation for the next session. We have deployed a variety of session structures. For the center-out movement task described below (Figure 2B), for example, animals had 6 30-minute training sessions per day spaced at 2 hour intervals (Figure 2A), whereas for the task in Figure 4, we employed 3 daily 60-minute sessions, each separated by 4 hours. Whether a particular session structure is superior to others has yet to be rigorously tested, but our experience thus far suggests that this is not a critical parameter.

Animals quickly learn to engage with the task (e.g. manipulating a joystick) predominantly during specified training sessions: in the third week of training in the center-out task, the likelihood of a rat pressing the joystick was, on average, 24 times higher in-session than out-of-session (n = 24 rats; Figure 2A). To prevent poorly performing animals from dehydrating, water is provided at the end of the night for animals that do not receive the prescribed minimum daily water amount during training.

### Validation of Arts: Center-Out Movement Task

A standard paradigm for studying neural control of movement in primates is the center-out reaching task[32,33], which involves moving a manipulandum to one of several possible cued locations. Rats trained with traditional methods can master a version of this task in a matter of weeks[15]. In our implementation of the task, rats are required to move a two-dimensional joystick along the arms of an inverted Y-shaped slot with their forepaws (Figure 2B, Methods). Trials are initiated by moving the joystick down the vertical arm of the slot in response to an LED cue. A second LED then prompts the animal to move the joystick either left or right. A correct trial is indicated by a short tone followed by water reward. Thirty rats were trained on the task in three sequential stages, each containing multiple sub-stages. All but one rat completed the first training stage (touching the joystick for a reward tone and collecting water reward) within 12 hours. Twenty-four out of 30 rats completed the second (moving the joystick vertically down on cue) and third (moving the joystick left and right) training stage to criterion (Figure 2C, Methods). Despite being trained using the same training protocol, animals learned at different rates (time to complete all three stages = 148 ± 78 hrs (mean ± S.D.) from start of training, range = 73 - 299 hrs, n = 24 rats). Furthermore, learning rates on one training stage was not a good predictor for mastery of other stages, which involved different sets of cognitive, learning and motor control challenges. The correlation coefficients between the time to complete different stages were -0.05 (stage 1, 2), -0.18 (stage 2, 3), and -0.34 (stage 1, 3) respectively (n = 24 rats; Figure 2D). Faced with such a substantial variation in the speed of learning across subjects and in distinct phases of learning, studies on complex learning that use learning rate as a behavioral readout will require large cohorts of animals trained in identical tasks, an approach that will be much helped by automated high-throughput training systems.

### Validation of Arts: Memory Guided Motor Sequence Execution

Having the capacity to simultaneously and effortlessly train large groups of animals, reduces the risk associated with -

and the investment made in – individual animals, making it feasible to train even very challenging tasks, i.e. ones that only a small fraction of animals may be capable of learning. We deployed our automated training set-up to explore whether rats can master sophisticated motor sequence learning paradigms previously used only in primates[2]. In particular we were interested in the extent to which rodents can execute action sequences from working memory[34]. We trained the 4 best rats in the center-out task (Figure 2) to make sequences of left/right joystick movements from memory (Figure 3A). At the beginning of each block of trials, visual cues (LEDs) were used to instruct the correct sequence of movements. After 2 consecutive correct visually guided trials, cues were removed and animals had to perform the same movement sequence from memory. Rats progressed to the next block (i.e. new sequence) after 2 consecutive correct memory guided trials or 10 trials, whichever occurred first.

Figure 3B shows an example of the star performer in this task once asymptotic performance was reached. The errors in the visually guided trials at the start of some blocks are typically due to the animal performing the sequence from the prior block.

To measure the extent of learning, we compared a week's performance on the task to simulated chance (Figures 3C,D), modeled as random left/right movements during the memory guided trials. All 4 rats completed significantly more blocks (i.e. got 2 consecutive correct memory guided trials within a span of 10 trials) than expected by chance (Figure 3C, fraction of completed blocks = 63% vs. 39% by chance; probability of observing performance by chance $< 2e{-4}$). Furthermore, the average number of memory guided trials required to complete a block (which can range from 2 to 10) was substantially smaller than chance levels for each animal (Figure 3D, 3.2 vs. 5.4 for chance; probability of observing performance by chance $< 1e{-4}$). The best rat completed over 75% of the blocks with, on average, only 3 memory guided trials per block. These results validate rodents as a model for working memory guided motor sequence generation, and ARTS as an efficient method for training such complex behaviors.

## Benchmarking Home-Cage Training Against Existing Training Methods

To benchmark the live-in training concept against more traditional methods, we compared the performances of rats trained in our home-cage set-up (n = 24 rats) with ones housed in social groups and exposed to the behavior apparatus only during daily training sessions (n = 13 rats) (Figure 4A). Both groups were trained in identical behavioral boxes using the same automated training protocol. Rats were trained to spontaneously press a lever twice with a 700 ms delay between presses (Figure 4A, Methods). Motivation to do the task, as measured by the number of trials initiated per day, was similar between the two groups (494 ± 243 (mean ± S.D.) trials per day for automated training vs. 426 ± 123 trials per day for manual training on day 15 of training; Figure 4B). Furthermore, learning rates, as characterized by the fraction of 'correct' trials (defined here as inter-press intervals within 30% of the 700 ms target) at 20,000 trials was also comparable (83% ± 8% for automated training vs. 76% ± 17% for manual training, $p=0.22$; Figure 4C). Beyond demonstrating the feasibility and non-inferiority of live-in training in terms of performance, our results also validate the use of our automated training system in cases when rats are transferred to behavior boxes only for the duration of training. While home-cage training has the obvious advantage of requiring no human involvement other than standard animal care, there may be scenarios in which the benefits of fully automated home-cage training outweigh the negative effects of social isolation[35,36]. In such instances ARTS can still automate all other aspects of training (as was done for the socially housed cohort in the precise lever pressing task, Figure 4). An added benefit of manually transferring animals to the behavior box during training sessions is that the same box can be multiplexed across many animals increasing the throughput of the system[19,26].

## DISCUSSION

We present a cost-effective, modular, and fully automated training system for rodents (ARTS, Figure 1) that dramatically decreases the effort required for implementing operant learning paradigms. Deploying the system in our animal facility enabled high-throughput training of rats with performance and learning rates similar to more traditional methods (Figure 4). While we benchmarked our system in a variety of motor learning tasks (Figures 2,3 and 4) we believe that its flexibility, modularity, and extensibility ensures that it can be used to automate virtually any training protocol relying on reward-based learning.

Though we designed and benchmarked ARTS for rats, a simple modification to the geometry of the home-cage should make the system applicable also to mice, though the extent to which mice are amenable to fully automated training in our system remains to be seen.

Simple behavioral tests in rodents have revolutionized our understanding of neurological function by allowing large-scale phenotyping of experimental animals[37]. Automated training further extends the power of rodent models in neuroscience by enabling standardized high-throughput studies of more complex behaviors[30]. Full automation also removes the vagaries inherent to human-assisted training by requiring explicit codification of all training steps, including contingencies and criteria for progressing from one stage to the next. Such a compact and complete description of the training process makes reproducing and comparing experimental outcomes across different animal cohorts and labs possible and meaningful.

Automated training protocols not only standardize the training process, but they ensure that incremental insights and improvements to training strategy accumulate. Indeed, our experience in setting up novel training tasks is that their implementation improves with time, as inefficiencies and 'bugs' in the training protocol get sorted out. In contrast to human-assisted training, where these experiential gains are largely confined to the researcher, automated training ensures that each improvement becomes part of an ever-evolving protocol.

Having well defined discrete training stages, each associated with its distinct set of cognitive, learning, perceptual, or motor control challenges, also enables increased specificity of the behavioral analysis. For example, when we analyzed learning rates in different phases of a multi-stage task we found no correlation between them, meaning that facility with associative learning aspects of a task, for example, may not translate into success on motor learning aspects (Figure 2D). Breaking down the learning process to its elementary components by evaluating each training stage independently will permit a more detailed phenotypic analysis and thus help better pinpoint how specific manipulations, genetic or otherwise, impact learning and performance of complex multi-faceted behaviors.

The advantages of home-cage training go beyond the benefits of full automation. It eliminates animal handling and the performance variability that goes with it[25] and fully automated continuous long-term neural recordings in behaving animals a feasible prospect. An initial practical concern with home-cage training, however, was the possible impact of social isolation on learning and performance[35,36]. In our benchmarking, however, we did not see a difference in either motivation or learning rates as compared to animals that were housed socially and exposed to the behavioral chamber only during training (Figure 4). It is possible that any detrimental effect of social isolation is compensated for by other factors unique to automated training, such as precise and regimented training schedules. Further experiments are needed to fully characterize the effects of social isolation on motivation and learning in a home-cage setting, with the understanding that different tasks may be impacted differently.

Lowering the barrier for training large number of animals on complex behavioral tasks, as ARTS does, has the potential to accelerate research towards understanding many fundamental questions in neuroscience.

## ACKNOWLEDGMENTS

The software architecture was inspired by BControl, a behavioral control system developed in the lab of Carlos Brody. We thank Edward Soucy, Joel Greenwood, Yohsuke Miyamoto, Adam Kampff and Claude Wang for help in building and assembling the system and Rene Chen for illustrations. We also thank David Cox, Naoshige Uchida, Ashesh Dhawale, Adam Kampff, Selmaan Chettih, and Edward Soucy for comments on the manuscript.

## REFERENCES

1. Platt ML, Glimcher PW (1999) Neural correlates of decision variables in parietal cortex. Nature 400: 233–238.10.1038/22268 PubMed: 10421364
2. Tanji J (2001) Sequential Organization of Multiple Movements: Involvement of Cortical Motor Areas. Annu Rev Neurosci 24: 631–651.10.1146/annurev.neuro.24.1.631 PubMed: 11520914
3. Shadlen MN, Newsome WT (2001) Neural Basis of a Perceptual Decision in the Parietal Cortex (Area LIP) of the Rhesus Monkey. J Neurophysiol 86: 1916–1936 PubMed: 11600651
4. Newsome WT, Britten KH, Movshon JA (1989) Neuronal correlates of a perceptual decision. Nature 341: 52–54.10.1038/341052a0 PubMed: 2770878
5. Goodman S, Check E (2002) Animal experiments: The great primate debate. Nature 417: 684–687.10.1038/417684a PubMed: 12066153
6. Zeeb FD, Robbins TW, Winstanley CA (2009) Serotonergic and Dopaminergic Modulation of Gambling Behavior as Assessed Using a Novel Rat Gambling Task. Neuropsychopharmacology 34: 2329–2343.10.1038/npp.2009.62 PubMed: 19536111
7. Murphy RA, Mondragón E, Murphy VA (2008) Rule Learning by Rats. Science 319: 1849–1851.10.1126/science.1151564 PubMed: 18369151
8. Viana DS, Gordo I, Sucena É, Moita MAP (2010) Cognitive and Motivational Requirements for the Emergence of Cooperation in a Rat Social Game. PLOS ONE 5: e8483.10.1371/journal.pone.0008483PubMed: 20084113
9. Blaisdell AP, Sawa K, Leising KJ, Waldmann MR (2006) Causal Reasoning in Rats. Science 311: 1020–1022.10.1126/science.1121872 PubMed: 16484500
10. Zoccolan D, Oertelt N, DiCarlo JJ, Cox DD (2009) A rodent model for the study of invariant visual object recognition. Proceedings of the National Academy of Sciences of the USA 106: 8748–8753.10.1073/pnas.0811583106
11. Uchida N, Mainen ZF (2003) Speed and accuracy of olfactory discrimination in the rat. Nat Neurosci 6: 1224–1229.10.1038/nn1142 PubMed: 14566341
12. Kepecs A, Uchida N, Zariwala HA, Mainen ZF (2008) Neural correlates, computation and behavioural impact of decision confidence. Nature 455: 227–231.10.1038/nature07200 PubMed: 18690210
13. Raposo D, Sheppard JP, Schrater PR, Churchland AK (2012) Multisensory Decision-Making in Rats and Humans. J Neurosci 32: 3726–3735.10.1523/JNEUROSCI.4998-11.2012 PubMed: 22423093
14. Ölveczky BP (2011) Motoring ahead with rodents. Curr Opin Neurobiol 21: 571–578.10.1016/j.conb.2011.05.002 PubMed: 21628098
15. Slutzky MW, Jordan LR, Bauman MJ, Miller LE (2010) A new rodent behavioral paradigm for studying forelimb movement. J Neurosci Methods 192: 228–232.10.1016/j.jneumeth.2010.07.040 PubMed:20691727
16. Brown VJ, Bowman EM (2002) Rodent models of prefrontal cortical function. Trends Neurosci 25: 340–343.10.1016/S0166-2236(02)02164-1 PubMed: 12079756
17. Nudo RJ, Frost S (2009) The Evolution of Motor Cortex and Motor Systems. Evolutionary Neuroscience; Kaas JH, editor. Academic Press
18. Sereno MI, Allman JM (1991) Cortical Visual Areas in Mammals (Leventhal AG, editor. The Neural Basis of Visual Function. Macmillan, London: pp. 160–172
19. Erlich JC, Bialek M, Brody CD (2011) A Cortical Substrate for Memory-Guided Orienting in the Rat. Neuron 72: 330–343.10.1016/j.neuron.2011.07.010 PubMed: 22017991
20. Dombeck DA, Khabbaz AN, Collman F, Adelman TL, Tank DW (2007) Imaging Large-Scale Neural Activity with Cellular Resolution in Awake, Mobile Mice. Neuron 56: 43–57.10.1016/j.neuron.2007.08.003PubMed: 17920014

21. Ghosh KK, Burns LD, Cocker ED, Nimmerjahn A, Ziv Y et al. (2011) Miniaturized integration of a fluorescence microscope. Nat Methods 8: 871–878.10.1038/nmeth.1694 PubMed: 21909102
22. Zhang F, Aravanis AM, Adamantidis A, de Lecea L, Deisseroth K (2007) Circuit-breakers: optical technologies for probing neural signals and systems. Nat Rev Neurosci 8: 577–581.10.1038/nrn2192PubMed: 17643087
23. Luo L, Callaway EM, Svoboda K (2008) Genetic dissection of neural circuits. Neuron 57: 634–660.10.1016/j.neuron.2008.01.002 PubMed: 18341986
24. Crabbe JC, Wahlsten D, Dudek BC (1999) Genetics of Mouse Behavior: Interactions with Laboratory Environment. Science 284: 1670–1672.10.1126/science.284.5420.1670 PubMed: 10356397
25. Hurst JL, West RS (2010) Taming anxiety in laboratory mice. Nat Methods 7: 825–826.10.1038/nmeth.1500 PubMed: 20835246
26. Clark RE, Reinagel P, Broadbent NJ, Flister ED, Squire LR (2011) Intact Performance on Feature-Ambiguous Discriminations in Rats with Lesions of the Perirhinal Cortex. Neuron 70: 132–140.10.1016/j.neuron.2011.03.007 PubMed: 21482362
27. Mechan AO, Wyss A, Rieger H, Mohajeri MH (2009) A comparison of learning and memory characteristics of young and middle-aged wild-type mice in the IntelliCage. J Neuroscience Methods 180: 43–51.10.1016/j.jneumeth.2009.02.018
28. Gess A, Schneider DM, Vyas A, Woolley SMN (2011) Automated auditory recognition training and testing. Animal Behaviour 82: 285–293.10.1016/j.anbehav.2011.05.003 PubMed: 21857717
29. Bari A, Dalley JW, Robbins TW (2008) The application of the 5-choice serial reaction time task for the assessment of visual attentional processes and impulse control in rats. Nat Protoc 3: 759–767.10.1038/nprot.2008.41 PubMed: 18451784
30. Schaefer AT, Claridge-Chang A (2012) The surveillance state of behavioral automation. Curr Opin Neurobiol 22: 170–176.10.1016/j.conb.2011.11.004 PubMed: 22119142
31. Harel D (1987) Statecharts: a visual formalism for complex systems. Science of Computer Programming8: 231–274.10.1016/0167-6423(87)90035-9
32. Georgopoulos AP, Schwartz AB, Kettner RE (1986) Neuronal population coding of movement direction. Science 233: 1416–1419.10.1126/science.3749885 PubMed: 3749885
33. Moran DW, Schwartz AB (1999) Motor Cortical Representation of Speed and Direction During Reaching. J Neurophysiol 82: 2676–2692 PubMed: 10561437
34. Tanji J, Shima K (1994) Role for supplementary motor area cells in planning several movements ahead.Nature 371: 413–416.10.1038/371413a0 PubMed: 8090219
35. Chida Y, Sudo N, Mori J, Kubo C (2006) Social isolation stress impairs passive avoidance learning in senescence-accelerated mouse (SAM). Brain Res 1067: 201–208.10.1016/j.brainres.2005.10.042 PubMed:16332359
36. Ouchi H, Ono K, Murakami Y, Matsumoto K (2013) Social isolation induces deficit of latent learning performance in mice: a putative animal model of attention deficit/hyperactivity disorder. Behav Brain Res238: 146–153.10.1016/j.bbr.2012.10.029 PubMed: 23103401
37. Crawley JN (2008) Behavioral Phenotyping Strategies for Mutant Mice. Neuron 57: 809–818.10.1016/j.neuron.2008.03.001 PubMed: 18367082

# CHAPTER 14 EQUIVALENT LATITUDE COMPUTATION USING REGIONS OF INTEREST (ROI)

Juan A. Añel [1,2], Douglas R. Allen[3] , Guadalupe Sa´enz[1,4], Luis Gimeno[2], Laura de la Torre[2]

[1]Smith School of Enterprise and the Environment, University of Oxford, Oxford, United Kingdom,

[2]EPhysLab, Facultade de Ciencias, Universidade de Vigo, Ourense, Spain,

[3]Naval Research Laboratory, Washington, District of Columbia, United States of America,

[4]Departamento de Fısica, Facultad de Ciencias, Universidad de Extremadura, Badajoz, Spain

## ABSTRACT

**This paper introduces a novel algorithm to compute equivalent latitude by applying regions of interest (ROI). The technique is illustrated using code written in Interactive Data Language (IDL). The ROI method is compared with the "piecewiseconstant" method, the approach commonly used in atmospheric sciences, using global fields of atmospheric potential vorticity. The ROI method is considerably more accurate and computationally faster than the piecewise-constant method, and it also works well with irregular grids. Both the ROI and piecewise-constant IDL codes for equivalent latitude are included as a useful reference for the research community.**

## INTRODUCTION

In atmospheric sciences Equivalent Latitude ($\phi_e$) is a Lagrangian coordinate defined as the geographical latitude enclosing the same area as the isoline of a given atmospheric field on a 2D (longitude by latitude) surface [1], [2]. It is computed as:

$$\phi_e = arcsin[1-(A/(2\cdot\pi\cdot R^2))]$$

$R$: radius of the sphere (e.g. Earth's radius).

Therefore computing $\phi_e$ is simply the problem of computing the area $A$ enclosed by the isoline of the studied property, which is essentially the determination of a function from a subset of data points.

**Citation:** Añel JA, Allen DR, Sáenz G, Gimeno L, de la Torre L. Equivalent Latitude Computation Using Regions of Interest (ROI). Convertino M, ed. PLoS ONE. 2013;8(9):e72970. doi:10.1371/journal.pone.0072970.

One common technique to compute $\phi_e$ works by assuming the value of the atmospheric field to be constant within each grid cell (hereafter the 'piecewise-constant' method). To determine $\phi_e$ for a given threshold value of the field, you simply sum the areas for all grid cells with field values less than the threshold value.

$$A(q_0) = \sum_{i=0}^{n} A_n(q<q_0)$$

$q$: value of the field. $q_0$: value to be evaluated. $n$: grid cell.

The piecewise-constant approach is only first-order accurate, not allowing the atmospheric field to vary across the cell. Increased accuracy could be attained by higher-order approximations for the field variation (e.g., linear, parabolic, cubic interpolation). In this paper, we develop a higher-order solution to the problem of calculating $\phi_e$ by using contour mapping techniques. This approach, known also as regions of interest (ROI), is a well known concept in medical imaging and is also used for geographical information systems. The general approach involves defining a region from a field (up to 4D), which is selected for a posteriori analysis. That is, given a field or sample, a subsample is selected which meets certain properties and that is the region in which we are interested for further analysis. Here we limit the field variation to the surface of a sphere (2D). The use of ROI based on interpolated contours is more accurate than the piecewise-constant method, since it is a better approximation to the real function (exact area). This is illustrated in figure 1, which maps the areas enclosed by a threshold value of potential vorticity (PV) using both the piecewise-constant and ROI methods. This is an advantage when considering, for example, small isolated and closed contours, since the size of the grid becomes more important in order to take them into account or not. For example, the ROI method is more accurate to assess the real area of a closed contour when it is slightly smaller or bigger than a cell or subset of cells of the grid.

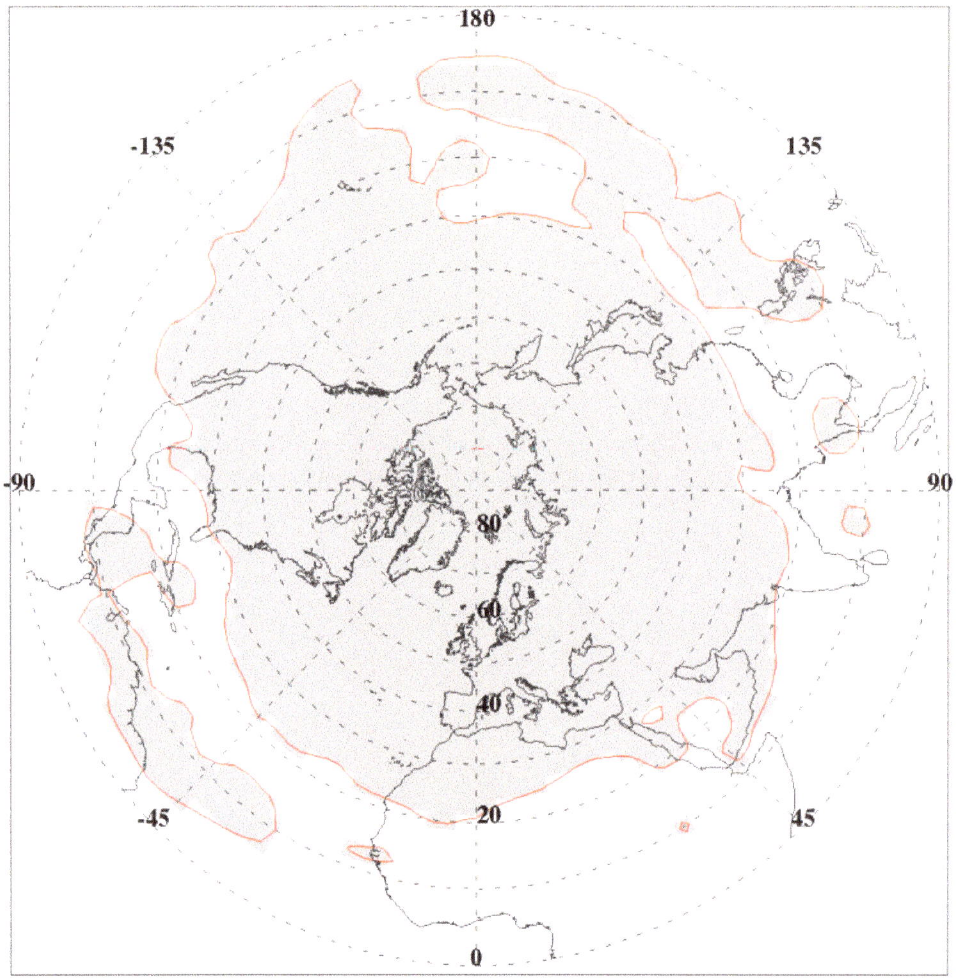


**Figure 1:** Comparison between the area used for the computation of $\phi_e$ by the piecewise-constant method (gray surface) and the ROI technique (surface inside red contours) for a grid size of 2.5°×2.5°.

The case corresponds to 1 January 1990 at OO UTC from NCEP1 for 2 PVU on an isentropic surface of 380 K.

In this paper we explore the ROI technique for the computation of $\phi_e$ and compare the performance and accuracy with that obtained using the piecewise-constant method. For the purposes of this paper the ROI will be a 2D field of atmospheric PV [3], usually measured in PV units (PVU), where

$$1PVU = 10^{-6}\frac{K\cdot m^2}{kg\cdot s}$$

The reason for this choice is that computation of $\phi_e$ from PV is commonly used in atmospheric sciences, applied for example to the study of the stratospheric polar vortex [4], [5], and the goal for which we originally developed this approach. The differences between both techniques and, explained in a basic way, the steps that we follow are:

- piecewise-constant technique (traditional):
    1. PV is assumed to be constant within each grid cell;
    2. compute the area of each cell which value is less than the PV threshold that we are interested in;
    3. sum the area of the cells from step 2
- ROI technique:
    1. PV is 'not' constant within each grid cell;
    2. make the contour mapping function 'draw' (interpolate) the isolines of PV;

3. compute the area enclosed by the isoline corresponding to the PV threshold value that we are interested in;

We developed the ROI code using the Interactive Data Language (IDL), a programming language extensively used for research in atmospheric sciences [6], and compare with piecewise-constant code also written in IDL. In this way we put the focus on the code and the technique, and do not take into account any dependence on programming language, corresponding libraries, or dependencies on hardware.

The following section describes the data used followed by the design and implementation of the ROI routine, addressing the ways in which we have solved the shortcomings of the computer language and subroutines affecting our implementation. This is followed by a results section that details the accuracy and performance of the ROI method relative to the piecewise-constant method. To conclude, we briefly discuss several ways of improving the solution here proposed, including using another programming languages and language interpreters.

## MATERIALS AND METHODS

### Previous Code and Data

Routines to compute $\phi_e$ are available through internet, e.g. the ones using the NCAR Command Language (http://www.ncl.ucar.edu/Applications/equiv_lat.shtml) or pascal (http://www.bodekerscientific.com/how-do-i/calculate-equivalent-latitude). To check our new methodology against the more traditional one, we use the code (not previously published) supplied as that applies the piecewise-constant method. This code takes as input a global gridded field with supplied latitude and longitude grids along with a desired threshold value of the field at which $\phi_e$ is calculated. The grid cells are sorted by the value of the field in each cell, and $\phi_e$ is calculated for every grid point on the globe. $\phi_e$ is then interpolated to the desired threshold value and is output to the user. A flow diagram is provided in figure 2.

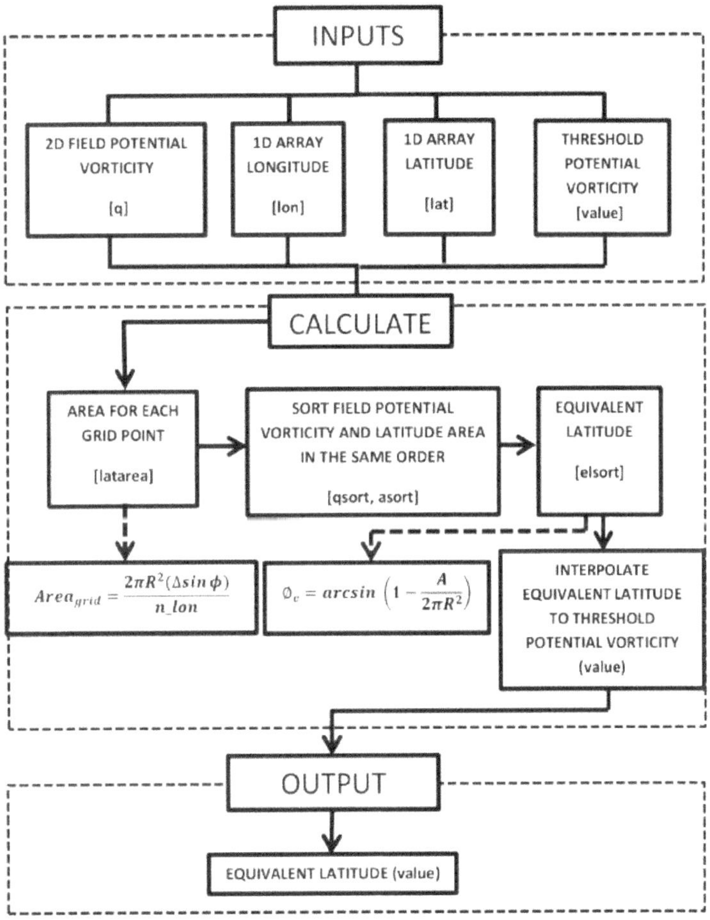


**Figure 2:** Flow diagram corresponding to the piecewise-constant code.

We have tested our new ROI routine using fields of PV computed for five sets of reanalyzed data (NCEP/NCAR (hereafter NCEP1) [7], NCEP/DOE (hereafter NCEP2) [8], JRA-25 [9], ERA-Interim [10]), MERRA [11] and one chemistry-climate model (WACCM3 [12]). Additional information about the computation of the fields of PV, the datasets and results obtained with this routine can be obtained from Añel et al. [13].

### Design and Implementation

The method here proposed is based on a simple idea: given the field that we want to study (PV), we just need to plot it using a global contour map and then to make use of the IDL tools to detect what parts of the field meet a criterion (in our case that the value is below a given PVU threshold). Then the area that meets the criterion is automatically computed by the ROI detection tools avilable in IDL and we just need to apply the corresponding equation to get $\phi_e$.

The first problem to be solved for the implementation of the computation of the area using ROI is to determine the configuration of a given isoline of a global field projected on a sphere (the planet). Depicting the field with a cylindrical projection, an isosurface of PV can show three different configurations, directly related to the shape of the isolines over this projection (seefigure 3):

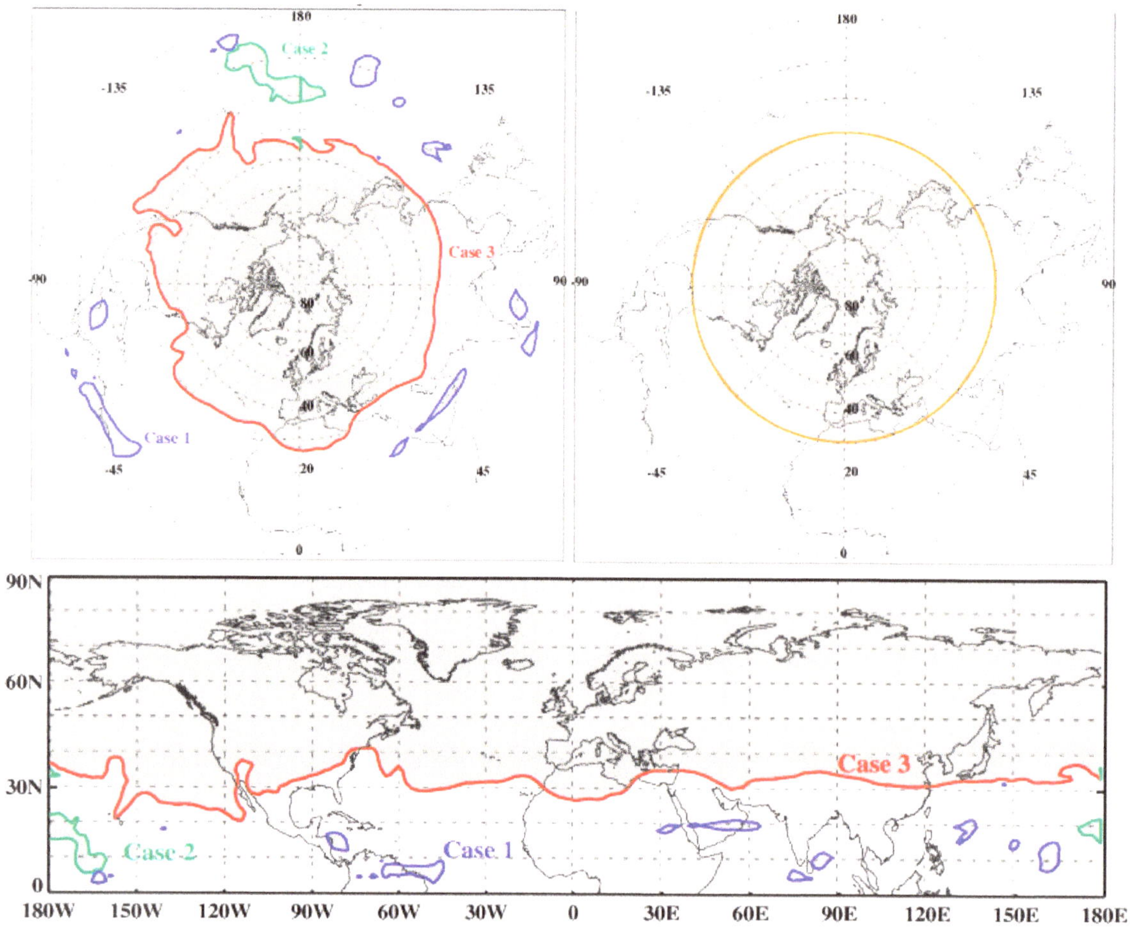


**Figure 3**: Upper left: global isosurface of 4 PVU on 1 January 1990 from ERA-Interim reanalysis data.

Upper right: $\phi_e$ corresponding to the area covered by the 4 PVU isosurface (in this case 30.41°). Lower panel: cylindrical projection corresponding to the upper left panel.

- case 1: contours closed for any region of the planet, the easiest problem as it requires just applying the computation of the area using the available routines for ROI;
- case 2: contours going through the meridian 180 and not enclosing the pole are not closed in a cylindrical projection, so they need to be split in two different contours (one in each hemisphere) and the area has to be computed as the sum of the two different areas;
- case 3: the contours around the poles are not closed in a cylindrical projection. They go from the the lowest to the highest value in longitude. They are closed using a large number of points (resolution of 0.1°) at the latitude near the pole (North or South) and then the enclosing area is calculated using routines for ROI.

Another problem addressed during the design of this code was that the computation of ROI in IDL gives erroneous negative values if one line of the isolines of PV drawn by the function 'contour' crosses itself. This happens mainly for latitudes near to the poles in rectangular grids where cell size and isolines get narrow and the IDL ROI implementation fails for unknown reasons. We solve this problem by increasing the latitudinal resolution in these regions, studying the ROI with a resolution of 0.1° to avoid the problem of crossing isolines.

It was also necessary to create new matrix of data in order to close the contours not closed in the cylindrical projection, just because for example they cut the meridian zero as we mentioned before. An additional problem was discovered for the computation of cosines for 90° and −90°. IDL presents a bug and the results are negative values instead of zero. To avoid this problem we close the contours in a latitude of 89.99° instead of 90°.

The IDLanROI class is used to determine the regions enclosing specified threshold values of PV, and it is combined with the application of the 'path_info' keyword in the Contour procedure. Also we had to take into account the difference between computation of the geometric area (the real value of the mathematical calculation) and the masked region (value from the pixels in the displayed area) when using ROI in IDL. Therefore we applied the Compute Geometry function to obtain the geometric area. Compute Geometry relies on the Contour procedure to get the function.

Finally, the total area to be passed to the routine to compute the equivalent latitude is considered as the addition of the values for the different partial areas obtained. We use −9999.99 for the total area when (according to 'path_info') there is not a corresponding contour for the threshold PV value that we try to evaluate.

The process is explained in a flow diagram in the figure 4.

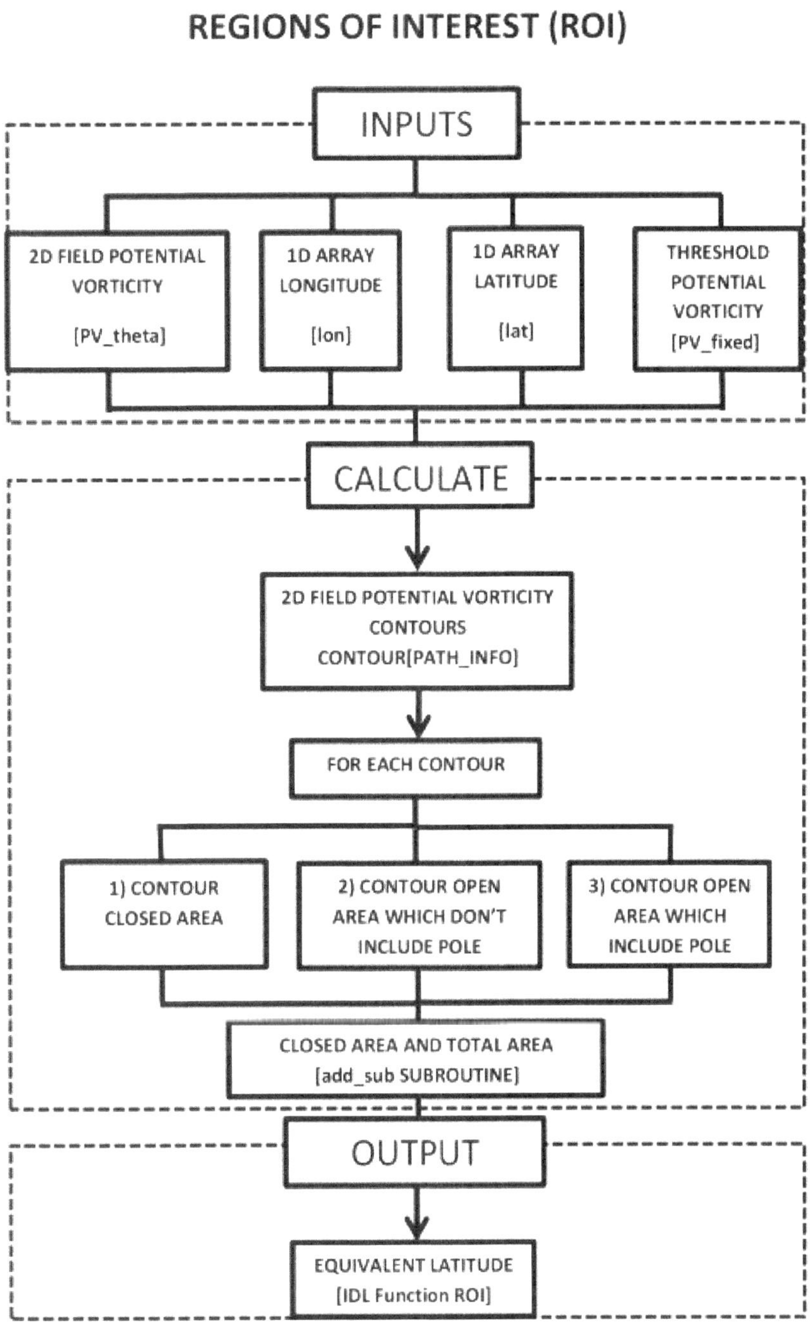


**Figure 4:** Flow diagram corresponding to the ROI code.

## RESULTS

### Precision

First, we checked that the ROI methodology produces reasonable results for $\phi_e$ at all latitudes and for different isentropic surfaces. Figure 5 shows $\phi_e$ calculated from ERA-Interim PV data on 1 January 1990 using both the piecewise-constant and ROI methods from 340 to 420 K potential temperature. It is clear that the two methods produce very similar results, although there are some differences (e.g., near 40°S at 340 K).

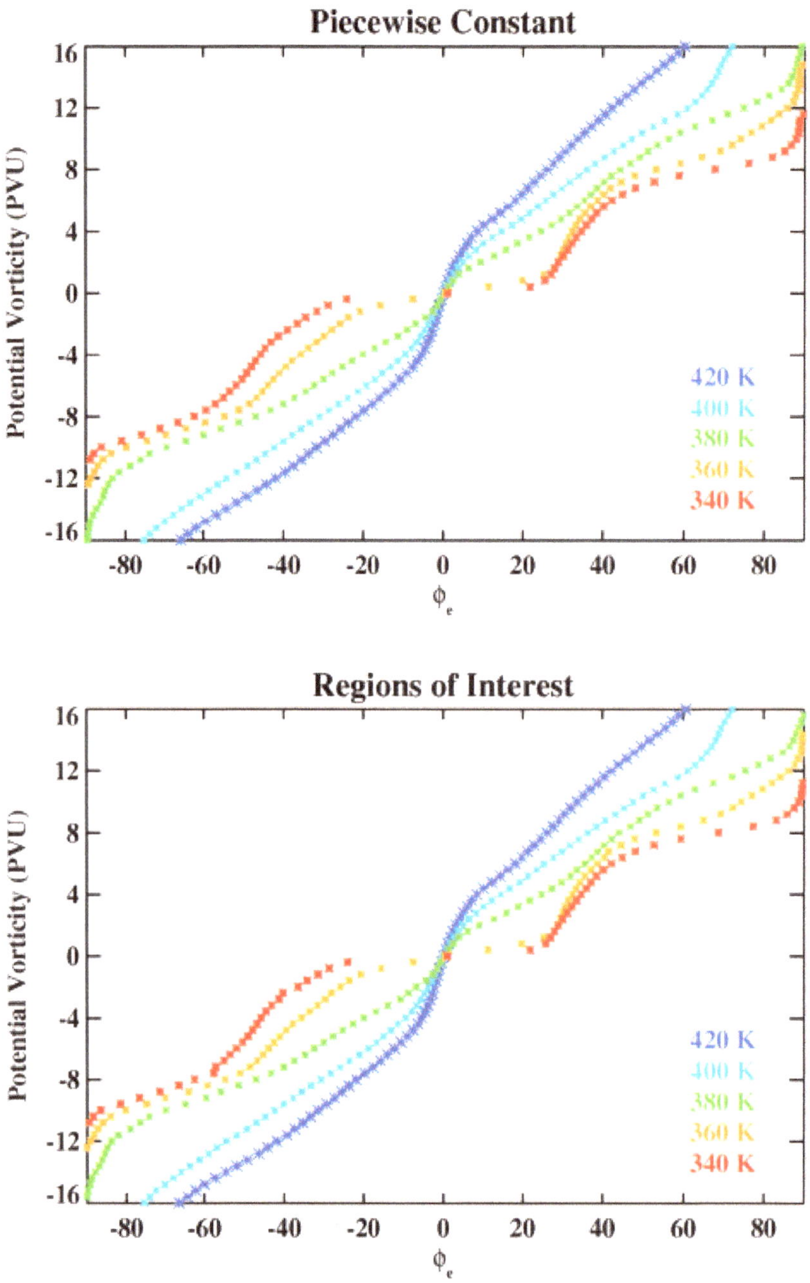


**Figure 5**: Comparison of PVU values for several isentropic surfaces and corresponding to different $\phi_e$.

Values computed using the piecewise-constant and ROI methods on 1 January 1990 from ERA-Interim data.

Next, in order to check the accuracy of both methods we computated $\phi_e$ for two different cases in which the PV field is not based on real data, but rather on an analytic function ($PV = latitude/10$ and $PV = ((latitude * sin(longitude))/10)$), so that we know the exact relationship between $\phi_e$ and PV. For the first case, the PV isolines form perfect circles around the pole and $\phi_e$ is simply equal to PV*10. In the second case we simply obtain a wavy field, but the relationship between $\phi_e$ and PV is the same. The PV fields generated in this way are then used as input for both methods and the results are compared. Figure 6 shows the results using the piecewise-constant and ROI routines for the first method and figure 7 for both of them. Also the tables 1 and 2 quantify the variation of the error for different grid sizes. As it can be seen for a grid of 1.5°×1.5° the piecewise-constant method shows a bias respect to the corresponding $\phi_e$ around a half degree for the first analytic function and 0.75 for the second one. This is greater than the bias for the ROI technique. Moreover the accuracy of the piecewise-constant method depends much more on the size of the grid (see both tables and figure 7).

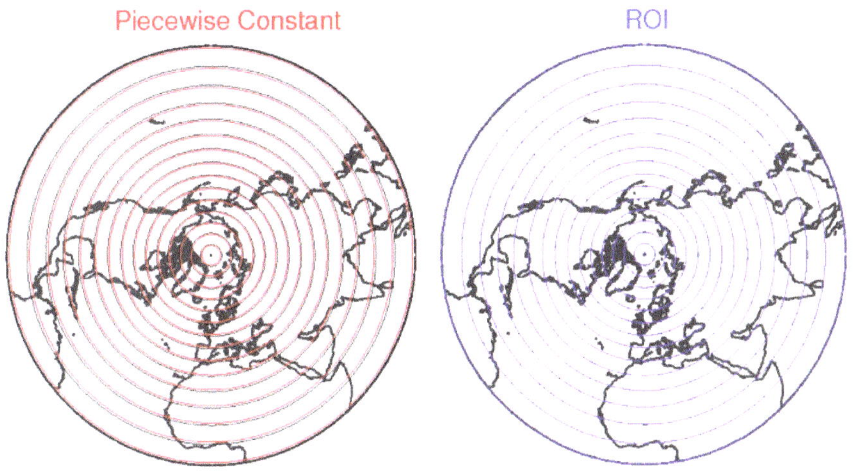


**Figure 6:** Red and blue circles: $\phi_e$ circles computed applying the piecewise-constant method and the ROI technique, respectively, from an ideal field of PV represented on a 2.5°×2.5° grid.

Black circles: real values of $\phi_e$ for the PV field studied (not seen for the case of the ROI technique as the blue ones are superimposed as they match perfectly the ideal field).

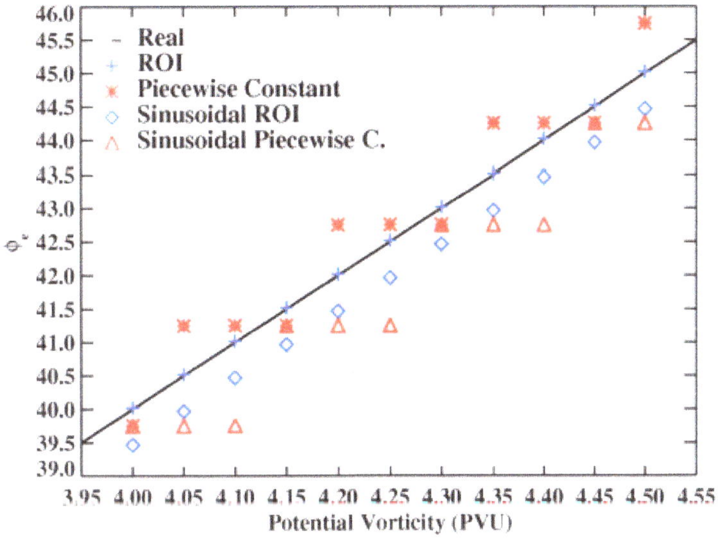


**Figure 7:** Accuracy of the ROI technique and the piecewise-constant method for different values of PV and latitude and for the two analytical functions.

**Table 1:** Precision dependence with technique and grid size in degrees for the PV field given by the first analytical function

| | ROI | piecewise-constant |
|---|---|---|
| 1,5°×1,5° | 0.030±0.025 | 0.415±0.237 |
| 3°×3° | 0.027±0.015 | 0.659±0.384 |
| 4,5°×4,5° | 0.029±0.020 | 1.145±0.660 |
| 6°×6° | 0.029±0.022 | 1.497±0.892 |

Mean absolute values computed as the difference between the $\phi_e$ given by each technique and the real one. Average and standard deviation resulting of the computation for 50 different PV isolines (25 in the Northern Hemisphere and 25 in the Southern Hemisphere).

**Table 2:** Precision dependence with technique and grid size in degrees for the PV field given by the second analytical function

| | ROI | piecewise-constant |
|---|---|---|
| 1,5°×1,5° | 0.540±0.010 | 0.746±0.415 |
| 3°×3° | 0.877±0.010 | 0.920±0.676 |
| 4,5°×4,5° | 0.801±0.010 | 1.255±0.836 |
| 6°×6° | 0.801±0.010 | 1.563±1.022 |

Mean absolute values computed as the difference between the $\phi_e$ given by each technique and the real one. Average and standard deviation computed following the same method that for table 1.

## Performance

As we can see in tables 3 and 4 the ROI technique computed in this way is faster than the piecewise-constant method for a grid of 1.5°×1.5°, and moreover the finer the grid the greater the advantage in computational time for the ROI technique. This is something to have into account as in the future we probably will be moving to smaller grid sizes. This result is probably because the piecewise-constant method relies for the evaluation of the values of the function in each point on several FOR loops, which makes especially slow any computation in IDL. However the ROI technique simply computes the function once.

**Table 3**: Computation time dependence with technique and grid size in $10^{-3}$seconds for the PV field given by the first analytical function.

| | ROI | piecewise-constant |
|---|---|---|
| 1,5°×1,5° | 4.09±0.16 | 36.97±0.25 |
| 3°×3° | 1.33±0.18 | 9.16±0.03 |
| 4,5°×4,5° | 0.83±0.18 | 4.18±0.02 |
| 6°×6° | 0.66±0.18 | 2.39±0.01 |

Average and standard deviation computed following the same method that for table 1.

**Table 4:** Computation time dependence with technique and grid size in $10^{-3}$seconds for the PV field given by the second analytical function.

| | ROI | piecewise-constant |
|---|---|---|
| 1,5°×1,5° | 4.13±0.17 | 43.13±0.79 |
| 3°×3° | 1.35±0.17 | 10.57±0.10 |
| 4,5°×4,5° | 0.85±0.17 | 4.82±0.04 |
| 6°×6° | 0.68±0.17 | 3.16±0.03 |

Average and standard deviation computed following the same method that for table 1.

The test was performed on a computer with the following hardware: Intel Quad 2 Core with cpu frequency of 2.66 GHz and 3 MB of cache memory, 3 GB of RAM memory. The operative system was Ubuntu GNU/Linux i686 with Linux kernel 2.6.32–37-generic. The IDL interpreter was provided by EXELIS and the version was 8.0.

## Availability and Future Directions

The ROI code described in this paper is publicly available from the URLhttps://github.com/eqlat/roi. As expressed in the code of the routine the code is under the GNU General Public License (GPL) (http://www.gnu.org/licenses). In this way we comply with the criteria on public availability of code for research purposes [14]. To work with it, it is just necessary to get the code and to have and IDL interpreter.

We suggest as potential future directions for development the possibility of writing an equivalent ROI code in Python or Fortran, two programming languages very used in the geociences community, but it should been had into account that very limited support for ROI computation seems to exist in both languages. To the authors knowledge just the NiPy library (http://nipy.sourceforge.net) for Python, currently under development, and some punctual implementations in Fortran. Also, currently is not possible to use the code based on ROI with GNUdatalanguage (http://gnudatalanguage.sourceforge.net), a free IDL compiler, as computation of ROI is not implemented in it.

## REFERENCES


1. Lary D, Chipperfield M, Pyle J, Norton W, Riishøjgaard L (1995) Three-dimensional tracer initialization and general diagnostics using equivalent PV latitude-potential-temperature coordinates. Q J R Meteorol Soc121: 187–210
2. Allen DR, Nakamura N (2003) Tracer equivalent latitude: A diagnostic tool for isentropic transport studies. J Atmos Sci 60: 287–304
3. McIntyre ME (2003) Potential Vorticity. In: Holton JR, Curry J, Pyle J, editors, Encyclopedia of Atmospheric Sciences, Academic Press, volume 2: 685–694
4. Butchart N, Remsberg E (1986) The area of the stratospheric polar vortex as a diagnostic for tracer transport on an isentropic surface. J Atmos Sci 43: 1319–1339
5. Schoeberl MR, Newman PA (2003) Polar Vortex. In: Holton JR, Curry J, Pyle J, editors, Encyclopedia of Atmospheric Sciences, Academic Press, volume 3: 1321–1328
6. Bowman KP (2006) An Introduction to programming with IDL: Interactive Data Language. Elsevier Academic Press, 286
7. Kalnay E, Kanamitsu M, Kistler R, Collins W, Deaven D, et al. (1996) The NCEP/NCAR 40-Year Reanalysis Project. Bull Amer Meteorol Soc 77: 437–471
8. Kanamitsu M, Ebisuzaki W, Woollen J, Yang S, Hnilo J, et al. (2002) NCEP-DOE AMIP-II Reanalysis (R-2). Bull Amer Meteorol Soc 83: 1631–1644
9. Onogi K, Tsutsui J, Koide H, Sakamoto M, Kobayashi S, et al. (2007) The JRA-25 Reanalysis. J Meteor Soc Japan 85: 369–432
10. Uppala SM, Kållberg PW, Simmons AJ, Andrae U, da Costa Bechtold V, et al. (2005) The ERA-40 re-analysis. Q J R Meteorol Soc 131: 2961–3012
11. Rienecker MM, Suarez MJ, Gelaro R, Todling R, Bacmeister J, et al. (2011) MERRA: NASA›s modern-era retrospective analysis for research and applications. J Clim 24: 3624–3648
12. Garcia RR, Marsh DR, Kinnison DE, Boville BA, Sassi F (2007) Simulation of secular trends in the middle atmosphere, 1950–2003. J Geophys Res 112: D09301
13. Añel JA, Gettelman A, Castanheira JM Tropical widening vs tropopause rising: a PV- perspective of the UTLS (submitted). PLoS ONE.
14. Añel JA (2011) The importance of reviewing the code. Communications of the ACM 54: 40–41

CHAPTER 15

# DISTMAP: A TOOLKIT FOR DISTRIBUTED SHORT READ MAPPING ON A HADOOP CLUSTER

Ram Vinay Pandey, Christian Schlötterer

Institut für Populationsgenetik, Vetmeduni Vienna, Vienna, Austria

## ABSTRACT

**With the rapid and steady increase of next generation sequencing data output, the mapping of short reads has become a major data analysis bottleneck. On a single computer, it can take several days to map the vast quantity of reads produced from a single Illumina HiSeq lane. In an attempt to ameliorate this bottleneck we present a new tool, DistMap - a modular, scalable and integrated workflow to map reads in the Hadoop distributed computing framework. DistMap is easy to use, currently supports nine different short read mapping tools and can be run on all Unix-based operating systems. It accepts reads in FASTQ format as input and provides mapped reads in a SAM/BAM format. DistMap supports both paired-end and single-end reads thereby allowing the mapping of read data produced by different sequencing platforms.**

## INTRODUCTION

Next Generation Sequencing (NGS) technologies have revolutionized biological research by producing an unprecedented amount of data in a cost effective manner. The rapid progress in NGS technology, however, has resulted in a subsequent increase in data volume that currently outpaces advances in computational power [1]. Hence there is a growing need for new software solutions that minimize the impact of increasing data volume on workflow duration. The first step in nearly all NGS workflows is the mapping of short sequence reads to a reference genome. As it may take several days to map NGS read data on a single computer, mapping is a potential bottleneck for most workflows. For this reason tools and software which support distributed computing are a powerful means to expedite mapping and the subsequent workflow.

At present several tools exist which support distributed mapping, each having specificities which may limit more general usage. For instance, Crossbow [2], Eoulsan [3] and FX [4], are designed for specific types of analyses, do not produce mapping output in SAM/BAM [5] format, and only support paired-end mapping. Similarly, SEAL [6] only supports paired-end BWA mapping using a sinlge version (0.5.8c), and is restricted to Linux operating systems. Other virtual machine workflows include Bio-Linux [7], Cloud Bio-Linux [8] and Galaxy [9]. Bio-Linux and Cloud Bio-Linux include a collection of useful bioinformatics tools, and the later has integrated MapReduce tools such as Crossbow [2], CloudBurst [10], SEAL [6] and bcbio-nextgen [11] but they have restrictions on mapper version and do not produce an

**Citation:** Pandey RV, Schlötterer C. DistMap: A Toolkit for Distributed Short Read Mapping on a Hadoop Cluster. Yan W, ed. PLoS ONE. 2013;8(8):e72614. doi:10.1371/journal.pone.0072614.

output in SAM/BAM format. Galaxy [9] is another powerful workflow system but supports only BWA and bowtie mapping and imposes version restrictions for both the mapper and the reference sequence.

Here we present a new tool, DistMap, a modular, scalable and user-friendly workflow, which facilitates the mapping of short reads on a Hadoop cluster [14]. DistMap supports nine different mappers – the most available in a single distributed mapping tool at present – and cover a wide range of NGS applications. Furthermore, DistMap allows mapping of paired-end and single-end reads from different sequencing platforms and produces mapping output in BAM/SAM file format, such that it can be used in conjunction with distributed downstream analytical tools such as GATK [12], and Hadoop-BAM [13]. Finally, the workflow has been developed specifically for adoption by non-expert users who wish to benefit from distributed NGS read mapping.

## RESULTS AND DISCUSSION

DistMap provides an integrated workflow for short read mapping against a user-specified reference genome. The whole workflow can be run with a single Perl command. This workflow is equipped with various customized parameters and provides detailed guidelines for its implementation. All components of DistMap and their inputs have been summarized in Figure 1. An overview of the key features are described below.

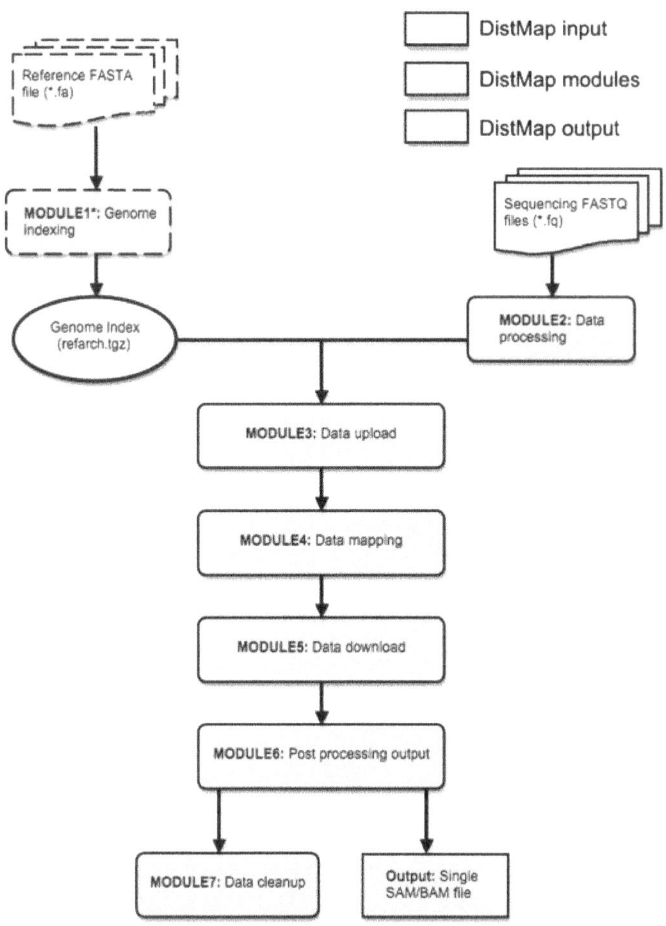


**Figure 1:** The workflow of DistMap.

The DistMap workflow has 7 modules. Modul 1 is to index reference fasta file. Module 2-6 are mandetory for each new FASTQ files. The DistMap entire workflow can be executed at once and if required each module can be executed one by one.

### An Integrated Workflow

DistMap provides a complete workflow that includes several modules. Each module has a start and stop point (shown in Figure 1). The user is provided with the flexibility to either execute the whole workflow or to execute individual modules one after another.

### Job Scheduler Support

DistMap is the only workflow, which supports the different job schedulers currently available for a Hadoop cluster. It supports three schedulers 1) FIFO [14] 2) Fair scheduler [15] and 3) Capacity scheduler [16]. The user can specify the scheduler information with the option *--hadoop-scheduler* within the Perl command.

### Custom Queue and Pool Support

DistMap is designed to manage the short read mapping on a large scale, whereby many custom queues and pools are available within the Hadoop cluster. Unlike other distributed mapping tools which only utilize a default queue, DistMap can also use customized queues and pools to run multiple mapping jobs in parallel. The queue assignment can be done with the option *–queue-name* to the Perl command.

## Custom Job Prioritization Support

DistMap supports a top-level job prioritization. The user can directly set job priority via the DistMap command line with the option *–job-priority*. Five priority levels are currently supported: VERY_LOW, LOW, NORMAL, HIGH and VERY_HIGH.

## Mapper Flexibility

The current version of DistMap (v 1.0) supports nine different mappers, covering a broad spectrum of NGS applications. Table 1 provides the corresponding version of all mapping software that has been used for testing. DistMap does not impose a version restriction for any mapper, whereby the user can download and compile any version for direct implementation within their specific workflow.

**Table 1:** List of mappers supported in current version of DistMap

| Mapper supported in DistMap | Version tested | Application |
|---|---|---|
| **BWA** | 0.5.8c | Short read mapping |
| **bowtie** | 0.12.7 | Short read mapping |
| **Bowtie2** | 2.0.6 | Short read mapping |
| **GSNAP** | 2012-07-20 | RNA-Seq Alignment DNA methylation |
| **SOAP** | 2.20 | Short read mapping |
| **STAR** | 2.2.0c | RNA-Seq Alignment |
| **Bismark** | v 0.7.7 | Bisulfite mapping |
| **BSMAP** | 2.73 | Bisulfite mapping |
| **TopHat** | 2.0.6 | RNA-Seq mapping |

Nine short read mappers for a wide range of NGS applications are supported. DistMap can use any version of these mappers.

## Flexibility and Transparency

DistMap imposes no restriction on the assembly version of the reference genome for mapping. Since DistMap does genome indexing itself during the execution of the workflow it is possible to map short reads with any reference genome assembly. DistMap collects all input files and parameters from a local computer and returns the final output to a local output directory as a single SAM or BAM file. There is no need to install the DistMap source code or mapper executables on all working nodes. The entire DistMap workflow can be run at once or in step-by-step fashion, such that the user can start from any step in the workflow. DistMap supports paired-end, single-end and mixed mapping of FASTQ formatted reads produced from various sequencing platforms. DistMap archives the genome index as a *. tgz file in the local output directory such that it can be re-used in subsequent mapping and thereby avoids unnecessarily re-indexing of the same genomes.

## Scalability

DistMap has no restriction on NGS data handling; it is specifically designed to map Gigabytes or Terabytes of sequencing data with a single command. The speed of DistMap scales with cluster size. Several different datasets ranging in size were used to test the scalability of the DistMap workflow on a Hadoop cluster (see Table 2)

**Table 2:** DistMap evaluation input datasets

| Number of read pairs (million) | Size (GB) | Read length (bp) |
|---|---|---|
| **5** | 2.46 | 100 |
| **50** | 24.7 | 100 |
| **100** | 49.4 | 100 |
| **200** | 98.82 | 100 |
| **500** | 247.04 | 100 |

These NGS data were generated from Illumina HiSeq sequencer. 100bp paired-end reads from *Drosophila melanogaster* genomes.

## \DistMap Evaluation

To evaluate the performance of DistMap we used paired-end genomic reads of 2x100bp from a*Drosophila melanogaster* pooled sequencing project [17] (see Table 2 for further information). The Hadoop cluster (version 1.0.3) consisted of 13 nodes running Mac OSX 10.6.8. For each node 10 CPUs, 32 GB RAM and 1TB SATA hard disk space was made available. All computer nodes were connected via Gigabit Ethernet.

We evaluated the performance of DistMap by comparing the execution time of four different mappers (BWA, bowtie, GSNAP and SOAP) for multiple datasets ranging in size, each time using a single worker node and a fixed set of parameters (see Figure 2 and Table 3). We found that DistMap execution time scales almost linearly with increase of input size, whereas single node execution increased exponentially. In particular, as data size increases beyond 500 million reads, DistMap had between 20-fold to 80-fold reduction in processing time relative to a single computer for the mappers tested. We reason that the non-linear scaling observed for the single node results from non-parallelized steps in the mapping procedure. For example, BWA only uses a single processor for the *sampe/samse* module, regardless of the number of processors on that computer. In contrast, DistMap can make use of all cluster nodes and their processors by splitting the data into subsets, which are later reassembled. Thus, by distributing mapping across several computers, DistMap avoids probable workflow bottlenecks caused by mapping on a single computer.

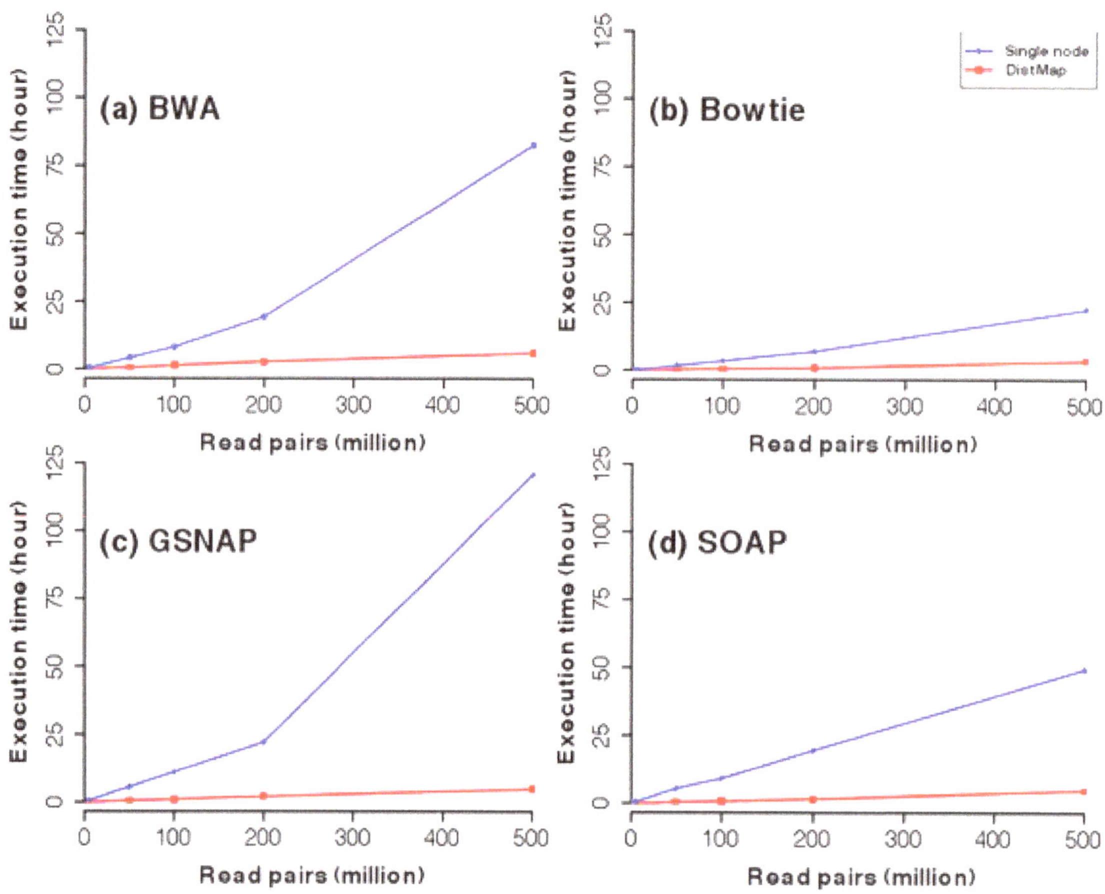


**Figure 2:** Evaluation of DistMap execution time with increase of data size.

Execution times were measured for different mappers using DistMap (red line) and compared to a single node (blue line). Datasets of different size (5, 50, 100, 200 and 500 million read pairs) from different pool-Seq experiments were used to estimate the scalability of DistMap. The hardware configuration of the single node was a Mac OSX 10.6.8 computer with 10 CPU, 32 GB RAM and 1TB Disk space available for mapping. The Hadoop cluster consists of 13 worker nodes with the same configuration. (**a**) BWA mapping (**b**) bowtie mapping, (**c**) GSNAP mapping, (**d**) mapping. All mappers were run with the same default parameters and datasets.

**Table 3:** Comparison of running time in hours of different mappers **on a single node with 10 cores and DistMap running on 13 nodes.**

| **Number of read pairs (million)** | **Mapper** | **DistMap time (hour, 13 nodes)** | **Mapper time (hour, 1 node)** |
|---|---|---|---|
| **5** | BWA | 0.12 | 0.47 |
| **50** | BWA | 0.70 | 4.22 |
| **100** | BWA | 1.40 | 8.33 |
| **200** | BWA | 2.78 | 19.35 |
| **500** | BWA | 6.05 | 82.73* |
| **5** | bowtie | 0.10 | 0.18 |
| **50** | bowtie | 0.30 | 1.77 |
| **100** | bowtie | 0.68 | 3.50 |

| | | | |
|---|---|---|---|
| **200** | bowtie | 0.97 | 7.10 |
| **500** | bowtie | 3.43 | 22.38 |
| **5** | GSNAP | 0.1 | 0.63 |
| **50** | GSNAP | 0.57 | 5.62 |
| **100** | GSNAP | 1.07 | 11.12 |
| **200** | GSNAP | 2.17 | 22.13 |
| **500** | GSNAP | 4.97 | 120.75* |
| **5** | SOAP | 0.08 | 0.52 |
| **50** | SOAP | 0.47 | 5.48 |
| **100** | SOAP | 0.87 | 9.2 |
| **200** | SOAP | 1.68 | 19.63 |
| **500** | SOAP | 4.88 | 49.4 |

## Reproducibility and Accuracy

We estimated the reproducibility, fault tolerance and data security of DistMap by mapping 5 million read pairs multiple times for each of the BWA, bowtie, GSNAP and SOAP mappers. Fault tolerance and data security were specifically tested by randomly deactivating nodes during an active mapping job. Even with random node deactivation, however, mapping results were found to be identical across the five independent runs for each mapper. Indeed, because DistMap makes a minimum of three copies of each data block, each distributed to a different node, data loss is highly improbable.

## Comparison with Existing Tools

DistMap can be run on any Unix system as a single Perl command and has many user-friendly features, which enable both advanced and non-expert users to map NGS reads using distributed computing. The workflow can be executed as a whole or individual modules can be executed one after another. A comparison of the most important features of DistMap to other available tools is given in Table 4.

**Table 4:** Comparison of various features of DistMap and other tools for distributed mapping

| Features | Crossbow v 1.2.0 | SEAL v 0.1.0 | Eoulsan v 1.1.6 | FX v 1.0.4 | DistMap v 1.0 | Galaxy |
|---|---|---|---|---|---|---|
| **SAM output** | no | no | no | no | yes | yes |
| **BAM output** | no | no | no | no | yes | yes |
| **Pair-end Mapping** | yes | yes | yes | yes | yes | yes |
| **Single-end Mapping** | yes | no | no | no | yes | yes |
| **Bisulfite Mapping** | no | no | no | no | yes | no |
| **Installation required** | yes | yes | yes | yes | no | yes |
| **Dependency** | yes | yes | yes | yes | no | yes |
| **Operating system** | All Unix | Only Linux | Only Linux | All OS | All Unix | All OS |
| **Mappers (complied)** | bowtie | BWA | BWA, bowtie, SOAP, GSNAP | GSNAP | BWA, bowtie, Bowtie2, GSNAP, SOAP, STAR, TopHat, TopHat2, Bismark, BSMAP | bowtie, BWA |
| **Mapper version dependency** | no | yes | yes | yes | no | yes |
| **Reference sequence version dependency** | no | no | no | no | no | yes |
| **Custom queue/pool support** | no | no | no | no | yes | no |
| **Fair scheduler and Capacity scheduler** | no | no | no | no | yes | no |

## MATERIALS AND METHODS

### Implementation

The DistMap was developed in Perl 5.8.8 [18] to map millions of short reads produced from a single NGS experiment in a distributed manner. The mapping module of DistMap is based on the MapReduce programming algorithm [19], which runs on the Hadoop cluster. There is no dependency required to use DistMap except a working Hadoop cluster. The minimum input requirements to run DistMap on any Unix operating system are (1) executables of the required mapping software, (2) MergeSamFiles.jar and SortSam.jar, two jar files from PICARD [20], (3) access to a Hadoop cluster, (4) FASTQ formatted reads (paired-end, single end or mixed) and (5) a FASTA formatted reference genome.

### Hadoop and MapReduce

Hadoop is an open source software framework, which can be installed and run on commodity computers and enables large-scale distributed data analysis. There are two components of Hadoop (1) a fault-tolerant and robust Hadoop Distributed File System (HDFS) and (2) MapReduce: a java-based API, which enables parallel computing across all nodes of a cluster.

Currently nine different mappers are supported in DistMap: BWA [21], bowtie [22], Bowtie2 [23], GSNAP [24], SOAP [25], STAR [26], Bismark [27], BSMAP [28] and TopHat [29], thereby supporting a wide range of biological applications (Table 1). While TopHat could be run on DistMap, we do not recommend this since the distributed mapping interferes with the identification of splice sites by TopHat. DistMap supports two different implementations of customized queuing systems: Capacity scheduler [26] and pool: Fair scheduler [27].

### DistMap Components

The DistMap workflow consists of seven main modules which can be executed either end-to-end by a single command, or each module can be executed by giving appropriate command line flags. The whole workflow is summarized in Figure 1.

### DistMap Input and Output

DistMap workflow takes the input from a local computer, performs the mapping of the reads on a Hadoop cluster, and stores the final output file on the local computer. No direct interaction between the user and the Hadoop cluster is needed. DistMap requires reference sequence data in FASTA format and short read data in FASTQ format. If the user has to map many datasets in a single DistMap run then it can be done via command line by using the option *–input* multiple times. The final output of DistMap is a single SAM or BAM file without any filtering. The user can request either a SAM or a BAM output file by using the DistMap command line option *–output-format*.

### Availability, Installation and Usage

DistMap is an open-source tool and is freely available for all researchers. The source code of the DistMap can be downloaded fromhttp://distmap.googlecode.com/files/DistMap_v1.0.tar.gz.

The user manual of DistMap is available on http://code.google.com/p/distmap/wiki/Manual.

Since DistMap was developed with easy use for non-expert researchers in mind, we provide a step-by-step guide to set up a Hadoop cluster on Linux computershttp://code.google.com/p/distmap/wiki/SetupHadoopLinux and on Macintosh computershttp://code.google.com/p/distmap/wiki/SetupHadoopMacintosh.

## CONCLUSIONS

DistMap is a user-friendly, modular, and integrated workflow for distributed mapping of NGS-generated short reads on a Hadoop cluster. Since in most NGS applications mapping is an essential and highly time intensive step, we believe that DistMap will be greatly expedite this process and the subsequent workflow. In comparison to other tools, DistMap stands out for its generality and flexibility, supporting nine different mappers that facilitate a range of different NGS-based analyses. The availability of multiple mappers means that DistMap can be readily integrated into many existing workflows without having to incorporate a new mapper. Similarly, the SAM/BAM output format was chosen to be compatible with the most widely used downstream analytical tools. Furthermore, unlike other distributed read mapping tools, DistMap supports customized queuing, multiple job schedulers, and job prioritization within a queue. Finally, DistMap was built to be accessible to novice and advanced users alike, being executed via a single Perl command. To help facilitate its use an extensive user manual and the step-by-step instructions for setting up a Hadoop cluster on Macintosh or Linux computers are provided alongside the source code.

## ACKNOWLEDGMENTS

We are grateful to E. Versace for helpful discussions and suggestions on manuscript. We thank all members of the 'Institut für Populationsgenetik' for the DistMap testing and feedback. Special thanks to R. Tobler and T. Hill for revising the manuscript.

## REFERENCES

1. Taylor R (2010) An overview of the Hadoop/MapReduce/HBase framework and its current applications in bioinformatics. BMC Bioinformatics 11(Suppl 12): S1.10.1186/1471-2105-11-S10-P1
2. Langmead B, Schatz MC, Lin J, Pop M, Salzberg SL (2009) Searching for SNPs with cloud computing. Genome Biol 10(11): R134.10.1186/gb-2009-10-11-r134 PubMed: 19930550
3. Jourdren L, Bernard M, Dillies MA, Le Crom S (2012) Eoulsan: a cloud computing-based framework facilitating high throughput sequencing analyses. Bioinformatics 28(11): 1542–1543.10.1093/bioinformatics/bts165 PubMed: 22492314
4. Hong D, Rhie A, Park SS, Lee J, Ju YS et al. (2012) FX: an RNA-Seq analysis tool on the cloud. Bioinformatics 28(5): 721–723.10.1093/bioinformatics/bts023 PubMed: 22257667
5. Li H, Handsaker B, Wysoker A, Fennell T, Ruan J et

al. (2009) The sequence alignment/map (SAM) format and SAMtools. Bioinformatics 25: 2078–2079.10.1093/bioinformatics/btp352 PubMed: 19505943

6. Pireddu L, Leo S, Zanetti G (2011) SEAL a distributed short read mapping and duplicate removal tool.Bioinformatics 27(15): 2159–2160.10.1093/bioinformatics/btr325 PubMed: 21697132
7. Field D, Tiwari B, Booth T, Houten S, Swan D et al. (2006) Open software for biologists: from famine to feast. Nat Biotechnol 24(7): 801-803.10.1038/nbt0706-801 PubMed: 16841067
8. Krampis K, Booth T, Chapman B, Tiwari B, Bicak M et al. (2012) Cloud BioLinux: pre-configured and on-demand bioinformatics computing for the genomics community. BMC Bioinformatics 13: 42.10.1186/1471-2105-13-42 PubMed: 22429538
9. Goecks J, Nekrutenko A, Taylor J, Galaxy Team (2010) Galaxy: a comprehensive approach for supporting accessible, reproducible, and transparent computational research in the life sciences. Genome Biol11(8): R86.10.1186/gb-2010-11-8-r86 PubMed: 20738864
10. Schatz MC (2009) CloudBurst: highly sensitive read mapping with MapReduce. Bioinformatics 25: 1363-1369.10.1093/bioinformatics/btp236 PubMed: 19357099
11. https://github.com/chapmanb/bcbio-nextgen bcbio-nextgen. Available: . Accessed 2013 Jun 14.
12. McKenna A, Hanna M, Banks E, Sivachenko A, Cibulskis K et al. (2010) The Genome Analysis Toolkit: A MapReduce framework for analyzing next-generation DNA sequencing data. Genome Res 20(9): 1297–1303.10.1101/gr.107524.110 PubMed: 20644199
13. Niemenmaa M, Kallio A, Schumacher A, Klemelä P, Korpelainen E et al. (2012) Hadoop-BAM: directly manipulating next generation sequencing data in the cloud. Bioinformatics 28(6): 876–877.10.1093/bioinformatics/bts054 PubMed: 22302568
14. http://hadoop.apache.org/ Apache. Hadoop. Available: . Accessed 2013 Jun 14.
15. http://hadoop.apache.org/docs/r1.2.0/capacity_scheduler.html Capacity scheduler. Available: . Accessed 2013 Jun 14.
16. http://hadoop.apache.org/docs/r1.2.0/fair_scheduler.html Fair scheduler. Available: . Accessed 2013 Jun 14.
17. Kofler R, Orozco-terWengel P, De Maio N, Pandey RV, Nolte V et al. (2011) PoPoolation: A Toolbox for Population Genetic Analysis of Next Generation Sequencing Data from Pooled Individuals. PLOS ONE6: e15925.10.1371/journal.pone.0015925 PubMed: 21253599
18. Perl Available: http://www.perl.org Accessed 2013 June 14.
19. Dean J, Ghemawat S (2004) MapReduce: simplified data processing on large clusters. In Proceedings of the 6th Symposium on Operating Systems Design & Implementation: 6-8 December 2004; San Francisco, California, USA. Volume 6. New York, NY, USA: ACM. pp. 137-150
20. PICARD Available: http://picard.sourceforge.net Accessed 2013 June 14.
21. Li H, Durbin R (2009) Fast and accurate short read alignment with Burrows-Wheeler transform. Bioinformatics 25: 1754–1760.10.1093/bioinformatics/btp324 PubMed: 19451168
22. Langmead B, Trapnell C, Pop M, Salzberg SL (2009b) Ultrafast and memory-efficient alignment of short DNA sequences to the human genome. Genome Biol 10(3): R25.10.1186/gb-2009-10-3-r25 PubMed:19261174
23. Langmead B, Salzberg SL (2012) Fast gapped-read alignment with Bowtie 2. Nat Methods 9(4): 357-359.10.1038/nmeth.1923 PubMed: 22388286
24. Wu TD, Nacu S (2010) Fast and SNP-tolerant detection of complex variants and splicing in short reads. Bioinformatics 26: 873–881.10.1093/bioinformatics/btq057 PubMed: 20147302
25. Li R, Li Y, Kristiansen K, Wang J (2008) SOAP: short oligonucleotide alignment program. Bioinformatics 24(5): 713–714.10.1093/bioinformatics/btn025 PubMed: 18227114
26. Dobin A, Davis CA, Schlesinger F, Drenkow J, Zaleski C et al. (2013) STAR: ultrafast universal RNA-seq aligner. Bioinformatics 29(1): 15–21.10.1093/bioinformatics/bts635 PubMed: 23104886
27. Krueger F, Andrews SR (2011) Bismark: a flexible aligner and methylation caller for Bisulfite-Seq applications. Bioinformatics27(11): 1571–1572.10.1093/bioinformatics/btr167 PubMed: 21493656
28. Xi Y, Li W (2009) BSMAP: whole genome bisulfite sequence MAPping program. BMC Bioinformatics10: 232.10.1186/1471-2105-10-232 PubMed: 19635165
29. Trapnell C, Pachter L, Salzberg SL (2009) TopHat: discovering splice junctions with RNA-Seq. Bioinformatics 25(9): 1105-1111.10.1093/bioinformatics/btp120 PubMed: 19289445

# CHAPTER 16 ACCELERATING COMPUTATION OF DCM FOR ERP IN MATLAB BY EXTERNAL FUNCTION CALLS TO THE GPU

Wei-Jen Wang[1], I-Fan Hsieh[2], Chun-Chuan Chen[2]

[1]Department of Computer Science and Information Engineering, National Central University, Taoyuan, Taiwan,

[2]Graduate Institute of Biomedical Engineering, National Central University, Taoyuan, Taiwan

## ABSTRACT

**This study aims to improve the performance of Dynamic Causal Modelling for Event Related Potentials (DCM for ERP) in MATLAB by using external function calls to a graphics processing unit (GPU). DCM for ERP is an advanced method for studying neuronal effective connectivity. DCM utilizes an iterative procedure, the expectation maximization (EM) algorithm, to find the optimal parameters given a set of observations and the underlying probability model. As the EM algorithm is computationally demanding and the analysis faces possible combinatorial explosion of models to be tested, we propose a parallel computing scheme using the GPU to achieve a fast estimation of DCM for ERP. The computation of DCM for ERP is dynamically partitioned and distributed to threads for parallel processing, according to the DCM model complexity and the hardware constraints. The performance efficiency of this hardware-dependent thread arrangement strategy was evaluated using the synthetic data. The experimental data were used to validate the accuracy of the proposed computing scheme and quantify the time saving in practice. The simulation results show that the proposed scheme can accelerate the computation by a factor of 155 for the parallel part. For experimental data, the speedup factor is about 7 per model on average, depending on the model complexity and the data. This GPU-based implementation of DCM for ERP gives qualitatively the same results as the original MATLAB implementation does at the group level analysis. In conclusion, we believe that the proposed GPU-based implementation is very useful for users as a fast screen tool to select the most likely model and may provide implementation guidance for possible future clinical applications such as online diagnosis.**

## INTRODUCTION

Dynamic Causal Modelling for Event Related Potentials (DCM for ERP) [1], [2] is a recently developed advanced method embedded in SPM (Statistical Parametric Mapping; a MATLAB software package; http://www.fil.ion.ucl.ac.uk/spm) as a module for studying neuronal effective connectivity measured with EEG. DCM for ERP has been used to address the issues about the brain plasticity and functional asymmetries [3]–[5]. The basic idea of DCM for ERP is to fit the observed time series data with a spatiotemporal model, of which the temporal dynamics is formulated based on a neuronally plausible model, the Jansen model [6], and

**Citation:** Wang W-J, Hsieh I-F, Chen C-C. Accelerating Computation of DCM for ERP in MATLAB by External Function Calls to the GPU. Chacron MJ, ed. PLoS ONE. 2013;8(6):e66599. doi:10.1371/journal.pone.0066599.

the neuronal network architecture is specified based on the prior knowledge of the user and the hypothesis been tested. The event related potentials are assumed as a result of the changes of the connection or coupling strength at each level of a cortical hierarchy in that spatiotemporal DCM model. This can be parameterized as a multiple-inputs multiple-outputs (MIMO) system, referred as the neuronal state equations in DCM for ERP. To solve these neuronal state equations, an iterative procedure named the expectation maximization (EM) algorithm [7], is employed to find the optimal model parameters that govern the underlying neuronal dynamics given a set of observed events (data) and the underlying probability model. The convergence will be reached when the likelihood function is maximized (for details, see [8]). Several models could be inverted according to the testing hypothesis, and Bayesian Model Comparison (BMS) allows one to select one winning plausible model that best explains the EEG data in terms of their model evidence. The computing workload is extremely heavy in DCM because of the compute-intensive EM algorithm and the possible combinatorial explosion of models to be tested [9]. Furthermore, while MATLAB could be efficient in numerical computations (for instance, matrices operations), it still has inherent limitation incurred by sequential execution. In fact, there are several attempts to parallelize the applications on MATLAB, such as image registration [10] and B-spline interpolation [11], and they have gained acceleration by a factor of about 4 to 13, depending on the applications.

Recently, the graphics processing units (GPUs) have been widely adopted as coprocessors to accelerate computation of CPUs, such as online biomedical applications [12], [13] and massive computing applications [13]–[20]. A GPU is an electronic device, which is initially developed for efficient manipulation of computer graphics. A GPU is notable for its multi-core architecture, and thus becomes a good tool to handle compute-intensive problems in parallel. A GPU contains several stream multi-processors (SMs) that can launch huge threads to process a computing task simultaneously in a single-instruction-multiple-data (SIMD) manner. The compute unified device architecture (CUDA) is a GPU programming model proposed by NVIDIA (CUDA C Programming Guide," Available: http://developer.nvidia.com/nvidia-gpu-computing-documentation). In CUDA, the data-parallel portion of a program is executed as the kernel on the NVIDIA GPU device. The kernel is executed as a grid of thread blocks, and threads from different thread blocks cannot cooperate. A thread warp is the basic unit of execution in a block, which contains 32 threads in CUDA Toolkit 4.2 and the earlier versions. That is, an NVIDIA GPU can only run 32 threads simultaneously per block. As the amount of cores in a GPU is different, the number of GPU blocks which can work simultaneously is also different.

Since a GPU is a physically independent device to a CPU, the only way to communicate with each other is by transferring data among them. Before the GPU starts computation, the CPU, referred as the host, has to copy data and sends them to the GPU, referred as the device. The data transfer procedure is necessary and may incur performance hit that reduces the performance improvement from GPU parallelism. When the data arrives at the GPU, the data have to be stored in the GPU memory hierarchy. The NVIDIA GPU hierarchy consists of registers, local memory, global memory, and constant memory, and different types of memories have different features, of which the details are described in the NVIDIA CUDA programming Guide. If the user's application does not specify the type of GPU memory for data storage, the GPU will save the data in the global memory on default. In the implementation of CUDA, a multiprocessor can execute multiple thread blocks in parallel; shared memory and registers are partitioned among the threads of all concurrent blocks accordingly. Since the shared memory and the registers are optimized for data access among a thread block, putting data in the shared memory and registers can reduce data access latency [21]. However, the size of the shared memory and the size of the registers are small. Only necessary and critical data should be put in the shared memory and the registers, while other data are put in the global memory or the memory in the host.

The goal of this study aims to use the GPU to reduce the execution time of DCM that is implemented in MATLAB. There are two kinds of approaches to do so. The first kind of approach is to use a high-level programming tool that supports direct GPU function invocations on MATLAB, such as JACKET (Jacket for GPU Computing – AccelerEyes. available at:http://www.accelereyes.com/products/jacket), parallel computing toolbox (PCT) (Parallel Computing Toolbox – Mathwork." available at: http://www.mathworks.com/products/parallel-computing/), and GPUmat (available at: http://sourceforge.net/projects/gpumat/). The second kind of approach is to call external CUDA programs from MATLAB. The major advantage of the first approach is that there exist no barriers between GPU and MATLAB. However, this also puts some constraints and limitations on a developer's code since one cannot design/optimize his own parallel strategy. On the contrast, the second approach allows a developer to design/optimize his own parallel strategy with better control on the GPU and the CPU. We have chosen the second approach in this study because it provides good flexibility and direct control on the GPC. We replaced part of the iterative EM algorithm, which is the most time consuming part of DCM for ERP, by invoking an external program written in CUDA and C++. In the implementation, we employed an adaptive computing thread allocation framework to fulfill a fast estimation of neural effective connectivity in DCM for ERP. To evaluate the performance efficacy of our proposed parallelism strategy, synthetic data with different model complexity and data length were generated. Ten sets of real experimental EEG data were used to test the computing accuracy and the speedup factor in practice. Both synthetic and experimental results showed that the proposed strategy can shorten the execution time.

## MATERIALS AND METHODS

### DCM for ERP

In this study, we propose to accelerate DCM for ERP with a GPU using CUDA. In this section, we briefly describe the theory of DCM for ERP, in particular, the neuronal model and the EM algorithm, which is the parallel processing target. The neuronal model consists several pre-specified cortical sources and each cortical source comprises four cell populations – superficial and deep pyramidal cells, spiny stellate cells and inhibitory interneurons. These populations are coupled through the intrinsic connectivity among cortical layers and the hierarchical cortico-cortical network model of cortical sources can be constructed through three kinds of inter-area connections (forward, backward and lateral) according to the belief of the users about the data (i.e. the prior), the experimental manipulation and the hypothesis been tested. The changes of the connection or coupling strength at each level of a cortical hierarchy result in the event-related responses and this can be formulated by a series of differential equations [22]:

$$\dot{x}_7 = x_8$$

$$\dot{x}_8 = \frac{H_e}{\tau_e}((C^B + C^L + \gamma_3 I)S(x_0)) - \frac{2x_8}{\tau_e} - \frac{x_7}{\tau_e^2}$$

$$\dot{x}_1 = x_4$$

$$\dot{x}_4 = \frac{H_e}{\tau_e}((C^F + C^L + \gamma_1 I)S(x_0) + C^U u) - \frac{2x_4}{\tau_e} - \frac{x_1}{\tau_e^2}$$

$$\dot{x}_0 - x_6$$

$$\dot{x}_2 = x_5$$

$$\dot{x}_5 = \frac{H_e}{\tau_e}((C^B + C^L)S(x_0) + \gamma_2 S(x_1)) - \frac{2x_5}{\tau_e} - \frac{x_2}{\tau_e^2}$$

$$\dot{x}_3 = x_6$$

$$\dot{x}_6 = \frac{H_i}{\tau_i}\gamma_4 S(x_7) - \frac{2x_6}{\tau_i} - \frac{x_3}{\tau_i^2}$$

**(1)**

where each $\dot{x}_i$ represents a state of neuronal subpopulations within one area, and the matrices$C^F$, $C^B$ and $C^L$ encode forward, backward and lateral extrinsic connections between areas, respectively. The deterministic inputs $u$ corresponded to experimental manipulations (i.e., presentation of stimuli) were introduced to the state equations via input connections $C^U$ to perturb the system and subsequently evoke the neuronal responses. In addition, the experimental factors (i.e., stimulus attributes or context) can be encoded in $C^B$.

The integration of the state equations gives the brain activities at the neuronal level and was transferred into the observation $h$ through a modality-dependent biophysical transfer function g(for example, the leadfield matrix for EEG in DCM for ERP):

$$\dot{x} = f(x, u, \theta)$$

$$h = g(x, \theta)$$

**(2)**

Inversion of this DCM for ERP model, given empirical data, makes possible the inferences about different models and the parameters of a particular model.

DCM utilizes an iterative procedure, the expectation maximization (EM) algorithm to search for the optimal parameters of the probability model in a heuristic manner, such that the likelihood function is maximized given a set of observed events (data) and the underlying probability model. The EM algorithm has two major steps, the expectation step (E-step) and the maximization step (M-step). The E-step calculates the current likelihood with the given/updated parameters; the M-step produces a new set of estimated parameters though maximizing the log-likelihood. The two steps continue in turn iteratively until convergence is reached, and then the EM algorithm outputs the searched optimal parameters (see [8] and [23]for details):

Until convergence {

E-step

$$\mathrm{J} = \frac{\partial h(\eta_{\theta|y})}{\partial \theta}$$

$$\bar{y} = \begin{bmatrix} y - h(\eta_{\theta|y}) \\ \eta_\theta - \eta_{\theta|y} \end{bmatrix}, \bar{J} = \begin{bmatrix} J & X \\ 1 & 0 \end{bmatrix}$$

$$C_{\theta|y} = (\bar{J}^T \bar{C}_\varepsilon^{-1} \bar{J})^{-1}$$

$$\begin{bmatrix} \Delta\eta_{\theta|y} \\ \eta_{\theta|y} \end{bmatrix} = C_{\theta|y}(\bar{J}^T \bar{C}_\varepsilon^{-1} \bar{J})$$

$$\eta_{\theta|y} \leftarrow \eta_{\theta|y} + \Delta\eta_{\theta|y}$$

M –step

$$P = \bar{C}_\varepsilon^{-1} - \bar{C}_\varepsilon^{-1} \bar{J} C_{\theta|y} \bar{J}^T \bar{C}_\varepsilon^{-1}$$

$$\frac{\partial F}{\partial \lambda_i} = -\frac{1}{2} tr\{PQ_i\} + \frac{1}{2} \bar{y}^T \bar{P}^T Q_i P \bar{y}$$

$$\langle \frac{\partial^2 F}{\partial \lambda_i^2} \rangle = -\frac{1}{2} tr\{PQ_i PO_i\}$$

$$\lambda \leftarrow \lambda - \langle \frac{\partial^2 F}{\partial \lambda_i^2} \rangle^{-1} \frac{\partial F}{\partial \lambda_i}$$

**(3)**

where the explicit system Jacobian J in the E-step will then used to calculate the numerical solution of the neuronal state equations (see Equation 1) as shown in the following update scheme:

## Parallelization Strategy

This study re-implemented part of DCM for ERP code using CUDA and improved the computing efficiency of DCM for ERP. As in DCM for ERP, the optimization scheme uses the MLE algorithm to iteratively update the model parameters and the computation inside each iterative loop of the MLE algorithm could be calculated in parallel [24]. Our strategy follows the above idea by first identifying the most time-consuming portion in the iterative loops of the EM algorithm and then parallelizing the calculation on the GPU. Specifically, the differential part that calculates the current estimates of the system Jacobin matrix J at neuronal source space in the E-step (see Equation 3) was selected to undergo the parallelism. This is because, by using synthetic data, our profiling records showed that this portion takes up to 80% of the total execution time in each EM loop in MATLAB, independent of data length and model complexity (i.e. the number of model parameters to be estimated) (figure 1). We further investigated this differential operation and found that, explicitly, the differential operation starts with the integration of the neuronal state equations given the current model parameters, followed by the mapping from neuronal states to cortical activities (Eq. 2) and then proceeds to the derivatives of the system Jacobian. It can be seen that the integration of the neuronal states is the best target for parallel computing given its usage and independency between states. Conceptually, we initiate the differential process in MATLAB, and then dispatch the computational tasks of state integrations to the GPU, along with the data for parallel processing. The result calculated by the GPU is then returned to MATLAB for subsequent calculation of the system Jacobian J. By the result, the EM algorithm continues to find a better set of parameters that maximizes the likelihood of the given model and the observed data. Figure 2 illustrates the scheme of the parallelism strategy. This strategy requires sending the data and assigning the computational tasks from the host (CPU) to the device (GPU). The communication between the host and the device is through NVIDIA NVMEX and the C++ code that executes the CUDA code (kernels) on the device. Figure 3 shows how the data are passed and computed between MATLAB and the GPU. To parallelize the E-Step for-loop, we first partition the for-loop into seven small for-loops, and then use CUDA to implement the four for-loops, Kernels 1~4, which are suitable for parallel processing in the GPU. The remaining sequential code pieces in the E-Step are not parallelized in CUDA because they are very fast in MATLAB. We have observed that, parallelizing these code pieces usually causes negative impacts on the performance.

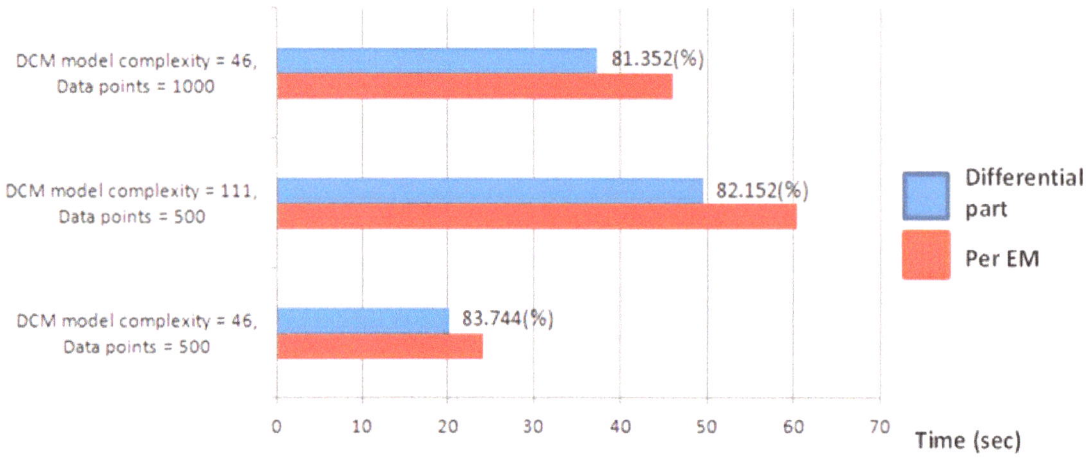


**Figure 1:** Evaluation of the most time-consuming portion in DCM for ERP (Per EM iteration) in Matlab.

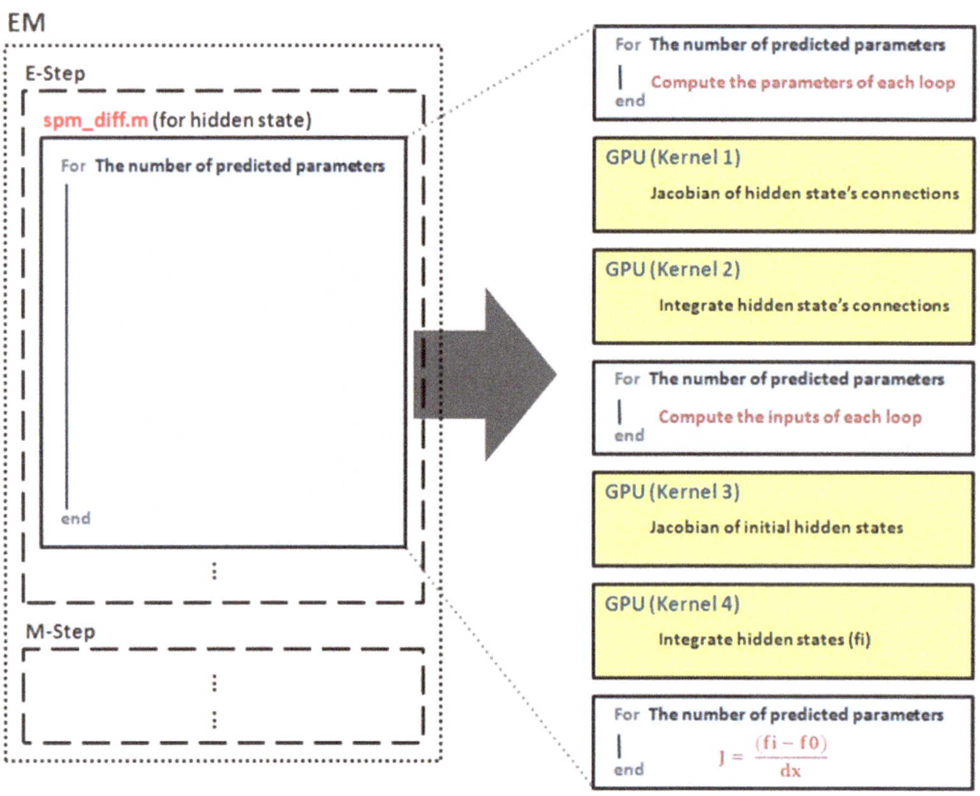


**Figure 2**: Schematic illustration of the parallelism strategy.

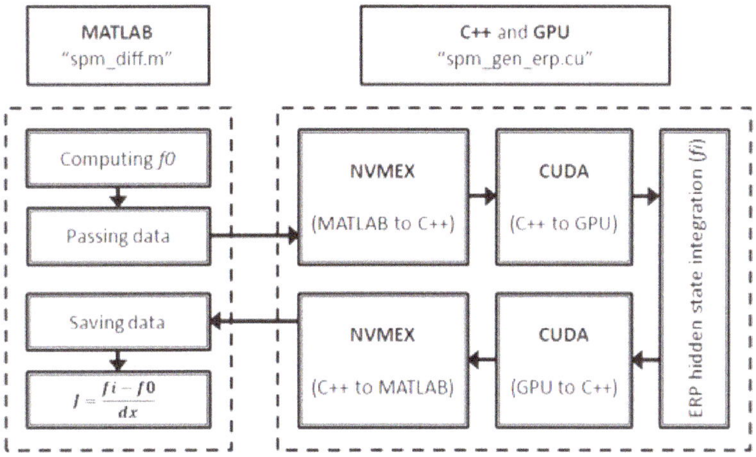


**Figure 3**: Schematic illustration of the data passing flow between the MATLAB and the GPU.

Note that the model to be inverted is specified by the users according to the hypothesis been tested, including the number of areas and the connection architectures. Therefore, the number of model parameters $C^F$, $C^B$ and $C^L$, reflecting the model complexity denoted as N in Figure 2, cannot be determined beforehand. So, in this study, we have to employ an adaptive parallel strategy, which dynamically assigns the tasks to the thread blocks to boost up the computation performance. That is, we dynamically assign each GPU thread to handle one integration task of inferring neuronal states.

## Adaptive Hardware-Dependent Thread Arrangement

In parallel computing, usually, each thread handles a computing task at a time. Without the knowledge of the underlying hardware, there are two naïve ways to arrange threads to computational tasks: (1) the thread-first arrangement strategy termed as thread and (2) the block-first arrangement termed as block. Figures 4(A) and 4(B) represents the concept of these two naïve arrangement strategies, respectively. Figure 4(A), the thread-first arrangement strategy, shows that two thread blocks are used to process 2048 independent tasks, where each thread block handles 1024 tasks. Under the thread-first arrangement, the threads are grouped as blocks, and a block must be fully occupied first and then the next block can be assigned to the remaining tasks. Because the maximum number of GPU threads per block is 1024 (or 512 for an older version of CUDA) and in this study the maximum number of tasks is seldom larger than 1024, we may use only one block by the thread-first arrangement strategy. Since a CUDA SM executes in the granularity of blocks, the thread-first strategy may not fully utilize the hardware resources of a GPU in this study. On the contrast, when employed the block-first arrangement strategy to process 2048 independent tasks, only the first thread of a block is used and each thread handles a task, as shown in Figure 4(B). Therefore, the number of blocks increases as the number of tasks increases.

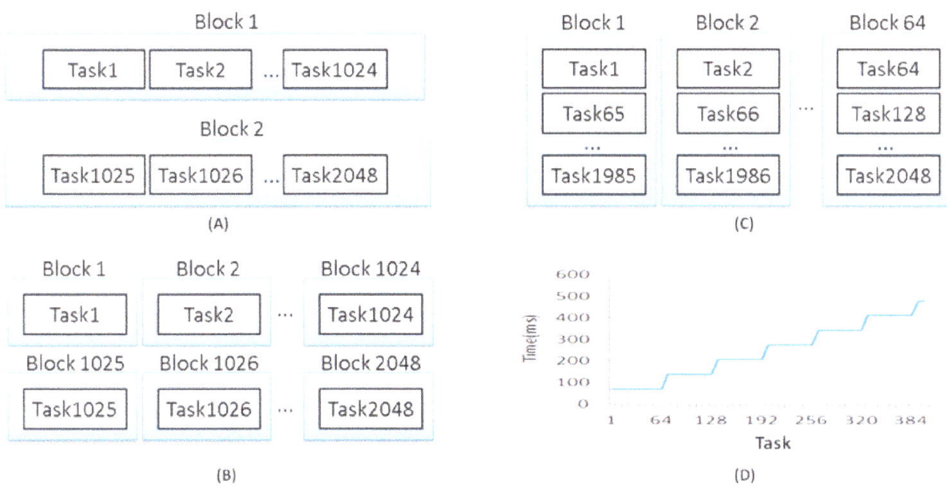


**Figure 4:** The architectures of three arrangements, (A) the block-first arrangement, (B) the thread-first arrangement, and (C) the block-64 arrangement, and the detection of the maximum number of simultaneous thread blocks using a small benchmark program (D).

The above two thread arrangement strategies are not efficient because they cannot utilize the hardware resources well. It has been observed that, the computation on the GPU becomes inefficient if the number of the blocks is not a multiple of the number of multiprocessors on the GPU [25]. Figure 4(D) shows the execution time of running a set of logarithm operations per thread block in the NVIDIA GTX 560 Ti GPU device, given different number of thread blocks. The execution time increases regularly as the number of thread blocks increases by a factor of 64. This means the maximum number of thread blocks that can be launched concurrently is 64. Since the maximum number of concurrent thread blocks is determined by the underlying GPU device, we can use a small program to detect the maximum number of concurrent thread blocks of the GPU device after the GPU device is installed in the computer. The detected value X is then used to assign threads to the computing tasks. The proposed thread arrangement strategy, termed as blockX, follows the concept of the block-first strategy, except that the number of blocks is limited to the detected value X. In the case that the number of tasks exceeds X, we use the round-robin approach to fairly assign threads to tasks until all of the X blocks reach the maximum number of threads per thread block, which is an inherent constraint in CUDA. When all the blocks are full of tasks, we will create another set of X thread blocks to handle the remaining tasks. Figure 4(C) shows the concept of the proposed blockX strategy for X=64, and thus we named it the block64 strategy. As in typical DCM For ERP studies, the number of parameters are usually over 64 but less than 1024, the proposed hardware-dependent thread arrangement strategy (the blockX strategy) is able to achieve good load balance among all the major computing components, the streaming multiprocessors. Therefore, the blockX strategy theoretically achieves better performance than the two naïve thread arrangement strategies.

Note that the value X can be calculated from the hardware specification of a GPU card. The maximum number of resident (simultaneous) thread blocks in a Streaming Multiprocessor is 8 for the GPU cards with CUDA computing capability 1.x or 2.x; the maximum number of resident thread blocks in a Streaming Multiprocessor is 16 for the GPU cards of CUDA computing capability 3.x. The GPU card used in our simulations complies with the CUDA computing capability 2.x, and the number of Streaming Multiprocessors on the card is 8. Therefore, the maximum number of resident (simultaneous) thread blocks is $8 \times 8 = 64$. As many users of the program DCM for ERP may not care to know the hardware specification of a GPU card, it would be more user-friendly and efficient to decide the maximum number of simultaneous thread blocks automatically by using a small benchmark program to detect it.

## Simulation Data

The data used in the simulation was downloaded from SPM website (http://www.fil.ion.ucl.ac.uk/spm/), in which 128 channel electroencephalography (EEG) signal was measured during an auditory oddball paradigm for eliciting Mismatch Negativity activities (see [3] for details). The model used for evaluating the execution time has five areas and reciprocal connections between low and higher areas and the task-specific modulations were set to be forward and backward (as FB model in [3]). This setting results in 46 model parameters to be estimated as shown in Figure 1. To increase the model complexity, we simply allow all possible connections and get the model complexity of 111 under this configuration (Figure 1). For more complex model (i.e. model parameters >111), we manually force the number of parameters to match our design. To increase the data length, we just concatenate the same epoch several times and truncate it to fit the desired data length. Note that, in these simulations, our design was only for evaluation of the execution time but not the accuracy.

## Empirical Data

The real experimental data were used to test the computing accuracy and the speedup factor in practice. The 32 channel EEG data were measured with 250 Hz sampling rate during a 3-D Virtual Reality based ball catch task. Ten healthy right-handed volunteer subjects participated in this experiment and part of the data will be published for addressing other scientific issues later. All subjects gave written informed consent for the experiment with a protocol approved by the institutional review board of the Taipei Veterans General Hospital. They were instructed to perform a ball catch task using their dominant hand under the virtual reality environment. The ball catch task has two conditions: standard and rare, which differ in their occurrence frequency. In the standard condition (80% of occurrence), the subjects have to catch a ball and when it is successful, the subjects will receive a sensational force through the hepatic device. For 20% of total events, there will have no force feedback even the subjects have caught the ball successfully. This oddball paradigm is to elicit a sensory P300 cortical activities. The data were epoched offline, with a peristimulus window of 0 to 900 ms, filtered with 30 Hz low-pass filter, artefact removal using the fully automated correction method [26]and averaged across artefact-free trials. For DCM for ERP analysis, we first specify six plausible models (Figure 5), differed in the areas and the inputs based on three previous literatures [27]–[29], to identify the most likely model hierarchy. The experimental data were used to evaluate the speedup factor and the estimation accuracy in practice in terms of the model evidence by Bayesian Model Selection (BMS).

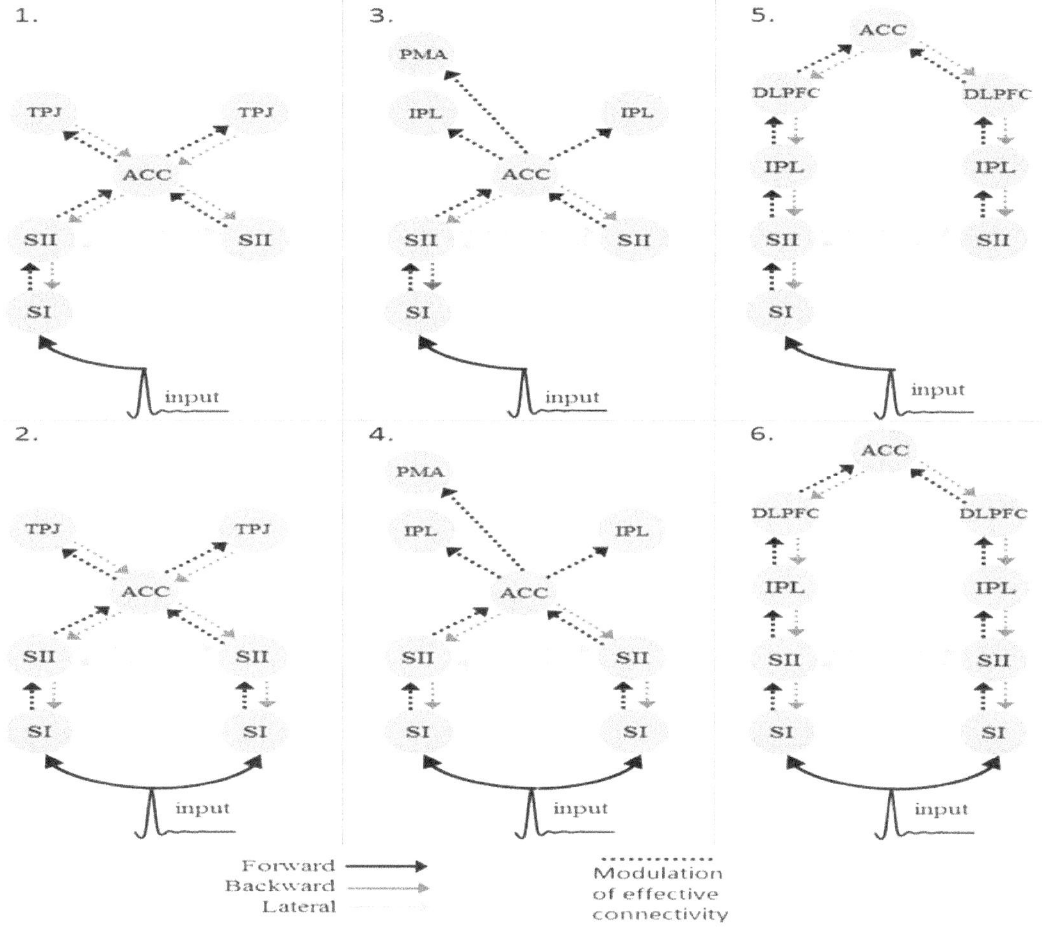


**Figure 5:** The models used in the performance evaluation (SI: primary sensory area; SII: secondary sensor area; ACC: Anterior cingulate cortex; TPJ: Temporoparietal junction; IPL: Inferior parietal lobule; PMA: Premotor area; DLPFC: Dorsolateral prefrontal cortex).

## RESULTS

In this study, we proposed a computing scheme using external calls from MATLAB to the GPU to achieve a fast estimation of neural effective connectivity in DCM for ERP. Synthetic data were used to evaluate the computing efficacy of the GPU in terms of the speedup factor and the experimental data were used to validate the accuracy of the computation in the GPU and quantified the speedup factor in practice.

## Simulation Result

### *Impact of Thread Arrangements on Execution Time*

We used the NVIDIA GTX 560 Ti GPU device to analyse the synthetic data for DCM for ERP in parallel. The NVIDIA GTX 560 Ti GPU device has 8 streaming multiprocessors and allows at most 8 resident thread blocks per streaming multiprocessor. Based on the result of our detection program, we found that $X$=64 achieves better performance for the proposed blockX thread arrangement strategy. The relationship between the number of tasks (complexities) and the performance of the proposed parallel computing strategies was first evaluated in terms of execution time per spm_diff function call (Figure 2) using synthetic data. Figure 6 shows the GPU efficiency resulting from the three thread arrangement strategies in comparison with the original MATLAB implementation, given 500 points of time series data. It can be seen that, with the external function calls to the GPU, the execution time reduces dramatically for all the three thread arrangement strategies (Figure 6(A)). We then further examine the superiority of the proposed blockX (block64 in this case) strategy in execution time while comparing it to the block-first strategy in Figure 6(B). The best speedup factor of them occurs when the number of tasks is a multiple of 64, and the block64 strategy performs better when the number of tasks exceeds 64. This is the evidence that the hardware constraints affect the performance of the software implementation. The speedup factors of the three arrangements are shown in Figure 7. The proposed hardware-dependent thread arrangement strategy (block64) can accelerate the computation by up to a factor of 31, depending on the model complexity.

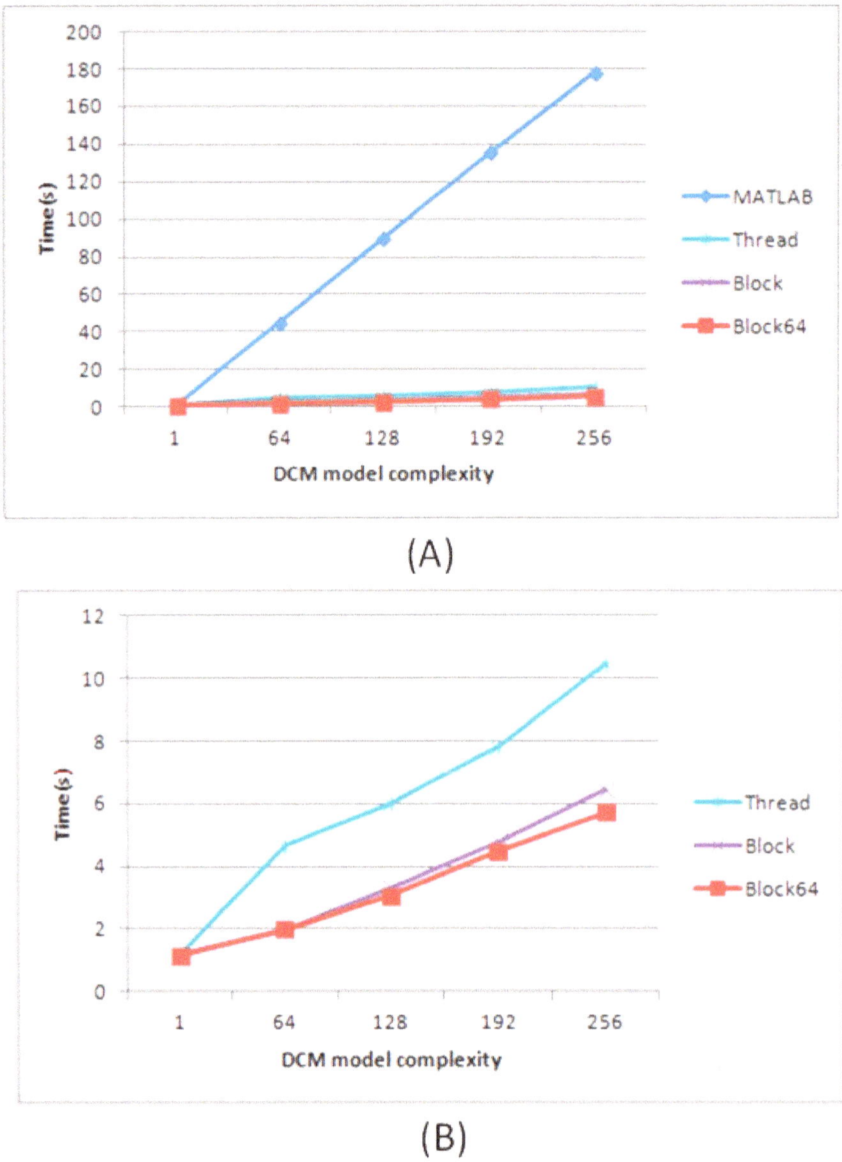


**Figure 6:** The GPU computing efficiency of the three different thread arrangements in comparison with the original MATLAB implementation.

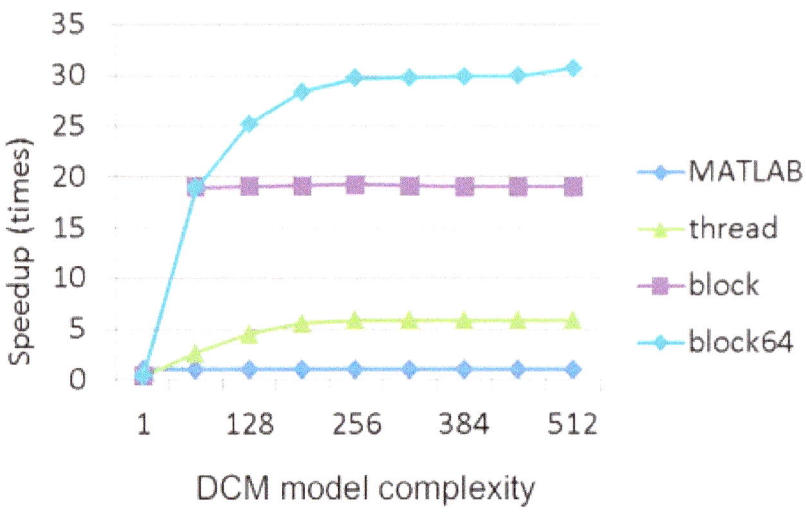


**Figure 7:** The effect of the number of tasks (model complexity) in relation to speedup factor.

The effect of data length in relation to the execution time is illustrated in Figure 8, given the model complexity of 128. The execution time increases linearly with the data length, and the block64 strategy has the slowest increasing slope, implying it has the best performance. This is confirmed by Figure 9, where the block64 strategy outperforms the others and reaches about 49 times of speedup based on the execution time of the MATLAB implementation. When we only compare the speedup of the code pieces that are parallelized by different thread arrangement strategies, as shown in Figure 10, the block64 strategy outperforms the others by a large margin and reaches about 155 times of speedup.

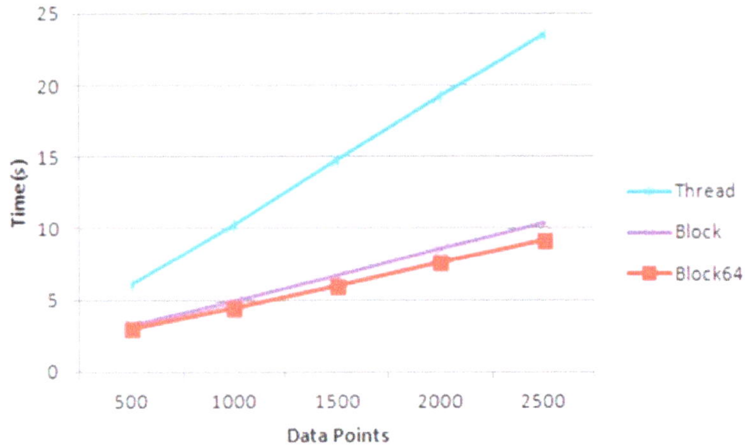


**Figure 8:** The effect of data length in relation to the execution time.

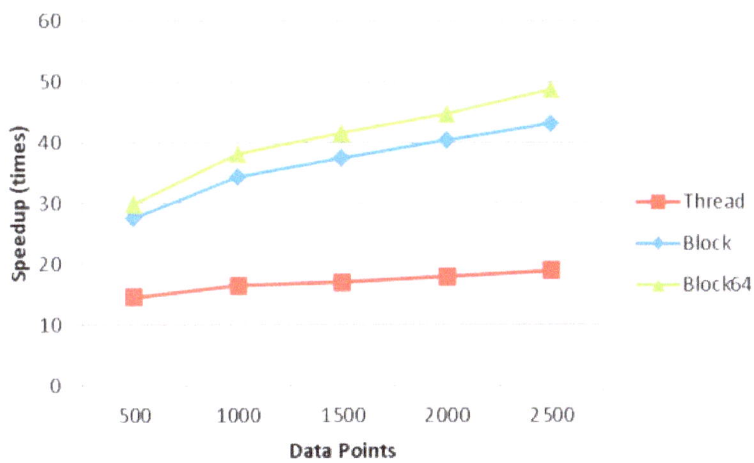


**Figure 9:** The effect of data length in relation to speedup factor.

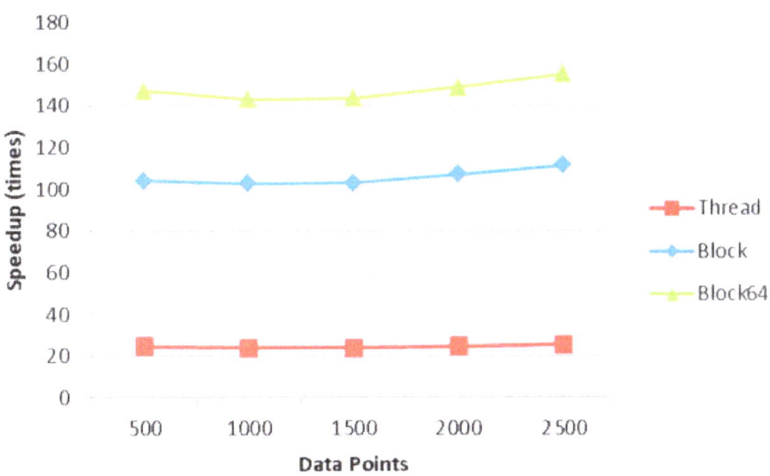


**Figure 10:** The effect of data length in relation to speedup factor for the parallelized part of DCM for ERP.

We further investigated the time span composition of the three thread arrangement strategies to reassure the efficiency of the block64 strategy. Figure 11 illustrates the breakdown of the execution time in different phases: computing, data transformation (from matrices to vectors for GPU computing) and data passing (between MATLAB and GPU). As the time for data transformation and data passing are the same for all the three thread arrangement strategies, the computing phase of block64 takes only up to 80% of the total execution time while the other two could use up 90 of it, though it relates to data length.

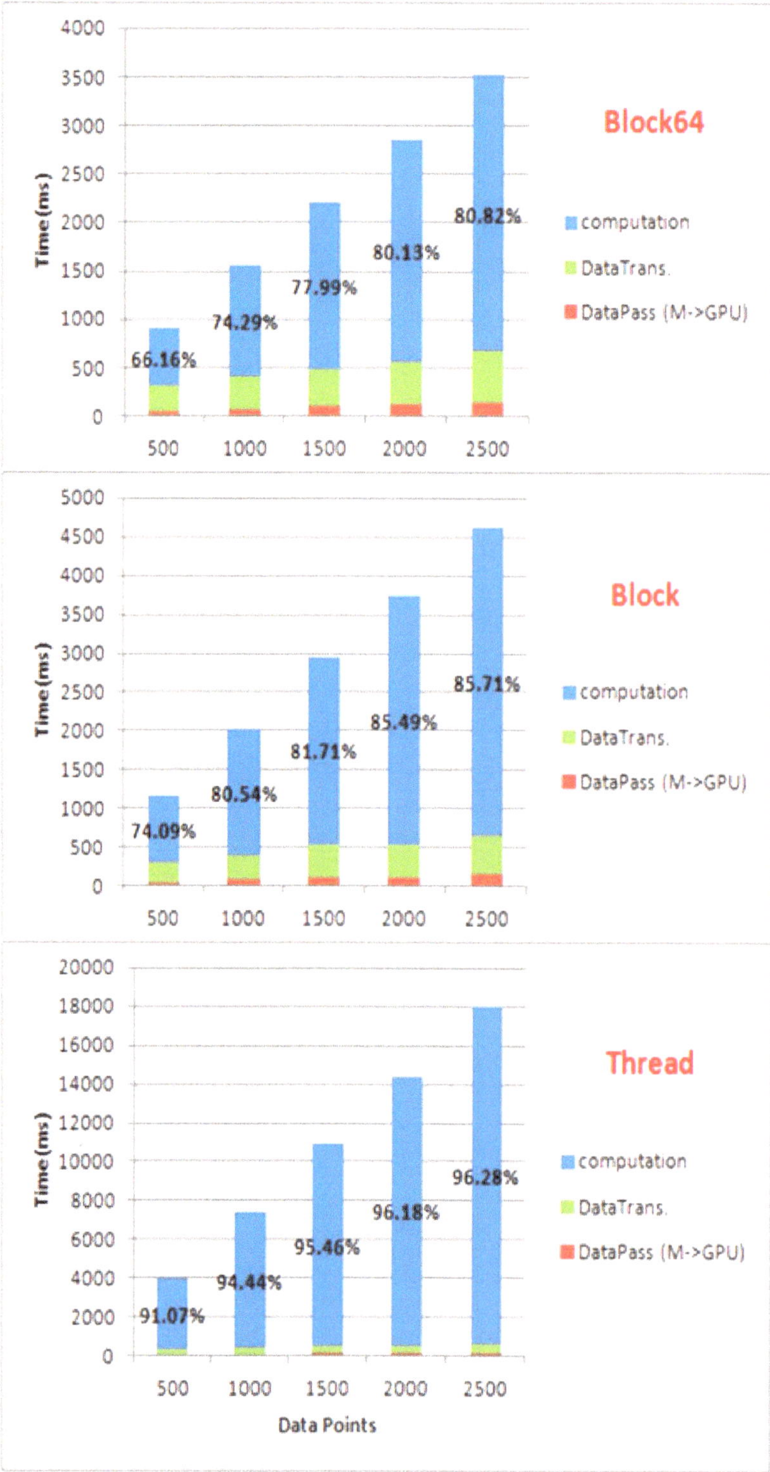


**Figure 11:** Time span composition, including computing time (in blue), data transformation (in green) and data passing (in red), of the three arrangements.

## EXPERIMENTAL RESULTS

### *Computational Accuracy and Efficiency*

Six DCM models were inverted using the MATLAB implementation and the CUDA-GPU (block64) implementation, for each subject as described in the previous section (see Figure 5). At the single subject level, six out of ten subjects have the model 6 as the best model from the results of the MATLAB implementation and only 4 subjects have Model 6 as the winning model from the results of the CUDA-GPU implementation. At the group level, the summed log-evidences over 10 subjects from the MATAB and the CUDA-GPU implementations are shown in Figure 12 (up panel). Bayesian model selection demonstrated that both, under fixed effect assumption, have chosen the model 6 (P > 0.99) as the best model, followed by model 5 and then model 2 (Figure 7, lower panel). When comparing the model-evidence of the same data and the same model between the MATLAB implementation and the CUDA-GPU implementation, the MATLAB implementation has 33 out of 60 (10 subjects * 6 models) greater values while the CUDA-GPU implementation has 27. Two sample t-test confirmed that, there has no significant difference (t=0.4362, p=0.66) on the model evidence between the results of both implementations. In other words, qualitatively, the CUDA-GPU implementation gives the same results as the MATLAB implementation does. We then compared the coupling parameters estimated by both implementations and found that, given the same initial priors, they didn't converge to the same results (Table 1). This may be due to the fact that, the two implementations have different numerical accuracy and lead to be trapped in different local maximum.

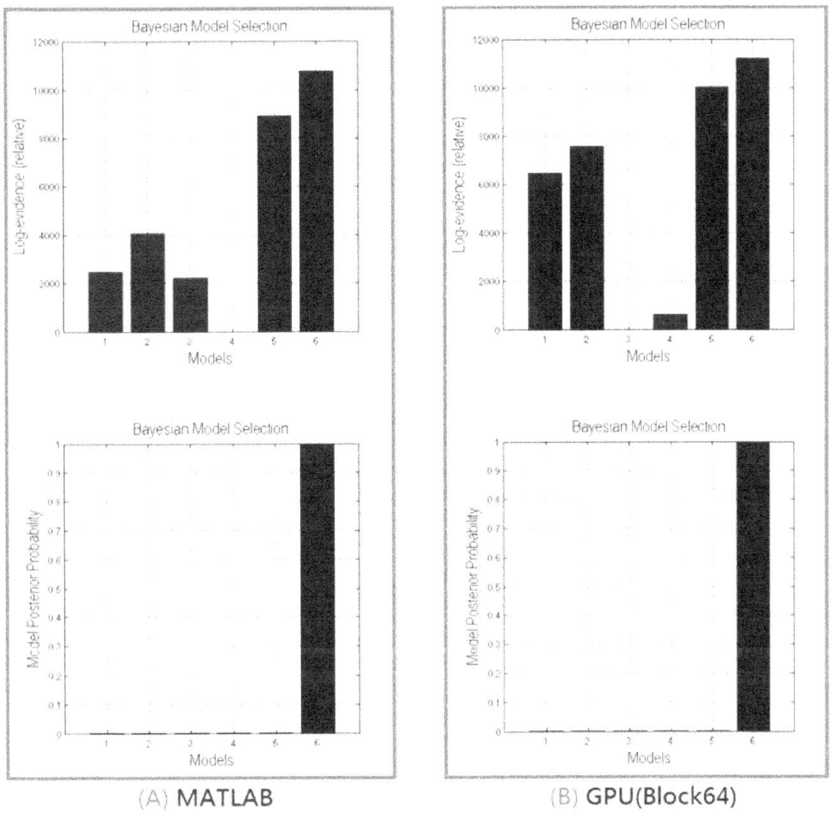


**Figure 12:** The group results of BMS under fixed effect assumption from MATLAB (A) and GPU (B).

**Table 1:** One example of the different estimates from MATLAB and GPU

| Forward | | | Backward | | |
|---|---|---|---|---|---|
| Connection | MATLAB (A. U.) | GPU (A.U.) | Connection | MATLAB (A. U.) | GPU (A.U.) |
| LS1 -> LS2 | −0.357 | −0.593 | LS2 -> LS1 | 0.099 | 0.059 |
| RS1 -> RS2 | −0.366 | −0.289 | RS2 -> RS1 | −0.023 | 0.134 |
| LS2 ->LIPL | −0.123 | −0.299 | LIPL -> LS2 | −0.091 | 0.081 |
| RS2 -> RIPL | −0.461 | −0.317 | RIPL -> RS2 | −0.194 | 0.024 |
| LIPL -> LDLPFC | −0.135 | 0.228 | LDLPFC -> LIPL | −0.517 | −0.062 |
| RIPL -> RDLPFC | −0.149 | −0.411 | RDLPFC -> RIPL | −0.123 | −0.006 |
| LDLPFC -> ACC | −0.111 | 0.520 | ACC -> LDLPFC | −0.046 | −0.148 |
| RDLPFC -> ACC | −0.469 | 0.314 | ACC -> RDLPFC | −0.031 | 0.127 |
| **Lateral** | | | **Input** | | |
| Connection | MATLAB (A. U.) | GPU (A.U.) | Connection | MATLAB (A. U.) | GPU (A.U.) |
| RS2 -> LS2 | −0.009 | 0.064 | Input -> LS1 | −0.505 | −0.541 |
| LS2 -> RS2 | −0.008 | −0.185 | Input -> RS1 | −0.859 | −0.329 |

In relation to the reduced execution time, the GPU can shorten the total execution time by a factor of 7 per model or 6 per EM loop on average. Table 2 shows the detailed information of the speedup factors of the GPU block64 strategy for each model. Note that the time saved by the GPU is data- and model- dependent since the EM algorithm may execute different number of loops for a different case.

**Table 2:** The speedup factor of the GPU block64 strategy for each model (of one representative subject)

| Model No. | Number of EM loops per model | | Execution time per EM loop | | | Total execution time per model | | |
|---|---|---|---|---|---|---|---|---|
| | MATLAB (loops) | GPU (loops) | MATLAB (s) | GPU (s) | Speedup[a] (times) | MATLAB (s) | GPU (s) | Speedup[b] (times) |
| 1 | 21 | 60 | 90.97 | 9.80 | 9.28 | 1910.30 | 588.28 | 3.24 |
| 2 | 15 | 49 | 85.56 | 12.18 | 7.02 | 4623.80 | 451.73 | 10.24 |
| 3 | 13 | 37 | 63.68 | 9.21 | 6.91 | 827.82 | 340.68 | 2.43 |
| 4 | 52 | 27 | 91.76 | 22.42 | 4.09 | 4771.70 | 605.31 | 7.88 |
| 5 | 48 | 28 | 96.33 | 16.13 | 5.97 | 4623.80 | 451.73 | 10.24 |
| 6 | 32 | 51 | 120.06 | 23.39 | 5.13 | 6123.10 | 748.37 | 8.18 |
| Avg. | 30.17 | 42.00 | 91.39 | 15.52 | 6.40 | 3813.42 | 531.02 | 7.04 |

speedup[a]: speedup factor per EM loop ; speedup[b]: speedup factor of total execution time.

## DISCUSSIONS

In this study, we proposed a computing scheme using external calls from MATLAB to the GPU to achieve a fast estimation of neural effective connectivity in DCM for ERP. Synthetic data were used to evaluate the computing efficacy of the GPU in terms of the speedup factor. The simulations show that this proposed GPU-based parallel computing strategy can accelerate the computation by a factor of about 155 for the parallel part and about 49 per EM loop. The impact of data length on the execution time in terms of speedup factor is minor, in the fact that the execution time increases linearly with the data length. The experimental data were then used to validate the accuracy of the computation in the GPU and quantified the speedup factor in practice. The speedup factor using real experimental data achieves about 7 per model, depending on the model complexity and the data length. This GPU-based implementation of DCM for ERP gives qualitatively the same results as MATLAB does in model selection though quantitatively the estimates of model parameters are not equal.

### GPU Computing Accuracy

Qualitatively, the GPU-based DCM for ERP gives the same results at the group level analysis as what MATLAB does. However, at the single subject level, the estimates of model parameters vary considerably. The reason for the difference between the MATLAB implementation and the GPU implementation, shown in Table 1, is due to the fact that the intrinsic numerical accuracy is different between MATLAB and the GPU, despite they both use double precision floating-point for computation. The difference is trivial in the beginning ($<10^{-5}$) but is further amplified by the iterative procedure in the EM algorithm. Furthermore, as in DCM for ERP, the Restricted maximum likelihood (ReML) approach was used in the optimization for degrading the importance of the nuisance parameters and this makes the likelihood function in DCM for ERP sensitive to the change of model parameters, i.e. the system Jacobian. Both together result in different gradient direction and convergence paths in MATLAB and the GPU as shown in the iteration number in EM in Table 2, for instance, 21 iterative loops in MATLAB and 60 iterative loops in the GPU for Model 1. Nevertheless, the accuracy of GPU computing is fair as there has no significant difference of model evidence between them at the group level.

### GPU Speedup Factor

The computing efficiency of our GPU implementation in terms of execution time is much better than the original MATLAB implementation of DCM for ERP, and the performance of the proposed blockX thread arrangement strategy is the best among the three thread arrangement strategies mentioned in the previous sections. The speedup factor varies significantly with a range from a few hundred in the parallel part using synthetic data down to about 7 per one plausible DCM model in real EEG data. The notable decrease of computing performance in practice using experimental data is because there are still many parts which can't be parallelized (or is not worthy) in the computing of DCM for ERP. These parts still take up a lot of computing time, for example, the matrix calculation, even though this part only takes less than 20% of the execution time in the original MATLAB implementation. As MATLAB has be known for its ability to handle complex matrix operations efficiently, we simply take this advantage by leaving the complex matrix operation in MATLAB to boost the most computing gain of both, as seen in Figure 2. This results in the best overall execution time per model. In addition, the different convergent paths also add the variability to the GPU speedup factor in practice. From the simulation, it can be inferred that the impact of data length on reducing execution time is minor in real data applications, as the typical EEG epoch is usually less than 2500 points. Nevertheless, the more complex the model is, the better the performance of the proposed blockX (block64 in all our simulation and experiment) strategy will achieve until all GPU resources are fully utilized.

Apart from the implementation consideration, the other important factor that affects the GPU performance is the time used for data transmission. We have observed that data transformation and data passing could be a performance bottleneck of our GPU implementations. It consumes a lot of time to pack and send data from the CPU to the GPU and this may reduce the benefits of GPU parallelism, especially when the data length is short. Furthermore, if the data type of the transmitted data is double-precision, the transmission speed can be 8 times as slow as that of single-precision data based on our measures. Because our goal is to maintain the same computing precision in the GPU as in MATLAB, our GPU implementation must suffer slow transmission speed to transmit double-precision data between the CPU and the GPU. In addition, the CUDA C programming guide also indicates that an NVIDIA GPU works much more efficient on single-precision data than on double-precision data. This means our GPU implementation can achieve better computing efficiency if we adopt single-precision data instead of double-precision data.

## GPU Memory Hierarchy and Data Layout

In the CUDA architecture, the data to be processed are sent from the main memory of the CPU to the global memory of the GPU. Each thread block has its shared memory, and all threads in a block can access the shared memory. Accessing the shared memory is much faster than accessing the global memory. However, to access the shared memory, one has to copy the data from the global memory to the shared memory. This procedure may incur overheads from data transmission and shared memory management. A GUDA program can be benefited from putting data in the shared memory if the data are frequently used and aligned well to reduce "bank conflicts" (a bandwidth problem caused by the hardware limitation) of the shared memory. Unfortunately, it is hard to use the GPU memory hierarchy to improve the efficiency of our parallel version of DCM of ERP. We have identified two difficulties in this problem domain. First, the data to be processed on the GPU by our DCM for ERP implementation consist of several data arrays of different sizes. The data are retrieved from the MATLAB computing environment and then sent to the GPU device. To avoid possible "bank conflicts" in the shared memory, the data have to be re-organized. However, data re-organization takes time, which may not be covered by the benefit of using the shared memory. Moreover, the data that are sent to GPU for parallel processing are not used frequently enough to reduce execution time. Importantly, the global memory becomes more efficient since CUDA computing capability 2.x. This may help to explain why our attempt of using shared memory does not work well. Nevertheless, in general, it is possible to use the shared memory to improve the execution time by putting some of the most frequent data items in the shared memory, though the cost of re-engineering is high and the gain is small in DCM for ERP.

## CONCLUSION

In conclusion, we have proposed a computing scheme using external calls to the GPU to achieve a fast estimation of neural effective connectivity in DCM for ERP. The speedup factor of GPU computing varies significantly with a range from 155 in the parallel part using synthetic data, and down to 7 per one plausible DCM model in real EEG data, depending heavily on the model complexity and the data length. This GPU-based DCM for ERP implementation gives qualitatively the same results as MATLAB does in model selection though quantitatively the estimates of model parameters are not equal. As the proposed hardware-dependent thread arrangement strategy could yield the computing efficiency of DCM for ERP while maintaining the accuracy and fidelity, we consider this a fast screen tool for users to select the most likely model and may provide implementation guidance for possible future clinical applications such as online diagnosis.

## REFERENCES

1. David O, Kiebel SJ, Harrison LM, Mattout J, Kilner JM, et al. (2006) Dynamic causal modeling of evoked responses in EEG and MEG. Neuroimage 30: 1255–1272
2. Kiebel SJ, Garrido MI, Moran R, Chen CC, Friston KJ (2009) Dynamic causal modeling for EEG and MEG. Hum Brain Mapp 30: 1866–1876
3. Garrido MI, Kilner JM, Kiebel SJ, Friston KJ (2007) Evoked brain responses are generated by feedback loops. Proc Natl Acad Sci U S A 104: 20961–20966
4. Garrido MI, Kilner JM, Kiebel SJ, Stephan KE, Baldeweg T, et al. (2009) Repetition suppression and plasticity in the human brain. Neuroimage 48: 269–279
5. Brown HR, Friston KJ (2012) Dynamic causal modelling of precision and synaptic gain in visual perception – an EEG study. Neuroimage 63: 223–231
6. Jansen BH, Rit VG (1995) Electroencephalogram and visual evoked potential generation in a mathematical model of coupled cortical columns. Biol Cybern 73: 357–366
7. Moon T, Stirling W (1999) Mathematical Methods and Algorithms for Signal Processing: Prentice Hall.
8. Friston KJ, Harrison L, Penny W (2003) Dynamic causal modelling. Neuroimage 19: 1273–1302
9. Lohmann G, Erfurth K, Muller K, Turner R (2012) Critical comments on dynamic causal modelling. Neuroimage 59: 2322–2329
10. Huang TY, Tang YW, Ju SY (2011) Accelerating image registration of MRI by GPU-based parallel computation. Magn Reson Imaging 29: 712–716
11. Dasgupta A, Kim H, Rorden C (2010) SPM & fMRI Medical Image Processing – GPU Computing Examples.
12. Men C, Gu X, Choi D, Majumdar A, Zheng Z, et al. (2009) GPU-based ultrafast IMRT plan optimization. Phys Med Biol 54: 6565–6573
13. Wilson JA, Williams JC (2009) Massively Parallel Signal Processing using the Graphics Processing Unit for Real-Time Brain-Computer Interface Feature Extraction. Front Neuroeng 2: 11.
14. Kim D, Trzasko JD, Smelyanskiy M, Haider CR, Manduca A, et al. (2010) High-performance 3D compressive sensing MRI reconstruction. Conf Proc IEEE Eng Med Biol Soc 2010: 3321–3324
15. Mousazadeh H, Marami B, Sirouspour S, Patriciu A (2011) GPU implementation of a deformable 3D image registration algorithm. Conf Proc IEEE Eng Med Biol Soc 2011: 4897–4900
16. Raimondo F, Kamienkowski JE, Sigman M, Fernandez Slezak D (2012) CUDAICA: GPU optimization of Infomax-ICA EEG analysis. Comput Intell Neurosci: 206972.

17. Yang J, Feng C, Zhao D (2013) A CUDA-based reverse gridding algorithm for MR reconstruction.Magn Reson Imaging 31(2): 313–323
18. Zhuge Y, Cao Y, Udupa JK, Miller RW (2011) Parallel fuzzy connected image segmentation on GPU.Med Phys 38: 4365–4371
19. Dudley JT, Butte AJ (2009) A quick guide for developing effective bioinformatics programming skills.PLoS Comput Biol 5: e1000589.
20. Pinto N, Doukhan D, DiCarlo JJ, Cox DD (2009) A high-throughput screening approach to discovering good forms of biologically inspired visual representation. PLoS Comput Biol 5: e1000579.
21. Nunna S, Bordoloi UD, Chakraborty S, Eles P, Peng Z (2010) Exploiting GPU On-Chip Shared Memory for Accelerating Schedulability Analysis. 2010: 147–152
22. Bastos A, Moran R, Litvak V, Fries P, Friston KJ (2011) A Dynamic Causal Model of how inter-areal synchronization is achieved in canonical microcircuits.; Society for Neuroscience 2011.
23. Friston KJ (2002) Bayesian estimation of dynamical systems: an application to fMRI. Neuroimage 16: 513–530
24. Wang WJ, Chang YS, Wu CH, Kang WX (2012) A Self-Adaptive Computing Framework for Parallel Maximum Likelihood Evaluation. Journal of Supercomputing 61: 67–83
25. Preis T, Virnau P, Paul W, Schneider J (2009) GPU accelerated Monte Carlo simulation of the 2D and 3D Ising model,. Journal of Computational Physics 228: 4468–4477
26. Schlogl A, Keinrath C, Zimmermann D, Scherer R, Leeb R, et al. (2007) A fully automated correction method of EOG artifacts in EEG recordings. Clin Neurophysiol 118: 98–104
27. Crottaz-Herbette S, Menon V (2006) Where and when the anterior cingulate cortex modulates attentional response: combined fMRI and ERP evidence. J Cogn Neurosci 18: 766–780
28. Downar J, Crawley AP, Mikulis DJ, Davis KD (2000) A multimodal cortical network for the detection of changes in the sensory environment. Nat Neurosci 3: 277–283
29. Huang MX, Lee RR, Miller GA, Thoma RJ, Hanlon FM, et al. (2005) A parietal-frontal network studied by somatosensory oddball MEG responses, and its cross-modal consistency. Neuroimage 28: 99–114

CHAPTER 17

# SCRIPTINGRT: A SOFTWARE LIBRARY FOR COLLECTING RESPONSE LATENCIES IN ONLINE STUDIES OF COGNITION

Thomas W. Schubert[1,2], Carla Murteira[2], Elizabeth C. Collins[2], Diniz Lopes[2]

[1]Department of Psychology, University of Oslo, Oslo, Norway,

[2]Centro de Investigac¸a˜o e Intervenc¸a˜o Social, Instituto Universita´rio de Lisboa (ISCTE-IUL), Lisboa, Portugal

## ABSTRACT

**ScriptingRT is a new open source tool to collect response latencies in online studies of human cognition. ScriptingRT studies run as Flash applets in enabled browsers. ScriptingRT provides the building blocks of response latency studies, which are then combined with generic Apache Flex programming. Six studies evaluate the performance of ScriptingRT empirically. Studies 1–3 use specialized hardware to measure variance of response time measurement and stimulus presentation timing. Studies 4–6 implement a Stroop paradigm and run it both online and in the laboratory, comparing ScriptingRT to other response latency software. Altogether, the studies show that Flash programs developed in ScriptingRT show a small lag and an increased variance in response latencies. However, this did not significantly influence measured effects: The Stroop effect was reliably replicated in all studies, and the found effects did not depend on the software used. We conclude that ScriptingRT can be used to test response latency effects online.**

## INTRODUCTION

There are two pervasive current trends in how to collect data in psychological studies: One is to take advantage of the Internet and collect data using online methods of various kinds, especially online questionnaires. This allows easier access to traditional participant samples, extension of research to hard-to-reach samples, and the adaptation of items to previous answers. The other trend is the long-standing but ever-increasing tendency to use response latencies as indices of cognitive processing. Such measures are utilized to examine both individual differences between participants, and differences elicited by experimental manipulations [1]–[3].

However, with a few notable exceptions, these two trends have not been merged: Only a fraction of online research measures response latencies to individual trials that last around a second or less. The reasons are of a rather technical nature, and repeated attempts to bridge the gulf demonstrate the need, while still falling short in many ways. The few projects that have bridged the gulf, however, show the great potential of online response latency collection.

In the present work, we offer a fresh approach to the problem. We design, implement, and evaluate an approach to measuring response latencies online that is based completely on open source or free technology, namely Adobe Flash

**Citation:** Schubert TW, Murteira C, Collins EC, Lopes D. ScriptingRT: A Software Library for Collecting Response Latencies in Online Studies of Cognition. Serrano-Gotarredona T, ed. PLoS ONE. 2013;8(6):e67769. doi:10.1371/journal.pone.0067769.

files created with Apache Flex [4] (formerly Adobe Flex), using concepts that are inspired by the free response latency software DMDX [5]. The software that we developed is itself open source and modular, inviting contributions from other laboratories and researchers.

## Previous Approaches to Online Response Latency Measurement

The typical response latency study presents the participant with a number of trials, somewhere between 50 and 300, and asks for as rapid responses as possible. The kind of stimuli in a trial and the task for the participant vary widely, and consequently the response latencies can vary immensely, from ca. 400 to 2000 ms for most tasks. The factors of interest are typically manipulated within participant, and latency differences in the literature range from a few to dozens of milliseconds.

In order to participate in a web-based survey, participants typically only need a standard computer with network connection and a recent browser program. In such surveys, the computer is doing little else besides showing the questionnaire and sending back the answers to the server. However, in order to collect response latencies to many individual trials, some kind of program needs to be executed on the participant's computer (i.e., client-side). This is because communication across networks and responses by servers takes time and the amount of time varies, and would introduce too much noise.

Thus, to run a response latency study online, one needs some program that runs on the participant's computer, and that presents the trials and collects the latencies. Several client side technologies have been used to create such programs: JavaScript, Java, Flash, and native (Windows PC or Mac) code that is downloaded. Let us briefly review some such attempts.

## Java Programs

Most attempts to measure response latencies in online studies have been based on Java. A decade ago, Eichstaedt [6] evaluated the performance of latency measurement by Java. Nosek, Banaji, and Greenwald [7] reported large datasets where the Implicit Association Test (IAT), a robust response latency paradigm, was applied online using applets programmed in Java. Eight of the nine reported IATs showed response latency differences between the critical blocks that were between 95 and 301 ms, with *SD*s lower than 224 ms, resulting in Cohen's *d*s between 0.72 and 1.42. Also working with Java, Keller, Gunasekharan, Mayo, and Corley [8]implemented a psycholinguistic study. Using a self-paced reading time paradigm that produces latencies between 1000 and 2000 ms, they replicated a study previously run in the lab. They estimated that their study had the power to detect reaction time differences above 183 ms. Von Bastian, Locher, and Ruflin recently [9] introduced Tatool, a Java-based open-source programming framework for psychological studies, however without an evaluation of its measurement precision.

## Flash Programs

It is worth noting that all recent online IATs run by "Project Implicit" [10] are programmed in Flash, replacing Java. Reimers and Stewart [11] varied whether participants completed a binomial choice paradigm with 30 trials in the lab using a test programmed in C++, in the lab with a Flash program, or with the same Flash program from outside the lab. They found that Flash added a delay of about 30 ms, but no additional standard deviation to the distribution of latencies.

## Scripting Programs: JavaScript and HTML

JavaScript and HTML 5 have been used by Mason [12] to implement a modular open source version of the IAT. No evaluation of that implementation has been published yet. Zwaan and Pecher [13] also relied on standard JavaScript to measure response latencies, but analysed median instead of mean values. Recently, Crump, McDonnell, and Gureckis [14] replicated several reaction time paradigms with JavaScript programs and participants recruited through Amazon MTurk [15]. They found solid replication of the chosen reaction time-based paradigms (Stroop, task-switching, flanker task, Simon, and Posner cuing). They also observed that control over stimulus presentation times could be achieved down to about 80 ms, but not shorter.

## Native Windows Programs

Two originally PC-based software packages designed to collect response times have made efforts to extend their reach to online data collection. The commercial software Inquisit enables running studies online. To participate in such a study, one must download either an executable file directly or one wrapped in Java Web Launch. Similarly, the free software package DMDX[5] offers a remote testing mode where participants must download an executable file. In both cases, the advantage is that well performing code is executed on the client's machine – in fact the same code as is used for desktop testing, except that the machines running this code will vary much more than a well-managed lab, adding error variance [16], [17]. The disadvantage is, in both cases, that participants must trust the source enough to allow the download of executable code. Security concerns, anti-virus software, and browser restrictions make this difficult, and possibly limit these packages to applications where participants know the entity conducting the study well enough (e.g., to students of a university).

## Comparison and Summary

In sum, Java, JavaScript, and Flash all have been used to measure response latencies online. The published evidence suggests that all three can be successfully used, but also that all three can be expected to increase noise in comparison to native programming on a PC, which can serve as an alternative.

The best comparison of these techniques to native programs that we are aware of has been published by Neath et al. [18]. They built a device that allowed the standardized evaluation of a system's latency and programmed a simple task where the screen turned from black to white. The onset of the white screen was detected by a light sensor placed on the screen, which was connected to a solenoid that was placed above the keyboard. When light was detected, the solenoid fired and pressed a button, given the answer in the trial. Using this system, Neath et al. evaluated four different hardware setups of Macintosh computers, and the same procedure using different software. When Neath et al. [18] programmed their task in Java, the average latency of their device was measured as 99.72 ms, with an average *SD* of 6.66 ms. Flash measured an average latency of 91.56 ms, with an average *SD* of 8.14. Javascript measured the reaction time as being on average 88.07 ms, with an average *SD* of 5.94 ms. As a comparison, when measuring with Matlab and Psychtoolbox and synchronized displays (i.e., native software), an average latency of 49.88, average *SD*=2.63, was obtained. The additional measurement error in Java, Flash and JavaScript seems acceptable for many paradigms.

## ScriptingRT

We developed a software library that supports programming response latency studies in Flash, called ScriptingRT (online at http://reactiontimes.wordpress.com/scriptingrt/). ScriptingRT studies run in a Flash plugin or in a Flash-supporting browser. They are programmed in Apache Flex and then compiled into Flash applications that can be distributed online and embedded in HTML pages.

Flex is a combination of an XML-based markup language (MXML) and a scripting language (ActionScript). Flex started as an Adobe product, but became open source in 2012, hosted by the Apache Foundation. Because ScriptingRT is also released under an open source license, developing ScriptingRT studies is thus completely based on open source and free software. In order to develop ScriptingRT studies, researchers need to install the Flex SDK (available for OS X and Windows), the ScriptingRT library [19], a text editor, a Flash-enabled browser, and a server running PHP on which data are stored.

The philosophy of ScriptingRT is to allow the programming of a response latency study using a simple set of markup tags in an XML file, while at the same time allowing the programming of additional functionality. The ScriptingRT markup tags and their functionality are defined in the ScriptingRT library, which is used to compile the studies into Flash files.

The concepts for this markup language are inspired by, but not identical to, the free response latency software DMDX. Studies are programmed as a combination of blocks, which consist of items; items, for their part, are made up of frames. A frame represents what is displayed on a single screen at one time. An item can consist of one or more frames. For instance, one item can include a blank intertrial interval frame, a frame with an asterisk to signal the next trial, a frame with a prime, and a frame with a target. Frames never change order within an item. Similarly, a block can be made up of one or multiple items. However, the order of items within a block can change (randomization). In their attributes, items save what the correct response should be.

Each of these structures is constructed with XML tags: A frame is created with the markup <Frame></Frame>, items are constructed with <Item></Item>, and blocks are constructed with <TestPart></TestPart>. Blocks that do not collect response latencies (e.g., for instructions) are constructed with <Part></Part>.

These XML tags are defined by the ScriptingRT library. In combination with such ScriptingRT-specific tags, standard Flex tags can be used. For instance, <Text> </Text> would be used to present text within a frame. As a result, every ScriptingRT code is a mix of tags from the ScriptingRT library and standard Flex tags. An item from a Stroop task could be coded as:

```
<TestPart id="stroop" positive="keyboard.Q.press" negative="keyboard.P.press" scramble="1" backgroundColor="0xffffff" color="0x000000">
<Item id="i1" type="+">
<Frame response="Time.2000" protocol="false">
<mx:Text verticalCenter="0" horizontalCenter="0" fontSize="48" text="+"/>
</Frame>
<Frame id="if1" protocol="true">
<mx:Text id="text100" verticalCenter="0" horizontalCenter="0" fontSize="36" color="0xff0000" text="red"/>
</Frame>
</Item>
</TestPart>
```

In this example, the <TestPart> tag sets the defaults for this block, including the expected answers (Q and P), randomization of items (scrambling), and default colors for background and text. Within this block one item with two frames is created. The type of the item is marked as positive with a plus sign, which means that the correct answer will be given with the key identified as correct for positive answers (O). The first frame stays on screen for 2000 ms and displays an asterisk, which is realized using a Text element from the regular Flex library. The second frame stays on screen until an answer is given. In this example, all XML tags except the <Text/> tag are defined by ScriptingRT. (That is also why the <Text/> tag has the prefix "mx:", which points to a previous definition of additional libraries in the opening <Application/> tag, not shown here.) Figure 1 shows an example of the structure of a complete experiment.

```
1 <?xml version="1.0" encoding="utf-8"?>
2 <Application
   xmlns="org.nad.dm.*"
   xmlns:mx="library://ns.adobe.com/flex/mx" … >

3        <WelcomeScreen … />

4        <Part …>
5                <Instruction …>
                 …
                 </Instruction>
         </Part>

6        <TestPart …>
7                <Item …>
8                        <Frame …>
9                                <mx:Text color="0xFF0000" text="red"/>
                         </Frame>
                 </Item>
10               <Item …>
11                       <Frame …>
12                               <mx:Text color="0x0000FF" text="blue"/>
                         </Frame>
                 </Item>
         </TestPart>

  </Application>
```

**Figure 1:** Outline of a Stroop study implemented in ScriptingRT.

Excerpt from a ScriptingRT source code file implementing a Stroop paradigm. The tags shown set preferences (tags 1 and 2), create an introductory screen and an instruction screen (3–5) as well as one experimental block with two items (6–12). Tags 1 and 2 are general Apache Flex components. Tags 9 and 12 also embed a general Flex object, a <Text/> object (referenced in the Application tag with the prefix mx). All other tags are part of the ScriptingRT library (referenced in the Application tag).

Other building blocks of ScriptingRT studies are special tags for instructions, feedback, and branching. A full list is given in Table 1. Except branching, all of these elements can be used without coding additional ActionScript. More information on the ScriptingRT library is available in the manual [19]. Additional capabilities that are neither in the standard nor the ScriptingRT library can be added by either importing other Flex libraries, or by writing ActionScript programs that are embedded in the XML file. ScriptingRT can contain any Flex object, such as text, html-coded text, vector graphics, images, or sound.

**Table 1:** Overview of main tags and attributes introduced by the ScriptingRT Library

| Tag | Explanation |
|---|---|
| <WelcomeScreen/> | Defines the contents of the first screen, which is equipped with a button to be pressed |
| <Part/> | Creates a block of items and instructions that are not collecting latencies |
| <Instruction/> | Displays an instruction |
| <TestPart/> | Creates a block of items that collect responses and latencies |
| <Item/> | Creates an item that can contain one or more frames |
| <Frame/> | Creates a frame, the basic unit of stimuli presentation |
| response | Attribute of <Part/> and <TestPart>, defines the way a frame can end. Can be keyboard event, mouse event, or time event. |
| positive, negative, noresponse | Attributes of <TestPart/>, define expected positive and negative response, and maximum time for answer |
| scramble | Defines way of item randomization in a <TestPart/> |
| outputURL, protocolFormatHead, protocolFormatItem, | Used in the opening <Application/> tag, define location and formatting of results output |
| debug | Used in the opening <Application/> tag, displays protocol for debugging at run time |
| finishedButtonValue | Used in the opening <Application/> tag, sets exit message |
| <repeat/> | Attribute of <TestPart/>, creates frames that are repeated before frames in every item |
| <Feedback/>, <correct/>, <incorrect/>, <miss/> | Creates feedback frames to be displayed after each item |
| <branches/>, <Branch/> | Attributes of TestParts, implementing branching between them |

For each answered item, ScriptingRT saves the response time and whether the response was correct or incorrect. Latency measurement is implemented with the standard Flex component flash.utils.Timer, and more specifically the flash. utils.getTimer, which measures in milliseconds.

ScriptingRT flash files can exchange data with the HTML page in which they are embedded. After the study is finished, the data are transmitted to a server that receives them using a PHP script. The format is fully customizable; additional information can be appended if programmed (e.g., order of randomized blocks, data transferred from the HTML page).

ScriptingRT focuses on measuring response latencies to specific stimulus presentations. Other response formats, such as text or scales, are available as standard components of Flex and could be incorporated in ScriptingRT studies. However, instead of adding other response formats, we rather envision ScriptingRT as one element of a larger web-based study, where open ended questions and rating scales that do not require latency measurement are implemented in HTML, and only the trial presentation is done with ScriptingRT in Flash. This approach can benefit from advanced HTML survey software.

One factor within Flash that we do not address empirically here is the frame rate specified in the Flex file. We used both the default (24 frames per second) and a modified rate of 60. Our current recommendation is to use 60 Hz.

In sum, a ScriptingRT study is programmed in Flex, compiled into a Flash file, and then embedded in an HTML page where it collects data that are sent back to a server. ScriptingRT studies are a combination of standard Flex and ScriptingRT-specific functionality for response time studies, and can also contain additional Flex libraries for special content, as well as additional ActionScript for special functionality. In combination, these building blocks provide a programming environment for creating many types of response latency studies, plus flexibility for more experienced programmers. The library is ready to be used, and available in source code. It should be noted that the functionality is under development and we hope will be continuously extended. A complete description of the philosophy, syntax, and capabilities of ScriptingRT is available online [19]. In the remainder of this paper, we present empirical investigations where we tested ScriptingRT using online samples, and also in the lab with independent timing equipment.

## OVERVIEW OF THE CURRENT RESEARCH

Six studies were run to evaluate the ScriptingRT software and to compare it to standard software packages. Studies 1 through 3 used hardware to evaluate the precision and accuracy of response latencies and presentation times in ScriptingRT. Studies 4 through 6 applied the Stroop paradigm, testing the replicability of the Stroop effect in ScriptingRT and comparing it to other software, both in the lab (Study 5) and online (Studies 4, 6).

We used a variety of hardware and software across the studies, and compared the performance of different software versions where possible. Table 2 gives an overview of the studies.

**Table 2**: Overview of the Studies

| Study | Data Collection | Hardware and Software |
|---|---|---|
| 1 | Timing study with external microcontroller | Arduino Leonardo board connected to Sony Vaio Core i5 laptop, ScriptingRT running in various browsers, and DMDX |
| 2 | Timing study with external microcontroller and solenoid | Arduino Uno board interacting with Intel Core i7 desktop computer, ScriptingRT and various other packages |
| 3 | Timing study with external microcontroller measuring presentation times | Arduino Uno board measuring Sony Vaio Core i5 laptop, ScriptingRT in Adobe Flash player and Flash plugin in Firefox, and DMDX |
| 4 | Online data collection with human participants | Various hardware and flash/browser software programs used by participants |
| 5 | Laboratory data collection with human participants | Sony Vaio Core i5 laptop, ScriptingRT running in Firefox with Adobe Flash plugin |
| 6 | Online data collection with human participants | Various hardware used by participants |

## Ethics Statement

Only Studies 4–6 dealt with human participants. The studies were conducted in concordance with the Ethics Guidelines issued in 2012 by the Scientific Commission (Comissão Científica) of the hosting institution Centro de Investigação e Intervenção Social, Lisboa, Portugal (CIS-IUL). These Ethics Guidelines provide a checklist to decide whether a formal review process is necessary. This checklist indicated that the current studies were exempt from formal ethics review because data were 1) collected anonymously with no pressure to complete, 2) did not involve questions about undesirable personal characteristics, 3) did not involve participants from a population of concern, 4) did not involve deception, 5) did not involve ingesting anything, 6) did not involve invasive measures, 7) did not collect personally identifying information (defined as name, IDs, physical or email addresses, or images), and 8) did not collect potentially endangering information.

All experiments were noninvasive, no false information was provided, and the results were analyzed anonymously. Data were collected sampling only adults. The participants in Study 4 were recruited online through a social network, those from Studies 5 and 6 were recruited at a Portuguese university (in person for Study 5 or through email for Study 6). Thus, all data were collected inside Portugal, the country of the hosting institution. In all three studies, participants read the description and purpose of the study on the initial screen, and were there informed that by proceeding, they consented to participating, but that they could withdraw at any stage of the study. In Study 5, which took place in the laboratory, this was repeated verbally.

## STUDY 1: COMPARING SCRIPTINGRT TO OTHER SOFTWARE USING AUTOMATED RESPONSES WITH AN EMULATED KEYBOARD

We start by examining how much variability in response times is introduced by the software ScriptingRT and Flash. Thus, in Study 1, we removed variance due to human variability and kept differences between trials to a minimum by automatizing the responses to a single stimulus. For this purpose, we employed an Arduino Leonardo Microcontroller board that detected the onset of stimuli on the screen with a light dependent resistor and sent virtual "key strokes" to the computer, emulating a participant's response on a keyboard. The latency of the board's "reactions" was then measured.

### Method

We connected an Arduino Leonardo microcontroller board to a computer by USB. The board can emulate a computer keyboard and send key strokes to the computer that are recognized as coming from a regular keyboard. The Arduino itself was equipped with a TinkerKit light dependent resistor (LDR) sensor, which was placed on the screen of a Vaio Core i5 laptop. The Arduino was programmed such that it checked the state of the LDR continuously. When the reading surpassed the threshold (i.e. was brighter than a certain programmed criteria), the Arduino communicated by USB with the computer, sending a SPACE key stroke, which appeared as a regular press of the space bar on the computer.

We programmed a simple task, which presented 100 trials, in both ScriptingRT and DMDX. The number of trials in this and the following two studies was derived from the typical cognitive science study, which has somewhere between 50 and 300 trials. In each trial, an inter-trial interval with a black screen was followed by the stimulus, a plain white screen, which remained until the press of the space bar was registered. The onset of this white screen was detected by the LDR. The length of time from the display of the white screen to the registration of the key press was measured as the latency. We ran the ScriptingRT task three times on the same laptop: in Chrome 24, Firefox 16, and IE9, all under Windows 7. All browsers relied on the Adobe Flash plugin 11.5.

### Results

The DMDX software set the benchmark in this study. It registered response rates from the Arduino Leonardo between 6.86 and 8.21 ms after the onset of the stimulus, $M$=7.60, $SD$=.30. Running ScriptingRT, Chrome detected responses between 50 and 97 ms later, $M$=72.21, $SD$=6.84. In IE9, response times ranged from 52 to 70 ms, $M$=60.92, $SD$=4.93. Firefox registered response times between 50 and 90 ms, $M$=64.31, $SD$=6.56.

When running $t$-tests to compare the means, they differed in all cases, $ts>4.13$, $ps<.001$. We compared the standard deviations with Levene's tests. They differed significantly between Firefox and IE9, $F(1,198)=14.54$, $p<.001$, and obviously between DMDX and the other three measures, but not between Chrome and the other two browsers (Chrome vs. IE9: $F(198)=2.72, p=.101$).

### Discussion

In Study 1 we used a well performing benchmark: DMDX in combination with an Arduino Leonardo board that detected stimulus onset with a light sensor and emulated a keyboard press as a response. DMDX detected this emulated response with a very low standard deviation of less than half a millisecond.

Not surprisingly, ScriptingRT was less precise. In three browsers, measured response latencies had ranges between 18 and 47 ms, and their averages differed significantly. On the other hand, the $SD$s of these responses stayed below 7 ms in all three browsers. That value is comparable to many regular keyboards and standard reaction time software. In addition, the constant added by measuring in ScriptingRT was about 60 ms. This result suggests that researchers using ScriptingRT should thus focus primarily on differences between RTs and be cautious when interpreting absolute latencies.

For researchers using ScriptingRT, knowing the size and the distribution of the offset is useful. In addition, it is instructive to know how this offset is produced. Several separate delays may feed into it. First, ScriptingRT starts measuring the latency as soon as the command to display the stimulus is issued, but the actual presentation on the screen might be delayed. A second possible delay occurs between the registration of the key press by the operating system and the activation of a key press event in the Flash software. A third delay may occur between the firing of that event and the recording of a time stamp in ScriptingRT.

We conclude that not surprisingly, ScriptingRT is less precise in the measurement of latencies than a natively run specialized response latency software program. Furthermore, different browsers result in somewhat different average latencies. Nevertheless, the offset produced by ScriptingRT seems acceptable.

## STUDY 2: COMPARING SCRIPTINGRT TO OTHER SOFTWARE USING AUTOMATED RESPONSES WITH A KEYBOARD

Study 1 used an emulated keyboard, and thus could not compare performance with a regular keyboard. That was the goal of Study 2. For this study, we built a machine that detected the appearance of a stimulus (a white screen following a black screen) with a photodiode, and then pressed a response button on an actual keyboard with a solenoid. It thus simulated a human participant in a reaction time task with the aim of getting constant external responses. With this setup, we compared various software packages to ScriptingRT using a standard keyboard[18], [20].

The same machine and procedure was used in previous work on response boxes by our laboratory [21]. In those tests, it was found that both a PST serial response box (connected to the serial port) and a new response device based on an Arduino microcontroller board resulted in standard deviations between 1 and 1.4 ms. This confirms that the machine used here had a rather low variance in its answers. The average reaction time as measured by E-Prime [22]was about 50 ms. This response time was a combination of the time the robot needed to register a change and to fire the solenoid, the pure travel time of the solenoid to the key, plus the time Windows and the software required to register the button press.

## Method

A simple test experiment was programmed in ScriptingRT, E-Prime 2.0.10.178, Inquisit 3.0[23], DMDX 4 [5], and SuperLab 4.0 [24]. Each trial consisted of a black screen presented for 2000 ms, followed by a white screen, representing the stimulus to which the robot should respond. The white screen remained until a response was detected. As response devices, we used a Microsoft keyboard (model 1047 KU-0459) or a PST Serial Response Box Model 200 (the latter only with E-Prime). Each experiment consisted of 100 trials, and we repeated each two times, resulting in 200 trials. For the sake of simplicity, in this paper we analyzed all 200 trials combined.

All tests were run on the same desktop computer (Intel Core i7, 3.4GHz) with an Nvidia GeForce GTX 560 graphics processor, running at 60 Hz frame rate, using Windows 7 (64-bit), on an Asus VE278 flat screen. The display resolution was set to 1920×1080 pixels, with a refresh rate of 60 Hz and 32 bit of true colors, maximum brightness.

The machine was built using a photodiode to sense stimulus onset, a solenoid to press the button, and an Arduino microcontroller board to connect the two. The photodiode was an Osram BPW 34, the solenoid an Intertec ITS-lz-2560 d-12vdc, and the controller an Arduino Uno, based on an Atmel ATmega328, running at 16 MHz. The Arduino was programmed to consecutively read the input from the photodiode. When a change of brightness was detected on two consecutive readings, the solenoid was fired, pressing a keyboard button positioned below it, and then turned off again after the next change. During the experiment, the machine was only connected to a power source; there was no communication between the computer running the study and the machine [34].

## Results

Table 3 summarizes the response latencies obtained using the machine, for each software and periphery. The benchmark here is the performance using the E-Prime PST serial response box (PreRelease =0; we also ran the same test with PreRelease =2000, which lead to worse performance. In E-Prime, PreRelease instructs the computer to prepare the next display while still executing the current display. In theory, setting PreRelease to the duration used to present the current display should allow the fastest performance, and this is thus the default in the most recent version of E-Prime. We do not know the reasons for this unexpected result in E-Prime. These data are identical those in Schubert et al. [21])

**Table 3:** Means and SDs of measured response times (in ms) by software (Study 2)

| | **Descriptives** | | **Comparison of Variances** | |
|---|---|---|---|---|
| **Software** | *M* | *SD* | ***F*(1,198)** | *p* |
| ScriptingRT | 92.80 | 4.21 | – | – |
| E-Prime SRB (PR = 0) | 56.91 | 1.37 | 131.89 | <.001 |
| E-prime SRB (PR = 2000) | 56.47 | 1.85 | 102.56 | <.001 |
| E-prime (PR = 0) | 84.58 | 6.25 | 12.84 | <.001 |
| E-prime (PR = 2000) | 70.96 | 3.30 | 7.57 | .006 |
| DMDX | 68.24 | 3.18 | 10.75 | .001 |
| Inquisit | 70.05 | 3.20 | 9.78 | .002 |
| Superlab | 98.18 | 4.17 | <1 | .822 |
| InquisitWeb | 66.21 | 2.74 | 24.04 | <.001 |

*Note.* Last two columns show comparisons of each variance to the variance measured by ScriptingRT (first row). All measures used a keyboard except those labelled SRB, indicating Serial Response Box. PR = PreRelease in E-Prime.

E-Prime in combination with a keyboard (and PreRelease =2000), Inquisit, DMDX and also the Web version of Inquisit all register somewhat longer overall averages than does E-Prime with a response box, but with acceptable *SD*s between 2.7 and 4 ms. Surprisingly, both E-Prime when using a keyboard and no PreRelease and Superlab produced higher averages and *SD*s larger than 4. ScriptingRT itself registered the machine's response latencies with an average of 93 ms and a *SD* of 4.21 – about 36 ms slower than E-Prime using the response box (the shortest reaction time), and with about three times the *SD*.

We analyzed these reaction times by submitting them to a mixed model with software as a fixed factor. (Note that the mixed model is in this case mathematically identical to a General Linear Model.) This model showed a highly significant effect of software on the average latency, $F(2786)=2374$, $p<.001$. We used the estimated marginal means to compare the average latency measured by ScriptingRT to each of the other software programs (using SIDAK corrections). The average of ScriptingRT's measurements was significantly different from every other software, all $ps<.001$. Thus, it was significantly slower than all, except Superlab, which it was significantly faster than. We also computed whether the standard deviations of ScriptingRT's measures differed from the *SD*s produced by the other software packages, by computing Levene's tests comparing the respective variances. The last two columns of Table 3 show that ScriptingRT's *SD* is significantly larger than those of every other program except Superlab and E-Prime in one configuration.

## Discussion

Study 2 evaluated ScriptingRT's performance when measuring reaction times in comparison to other software packages. For this purpose, we created a machine that pressed a button in response to a stimulus onset. Previous tests confirmed that measurements with this machine produce standard deviations below 1.5 ms with precise hard- and software [21].

ScriptingRT resulted in both longer response latencies and a larger standard deviation than all other packages except SuperLab and E-Prime in one configuration. Nevertheless, in absolute terms, the *SD* of 4.21 is comparable to what was standard for keyboards for a long time [16]. It is thus clear that any test with ScriptingRT should be well powered and used to assess primarily paradigms with a large effect size. At the same time, the differences between the other tests show that differences are also present between different native software packages (e.g, Superlab vs. DMDX), or can be due to specifics of programming (e.g., the pre-release in E-Prime) and hardware (keyboard vs. response box). Thus, researchers should always be aware that their choice of software, programming, and hardware results in a specific amount of error variance that often can only be evaluated through empirical testing.

## STUDY 3: MEASURING REFRESH RATE IN SCRIPTINGRT

In addition to the measurement performance of ScriptingRT, it is useful to know how precise the timing of presentations can be. For this purpose, we programmed varied duration, quickly changing presentations in both ScriptingRT and DMDX, and measured the duration of each presentation with an external photodiode. As we anticipate that ScriptingRT will not be used for millisecond-accurate or subliminal presentations, but rather with presentations that have a minimum of about 100 ms, this was our lowest presentation time.

## Method

We programmed ScriptingRT and DMDX (as a comparison) scripts that switched between a white and a black screen 250 times, with varying presentation durations. In ScriptingRT screen presentation durations were 100, 200, or 300 ms. We ran these with the standalone Flash player and also with the plugin running in Firefox. The timing method used in DMDX is based on units of so-called tics – one refresh cycle of the screen. We used a screen with 60 Hz refresh rate, which resulted in single tics that were 16.664 ms long. Each screen was displayed for 1, 2, 3, 4, 5, or 10 tics. All tests were done on a Vaio Core i5 Laptop. The ScriptingRT tasks ran with a display resolution of 1366×768 pixels.

To measure the duration of each black and white screen, we used the photodiode component of the machine used in Study 2. The Arduino microcontroller to which the photodiode was connected registered a change in brightness when two consecutive readings indicated it, and saved the duration in ms between the changes in its internal memory. It did this for 250 changes, and then sent all measurements via the USB connection to the attached PC. In other words, the Arduino measured and recorded the measurements stand-alone and offline during the test, and only transmitted them afterwards.

## Results

Table 4 summarizes the results. The first six lines confirm that the apparatus measured presentation duration rather precisely and with low standard deviations: We obtained absolute differences between 0.03 and 0.21 ms between how long DMDX and the screen ideally should have presented for and what was measured, and *SD*s varied between 1.11 and 2.81 ms.

**Table 4:** Presentation times by DMDX and ScriptingRT (in ms, Study 3)

| Software | Target Time | *M* | *SD* |
|---|---|---|---|
| DMDX | 16.66 (1 tic) | 16.63 | 1.11 |
| | 33.33 (2 tics) | 33.20 | 2.56 |
| | 49.99 (3 tics) | 49.78 | 2.17 |
| | 66.56 (4 tics) | 66.42 | 2.20 |
| | 83.32 (5 tics) | 83.20 | 1.53 |
| | 166.64 (10 tics) | 166.43 | 2.81 |
| Flash Standalone Player, 60 Hz refresh rate | 100 | 124.57 | 10.86 |
| | 200 | 223.43 | 11.70 |
| | 300 | 323.64 | 10.45 |
| Flash plugin in Firefox, 24 Hz refresh rate | 100 | 124.84 | 11.45 |

*Note.* Measured with an Arduino connected to a photodiode, for 250 switches between a black and a white screen (Study 3).

ScriptingRT produced a rather constant lengthening of about 24 ms in its presentation duration. This was independent of the programmed presentation duration. Likewise, there was a standard deviation of around 11 ms that did not depend on the programmed duration. The plugin and the standalone player did not differ.

## Discussion

In contrast to specialized experimentation software (DMDX), Flash/ScriptingRT adds a constant duration of about 24 ms to each presentation, and the standard deviation of the measured presentation duration was about 11 ms, or 5 times higher. Note that this test switched the screen consecutively between white and black about 250 times, which is probably a rather straining test. Note also that these results might be specific to the display monitor used in this study. Nevertheless, the conclusion is that stimulus presentations in Flash/ScriptingRT cannot be relied upon to be more precise than the above numbers, and that the choice of paradigm should follow these constraints.

# STUDIES 4–6 OVERVIEW: STROOP TASK

Studies 1–3 outlined the basic capabilities of ScriptingRT, leading to the conclusion that it will be safely replicating robust paradigms that do not require very short presentation times. The following three studies apply such a paradigm to evaluate and compare ScriptingRT to various other software packages.

We adapted a standard color Stroop task for our evaluation purposes [25]. This is one of the most robust findings in cognitive psychology [26]. We used the version employed by Jostmann and Koole [23].

## Method

We created a Portuguese version of the Stroop task. The stimuli were either words (*vermelho* = red, and *azul* = blue) or a neutral letter string (XXXX), that appeared either in red or blue script on a white background. Each color word was presented in both colors ten times, and the neutral string was presented in each color ten times, resulting in a total of 60 trials. Trial order was randomized. In addition, there were 10 practice trials. Congruent trials were those where the word named the color it was written in. Incongruent trials were those where the word named the other color.

Each trial consisted of a blank frame (2000 ms), followed by a frame with a central fixation cross "+" (1000 ms), followed by the target, which stayed on screen until a response was detected. Participants were instructed to press Q if the word was written in red and P if was printed in blue. In order to reduce additional variance, the response keys were not counterbalanced.

## Analytical Strategy

Jostmann & Koole [23] focused on the Stroop interference alone (i.e., the difference between incongruent and neutral trials) for theoretical reasons. We decided to focus our analyses on the combined interference and facilitation effect (the comparison of congruent and incongruent trials) because a) we are not interested in the difference between interference and facilitation here, b) in preliminary analyses, facilitation effects were much smaller and mostly insignificant, while interference effects were strong and always significant [27]. When comparing congruent and incongruent trials, it is possible to include judged color as another factor (which in our case is confounded with which hand is used to answer). Preliminary analyses showed that this factor did not explain a significant amount of variance here, and we thus also dropped it from our reports for ease of presentation. (Analyses including neutral trials and color as an additional factors can be requested from the first author.)

We report the significance of each statistical test, the 95% confidence interval for the difference, and an effect size. Both the significance tests and confidence intervals were computed by submitting the data to a mixed model (also known as hierarchical linear model) in SPSS 20. In mixed models, individual response latencies are the units of analyses, instead of averaging them to create composite scores, which is the traditional practice. Mixed models have recently been recommended over the standard practice because of more precise and often more conservative testing, and because of enhanced modeling options [28], [29]. However, effect size estimation remains difficult in mixed models. For this reason, after reporting test and confidence intervals estimated from the mixed model, we then averaged response latencies for each participant and computed effect sizes in the traditional manner to report here.

In order to have an *a priori* estimate of the effect size of the Stroop effect, we computed a weighted average of the Stroop interference Jostmann and Koole [23] reported in their Study 1: a difference of 85 ms with an *SD* of 84 ms, a large effect. To replicate such an effect at a significance level $\alpha<.05$ and with a test power of .80, one would need ten participants. The combined effect of facilitation and interference, which we are going to test, is likely larger. We sampled more than ten participants in each study to assure sufficient power.

# STUDY 4: REPLICATING STROOP WITH SCRIPTINGRT ONLINE

## Method

### Overview and Design

Study 4 was conducted online. Participants performed the Stroop task programmed in ScriptingRT with the following design: 3 (target word: blue vs. red vs. xxxx, within) ×2 (color: red vs. blue, within) design.

### Participants

All participants volunteered to take part in the experiment. Recruiting was done on Facebook from a Portuguese community. After removing cases with missing values, 19 participants remained in the sample (Age: $M$=28.3, $SD$=6.3).

### Materials and Procedure

The Flash applet running the ScriptingRT task was 600 pixels high and 800 pixels wide. The frame rate was set to the Flex/Flash default of 24 Hz. The flash applet was embedded in an HTML page. Initial survey instructions requested that participants switch the browser into full screen mode and explained the task: particularly to answer as fast as possible, but also as correctly as possible.

## Results

### *Response Latencies*

All participants answered more than 48 of the 60 trials correctly. Incorrect responses and latencies above 1600 ms or below 300 ms (together 5% of all trials) were removed from the analyses.

We submitted the response latencies to a mixed model, entering congruency as a fixed effect, and participants as the grouping variable. Congruent trials were answered faster ($M$=577.32,$SD$=195.58) than incongruent trials ($M$=632.59, $SD$=246.26), showing the classical Stroop effect. This difference was statistically significant, $F(1,702)=18.81$, $p<.001$.

The traditional way to analyse these data would be to average trials of one type for each participant, and then to subject them to a GLM or equivalent analysis. For comparison purposes, we did this for this sample, averaging for each participant congruent and incongruent trials into two separate scores. When we tested this as a repeated factor in a GLM, we found that congruency had a significant effect, $F(1,18)=9.18$, $p=.007$.

We estimated confidence intervals for this difference with the/EMMEANS ... COMPARE command in SPSS Mixed Models. The estimated mean difference of 59.92 has a confidence interval from 32.79 to 87.05 (Figure 2). After averaging the response latencies for each participant and condition, the effect size for congruency was estimated as $\eta_p^2=.338$.

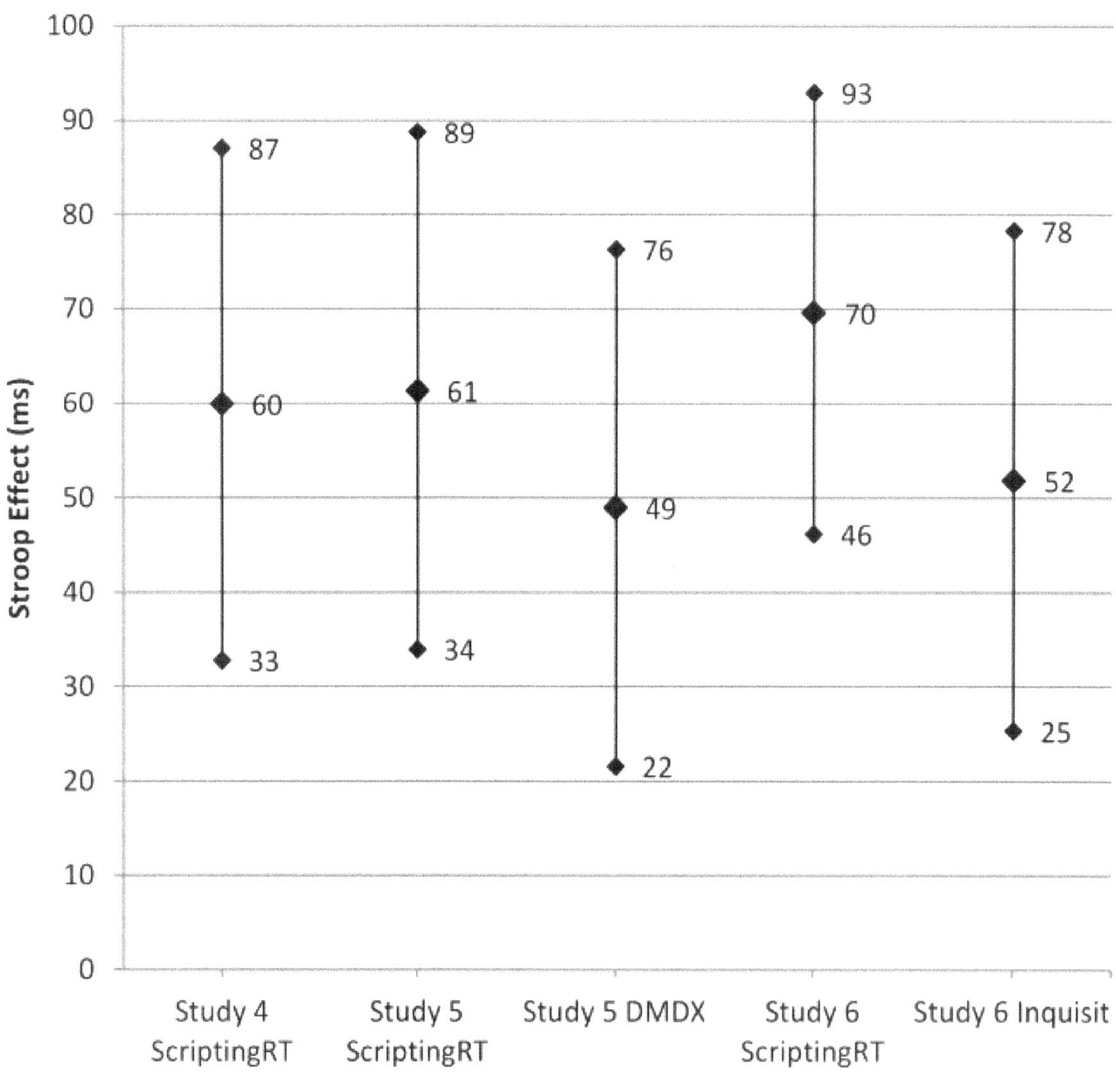


**Figure 2:** Stroop effects and confidence intervals.

Estimated mean Stroop effect (average difference between response latencies in incongruent and congruent trials in ms) and their 95% confidence intervals, obtained in three studies with five samples. Studies 4 and 6 were run online, Study 5 in the laboratory. Software varied within participants in Studies 5, and between participants in Study 6.

## Discussion

The goal of Study 4 was to validate ScriptingRT with a well know paradigm, the Stroop Effect. Participants had to decide which color a target series of letters was written in, responding to 60 trials. The results showed that responses on incongruent trials were about 60 ms slower than those on congruent trials, and that ScriptingRT measured this difference precisely enough to be significant in the sample of 19 participants.

## STUDY 5: COMPARING SCRIPTINGRT AND DMDX IN THE LABORATORY

Study 5 tested the precision of ScriptingRT by comparing it to DMDX [5] with both running on the same computer in a controlled laboratory setting.

### Method

#### *Overview and Design*

All participants completed a Stroop task twice on the same PC, once in ScriptingRT and once in DMDX. The order of software was counterbalanced. The complete design was thus 3 (targets words, within) ×2 (color, within) ×2 (software: ScriptingRT vs. DMDX, within) ×2 (first task: DMDX vs. ScriptingRT, between).

#### *Participants*

Nineteen undergraduates students from a Portuguese university took part in the experiment and were compensated with a 5 € gift voucher (Age: *M*=25.3, *SD*=9.1). The data from one participant had to be excluded because 27 responses were either incorrect or outside of the response window. Thus, data from 18 participants were analyzed.

### Materials and Procedure

Participants were informed that we were testing several software packages and therefore they had to perform the same task twice. Between the two versions of the task there was a short break. Participants were run individually. The Stroop task was programmed as before and conducted in Portuguese. The DMDX procedure matched the one in ScriptingRT as closely as possible. In ScriptingRT, the size of the Flash app in the browser was set to 1366×768 pixels, with a frame rate of 24 Hz, run in Mozilla Firefox with the Adobe Flash plugin. In DMDX, the task was displayed with the same resolution, but DMDX used the standard frame rate of 60 Hz. This study was run in the laboratory on Sony Vaio Core i5 laptops, running Windows 7 (64-bit). These laptops have 13 inch screens, with a refresh rate of 60 Hz.

### Results

We first removed incorrect trials and trials with latencies above 1600 ms and below 300 ms (a total of 4.03%).

We submitted the individual response latencies to a mixed model, with congruency, software, order of software, and all their interactions as fixed effects, and participant as the grouping variable.

Congruent trials were faster than incongruent trials in both ScriptingRT (*M*=629.66, *SD*=234.17 and *M*=729.04, *SD*=301.44, respectively) and DMDX (*M*=504.85, *SD*=172.98 and *M*=565.73,*SD*=229.88, respectively). The main effect of congruency was significant in the mixed model,$F(1,1358)=21.23$, $p<.001$. In addition, there was a main effect of software, $F(1,1358)=58.47$,$p<.001$. DMDX recorded responses as faster, *M*=551.98, *SD*=201.38, than ScriptingRT did, *M*=631.63, *SD*=243.42. Importantly, the congruency effect was not moderated by software, $F<1$.

In addition there were some effects that are irrelevant given the present purposes. Software and order interacted, indicating that the second software run produced faster answers (presumably because of practice). We also found a moderation of the overall Stroop effect by which software was run first, which is most likely a randomization artifact.

Turning to confidence intervals of the estimated mean differences, we found that the difference due to congruency in ScriptingRT was 61.35, ranging from 33.96 to 88.75 (Figure 2). Responses in DMDX resulted in a smaller difference of 48.96, ranging from 21.59 to 76.33.

Effect sizes were computed after averaging latencies, for each participant, software, and congruency separately. We used two separate GLMs with congruency as a repeated measure. The effect size for congruency was $\eta_p^2=.37$ in ScriptingRT and $\eta_p^2=.24$ in DMDX.

### Discussion

Study 5 compared ScriptingRT and DMDX, using again the classic Stroop effect. All participants performed the task in both programs in the laboratory on the same computer. We found that the size of the Stroop effect was not affected by which software was used. If there was a difference at all, ScriptingRT showed larger interference effects than did DMDX. However, that ScriptingRT indicated significantly longer response latencies. The difference is close to the differences observed in Studies 1 and 2. Note that it seems impossible to state exactly how much measuring in Flash with ScriptingRT adds as a constant to the latency, as this seems to differ between browsers (Study 1) and presumably also depending on hardware[18].

## STUDY 6: COMPARING SCRIPTINGRT TO INQUISIT WEB EDITION, RUNNING ONLINE

### Method

#### *Overview and Design*

Study 6 went beyond the previous studies by comparing ScriptingRT to the only currently available commercial solution for online data collection, namely Inquisit Web Edition. We ran this study online, directing voluntary participants to a website and assigning them randomly to either a ScriptingRT or an Inquisit Web Edition version of the same Stroop task that was used before. Software thus varied between participants in this study.

#### *Participants*

Undergraduates of a Portuguese university were contacted by e-mail and asked to perform the experiment voluntarily. The E-mail contained a brief explanation of the experiment's goal (not mentioning interference) and a link to the web page. Each participant was assigned randomly to either ScriptingRT or Inquisit. Data from 43 participants were collected, but one had technical problems, leaving 42 in the final sample; 18 performed the task in Inquisit and 24 in ScriptingRT (Age: *M*=25.8 *SD*=7.78).

### Materials and Procedure

ScriptingRT used a resolution of 600×800 pixels. The frame rate in Flex was set to 60 Hz. The task was programmed in Inquisit and deployed using the web edition version. The experiment ran on the participant's computer with their specific resolution and frame rate.

### Results

Again, we first removed trials with incorrect responses and responses outside the 300 to 1600ms time window (in total 6.9%). Individual latencies were subjected to a mixed model with software, congruency, and their interaction as fixed factors, and participant as grouping variable.

Congruent trials were faster than incongruent trials in both ScriptingRT ($M$=569.16, $SD$=224.79 and $M$=630.10, $SD$=269.74) and Inquisit ($M$=526.58, $SD$=184.26 and $M$=576.24, $SD$=250.66). The main effect of congruency was significant, $F(1,1520)=45.40, p<.001$. Software had neither a main effect, nor did it interact with the congruency effect, both $Fs<1$.

When we estimated means and confidence intervals, the congruency effect in ScriptingRT was estimated as 69.57, with an interval from 46.19 to 92.94. In Inquisit, the congruency effect was estimated as 51.82, with an interval from 25.32 to 78.32 (Figure 2).

We again averaged latencies for participants to two scores for congruent and incongruent trials, and then ran two GLMs to estimate effect sizes. The effect size in ScriptingRT was $\eta_p^2=.33$, and in Inquisit $\eta_p^2=.28$.

### Discussion

In an online study, we compared ScriptingRT to the only commercially available software that measures response latencies online. Again, the Stroop effect replicated in ScriptingRT, and again we found no difference from another software, this time Inquisit Web Edition. The latencies measured by ScriptingRT were again somewhat longer, but the difference was not significant here. Note that this study used a between subjects design, which added more error variance to the between software comparison.

## GENERAL DISCUSSION

ScriptingRT is an open source software framework for developing online response latency studies running in Adobe Flash. ScriptingRT studies are programmed in Apache Flex, with a combination of four elements: (1) ScriptingRT-provided components (in MXML) that create the building blocks of a latency study (e.g., blocks, items, and frames), (2) standard Flex components (in MXML) that describe general content such as text, graphics, images, or sound, (3) additional Flex components that add custom components, and (4) programs (in ActionScript) that add custom functionality.

Flash has been used to conduct response latency studies before, notably using the IAT [7]. In the current paper, we show that the precision and accuracy provided by Flash in the form of ScriptingRT is not perfect, but suitable for many paradigms. As Figure 2 shows, using ScriptingRT, we replicated in three studies the classic Stroop interference effect with samples of around 20 participants. In two of those studies, we compared the combined interference and facilitation effect obtained in ScriptingRT to the same effect in a different software (DMDX, Inquisit Web Edition), without finding a significant difference. Figure 2 also shows that all five computed Stroop differences fall within the 95% confidence intervals of all other studies and conditions, suggesting a solid replication of the effect across software. Notably, when computing effect sizes, we found somewhat larger effects in ScriptingRT in all three comparison studies. Even though the differences between software were never significant, this assures that we did not simply have too little power in the tests of an inferior software, when measuring ScriptingRT against the competitors.

The solid replication and the missing significant differences across software might be surprising given the offsets documented in Studies 1–3. To understand this, one should keep in mind that the delays have a random distribution with a standard deviation that is much smaller than the studied effect itself. In addition, other sources of error variance, in particular due to participants, are distributed randomly. In the current paper, we did not address the question of how smaller experimental effects may hold up in the same comparison. In other words, can we expect to replicate response latency differences around 20 or even 10 ms? It can be expected that the smaller the effect, the more problematic the noise introduced by ScriptingRT (and online experimentation more generally). Both pilot testing and simulation can be used to estimate the impact on a particular paradigm with given number of trials and variance in materials. For researchers interested in using ScriptingRT to study smaller effects, we recommend to a) include conditions that replicate well known effects as a comparison condition, and b) use pilot studies to estimate effect sizes and required sample size for sufficient power.

Tests using special hardware designed to register the precise timing of stimulus presentations found evidence that as a stimulus presentation vehicle, Flash is not precise to the millisecond; we found constant lags of about 24 ms using the Flash-based ScriptingRT software. We also saw that compared to standard software packages, the standard deviation of the measures was larger; but because these deviations were below 5 ms, it still seems to be useful for most purposes. This amount of additional variance is comparable to what was standard for many years when regular keyboards were used. Finally, ScriptingRT overestimates the response latencies by a constant amount of about 60 ms. These issues must be taken into account when planning a study using ScriptingRT and interpreting results.

Importantly, variance added by measuring response latencies in Flash rather than a native software is only one source of added variance when collecting data online. In addition, it is quite likely that different implementations (e.g., Flash plugin vs. Flash support integrated into Chrome), different operating systems (e.g., Windows vs. OS X), additional programs running on the computer, and the quality of the hardware, can influence both the presentation timing and the time measurement, and will add error variance that is indistinguishable from variance due to interindividual differences. The present data do not yet allow conclusions on this beyond the differences found in Study 1, but as a precaution, any online data collection project should collect as much technical data on the client machine as possible. We will continue with formal tests to find out more about these variances.

With the current evaluation we show that ScriptingRT can replicate strong effects. What remains a task for future work is to provide exact guidelines for a priori judgments of how added noise in latency measures, combined with variability by assessing more diverse samples, will affect test power and the occurrence of false positive findings.

ScriptingRT can be used in its current form to implement many different paradigms, and it is under further development. Its source code is available, and we invite contributions to it. We will actively continue to develop it, document programmed enhancements online, and empirically test them.

## CONCLUSION

ScriptingRT is a software library that allows programming response latency studies using Apache Flex and Adobe Flash. ScriptingRT offers the building blocks for typical response latency paradigms in XML, while additional functionality can be added with programming a scripting language. The testing reported herein suggests that it is, in its present form, a viable software for using standard response latency paradigms online. Our evidence suggests that for a robust paradigm like Stroop, ScriptingRT is comparable to the other available options (i.e., Java, and HTML/JavaScript, and Inquisit Web Edition).

Future research will ideally run studies with a variety of software in a variety of environments, for instance using Flash and JavaScript to access large samples, native software running on a desktop computer and Java to get more precise measures, and accompanying replications in the lab with precise equipment. We see Flash and ScriptingRT as an important component in this mix, because it is free and accessible, and thus allows smaller labs to run large studies.

We contend that running response latency studies online can contribute to overcoming a number of problems that trouble current psychological research: First, many studies have low power. Here, easy access to participants online can help [15], [30], even though power will be slightly decreased by the additional noise from using Flash compared to native PC software. Second, many studies are conducted by sampling only from Western, educated, industrialized, rich, and democratic societies [31]. Running online naturally restricts sampling to educated and industrialized populations that have access to computers and the Internet, but it may go a long way towards getting more cultural variability into cognitive and social science studies. Finally, replication is becoming increasingly important in psychological research [32], [33]. Response latency studies may be especially difficult to replicate because their material is often programmed in proprietary software, and not easily shareable. ScriptingRT is completely open source, and its source files are simple text, and thus easily shareable.

ScriptingRT is already being used by various researchers to run studies. We believe it is quite accessible for the average researcher. Because ScriptingRT is an open source software program, developed to be used in conjunction with other open source programs, we look forward to its growth in many directions, with wide applications. The results obtained and reported in this article and the expansion possibilities allowed by the software's open source nature, make us confident that ScriptingRT will gain researchers' interest and we hope that its usage will be widespread.

## ACKNOWLEDGMENTS

We thank Frank Friedmann for programming ScriptingRT, Gonçalo Paiva, Pedro Antunes, João Fonseca, and Robert Richards for their help with building the photodiode and solenoid hardware, and Yoav Bar-Anan for helpful comments on this manuscript.

## REFERENCES

1. Kraut R, Olson J, Banaji M, Bruckman A, Cohen J, et al. (2004) Psychological research online: Report of Board of Scientific Affairs' Advisory Group on the conduct of research on the Internet. Am Psychol 59: 105–117doi:10.1037/0003-066X.59.2.105
2. Fraley RC (2007) Using the Internet for personality research: What can be done, how to do it, and some concerns. In: Robins RW, Fraley RC, Krueger RF, editors. Handbook of research methods in personality psychology. New York, NY, US: Guilford Press. 130–148.
3. Sargis EG, Skitka LJ (2012) The Internet as psychological laboratory revisited: Best practices, challenges, and solutions. In: Amichai-Hamburger Y, editor. The Internet as psychological laboratory revisited: Best practices, challenges, and solutions (2nd ed.). Oxford University Press. 253–270.
4. Apache Flex (2013) Available: http://flex.apache.org/ Accessed 2013 May 1.
5. Forster KI, Forster JC (2003) DMDX: A Windows display program with millisecond accuracy. Behav Res Methods Instrum Comput 35: 116–124
6. Eichstaedt J (2001) An inaccurate-timing filter for reaction time measurement by JAVA applets implementing Internet-based experiments. Behav Res Methods Instrum Comput 33: 179–186
7. Nosek BA, Banaji M, Greenwald AG (2002) Harvesting implicit group attitudes and beliefs from a demonstration web site. Group Dyn 6: 101–115doi:10.1037//1089-2699.6.1.101
8. Keller F, Gunasekharan S, Mayo N, Corley M (2009) Timing accuracy of Web experiments: a case study using the WebExp software package. Behav Res Methods 41: 1–12doi:10.3758/BRM.41.1.12
9. Von Bastian CC, Locher A, Ruflin M (2013) Tatool: A Java-based open-source programming framework for psychological studies. Behav Res Methods 45: 108–115doi:10.3758/s13428-012-0224-y
10. Project Implicit (2011). Available: https://implicit.harvard.eduAccessed 2013 May 1.
11. Reimers S, Stewart N (2007) Adobe Flash as a medium for online experimentation: A test of reaction time measurement capabilities. Behav Res Methods 39: 365–370
12. Mason W (2011) Open-source, Web-based IAT. Available: http://github.com/winteram/IAT Accessed 2013 May 1.

13. Zwaan RA, Pecher D (2012) Revisiting mental simulation in language comprehension: six replication attempts. PloS ONE 7: e51382.doi:10.1371/journal.pone.0051382
14. Crump MJC, McDonnell JV, Gureckis TM (2013) Evaluating Amazon›s Mechanical Turk as a tool for experimental behavioral research. PLoS ONE 8: e57410.doi:10.1371/journal.pone.0057410
15. Buhrmester M, Kwang T, Gosling SD (2011) Amazon›s Mechanical Turk: A new source of inexpensive, yet high-quality, data? Perspect Psychol Sci 6: 3–5doi:10.1177/1745691610393980
16. Plant RR, Turner G (2009) Millisecond precision psychological research in a world of commodity computers: New hardware, new problems? Behav Res Methods 41: 598–614doi:10.3758/BRM.41.3.598
17. Plant RR, Hammond N, Whitehouse T (2003) How choice of mouse may affect response timing in psychological studies. Behav Res Methods Instrum Comput 35: 276–284
18. Neath I, Earle A, Hallett D, Surprenant AM (2011) Response time accuracy in Apple Macintosh computers. Behav Res Methods 43: 353–362doi:10.3758/s13428-011-0069-9
19. Schubert TW (2012) ScriptingRT. Available: http://reactiontimes.wordpress.com/scriptingrt/ Accessed 2013 May 1.
20. Forster JC (2012) DMDX Help Input. Available:http://www.u.arizona.edu/~jforster/dmdx/help/dmdxhinput.htm Accessed 2013 Aug 16.
21. Schubert TW, D'Ausilio A, Canto R (2013) Using Arduino microcontroller boards to measure response latencies. Behav Res Methods. 10.3758/s13428-013-0336-z.
22. E-Prime (2012) Computer software. Pittsburth, PA: Psychology Software Tools.
23. Inquisit (2011) Computer software. Seattle, WA: Millisecond Software.
24. SuperLab (2011). Computer software. San Pedro, CA: Cedrus Corporation.
25. Stroop JR (1935) Studies of interference in serial verbal reactions. J Exp Psychol 18: 643–662
26. MacLeod CM (1991) Half a century of research on the Stroop effect: an integrative review. Psychol Bull109: 163–203
27. Jostmann NB, Koole SL (2007) On the regulation of cognitive control: Action orientation moderates the impact of high demands in Stroop interference tasks. J Exp Psychol Gen 136: 593–609doi:10.1037/0096-3445.136.4.593
28. Hoffman L, Rovine MJ (2007) Multilevel models for the experimental psychologist: foundations and illustrative examples. Behav Res Methods 39: 101–117
29. Judd CM, Westfall J, Kenny DA (2012) Treating stimuli as a random factor in social psychology: A new and comprehensive solution to a pervasive but largely ignored problem. J Pers Soc Psychol 103: 54–69doi:10.1037/a0028347
30. Mason W, Suri S (2012) Conducting behavioral research on Amazon›s Mechanical Turk. Behav Res Methods 44: 1–23doi:10.3758/s13428-011-0124-6
31. Henrich J, Heine SJ, Norenzayan A (2010) The weirdest people in the world? Behav Brain Sci 33: 61–135doi:10.1017/S0140525X0999152X
32. Asendorpf JB, Conner M, De Fruyt F, De Houwer J, Denissen JJA, et al. (2013) Recommendations for increasing replicability in psychology. Eur J Pers 27: 108–119doi: 10.1002/per.1919
33. Pashler H, Wagenmakers EJ (2012) Editors› Introduction to the Special Section on Replicability in Psychological Science: A Crisis of Confidence? Perspect Psychol Sci 7: 528–530doi:10.1177/1745691612465253
34. Schubert TW (2012) Electro-Mechanical Turk. Available: http://reactiontimes.wordpress.com/electro-mechanical-turk/ Accessed 2012 Oct 30.

CHAPTER 18

# AUTOMATICALLY GENERATED ALGORITHMS FOR THE VERTEX COLORING PROBLEM


Carlos Contreras Bolton[1] , Gustavo Gatica[2] , Vı´ctor Parada[1]

[1]Departamento de Ingenierı´a Informa´tica, Universidad de Santiago de Chile, Santiago, Chile,

[2]Escuela de Informa´tica, Universidad Andre´s Bello, Santiago, Chile



## ABSTRACT

**The vertex coloring problem is a classical problem in combinatorial optimization that consists of assigning a color to each vertex of a graph such that no adjacent vertices share the same color, minimizing the number of colors used. Despite the various practical applications that exist for this problem, its NP-hardness still represents a computational challenge. Some of the best computational results obtained for this problem are consequences of hybridizing the various known heuristics. Automatically revising the space constituted by combining these techniques to find the most adequate combination has received less attention. In this paper, we propose exploring the heuristics space for the vertex coloring problem using evolutionary algorithms. We automatically generate three new algorithms by combining elementary heuristics. To evaluate the new algorithms, a computational experiment was performed that allowed comparing them numerically with existing heuristics. The obtained algorithms present an average 29.97% relative error, while four other heuristics selected from the literature present a 59.73% error, considering 29 of the more difficult instances in the DIMACS benchmark.**


## INTRODUCTION

The vertex coloring problem (VCP) consists of identifying the lowest number of colors required to color a graph. Let $G=(V, E)$ be an undirected graph, where $V$ is a set of vertices and $E$ is a set of edges. A function $F$: $V \mapsto$ <$>\raster="rg1"<$> is defined, where <$>\raster="rg1"<$> is a finite set of colors such that if $u$ and $v \in V$ and $(u,v) \in E$, then $F(u) \neq F(v)\ \forall u,v$. The objective is to find the chromatic number, $\chi(G)$, corresponding to the minimum number of colors needed to color $G$ [1].


**Citation:** Contreras Bolton C, Gatica G, Parada V. Automatically Generated Algorithms for the Vertex Coloring Problem. Golden AA-J, ed. PLoS ONE. 2013;8(3):e58551. doi:10.1371/journal.pone.0058551.


Because of its NP-hardness [2], the VCP has been treated using various methods: exact, constructive heuristics, and metaheuristics [3]. The exact methods consider different integer programming formulations. Its solution, however, does not completely consider the problem as certain instances belong to the known benchmarks that cannot be solved in reasonable times and their $\chi(G)$ values remain unknown. To obtain results with low computational times, Méndez-Díaz and Zabala [4], [5] combine linear integer programming with instance preprocessing methods, while Malagutti et al. [6] combine branch-and-price with an algorithm that integrates tabu search, greedy, and evolutionary algorithm components and reports 33 optimum values, of which five were "open for several years", leaving 28 problems with unknown $\chi(G)$ among the 115 analyzed instances.

Constructive heuristic methods integrate elementary heuristic functions that color a graph step-by-step, considering decisions on the next vertex to color and color to use [7]–[9]. Because the heuristics can be easily implemented in polynomial time, they are also used as tools within other algorithms. Malaguti et al. [10] propose an evolutionary algorithm that combines tabu search, generating a set of initial solutions through the well-known greedy constructive heuristics SEQ [3], DSATUR [7] and Recursive Largest First (RLF) [8]. The initial solutions are then improved by solving a set-covering problem. Although such hybridization obtains better solutions than other methods, several hours of computational time are required to achieve them.

Various metaheuristic approaches have resulted from heuristic combinations to solve the VCP. Combining evolutionary techniques with simulated annealing has allowed finding new chromatic numbers for various test instances [11], [12]. Another interesting combination of a genetic algorithm with the classical tabu search [13] provides a method with five different versions, obtaining optimum solutions for some hard instances of the DIMACS benchmark, with a computational time limit of 12 hours [14]. The existing VCP results indicate that an adequate method combination can solve some of the more difficult instances, but the combinations revised so far represent a small part of those that can possibly be revised.

The selection of an appropriate combination of heuristics to solve a problem, can be performed automatically. In fact, Minton [15] proposed an analytical learning system, which from a set of generic heuristics, produces specific heuristic combinations for the constraint-satisfaction problem. For the same problem, Epstein et al. [16] have proposed an adaptive engine that, from a set of elementary methods, produces a combination of heuristics that learn from their past decisions, as the search progresses. The engine is not only capable of finding novel heuristic for the problem, but also it rediscovers existing heuristics. Also, Nareyek [17]proposed a method that uses reinforcement learning to discover the best heuristic to be adopted at each stage of a search process. A particular case of the constraint satisfaction problem is the MAX-SAT, which is to determine a solution that satisfies a maximum number of constraints, therefore, it can be seen as a typical combinatorial optimization problem. Bain et al. [18] proposed a novel way to solve the problem by means of genetic programming [19],[20], i.e., evolving algorithms that are combinations of elementary heuristics already known for the problem. Also, Fukunaga [21], [22] proposed a heuristic evaluation system for solving the satisfiability problem. The new heuristics produced are competitive with some of the existing ones, showing that for this problem, genetic programming can automatically produce new algorithms. In the field of combinatorial optimization, the hyper-heuristics [23] are a generalization of metaheuristics. Such techniques also can combine heuristics to solve difficult optimization problems. These have been tested with various problems such as timetabling [24] problem and strip packing problem [25].

In this paper, we suggest that a combination of heuristics for VCP can be performed using evolutionary computation, which allows new algorithms to be produced that use already existing techniques constructed from elementary heuristic components and control structures typical of any algorithm type, producing procedures that can compete with existing heuristics. The participation of the elementary heuristics and control structures are coded using binary*strings* that are subjected to selection, crossover and mutation operations at each stage [26],[27]. Using some control parameters, we detected that the new algorithms have characteristics common to existing heuristics.

The automatic revision of heuristic combinations enables studying the potential algorithms that solve the VCP with low computational requirements and obtain high-quality solutions. The algorithms that can be generated would thus allow detecting heuristic combinations with good performance for given groups of VCP instances.

The following section of this paper describes the procedures involved in generating the new algorithms, while the third section presents and discusses the computational results of the generated algorithms. The last section presents the conclusions of the study.

## Procedure for Generating the Algorithms

This section presents the evolutionary process used to obtain algorithms for the VCP. The process follows similar steps to those used in genetic programming to represent a problem[19], [20]. This means that it has to be defined the representation used, the data structures, the fitness function definition, the corresponding functions and terminals with elementary heuristics used to generate algorithms, the testing and validation instances, the parameter calibration procedure, and the hardware and software used.

## Evolutionary Process

To perform algorithm evolution, we designed and implemented an evolutionary algorithm that operates in a genotype-phenotype mode [28]. As genotype, we use a structure that specifies the participation of each heuristic component and typical instructions, and as phenotype, a tree structure that corresponds to the algorithm to be constructed. The evolution of a population with fixed size is performed using binary tournament selection operators between 2 individuals selected randomly, two-point crossover, and binary mutation [27]. Each new population contains binary strings obtained from the current population. Every time a string is generated, the fitness function evaluates the individual, constructs an instructions tree and validates its performance on a set of test instances. Figure 1 describes the evolutionary algorithm scheme, showing the stages involved in the generation of population $P(t+1)$ from population $P(t)$.

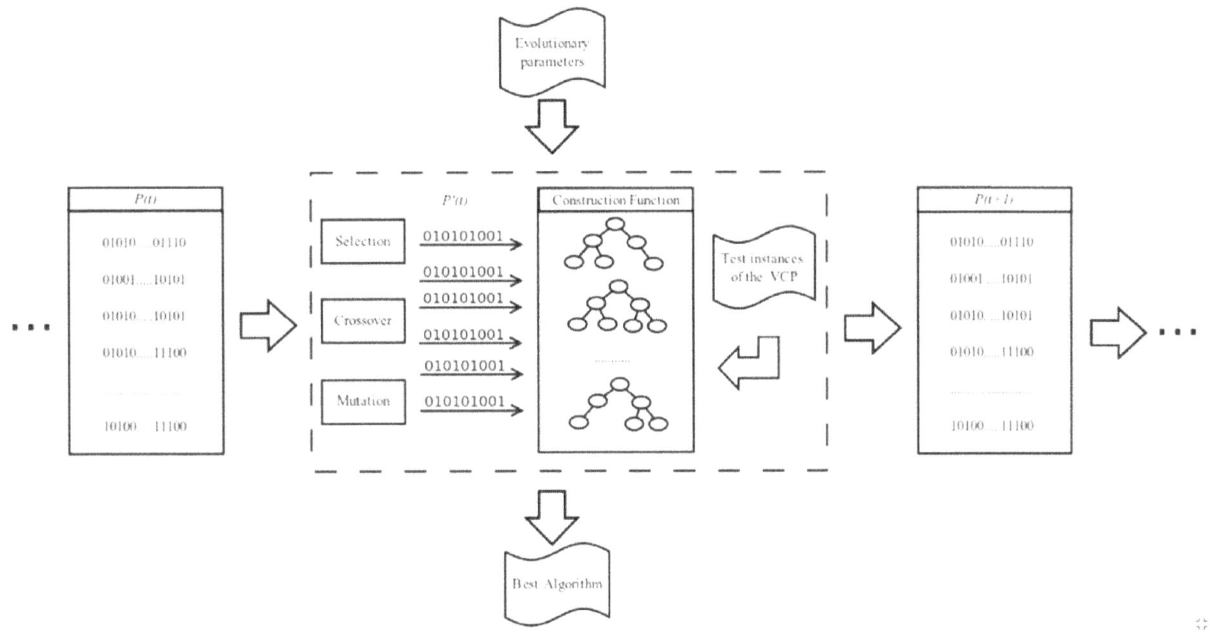


**Figure 1:** Evolutionary process.

The evolutionary process considers 10 executions of 12 problem groups: DSJ, LEI, GOM, MYC, HOS, KOZ, CAR, LAT-SCH, SGB, REG, MYZ and CUL, available athttp://mat.gsia.cmu.edu/COLOR/instances.html. Consequently, 120 evolutionary processes are performed with populations of 50 individuals and a stopping criterion of 100 generations. To decrease the computational time used in the implementation, the fitness function is evaluated in parallel, considering 6 processors with shared memory. The evaluations are distributed among the parallel processors from a waiting queue.

## Representing the Genotype and Phenotype

The elementary components of the artificially generated algorithms are identified using an integer number that is transformed into a binary number. Five bits are thus used to represent 32 different components. A binary string indicates the components and the order in which they are selected to construct the corresponding artificial algorithm (phenotype), represented using a preordered binary tree [29]. Figure 2 describes a string with 30 bits and a binary tree with six nodes.

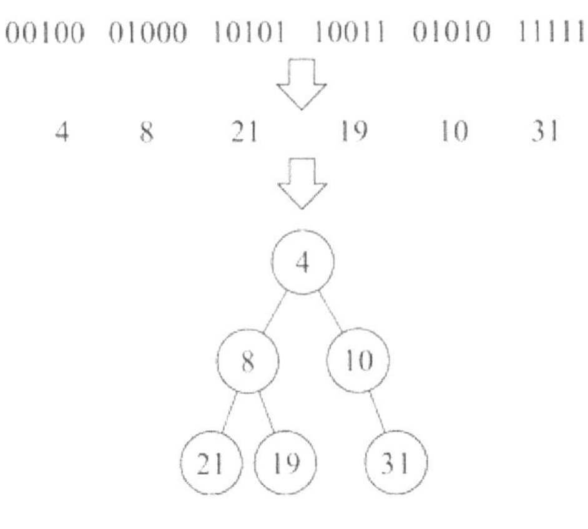


**Figure 2:** Decoding a binary string.

## Data Structure

The data structure from which the artificial algorithms are created stores the graph to be colored. The graph is stored in an adjacent list. Implementation uses the Boost Graph Library[30], which contains functions optimized for recurrent operations on graphs.

## Fitness Function

We define a fitness function containing three terms: the first measures the coloring degree of the graph, the second represents the number of colors used, and the third corresponds to the tree size.

Let $I = \{1, 2, \ldots, n_I\}$ be a set of instances in the VCP, and let us introduce the following definitions:

$\vartheta_i$: number of colors used to color graph $i$,

$h$: tree depth,

$n_{c_i}$: number of vertices with a color assigned to graph $i$,

$n_{v_i}$: total number of vertices in graph $i$,

$\chi_i(G)$: best known chromatic number for graph $i$,

$\delta_i$: number of nodes in algorithm $i$.

Let $\varphi_i$ be the relative error of the number of colored vertices with respect to the number of vertices in problem $i$ (Eq. 1).

$$\varphi_i = \frac{n_{v_i} - n_{c_i}}{n_{v_i}} \quad \forall i \in I \tag{1}$$

Equation 2 corresponds to the fitness function. The first internal term of the summation represents the average relative error of the number of colors used for all instances, the second weights the average deviation of the best chromatic number known, and the third weights a deviation of the tree size for a height defined by $h$. The values of $f(G)$ are in the [0,1] range. The terms are weighted parametrically by values $a$, $b$ and $c$.

$$f(G)=\frac{\sum_{i=1}^{n_f}\left(a\cdot\varphi_i\cdot\lceil\varphi_i\rceil+b\left(\lceil\varphi_i\rceil+(1-\lceil\varphi_i\rceil)\cdot(\frac{\chi_i(G)-\varphi_i}{\chi_i(G)})\right)+c\cdot\left(\frac{\delta_i}{2^{h+1}-1}\right)\right)}{N_f} \quad (2)$$

## Function and Terminal Definitions

As elementary components of the produced algorithms, function and terminal sets are defined. Executing a function requires one or two arguments that can also be functions or terminals, denoted *function(argument1,argument2)*. Each graph vertex is numbered, as are the colors available for coloring. The functions are subdivided into coloring and generic functions. The former assign a color to the vertex based on a defined criterion and require a terminal that returns a vertex as an argument, while the latter receive a Boolean value as an argument that corresponds to the evaluation of a subtree.

## Coloring Functions

- ***Greedy (v)*:** It assigns the least feasible color to vertex *v*. When changing the vertex color, the function returns the value true, otherwise it returns false. It is based on the*Iterated Greedy* algorithm [9].
- ***More-frequent-color(v)*:** It assigns the feasible color with higher frequency in the graph to vertex *v*. If this is not possible, it assigns a color to the vertex using *Greedy* (*v*). If the function changes the color assigned to the vertex, it returns true; otherwise, it returns false.
- ***Less-frequent-color(v)*:** It assigns a less frequent feasible color in the graph to vertex*v*. If this is not possible, it assigns a feasible color that does not generate conflicts using *Greedy* (*v*). If the function changes the color assigned to the vertex, it returns true; otherwise, it returns false.
- ***Swap-color($v_1$,$v_2$)*:** It exchanges the color of vertex $v_1$ with that of vertex $v_2$. If no conflicts are generated, it returns true; otherwise, it returns false.
- ***Greedy-adjacents(v)*:** It assigns a feasible color to the vertices adjacent to *v* using*Greedy*(*v*) and returns the value true if it assigns at least one color to an adjacent vertex; otherwise, it returns false.
- ***Uncoloring(v)*:** It removes the current color of *v*, returning the true value; if *v* has no color assigned, it returns false.
- ***Uncoloring-adjacents(v)*:** It removes the color of each vertex adjacent to *v* and returns a true value if removing at least one color is feasible; otherwise, it returns false.

## Generic Functions

A set of generic functions, i.e., those that participate in the algorithms as control structures, is defined; they are denoted using arborescent arguments: *Equal*($P_1$,$P_2$), *And*($P_1$,$P_2$), *Or*($P_1$,$P_2$), and *Not* ($P_1$,$P_2$). The following two functions are also used:

- ***If ($P_1$,$P_2$)*:** It executes *subtree* $P_2$ if *subtree* $P_1$ has a true value. It returns a true value if executing the second argument is feasible (regardless of its return); otherwise, it returns false.
- ***While($P_1$,$P_2$)*:** It performs a cycle on *subtree* $P_2$ if the condition of *subtree* $P_1$ remains true. It returns true when it modifies the graph color; otherwise, it returns false. *Subtree* $P_1$ corresponds to the condition and *subtree* $P_2$ to the body. The stop criterion is met when $P_1$ returns false, or when a number of iterations (10) elapses without any change in the data structure or when it is exceeded a predefined maximum number of iterations equal to number of vertices of the instance. Figure 3*a* shows a tree with a cycle whose left offspring is the condition and right offspring the body. Fig. 3*b* shows its equivalent pseudocode.

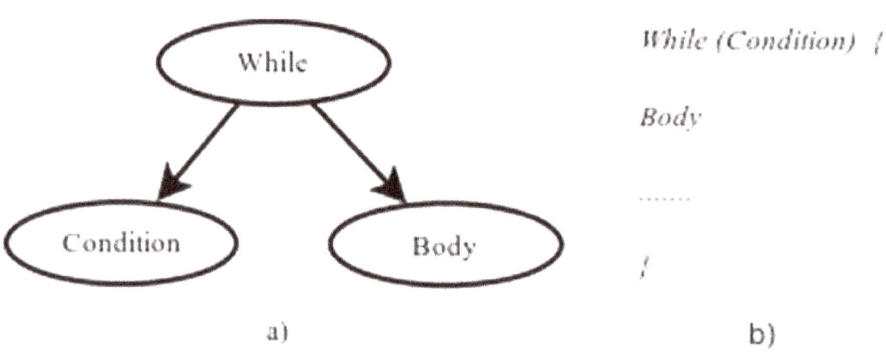


Figure 3: While cycle and its equivalence in pseudocode.

## Set of Terminals

The terminals are subdivided into vertex identifiers and state indicators. The vertex identifiers aim to identify particular vertices in the graph. If no vertex is found that fulfills the desired characteristic, it returns false. Conversely, the latter return true or false, and they are used as arguments of the condition of generic functions.

### Vertex Searching Terminals

- ***First-vertex***: It identifies the lowest numbered vertex, uses the First-Fit [31] vertex selection criterion, and returns false if it does not find a vertex with that characteristic.
- ***More-frequent-color-vertex***: It identifies the highest numbered vertex with the most frequently used color in the graph; if it does not exist, it returns false.
- ***Less-frequent-color-vertex***: It identifies the lowest numbered colored vertex with a less frequent color; if it does not exist, it returns false.
- ***Lowest-numbered-color-vertex***: It identifies the highest numbered vertex with the lowest numbered color; if it does not exist, it returns false.
- ***Highest-numbered-color-vertex***: It identifies the highest numbered vertex with the highest numbered color; if it does not exist, it returns false.
- ***Minimum-degree-vertex***: It identifies the lowest numbered vertex with the fewest adjacent vertices, based on the Minimum Degree Ordering [32] vertex selection criterion; if the vertex does not exist, it returns false.
- ***Largest-degree-vertex***: It identifies the vertex with the most adjacent vertices. If there is more than one vertex that fulfills this characteristic, it returns the lowest numbered vertex that fulfills this condition, based on the Modified Largest Degree Ordering [31]vertex selection criterion; if the vertex does not exist, it returns false.
- ***Saturation-degree-vertex***: It identifies the vertex with the most adjacent vertices with different assigned colors, based on the Saturation Degree Ordering vertex selection criterion used by the *DSATUR* algorithm. If more than one vertex has this characteristic, it returns the lowest numbered vertex; otherwise, it returns false.
- ***Incidence-degree-vertex***: It identifies the lowest numbered vertex with the most colored adjacent vertices, based on the Incidence Degree Ordering [31] vertex selection criterion; if it does not find a vertex, it returns false.
- ***More-uncolored-adjacents-vertex***: It identifies the lowest numbered vertex with the most uncolored adjacent vertices, according to the vertex selection criterion of the RLF algorithm; if it does not find a vertex, it returns false.

### Boolean Terminals

These are variables that indicate the coloring state of the graph at any construction stage. The first, *Not-increase,* indicates if there is an increase of the number of colors used to color the graph. The other variable, *Exist-uncolored-vertex*, indicates if uncolored vertices remain in the graph.

### Adaptation and Test Cases

The problems used to test and adapt the individuals comprise a problem set from the DIMACS benchmark, which compiles instances considered as a standard set for the VCP [33].

### Parameter Calibration

The evolutionary algorithms' computational performance has a direct relationship with the parameters used in the experimental stage. The parameters involved are the probabilities of crossover and mutation, the number of generations, the chromosome length and the parameters $a$, $b$ and $c$ of the fitness function. Based on the studies by Grefenstette [34], the crossover probability is set to 0.9. The mutation probability was fine-tuned with the following values: {0.005, 0.01, 0.02, 0.04, 0.08, 0.10, 0.12, 0.14, 0.16, 0.18, 0.20}, and it delivered a value of 0.16. In preliminary experiments, no improvements are detected after 100 iterations; the detention criterion of the evolutionary algorithm is thus set to 100 generations. In contrast with other problems approaches using evolutionary algorithms, where chromosome length is automatically defined by considering the problem to solve as the basis, e.g., in the travelling salesman problem, which is based on the number of cities [35], for this approach we must determine the chromosome length parameter. A fine-tuning is thus performed using the values {40, 80, 160, 320}, which delivers the value 160. Finally, the weights of the fitness function were adjusted in preliminary tests to give greater importance to the minimization of the error; the values adopted were: $a$=0.3, $b$=0.6 and $c$=0.1.

### Hardware Used

A computer cluster was used, containing two machines with *Intel Xeon* E5045 2 *GHz*processors with 16 GB *RAM*, and six other machines with *AMD Opteron* 2210 1.8 *GHz*processors with 2 GB *RAM*. All used the *GNU/Linux Ubuntu* 10.10 distribution.

## RESULTS AND DISCUSSION

As the evolutionary process advances, increasingly better individuals are generated until reaching the final stages, where there is a convergence to populations with individuals of diverse quality; most of these populations have a fitness value close to the best value of the population. Figure 4 shows a typical case of the evolutionary process, considering 5,000 individuals that correspond to one of the 10 runs made on a problem group. The ordinate shows the fitness value, and the abscissa indicates the generation number. In this case, the randomly generated population had fitness values approximately between 0.6 and 0.9; in the first generations, there is already a strong decrease in the fitness value of the best individual of each population. Starting in generation 27, the average value and the value of the best individual are close to one another. The best individual obtained in this run was found in generation 42. The curve of the worst individual during the process shows an individual with a fitness value close to 0.9 in many generations, which corresponds to individuals that do not color the graph correctly, according to our fitness definition, and therefore have a positive penalty value. However, their presence is detected with increasingly lower frequencies because the number of individuals that correctly color each graph typically increases, following the trend in Figure 5 for the same run.

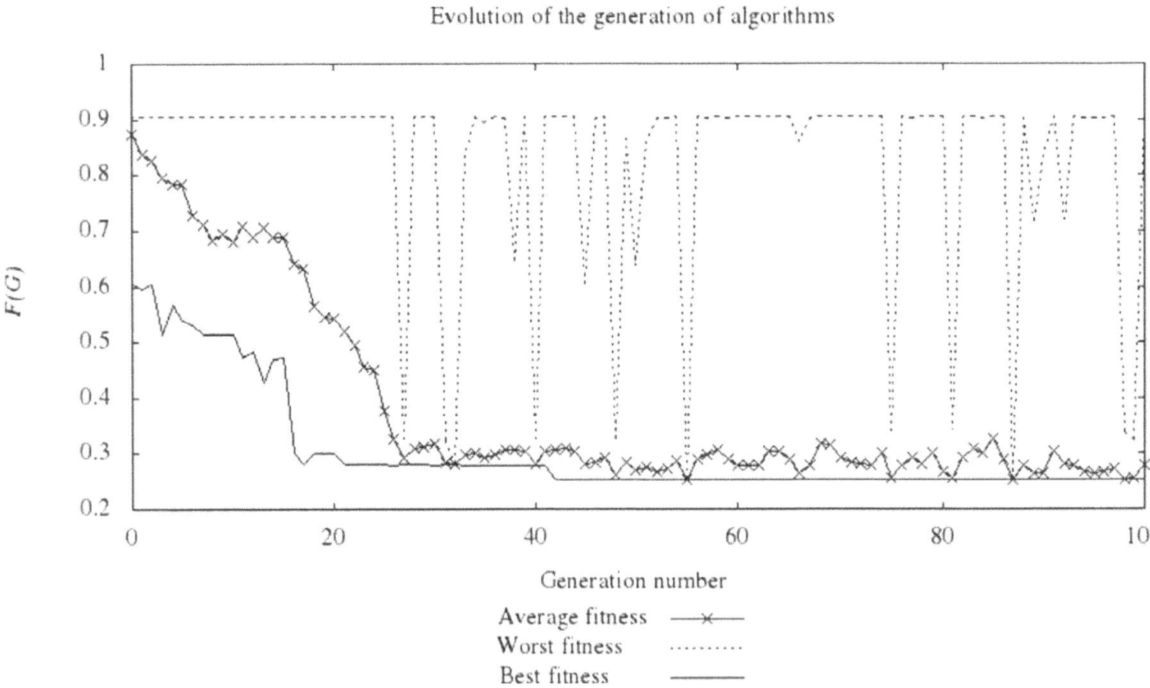


**Figure 4:** Evolving VCP algorithms.

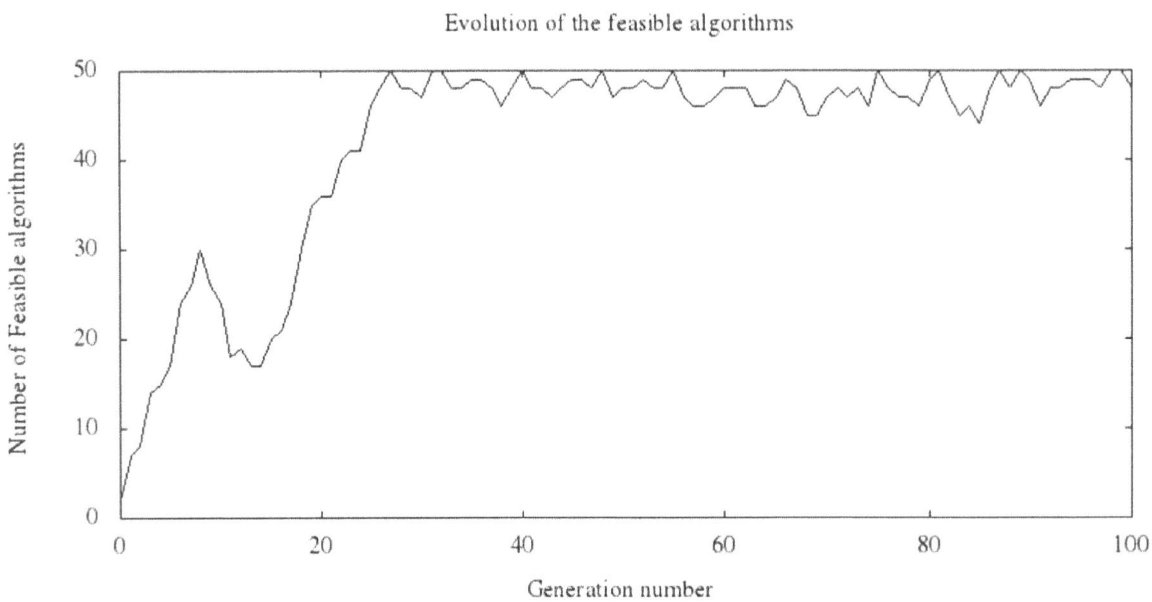


Figure 5: Evolution of feasible algorithms.

The different individuals generated during the evolutionary process can be manually decoded from their tree structure into their corresponding algorithms, described in pseudocode. The computational experiment was carried out using $h$=9 in Eq. 2, thus ensuring that we obtain individuals with a legible and decodable structure in their algorithms. Algorithm 1 presents an illustrative case, which is obtained from the individual shown in Figure 6; its nodes correspond to the defined functions and terminals, and the arcs of each function or terminal define how the procedure works. According to the defined functions and terminals, Algorithm 1 is a constructive and greedy algorithm because it gradually colors the graph every time it applies a color and tries to not increase the number of colors. In its main stage, the algorithm selects a vertex using a criterion similar to the DSATUR algorithm to color it with the most frequent color. It performs this task within a *while* cycle (instructions 3 to 5), and refines the solution found (instructions 6 to 10), either by coloring the remaining vertices or exchanging already assigned colors.

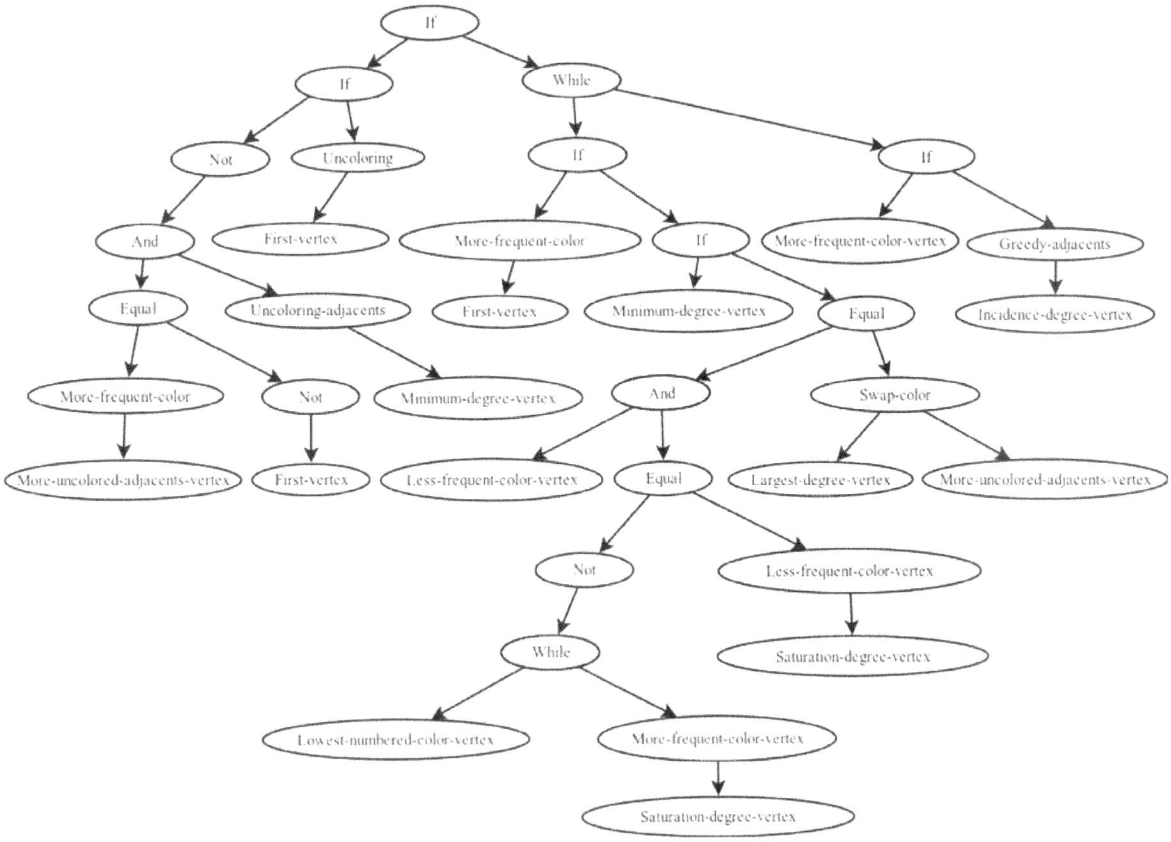


**Figure 6:** Representation tree of algorithm A3.

Algorithm 1: Pseudocode of A3

**Input:** Graph

**Output:** ColoredGraph

More-frequent-color (More-uncolored-adjacents-vertex)

**while** More-frequent-color (First-vertex) **do**

**while** Lowest-numbered-color-vertex **do**

More-frequent-color (Saturation-degree-vertex)

**end while**

Less-frequent-color (Saturation-degree-vertex)

Greedy-adjacents (Incidence-degree-vertex)

Swap-color (Largest-degree-vertex, More-uncolored-adjacents-vertex)

**If** More-frequent-color-vertex **then**

Greedy-adjacents (Incidence-degree-vertex)

**end if**

**end while**

**return** Graph Colored

The size of the individuals measured using tree height tends to stabilize at a value close to the height parameterized at the beginning of the evolutionary process. The initial randomly generated population determines a disperse range of possible heights for the individuals, and this range tends to decrease gradually as the evolutionary process occurs. Figure 7 illustrates a typical case, which corresponds to the same run presented in Figures 4 and 5. The figure shows the maximum, minimum and average height values in each population. Some stability can be identified in the individuals produced, with a value of 9, during 50 consecutive generations. This behavior is essentially due to the penalty considered in the fitness function.

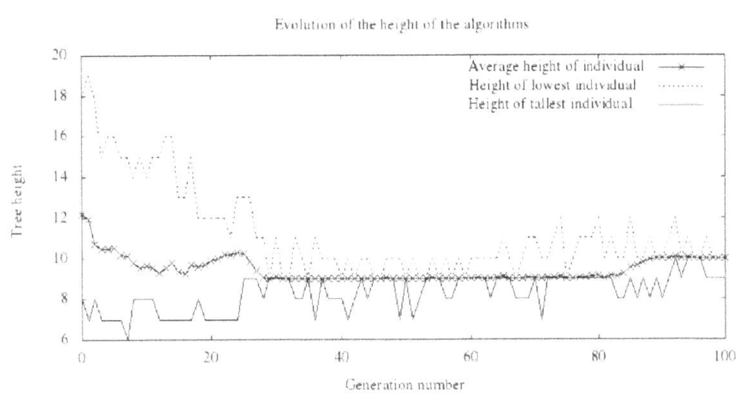


**Figure 7:** Evolution of the tree height.

The various algorithms demonstrate the presence of common structures with characteristics similar to the existing heuristics for the VCP. Figure 8 shows two such structures. The first one (8a) corresponds to a greedy coloring of a vertex selected using the criterion of neighboring vertices with different colors, which is similar to the *DSATUR* heuristic algorithm; the second (8b) corresponds to a greedy coloring of the vertex with the highest degree, as in the Largest First algorithm [31].

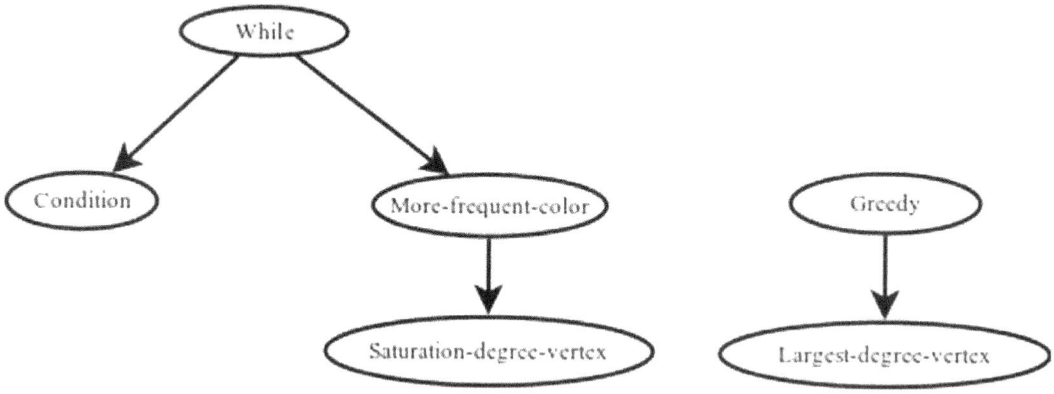


a) b)

**Figure 8:** Repetitive constructions observed in the obtained individuals.

The algorithms obtained through the evolutionary process are numerically competitive with elementary heuristics that solve the VCP. The generated algorithms find optimum solutions for some problems, as do existing heuristics. Table 1 presents the numerical results of three algorithms: the first produced with the DSJ instances, and the second and third with LEI. They are tested using 29 problems from the *DIMACS* benchmark. The first six columns correspond to the problem name, number of vertices, number of edges, density, optimum chromatic number, and best known chromatic number. The following four columns correspond to results obtained from heuristics presented in the literature: *Greedy Sequential*, *Largest First*, *Smallest First*, and *DSATUR*, which we consider as the conceptual bases for constructing our functions and terminals. The last six columns correspond to the chromatic number and computational time of our three algorithms, which we call A1, A2 and A3. The symbol "?" indicates that $\chi(G)$ is unknown for the corresponding instance, and bold characters are used when the best known chromatic number was obtained.

**Table 1:** Numerical results

| Instance | *n* | *m* | *d(G)* | $\chi(G)$ | Best($\chi$) | *Greedy Sequential* | *Largest First* | *Smallest First* | *DSATUR* | A1 | | A2 | | A3 | | Best $\chi$ |
|---|---|---|---|---|---|---|---|---|---|---|---|---|---|---|---|---|
| | | | | | | | | | | $\chi$ | Time (s) | $\chi$ | Time(s) | $\chi$ | Time(s) | |
| DSJC125.1 | 125 | 736 | 0.095 | ? | 5 | 8 | 8 | 8 | 6 | 6 | 0.016 | 6 | 0.020 | 7 | 0.012 | 6 |
| DSJC125.5 | 125 | 3891 | 0.502 | ? | 17 | 26 | 24 | 29 | 22 | 22 | 0.073 | 22 | 2.890 | 23 | 2.921 | 22 |
| DSJC125.9 | 125 | 6961 | 0.898 | ? | 44 | 56 | 56 | 59 | 51 | 52 | 0.161 | 52 | 10.315 | 52 | 10.696 | 52 |
| DSJR500.1 | 500 | 3555 | 0.028 | 12 | 12 | 15 | 15 | 16 | 13 | 13 | 0.142 | 13 | 0.205 | **12** | 0.099 | **12** |
| DSJR500.1c | 500 | 121275 | 0.972 | ? | 85 | 109 | 107 | 121 | 90 | 93 | 12.613 | 93 | 30.524 | 93 | 18.536 | 93 |
| DSJR500.5 | 500 | 58862 | 0.472 | 122 | 122 | 143 | 143 | 159 | 130 | 127 | 4.219 | 127 | 41.784 | 126 | 26.962 | 126 |
| r125.1c | 125 | 7501 | 0.968 | 46 | 46 | 51 | 50 | 51 | 46 | **46** | 0.241 | **46** | 11.497 | **46** | 10.735 | **46** |
| r125.5 | 125 | 3838 | 0.495 | 36 | 36 | 44 | 44 | 47 | 38 | 39 | 0.091 | 39 | 9.305 | 39 | 11.222 | 39 |
| r250.1 | 250 | 867 | 0.028 | 8 | 8 | 9 | 9 | 11 | **8** | **8** | 0.054 | **8** | 0.043 | **8** | 0.017 | **8** |
| r250.1c | 250 | 30227 | 0.971 | 64 | 64 | 76 | 77 | 78 | 65 | 67 | 1.827 | 67 | 14.843 | 67 | 20.321 | 67 |
| r250.5 | 250 | 14849 | 0.477 | 65 | 65 | 79 | 79 | 84 | 68 | 69 | 0.580 | 69 | 14.803 | 67 | 10.519 | 67 |
| r1000.1 | 1000 | 14378 | 0.029 | 20 | 20 | 26 | 26 | 28 | **20** | **20** | 1.339 | **20** | 2.985 | **20** | 1.620 | **20** |
| r1000.5 | 1000 | 238267 | 0.477 | 234 | 234 | 275 | 276 | 317 | 250 | 243 | 36.791 | 245 | 51.879 | 252 | 34.181 | 243 |
| le450_15a | 450 | 8168 | 0.081 | 15 | 15 | 22 | 21 | 27 | 17 | 17 | 0.449 | 17 | 0.746 | 16 | 0.603 | 16 |
| le450_15b | 450 | 8169 | 0.081 | 15 | 15 | 22 | 22 | 27 | 16 | 17 | 0.452 | 16 | 0.734 | 17 | 0.573 | 16 |
| le450_15c | 450 | 16680 | 0.165 | 15 | 15 | 30 | 31 | 40 | 23 | 24 | 1.238 | 24 | 5.067 | 24 | 5.207 | 24 |
| le450_15d | 450 | 16750 | 0.166 | 15 | 15 | 31 | 30 | 37 | 24 | 24 | 1.241 | 24 | 5.135 | 25 | 5.594 | 24 |
| le450_25a | 450 | 8260 | 0.082 | 25 | 25 | 28 | 28 | 31 | **25** | **25** | 0.409 | **25** | 1.109 | **25** | 1.009 | **25** |
| le450_25b | 450 | 8263 | 0.082 | 25 | 25 | 27 | 27 | 34 | **25** | **25** | 0.391 | **25** | 0.971 | **25** | 0.889 | **25** |
| le450_25c | 450 | 17343 | 0.172 | 25 | 25 | 37 | 36 | 45 | 29 | 29 | 1.178 | 29 | 11.148 | 30 | 10.786 | 29 |
| le450_25d | 450 | 17425 | 0.172 | 25 | 25 | 35 | 35 | 43 | 28 | 29 | 1.205 | 29 | 11.181 | 28 | 10.663 | 28 |
| le450_5a | 450 | 5714 | 0.057 | 5 | 5 | 14 | 14 | 16 | 10 | 9 | 0.371 | 10 | 0.425 | 10 | 0.291 | 9 |
| le450_5b | 450 | 5734 | 0.057 | 5 | 5 | 13 | 13 | 18 | 9 | 10 | 0.363 | 10 | 0.428 | 10 | 0.281 | 10 |
| le450_5c | 450 | 9803 | 0.097 | 5 | 5 | 17 | 15 | 22 | 10 | 7 | 0.655 | 8 | 0.825 | 10 | 0.741 | 7 |
| le450_5d | 450 | 9757 | 0.097 | 5 | 5 | 18 | 17 | 24 | 12 | 7 | 0.654 | 7 | 0.823 | 6 | 0.827 | 6 |
| anna | 138 | 493 | 0.052 | 11 | 11 | 12 | 12 | 13 | **11** | **11** | 0.011 | **11** | 0.018 | **11** | 0.013 | **11** |
| david | 87 | 406 | 0.109 | 11 | 11 | 12 | 12 | 12 | **11** | **11** | 0.006 | **11** | 0.011 | **11** | 0.007 | **11** |

doi:10.1371/journal.pone.0058551.t001

Of the 5,000 total algorithms revised in each evolution, an average of 83.47%, completely color the 12 evolution groups, i.e., approximately 500,810 algorithms feasible in the 120 executions are generated. The average computational time required to evolve the three algorithms from the 12 groups of instances used, considering the 10 executions for each group, is 43.85 hours for each algorithm. Two of the automatically generated algorithms obtain the optimum solution in 24.14% of the test problems, while the third one obtains 27.59% of the optimum solutions. Compared to the selected heuristics, the three algorithms present the same computational performance level, with 29.97% average relative error, while the other four heuristics present 59.73% considering the 29 testing instances. Algorithm A1 obtains 27.56% average relative error, while the DSATUR heuristic obtains 34.30%. For computational time, algorithms A1, A2 and A3 solve the 29 instances in an average of 5.54 seconds. We avoid a computational time comparison between the generated algorithms and the existing heuristics since both are in different languages (interpreted and compiled, respectively).

## CONCLUSIONS

This paper presents the results of three new algorithms to solve the VCP. The algorithms were produced using an evolutionary computation procedure designed and implemented for that purpose that combines components of the elementary heuristics and control structures. To evolve the algorithms, 12 groups of instances selected from the DIMACS benchmark were used, and a set of 29 instances was considered to test them.

The algorithms evolved from an initial population and improved gradually as the evolutionary process occurred. The algorithm sizes stabilized at a value near the size originally given as a reference. The new algorithms are competitive in the quality of the obtained solutions to the previously existing heuristics for solving the problem; the average relative error for the testing problems is lower than the average error of the heuristics considered in the research. The new algorithms are characterized by the presence of structures similar to those in the existing heuristics for the problem.

## REFERENCES


1. Matula DM, Marble G, Isaacson JD (1972) Graph coloring algorithms. In: Read RC, editor. Graph theory and Computing. (pp 109–122). New York: Academic Press.
2. Garey M, Johnson D (1979) Computers and Intractability: A Guide to the theory of NP-completeness. New York: W. H. Freeman & Co.
3. Malaguti E, Toth P (2010) A survey on vertex coloring problems. International Transactions in Operational Research 17: 1–34
4. Méndez-Díaz I, Zabala P (2006) A branch-and-cut algorithm for graph coloring. Discrete Applied Mathematics 154: 826–847
5. Méndez-Díaz I, Zabala P (2008) A cutting plane algorithm for graph coloring. Discrete Applied Mathematics 156: 159–179
6. Malaguti E, Monaci M, Toth P (2011) An exact approach for the Vertex Coloring Problem. Discrete Optimization 8: 174–190
7. Brélaz D (1979) New methods to color the vertices of a graph. Communications of the ACM 22: 251–256
8. Leighton FT (1979) A graph coloring algorithm for large scheduling problems. Journal of Research of the National Bureau of Standards 84: 489–503
9. Culberson JC, Luo F (1996) Exploring the k-colorable landscape with iterated greedy. In Johnson DS, Trick MA, editors. Cliques, Coloring and Satisfiability. DIMACS Series in Discrete Mathematics and Theoretical Computer Science. (Vol 26, 245–284). Providence: American Mathematical Society.
10. Malaguti E, Monaci M, Toth P (2008) A metaheuristic approach for the vertex coloring problem.INFORMS Journal on Computing 20: 302–316
11. Titiloye O, Crispin A (2011) Graph coloring with a distributed hybrid quantum annealing algorithm. In: O'Shea J, Nguyen NT, Crockett K, Howlett RJ, Jain LC, editors. Agent and multi-agent systems: technologies and applications. (Vol 6682, 553–562) Berlin, Heidelberg: Springer Berlin Heidelberg.
12. Titiloye O, Crispin A (2011) Quantum annealing of the graph coloring problem. Discrete Optimization 8: 376–384
13. Hertz A, Werra D (1987) Using tabu search techniques for graph coloring. Computing 39: 345–351
14. Porumbel DC, Hao JK, Kuntz P (2010) An evolutionary approach with diversity guarantee and well-informed grouping recombination for graph coloring. Computers & Operations Research 37: 1822–1832
15. Minton S (1993) An analytic learning system for specializing heuristics. Proceedings of the 13th International Joint Conference on Artifical Intelligence - Volume 2. IJCAI'93. San Francisco: Morgan Kaufmann Publishers Inc. 922–928.
16. Epstein SL, Freuder EC, Wallace R, Morozov A, Samuels B (2006) The Adaptive Constraint Engine. In: Hentenryck PV, editor. Principles and Practice of Constraint Programming - CP 2002. Lecture Notes in Computer Science. Heidelberg: Springer Berlin, 525–540.
17. Nareyek A (2004) Choosing search heuristics by non-stationary reinforcement learning. In: Resende MGC, de Sousa JP, Viana A, editors. Metaheuristics. Norwell: Kluwer Academic Publishers, 523–544.
18. Bain S, Thornton J, Sattar A (2005) Evolving variable-ordering heuristics for constrained optimisation. In: Beek P van, editor. Principles and Practice of Constraint Programming - CP 2005. Lecture Notes in Computer Science. Heidelberg: Springer Berlin, 732–736.
19. Koza JR (1992) Genetic programming: on the programming of computers by means of natural selection complex adaptive systems. Cambridge: MIT Press.
20. Koza, JR, Keane MA, Streeter MJ, Mydlowec W, Yu J, Lanza G (2003) Genetic Programming IV: Routine Human-Competitive Machine Intelligence. Norwell: Kluwer Academic Publishers.
21. Fukunaga A (2002) Automated discovery of composite

SAT variable-selection heuristics. Eighteenth National Conference on Artificial intelligence. Menlo Park: American Association for Artificial Intelligence. 641–648.

22. Fukunaga A (2008) Automated discovery of local search heuristics for satisfiability testing. Evolutionary Computation 16: 31–61 [PubMed]
23. Burke EK, Hyde MR, Kendall G, Ochoa G, Özcan E, et al. (2010) A classification of hyper-heuristic approaches. In: Gendreau M, Potvin J-Y, editors. Handbook of Metaheuristics. Springer US, Vol. 146: 1–21
24. Burke EK, McCollum B, Meisels A, Petrovic S, Qu R (2007) A graph-based hyper-heuristic for educational timetabling problems. European Journal of Operational Research. 176: 177–192
25. Burke EK, Hyde M, Kendall G, Woodward J (2010) A genetic programming hyper-heuristic approach for evolving 2-d strip packing heuristics. IEEE Transactions on Evolutionary Computation 14: 942–958
26. Poli R, Langdon W, McPhee N (2008) A Field Guide to Genetic Programming. Published viahttp://lulu.com and freely available at http://www.gp-field-guide.org.uk
27. Affenzeller M, Winkler S, Wagner S, Beham A (2009) Genetic algorithms and genetic programming: modern concepts and practical applications. 1st ed. Boca Raton: Chapman and Hall/CRC.
28. Falkenauer E (1998) Genetic algorithms and grouping problems. New York: John Wiley & Sons, Inc.
29. Aho AV, Hopcroft JE, Ullman J (1983) Data structures and algorithms. 1st ed. Boston: Addison-Wesley Longman Publishing Co., Inc.
30. Siek J, Lee LQ, Lumsdaine A (2001) The boost graph library: user guide and reference manual. Boston: Addison-Wesley Longman Publishing Co., Inc.
31. Al-Omari H, Sabri KE (2006) New graph coloring algorithms. Journal of Mathematics and Statistics 2: 739–741
32. George A, Liu JWH (1989) The evolution of the minimum degree ordering algorithm. SIAM Review 31: 1–19
33. Johnson DS, Trick MA (1996) Introduction to the second DIMACS challenge: Cliques, coloring, and satisfiability. In: Johnson DS, Trick MA, editors. Cliques, coloring, and satisfiability, DIMACS Series in Discrete Mathematics and Theoretical Computer Science. (Vol 26, 1–7). Providence: American Mathematical Society.
34. Grefenstette JJ (1986) Optimization of control parameters for genetic algorithms. IEEE Transactions on Systems, Man and Cybernetics 16: 122–128
35. Rothlauf F (2006) Representations for genetic and evolutionary algorithms. 2nd ed. Secaucus: Springer-Verlag New York, Inc.

CHAPTER 19

# NETMODE: NETWORK MOTIF DETECTION WITHOUT NAUTY

Xin Li[1], Douglas S. Stones[2,3], Haidong Wang[1] , Hualiang Deng[1], Xiaoguang Liu[4], Gang Wang[1]

[1]Nankai-Baidu Joint Laboratory, College of Information Technical Science, Nankai University, Tianjin, China,

[2]Clayton School of Information Technology, Monash University, Victoria, Australia,

[3]School of Mathematical Sciences, Monash University, Victoria, Australia,

[4]College of Software, Nankai University, Tianjin, China

## ABSTRACT

**A motif in a network is a connected graph that occurs significantly more frequently as an induced subgraph than would be expected in a similar randomized network. By virtue of being atypical, it is thought that motifs might play a more important role than arbitrary subgraphs. Recently, a flurry of advances in the study of network motifs has created demand for faster computational means for identifying motifs in increasingly larger networks. Motif detection is typically performed by enumerating subgraphs in an input network and in an ensemble of comparison networks; this poses a significant computational problem. Classifying the subgraphs encountered, for instance, is typically performed using a graph canonical labeling package, such as Nauty, and will typically be called billions of times. In this article, we describe an implementation of a network motif detection package, which we call** *NetMODE*.**NetMODE can only perform motif detection for $k$-node subgraphs when $k \leq 6$, but does so without the use of Nauty. To avoid using Nauty, NetMODE has an initial pretreatment phase, where $k$-node graph data is stored in memory ($k \leq 5$). For $k = 6$ we take a novel approach, which relates to the Reconstruction Conjecture for directed graphs. We find that NetMODE can perform up to around 30 times faster than its predecessors when $k \leq 5$ and up to around 20 times faster when $k = 6$ (the exact improvement varies considerably). NetMODE also (a) includes a method for generating comparison graphs uniformly at random, (b) can interface with external packages (e.g. R), and (c) can utilize multi-core architectures. NetMODE is available from netmode.sf.net.**

## INTRODUCTION

A *network motif* in a network $G$ is a connected graph $H$ that occurs significantly more frequently as an induced subgraph than would be expected in a "similar" random network. The term "network motif" was coined by [1], [2], who discovered that they occur in several biological and artificial networks. Recently, network motifs have been found in a vast range of networks, and, in some cases, have been identified as functionally important. One prominent example is the 3-node feed-forward loop  in the E. coli transcription factor network [3]. For further reading, see [4], [5].

**Citation:** Li X, Stones DS, Wang H, Deng H, Liu X, Wang G. NetMODE: Network Motif Detection without Nauty. Amaral LAN, ed. PLoS ONE. 2012;7(12):e50093. doi:10.1371/journal.pone.0050093.

## Definition in Practice

In practice, the detection of network motifs is typically implemented in the following way.

- *Step 1*: Compute the number of times that $H$ occurs in $G$ as an induced subgraph, call this number $f_G(H)$. We will assume that distinct copies of $H$ may overlap (although, this is topical).
- *Step 2*: Generate an ensemble $\Omega$ of random graphs "similar" to the input network.
- *Step 3*: For each graph $R \in \Omega$, we compute the number of times $H$ occurs in $R$, which we will denote $f_R(H)$.
- *Step 4*: Compute the probability $p$ (called the *P-value*) that a similar graph $R \in \Omega$contains the same or more copies of $H$ than $G$. If the estimate for $p$ is less than some user-defined threshold $\chi$, we declare $H$ a network motif.

Performing these steps for all $k$-node connected subgraphs will be referred to as performing a $k$-node *subgraph census*.

In some motif detection programs, a *Z-score* is used instead of, or together with, the $P$-value above; it is given by $\frac{1}{\hat{\sigma}_H}(f_G(H) - \hat{\mu}_H)$ where $\hat{\mu}_H$ and $\hat{\sigma}_H$ are the sample mean and standard deviation of the dataset $\{f_R(H) : R \in \Omega\}$. However, we caution the reader that, in this context, the use of a "Z-score" does not imply a corresponding normal distribution.

Typically, a graph is described as *similar* to $G$ if it has the same vertex set as $G$ and if its vertices have the same in-degrees and out-degrees as in $G$. However, the treatment of loops and bidirectional edges can be addressed in different ways. We will describe how we address these issues in the "Modifications" section. In any case, we will refer to the similar graphs in $\Omega$ as the *comparison* graphs.

In practice, additional criteria are added, such as a minimum value for $f_G(H)$. Instead of frequency, concentration might also be considered [6], that is, the proportion of $H$ amongst all $k$-node connected induced subgraphs in the network. The decision of which statistic to use can have a significant impact on whether or not $H$ is declared a motif.

## Software

Many packages have been developed that enable motif detection. Mainstream packages, those that can perform a $k$-node subgraph census, include Mfinder [7], MAVisto [8], [9], FanMod [6], [10], [11], MODA [12], and Kavosh [13]. This is the family of network motif detection packages to which our program, NetMODE, belongs.

Of these, we will focus on FanMod and Kavosh, which are the most relevant: Mfinder and MAVisto are largely subsumed by FanMod; the authors of MODA have asked us to consider Kavosh instead (via private communication). We find Kavosh is typically faster than FanMod (see Table 1).

**Table 1:** Speedup of NetMODE vs. Kavosh

| *G* | *v* | *e* | *k* | **run-time (sec.)** | **K-speedup** | |
|---|---|---|---|---|---|---|
| | | | | **Kavosh** | **serial** | **4-core** |
| 1 | 67 | 182 | 3 | 0.5 | 0.5 | 1.8 |
| Social | | | 4 | 1.5 | 1.5 | 2.1 |
| | | | 5 | 8.5 | 3.2 | 2.4 |
| | | | 6 | 50.5 | 1.5 | 4.9 |
| 2 | 672 | 1276 | 3 | 3.9 | 1.0 | 7.1 |
| E. coli | | | 4 | 11.7 | 3.5 | 20.0 |
| | | | 5 | 79.6 | 6.2 | 15.7 |
| | | | 6 | 752.1 | 4.2 | 16.1 |
| 3 | 688 | 1079 | 3 | 10.5 | 4.4 | 13.2 |
| Yeast | | | 4 | 214.2 | 17.7 | 74.6 |
| | | | 5 | 5990.8 | 31.8 | 123.5 |
| | | | 6 | 119359.3 | 11.4 | 46.1 |
| 4 | 50 | 2540 | 3 | 20.7 | 7.6 | 27.0 |
| Complete graph | | | 4 | 460.7 | 25.5 | 107.6 |
| | | | 5 | 6971.7 | 31.7 | 122.1 |
| | | | 6 | 88025.3 | 20.4 | 81.0 |

G-Tries [14]–[17] (see also [18]) is a data structure whose authors claim impressive speedups vs. FanMod. We do not include G-tries in the experiments in this paper since the G-tries data structure comprises only part of motif detection, although we give a theoretical analysis in the Theory section. Moreover, only recently has a "preliminary" program, called gtrieScanner, that implements the G-tries data structure become available; we make some remarks about gtrieScanner in the Conclusion.

There is also a range of other algorithms and packages that have some specialized functionality, or functionality related to motif detection, such as NeMo [19], which considers non-induced subgraphs.

There are also several papers that compare algorithms and software for network motif detection [20]–[26].

## NetMODE

We will now introduce our network motif detection package NetMODE, **Net**work **MO**tif**DE**tection, designed to improve upon Kavosh for $k \leq 6$.

## Modifications

NetMODE began development as a modified version of Kavosh, but over time was modified so substantially that we no longer consider it a Kavosh variant. We will now explain the differences.

### *Canonical Labeling*

In packages such as FanMod and Kavosh, the highly-optimized graph isomorphism package Nauty (available from cs.anu.edu.au/bdm/nauty/) is used to provide canonical labels for all of the $k$-node subgraphs encountered. Typically, they make millions, or even billions, of calls to Nauty. However, in small cases, the number of isomorphism classes of directed graphs is not overly large. Consequently, Nauty is called to perform the exact same task many times over. Moreover, often the majority of $k$-node subgraphs encountered fall into a handful of isomorphism classes.

NetMODE instead stores all canonical labels in memory. This scheme works easily for $3 \leq k \leq 5$, but for $k = 6$ we need to be a bit more clever, and for $k \geq 7$, this scheme seems totally impractical. Any significant run-time improvement achieved by NetMODE is the result of this preprocessing scheme.

### *Generating Similar Graphs*

NetMODE has several methods for sampling similar graphs; which one to use should be determined based on the input network.

We employ several variants of a switching method similar to that described in [27]. The switching operation is quite simple: two edges $(a,c)$ and $(b,d)$ are randomly chosen, and are replaced by $(a,d)$ and $(b,c)$ provided no loops or parallel edges are introduced.

Kavosh uses a modified version of this switching process which has some unfortunate drawbacks. FanMod has three different options for the handling of bidirectional edges. In NetMODE, we modify Kavosh's switching method to allow FanMod-like functionality while still using Kavosh's edge selection method. Additional details regarding comparison graph generation methods used in Kavosh, FanMod, and NetMODE.

In all of the above cases, the random graphs are sampled from a non-uniform distribution [28]. Furthermore, Ginoza and Mugler [29] discussed how the switching operations can change subgraph counts in a highly correlated manner. However, in practice, the switching method seems reasonable enough (when compared to uniform sampling). Note that different switching methods will incur different run-times.

An alternative method for sampling similar graphs has also been enabled in NetMODE. This option generates similar graphs uniformly at random, but is typically much slower than the switching methods. It implements the "local constant mode" using a variant of the Configuration Model. In some cases, it is extremely slow, but if the user finds it infeasible for a given input network, they may revert to a switching method. A related "stubs" method was implemented in Mfinder.

### *Subgraph Enumeration*

Kavosh utilizes a "revolving door" routine to iterate through combinations of vertices. (The "revolving door" routine minimizes the number of changes between each iteration, with the aim to improve computational efficiency.) NetMODE utilizes Kavosh's subgraph iteration procedure, except it does not use the revolving door algorithm; it does not seem to have any significant benefit for our purposes.

## Structure

When NetMODE is run, it will first enter a *pretreatment phase*. If $3 \leq k \leq 5$, then a list of all $2^{k(k-1)}$ possible loop-free $k$-node directed graphs are stored in memory along with their canonical labels (obtained via a brute-force search). For $k \leq 4$, we experience negligible overhead, while for $k = 5$, we experience around 5 seconds overhead (this will differ on varying platforms). For $k = 6$ this approach is infeasible, so we take an alternative approach that involves a special case of a variant of the Reconstruction Conjecture in graph theory.

From a k-node graph $G$, we can generate k induced subgraphs on $k-1$ vertices, called*cards*, by deleting one vertex v (and the edges that have v as an endpoint). The multiset of cards from a given graph is called the *deck*, which we will denote $\text{deck}(G)$. Note that if G and G are isomorphic graphs, then $\text{deck}(G) = \text{deck}(G')$. By two independent computer searches we find that the converse is true for 6-node directed graphs barring a few exceptions, as detailed in Theorem 1.

**Theorem 1** *If $G$ and $G'$ are two non-isomorphic loop-free 6-node directed graphs, then $\text{deck}(G) \neq \text{deck}(G')$, except when $\{G,G'\}$ belongs to the following list of exceptions:*

$$\{56044064,56036128\},\{1133217864,1133217802\},$$
$$\{1640468230,1640206094\},\{1657244500,1656986394\},$$
$$\{1657252436,1656990300\},\{3311111272,3311111210\},$$
$$\{3788211532,3788211470\},\{3838293818,3838289726\},$$
$$\{3856371052,3856370990\}.$$

Theorem 1 asserts that, with a few exceptions, loop-free 6-node directed graphs are determined (up to isomorphism) by their 5-node induced subgraphs. Thus, we instead store in memory the canonical labels for 5-node directed graphs, and use this data for canonical labeling 6-node subgraphs. In Theorem 1, graphs $H$ are listed as their*graphID*, the number defined when the adjacency matrix is read as a binary number; it is also *canonical*, the minimum such number in the isomorphism class. The computation required to prove Theorem 1 has been performed independently by the authors Li and Stones (the code used has also been made available).

When running NetMODE for $3 \leq k \leq 5$, on both the input network and the random comparison graphs, we iterate through all $k$-node subgraphs $H$, and simply increase the count corresponding to its canonical label. Running NetMODE for 6-node subgraphs is more complicated and involves two distinct stages. In Stage 1, we process the input network. We start with an empty list $L$, and as the algorithm proceeds:

- If $H$ is an exception, we account for it separately.
- If $\text{deck}(H)$ does not appear in L, we add a new entry to L (with count 1). Otherwise, $\text{deck}(H)$ appears in L, so we simply increase its count. Searching through L is facilitated by a hash function.

In Stage 2 we process the comparison graphs. When a 6-node subgraph H is found, we compute $\text{deck}(H)$ and search for its hash value in L. If found, then we search for $\text{deck}(H)$amongst all entries with that hash value, and if $\text{deck}(H)$ is found, we then increase its count. Otherwise, if its hash value or $\text{deck}(H)$ is not found in L, we do nothing.

For $k=6$, note that we store, and hence return, the first graph isomorphic to H found in the input network, which is not necessarily in canonical form. Note also that, in all cases, NetMODE only returns the counts of subgraphs that are found in the input network.

## Other Features

### *Usability*

The theory of network motifs is relatively new and has received some criticism, e.g. [30]. Consequently, we should be careful when making claims relating to network motifs. With this in mind, we have included a *verbose mode* in NetMODE, where we return the number of subgraphs isomorphic to H in both the input network G and the comparison graphs. This allows the user access to all of the data encountered during run-time, so that the user can perform their own independent analysis. Typically, this is a large amount of data, so verbose mode is intended for analysis via a separate program.

NetMODE uses stdin/stdout so that it can interface with well-established packages, such as R. We also provide some R code that can be run to enable interfacing with NetMODE in verbose mode (using the igraph extension). The user can therefore use R to e.g. draw motifs, check whether or not sufficiently many comparison graphs have been used, check whether the comparison graph counts are approximately normally distributed, and so on.

We also introduce a *burnin* feature, whereby the first few comparison graphs generated by the switching operation are discarded, resulting in a better ensemble of comparison graphs. The benefit of using burnin is that it essentially allows the switching process to start at a random starting point (rather than the input network); its use is standard practice in MCMC algorithms. In general, it is unclear what amount of burnin to use, but we found that 1000 discarded comparison networks seems reasonable in most cases.

### *Parallelism*

We also design NetMODE to be capable of utilizing parallel processing in multi-core computers. We use a basic coarse-grained parallelism where an individual thread is responsible for performing subgraph census on one of the comparison graphs. Parallelism is only invoked for the comparison graphs, whereas the input graph is processed in serial. At this level, it is an embarrassingly parallel problem, in that no communication is required between individual threads once they are created. Message passing is handled by the pthread library. Each comparison graph computation is added to a queue, which is managed by a *thread manager*. The thread manager limits the number of simultaneous threads to some user-defined threshold.

## EXPERIMENTAL RESULTS

In this section we report the experimental results obtained from testing the various algorithms described in this paper.

## Experimental Setup

Unless otherwise specified, the platform used in these experiments is: AMD Phenom II X4 945 (4 cores) with 2×2 GB RAM running Red Hat Enterprise Linux 5.

The number of similar graphs generated for comparison is always 1000 (we do not endorse this number of comparison graphs be used in practice; users should decide for themselves based on the input network and value of k), and we use zero burnin. Each experiment is performed only once, since differences in run-times are negligible.

In its downloadable form, Kavosh wastes a lot of time printing to the screen and writing to files. To obtain a more reasonable comparison, all computations involving Kavosh are performed using a modified version in which printing is disabled; similarly we disable writing to the disk. The difference can be significant: e.g. 50 minutes vs. 80 seconds on the E. coli dataset, $k=5$.

## Speedup

We define the *K-speedup* (resp. *F-speedup*) of NetMODE to be the number of times faster NetMODE is than Kavosh (resp. FanMod) when processing a given dataset. All variables (platform, number of comparison networks, etc.) are kept the same, except possibly for the number of threads (which we will explicitly highlight, when relevant).

In Table 1, we list the K-speedup in a range of instances. For Table 1 we use the "fixed bidirectional edges" switching method, since it matches Kavosh's switching method. For the given input network, we use $v$ to denote the number of nodes and $e$ to denote the number of directed edges. We test NetMODE using four input networks: (a) a social network, (b) the metabolic pathway of E. coli, (c) the transcription network of S. cerevisiae (yeast), and (d) the complete directed graph on 50 vertices. Input networks (a), (b), and (c) were used in testing Kavosh and were packaged with the Kavosh source code. No description other than "a real social network" was given for input network (a) in [13].

The fourth input network was chosen since it has some easy-to-compute properties, e.g. in each of the 1001 networks (the input network and all 1000 comparison networks), there are exactly $\binom{50}{k}$ copies of $\vec{K}_k$. Therefore, the number of calls to Nauty by Kavosh is $1001 \cdot \binom{50}{k}$.

Table 2 gives some example run-times for FanMod and NetMODE under various switching methods. Notation: F=fixed bidirectional edges; NR=no regard; GC=global constant; LC=local constant; ULC=uniform local constant. In some instances, ULC mode is impractically slow.

**Table 2:** Run-times (sec.) for Kavosh, FanMod, and NetMODE under various switching methods

| | **Yeast; 4-node subgraph census** | | | | |
|---|---|---|---|---|---|
| | **F** | **NR** | **GC** | **LC** | **ULC** |
| Kavosh | 214.2 | - | - | - | - |
| FanMod | - | 318.0 | 319.0 | 318.0 | - |
| NetMODE | 12.1 | 12.6 | 12.0 | 12.3 | - |
| NetMODE 4-core | 2.9 | 2.9 | 3.0 | 3.0 | - |
| | **Social; 6-node subgraph census** | | | | |
| | **F** | **NR** | **GC** | **LC** | **ULC** |
| Kavosh | 50.5 | - | - | - | - |
| FanMod | - | 464.0 | 139.0 | 147.0 | - |
| NetMODE | 33.5 | 87.2 | 31.4 | 34.9 | 34.5 |
| NetMODE 4-core | 10.3 | 24.1 | 10.1 | 10.8 | 11.6 |

## Scalability

In this section we describe the results of experiments designed to test the scalability of NetMODE. For these experiments, we use the local constant switching method (LC), which is probably the most reliable of the possibilities. Other switching methods can take longer, cf.Table 2.

### *Size of Input*

Figure 1 plots the run-times of NetMODE and FanMod in a range of circumstances. In these experiments, we use "protein structure networks" (as defined in [1]), for a range of proteins, whose structures were obtained from the Protein Data Bank [31]. The protein ID numbers are: 1IEG, 1DNP, 1VR0, 1F3U, 1OLM, 1HI9, 2IDB, 2VV5, 7AHL, 1B65, 2UUB, 1V54, 1HBN, 1SUV, 1K1E, 1UW6, 1RVV, 1KP8, 1GR5, 2FUG, 1TZN (although, only 1IEG, 1DNP, 1VR0, and 1F3U were used for the $k = 6$ experiments). These networks are undirected, where undirected edges are treated as bidirectional edges. In several instances, we were unable to run Kavosh for these networks, so we use FanMod for the run-time comparison. The networks are also available for download with NetMODE.

A

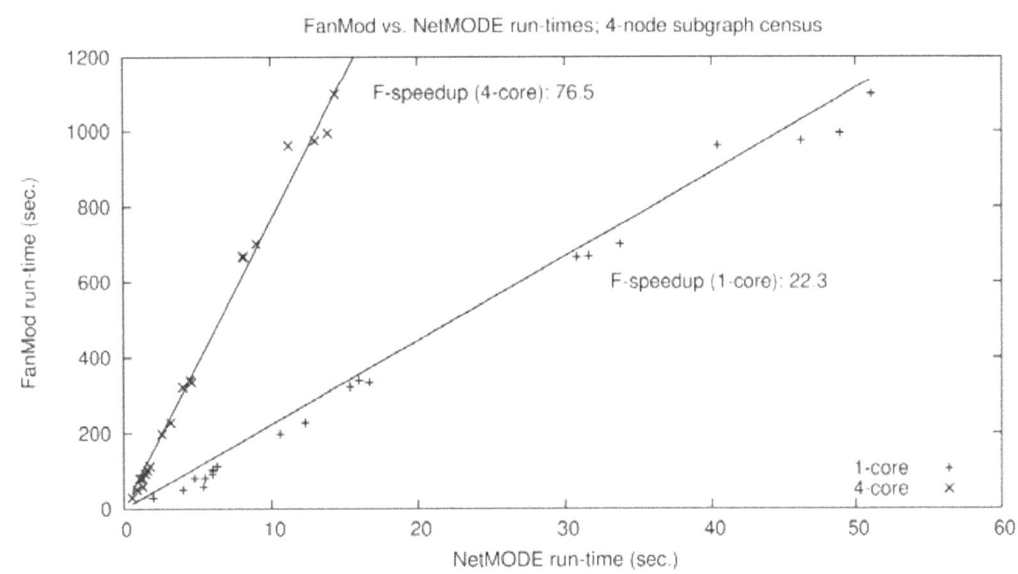

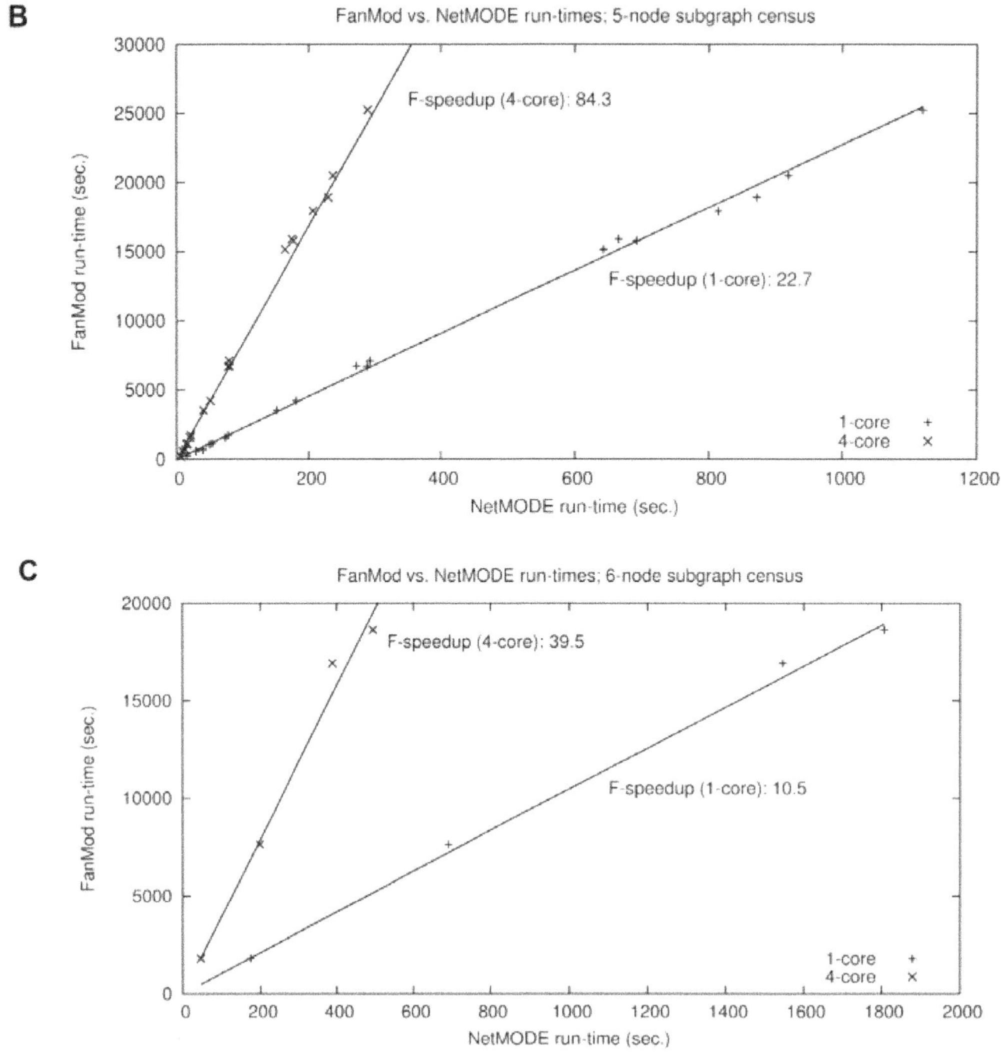


**Figure 1:** Run-times of NetMODE and FanMod on various protein structure networks

## Number of Cores

Figure 2 plots the run-time by the multi-core version of NetMODE as the number of utilized CPU cores varies. To perform this experiment, we switch to a platform with more cores: Red Hat Enterprise Linux 5; AMD Opteron Processor 6168 ($4 \times 12$ cores); $16 \times 4$G RAM. The input network was the complete directed graph on 50 vertices.

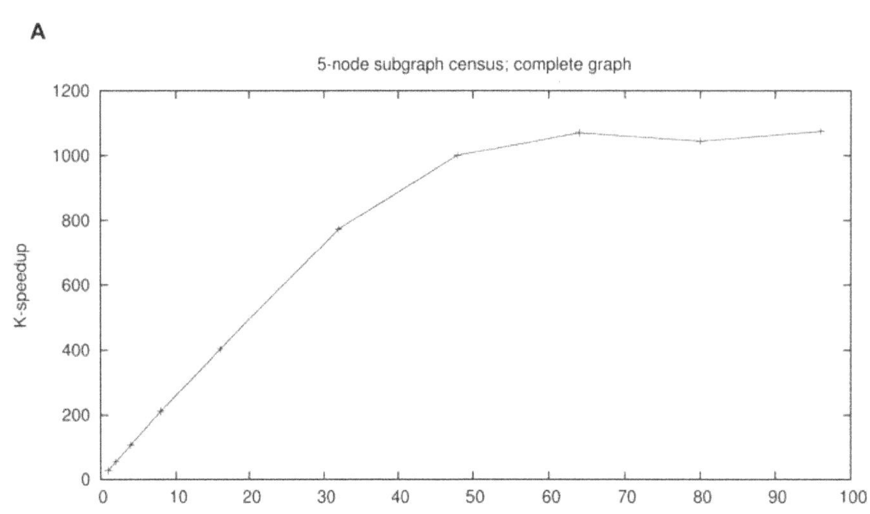

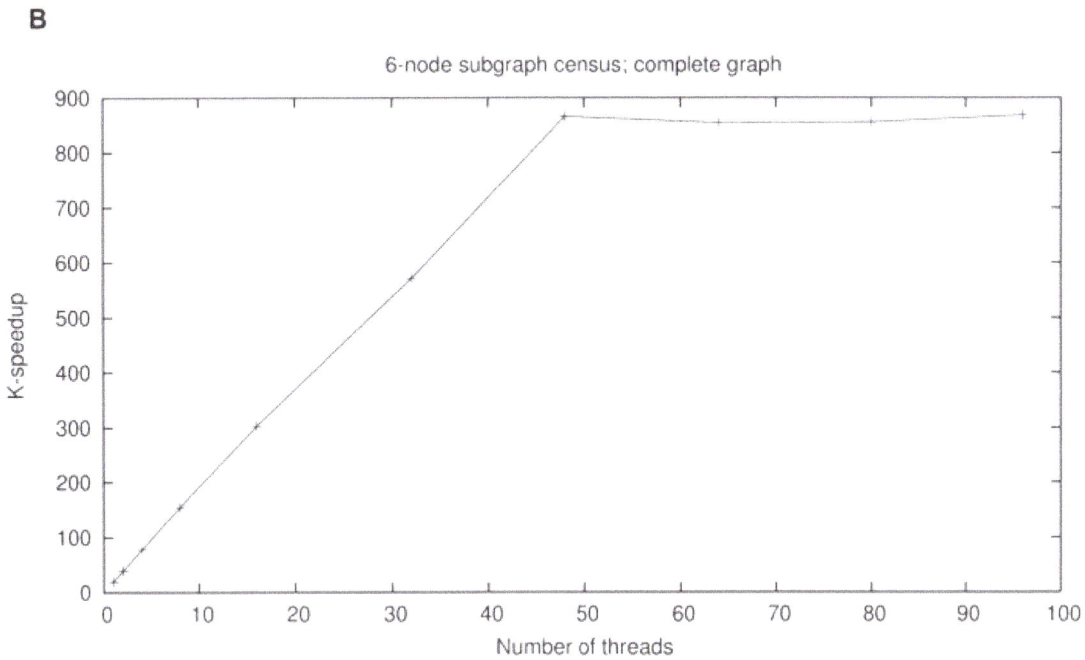


**Figure 2:** Speedup of NetMODE vs. Kavosh as the number of threads varies.

Kavosh took 713 seconds and 134670 seconds, respectively.

## Accuracy

Since NetMODE allows uniform local constant (ULC) random comparison graph sampling, we can inspect the accuracy of NetMODE's results. In Table 3 we list some concentration-based Z-scores returned by Mfinder in local constant mode, estimated using $10^7$ samples (denoted LCs), FanMod in local constant (LC) mode, and NetMODE in both LC and ULC modes. We also list some frequency-based Z-scores returned by Mfinder in LC mode, and NetMODE in both LC and ULC modes.

**Table 3:** Concentration and frequency Z-scores returned by FanMod, Mfinder, and NetMODE; E. coli network, 3-node subgraph census

| | Concentration | | | | Frequency | | |
|---|---|---|---|---|---|---|---|
| | Mfin. | FanM. | NetM. | NetM. | Mfin. | NetM. | NetM. |
| gID | LCs | LC | LC | ULC | LC | LC | ULC |
| 6 | −3.65 | −3.35 | −3.49 | −3.66 | −11.94 | −11.60 | −11.86 |
| 12 | −4.10 | −4.25 | −4.54 | −4.27 | −13.13 | −12.60 | −12.02 |
| 14 | 2.66 | 2.98 | 2.50 | 2.55 | −10.18 | −9.49 | −9.65 |
| 36 | −5.96 | −6.09 | −6.14 | −6.34 | −12.80 | −12.70 | −13.17 |
| 38 | 16.34 | 16.40 | 16.75 | 16.75 | 15.47 | 15.59 | 16.08 |
| 46 | 1.12 | 1.22 | 1.17 | 1.25 | 1.20 | 1.09 | 1.18 |
| 74 | 3.55 | 3.76 | 3.26 | 3.42 | −8.92 | −8.33 | −8.61 |
| 78 | −16.56 | **−46.11** | −15.97 | −16.24 | −21.94 | −21.60 | −20.62 |
| 98 | 5.16 | 5.01 | 5.08 | 4.73 | 5.42 | 4.95 | 4.53 |
| 102 | 3.42 | 3.06 | 3.32 | 3.25 | 3.21 | 2.80 | 3.09 |
| 110 | 11.91 | 11.84 | 11.65 | 11.62 | 11.71 | 11.56 | 11.14 |
| 238 | 19.05 | **98.99** | 18.37 | 18.98 | 18.83 | 18.77 | 18.23 |

# DISCUSSION

## Experiment

In the experiments in this paper, the primary focus is on run-time, since this is the main advantage for the end user. Memory requirements will typically be easily met, even on modest computers.

From our experiments, we find that Kavosh is usually faster than FanMod (i.e. the speedup vs. FanMod will typically be slightly greater than a speedup vs. Kavosh). To put this into a broader context, FanMod admits a host of functionality, such as allowing colored graphs as input networks, and the use of a sampling method (rather than complete enumeration). Neither Kavosh nor NetMODE have these features. NetMODE specializes on one specific task, and is faster than FanMod at this one task. However, NetMODE also offers multi-core parallelism, a uniform method for generating comparison graphs, and the ability to access the comparison graphs' subgraph counts, which are all important features that are absent from FanMod.

Tables 1 and 2 give run-times and speedups of NetMODE in a range of circumstances. We see that NetMODE can attain substantial speedups vs. Kavosh and FanMod. We also see a noticeable drop in speedup from $k=5$ to $k=6$ as NetMODE switches to a different mode.Table 2 also compares the run-times of NetMODE and FanMod under different methods for generating comparison graphs. We see that, while some switching methods are slower in NetMODE, they are also correspondingly slower in FanMod.

Figure 1 shows that the speedup achieved by NetMODE is roughly constant with the size of the input network. Figure 2 shows a near-linear increase of speedup with the number of cores utilized. In some instances, we see speedups of over 1000, and expect that this would be increased further if we were to use more cores.

We give a comparison of Z-scores returned by FanMod, Mfinder, and NetMODE in Table 2. We see that NetMODE's results resemble that of the uniform null model. FanMod's results, which typically resemble the uniform null model, are sometimes wildly different. Specifically, the graphs with graphID 78  and 238  have surprising Z-scores. We can exclude the possibility of this discrepency being the result of a bug with NetMODE since NetMODE and Mfinder's results are comparable. This indicates a bias in FanMod's results in some cases. Further experimentation relating to FanMod's bias.

## Theory

## Maximum Theoretical Speedup

If S, I, and N are the run-times of the components "generate similar graphs", "iterate through subgraphs", and "canonically label subgraphs", then NetMODE could achieve a speedup vs. Kavosh (or FanMod) of at most

$$\text{speedup} \leq \frac{S+I+N}{S+I}, \tag{1}$$

since these programs share the S and I components.

Methods for decreasing I (along with N) are already available, such as estimating the concentration of subgraphs via sampling, or searching for only a single k-node subgraph. These approaches offer a trade-off of accuracy or scope for run-time. These methods will still have a theoretical best speedup of $(S+I+N)/S$.

An alternative approach is to compute the P-values analytically, which is not easy to do with the established definition of a "similar" graph. Such an approach was use in NeMo [19], but for a different distribution of comparison graphs.

Some other programs avoid the use of Nauty by using symmetry breaking. These include the program by Grochow and Kellis, which searches for one k-node subgraph at a time, and both MODA and G-tries, which utilize a tree-like data structure to guide their subgraph searching (although in dissimilar ways). Another approach was offered by Baskerville and Paczuski [32], which uses a heuristic based on vertex invariants; it is able to distinguish all isomorphism classes of undirected graphs for $k \leq 6$ and most isomorphism classes for $k \leq 8$.

Another bound dominates when $N \to \infty$ and $S = o(N)$. In these instances, if s and t are respectively the average times taken to canonically label a given subgraph by NetMODE and Kavosh, then the speedup will be bounded above by $t/s$. To estimate $t/s$, we ran NetMODE and Kavosh on the input network $\bar{K}_{200}$ (with 0 comparison graphs), which gave speedups of $21.2,\quad 31.7,\quad 35.3,\quad 23.2$for $k=3,4,5,6$, respectively.

### *Remarks on G-Tries*

Ribeiro and Silva [15] claimed speedups of G-tries vs. their own version of FanMod of over 1000 in some cases. However, there are several properties of their experimental design and results that indicate these results would not be applicable to an end user.

Since G-tries describes a data structure rather than a full program, we will discuss Program G, a hypothetical program which incorporates G-tries, as described by [15].

### *G-tries vs. NetMODE*

In order to perform a k-node subgraph census, Program G generates random comparison graphs and iterates through all $k$-node connected subgraphs, thus its run-time contains the components measured by S and I. Any significant speedup of Program G vs. FanMod is therefore achieved wholly by reducing $N$ (i.e. by avoiding the use of Nauty), but this is achieved in a much more straightforward fashion in NetMODE.

### *Excluding S.*

The experiments for benchmarking G-tries were designed to test only the components improved by G-tries. As such, the authors have excluded the time it takes to generate similar graphs (i.e. S).

To illustrate the discrepancy, in the power network tested in [15], we find that S amounts to more than 47% and 12% of the total run-time in FanMod, when performing a 3-node and 4-node subgraph census, respectively (undirected graphs, complete enumeration). Consequently, it is theoretically impossible for Program G to achieve a speedup vs. FanMod of more than around 3 or 9, respectively, in this example (which is much less than the 100+speedups reported). This issue reduces as k increases, since S becomes relatively smaller.

### Measurements

The run-times by the version of FanMod used in [15] appear to be much larger than can be achieved by an authentic version of FanMod. For example, in Table 4 we list the average run-time (sec.) per comparison graph to perform a $k$-node subgraph census given by [15] on the "power" network, along with that achieved by an authentic version of FanMod run on a slower computer (Windows XP, 1.66 GHz, 1 GB RAM).

**Table 4:** Examples of run-time discrepency between G-tries's FanMod and the authentic version of FanMod

| k | G-tries's FanMod | authentic FanMod | articial speedup |
|---|---|---|---|
| 3 | 0.91 | 0.052 | ≥17.6 |
| 4 | 3.01 | 0.202 | ≥14.9 |
| 5 | 12.38 | 1.043 | ≥11.9 |

## Parallelism

NetMODE can utilize multi-core architecture, such as in many modern computers. Considering that multi-core hardware has been widespread for some time (particularly in bioinformatics), the inability of other programs to utilize parallel hardware is a serious limitation.

Figure 2 illustrates that the multi-core version achieves a near-linear speedup (which should be expected in such embarrassingly parallel problems). The computer used in this experiment has 48 CPU cores, so increasing the number of threads used beyond 48 did not achieve anything significant.

We also made an attempt to accelerate the subgraph searching method on a graphics processing unit (GPU). We use NVIDIA's CUDA parallel computing architecture, and testing was performed on the NVIDIA GeForce GTX 480. We tried two approaches:

- We collect a number of graphs and distribute them to the GPU's blocks; each kernel performs a separate subgraph searching procedure. After the kernel exits we combine the results from several graphs.
- We search a single graph in one call, requiring each block to search a subset of the vertices. When one random graph is generated, we launch a kernel. After the kernel exits we combine the results from that single graph, and move onto the next graph. This method was also carefully optimized with the kernel stream.

Unfortunately, neither method displayed significant performance. This comes as a surprise, considering how useful the GPU is for detecting "sequence motifs" (see e.g. [33]–[35]). We believe this is mainly a result of the divergence within the subgraph searching procedure. The GPU is optimized for performing similar operations in different threads, so the differences between the searching procedure (caused by the randomness of the comparison graphs) together with the enormous memory requirements slow down the kernel. To help future researchers, these programs are made available for download with NetMODE.

## Combinatorial Explosion

There are extremely many connected digraphs on k nodes for large k. The number of non-isomorphic connected k-node digraphs is given by Sloane's A003085 and the number of non-isomorphic connected k-node undirected graphs is given by Sloane's A001349; see oeis.org. The first few values are listed in Table 5.

**Table 5:** The number of k-node connected digraphs and undirected graphs, respectively

| k | A003085 | A001349 |
|---|---|---|
| 1 1 1 | 1 | 1 |
| 2 | 2 | 1 |
| 3 | 13 | 2 |
| 4 | 199 | 6 |
| 5 | 9364 | 21 |
| 6 | 1530843 | 112 |
| 7 | 880471142 | 853 |
| 8 | 1792473955306 | 11117 |

This property is sometimes referred to as "combinatorial explosion". If we were to run e.g. a 7-node subgraph census on a directed graph, the sheer number of non-isomorphic 7-node digraphs will give rise to many estimated P-values of 7 (the reader can readily verify this with FanMod). Unless we use extremely many comparison graphs, mixed in the list of subgraphs with an estimated P-value of 0 will be many insignificant subgraphs. In fact, this problem is still a significant concern at $k = 6$.

An alternative is to use Z-scores instead of P-values, but this was shown to be an unreliable statistic by Picard et al. [36] (and more about this will appear in [37]); we include Z-scores in NetMODE mainly for reasons of comparison. Thus, to distinguish between the subgraphs with an estimated P-value of 0, the user should repeat the experiment using a larger number of comparison graphs. Practically, this is a double blow, not only does the computational time increase rapidly with k, but also increases linearly with N (which should be chosen to increase rapidly with k).

In NetMODE, we enable the user to use more comparison graphs through parallelism (and by simply being faster than previous programs). FanMod (and Mfinder) instead offers the option of estimating subgraph concentrations via subgraph sampling (rather than complete enumeration).

## CONCLUSION

We have implemented a network motif detection package, NetMODE, designed to improve on Kavosh and FanMod by minimizing the time taken for canonical labeling. While other packages, such as FanMod, offer a host of functionality, NetMODE's function is more specialized: it consideres only uncolored graphs, performs only complete enumeration and searches for k-node motifs for $3 \leq k \leq 6$. The goal for NetMODE is to perform this task faster than its predecessors, which has been achieved through a preprocessing scheme.

We have also designed NetMODE to be functional on multi-core parallel architectures. Running NetMODE on multi-core hardware should be straightforward to use even for less computer savvy users: just add e.g. "-t 2" to the command line to use two threads. For portability, we have developed NetMODE to use stdin/stdout, and allow interfacing with the popular R statistical package. Since NetMODE is substantially faster than FanMod (and can be run in parallel), it offers the ability to search for k-node motifs for $3 \leq k \leq 6$ (using complete enumeration) within larger input networks than FanMod would practically cope with.

One apparent technique for practically extending NetMODE's functionality to $k \geq 7$ is, in the preprocessing phase, store in memory only the canonical labels of the subgraphs that are likely to be encountered (reverting to calling Nauty whenever other subgraphs are encountered). In this case, which subgraphs to preprocess could be determined from testing, or from an auxiliary file. However, we have not explored this avenue in NetMODE since we consider the problem of combinatorial explosion to be overwhelming at this stage, and, in any case, the majority of research interest so far has been for subgraphs with 6 or fewer nodes.

Brendan McKay suggested another way to improve preprocessing times: generating and storing in memory only the k-node digraphs whose degree sequences are in "order" with respect to the vertex labels (for directed graphs, the "order" could be the lexicographic order on in-degree/out-degree pairs). In this scheme, when we encounter a $k$-node subgraph, we first permute its vertices so that its degree sequence is in order, then recall its canonical label from memory.

## G-tries Run-Time

After the submission of this paper, gtrieScanner, a network motif detection package based on G-tries was released on Ribeiro's webpage (http://www.dcc.fc.up.pt/gtries/). This gave the present authors an opportunity to compare the two programs. Recall that both programs improve upon previous methods by minimizing the canonical labeling component, i.e. N in (1).

Ribeiro commented that the current release of gtrieScanner (version 0.1) is a "preliminary" version of a program that implements the G-tries data structure. Thus, we feel it would be misleading to give a full-blown comparison of this version of gtrieScanner vs. NetMODE. However, we make the following observations:

- For the experiments we performed, the relevant subgraph counts, Z-scores, and P-values between NetMODE and gtrieScanner were consistent.
- For performing a k-node subgraph census with $3 \leq k \leq 5$ , the run-times of gtrieScanner and NetMODE were comparable. This suggests that both methods have improved upon previous methods by minimizing the time taken to canonically label subgraphs. Differences in e.g. preprocessing times and memory usage causes some fluctuation between the run-times of gtrieScanner and NetMODE.
- For a 6-node subgraph census, gtrieScanner performed much faster than NetMODE for undirected networks (but returned a segmentation fault for directed networks). Moreover, unlike NetMODE, gtrieScanner can also perform 7-node to 9-node subgraph census for undirected networks.
- For large input networks, gtrieScanner used a considerable amount more memory than NetMODE. We gleam from the source code, that gtrieScanner stores e.g. the input network's adjacency matrix in memory, thereby requiring $O(v^2)$ memory, where $v$ is the number of nodes in the input network. This approach is not scalable, and gtrieScanner is virtually unusable for graphs with $10^5$ or more nodes.

Note also that, unlike NetMODE, gtrieScanner is not (yet) a parallelized program.

## ACKNOWLEDGMENTS

The authors would like to thank Rosemary Bailey and Peter Cameron for helpful discussions regarding the uniform sampling method, and Sebastian Wernicke for a helpful discussion regarding the switching method.

## REFERENCES

1. Milo R, Shen-Orr S, Itzkovitz S, Kashtan N, Chklovskii D, et al. (2002) Network motifs: Simple building blocks of complex networks. Science 298: 824–827
2. Shen-Orr S, Milo R, Mangan S, Alon U (2002) Network motifs in the transcriptional regulation network of Escherichia coli. Nature Genetics 31: 64–68
3. Alon U (2007) Network motifs: theory and experimental approaches. Nature Reviews Genetics 8: 450–461
4. Maslov S, Sneppen K, Alon U (2003) Handbook of Graphs and Networks: From the Genome to the Internet, Wiley-VCH, chapter Correlation profiles and motifs in complex networks. pp. 168–198.
5. Schwöbbermeyer H (2008) Network motifs. In: Analysis of Biological Networks. Hoboken, NJ: Wiley. pp. 85–111.
6. Wernicke S, Rasche F (2006) FANMOD: a tool for fast network motif detection. Bioinformatics 22: 1152–1153
7. Kashtan N, Itzkovitz S, Milo R, Alon U (2004) Efficient sampling algorithm for estimating subgraph concentrations and detecting network motifs. Bioinformatics 20: 1746–1758
8. Schreiber F, Schwöbbermeyer H (2004) Towards motif detection in networks: frequency concepts and exible search. In: Merelli E, et al. ., editors. Proc International Workshop on Network Tools and Applications in Biology (NETTAB'04). pp. 91–102. Available: http://www2.ipk-gatersleben.de/~schreibe/publications/SchreiberS04.pdf Accessed 2012 Nov 21.
9. Schreiber F, Schwöbbermeyer H (2005) MAVisto: a tool for the exploration of network motifs.Bioinformatics 21: 3572–3574
10. Wernicke S (2005) A faster algorithm for detecting network motifs. In: Casadio R, Myers G, editors. Proc

Of the 5th International Workshop on Algorithms in Bioinformatics. Lecture Notes in Computer Science, volume 3692. Berlin: Springer. pp. 165–177.

11. Wernicke S (2006) Efficient detection of network motifs. IEEE/ACM Transactions on Computational Biology and Bioinformatics 34: 347–359
12. Omidi S, Schreiber F, Masoudi-Nejad A (2009) MODA: An efficient algorithm for network motif discovery in biological networks. Genes Genet Syst 84: 385–395
13. Kashani ZRM, Ahrabian H, Elahi E, Nowzari-Dalini A, Ansari ES, et al. (2009) Kavosh: a new algorithm for finding network motifs. BMC Bioinformatics 10
14. Ribeiro P, Silva F (2010) Efficient subgraph frequency estimation with g-tries. In: Proceedings of the 10th International Conference on Algorithms in Bioinformatics (WABI '10). Berlin: Springer-Verlag. pp. 238–249.
15. Ribeiro P, Silva F (2010) G-tries: an efficient data structure for discovering network motifs. In: Proc. 25th ACM Symposium On Applied Computing – Bioinformatics Track. New York: ACM. pp. 1559–1566.
16. Ribeiro P, Silva F, Lopes L (2010) Efficient parallel subgraph counting using g-tries. In: IEEE Cluster. pp. 217–226. Available: http://doi.ieeecomputersociety.org/10.1109/CLUSTER.2010.27 Accessed 2012 Nov 21.
17. Ribeiro P, Silva F, Lopes L (2010) Parallel calculation of subgraph census in biological networks. In: Proc 1st International Conference on Bioinformatics. pp. 56–65. Available:http://dblp.dagstuhl.de/db/conf/biostec/bioinformatics2010.html Accessed 2012 Nov 21.
18. Ribeiro P, Silva F, Lopes L (2011) A parallel algorithm for counting subgraphs in complex networks. In: Fred A, Filipe J, Gamboa H, editors, Biomedical Engineering Systems and Technologies, volume 127. Berlin: Springer. pp. 380–393.
19. Koskas M, Grasseau G, Birmelé E, Schbath S, Robin S (2011) NeMo: Fast count of network motifs. In: Book of Abstracts for Journées Ouvertes Biologie Informatique Mathématiques (JOBIM) 2011. pp. 53–60.
20. Bruno F, Palopoli L, Rombo SE (2010) New trends in graph mining: Structural and node-colored network motifs. International Journal of Knowledge Discovery in Bioinformatics 1: 81–99
21. Ciriello G, Guerra C (2008) A review on models and algorithms for motif discovery in proteinprotein interaction networks. Brief Funct Genomic Proteomic 7: 147–156
22. Hu JL, Gao L, Qin GM (2009) Evaluation of subgraph searching algorithms for detecting network motifs in biological networks. Front Comput Sci China 3: 412–416
23. Qin GM, Gao L, Hu JL (2009) A review on algorithms for network motif discovery in biological networks. Acta Electronica Sinica 37: 2258–2265
24. Ribeiro P, Silva F, Kaiser M (2009) Strategies for network motifs discovery. In: Proc E-SCIENCE ‹09. pp. 80–87.
25. Wan R, Mamitsuka H (2009) Biological Data Mining in Protein Interaction Networks, IGI Global, chapter Discovering Network Motifs in Protein Interaction Networks. pp. 117–143. doi:10.4018/978-1-60566-398-2.ch008.
26. Wong E, Baur B, Quader S, Huang CH (2011) Biological network motif detection: principles and practice. Brief Bioinform doi:10.1093/bib/bbr033
27. Milo R, Kashtan N, Itzkovitz S, Newman MEJ, Alon U (2003) On the uniform generation of random graphs with prescribed degree sequences. Available: http://arxiv.org/pdf/condmat/0312028.pdf Accessed 2012 Nov 21.
28. Artzy-Randrup Y, Stone L (2005) Generating uniformly distributed random networks. Phys Rev E 72: 056708
29. Ginoza R, Mugler A (2010) Network motifs come in sets: Correlations in the randomization process.Phys Rev E 011921
30. Konagurthu AS, Lesk AM (2008) On the origin of distribution patterns of motifs in biological networks. BMC Systems Biology 2
31. Berman HM, Westbrook J, Feng Z, Gilliland G, Bhat TN, et al. (2000) The protein data bank. Nucleic Acids Res 28: 235–242
32. Baskerville K, Paczuski M (2006) Subgraph ensembles and motif discovery using an alternative heuristic for graph isomorphism. Phys Rev E 74: 051903
33. Chen C, Schmidt B, Weiguo L, Müller-Wittig W (2008) GPU-MEME: Using graphics hardware to accelerate motif finding in DNA sequences. In: Chetty M, Ngom A, Ahmad S, editors. Pattern Recognition in Bioinformatics, Third IAPR International Conference Proceedings (PRIB 2008). Lecture Notes in Computer Science, volume 5265. Berlin: Springer. pp. 448–459.
34. Liu Y, Schmidt B, Liu W, Maskell DL (2010) CUDAMEME: Accelerating motif discovery in biological sequences using CUDA-enabled graphics processing units. Pattern Recognition Letters 31: 2170–2177
35. Yu L, Xu Y A parallel Gibbs sampling algorithm for motif finding on GPU. In: 2009 IEEE International Symposium on Parallel and Distributed Processing with Applications. New York: IEEE. pp. 555–558.
36. Picard F, Daudin JJ, Koskas M, Schbath S, Robin S (2008) Assessing the exceptionality of network motifs. J Comput Biol 3: 347–359
37. Brand M, Stones DS (2012) The trouble with network motifs: an analytical perspective. In preparation

CHAPTER 20

# PARAMETER TUNING PATTERNS FOR RANDOM GRAPH COLORING WITH QUANTUM ANNEALING

Olawale Titiloye and Alan Crispin

School of Computing, Mathematics and Digital Technology, Manchester Metropolitan University, Manchester, United Kingdom

## ABSTRACT

**Quantum annealing is a combinatorial optimization technique inspired by quantum mechanics. Here we show that a spin model for the k-coloring of large dense random graphs can be field tuned so that its acceptance ratio diverges during Monte Carlo quantum annealing, until a ground state is reached. We also find that simulations exhibiting such a diverging acceptance ratio are generally more effective than those tuned to the more conventional pattern of a declining and/or stagnating acceptance ratio. This observation facilitates the discovery of solutions to several well-known benchmark kcoloring instances, some of which have been open for almost two decades.**

## INTRODUCTION

Quantum annealing [1]–[6] is a combinatorial optimization technique that employs a quantum fluctuation parameter $\Gamma$ for the purpose of escaping local minima. The parameter $\Gamma$ is often a transverse magnetic field in the presence of a low temperature $T$ [3]. Quantum annealing studies have been carried out on NP-hard [7] problems such as the traveling salesman problem [8] and the graph coloring problem [9], [10]. Our version of quantum annealing is close to that in ref. [8] in terms of the approximations employed in the formulation. The algorithms in refs. [2], [5] prioritize simulating a quantum system as strictly as possible, while ours is more flexible in incorporating known classical optimization techniques, with the main aim of solving large and difficult combinatorial optimization problems on a classical computer. The graph k-coloring problem requires a determination of whether every vertex of a given graph can be colored differently to all its adjacent vertices, when only k colors are available. In order to get the best performance out of quantum annealing, the main parameters $\Gamma$ and $T$ need to be tuned according to the particular problem instance under consideration. Although suitable values for the parameters can usually be found by trial runs [8], [9], a study of why certain values work better than others is desirable. Our findings show that the best parameter settings for dense random graphs are those that induce a continuously increasing acceptance ratio during Monte Carlo quantum annealing. Achieving this involves setting a low value for $T$, and tuning $\Gamma$ to within a critical range.

**Citation:** Titiloye O, Crispin A. Parameter Tuning Patterns for Random Graph Coloring with Quantum Annealing. Adesso G, ed. PLoS ONE. 2012;7(11):e50060. doi:10.1371/journal.pone.0050060.

## METHODS

Given an undirected graph $G=(V,E)$ with a vertex set $V$of size $n$, an edge set $E$, and a set $K$ consisting of $k$ colors, $G$ is said to be k-colorable if there exists a mapping $\varphi : V \rightarrow K$such that $\varphi(i) \neq \varphi(j)$, for all $\{i,j\} \in E$. To decide k-colorability, we can minimize a cost function or problem Hamiltonian $H_P$, given by the number of edges with conflicts. A graph is k-colorable if and only if some configuration $\omega(\varphi(1),\varphi(2),\ldots,\varphi(n))$ exists such that $H_P=0$. Any $\omega$ with $H_P(\omega)=0$ is also a global minimum. A configuration $\omega$ can be expressed in terms of $N$constrained Boolean variables $\{x_{ij}\}$, where $ij$ represents a pair of vertices with $i>j$, and $N=n(n-1)/2$ [9]. The Boolean variables are such that $x_{ij}=0$ when $\varphi(i) \neq \varphi(j)$, and $x_{ij}=1$ otherwise [9], [10]. To create an Ising model, we define the set of spins $\{S_{ij}\}$, where $S_{ij}=1-2x_{ij}=\pm 1$. When the spins are defined this way, not all of the $2^N$possible spin configurations correspond to a valid member of the k-coloring search space. Therefore thek-coloring search space cannot be explored by starting from just any spin configuration, and moving to a different one with a single spin flip. Instead, we first obtain an initial $\{S_{ij}\}$ from a uniformly random assignment of one of the k colors to each of the vertices. Afterwards, a new valid configuration can be obtained by changing the color of a vertex, thereby implicitly performing specific multiple spin flips that maintain validity. The problem Hamiltonian can be represented as

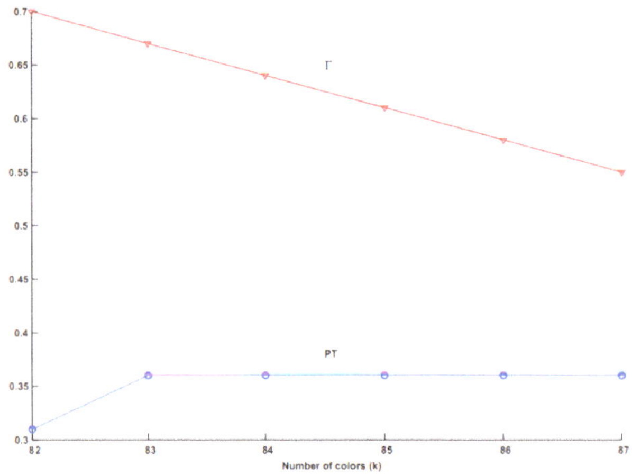


**Figure 1:** Parameter tuning variance with the number of colors for the graph DSJC1000.5

The field strength Γ (red), and the effective temperature PT (blue), plotted against the number of available colors k.

$$H_P(\{S_{ij}\}) = \sum_{ij \in E} (1-S_{ij})/2 \quad \textbf{(1)}$$

The classical Hamiltonian in equation (1) can be converted to a quantum Hamiltonian with a transverse field to give

$$H_q = H_P\left(\left\{\sigma_{ij}^z\right\}\right) - \Gamma \sum_{ij} \sigma_{ij}^x \quad \textbf{(2)}$$

where $\sigma_{ij}^z$ and $\sigma_{ij}^x$ are Pauli matrices, and Γ is a parameter representing the strength of a magnetic field providing quantum fluctuations. To address large problem instances feasibly on a classical computer, we use path integral Monte Carlo. This involves applying a Suzuki-Trotter transformation to $H_q$ in equation (2) to give a new classical Hamiltonian.

$$H = \frac{1}{P}\sum_{\rho=1}^{P} H_P(\{S_{ij,\rho}\}) - J_\Gamma \sum_{\rho=1}^{P}\sum_{ij} S_{ij,\rho}S_{ij,\rho+1} \quad \textbf{(3)}$$

The Hamiltonian H in equation (3) consists of P replicas of the original problem Hamiltonian, simulated at a fixed effective temperature $PT$, with $S_{ij,\rho}$ representing the $ij$-th spin of the $\rho$-th replica, and $J_\Gamma$ given as $-T/2 \ln \tanh(\Gamma/PT)$ [9], [11]. Just as in the quantum annealing of the traveling salesman problem [8], the use of a single spin-flip transverse term in equation (2) is an approximation enabling a straightforward application of the Suzuki-Trotter transformation. In our implementation, only conflicting vertices are eligible for a color change with the Metropolis criterion [9], [10].

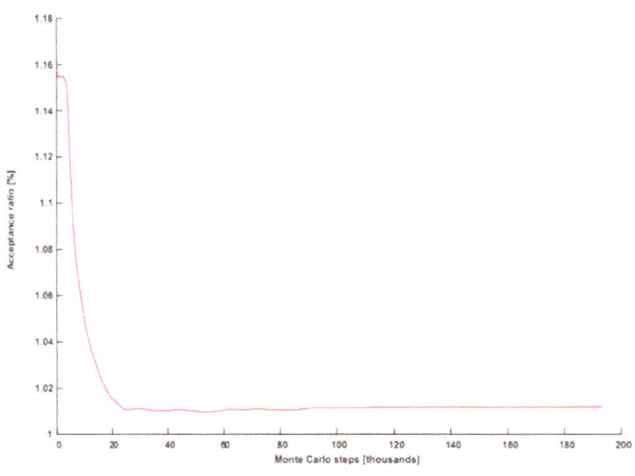


**Figure 2:** An unsuccessful simulation with a declining and stagnating acceptance ratio.

The acceptance ratio plotted against Monte Carlo steps for (G=DSJC1000.5, k=82) with parameters Γ=0.7 and PT=0.36.

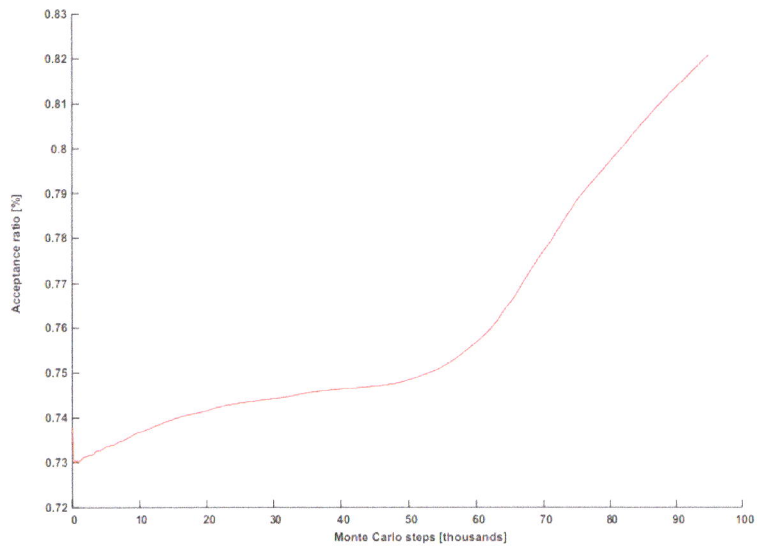


**Figure 3:** A successful simulation with a continuously rising acceptance ratio.

The acceptance ratio plotted against Monte Carlo steps for (G=DSJC1000.5, k=82) with parameters Γ=0.7 and PT=0.31.

Parameter tuning is crucial to the success of quantum annealing. In addition to the tuning of the temperature $T$ and the field strength Γ, a decrement rate for Γ is usually required [8], [9],[11], [12]. If the initial value of Γ is too high, then a slow decrement rate can become impractical. On the other hand, decreasing Γ too quickly can result in the system being trapped by local minima. But if $T$ and $\Gamma$ are heuristically chosen to fit the problem instance, we have recently experimentally demonstrated for graph coloring that successful simulations can be achieved with Γ fixed throughout the duration of a particular simulation [10]. This is the variant of quantum annealing that we use in the current work. A good value of $T$ for a problem instance $(G,k)$ is usually a suitable value for the more difficult instance $(G,k-1)$. Additionally, a good value of $\Gamma$ for $(G,k-1)$ can usually be obtained from that of $(G,k)$ by incrementing it slightly [9], [10].

**Table 1:** Quantum annealing (QA) coloring results compared with the best algorithms

| Graph | QA | Evolutionary-Tabu | Extraction pre-processing |
|---|---|---|---|
| DSJC500.5 | **47** | 48 refs. [17,21,23,24] | 48 ref. [22] |
| DSJC1000.5 | **82** | 83 refs. [17,21,23,24] | 83 ref. [26] |
| DSJC1000.9 | **222** | 223 refs. [21,24] | 222 ref. [26] |
| C2000.5 | **145** | 148 refs. [21,24] | 145 ref. [27] |
| C4000.5 | 262 (**259***) | 271 ref. [21] | 259 ref. [27] |
| C2000.9 | **400** | 413 ref. [26] | 408 ref. [27] |
| flat1000_76_0 | **81** | 82 refs. [21,23,24] | 81 ref. [27] |

*We found 259-colorings for C4000.5 by performing quantum annealing on a residual graph obtained from the independent set extraction experiments in ref. [26].

**Table 2:** Detailed quantum annealing results

| Graph | k | PT | Γ | Attempted | Accepted | Time | Success |
|---|---|---|---|---|---|---|---|
| DSJC500.5 | **47** | 0.30 | 0.70 | $2.8\times10^{11}$ | $4.1\times10^{9}$ | 36 min | 2/10 |
| DSJC1000.5 | **82** | 0.31 | 0.70 | $5.6\times10^{11}$ | $4.4\times10^{9}$ | 1.2 hr | 10/10 |
| DSJC1000.9 | **222** | 0.20 | 0.40 | $5.9\times10^{11}$ | $3.1\times10^{9}$ | 1.1 hr | 6/10 |
| C2000.5 | 146 | 0.32 | 0.65 | $2.5\times10^{12}$ | $1.1\times10^{10}$ | 5.4 hr | 5/5 |
| | **145** | 0.32 | 0.69 | $1.4\times10^{13}$ | $6.7\times10^{10}$ | 31.6 hr | 2/2 |
| C4000.5 | 270 | 0.28 | 0.51 | $1.2\times10^{14}$ | $2.0\times10^{11}$ | 11 days | 1/1 |
| | 262 | 0.28 | 0.57 | $1.3\times10^{15}$ | $1.8\times10^{12}$ | 4 mo. | 1/1 |
| C2000.9 | 403 | 0.18 | 0.29 | $1.2\times10^{13}$ | $2.0\times10^{10}$ | 24 hr | 5/5 |
| | 402 | 0.18 | 0.295 | $2.8\times10^{13}$ | $4.5\times10^{10}$ | 54 hr | 1/1 |
| | 401 | 0.18 | 0.30 | $8.8\times10^{13}$ | $1.4\times10^{11}$ | 174 hr | 1/1 |
| | **400** | 0.18 | 0.31 | $1.3\times10^{14}$ | $2.0\times10^{11}$ | 505 hr | 1/1 |
| flat1000_76_0 | **81** | 0.31 | 0.70 | $1.0\times10^{12}$ | $8.7\times10^{9}$ | 2.2 hr | 10/10 |

Columns 5 and 6 contain the average number of attempted and accepted color changes respectively for successful runs. The average time for a successful simulation is displayed in column 7, while the success rate is in column 8. Proofs of our colorings can be found at https://sites.google.com/site/olawaletitiloye/graphcoloring/qacol

An exact simulation of quantum computation with path integral Monte Carlo requires that the number of replicas P approach infinity [3]. In practice, P has to be set to a low value. A value of 30 has been used for the traveling salesman problem [8], while we have used values such as 10 and 20 for large instances of the graph coloring problem [9], [10]. Each of the P replicas was independently initialized by assigning to each vertex one of the k available colors uniformly at random. To alleviate the drawback of using only a small number of replicas, we implemented a similarity control mechanism of preventing directly connected replicas from prematurely becoming too similar, by randomly perturbing a fraction of the spins at critical moments [10]. Specifically, two replicas were considered too similar when one could be made identical to the other by changing the colors of less than 10% of all vertices in one of them[10]. Also, in order to perturb a configuration, we randomly selected 10% of all vertices and assigned a new randomly selected color for each of them [10]. The procedure usually activated itself towards the end of a simulation involving difficult instances. For many of the easier instances, a solution was often already reached before such measures were needed.

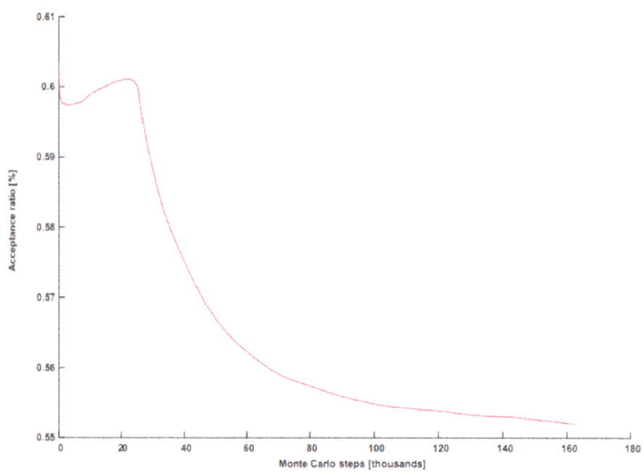


**Figure 4:** An ineffective simulation for (G= C2000.5, k=146) with an increased temperature PT =0.35.

The acceptance ratio persistently declines in a manner very similar to thermal annealing.

http://dx.doi.org/10.1371/journal.pone.0050060.g004

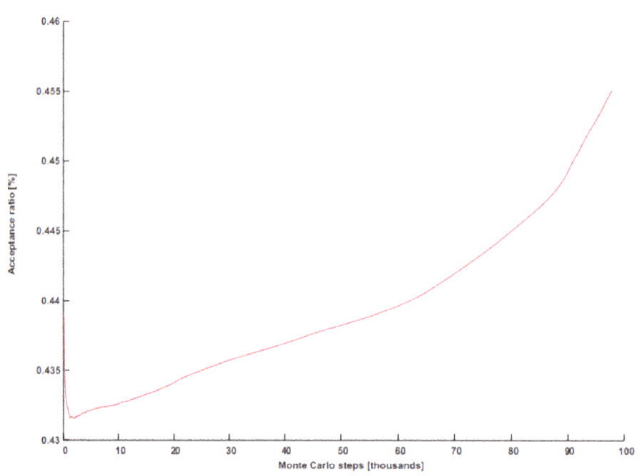


**Figure 5:** Acceptance ratio plot for (G=C2000.5, k=146) with $\Gamma$=0.65 and PT =0.32.

A successful simulation shows a continuously rising pattern for the acceptance ratio over time.

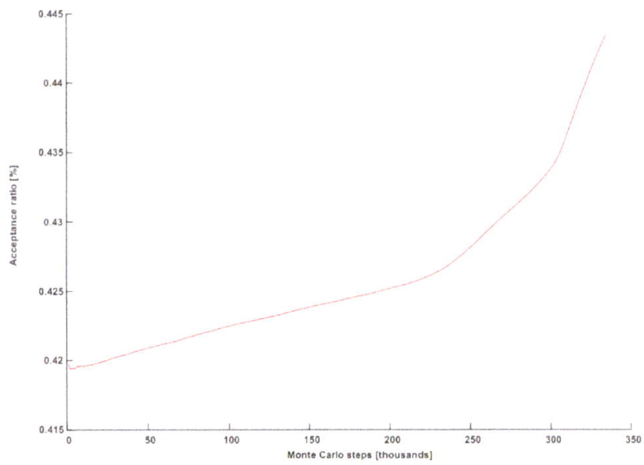


**Figure 6:** Acceptance ratio plot for (G=C2000.5, k=145) with **Γ**=0.69 and PT=0.32

A successful simulation shows a continuously rising pattern for the acceptance ratio over time.

Our computer hardware setup consisted of 12 CPU cores distributed across two identical desktop computers (having 6 CPU cores each), with each of the 10 replicas running on its own core, and one core left free on each desktop. Each core had a frequency of 2.6GHz, and each desktop had 6GB of RAM. The programming environment was GNU C++ on Linux. Communication between the two computers was achieved with MPI (Message Passing Interface), while intra-computer parallelism was performed with OpenMP (Open Multi-Processing). We considered one Monte Carlo step to be complete after all P replicas had each completed $8|V|k$ color change attempts [10]. After each Monte Carlo step, each replica received the configuration of directly connected replicas. The configuration of each replica was stored and transmitted as an assignment of vertices to colors. From this, the value of any spin $S_{ij}$ can be deduced. Rather than try to keep track of the instantaneous state of other replicas, each replica simply used an old copy in its computations, until it received an update [10].

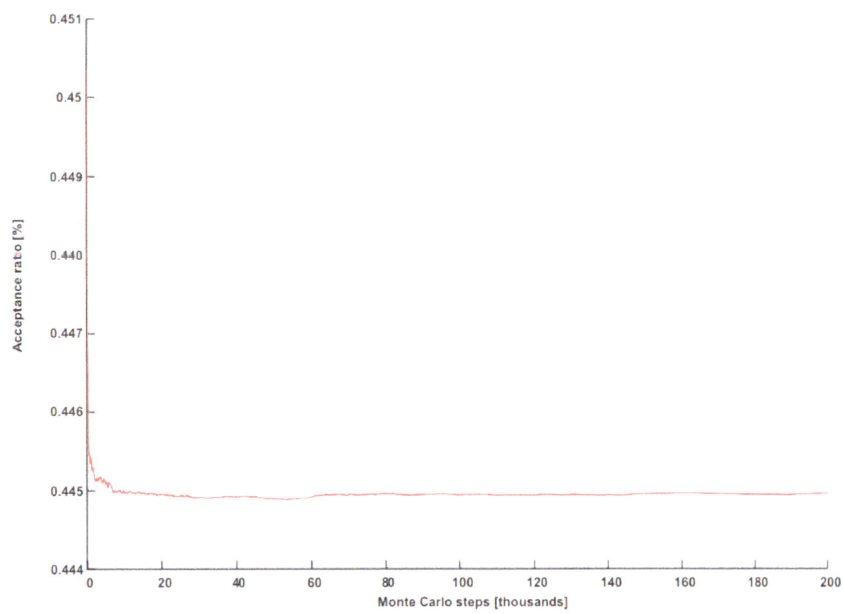


**Figure 7:** Acceptance ratio plot for (G=C2000.5, k=146) with **Γ**=0.8 and PT=0.32.

When the field strength is set higher than the critical value of Γ=0.65, the simulation becomes ineffective. It also shows a persistent stagnation in the evolution of the acceptance ratio.

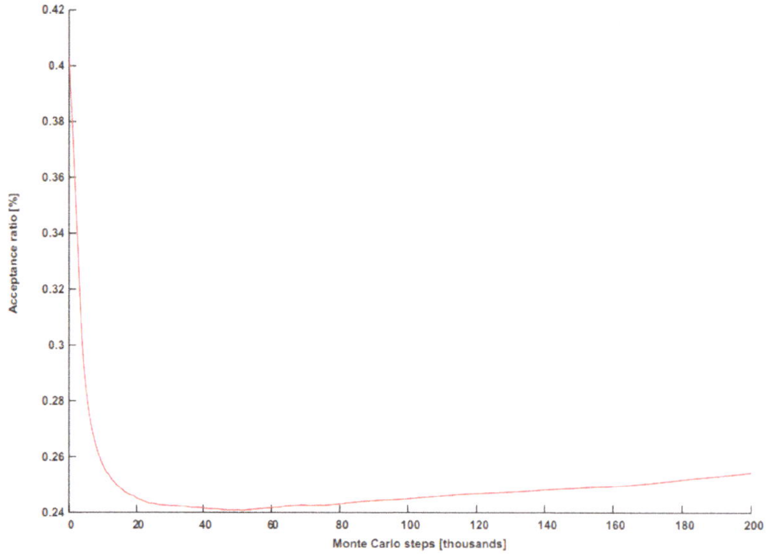


**Figure 8:** Acceptance ratio plot for (G=C2000.5, k=146) with $\Gamma$=0.5 and PT=0.32.

The simulation becomes ineffective when the field strength is set lower than the critical value of $\Gamma$=0.65. The evolution of the acceptance ratio shows a long period of decline and a very weak growth afterwards.

## RESULTS AND DISCUSSION

We considered the Erdös-Rényi $G(n,p)$, which is a standard model of random graphs in which an n-vertex graph is formed by independently including each possible edge with a probability P. The graph coloring problem is still hard, even when restricted to such random graphs, provided instances are chosen near the uncolorable transition [13], [14], where k is very close or equal to the chromatic number X. The chromatic number is the smallest possible value of k for which a proper coloring exists. In fact, no known polynomial time algorithm is guaranteed to color random graphs with $(2-\varepsilon)\chi$ where $\varepsilon > 0$ is fixed [15]. We used DIMACS [16] as our source of benchmark graphs, as numerous algorithms have been tested against them. DIMACS random graphs have P ranging between 0.1 and 0.9, and can all be considered dense in comparison to very sparse graphs that might be 3-colorable [14]. The graph DSJC1000.5 is a member of the $G(1000,0.5)$ family of graphs. An upper bound of 83 was reported for the chromatic number of DSJC1000.5 in the year 1999 [17], and no algorithm has been able to do better since then. We used our Monte Carlo quantum annealing algorithm given in ref. [10] to easily find colorings for instances in the range $83 \le k \le 87$, for which the effective temperature $PT = 0.36$ appears to be optimal [9], [10]. Although we set the value of P to 10 for all experiments in this paper, different values of P can be used by adjusting T to maintain the same value for $PT$ [8], [10]. The acceptance ratio is the number of completed moves (or color changes) divided by the number of attempted moves. We know that $PT = 0.36$ corresponds to a low temperature because the starting acceptance ratio [9], [18] during the Monte Carlo simulation is about 1.3% with $k = 83$. In contrast, a value of $PT = 500$ is needed to bring the acceptance ratio to about 50%, which was the starting ratio for comparable experiments with thermal annealing for graph coloring in ref. [18]. Each time we solved for a smaller value of k, we chose a larger, fixed value for the magnetic field strength $\Gamma$ from the range between 0.55 and 0.68, to allow for the increase in difficulty [9].

Since probabilistic counting arguments [18], [19] suggest that colorings with $k = 82$ might exist for the $G(1000,0.5)$ family of graphs, we tried to find the first ever 82-coloring for DSJC1000.5 by setting an increased value for $\Gamma$. Parameter settings of $PT = 0.36$ and $\Gamma = 0.7$ repeatedly failed to produce an 82-coloring, and setting an even larger $\Gamma$ did not improve the situation. When k is close to the chromatic number, we are likely to encounter phase transitions in the structure of the solution space [13], [15] characterized by the clustering of solutions, and the subsequent emergence of frozen vertices [14], which might require a change in approach. A further series of experiments with a reduced effective temperature of $PT = 0.31$ and a field strength $\Gamma = 0.7$ surprisingly produced 82-colorings for DSJC1000.5 with a 100% success rate from 10 independent runs. The successful tuned values of $PT$ and $\Gamma$ for the DSJC1000.5 graph with $82 \le k \le 87$ are presented in Fig. 1.

For each successful run with the instance (G=DSJC1000.5, k=82), quantum annealing made an average of $5.6 \times 10^{11}$ color change attempts and $4.4 \times 10^{9}$ color changes before a solution was found. Our algorithm took an average wall-clock time of 1.2 hours to find an 82-coloring for DSJC1000.5. This is comparable to the computational resources other researchers have dedicated to this problem. For example, in some experiments in ref. [20] and ref. [21], their single-threaded algorithms took up to 10 and 12 hours respectively for each run on the same DSJC1000.5 graph, without reporting any 82 colorings.

Fig. 2 and Fig. 3 show the evolution of the acceptance ratio with time measured in Monte Carlo steps, for the simulations involving (G=DSJC1000.5, k=82), with $PT = 0.36$ and $PT = 0.31$ respectively. In the ineffective simulation with the higher temperature in Fig. 2, there is a persistent decline and stagnation of the acceptance ratio. This is also what often happens in a thermal annealing algorithm [18]. However, the successful simulation for the instance (G=DSJC1000.5, k=82) with the lower temperature of $PT = 0.31$ shows an unusual pattern of a continuously rising acceptance ratio (in Fig.

3), which persists until a solution is found. While quantum annealing with a persistently declining acceptance ratio can solve the easier cases of $k \geq 83$ with $PT = 0.36$ [9], the higher temperature turns out to be problematic for $k = 82$, no matter the value of $\Gamma$. The lower temperature of $PT = 0.31$ also works for $k \geq 83$, but the required computational effort is unnecessarily increased. Almost our entire past quantum annealing results for random graph coloring [10] used parameter settings which led to stagnating and/or declining acceptance rates. Tuning quantum annealing that way was competitive in its own right. However, parameters that induce a continuously increasing acceptance seem to be necessary for an improved result.

In order to verify that the continuously rising acceptance ratio was not simply due to the perturbation from the similarity control, we first noted that a typical successful run for the simpler instance (G=DSJC1000.5, k=83) with $PT = 0.36$ and $\Gamma = 0.68$ results in about 4000 perturbations out of a total of about 5000 Monte Carlo steps required to solve the problem. A perturbation acts on one replica, while each Monte Carlo step refers to the iteration over P replicas. A declining pattern for the acceptance ratio similar to Fig.2 was observed. However, we found that by setting the reduced temperature of $PT = 0.31$ and keeping everything else the same in the aforementioned problem, no perturbations were needed at all to solve the problem, although a much larger number of Monte Carlo steps of about 30,000 were necessary. More importantly, in this case, the acceptance ratio continuously rises as in Fig. 3. Furthermore, even though the more difficult instance (G=DSJC1000.5, k=82) with settings $PT = 0.31$ and $\Gamma = 0.70$ typically requires about 10,000 perturbations out of a total of about $10^5$ Monte Carlo steps, we observed that another successful experiment with the settings of a lower temperature $PT = 0.30$, and $\Gamma = 0.70$ resulted in only 5 perturbations out of about $2.5 \times 10^5$ Monte Carlo steps. Nevertheless, this also produced a continuously rising pattern in the acceptance ratio similar to that in Fig. 3. This shows that the longer simulations with slightly lower temperatures and much less perturbations can still produce a continuously rising acceptance ratio. Therefore we can be confident that the phenomenon is not due to the perturbations used to control similarity.

The continuously rising pattern of Fig. 3 can be induced for other random graphs to produce results that we have not been able to achieve with parameters that exhibit a declining or stagnating pattern. In some cases, our results are the best ever found by any algorithm. For example, in the case of DSJC500.5, a $G(500, 0.5)$ graph that had the upper bound on its chromatic number improved to 48 in the year 1996 [22], we have been able to find 47-colorings for the first time. We did this by setting a reduced temperature of $PT = 0.3$ for $k = 47$, instead of $PT = 0.35$ used for $k = 48$ [9], while maintaining the field strength at $\Gamma = 0.7$. With an appropriately low temperature, and a carefully tuned field strength, quantum fluctuations dominate thermal ones, and quantum annealing is able to escape the deceptive local minima that have confounded all previous algorithms on the (G= DSJC1000.5, k=82) and (G=DSJC500.5, k=47) instances for almost two decades. The main competitors of quantum annealing for the coloring of dense graphs are evolutionary algorithms incorporating Tabu local search [17], [21], [23], [24]. Simpler approaches such as thermal annealing [18] and plain Tabu search [25] are generally less competitive for coloring dense random graphs. The preprocessing technique of independent set extraction [19] has been improved [26], [27] to produce good results for very large random graphs, but quantum annealing can also incorporate this idea when necessary.

We have improved on the recent result of 409-colorings in ref. [26] for C2000.9, a $G(2000, 0.9)$ graph, by finding 400-colorings. Quantum annealing also found 145-colorings for C2000.5, a $G(2000, 0.5)$ graph, thereby improving on the 146-colorings of ref. [26]. Our results were obtained by selecting parameters that exhibited a continuously rising acceptance ratio. Simulations with parameters that produced a declining acceptance ratio were repeatedly unsuccessful in several independent runs. The graphs C2000.9 and C2000.5 are large, and consist of about 1.8 million and 1 million edges respectively. But unlike in ref. [26], our experiments with C2000.9 and C2000.5 did not need to employ pre-processing by set extraction in order to obtain or improve on the best known results for these particular graphs.

The largest Erdös-Rényi graph from the DIMACS benchmarks is C4000.5, which is a $G(4000, 0.5)$ graph with about 4 million edges. It is not often used in experiments due to its very large size. The best result obtained without independent set extraction was a 271-coloring by an evolutionary algorithm incorporating Tabu search [21]. This was recently improved to $k = 260$ by coloring a residual graph of about 800 vertices obtained after extracting several large independent sets [26]. Encouraged by the superior results of quantum annealing on $G(1000, 0.5)$, we extracted 163 large independent sets from C4000.5 that were obtained in the experiments of ref. [26] in about 5 days of single processor time. We found 96-colorings of the resulting residual graph of about 1200 vertices by quantum annealing in 12 hours on our hardware setup, thereby providing 259-colorings for C4000.5. Without the aid of set extraction pre-processing, quantum annealing located a 270-coloring in 11 days and a 262-coloring in 4 months. C4000.5 is the only random graph in the DIMACS benchmark for which we had to employ set extraction pre-processing in order to obtain the best results.

Although the graph flat1000_76_0 from the DIMACS benchmarks is not an Erdös-Rényi graph, we have previously observed that quantum annealing required similar parameters to a $G(1000, 0.5)$ graph when solving instances in the range $87 \leq k \leq 82$ [9]. Specifically, $PT = 0.36$ and $\Gamma = 0.67$ are good parameters for finding 82-colorings of flat1000_76_0, as well as 83-colorings for DSJC1000.5 [9], [10]. Both graphs are also of similar density, and consist of the same number of vertices. Even though flat1000_76_0 is a flat graph with a hidden 76-coloring [28], it tends to behave similarly to DSJC1000.5 when k is large enough. For example, algorithms in refs. [17], [20]–[24] produce a similar upper bound for the chromatic number $\chi$ on both flat1000_76_0 and DSJC1000.5, often by using similar parameters and a comparable computational effort for both graphs. It was therefore natural to investigate whether the parameters $PT = 0.31$ and $\Gamma = 0.7$ for (G=DSJC1000.5, k=82), could also be used to improve the results of the flat graph by solving (G= flat1000_76_0, k=81). Our experiments show that this is indeed the case. After completing our computations, we learned that successful solutions to (G=C2000.5, k=145), (G=C4000.5, k=259), (G=flat1000_76_0, k=81) and (G=C2000.9, k=408) have recently been mentioned in ref. [27]. They were obtained by improving the synergy between the set extraction preprocessing in ref. [26] and their main graph coloring algorithm in [24]. Quantum annealing still maintains a lead of eight colors on the very dense C2000.9 by finding 400-colorings. Additionally, our approach is still the only one that successfully solves (G= DSJC1000.5, k=82) and (G=DSJC500.5, k=47). The results of our colorings are summarized in Table 1. Additional details such as the parameter settings, number of attempted color changes, wall clock time taken, and the frequency of success can be found in Table 2.

During the quantum annealing of our artificial spin model, even though the state of an individual spin at a future time is highly unpredictable, the acceptance ratio is an easily tracked property describing the collective activity of the spins. We were unable to find any set of parameters producing a declining and/or stagnating acceptance ratio such as in Fig. 2, that nevertheless solves the problem instance (G=DSJC1000.5, k=82). Instead the continuously rising pattern inFig. 3 appears to be crucial for success with that particular instance. Extensive experiments suggest that the temperature $PT=0.36$ is not low enough for $k=82$, even though it is adequate for the easier instances with $k \geq 83$, despite the production of a declining and stagnating pattern for the acceptance ratio in those cases. Lowering the temperature to $PT=0.31$ turns out to be useful and important, both in solving the instance (G=DSJC1000.5,k=82), and in producing a continuously rising pattern for the acceptance ratio. We also generated five new $G(1000,0.5)$ graphs and found that they were all 82-colorable with the same parameter settings of $PT=0.31$ and $\Gamma=0.7$. This is not surprising, as Erdös-Rényi graphs with the same values for P and n are known to possess very similar characteristics[29].

Additionally, we observed that the larger the graph, the earlier one is forced to start using lower temperatures, even when $k$ is still far from the chromatic number. For example, the temperature parameter used in ref. [10] to find 147-colorings for C2000.5 was $PT=0.32$, and any attempts to use anything higher causes problems. In our experiments, we used this same temperature value to successfully solve for $k=146$ and $k=145$, by setting a field strength of $\Gamma=0.65$ and $\Gamma=0.69$ respectively. We also performed several experiments on (G=C2000.5, k=146) with a higher temperature $PT=0.35$, and the field strength maintained at $\Gamma=0.65$. They were all ineffective. Fig. 4 depicts a typical acceptance ratio plot for this experiment. In addition to not locating a solution, the simulations exhibited a persistently declining acceptance ratio reminiscent of thermal annealing. In contrast, the experiments with $PT=0.32$ depicted in Fig. 5 and Fig. 6 were effective, and produced a continuously rising acceptance ratio. This strongly suggests that it is necessary for the temperature to be as low as $PT=0.32$. Nevertheless we have observed that random graphs of various sizes with the same probability P can often be approached with the same (or very close) value for the temperature $PT$. For example, when$p=0.9$, good values for $PT$ tend to be very close to 0.2 for different values of n, as can be seen from Table 2 and our past graph coloring studies in refs. [9], [10].

The field strength $\Gamma=0.65$ appears to be a special value of the field strength for the instance (G= C2000.5, k=146). Experiments with a higher value of $\Gamma=0.8$ produced an acceptance ratio curve with a persistently stagnating pattern following an initial brief period of decline, as shown in Fig. 7. The simulations with this setting repeatedly failed to reach a solution in several independent runs, even though we allocated three times the amount of Monte Carlo steps as was used for $\Gamma=0.65$. Similarly, simulations with the lower value of $\Gamma=0.5$ proved to be ineffective. As shown in Fig. 8, the acceptance ratio underwent a long period of decline and only rose very weakly afterwards. The diverging pattern of the acceptance ratio seen inFig. 5 did not appear. When $\Gamma$ is on either side of 0.65, the behavior of the system starts becoming unfavorable for locating solutions.

The least dense family of $G(n,p)$ graphs from the DIMACS benchmarks is $G(n,0.1)$. The largest such graph from the benchmarks is DSJC1000.1 with $n=1000$. Quantum annealing can match the best algorithms in coloring DSJC1000.1 with $k=20$: the lowest ever used [9]. However, when we repeated the experiments with various parameter settings, we noticed that unlike denser graphs, we could not find settings which solved the problem with a diverging acceptance ratio. Instead, success for this sparse graph appeared to require a declining acceptance ratio, which started from values as high as 5%. We proceeded to generate several sparser random graphs, some of which were likely to be 3-colorable, and were up to 5000 vertices. A similar behavior to that of DSJC1000.1 was observed during quantum annealing. In fact, the sparser the graph, the closer the performance and behavior of our quantum annealing was to thermal annealing. In our k-coloring spin model, all graphs with the same number of vertices possess the same number of spins. But the denser graphs have more constraints, and hence more interaction between their spins. We observed that the appearance of a diverging acceptance ratio correlated with the density of the graph.

By studying the effects of parameter tuning on a Monte Carlo quantum annealing algorithm for the coloring of dense random graphs, we have solved some well known k-coloring problem instances that no other approach has been able to. As more insight is gained into parameter tuning, Monte Carlo quantum annealing may be able to improve on other heuristics for different types of combinatorial optimization problems.

## ACKNOWLEDGMENTS

We thank Z. Bandar for discussions and P. Brown for the help in setting up the Beowulf cluster used for simulations.

## REFERENCES

1. Finnila AB, Gomez MA, Sebenik C, Stenson C, Doll JD (1994) Quantum annealing: A new method for minimizing multidimensional functions. Chemical Physics Letters 219: 343–348
2. Kadowaki T, Nishimori H (1998) Quantum annealing in the transverse Ising model. Physical Review E58: 5355–5363
3. Das A, Chakrabarti BK (2008) Quantum annealing and analog quantum computation. Reviews of Modern Physics 80: 1061
4. Martoňák R, Santoro GE, Tosatti E (2002) Quantum annealing by the path-integral Monte Carlo method: The two-dimensional random Ising model. Physical Review B 66: 094293

5. Farhi E, Goldstone J, Gutmann S, Lapan J, Lundgren A, et al. (2001) A quantum adiabatic evolution algorithm applied to random instances of an NP-complete problem. Science 292: 472–475
6. Santoro GE, Tosatti E (2006) Optimization using quantum mechanics: quantum annealing through adiabatic evolution. Journal of Physics A: Mathematical and General 39: 393–431
7. Garey MR, Johnson DS (1979) Computers and intractability: A guide to the theory of NP-completeness. New York: W.H. Freeman & Co.
8. Martoňák R, Santoro GE, Tosatti E (2004) Quantum annealing of the traveling salesman problem.Physical Review E 70: 057701
9. Titiloye O, Crispin A (2011) Quantum annealing of the graph coloring problem. Discrete Optimization8(2): 376–384
10. Titiloye O, Crispin A (2011) Graph coloring with a distributed hybrid quantum annealing algorithm. In: O'Shea J, Nguyen NT, Crockett K, Howlett RJ, Jain LC, editors. Agent and multiagent systems: technologies and applications, Springer-Verlag, Berlin, Heidelberg. pp 553–562.
11. Battaglia DA, Santoro GE, Tosatti E (2005) Optimization by quantum annealing: Lessons from hard satisfiability problems. Physical Review E 71: 66707
12. Santoro GE, Martoňák R, Tossati E, Car R (2002) Theory of quantum annealing of an Ising spin glass.Science 295: 2427–2430
13. Achlioptas D, Naor A, Peres Y (2005) Rigorous location of phase transitions in hard optimization problems. Nature 435: 759–764
14. Zdeborova L, Krzakala F (2007) Phase transitions in the coloring of random graphs. Physical Review E76: 031131
15. Achlioptas D, Coja-Oghlan A (2008) Algorithmic barriers from phase transitions. In: Proceedings of the 49th Annual IEEE Symposium on Foundations of Computer Science. pp 793–802.
16. Johnson DS, Trick M, editors (1996). Cliques, coloring, and satisfiability: Second DIMACS Implementation challenge. DIMACS series in Discrete Mathematics and Theoretical Computer Science 26. American Mathematical Society.
17. Galinier P, Hao JK (1999) Hybrid evolutionary algorithms for graph coloring. Journal of Combinatorial Optimization 3(4): 379–397
18. Johnson DS, Aragon RC, McGeoch LA, Schevon C (1991) Optimization by simulated annealing: an experimental evaluation; part II, graph coloring and number partitioning. Operations Research 39(3): 378–406
19. Bollobas B, Thomason A (1985) Random graphs of small order. Annals of Discrete Mathematics 28: 249–255
20. Blöchliger I, Zufferey N (2008) A graph coloring heuristic using partial solutions and a reactive tabu scheme. Computers and Operations Research 35(3): 960–975
21. Porumbel DC, Hao JK, Kuntz P (2010) An evolutionary approach with diversity guarantee and well-informed grouping recombination for graph coloring. Computers and Operations Research 37(1), 1822–1832.
22. Morgenstern C (1996) Distributed coloration neighborhood search. In: Johnson DS, Trick M, editors. Cliques, coloring, and satisfiability: Second DIMACS Implementation challenge. DIMACS series in Discrete Mathematics and Theoretical Computer Science 26. American Mathematical Society. pp 335.
23. Malaguti E, Monaaci M, Toth P (2008) A metaheuristic approach for the vertex coloring problem.INFORMS Journal on Computing 20(2): 302–316
24. Lü Z, Hao JK (2010) A memetic algorithm for graph coloring. European Journal of Operational Research 203(1): 241–250
25. Hertz A, De Werra D (1987) Using tabu search techniques for graph coloring. Computing 39: 345–351
26. Wu Q, Hao JK (2012) Coloring large graphs based on independent set extraction. Computers and Operations Research 39(2): 283–290
27. Galinier P, Hamiez JP, Hao JK, Porumbel DC (2012) Recent advances in graph vertex coloring. In: Zelinka I, Abraham A, Snasel V, editors. Handbook of Optimization: From classical to modern approach. Springer New York.
28. Culberson JC, Luo F (1996). Exploring the k-colorable landscape with iterated greedy. In: Second DIMACS Implementation challenge. DIMACS series in Discrete Mathematics and Theoretical Computer Science 26. American Mathematical Society. 245 p.
29. Bollobas B (1985). Random Graphs. London: Academic Press.

CHAPTER 21

# PEPESEARCH: SEMANTIC DATA FOR THE MASSES

Guillermo Vega-Gorgojo[1], Martin Giese[1] , Simen Heggestøyl[1] , Ahmet Soylu[2] , Arild Waaler[1]

[1]Department of Informatics, University of Oslo, Oslo, Norway,

[2]Faculty of Computer Science and Media Technology, Norwegian University of Science and Technology, Gjøvik, Norway

## ABSTRACT

**With the emergence of the Web of Data, there is a need of tools for searching and exploring the growing amount of semantic data. Unfortunately, such tools are scarce and typically require knowledge of SPARQL/RDF. We propose here PepeSearch, a portable tool for searching semantic datasets devised for mainstream users. PepeSearch offers a multiclass search form automatically constructed from a SPARQL endpoint. We have tested PepeSearch with 15 participants searching a Linked Open Data version of the Norwegian Register of Business Enterprises for non-trivial challenges. Retrieval performance was encouragingly high and usability ratings were also very positive, thus suggesting that PepeSearch is effective for searching semantic datasets by mainstream users. We also assessed its portability by configuring PepeSearch to query other SPARQL endpoints.**

## INTRODUCTION

The last few years we have witnessed the emergence of the Web of Data [1]–a giant, global and interconnected data space spanning all sorts of topics, such as media, publications or geographic locations. Following the so-called Linked Data principles [2], publishers of any kind can contribute, with their datasets, to the Web of Data. Briefly, this process involves minting URIs for naming resources, preparing RDF [3] (Resource Description Framework) representations for lookup and linking to other related resources. Once a dataset is ready, a triple store is commonly employed for publishing Linked Data. Besides URI lookup, triple stores provide a SPARQL endpoint, a popular and convenient mechanism for querying a dataset using the SPARQL query language [4]. Although publishing Linked Data requires a non-trivial effort, it provides a generic and flexible mechanism for accessing, discovering and integrating data from different sources. As a result, there is an ongoing trend to publish Linked Data by private organizations and public bodies such as universities, broadcasters and governments [1].

With such a large volume of structured data available, it is possible to formulate semantic searches, i.e. referring to concepts instead of word occurrence as in text searches, for any imaginable topic. For example, we can ask *which Norwegian companies have ever had a net income of more than one billion*

**Citation:** Vega-Gorgojo G, Giese M, Heggestøyl S, Soylu A, Waaler A. PepeSearch: Semantic Data for the Masses. Kamps J, ed. PLoS ONE. 2016;11(3):e0151573. doi:10.1371/journal.pone.0151573.

*Norwegian kroner, but no more than 4 employees* to the RDF version of the Norwegian Register of Business Enterprises (http://data.computas.com). Unfortunately, posing this query requires knowledge of SPARQL and of the underlying data structure, thus severely limiting the target audience. This is especially unfortunate in the case of Linked Open Government Data [5] since citizens have funded these initiatives and they should be able to take profit of them.

Given the effort invested in setting up a dataset in the Web of Data—assigning URIs, creating and reusing vocabularies, defining mappings and interlinking to other datasets—we should find new ways of facilitating the search of semantic data by mainstream users [6], i.e. novice to casual users that are computer literate and do not necessarily have knowledge of RDF or SPARQL. Unfortunately, most tools available are not appropriate for searchers having few-to-no technical skills [7]. Most are SPARQL query interfaces that require a user to learn how to write SPARQL syntax. We address this problem here with PepeSearch, a form-based tool for querying arbitrary SPARQL endpoints. PepeSearch is intended for mainstream users, so the user interface has been carefully designed to be highly usable, while at the same time supporting a considerable degree of expressivity. *Pepe* is the pet form of José, a common Spanish name; PepeSearch is thus a search tool for "the common man".

The rest of the paper is organized as follows. In Section 2 we analyze the different approaches for querying semantic datasets. We depict the novel form-based interface of PepeSearch in Section 3. We present the results of a user study with PepeSearch and showcase its portability in Section 4. Finally, we include a discussion and plans for future work in Section 5.

## Related Work

We can find different types of query specification interfaces for semantic datasets in the literature: SPARQL query editors, information retrieval-based interfaces, natural language interfaces and visual approaches. When analyzing the different alternatives, we are mainly interested in the usability and expressiveness criteria. Usability refers to learnable, efficient and intuitive user interfaces, while expressivity indicates the variety of queries that can be posed. Since there is a trade-off between both dimensions [8], some query expressivity is commonly sacrificed to achieve a usability gain. Besides, a search system for the Web of Data needs to be portable, i.e. no code changes should be required to be used in a new domain.

Table 1 summarizes the different alternatives found in the literature. A SPARQL editor is a simple solution that allows the use of the full expressivity of the query language. However, this is not an option in most cases since users have to know the SPARQL syntax. Further, querying a triple store needs familiarity with the underlying data schema. To overcome this limitation, context-aware editors like SparQLed [9] extract a structural summary of a dataset and then provide autocompletion and recommendations of structure elements such as class or property names—though knowledge of SPARQL is still required.

**Table 1:** Approaches for querying semantic datasets

| General approach | Approach | Usability | Expressivity | Examples | Comments |
|---|---|---|---|---|---|
| Formal query language | SPARQL editor | Very low | High | SparQLed [9] | Requires SPARQL knowledge<br>Users are not aware of the data structure<br>Simple solution |
| Information retrieval | Keyword-based search interfaces | High | Very low | SWSE [10] | Well-known approach<br>Users are not aware of the data structure |
| Natural language processing | Question-answering systems | High | Natural language approximation | PowerAqua [11] | Ambiguities and linguistic variability<br>Users are not aware of the data structure<br>Complex solution |
| Visual | Graph-based query editors | Medium | High/Medium | NITELIGHT [13], QueryVOWL [14] | Natural choice for RDF data<br>Not very usable for mainstream users |
| | Form-based query editors | High | Medium | Virtuoso facets [15], Explorator [16], tFacet [17], Rhizomer [18] | Difficult to translate SPARQL query patterns into a generic form interface<br>Well-known approach |

Information retrieval approaches mimic traditional keyword-based search, allowing users to pose bags-of-words as queries—hence expressivity is limited. The search system tries to match keywords to classes or instances, possibly exploiting relations in the dataset to create a structured SPARQL query—see SWSE [10] for an example. As an evolution, natural language approaches, e.g. PowerAqua [11], interpret the query as a whole with the aim of achieving the expressivity of natural language. However, ambiguities and linguistic variability limit its effectiveness [12], so existing approaches typically engage the user in feedback cycles or try to get approximate results. The challenges of information retrieval and natural language approaches for querying the Web of Data are thoroughly analyzed in [8].

Visual approaches comprise a wide range of user interfaces that allow the construction of SPARQL queries through the interaction with visual elements. The syntax of the language is hidden from the user, while available actions are limited so as to only produce valid queries. The majority of visual approaches can be classified either as graph-based or form-based. Graph-based query editors allow to visually construct a query by adding nodes (representing RDF classes or individuals) and arcs (representing RDF properties). There are many examples of graph-based interfaces, e.g.

NITELIGHT [13] or QueryVOWL [14], since Linked Data can be represented as graphs. Nevertheless, there is evidence that mainstream users are not particularly comfortable with graph visualizations [19, 20], making this approach questionable for this user group from a usability point of view.

Finally, form-based interfaces allow the specification of queries through the use of text boxes, drop-down menus, radio buttons and other form elements. This approach is appealing to mainstream users, since they are commonly employed in everyday tasks such as flight booking. However, the challenge is the translation of SPARQL query patterns into a generic form interface. Preliminary attempts have reproduced faceted search [21] for semantic data by exploiting the vocabulary structure, e.g. Virtuoso Facets [15]. Unfortunately, expressivity is typically low, since queries can only include one concept. More recent developments have tried to overcome this limitation: Explorator [16] includes Boolean operators for combining facets; tFacet [17] supports so-called hierarchical facets by using additional menu forms to include facets from other classes; Rhizomer [18] provides pivoting operations, i.e. changing the focus of a query from one class to another. Overall, the effectiveness of these approaches is questionable for mainstream users, given their increased complexity and the scarcity of user studies to assess their benefits.

## PepeSearch: A Portable Form-Based Search Interface for Semantic Datasets

We pursue to provide a highly usable search tool that actually hides the complexity of SPARQL/RDF, while ensuring syntactic correctness and making the user conscious of the data structure. Further, expressivity should be enough to cover a wide range of query types, although we do not aim to support all the SPARQL expressivity. In addition, the proposed search tool should be portable to an arbitrary dataset without requiring changes in the code.

## System Architecture

PepeSearch is the tool we have devised to fulfill the aforementioned requirements. Its user interface corresponds to the category of form-based query editors (see Table 1). PepeSearch provides a multi-class search form that allows the searcher to set multiple constraints on any of the classes in the dataset.

The system architecture of PepeSearch is depicted in Fig 1. The SPARQL analyzer is employed in a bootstrapping stage to gather information about the dataset. A data schema in the standardized JavaScript Object Notation (JSON) format is generated from this process. This data schema is the basis for the creation of the multi-class form in the user interface component. For a given class, the data schema can be inspected to get a readable label, its datatype properties with appropriate ranges, and the connections to other classes through an object property or through a subclass relation. Furthermore, the SPARQL analyzer can optionally retrieve the string values of datatype properties which are then sent to a text search engine.

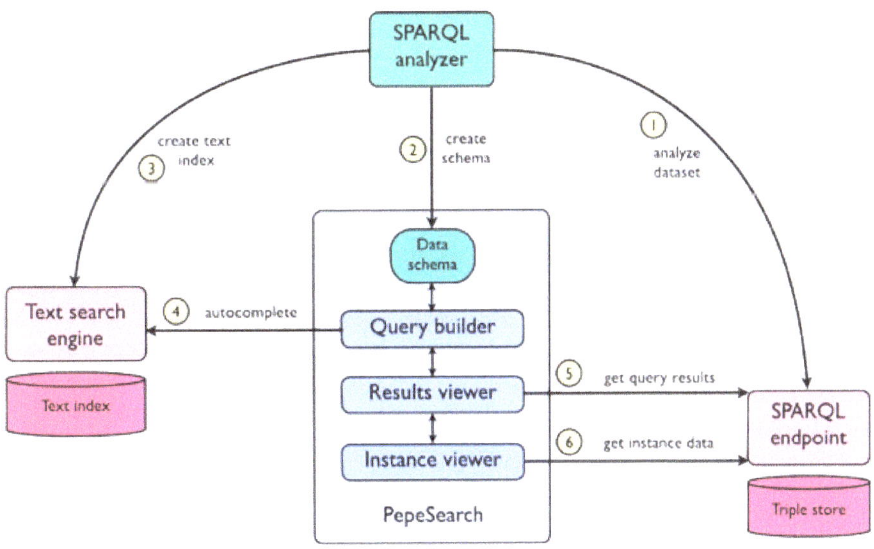


**Figure 1:** Logical architecture of Pepesearch.

A system administrator will typically carry out this bootstrapping process and then set up a PepeSearch instance with the obtained data schema. There is no need to rerun the SPARQL analyzer unless there are unreflected structural changes in the RDF model of the triplestore, e.g. a new class is introduced, or new data that invalidates the obtained ranges of a numerical datatype. In any case, the data schema will still be usable and it is possible (and advisable) to schedule periodical updates based on the frequency of data changes.

Once a PepeSearch instance is configured, the query builder relies on the obtained data schema to construct the view—see Fig 2. The user can restrict any of the fields of the presented classes in the form; appropriate ranges and term suggestions are exploited to reduce input errors. The text search engine is employed to make dynamic term suggestions during query specification—for example, after typing "os" in the municipality textbox, PepeSearch will suggest OS, OSLO, ØSTRE TOTEN, OSTERØY, and OSEN. In case of subclasses, the form includes controls for selecting a more general/specific concept—see the filter and the collapsible of "Computer programming, consultancy and related activities" in Fig 2.

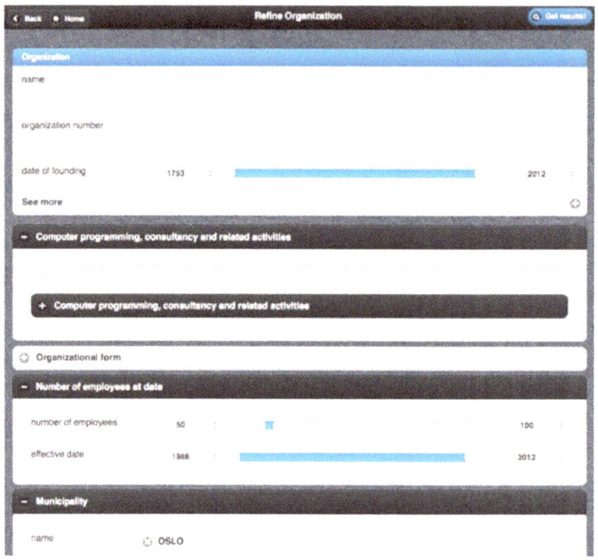


**Figure 2:** Snapshot of PepeSearch (query).

After pushing the search button, the query builder generates a valid SPARQL conjunctive query containing all the user restrictions. The results viewer sends the query to the SPARQL endpoint and obtained results are then presented to the user in a tabular representation; this includes controls to paginate, add/remove columns and sort by any field—see Fig 3. Moreover, class instances are clickable, and the instance viewer is in charge of obtaining all the information available in the dataset and creating a corresponding view—see Fig 4.

**Figure 3:** Snapshot of PepeSearch (results)

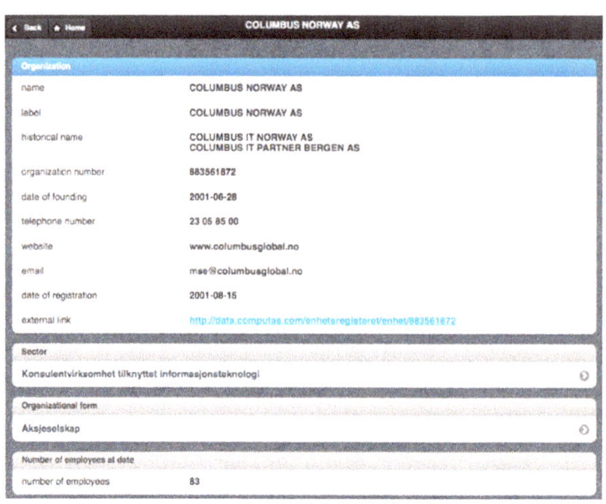


**Figure 4:** Snapshot of PepeSearch (instance).

## User Interface Design

For an arbitrary RDF class, PepeSearch creates a form block in which datatype properties are mapped to widget elements, e.g. text boxes for string literals or slide ranges for integers. In this way, a searcher can easily set restrictions on a class by manipulating the visual elements of the block form. Beyond refining a single class, further expressivity is required in many cases. In PepeSearch we address this challenge by providing new form blocks for each RDF class that is connected with an object property to the selected RDF class: for the vocabulary in Fig 5, PepeSearch will create a block form for the concept "Role" when selected, as well as additional block forms for "Company" and "Person". Since form-based interfaces can become bloated with many form elements, we use collapsibles for these additional block forms—seeFig 2. The corresponding collapsibles can be expanded, thus allowing the searcher to set restrictions to the class attributes. Moreover, we provide controls for selecting a class type in the case of concept taxonomies. For instance, Fig 2 shows the "Computer programming, consultancy and related activities" form block, one of the 380 subtypes of "Sector" in the test vocabulary.

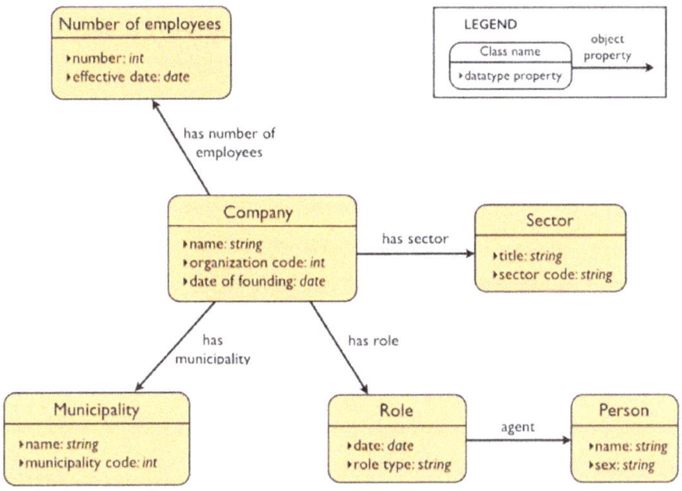


**Figure 5:** Vocabulary excerpt of the Norwegian Register of Business Enterprises.

We illustrate our approach for the user interface with the following example: we want to find*which information technology consultancy companies in Oslo have between 50 and 100 employees*? The SPARQL analyzer has previously extracted the data structure from the Norwegian Register of Business Enterprises triple store—an excerpt of the vocabulary is shown in Fig 5. After that, the interaction with the system can be the following:

- PepeSearch presents a list of the available classes.
- The user selects "Company".
- PepeSearch presents a form composed of different classes: one for "Company" and another one for each directly connected concept in Fig 5. Each class includes controls for refining its attributes.
- The user sets the following restrictions: "Computer programming, consultancy and related activities" in the sector hierarchy, "Oslo" in municipality, and "50–100 range" in the number of employees. Fig 2 shows a snapshot of this query.
- The user pushes the search button.
- PepeSearch generates a SPARQL query from the user input and sends it to the SPARQL endpoint.
- With the response, PepeSearch prepares a suitable representation of the results—seeFig 3.
- The user can navigate through the results by following the links, e.g. Fig 4 shows the information of one of the companies found.

## The SPARQL Analyzer

The SPARQL analyzer is in charge of creating the data schema that will be employed to create the multi-class search form. Remarkably, this process is generally applicable to an arbitrary triplestore due to the self-describing nature of RDF, the schema-level queries in SPARQL, and to the generality of the mapping assumptions.

In a bootstrapping stage, the SPARQL analyzer submits a sequence of queries to the target triplestore in order to collect information about the dataset. First, a list of all the non-empty classes is obtained—this filtering is intended to limit the formulation of zero-results queries during user operation. Then, for each retrieved class the SPARQL analyzer get its subclass relations, object properties and datatype properties. In the case of numerical datatype properties, the SPARQL analyzer also collects the minimum and maximum values for each class in order to set appropriate slide ranges. Specifically, the main SPARQL queries employed for gathering that information are the following:

- Get the non-empty classes:

```
SELECT DISTINCT ?class
WHERE { ?instance a ?class . }
```

- Get the subclasses of a given class with URI class_uri

```
SELECT DISTINCT ?subclass
WHERE { ?subclass rdfs:subClassOf <class_uri>
. }
```

- Get the distinct object properties and corresponding object classes for a given class with URI class_uri

```
SELECT DISTINCT ?object_prop ?object_class
WHERE { ?subject a <class_uri> .
        ?subject ?object_prop ?object .
        ?object a ?object_class . }
```

- Get the distinct datatype properties for a given class with URI class_uri

```
SELECT DISTINCT ?literal_prop
WHERE { ?subject a <class_uri> .
        ?subject ?literal_prop ?literal .
        FILTER (isLiteral(?literal))
```

### Implementation

The SPARQL analyzer is offered as a standalone component athttps://github.com/simenheg/sparql-endpoint-analyzer. It analyzes the data structure of an arbitrary SPARQL endpoint and automatically generates the data schema and a term suggestions document. Although not required, some manual customization can be performed, especially to annotate secondary properties—for example, the company website is not available for search in Fig 2, but can be shown by pressing the "See more" button.

PepeSearch is coded in JavaScript and available at https://github.com/guiveg/pepesearch. We have employed the JQuery Mobile framework to simplify the development of the user interface, as well as to facilitate its deployment in most smartphone, tablet and desktop platforms. As for the text search engine, we have employed Apache Solr (http://lucene.apache.org/solr/), though this component is not required to run PepeSearch.

## PEPESEARCH IN PRACTICE

### The Norwegian Register of Business Enterprises

As part of the Semicolon II project, a collaboration of a number of public sector, industry, and academic partners in Norway, the Norwegian Register of Business Enterprises was published as Linked Open Data [22], (http://data.computas.com).

The triplestore contains administrative and accountancy data of more than 300K companies, amounting to almost 50M triples. The complexity of the schema is moderate/low, consisting of 11 classes, 16 object properties and 59 datatype properties (see an excerpt in Fig 1). We have set up a PepeSearch instance to query this triplestore, available athttp://sws.ifi.uio.no/project/semicolon/search/.

In order to assess the effectiveness of PepeSearch, we arranged a search challenge with an award of a 1000 kroner book voucher for the best performer. This competition was advertised at the University of Oslo and at the Oslo Akershus University College. Eventually, 14 students and 1 postdoctoral researcher (6 female and 9 male) participated. 10 of them had a background in informatics and 5 in library studies. The average age was 25, ranging from 18 to 44. Participants sporadically made searches of Norwegian companies, although 2 of them reported higher frequency of searches. All of them were heavy users of computers and were very used to web searches. They had to register through a web questionnaire in order to participate in the study, and we sent them a link to five slides of PepeSearch a few days before the experiment.

The search challenge was carried out in a single session. We followed the ethics guidelines for conducting usability studies that are common in the field—see for instance [23]—and for this reason we did not seek approval of an institutional review board. As a result, participants in the study were informed that all their data would be anonymized and exclusively used for a research project on search interfaces. All of them gave their oral consent and carried out the scheduled search tasks. Participant consent was not recorded and we considered it was not necessary to do it, given that participants had previously registered in order to conduct the usability study. Indeed, they were volunteers and free to withdraw at any time.

We gave them some basic instructions for signing up and submitting the results of a search task. Each participant had to respond to three search tasks. These were randomly selected from the following pool:

- *Which Norwegian companies had a net income of more than 1,000,000,000 (one billion) Norwegian kroner in 2008, but no more than 4 employees?*
- *Which are the eight oldest accommodation establishments (hotels or other) in Tromsø?*
- *Which companies are settled in Brønnøy, street Industriveien 30?*
- *Which were the seven manufacturing companies of dairy and ice-cream products with the highest net income in 2010?*
- *Which wireless telecommunications companies settled in Oslo have above 40 employees?*
- *Which companies does "Svein Rennemo" lead?*

They had 45 minutes to carry out the search tasks, although all participants were able to finish before the deadline; in fact, the average time for a search task was 8 minutes and 20 seconds (including the time employed filling the search form)–note that participants did not receive any training of PepeSearch.

We used the *F*-measure to assess the retrieval performance, a popular single-valued metric for interactive evaluations [24]. The *F*-measure is calculated as the harmonic mean of recall and precision, ranging from 0 (worst case) to 1 (perfect response). Remarkably, the mean *F*-measure was 0.82 with a standard deviation of 0.17. Participants were also asked to fill a usability questionnaire for assessing subjective reactions to interactive interfaces. We then computed the System Usability Scale (SUS) [25] score, obtaining 75.3 points with a standard deviation of 18.1.

To put our results into context, we have reviewed the literature in order to find user studies on semantic search that could serve as a baseline comparison for PepeSearch. [20] is a comprehensive semantic search usability study with five different user interfaces (2 natural language, 2 graph-based and 1 form-based interfaces). The obtained SUS scores ranged from 32.5 to 63.8 (41.3 in the case of form-based interfaces). Since these SUS scores are not particularly high, we set a goal of 67.0 that is the mean value for web user interfaces found in an extensive study on the use of the SUS questionnaire [26]. We then employed a one-sample*t*-test to assess whether this goal had been accomplished. The observed difference of 8.3

SUS points is 1.8 standard errors from the benchmark, while the obtained $p$-value is 0.048, which is a statistically significant result.

Concerning retrieval performance, we could not use the figures from [20] because the employed dataset was much smaller and the search tasks less complex than in our user study. Instead, we employed as a basis the results from the first and second editions of a public evaluation challenge for question answering systems over linked data (QALD) [27]. Since the focus relies on evaluating natural language processors that automatically translates textual questions into SPARQL queries, users were not involved in the QALD challenges. However, the complexity of the questions are comparable to the ones employed in our case study, e.g. "Give me all live albums by Michael Jackson", the size of the datasets is comparable, e.g. 15M triples for the MusicBrainz dataset, and the F-measure is also employed for measuring retrieval performance, ranging from 0.38 to 0.71 for the best system with the MusicBrainz dataset in QALD-1. We set this maximum value as a comparison goal in our study, obtaining a difference of 0.11 with a $t$ of 2.56 and a $p$-value of 0.011, thus indicating a statistically significant difference.

All in all, this analysis suggests that the usability-expressivity tradeoff of PepeSearch is well balanced, given the high scores for retrieval performance and usability that significantly surpasses the goals we set. Since the comparison with other approaches is mediated through benchmark scores, we aim to conduct further user studies with PepeSearch and other representatives of semantic search interfaces to confirm these results.

### Other Settings

Since PepeSearch is designed to be portable, we have tested this tool in other settings. The Semantic Web Dog Food Corpus (http://data.semanticweb.org/) provides information about the main conferences and workshops in the Semantic Web research field. Overall, this dataset is of medium size (about 600K triples) and of moderate complexity (118 classes, 48 object properties and 72 datatype properties). Though the endpoint is not very responsive, it was easy to query and browse this triplestore with PepeSearch, e.g. to find the papers of a researcher in a specific conference.

We also configured PepeSearch to query the Linked Open NPD FactPages [28] dataset (http://sws.ifi.uio.no/project/npd-v2/), which is an RDF representation of a wide range of public information about petroleum related activities on the Norwegian Continental Shelf. This is a large dataset (more than 7M triples) with a rather complex schema about oil fields, involved companies, wells and wellbores—totaling 173 classes, 99 object properties and 349 datatype properties. As in the other cases, no code changes were required to set up PepeSearch. We were also able to query this triplestore, although some domain knowledge is required to understand the FactPages schema.

## DISCUSSION

Given the difficulties that mainstream users have for searching and exploring semantic datasets, we aimed to propose an adequate user interface for their needs. Our preliminary results with PepeSearch show that mainstream users were able to solve non-trivial search challenges with PepeSearch without previous training and that the usability-expressivity tradeoff seems adequate.

The majority of form-based interfaces are still very complicated for lay users, as criticized in [18]. For instance, Explorator [16] shows the subject, property and object constructs of RDF at the user interface, while tFacet [17] employs a hierarchical structure of facets that becomes easily impractical when traversing many classes.

Regrettably, there is a lack of empirical evidence of the effectiveness of query interfaces for the Semantic Web [29]. Rhizomer [18] is one of the scarce proposals that include a user evaluation aimed to test the validity of facet pivoting—this technique allows the formulation of queries with more than one concept (see Section 2). However, they report usability problems as users found problems identifying the pivoting button and making sense of it. In comparison, the interface design of PepeSearch offers a clear separation of classes and additional expressivity, since an arbitrary number of constraints can be set for each query concept.

While dynamic term suggestion is a very popular technique in search interfaces [21], they are not so common in semantic search systems. Participants in our user study profusely employed suggested terms for setting literal string values. As a result, dynamic term suggestion avoided spelling errors and contributed to reduce the number of zero results.

Future work for PepeSearch includes further comparisons with other approaches. In addition, we plan to leverage this tool by supporting new result visualizations and to increase query expressivity without compromising usability. We are also working on supporting basic federation through the use of the SERVICE operator of SPARQL 1.1.

## REFERENCES

1. Heath T, Bizer C. Linked Data: Evolving the Web into a Global Data Space. Morgan & Claypool; 2011.
2. Berners-Lee T. Linked Data. 2006. Available: http://www.w3.org/DesignIssues/LinkedData.html
3. Klyne G, Carroll J, eds. Resource Description Framework (RDF): Concepts and Abstract Syntax. W3C Recommendation. Feb. 2004. Available: http://www.w3.org/TR/rdf-concepts/
4. Prud'hommeaux E, Seaborne A, eds. SPARQL Query Language for RDF, W3C Recommendation, Jan. 2008. Available: http://www.w3.org/TR/rdf-sparql-query/
5. Ding L, Peristeras V, Hausenblas M. Linked Open Government Data. IEEE Intelligent Systems. 2012.27(3):11–15.
6. Dadzie A, Rowe M. Approaches to visualising linked data: A survey. Semantic Web. 2011. 2(2):89–124.
7. Bizer C, Heath T, Berners-Lee T. Linked Data—The story so far. International Journal on Semantic Web and Information Systems, Special Issue on Linked Data. 2009. 5(3):1–22.
8. Freitas A, Curry E, Oliveira JG, O'Riain S. Querying Heterogeneous Datasets on the Linked Data Web:

Challenges, Approaches, and Trends. IEEE Internet Computing. 2012. 16(1):24–33.

9. Campinas S, Perry TE, Ceccarelli D, Delbru R, Tummarello G. Introducing RDF Graph Summary with Application to Assisted SPARQL Formulation Proc. 23rd International Workshop on Database and Expert Systems Applications (DEXA12). 2012. 261–266.
10. Hogan A, Harth A, Umbrich J, Kinsella S, Polleres S, Decker S. Searching and browsing linked data with SWSE: The semantic web search engine. Web Semantics: Science, Services and Agents on the World Wide Web. 2011. 9(4):365–401.
11. Lopez V, Motta E, Uren V. PowerAqua: Fishing the Semantic Web Proc. 3rd European Semantic Web Conference (ESWC04). 2004. 4011:393–410.
12. Kaufmann E, Bernstein A. Evaluating the usability of natural language query languages and interfaces to Semantic Web knowledge bases. Web Semantics: Science, Services and Agents on the World Wide Web. 2010. 8(4):377–393.
13. Russell A, Smart PR, Braines D, Shadbolt NR. Nitelight: A graphical tool for semantic query construction. Proc. Semantic Web User Interaction Workshop (SWUI 2008). 2008.
14. Haag F, Lohmann S, Siek S, Ertl T. QueryVOWL—Visual Composition of SPARQL Queries. Proc. 12th European Semantic Web Conference (ESWC2015). 2015.
15. OpenLink. Faceted Browsing Service. Available:http://www.openlinksw.com/dataspace/doc/dav/wiki/Main/VirtuosoFacetsWebService
16. Araujo S, Schwabe D. Explorator: a tool for exploring RDF data through direct manipulation. Proc. of Linked Data on the Web (LODW 2009) Workshop at WWW 2009. 2009.
17. Brunk S, Philipp H. tFacet: Hierarchical faceted exploration of semantic data using well-known interaction concepts. Proc. International Workshop on Data-Centric Interactions on the Web (DCI 2011). 2011.
18. Brunetti JM, Garcia R, Auer S. From overview to facets and pivoting for interactive exploration of semantic web data. International Journal on Semantic Web and Information Systems. 2013. 9(1):1–20.
19. Viégas FB, Donath J. Social network visualization: Can we go beyond the graph? Proceedings of the 2006 20th anniversary conference on Computer Supported Cooperative Work (CSCW'06), Workshop on Social Networks. 2014. 4:6–10.
20. Elbedweihy K, Wrigley SN, Ciravegna F. Evaluating semantic search query approaches with expert and casual users Proc. of the 11th International Conference on The Semantic Web (ISWC 2012). 2012. 274–286.
21. Hearst M. Search user interfaces. Cambridge University Press; 2009.
22. Roman D, Norheim D. An Overview of Norwegian Linked Open Data Proc. 4th International Conference on Information, Process, and Knowledge Management (eKNOW). 2012. 93–96.
23. Miller CS. Ethics for conducting a usability test. DePaul University; Available:http://facweb.cs.depaul.edu/cmiller/eval/ethics.html
24. Oard DW. Evaluating interactive cross-language information retrieval: Document selection. Proc. of the First Cross-Language Evaluation Forum (CLEF 2001). 2001. 2069:57–71.
25. Brooke J. SUS—A quick and dirty usability scale In: Usability evaluation in industry. Taylor & Francis; 1996.
26. Sauro J, Lewis JR, "Quantifying the user experience: Practical statistics for user research," Morgan-Kaufmann, 2012.
27. Lopez V, Unger C, Cimiano P, Motta E. Evaluating question answering over linked data. Web Semantics. 2013. 21:3–13.
28. Skjæveland MG, Lian EH, Horrocks I. Publishing the Norwegian Petroleum Directorate's FactPages as Semantic Web Data. Proc. of the 12th International Semantic Web Conference (ISWC 2013). 2013.8219:162–177.
29. Hachey G. Semantic Web User Interfaces: A Systematic Mapping Study Master's thesis. Athabasca University; 2011. Available: http://dtpr.lib.athabascau.ca

# INDEX